THE WAITE GROUP®

Workout C

DAVID HIMMEL

Corte Madera, CA

Development Editor	Mitchell Waite
Editorial Director	Scott Calamar
Production Manager	Julianne Ososke
Content Editor	Jim Stockford
Technical Reviewers	Dennis Saunders, Harry Henderson, Stephen Prata
Designer	Barbara Gelfand
Illustrator	Pat Rogondino
Managing Editor	Joel Fugazzotto

FIRST EDITION

ISBN: 1-878739-14-X

Printed in the United States of America

94 95 • 10 9 8 7 6 5 4

Himmel, David.
The Waite Group's Workout C / David Himmel. -- 1st ed.
p. cm.
Includes index.
ISBN 1-878739-14-X (trade paper) : $39.95
1. C (Computer program language) I. Waite Group. II. Title. III. Title: Workout C.
QA76.73.C15H56 1992 <MRCRR>
005.13'3--dc20

DEDICATION

For Marilyn,
who always wanted the best for me,
and then gave it.

ACKNOWLEDGMENTS

As the author sits to write
in the early morning light,
he feels he has a lonely task.
But this is only how things seem,
'cause the author has the help
of a great publishing team.

Thanks to the following members of The Waite Group: Scott Calamar, for his attention and guidance in managing the project; Joel Fugazzotto, for finishing it off in good style; Stephen Prata, for his in-depth knowledge of C and editing suggestions; Jim Stockford, for his dynamite reviews and great ideas; Mitch Waite, for formulating the concept and giving me the opportunity to write the book.

I also wish to extend thanks to my wife, who supplemented my knowledge of the C language with her knowledge of the English language, to my son Todd for his direct contribution, and to my son Chad for his indirect contribution.

TABLE OF CONTENTS

TABLE OF CONTENTS

FOREWORD

After publishing more than seventy titles, The Waite Group has earned a reputation for producing high quality computer books. The care and attention to detail that they put into each book results in a very distinctive Waite Group look and feel. An excellent example is *The Waite Group's New C Primer Plus,* the best-selling C language programming book and winner of the 1990 Computer Press Association Award: BEST HOW-TO BOOK.

Because of their very successful track record, we were delighted to team up with The Waite Group to produce the product you are now holding. *Workout C* combines The Waite Group's excellent new C language tutorial with our ANSI standard **Power C** compiler. The result is a complete, self-contained training system that offers you a hands-on approach to learning C.

The only truly effective way to learn any programming language is to write lots of programs. You learn by making, discovering, and then correcting your programming errors. *Workout C* provides you with a series of small but interesting C programs, each designed to illustrate specific features of the C language. As you work through these example programs, you will learn by actually editing, compiling, executing, and correcting any programs that contain errors.

After going through all of the exercises presented in *Workout C,* you will have a very solid foundation on which to build additional C language experience. If you decide that the C language is for you and you want to find out more about the commercial version of the **Power C** compiler, see the tear-out card at the back of this book. We hope that you enjoy *Workout C* as much as we've enjoyed participating in its development.

Dennis Saunders
Marketing Director
Mix Software, Inc.

February 1992

PREFACE

Inspiration for *Workout C* came from two sources: First, users of *The Waite Group's Master C* training package asked for a book with additional reader exercises, and second, our readers asked for a tutorial that would give them a chance to learn C by direct experience. Accordingly, we designed *Workout C* to be full of exercises that you work from beginning to end. Each exercise presents a program for you to enter or modify and explains exactly what you need to do to get the program running. We have taken care that the exercises cover one topic at a time, but we have also structured many of the examples so that you gradually add features to develop programs of some complexity. We strove to make the examples interesting and useful—there are card playing programs, calculator programs, programs that dump files, and programs that illustrate animated graphics.

There is no substitute for practice, and with this book you gain programming experience while learning C. Under the guidance of *Workout C*, you go through all the steps of programming in a real environment—you enter, compile, link, and run programs. You also modify programs to expand and improve their performance, and you even purposely introduce and analyze some programming errors. Not only do you learn the elements of C programming, but you learn about programming style. *Workout C* is packed with tips and suggestions, gleaned from decades of programming experience, about how to write good programs and how to write them efficiently.

Workout C is written for C language beginners, but if you have programming experience, with C or any other language, so much the better—you will progress faster and deeper into the material. We make no assumption that you are "computer savvy" and endeavor to use straight talk throughout. *Workout C* comes bundled with an excellent and easy-to-use compiler, Power C. So by the time you have finished the book, you will not only have new skills in C, but you will also have a compiler that you can continue to use.

You should approach this book in the spirit of learning while doing. By working each and every example, you will become familiar with important features of the editor, the compiler, and the linker. You will also become proficient in all of the steps of programming—the knowledge will be in your fingers as well as your head. We encourage you to experiment; perhaps you will have ideas about how to modify or improve many of the programs presented and you should follow the urge to enhance the programs on your own.

The best way to use this book is to start at the beginning and progress through the chapters in order, but you can also select a specific topic and go directly to that chapter. Here is what you will find in the chapters:

Chapter 1, "Getting Started," guides you through simple installation procedures for the Power C compiler and then familiarizes you with the steps involved in C programming.

Chapter 2, "The C Language," gives you an overview of C and guides you through the development of an example that illustrates the structure of a basic C program.

The next four chapters (3 through 6) present small programs to get you primed with enough information to progress to larger endeavors. Chapter 3, "Working with Data," introduces and shows you how to use the different kinds of data that C can handle.

Chapter 4, "Input from the Keyboard and Output to the Screen," explains the difference between external character data that you normally deal with at the keyboard and screen, and internal data, stored in the computer memory. In this chapter you will practice using input and output functions that you will frequently need.

In Chapter 5, "Operators and Expressions," you will use arithmetic operators to manipulate data and you will learn the rules of writing and evaluating expressions.

The next two chapters represent your first real opportunity to assume command of programs, because the topic is control statements. With Chapter 6, "Looping Control Statements," and Chapter 7, "Branching Control Statements," you will have accumulated sufficient skills to program a calculator and to begin the development of a card playing program.

Chapter 8, "Functions," addresses the heart of C programming. This chapter discusses software design strategies and uses different aspects of the card playing program, begun in Chapter 7, to illustrate how to set up functions.

Chapters 9, 10, and 13 present ways to deal with grouped or connected data. Chapter 9, "Arrays," shows you how to set up storage for large amounts of data, and culminates the card playing examples with a program for playing solitaire.

Chapter 10, "Strings," explains how to store text data in arrays, and provides a series of examples that illustrate the most important functions for processing text information.

In Chapter 11, "Pointers," we once again use smaller programs to explain, in clear terms, the important concept of using addresses to access data.

Chapter 12, "File I/O," extends the discussion of input and output functions to include disk files. Here you will create and read files in different ways, and you will develop a program (a dump utility) that allows you to see the contents of disk files.

In Chapter 13, "Structures and Unions," you will progressively develop a program that stores data for a fleet of automobiles. Through this series of examples, you will learn the advantages of using data structures to store diverse but related pieces of information.

In Chapter 14, "Bit Manipulation," we introduce some new operators for changing the smallest element of data, the bit, and then use the operators to perform some animated graphics.

Chapter 15, "Preprocessor," shows you how to tailor a program at compile time by inserting C *directives* into your source code.

Chapter 16, "More About Data Types," winds up the lessons on the features of C with a discussion of the important concept of data class.

Chapter 17, "Programming Technique and Style," summarizes many of the rules and suggestions presented throughout *Workout C* on how to write better programs, and covers some programming techniques not discussed elsewhere. This is not a long chapter, but you should not slight it; style is important and this topic deserves your attention.

We think you will like the hands-on approach that *Workout C* provides, and we wish you an enjoyable and successful learning experience with the materials.

CHAPTER 1
GETTING STARTED

Congratulations on your purchase of Workout C! C is an exciting programming language because it is in the mainstream of today's software products and tomorrow's new developments. Workout C will give you solid preparation for a rewarding future with this important language. This book is a tutorial that concentrates on programming examples. It includes the high-performance C compiler, Power C, so you have a complete package for a successful learning experience. Whether you are being introduced to C programming or are expanding your knowledge, the Power C compiler combined with the hands-on examples provide an excellent way to learn about C. With Workout C, not only will you see how correct C programs operate, but you will gain experience that will help you avoid many common programming mistakes. The examples show you how to use all of the great features of the C language. Some of them also illustrate problems that lead to compile and execution errors, so you can learn to recognize and avoid the pitfalls of this powerful language. You will have some fun with programs that play cards and illustrate animation, and you will also design some utilities to do such things as handle keyboard input and view (or dump) the contents of data files. Workout C also contains many tips on programming technique and style that lead to better programs.

You can readily work the examples with any C compiler, but the Power C compiler supplied is particularly easy to use, and the Workout C instructions contain Power C commands and responses. If you intend to use your own compiler, you can skip the next section.

INSTALLING Power C

The first thing you need to do is install the Power C compiler. To use Power C, you need an IBM PC, XT, AT, PS/2, or compatible computer with at least 320KB of memory. At minimum, you need two floppy disk drives, but we recommend a hard disk drive. The operating system must be MS DOS or PC DOS Version 2.0 or later. The Power C files come in a packed form on two 5.25-inch diskettes; we will refer to the first diskette as *disk 1* and the second diskette as *disk 2*. The installation program, INSTALL.EXE, on disk 1 unpacks the files and copies them to your directories. If you place disk 1 in drive A and type in the DOS directory command, dir A:, you will see the packed files:

```
C:\>dir A:

 Volume in drive A has no label
 Directory of  A:\

READ      ME          530  03-06-92    4:14P
INSTALL   EXE       15616  01-10-92    7:42p
COMPILER  ARC      218775  01-13-92    5:56p
EDITOR    ARC       61945  03-06-92    4:17p
          2 File(s)    126976 bytes free
```

The Power C compiler consists of several files that are packed into the large file, COMPILER.ARC. The file, EDITOR.ARC, contains the packed files for the Power C editor, which you can use to enter the source programs. If you already have a favorite editor that you are familiar with, you may choose to use it instead. Now place disk 2 in drive A and repeat the DOS directory command:

```
C:\dir A:

 Volume in drive A has no label
 Directory of  A:\

LINKER    ARC    154270    01-13-92   5:57p
HEADERS   ARC     24023    01-13-92   5:57p
EXAMPLES  ARC       752    03-06-92   3:32p
WC01      ARC       108    03-06-92   3:32p
```

```
          .
          .
          .
WC017     ARC       2380     03-06-92   3:32p
          3 File(s)      120832 bytes free
```

The file, LINKER.ARC, contains packed files that make up the Power C linker, a program that you will use to make the final, executable version of your programs. The second file on disk 2, HEADERS.ARC, contains the C header files (.h extensions). These files are not normally needed since the compiler uses a single packed header file named HEADERS.HHH by default. The remaining files contain the example programs for chapters 1 through 17.

In the procedures below, we represent the DOS prompt as C:\>. Following this prompt, we show the command entries that you should enter. The keys that you should press will appear as key symbols: for example, (ENTER) or (3).

Instructions for installation on a hard disk

By performing the following steps, you can install the compiler in a directory called WORKOUTC on your hard disk; you can substitute another name for WORKOUTC if you prefer. The Workout C files will take approximately 1.2 megabytes of disk space.

1. Run the installation program to copy files from the Power C disks to directories on your hard disk.
2. Include the new WORKOUTC directory in the PATH command of your AUTOEXEC.BAT file.

DETAILED INSTRUCTIONS FOR HARD DISK INSTALLATION:
Run the install program and respond to the installation prompts by pressing the Enter key after each one (this accepts the default selections shown in square brackets). The install program will unpack and copy all the files from disk 1, then prompt you to insert disk 2, after which it will unpack and copy all the files from disk 2.

```
C:\>A:INSTALL

Workout C requires approximately 1.2 Megabytes of disk space

Install on hard disk (H), 5.25 inch (5) or 3.5 inch (3)
[default=H]: (ENTER)

Name of directory in which to install the files
[default=c:\workoutc]: (ENTER)
c:\workoutc\read.me
c:\workoutc\pc.exe
c:\workoutc\pco.exe
c:\workoutc\headers.hhh
```

```
c:\workoutc\edit.com
     .
     .
     .
c:\workoutc\setup.edit
Insert Workout C Disk 2 in drive A
Press any key when ready ENTER
c:\workoutc\pcl.exe
c:\workoutc\pclib.mix
     .
     .
     .
c:\workoutc\examples\wc17\errors4.c

Installation complete
```

Now you have all the Workout C files on your hard disk. You need to make them accessible from any other directory by inserting a DOS PATH command in the AUTOEXEC.BAT file. If you have an AUTOEXEC.BAT file, it is located in the root directory, C:\. If it doesn't exist, you need to create it with the Power C editor. Bring up the AUTOEXEC.BAT file in the editor:

```
C:\>cd WORKOUTC

C:\>edit C:\AUTOEXEC.BAT
```

Then add the directory C:\WORKOUTC to the path command so that it reads:

```
PATH=<previous path command>;C:\WORKOUTC;
```

If there was no previous path command you should enter:

```
PATH=C:\WORKOUTC;
```

Save the file (by pressing ALT-F5) and leave the editor (by pressing ALT-F8). (The notation ALT-F5 means to hold down the Alt key while pressing the F5 key.) Finally, activate the path by running the AUTOEXEC batch file:

```
C:\>C:\AUTOEXEC
```

Instructions for installation with two floppy drives

By performing the steps outlined below, you can install Power C on a system with two 5.25-inch floppy disk drives. If you have high-density (1.2MB) disk drives, you will need two empty formatted disks. If you have lower-density (360KB) drives, you will need four empty formatted disks.

1. Format the new blank disks.
2. Run the installation program to unpack and copy files from the Workout C disks to your new disks.
3. Put the DOS command PATH=B: in the AUTOEXEC.BAT file on your boot disk so that compile and link commands can find the Power C files in drive B.

DETAILED INSTRUCTIONS FOR INSTALLATION ON TWO 1.2MB FLOPPY DISKS:

To format the new disks, place them one at a time in drive B and enter the DOS format command:

```
A:\>format B:
```

Label one of the new disks "Compiler/Linker/Editor," because you will use it while compiling, linking, and editing, and label the other disk "Headers/Examples," because it will contain Power C header files and source code for the examples that you work.

To install the Power C files, insert Workout C disk 1 in drive A, then run the install program and respond to the installation prompts as shown. You should fool the installation program by answering the first prompt as if you had 3.5-inch disks, because these are high density disks and the installation program will copy more files onto each of your 5.25-inch high density disks.

```
A:\>INSTALL

Workout C requires approximately 1.2 Megabytes of disk
space

Install on hard disk (H), 5.25 inch (5) or 3.5 inch (3)
[default=H]: (3)

You should have 2 formatted blank floppy disks.
Are you ready? (Yes or No)
[default=Y]: (ENTER)

Name of drive containing formatted disk
[default=B]: (ENTER)

Insert blank formatted disk #1 "Compiler/Linker/Editor" into
     drive B
Press any key when ready (ENTER)
```

```
B:pc.exe
B:pco.exe
B:headers.hhh

B:edit.com
      .
      .
      .
B:setup.edt

Insert Workout C Disk 2 into drive A
Press any key when ready (ENTER)
B:pcl.exe
B:pclib.mix
      .
      .
      .
B:setup.edt

Insert blank formatted disk #2 "Headers/Examples" into drive B
Press any key when ready (ENTER)
B:\headers\assert.h
B:\headers\bios.h
      .
      .
      .
B:examples\WC17\ERRORS4.c

Installation complete
```

This arrangement allows you to keep your source files on the Headers/Examples disk in drive A and the Compiler/Linker/Editor disk in drive B without changing disks between steps. You will normally make drive A the default drive, and you need to make the files in drive B accessible by issuing a DOS PATH command:

```
A:\>PATH B:
```

You may want to place this command in the AUTOEXEC.BAT file on your boot disk to avoid typing it each time you start up.

DETAILED INSTRUCTIONS FOR INSTALLATION ON FOUR 360KB FLOPPY DISKS:

To format the new disks, place them one at a time in drive B and enter the DOS format command:

```
A:\>format B:
```

Label one of the new disks "Compiler," because you will use it while compiling, label another disk "Linker/Editor," because you will use it while linking or editing, and label the third disk "Headers/Examples," because it will contain Power C header files and source code for the examples that you work. Label the Fourth disk "More Examples" because it will contain the remaining examples.

To install the Power C files, insert Workout C disk 1 in drive A, then run the install program and respond to the installation prompts as shown:

```
A:\>INSTALL

Workout C requires approximately 1.2 Megabytes of disk space

Install on hard disk (H), 5.25 inch (5) or 3.5 inch (3)
[default=H]: 5

You should have 4 formatted blank floppy disks.
Are you ready? (Yes or No)
[default=Y]: ENTER

Name of drive containing formatted disk
[default=B]: ENTER

Insert blank formatted disk #1 "Compiler" into drive B
Press any key when ready ENTER
B:read.me
B:pc.exe
B:pco.exe
B:headers.hhh

Insert blank formatted disk #2 "Linker/Editor" into drive B
Press any key when ready ENTER
B:edit.com
B:file.hlp
     .
     .
     .
B:setup.edt

Insert Workout C Disk 2 into drive A
Press any key when ready ENTER

B:pcl.exe
B:pcl:b.mix
     .
     .
     .
```

```
B:merge.exe

Insert blank formatted disk #3 "Headers/Examples" into drive B
Press any key when ready (ENTER)
B:\headers\assert.h

B:\headers\bios.h
      .
      .
      .
B:examples\WC08\TYPES.C

Insert blank formatted disk #4 "More Examples" into drive B
Press any key when ready (ENTER)
B:examples\wc09\ARRAY.C
      .
      .
      .
B:examples\WC17\ERRORS4.C
Installation complete
```

This arrangement allows you to keep your source files on the "Headers/Examples" disk in drive A and the Power C edit, compile, and link files in drive B. You will have to change disks in drive B for the edit, compile, and link steps because the first, "Compiler" disk contains the compiler, whereas the second, "Linker/Editor" disk contains the linker and the editor. You will normally make drive A the default drive, and you need to make the files in drive B accessible by issuing a DOS PATH command:

```
A:\>PATH B:
```

You may want to place this command in the AUTOEXEC.BAT file on your boot disk to avoid typing it each time you start up.

PROGRAMMING WITH Power C

Programming is a series of steps beginning with an idea of what a program should do and culminating with an operational program. There are seven distinct steps to programming, and if everything were to go right, you would progress directly from beginning to end, performing each step only once. However, programming is seldom that simple, so you will normally repeat the steps in a cyclical fashion. Software programming is very much a process of design, trial, and refinement. There are three major cycles in the lifetime of a program, as illustrated in Figure 1-1.

The design cycle

The first two steps in Figure 1-1 constitute the programming *design cycle*. We cannot overemphasize the importance of this phase of programming; time spent here is a wise

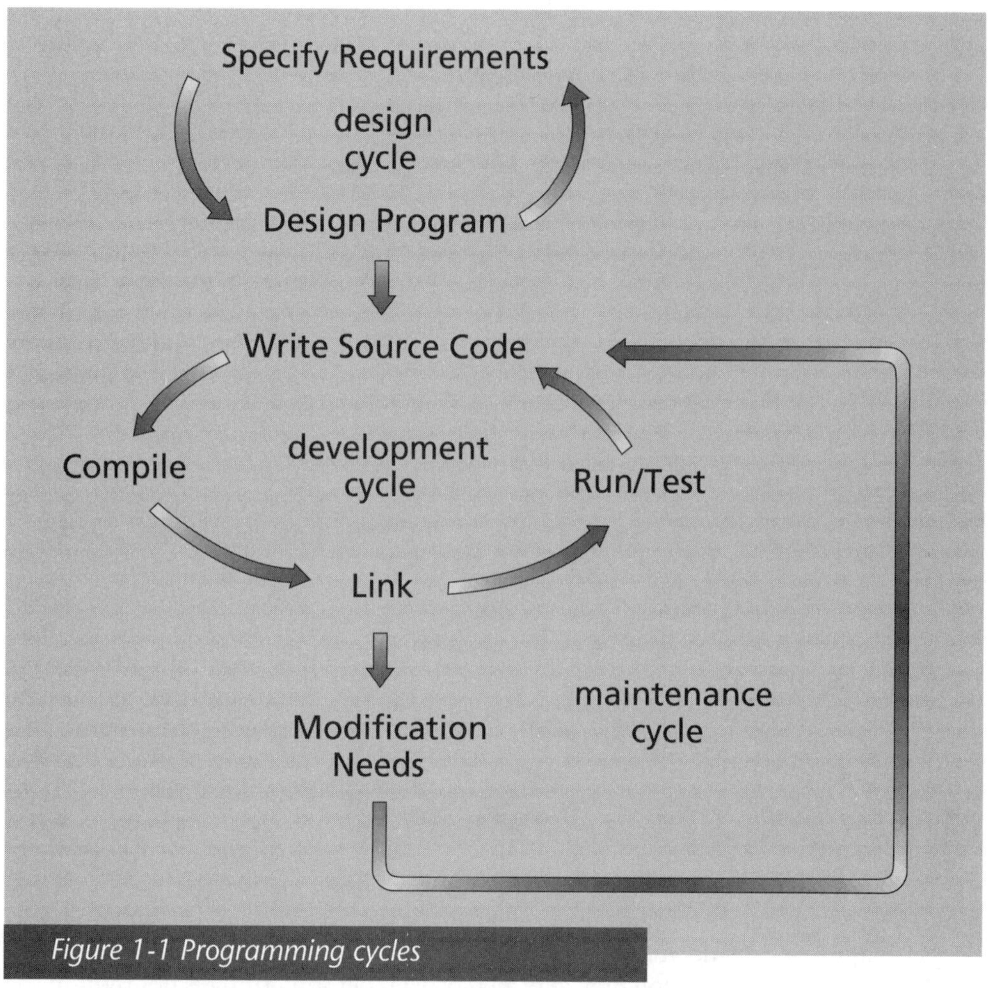

Figure 1-1 Programming cycles

investment. There is always great temptation to start writing code immediately, but you should resist and make sure you do not jump out of the design cycle too early. The time spent thinking about alternative ways to structure data and accomplish processing operations can be the most productive and enjoyable period of a programming project.

The design cycle consists of specifying the requirements and sketching out the design of a program. Requirements are determined by answering questions such as:

- Where does the program get data?
- What operations must be performed?
- What equipment must the program use?
- What does the program display on the screen, and when?

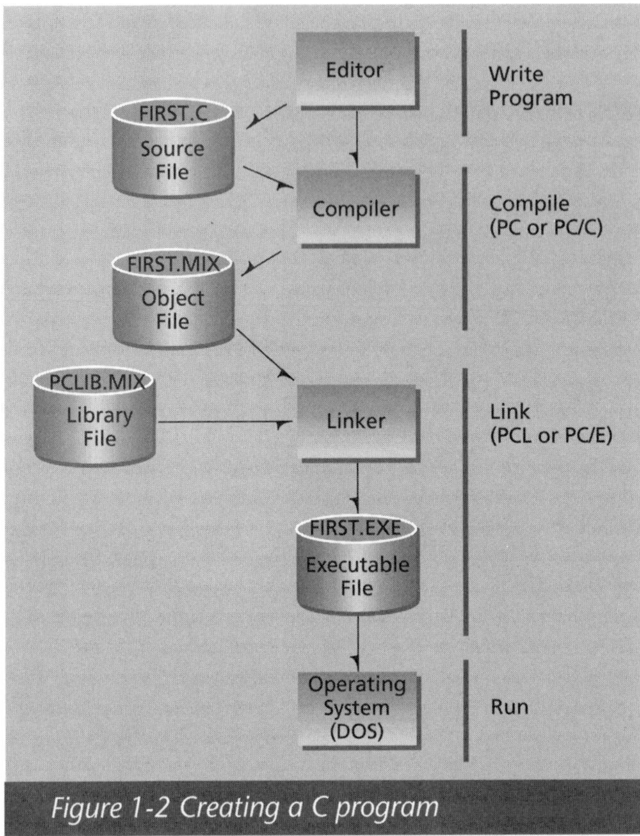

Figure 1-2 Creating a C program

For very simply programs you can just run through the requirements in your head (most of the examples in the book fit this category); for slightly larger programs you will probably need to make a list of requirements (only a couple of the examples in the book fit this category), and for complex projects that involve more than one programmer, you will need to develop a requirements document (there are no examples of this type in Workout C).

Once the requirements are known, you can design the program; this involves defining the data in some detail and laying out the sequence of operations. You might use a detailed data file layout, a list of program variables, and a program flow diagram to specify the design. The complexity of the design will match the complexity of the program; for very small programs, you can keep the design in your head, whereas large projects require formal documents.

During the design step, you may very well realize that something is not right in the requirements specification, so you go back and improve the requirements and then continue designing. Programming projects seldom have final specifications before programming begins—significant changes almost always occur. Don't be disturbed about this; be prepared for it by realizing that programming is a cyclical process. You can always jump back to the design cycle from the development cycle.

The development cycle

During the development cycle, you use software tools to create, test, and modify a program so that it matches your design. The basic tools that you need to build a C program are an *editor*, a *compiler*, and a *linker*. You use the editor to generate program statements in the form of lines of text, known collectively as *source code*. Then you run the source code through a compiler that generates *object code*. The object code is a translation of your program statements that the computer can understand. Finally, you use a linker to combine the object code for your program with other pieces of object code to produce the final, *executable code*. The source code, object code, and executable code all reside in different files. Figure 1-2 shows how to use these software tools to produce the different files that constitute your program.

The steps in the development cycle (Figure 1-1) correspond with the software tools shown in Figure 1-2. You **write** the source code with an **editor**, you **compile** the source code with a **compiler**, and you **link** the object code with a **linker**. In the fourth step, you **test** the program by running it with an operating system command. During the first series of runs, you will usually discover errors (also called *bugs*). You go back and repeat the **edit**, **compile**, and **link** steps to correct the bugs, then run again. You continue this process until the program has been thoroughly tested and performs according to its specifications. In the next three sections, we will discuss how to use the Power C tools that come with Workout C.

Using the Power C editor

You use an editor to create and modify source files. A C source file is a file of text characters, so any editor that produces a character file will work. If you have a favorite editor, you may prefer to use it, but the editor supplied with Workout C will serve quite nicely for the examples in this book. You may refer to Appendix A for complete instructions on how to use this editor, but you can easily create a C program with this editor by following the instructions below. If you have installed Power C on your hard disk according to the instructions earlier in this chapter, you have the examples for each chapter in a seperate directory. You can get some practice with the editor by repeating the first program example as follows:

1. Make C:\WORKOUTC\EXAMPLES\WC01 the current directory with the following DOS commands (the current directory is the disk directory that is currently active):

   ```
   C:\>cd WORKOUTC\EXAMPLES\WC01
   ```

   Note: As you progress through the book, you will access the examples for each directory in a similar fashion–by making the directory for that chapter the current directory.

   FLOPPY DISK OPERATION

   If you are working from floppy disks, insert the Headers/Examples disk into drive A and make it the current drive (enter A:)

2. Rename the original first example by entering the following DOS command:

   ```
   C:\>rename FIRST.C SAVE.C
   ```

3. Start up the editor and create a new source file named FIRST.C with the DOS command:

   ```
   C:\>edit FIRST.C
   ```

The characters, *EOB, mark the end of the file, which will move as you type in new text.

4. Type in these five lines using all lowercase characters exactly as shown:

```
#include <stdio.h>
main()
{
   printf("hello, world\n");
}
```

5. If you make a mistake, use BACKSPACE, INS, DEL, and the cursor keys (or Arrows) to make corrections.

6. Save the file by pressing ALT-F5.

You have just created a C program that will display a greeting. The program lines may be a bit mysterious to you, but we will defer discussion of the details until the next chapter. For now, let's get a little more practice with the editor. There are many features to the editor that you can become familiar with by referring to Appendix A or by browsing through the help screens listed when you press ALT-F1. Most of the editor operations you need are the ones you have just used—that is, open a file, enter text lines, modify characters, and save the results to a file. Sometimes you can more efficiently enter a program by duplicating similar sections of code rather than by typing them separately. You will find that the *block copy* feature is handy for this. You first mark a block of text, then you place the cursor at the beginning of the destination and copy the block of text. You activate the block commands by pressing CTRL-K and one other key. Here is an example of how you do it:

1. Move the cursor to the first column on row 4 (the beginning of the line with *printf*). Notice that the editor displays the current row and column for the cursor at the bottom of the screen. Now press CTRL-K-B to mark the beginning of the block. That is, hold down CTRL while pressing K, then B. The message "Marked beginning" should appear at the bottom of the editor screen.

2. Move the cursor down to the first column in row 4 (press the down arrow once), then press CTRL-K-K. The message "Marked end" should appear at the bottom. At this point, you have marked one line of text.

3. Leave the cursor where it is so that the next command will copy the line above the closing curly brace of the program. Press CTRL-K-C and the editor should duplicate the *printf* line.

You can mark and copy any desired section of text to any other location. Delete the line that you just duplicated by pressing CTRL-Y, and leave the editor by pressing ALT-F8. You previously saved the file, so you can quit without saving any of the recent changes—answer Y to the prompt <QUIT>REALLY? Now let's move ahead and learn how to use the compiler so that you can run this program.

Using the Power C compiler

The Power C compiler is a program named PC.EXE that you previously installed. This program reads your source file, compiles the source code into object code, and writes the result to an object file with the same base name and an .MIX file extension. You specify the name of the source file on the line with the compile command; if you don't specify a file extension, the compiler assumes it's a .C extension. Compile your new program by entering the following command:

```
C:\>PC FIRST
```

You should see the result:

```
Power C - Version 2.1.3
(C) Copyright 1989-1991 by Mix Software
Compiling ...
  112 lines compiled
Optimizing ...
    1 function optimized in 1 file
```

> **FLOPPY DISK OPERATION**
> If you are working from floppy disks, be sure that the Headers/Examples disk is in drive A, the Compiler disk is in drive B, and the current directory is drive A before entering the compile command.

The Power C compiler has an automatic *make* feature; it will only compile a source file that is newer (has a more recent date) than its object file. If the object file (.MIX) has a more recent date, then the source file (.C) has already been compiled, and a repeat compilation is unnecessary.

When the compiler ends without an error, it automatically runs the Power C optimizer, the PCO.EXE program. This program makes the object code smaller and faster. The object file FIRST.MIX should now be present in directory WC01; list the directory to see which files are present:

```
C:\>DIR

Volume in drive C has no label
```

```
Directory of  C:\WC01

.           <DIR>          11-02-91   1:17p
..          <DIR>          11-02-91   1:17p
FIRST    C           66    11-01-91   8:21p
FIRST    MIX        190    11-02-91   1:19p
      4 File(s)   8808448 bytes free
```

IF YOU HAVE PROBLEMS
If the compile result indicates an error or the object file is not present, then the source code is wrong—you should go back into the editor and make sure the source program is correct. If the compiler will not run, then the installation was not correctly completed—you should check to be sure that the WORKOUTC directory is specified in the PATH command of your AUTOEXEC.BAT file, and repeat the installation procedure if necessary.

You are now ready to link the object file to make an executable file. If you are working from a hard disk, you can combine the compile and link steps into one command. The compiler has options which you specify with a slash followed immediatly by an option letter (/option) on the compile command line; the option letter can be either uppercase or lowercase—it makes no difference. Appendix B lists all of the available options, but we will discuss only two of them here. If you specify the **/E** option when you run the compiler, it will execute the linker to create an executable file (.EXE). In this case, the compiler will only compile your program if the source file is more recent than the object file. If you also specify the **/C** option, the compiler will compile the source code before it links, regardless of the source file date. Thus, you can command a combined compile and link with the command:

```
C:\>PC/C/E FIRST
```

The result should be:

```
Power C - Version 2.1.3
(C) Copyright 1989-1991 by Mix Software
Compiling ...
  112 lines compiled
Optimizing ...
   1 function optimized in 1 file
Linking ...
FIRST.EXE created
```

This is the form of compile that you will use most often while working the examples in Workout C—a combined compile and link.

You can examine the sizes of the source (FIRST.C), object (FIRST.MIX), and executable (FIRST.EXE) files with a DOS directory command:

```
C:\>DIR

Volume in drive C has no label
Directory of  C:\WC01

.           <DIR>          11-02-91    1:17p
..          <DIR>          11-02-91    1:17p
FIRST   C          66      11-02-91    1:18p
FIRST   MIX       190      11-02-91    1:19p
FIRST   EXE      3008      11-02-91    1:19p
    5 File(s)    8808448 bytes free
```

The executable file is much larger than the source or object file because it includes code linked from the Power C library, PCLIB.MIX.

Using the Power C linker

The Power C linker is a program named PCL.EXE which you previously installed. This program combines your object files with existing Power C library files to create an executable file having the extension .EXE. When you run the compiler with the /E option, it executes the PCL program. You can also run the linker separately with the command:

```
C:\>PCL FIRST
```

The result should be:

```
Power C Linker - version 2.1.2
FIRST.EXE created
```

> **FLOPPY DISK OPERATION**
> If you are working from floppy disks, be sure that the linker disk is in drive B and that the current directory is drive A before entering the link command.

> **IF YOU HAVE PROBLEMS**
> If this step was not successful, check the WORKOUTC directory for the presence of the linker (PCL.EXE) and the Power C library file (PCLIB.MIX), and check directory WC01 for the presence of your object file (FIRST.MIX). If the linker or the library file is not present, then you need to reinstall Power C. If your object file is missing, then something went wrong in the previous compile step.

You will use PCL to perform a separate link step if you are working with 360KB floppy disks or you have more than one object file (in addition to the Power C library files). In this case, you specify all of your object files on the command line:

```
C:\>PCL FILE1.MIX, FILE2.MIX, FILE3.MIX
```

Running your program

You can run your program and obtain the display output just by typing the name:

```
C:\>FIRST
hello, world
```

With Power C, it is extremely simple to compile, link, and run a program—to summarize, you just issue the following two commands:

```
C:\>PC/C/E FIRST

C:\>FIRST
```

At this point, the program is complete and ready for continued use, but changes do not stop even then—this is where the maintenance cycle begins.

The maintenance cycle

Most programs are modified many times during their lifetimes, and the better programs have longer lives, so they are modified the most. The maintainence cycle, shown at the bottom of Figure 1-1, encompasses the development cycle, because once you decide to alter a program, you go through the same steps that occur in the original development cycle (modifying the source code, compiling, linking, and testing). Maintenance can be initiated by a need to modify how a program operates, by the discovery of a previously unknown bug, or by a requirement to transfer the program to another computer system. Maintenance only ends when a program ceases to be useful and is discarded. In the business world, it is very common for 80% of the total programming time to be devoted to maintenance. Thus, it is important to write programs that are easy to maintain by paying proper attention to structure, style, and commmenting.

In Chapter 2, you will become familiar with the structure of C programs and have a chance to develop a program from a very simple beginning.

CHAPTER 2
THE C LANGUAGE

This chapter begins with the "big picture" and sketches the basic form of a C program. It shows you the key ingredients of a C program and how the parts relate to one another. Then you will develop a program example, starting with the simplest possible form, and flesh it out with some specific C features that you will use throughout the book.

The last part of the chapter sketches the beginnings of C and discusses the current status of the language. C has become an enormously popular programming language; you will understand why if you know something about where C came from and how it developed. You will learn about the many advantages that brought C to its current prominence, and you will also learn about the few inevitable disadvantages.

ANATOMY OF A C PROGRAM

In this section, we will outline a C program and look at some of its important pieces. You needn't worry about grasping too much detail as you read through the material; the intent is to present an overview of a total C program that you can refer to later if necessary.

The basic building block of C programs is the *function*. A function is a separate block of code that performs a specific task. When you write a C program, you write it in terms of functions. A program goes back and forth between functions in a sequence that you specify by having one function *call* another. Within each function are *statements* that carry out the task of the function; certain statements and *directives* can also exist outside functions. Figure 2-1 shows how the source code for functions and groups of statements fit together to form a whole program. This is a program that displays a message informing you that it is executing, then it calls a second function that also displays a message when it executes.

The source code for this program resides in two files. The SIMPLE.C file contains the program statements that you would enter, and file stdio.h is a standard header file that is supplied with the compiler. Preprocessor #include directives are normally the very first items in a C source file. The *preprocessor* is the first stage of the compiler, and when it encounters an #include directive, it copies an external header file into the source file at that location. Figure 2-1 illustrates this by inserting stdio.h into a cutout at the top of the program—in actual practice, the preprocessor would replace the *#include* directive with the file contents.

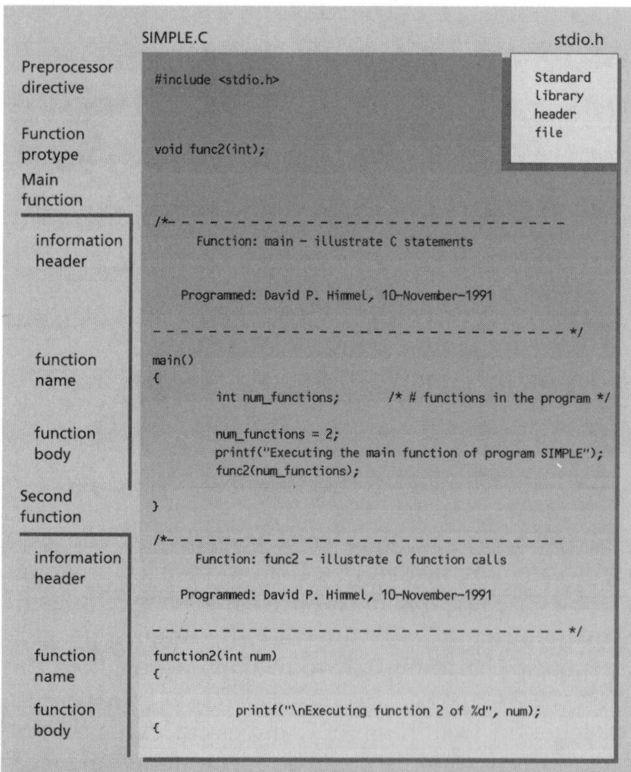

Figure 2-1 Anatomy of a C program

Other preprocessor directives, such as *#define*, also normally appear near the top of a source file. You use #define directives to replace certain items in the source code before the compiler begins its real work. These directives take effect from the place where they appear down to the bottom of the file, so it is reasonable to put them near the beginning.

Function *prototype* statements provide information that describes each function (except main()) so that the compiler can check for proper function calls before the link step. These prototype statements should be grouped into a section near the top of the program, as shown in Figure 2-1. Alternatively, you can place them in one or more separate *header* files that are referenced by *#include directives*.

Every C program must have a function named *main* such as that in Figure 2-1, because this is where the program begins executing. You can give other functions any name you wish, and you normally place them beneath main() in the source file. You can also place functions in separate files, in which case you compile more than one source file into an object file. When you link the object files, the linker makes the separate functions known to one another so that your programmed function calls can occur.

In C, you declare variables by stating *identifiers* (names) and *data types* for the variables; the data type determines how the variable will be handled, how much memory the compiler will allocate, and what kind of data can be stored in the variable.

Basically you define variables in one of two places: either inside a function, or outside all functions. When you define a variable outside all functions, it is known as a *global* variable, because it is accessible to all functions. When you define one inside a function, it is *local*, because the variable is accessible only to that function. The preferred location for global definitions is just above the main function, and local variable definitions belong at the beginning of each function.

All the program sections described so far serve as a "stage setting" for the functions, where the work actually occurs. The central part of each function is called the body, and this is where most of the executable statements appear. Curly braces { } mark the beginning and end of the body of a function. Every function, including the main function, has three necessary elements: a name, parentheses for calling parameters, and curly braces for the body. You arrange these elements like this:

```
func_name()
{
}
```

As you might expect, a program executes statements in the body of a function in the order in which they appear from top to bottom. There are control statements that can cause looping and branching to occur, which will alter the flow of execution, but the natural progression is from top to bottom.

We shouldn't overlook a very important item connected to every function—the information header. You should precede every function with a section of comments that explains the purpose and operation of the function; this is invaluable for future program maintenance.

C allows a great deal of freedom in the placement of program sections, and there is no single, correct way to order the sections of a C program. The layout of Figure 2-1 has proven to be effective, but it is only recommended—you can deviate from this placement of sections and statements when it is necessary or desirable.

USING WORKOUT C EXAMPLES

The heart of Workout C is the examples, which give you the opportunity to learn C through direct experience. Each example shows how to use a particular feature of C, and many examples start as a small program that grows as programming features are added. These so-called "focus" programs allow you to work with one topic at a time, yet build more complex programs. Some examples purposely ask you to induce an error in a program to become familiar with the appearance and effects of common programmming mistakes.

To get the maximum benefit, you should enter and run each example—do not rely on just reading the material. There is no substitute for the actual experience of typing in program statements, then compiling and running the program—this is a key factor in absorbing the details of each topic. During this process, you will think about the programs and gain some familiarity through repetition; you will also become familiar with the editor, compiler, and operating system commands.

Listing | Program name | Title phrase

Example number → 1.1 | FIRST.C | First C program

Action request → DO: Enter, compile, and run FIRST

Source code →

```
#include <stdio.h>
main()
{
      printf("hello, world\n");              /*1*/
}
```

Change marker → /*1*/

Results section → RESULT:

Compile command → C:\>p/c/e FIRST ← Not shown unless a compile error occurs

Compile result →

```
Power C - Version 2.0.1
(c) Copyright 1989 by Mix Software
Compiling ...
  119 lines compiled
Optimizing ...
    1 function optimized in 1 file
Linking ...
FIRST.EXE created
```

Run command → C:\>FIRST

Run result → hello, world

Discussion →

1. This is the famous first C program from the Kernighan and Ritchie book, "The C Programming Language".

2. The first line in the program, #include, pulls in some information about the standard input/output library.

3. Three of the lines are essential to any C program: main()
{
}

4. The printf() statement on line /*1*/ displays a greeting.

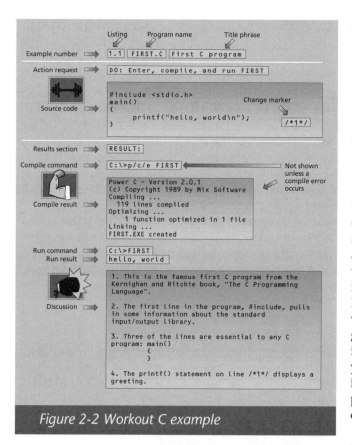

Figure 2-2 Workout C example

You can use all of the examples supplied by the installation, or you can choose to gain more experience with the editor and enter of modify examples. This installation program makes a separate directory to hold the example programs for each chapter (with names WC01, WC02, etc.). For example, the full name of the directory for Chapter 2 is:

```
C:\WORKOUTC\EXAMPLES\WC02
```

We suggest that you retain the examples (don't delete them) as you go through each chapter. Very often you will be asked to modify a program used earlier in the chapter, and occasionally even used in an earlier chapter. If you run short of disk space, you can delete the object (.MIX) and executable (.EXE) files and retain the source (.C) files.

Figure 2-2 shows a typical Workout C example.

The first line of each example contains an identifying number (a serial number attached to the chapter number), a program name (in capital letters), and a title phrase. You should use the program name for the name of the source file when you enter the program with the editor or when you select a supplied source file.

The second, action request line (DO:) contains brief instructions that you should follow to work the example. Usually these instructions will ask you to enter or modify the program, then compile and run it.

The source code for the program follows the action line. When the example asks you to enter a program, you should duplicate the program lines with the editor. When it asks you to modify a program, the lines to be modified will usually be marked with a numbered comment /*n*/ near the right margin. These marked lines are either new or they contain changes from the previous program. Unmarked lines in a modified program are unchanged and you don't need to edit them. The numbered comments also serve to identify program lines for the discussion that follows the example.

Following the source code is a section (beginning with the word RESULT:) that shows the results of compiling and running the program. Because successful compile results are so similar between programs, the compile messages are usually not shown unless a compile error is expected.

Below the result (in the ANALYSIS section), some numbered discussion lines explain important details of each example program; the discussion will often refer to numbered change comments in the source code.

Occasionally you will be asked to run a program several times to see the result of executing a program with different data. These requests will appear in separate action sections (DO: requests) that are followed by a RESULT: section and a ANALYSIS: section.

SOME FIRST EXAMPLES

In this section you will "get your feet wet" with some actual programs. You can start with the simplest possible C program and build it up to resemble the program shown in Figure 2-1.

The simplest possible C program

Here is the shortest C program that you can write; it does not do anything, but it will successfully compile and run. We present this program in the form of a Workout C example that shows you a title, an action request (DO:), the program, the results (RESULT:), and finally, a discussion (ANALYSIS:). This is your first Workout C example, but there are many more to follow.

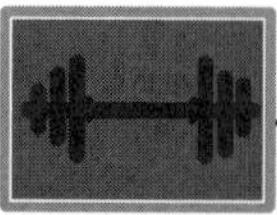

Listing 2.1 SIMPLE.C A simple C program

DO: Enter, compile, and run SIMPLE

```
main()
{
}
```

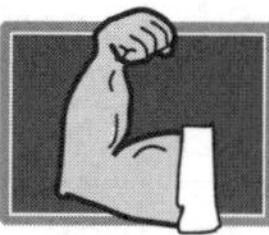

RESULT:

```
C:\>pc/c/e SIMPLE
Power C - Version 2.1.3
(C) Copyright 1989-1991 by Mix Software
Compiling ...
   3 lines compiled
Optimizing ...
   1 function optimized in 1 file
Linking ...
SIMPLE.EXE created

C:\>SIMPLE
```

ANALYSIS:

1. This program has the barest essentials of a C program; it has the name *main*, which tells the linker and operating system where to begin executing, it has the parentheses required of all functions even though there are no parameters, and it has curly braces to mark the boundaries of the body, which is empty.
2. When executed, the program does nothing.

C statements

A C *statement* is a sequence of identifiers, keywords, operators, and punctuation, ending with a semicolon (;). Not just any sequence will do; the order of the parts of a statement is called *syntax*, and the compiler checks for valid syntax. For instance, this is a valid statement:

```
age = 21;
```

But this is not:

```
= age 21;
```

The last statement will cause a compiler error. Some programming languages dictate the placement of source statements on lines in a source file—C does not. You can start a statement at the beginning of a line, or in the middle; you can have more than one statement on a line, or you can even split a statement into two or more lines. Of course, you don't want to just place statements willy-nilly in a source file—it would be a mess. As you go through Workout C, we will provide style guidelines that will help you to write quality programs.

The printf() function

Perhaps the most frequently used function from the standard I/O library is printf(). The purpose of printf() is to display formatted data, and it is used throughout the Workout C examples to illustrate operations and show results. When you call printf() and place some text surrounded by double quotes inside the parentheses, the text is displayed on the screen. Let's add such a printf() call to the SIMPLE program.

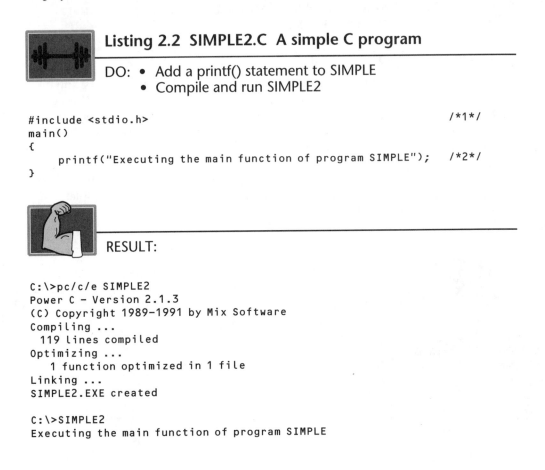

Listing 2.2 SIMPLE2.C A simple C program

DO:
- Add a printf() statement to SIMPLE
- Compile and run SIMPLE2

```
#include <stdio.h>                                          /*1*/
main()
{
     printf("Executing the main function of program SIMPLE");    /*2*/
}
```

RESULT:

```
C:\>pc/c/e SIMPLE2
Power C - Version 2.1.3
(C) Copyright 1989-1991 by Mix Software
Compiling ...
  119 lines compiled
Optimizing ...
   1 function optimized in 1 file
Linking ...
SIMPLE2.EXE created

C:\>SIMPLE2
Executing the main function of program SIMPLE
```

ANALYSIS:

1. This program contains numbered comments /*1*/ and /*2*/ to mark new lines that you should add to the previous program. Throughout Workout C, we will use these comments to show you where to add or change program lines.
2. On line /*1*/ a preprocessor *#include* directive copies the standard I/O header, stdio.h, into the program. Among other things, this header contains the function prototype for printf(), so the compiler can check the printf() statement.
3. Line /*2*/ is a statement that calls the printf() function to display some text on the screen. Notice that when the program executes, it does not display the double quotes ("); they only serve to indicate that the enclosed text is a *string constant.*

Identifiers and keywords

Identifiers are names that you give to constants, labels, variables, parameters, and functions. You compose identifiers by putting letters (A through Z), digits (0 through 9), and underscores (_) together in any combination that you wish, as long as you don't begin with a number. C is *case sensitive*—that is, a C compiler knows the difference between uppercase and lowercase characters—a variable named *age* is not the same as one named *AGE.*

C has 32 *keywords* that have special meaning to the compiler; keywords are always lowercase, and you cannot use them as identifiers. See Appendix F for a complete list of C keywords. You can use a keyword (*int*) and an identifier *(num_functions)* to add a variable to the program.

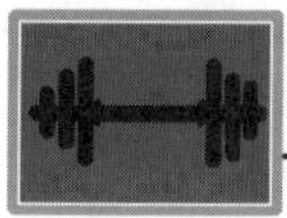

Listing 2.3 SIMPLE3.C A simple C program

DO:
- Add an assignment statement to SIMPLE2
- Compile and run SIMPLE3

```
#include <stdio.h>
main()
{
    int num_functions;                                      /*1*/

    num_functions = 1;                                      /*2*/
    printf("Executing the main function of program SIMPLE");
}
```

RESULT:

```
C:\>pc/c/e SIMPLE3
Power C - Version 2.1.3
(C) Copyright 1989-1991 by Mix Software
Compiling ...
 122 lines compiled
Optimizing ...
   1 function optimized in 1 file
Linking ...
SIMPLE3.EXE created

C:\>SIMPLE3
Executing the main function of program SIMPLE
```

ANALYSIS:

1. Line /*1*/ defines the local variable *num_functions*; the keyword *int* instructs the compiler to make it an integer data type and to allocate the amount of memory space appropriate for an integer (two bytes in this case).
2. Line /*2*/ assigns a value of 1 to variable *num_functions*; this is an *assignment statement.*

Comments

You can, and should, insert explanatory text into programs in the form of C *comments*. Comments are bounded by slash-asterisk sequences like:

```
/* This is a comment */.
```

A comment can share a line with a statement, occupy its own line, or even extend over several lines. Continue expanding the program by adding an information header that spans several lines and a comment that shares a line with a statement.

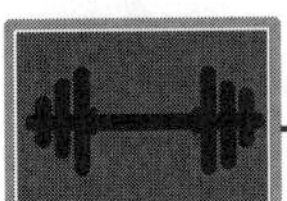

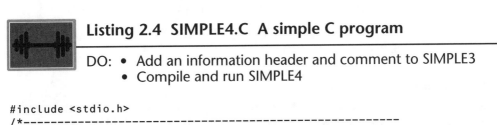

Listing 2.4 SIMPLE4.C A simple C program

DO: • Add an information header and comment to SIMPLE3
• Compile and run SIMPLE4

```
#include <stdio.h>
/*-----------------------------------------------------------
   MAIN FUNCTION - Illustrate C statements
```

```
   Programmed: David P. Himmel, 10-November-1991
   -------------------------------------------------------*/
main()
{
      int num_functions;       /* # of functions in the program */

      num_functions = 1;
      printf("Executing the main function of program SIMPLE");
}
```

RESULT:

```
C:\>pc/c/e SIMPLE4
Power C - Version 2.1.3
(C) Copyright 1989-1991 by Mix Software
Compiling ...
  125 lines compiled
Optimizing ...
    1 function optimized in 1 file
Linking ...
SIMPLE4.EXE created

C:\>SIMPLE4
Executing the main function of program SIMPLE
```

ANALYSIS:

1. There are two comments in this program; both comments begin with a slash-asterisk character pair (/*) and end with an asterisk-slash (*/).
2. The first comment spans the first five lines and is the information header for the main function. This is an abbreviated information header, but we want to keep this example short. Chapter 17 will explain all the things that should go into an information header.
3. The second comment briefly explains the purpose of variable *num_functions*.

Functions

Let's round out the last example of the chapter by adding a function to the SIMPLE program. The main function will call the new function, func2(), while passing a value to it, and the new function will display the value using printf().

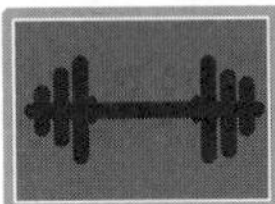

Listing 2.5 SIMPLE5.C A simple C program

DO:
- Add a function to SIMPLE4
- Compile and run SIMPLE5

```
#include <stdio.h>

void func2(int);
                                                              /*1*/
/*-----------------------------------------------------
    Function: main - Illustrate C statements

 Programmed: David P. Himmel, 10-November-1991
-----------------------------------------------------*/
main()
{
    int num_functions;           /* # functions in the program */

    num_functions = 2;                                        /*2*/
    printf("Executing the main function of program SIMPLE");
    func2(num_functions);                                     /*3*/
}

/*-----------------------------------------------------
    Function: func2 - Illustrate C function calls

 Programmed: David P. Himmel, 10-November-1991
-----------------------------------------------------*/
void func2(int num)                                           /*4*/
{                                                             /*5*/
     printf("\nExecuting function 2 of %d", num);             /*6*/
}                                                             /*7*/
```

RESULT:

```
C:\>pc/c/e SIMPLE5
Power C - Version 2.1.3
(C) Copyright 1989-1991 by Mix Software
Compiling ...
  133 lines compiled
Optimizing ...
   1 function optimized in 1 file
Linking ...
SIMPLE5.EXE created

C:\>SIMPLE5
Executing the main function of program SIMPLE
Executing function 2 of 2
```

ANALYSIS:

1. Seven changes were required to add the function to this program. Line /*1*/ is the prototype for the new function.
2. The total number of functions is now two, so you change line /*2*/ to assign a value of 2 to *num_functions*.
3. Line /*3*/ calls the new function with one *argument*, variable *num_functions*.
4. Lines /*4–7*/ define the new function; it has one parameter, *num* on line /*4*/, which takes its value from the calling argument.
5. The body of the function lies between the curly braces of lines /*5*/ and /*7*/—the single printf() statement on line /*6*/. This printf() statement introduces two new display features: the first is the newline character (\n), which causes the display cursor to move to the next line, and the second is the format specifier (%d), which causes the value of variable *num* to be displayed on the screen.

The examples in this chapter amount to a brief introduction to C programming. In the chapters that follow, you will probe deeper into the topics presented here and have a chance to explore all of the important features of C. The next two sections close out this introduction with a short narrative on the evolution of C and a few insights about the advantages of the language.

HISTORICAL PERSPECTIVE

C was developed in 1972 by Dennis Ritchie at AT&T's Bell Laboratories. He needed a new programming language suitable for writing the UNIX operating system; this operating system (and by extension the new language) had to be efficient and it had to be portable (easily run on different computers). Ritchie derived C from a language called B, which Ken Thompson had written in 1970 for the first UNIX operating system. In turn, B was based on many concepts from an earlier language called BCPL, developed by Martin Richards. Therefore, C inherited important characteristics from prior designs that intentionally addressed the real needs of professional programmers.

Throughout the '70s, the UNIX operating system, written in C, was improved and transported to many different computer systems. The popularity of C really took off after the introduction of the IBM personal computer (PC) in the 1980s. Whereas BASIC became popular because it was easy to learn, C gained acceptance because it was particulary suitable for developing small, fast programs for the PC. As PCs grew in speed and capability, C proved able to grow with them. Today the vast majority of commercial programs for PCs are written in C—business programs like word processors and spreadsheets, programs for scientific and engineering analysis, compilers for other programming languages, and even games and movie special-effects programs.

For years, the definitive reference for C was the first edition of a book written by Brian Kernighan and Dennis Ritchie, *The C Programming Language*. This book served as the de facto standard for the version of C known both as *common C* and as *K&R C*. In 1983, the American National Standards Institute (ANSI) established a committee to develop an official version of C. The committee finalized a document in 1988 that is now the accepted standard for the version of the language known as *ANSI C*. ANSI C includes virtually all of the features of common C so that older programs can continue to be used. Most C compilers (including Power C) now conform to the ANSI standard, and the material in Workout C is based on the ANSI standard.

CHARACTERISTICS OF C

Other programming languages are suited to particular applications for various reasons: ADA is required for military contracts, BASIC is easy to learn, COBOL has long been used for business purposes, FORTRAN is for scientific calculations, and PASCAL is a teaching language. C had its beginnings as a language for operating systems, but now it is used for a very wide range of applications and it is the language of choice for professional programmers and hobbyists alike. Here are the reasons:

C is portable

When you move a program from one computer system to another, some changes are always required; programs written in some languages require a lot of modification. C programs are often transported with little or no modification. C is the most portable language because it was initially designed to be so, and because from the beginning a de facto standard existed—the Kernighan and Ritchie book, *The C Programming Language*. As part of the design strategy for making C portable, the authors placed the I/O operations outside the central definition of the language. Most programming languages have I/O commands that are an inherent part of the language, but in C, the I/O operations are performed by calling separate functions located in a standard library. As separate functions, these operations can be easily tailored by compiler software companies to accomodate the needs and peculiarities of different computer systems.

C is fast

C source code compiles quickly, and the executable programs run fast. One reason is that many of the C operators correspond to hardware operations that are designed into the central processing unit (CPU) of any computer. Some examples are the operators that do arithmetic, the increment and decrement operators (++, --), and the operators that work with bits. Another reason for C's quickness is that it uses *pointers* to reference data. Pointers relate directly to how addressing is accomplished in computer hardware, leading to rapid data access. Also aiding fast data access is the rich set of C data types that match the natural organization of computer memory elements.

C is compact

C source code is terse. The statements are short but potent; you can write statements that carry out combined operations, and some operators perform two tasks (for instance, += does both addition and assignment). C source code compiles to small oject files for the same reasons that the programs run fast—because the data and operators correspond closely to hardware constructs.

C allows both low-level operations and high-level constructions

C places the programmer close to the computer CPU with low-level operations, but it also provides for higher-level constructions built around control statements like *for, if,* and *while*. There is an *80-20 rule* in programming that says a program often spends 80% of its time executing only 20% of the code. The robustness of C allows you to write 80% of a program using high-level statements that have a good, clear structure, yet you can optimize the critical 20% where necessary.

Disadvantages

There are two sides to every coin, and the freedom that C grants you to write powerful programs can also lead to dangers. The designers of C worked from the premise that a C programmer would be well aware of what he or she is doing and should be given wide latitude. As a consequence, there are aspects of C, particularly related to pointers, where it is all too easy to make serious mistakes.

Many programmers find the syntax of C to be difficult to learn, but this becomes a temporary objection that quickly recedes as you become used to the language.

Some of the symbols in C have more than one meaning; the ampersand (&), for example, plays a role in three different operators, the address operator (&), the logical AND operator (&&), and the bitwise AND operator (&). Although the symbols are not really ambiguous because of context, they often cause some initial confusion when you are learning the language, and they can cause inadvertent programming errors.

Taken in perspective, the disadvantages outlined here are relatively minor, and you can go a long way toward avoiding the problems related to them by following good programming style.

Programming in C can be an exciting art. Programming is mundane if you merely write programs; the pursuit of **good** programs makes programming interesting and exciting. A good program goes beyond fulfilling its basic purpose. A good program is efficient, easy to learn, and forgiving of a user's mistakes—generally a pleasure to run. The source code is also clear, readable, and a pleasure to work with. A quality program is the result of attention to design during the early stages of programming and the constant practice of good programming style. Workout C will help you gain the skills that will allow you to successfully pursue the art of C programming.

CHAPTER 3
WORKING WITH DATA

Data is the basic material that a computer program uses to do its work. Computers are capable of processing enormous amounts of data, and as a programmer, you control that processing. An important part of this control is choosing how to allocate computer memory to hold data. In this chapter you will learn that there are different types of data suited for different purposes. You will also see that there are tradeoffs between memory size and speed that are associated with choosing certain data types.

C uses identifiers to refer to sections of memory that you allocate for data, and you will learn how to name *variables* with identifiers.

A program must load data into memory to use it. This chapter concentrates on how to set data values in memory with *constants*, whereas the next chapter will cover some methods for transferring data into and out of memory.

DATA IN COMPUTER MEMORY

Data usually resides either in computer memory or in disk storage. Computer memory is also called random access memory (RAM), and it takes the form of electronic chips mounted on printed circuit boards inside your computer chassis, as shown in Figure 3-1.

Disk storage is available either on your hard disk unit or diskettes that you place in the removable disk drives. Both types of disks store data on a spinning magnetic sur-

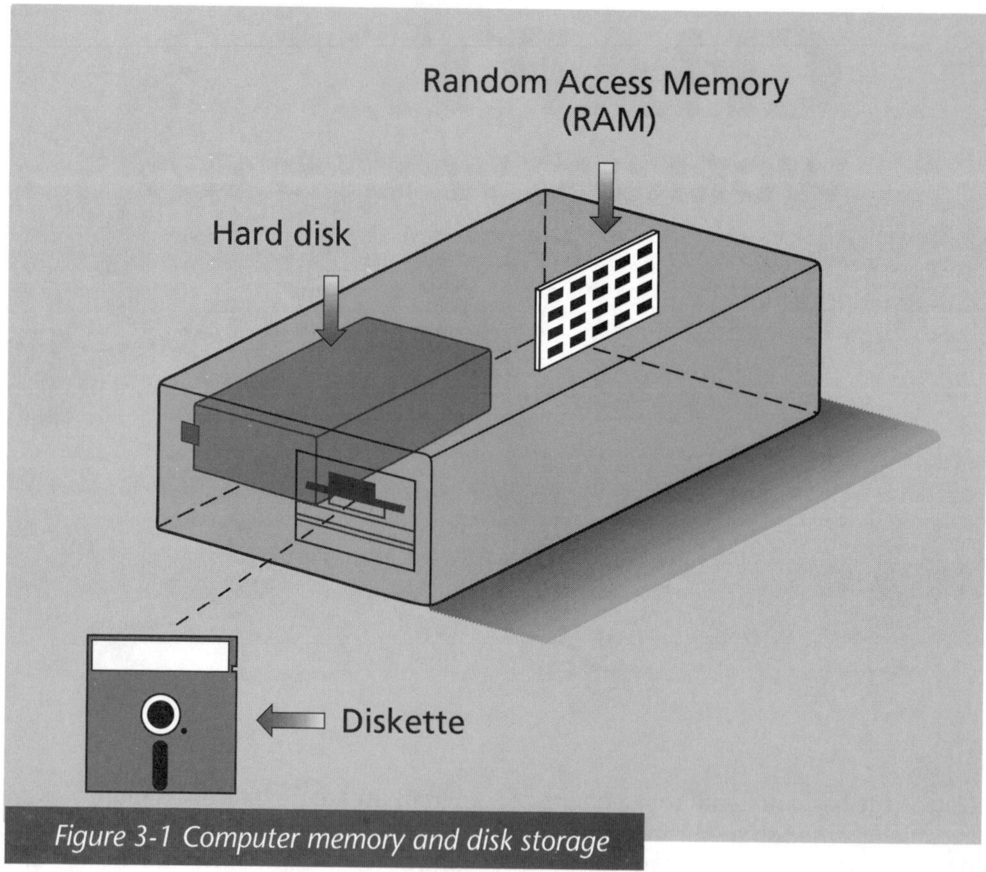

Figure 3-1 Computer memory and disk storage

face. Recently, optical disks have also become a practical alternative for storing large amounts of data. Disk storage is nonvolatile—the data remain there after you turn the computer off, so this is where the programs and data are kept for long-term storage. In contrast, the computer memory is volatile—all the programs and data that reside there are lost when you turn the power off. Before you can run a program, you must first load

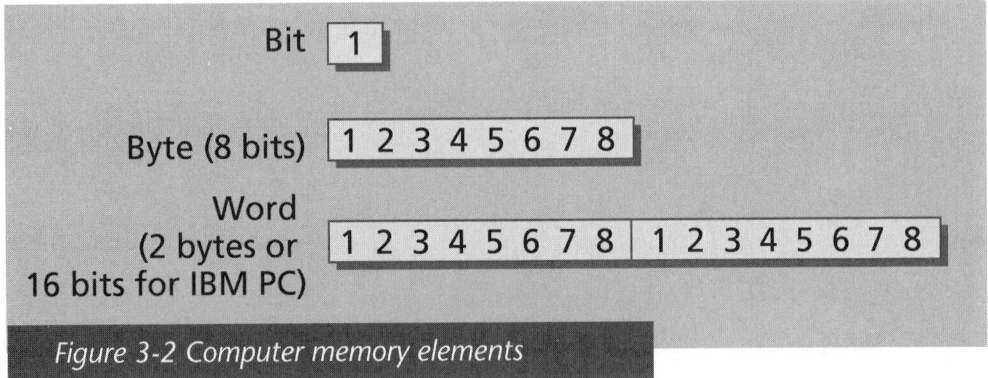

Figure 3-2 Computer memory elements

it from disk storage into computer memory; the operating system (DOS) loads a program in response to your command to run the program. Data must also be brought into computer memory before a program can make use of it; you make this happen by specifying constants within a program or by writing statements that read data from the keyboard or disk files.

Computer memory is composed of small pieces, or elements, and C provides different types of data built from these elements. Figure 3-2 shows the basic elements of computer memory.

The smallest element of computer memory is the binary digit, or *bit*. A bit can have a value of either 0 or 1 (the only binary digits allowed). The next larger memory element is the *byte*, which is made up of 8 bits. A byte can hold any one of 256 different values. The next larger computer memory element is the *word*, which is made up of 2, 4, or more bytes. The number of bytes in a word depends on the computer model—an IBM PC has 2 bytes (16 bits) per word, whereas a DEC VAX has 4 bytes (32 bits) per word.

DIFFERENT TYPES OF DATA

There are four basic data types in C: integers, characters, floating-point numbers, and large floating-point numbers. Except for size, the latter two types of floating-point numbers are much alike, but C classifies them separately. The data type determines what kind of data you can use in a variable, the amount of memory the compiler allocates for a variable, and how the program treats the data. The data type of a variable is set by the keyword (*int, char, float, double*) that you use in the declaration of the variable. You can use other keywords (*long, short, signed, unsigned*) to qualify specific types of variables within the four basic groups. Table 3-1 summarizes the basic data types and the keywords that you can use to declare them.

Data type	Declaration keyword	Size	Power C size
Short integer	short int short	Less than or equal to int— Minimum of 2 bytes for ANSI C	2 bytes
Integer	int	Less than or equal to long	2 bytes
Long integer	long int long	Minimum of 4 bytes for ANSI C	4 bytes
Character	char	1 byte	1 byte
Floating-point	float	Less than or equal to double	4 bytes
Large floating-point	double float double		8 bytes

Table 3-1 Data types

Notice that C specifies the size of *int* and *float* as less than that of *long* and *double,* respectively—and different compilers are free to set these sizes differently within the prescribed limits.

The first program, SIZE, shows how to use the sizeof() operator to discover the amount of memory that your compiler allocates to each data type. An *operator* is a special symbol in C that processes some data (operands) and returns a result. The very useful sizeof() operator returns the size in bytes of any data type inserted in the parentheses. For instance, you could obtain the size of *int* with:

```
sizeof(int)
```

The parentheses are optional, so you could just as well write:

```
sizeof int
```

However, we recommend you use parentheses because they clearly associate the data type with the *sizeof* operator and separate the whole item from other items.

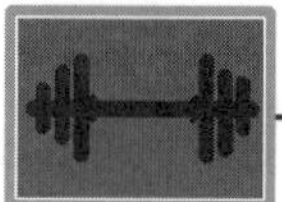

Listing 3.1 SIZE.C Sizes of data types

DO: Enter, compile, and run SIZE

```
main()
{
     printf("\n# bytes for a short integer = %d", sizeof(short));
     printf("\n# bytes for a basic integer = %d", sizeof(int));
     printf("\n# bytes for a long integer = %d", sizeof(long));

     printf("\n\n# bytes for a character = %d", sizeof(char));
```

```
    printf("\n\n# bytes for a floating-point number = %d",
           sizeof(float));
    printf("\n# bytes for type double = %d", sizeof(double));
}
```

RESULT:

```
C:\>PC/C/E SIZE
Power C - Version 2.1.3
(C) Copyright 1989-1991 by Mix Software
Compiling ...
   12 lines compiled
Optimizing ...
   1 function optimized in 1 file
Linking ...
SIZE.EXE created

C:\>SIZE

# bytes for a short integer = 2
# bytes for a basic integer = 2
# bytes for a long integer = 4

# bytes for a character = 1

# bytes for a floating-point number = 4
# bytes for type double = 8
```

ANALYSIS:

1. The SIZE program introduces two new items: the sizeof() operator and some keyword abbreviations (*short* and *long*).
2. In the first three printf() statements, the program asks for the sizes of the data types *short, int,* and *long*. Here the program has abbreviated *short int* to *short* and *long int* to *long*—both abbreviations are allowed by the compiler and both are commonly used. You can see from the output of program SIZE that Power C has chosen to make *short* and *int* data types the same size—it allocates 2 bytes of memory for each; however, type *long* has a size of 4 bytes.
3. The next printf() statement displays the size of type *char,* which is 1 byte.
4. The last two printf() statements display the sizes of data types *float* and *double,* which are 4 bytes and 8 bytes, respectively, for Power C on an IBM PC.

With Power C your compiled results should look exactly like the lines that follow the caption RESULT: in the previous program. This is what you will see when a program successfully compiles and links. Power C displays each step of the process (Compiling..., Optimizing..., Linking...) and then displays the result of each step (12 lines of code were compiled, one function was optimized, and SIZE.EXE was created by the linker). The compiler will display this same block of information for each error-free program that it compiles. This would become very repetitious if we included it with every example, so we will include it with this program example only and leave it out from now on unless an error occurs. When you have errors in a program, the compiler gives specific messages with information about the error and which line of your program was responsible. You will experience some compile errors a little later in this chapter.

As you work the examples, you will gain first-hand knowledge about the kind of information for which each data type is most suited, and you will learn that there are tradeoffs between memory size and processing speed for the different types. Generally, the integer data types (*char, int, long*) require less memory, allow faster processing, and have a more limited range of values, whereas floating-point data types (*float, double*) can hold very large or very small values, but require more memory and are slower.

CONSTANTS AND VARIABLES

In C you refer to data in computer memory by using *constants* and *variables*. Variables are memory locations that can change value. You can set or change the value of a variable in any number of ways—by assigning (copying) the value of another variable, by setting it to the value of a constant, by reading data from the keyboard, or by taking a value from a file. Constants are also values stored in computer memory, but they do not change. You can assign the values of constants to variables, but you cannot assign new values to constants.

Defining variables

Before you can use a variable, you must *define* it. Defining a variable accomplishes three things: (1) It establishes the data type, (2) it gives the variable an identifier (a name), and (3) it reserves memory for the variable. Normally you will define variables at the beginning of a program, as shown in the following two programs. The programs do not generate any output, so there is no need to compile or run them. These programs just give a few quick examples of how to define variables. The first program allocates storage in memory for an integer number, an alphabetic character, and a floating-point number.

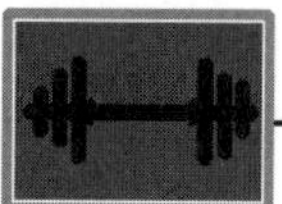

Listing 3.2 DEFINE.C Define some variables

DO: Examine program DEFINE while reading the analysis

```
main()
{
```

```
    int   number;          /* int allocates two bytes of memory    */
    char letter;           /* char allocates one byte of memory    */
    float fraction;        /* float allocates four bytes of memory */

                           /* These memory allocation sizes apply
                              to IBM PCs--they could be different
                              for other computer systems. */
}
```

ANALYSIS:

1. The statement beginning with the keyword *int* (the abbreviation for integer) defines a variable of the data type *integer* and gives it the identifier *number*. Similarly, the keywords *char* and *float* declare variables of the data type *character* and *floating-point* with identifiers *letter* and *fraction*, respectively.
2. The three definitions also allocate memory to hold values that may be assigned to the variables: for Power C, *int* allocates 2 bytes, *char* allocates 1 byte, and *float* allocates 4 bytes.
3. To the right of each definition statement is a *comment* that explains something about the statement.

Comments are enclosed by slash-asterisk (/*) and asterisk-slash (*/) symbols, and they are allowed anywhere within a C program. You should use comments to clarify what is occurring in your program. Comments can start and end anywhere, and they can span several lines between start and finish if you have a lot to say, as in the last comment in the program DEFINE.

You can define as many variables of as many different types as you need for your program. There is more than one way to define several variables, and some ways are better than others. The following program shows three ways to present variable definitions; all three forms are acceptable to the compiler, but not all are recommended.

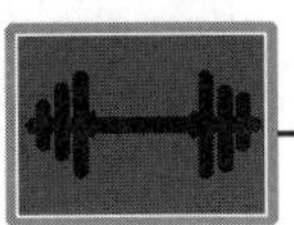

Listing 3.3 DEFINE2.C Define more than one variable of the same type

DO: Examine program DEFINE2 while reading the explanations

```
main()
{
    int number;              /* Number of pizzas ordered   */
    int number_delivered;    /* Number of pizzas delivered */

    char letter,             /* A letter of the alphabet      */
```

```
          next_letter;        /* The next letter of the alphabet */

    float fraction, tiny_fraction;  /* Not recommended */
}
```

ANALYSIS:

1. The preferred form of defining multiple variables is used for *number* and *number_delivered,* in which the program declares each variable with a separate statement. This makes future changes easier and allows individual comments to be attached.
2. You can define two or more variables of the same type with one statement by separating variable names with commas, even if the variables are on different lines, as with the declaration of *letter* and *next_letter*. This is an alternative form that allows a separate comment to be attached to each variable, and it is also recommended.
3. The style used in defining the floating-point variables *fraction* and *tiny_fraction* is **not** recommended because the variables are crowded onto a single line with limited opportunity for comments.

Names of variables—identifiers

The names that you use to declare variables are called *identifiers*. You can use almost any combination of letters and numbers in an identifier; however, there are a few simple rules to observe when choosing identifiers.

First of all, case is important with identifiers. If two identifiers contain the same letters, but one is uppercase and the other is lowercase, then the C compiler will treat them as different identifiers. For example, *letter* is not the same identifier as *LETTER*, and *Letter* is different from either of the first two identifiers.

An identifier must begin with either a letter (A through Z, uppercase or lowercase) or an underscore (_), and it must contain only letters, digits (0 through 9), and underscores. The program DEFINE3 does not attempt to do anything except define several variables; it will not execute even if you try to execute it, because the program contains some errors. See the next section, "Looking at compile errors," for information about the compile error messages.

Listing 3.4 DEFINE3.C Try some different identifiers

DO: Add some lines to the previous program and compile

```
main()
{
```

```
    int number;
    int number_delivered;
    int Number;      /* Different from "number", above          */
    int Number_1;    /* Digit is ok anywhere but the beginning  */
    int 1_Number;    /* Illegal--must begin with a letter       */
    int Number_#;    /* Illegal--# is not a letter or digit     */
    INT Number_1;    /* Illegal--keyword int must be lowercase  */
    int _Number_;    /* Not recommended--reserved for system IDs */
    int int;         /* Keyword cannot be used as an identifier  */

    char letter;
    char next letter;       /* Spaces are not allowed */

    float fraction;
    float tiny-fraction;    /* Illegal--hyphen is not allowed */
}
```

RESULT:

```
C:\PC/C/E DEFINE3
Power C - Version 2.1.3
(C) Copyright 1989-1991 by Mix Software
Compiling ...
DEFINE3.C(7):  int 1_Number;   /* Illegal--must begin with a letter */
************        ^  2  ^104
    2: Identifier expected in a type declaration
  104: Undeclared identifier
-------------------------------------------------------------------
DEFINE3.C(8):  int Number_#;   /* Illegal--# is not a letter or digit */
************        ^  9
    9: Right braces expected
-------------------------------------------------------------------
DEFINE3.C(9):  INT Number_1;   /* Illegal--keyword int must be lowercase */
************        ^ 14, 14
   14: ';' expected
-------------------------------------------------------------------
DEFINE3.C(11): int int;        /* Keyword cannot be used as an identifier */
*************       ^  2
    2: Identifier expected in a type declaration
-------------------------------------------------------------------
DEFINE3.C(14): char next letter;      /* Spaces are not allowed */
*************       ^ 14   ^158
   14: ';' expected
  158: Redefinition of a global variable
-------------------------------------------------------------------
DEFINE3.C(17):  float tiny-fraction;   /* Illegal--hyphen is not allowed */
*************       ^ 14   ^158
   14: ';' expected
  158: Redefinition of a global variable
-------------------------------------------------------------------
```

```
DEFINE3.C(18):}
*************       ^ 3
   3: Variable or function declaration expected
--------------------------------------------------------------------
     18 lines compiled
     11 Compile errors
```

ANALYSIS:

1. The compiler accepts the identifiers *number* and *Number* as being distinct from one another because they differ in the use of uppercase letters.

2. The compiler accepts an identifier ending with a digit, *Number_1*, but it does not accept an identifier **starting** with a digit, *1_Number*, on line 7. The error message says, "Identifier expected in a type declaration," meaning the compiler did not recognize the name as an identifier.

3. Using a special character (#) that is not a letter or digit causes the error message on line 8.

4. The compiler is case-sensitive regarding keywords, as evidenced by the error from line 9—the keyword *int* must be lowercase. As a matter of fact, all C keywords are lowercase.

5. It is not a good idea to start or end an identifier with an underscore, as with *_Number_*, even though the compiler has no trouble with it. This form usually signifies an identifier used by systems programmers for the internal operating system.

6. You cannot use a keyword for the name of a variable, as on line 11.

7. Spaces are not allowed within identifiers, so the compiler has found an error on line 14.

8. Don't confuse the hyphen (-) with the underscore (_) as on line 17; they are distinctly different characters and the compiler knows the difference.

9. The final error on line 18 was induced by one or more of the other errors that occurred.

In C, you use these same rules of composition to form identifiers wherever they are needed—not just for variables, but also to name symbolic constants, functions, and structures.

Looking at compile errors

The sidebar below explains how to interpret the error messages generated by the Power C compiler.

You may notice that a compiler sometimes generates error messages that are side effects of another error and don't necessarily tell you anything significant (like the last error in the program DEFINE3). Knowing this, when you can't figure out the reason for an error and have already corrected other errors, you should just recompile and see if the mystery error will disappear.

A compiler does its work in several phases (preprocessor, compilation, optimization, link) and errors can occur during any phase. During the preprocessor and compilation stages, the compiler can detect *syntax* errors but not *logic* errors. The errors from program DEFINE3 are syntax errors. Syntax refers to the way keywords, variables, constants, and punctuation relate to each other. The compiler knows how legal C statements should be composed, and it can report such errors, but it cannot predict what you intend the overall program to accomplish, so it cannot report logic errors.

Anatomy of a Power C compile error

When a compile error occurs, the compiler displays several lines of information similar to the following, which is the first error from the program DEFINE3:

```
DEFINE3.C(7):  int 1_Number; /* Illegal--,uist begin with a letter*/
************       ^ 2  ^ 104
     2: Identifier expected in a type delcaration
   104: Undeclared identifier
------------------------------------
```

The first line lists the name of the program followed immediately by the source line number of the error in parentheses. Then a colon appears and Power C displays the text of the offending source line. Just below the source text, a caret symbol (^) marks the approximate location of the error(s), and an error message number appears along side the caret marker. The compiler repeats the message number(s) below this, and attaches an explanation of the nature of the error. Finally, Power C delineates the error with an underline running across the display. Power C also writes the errors to a file (c.err) so that you can print or examine them at leisure.

Storing data values in memory with constants

Once you have defined a variable, it is ready to take on values. Perhaps the simplest way to assign a value is to use a constant. To assign a constant, you simply put the variable on the left side of an equal sign and the constant on the right. When you assign a constant to a variable, you store that value in the memory area that is allocated for the variable. The following program shows two ways to assign integer constants.

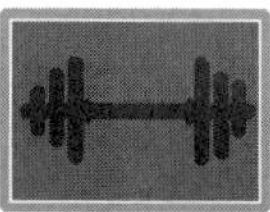

Listing 3.5 INIT.C Initialize the value of some integers

DO: Enter, compile, and run INIT

```
main()
{
      int cokes;
      int eggs = 12;

      cokes = 6;
      printf("We bought %d cokes and %d eggs.", cokes, eggs);
}
```

RESULT:

```
C:\>INIT
We bought 6 cokes and 12 eggs.
```

ANALYSIS:

1. The compiler interprets the numbers 6 and 12 in this program as decimal integer constants.
2. The program defines the variable *cokes,* then it defines variable *eggs* and assigns the value 12 to it at the same time.
3. The next statement assigns a constant to the variable *cokes,* causing the value 6 to be stored in the previously allocated memory word.
4. The printf() function displays data on the screen. Some of the characters used with printf() are format control characters (such as %d)—they determine how the data will be displayed. You need one such specifier for each variable you display. You will learn all about the printf() function and its format control characters in Chapter 4.

If you initialize a variable in the definition statement (like the statement, *int eggs = 12;*), you save a line of code and initialize the variable at the earliest possible opportunity. Sometimes, though, you need to set the initial value of a variable more than once in different parts of a program, or you may want to initialize a variable close to where it will be used instead of at the very beginning of the program. Under these circumstances, a separate assignment statement is needed (like the statement, *cokes = 6;*).

Defining symbolic constants

Symbolic constants are identifiers (names) that are synonymous with associated constants. The same rules apply to both symbolic identifiers and variable identifiers. Symbolic constants are handled by the compiler *preprocessor*, which, as its name implies, is a process that occurs before actual compilation begins. The preprocessor is a part of the compiler, but it is a step that only alters the source code in preparation for the main compile steps. Preprocessor *directives* are statements that begin with the pound sign (#). The define directive, consisting of *#define* followed by an identifier and then a value, sets up a symbolic constant. The following directive defines the symbolic constant *TRUE* to have the value 1.

```
#define TRUE 1
```

During the preprocessor step, the compiler replaces the identifiers of all the symbolic constants in the program with the corresponding defined values. Symbolic constants make a program much more readable and provide a way to centralize values that you can use in many places. Unlike a variable, the value of a symbolic constant is fixed during compilation and you cannot change it later in the program. The next program shows you how to use symbolic constants.

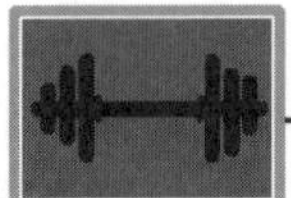

Listing 3.6 INIT2.C Define symbolic constants

DO:
- Add symbolic constants to the previous program
- Compile and run INIT2

```
#define DOZEN    12                                          /*1*/
#define SIX_PACK  6                                          /*2*/
main()
{
      int cokes;
      int eggs = DOZEN;                                      /*3*/

      cokes = SIX_PACK;                                      /*4*/
      printf("\nWe bought %d cokes and %d eggs.", cokes, eggs);
}
```

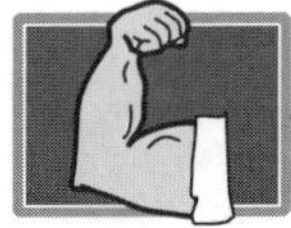

RESULT:

```
C:\>INIT2
We bought 6 cokes and 12 eggs.
```

ANALYSIS:

1. The numbered comments /*n*/ out to the right mark the lines that you should add or change.
2. The first two lines of the program define the symbolic constants *DOZEN* and *SIX_PACK*, which are synonymous with 12 and 6, respectively.
3. The preprocessor will replace any occurrence of *DOZEN* with the value 12 and any occurrence of *SIX_PACK* with 6, so that the program INIT2 is really the same as the previous program, INIT, when the preprocessor is finished with it.

You must use a separate preprocessor statement to define each symbolic constant. You should usually locate preprocessor directives above the opening *main* statement. It is a universal convention to use uppercase letters for the names of symbolic constants in C; notice that the underline (_) character is perfectly acceptable, as with *SIX_PACK*.

Types of constants

C provides different types of constants: integer constants are formed by using the digits 0–9; character constants are enclosed in single quotes (like 'A'), and floating-point constants use the ten numeric digits and a decimal point (like 98.6). The next progam gives you a chance to use these different types of constants.

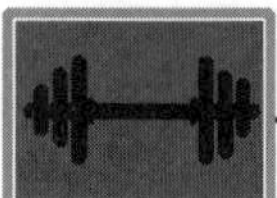

Listing 3.7 INIT3.C Use different constant types

DO:
- Add character and floating-point constants to INIT2
- Compile and run INIT3

```
#define DOZEN        12     /* Integer constant        */
#define SIX_PACK     6      /* Integer constant        */
#define DOLLAR_SIGN '$'     /* Character constant      */
#define PRICE        8.37   /* Floating-point constant */
main()
{
        int  cokes;
        int  eggs   = DOZEN;
        char  dollar = DOLLAR_SIGN;                          /*1*/
        float amount = PRICE;                                /*2*/

        cokes = SIX_PACK;
        printf("\nWe bought %d cokes and %d eggs for %c%.2f.",
               cokes, eggs, dollar, amount);                 /*3*/
}
```

RESULT:

```
C:\>INIT3
We bought 6 cokes and 12 eggs for $8.37.
```

ANALYSIS:

1. The program defines the symbolic constant *DOLLAR_SIGN* to be the character '$', and it defines the symbolic constant *PRICE* to be the floating-point constant 8.37.
2. The definition statements just below main() in this program use the keywords *int*, *char*, and *float* to declare different variable types.
3. Notice how we have taken pains to line up certain items in this program—the comments, the constants in the #define directives, and the variable identifiers. Readability is important, especially with larger programs, and good programmers are neat freaks in this regard.

We emphasize symbolic constants in this section because you can write better programs if you are in the habit of using them. Symbolic constants give names to values in a program so that anyone looking at the program can better understand the purpose and meaning of the constants. Symbolic constants also localize values so that changes are easier to make. Whenever you need a number in a progam, you will always be tempted to just insert a numeric constant, but you should rarely do this. If you practice good programming, you will almost always use symbolic constants.

Declaring a variable constant

You can make a variable act like a constant by declaring it with the qualifier *const*. You can initialize a variable declared this way, but after doing so you cannot change it. For instance, you could make the variable *cokes* in program INIT a constant, and a compiler should generate an error when the program tries to assign another value to it. The qualifier *const* was added to C by the ANSI specification to allow a compiler to assign a variable to high-speed, read-only memory (if this type of memory is available) to optimize a program.

INTEGERS

Integer data types are whole numbers—that is, numbers without fractions, such as 1492, 365, and 7. Integers can be positive, negative, or zero, but they can never contain a fractional part of a number. Variables declared with the *int* keyword are perhaps the most commonly used variables in C. The amount of memory storage allocated for an *int* variable depends on which compiler is being used, but it is usually either 2 bytes

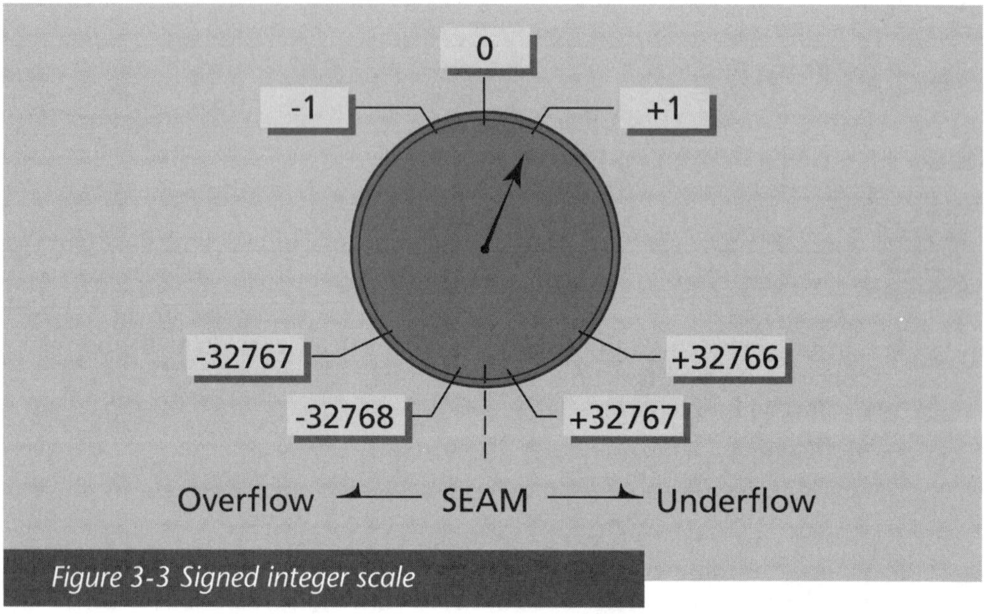

Figure 3-3 Signed integer scale

(for Power C on an IBM PC) or 4 bytes (for the C compiler on a DEC VAX). You can declare integers of other sizes by preceding *int* with the qualifying keyword *short* or *long*. The amount of memory allocated for different data types varies, but each type gets a fixed amount, so it should not be surprising that there are definite limits to how large and how small integer numbers can be.

Integer limits

The decision as to which integer type to declare involves a tradeoff between the amount of computer memory used and the sizes of the integer numbers to be computed. For this reason, it is important that you know the smallest and largest values that can fit into each type of integer. The limits are listed in Table 3-2:

Power C type	Integer length (bytes)	Minimum value	Maximum value
char	1	-128	+127
int	2	-32768	+32767
long	4	-2147483648	+2147483647

Table 3-2 Limits of signed integer values

What happens when you try to put a number larger than the maximum limit into an integer variable? The value *overflows* and, as with a clock, it moves past the maximum allowed value back to smaller values. Figure 3-3 illustrates the circular nature of a 16-bit, signed integer. Even though integer values flow continuously in a circle, there is a "seam" in the circle between +32767 and -32768 where the values jump by more than one.

The next program takes you around the clock to where integer overflow occurs.

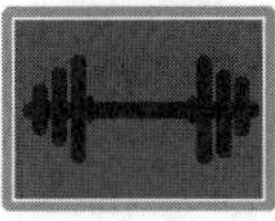

Listing 3.8 LIMITS.C Integer overflow

DO: Enter, compile, and run OVERFLOW

```
main()
{
     int number=32767;

/* INTEGER OVERFLOW */

     printf("\nMaximum value of number = %d", number);
     number = number + 1;
     printf("\nValue of number after positive overflow = %d",
          number);
     number = number + 1;
     printf("\nValue of number after adding one more = %d", number);

/* INTEGER UNDERFLOW */

     number = -32768;
     printf("\n\nMinimum value of number = %d", number);
     number = number - 1;
     printf("\nValue of number after negative underflow = %d",
          number);
     number = number - 1;
     printf("\nValue of number after subtracting one more = %d",
          number);
}
```

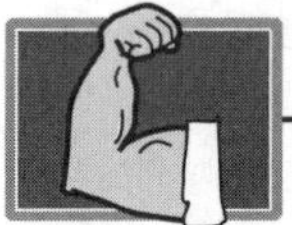

RESULT:

```
C:\>OVERFLOW

Maximum value of number = 32767
Value of number after positive overflow = -32768
Value of number after adding one more = -32767

Minimum value of number = -32768
Value of number after negative underflow = 32767
Value of number after subtracting one more = 32766
```

1. The program first displays the integer *number*, having the maximum positive value of 32767. Then it prints *number* again after adding one to its value, and you can see it overflow to -32768. When the program adds one more to its value, the result is -32767.
2. Next the LIMITS program shows an *underflow* in the opposite direction by assigning the minimum negative value and displaying *number* after **subtracting** one from its value. You can see that it underflows back to the maximum positive value. Then when the program subtracts one more, the value simply counts down.

Unsigned integer limits

The keyword qualifier *unsigned* provides another variation on integers. An *unsigned int, unsigned short,* or *unsigned long* is an integer that can take on only positive values—negative numbers are not allowed. Thus the minimum value is 0 and the maximum value is twice that of the comparable signed integer, plus 1. Table 3-3 shows the limits of unsigned integers.

Power C type	Unsigned integer length (bytes)	Minimum value	Maximum value
unsigned char	1	0	+255
unsigned int	2	0	+65535
unsigned long	4	0	+4294967295

Table 3-3 Limits of unsigned integer values

Figure 3-4 illustrates the continuous positive scale of 16-bit, unsigned integer values, with the seam appearing between 0 and 65535.

You can use unsigned integers when you need larger numbers as long as those numbers will never be negative. You can also use them for special purposes when you need to process the individual bits of a variable separately (see Chapter 14, "Bit Manipulation"). The next program illustrates the limits of an *unsigned int.*

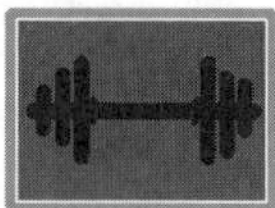

Listing 3.9 LIMITS2.C Value limits of an unsigned int

DO:
- Modify the previous program by changing the definition of number to unsigned and changing the initialization values in two places. Also change the conversion specifier **%d** to **%u** (for displaying unsigned int) in the printf() statements.
- Compile and run LIMITS2

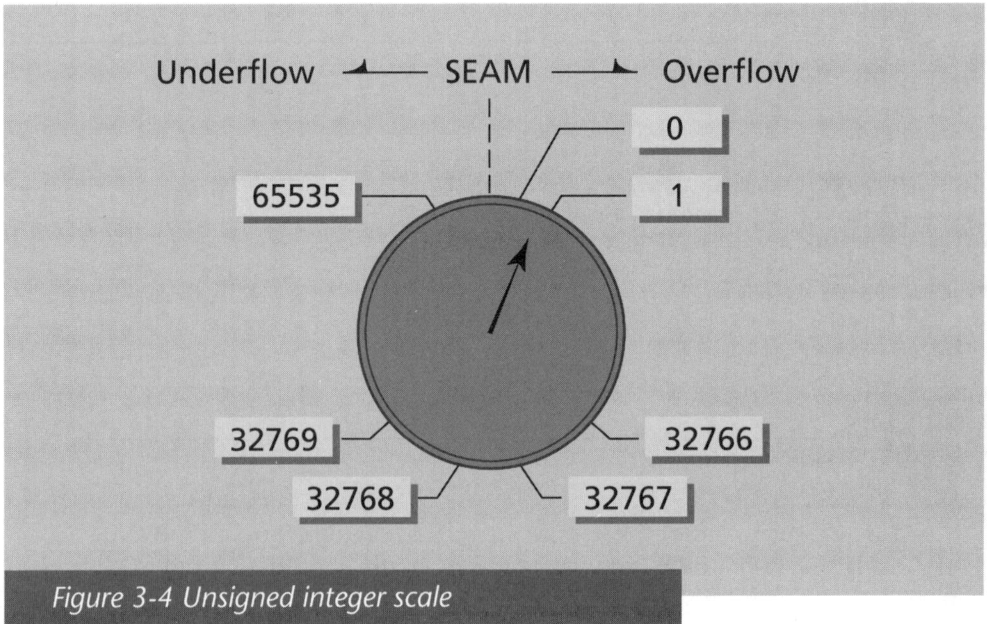

Figure 3-4 Unsigned integer scale

```
main()
{
     unsigned int number = 65535;                               /*1*/

/* INTEGER OVERFLOW */

     printf("\nMaximum value of number = %u", number);          /*2*/
     number = number + 1;
     printf("\nValue of number after positive overflow = %u",   /*3*/
          number);
     number = number + 1;
     printf("\nValue of number after adding one more = %u",     /*4*/
          number);

/* INTEGER UNDERFLOW */

     number = 0;                                                /*5*/
     printf("\n\nMinumum value of number = %u", number);        /*6*/
     number = number - 1;
     printf("\nValue of number after negative underflow = %u",  /*7*/
          number);
     number = number - 1;
     printf("\nValue of number after subtracting one more = %u", /*8*/
          number);
}
```

RESULT:

```
C:\>LIMITS2

Maximum positive value of number = 65535
Value of number after positive overflow = 0
Value of number after adding one more = 1

Minimum value of number = 0
Value of number after negative underflow = 65535
Value of number after subtracting one more = 65534
```

ANALYSIS:

1. The display output shows that an *unsigned int* overflows in the same way as an *int* at the limits of its values; it just has different limits.

Different kinds of integer constants

Besides decimal integer constants, C provides long integer constants, octal constants, and hexadecimal constants—all variations of integer constants. You must use long integer constants when assigning numbers to variables of the data type *long*. Integers represented in *octal* or *hexadecimal* (abbreviated *hex*) form often reveal more about the underlying bit pattern than does the usual decimal form.

Octal and hexadecimal integer constants

A decimal constant represents numbers in the familiar base 10 notation in which you count up to 9 and then add a 10's digit to represent the value of 10. Octal constants represent numbers in the base 8 notation by counting up to a maximum value of 7 and then adding an octal digit so that 10 represents the value of decimal 8. Similarly, hex constants represent numbers in base 16 notation by counting up to a maximum value of 15 (using letters A through F for values 10 through 15) and then adding a hex digit so that 10 represents the value of decimal 16. Table 3-4 illustrates counting up from 0 in these three integer representations.

In the following table, the decimal value 11 is equivalent to an octal value of 13 and a hex value of B. Computer words are composed of bits (binary digits), so the number 2 is very significant when storing values in memory. Because the base numbers 8 and 16 are powers of two (formed by multiplying 2 by itself), octal and hex numbers are often more useful than decimal numbers for computer arithmetic. Because a hex digit is composed of 4 bits, a byte of data is represented by exactly 2 hex digits, making it easy for you to examine the bit configuration of a 16-bit word. For example, the decimal value 32768 is 8000 in hex notation, and it is easy to see that the lower 12 bits of the memory word are 0.

Decimal (base 10)	Octal (base 8)	Hexadecimal (base 16)
0	0	0
1	1	1
2	2	2
3	3	3
4	4	4
5	5	5
6	6	6
7	7	7
8	10	8
9	11	9
10	12	A
11	13	B
12	14	C
13	15	D
14	16	E
15	17	F
16	20	10

Table 3-4 Integer counting

To use a decimal integer constant, you simply write a decimal value. To designate that a constant is octal, you precede the value with a zero (0). To designate a hex constant, you precede the value with a zero and an x (0x), as in the next program.

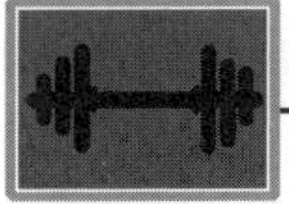

Listing 3.10 INTCON.C Integer constants

DO: Enter, compile, and run INTCON

```
main()
{
     int dec = 16;
     int oct = 020;          /* Octal constants begin with 0 */
     int hex = 0x10;         /* Hex constants begin with 0x */

     printf("\nValues printed in decimal format = %d %d %d",
          dec, oct, hex);
     printf("\nValues printed in octal format = %o %o %o",
```

```
        dec, oct, hex);
    printf("\nValues printed in hexadecimal format = %X %X %X",
        dec, oct, hex);
}
```

RESULT:

```
C:\>INTCON

Values printed in decimal format = 16 16 16
Values printed in octal format = 20 20 20
Values printed in hexadecimal format = 10 10 10
```

ANALYSIS:

1. The program INTCON initializes three integer variables to the same value using decimal, octal, and hexadecimal constants.
2. The values of the three variables (dec, oct, hex) are the same after initialization because the three constants represent the same value. You can see this in the displayed result. The first printf() statement outputs each of the three variables in decimal format (because of the format specifier %d), then the second and third printf() statements output the variables in octal (%o) and hexadecimal (%X) formats, respectively.

An octal constant cannot contain any digits larger than 7; the compiler will generate an error if you precede a constant that includes an 8 or 9 with the octal specifier 0. Octal constants are not often used, but it is easy to confuse them with decimal constants because the zero prefix is the only difference, so beware. Change the octal constant in the previous program to include an 8 and see how the compiler reacts.

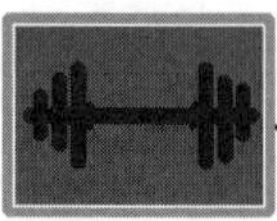

Listing 3.11 INTCON2.C Octal constant error

DO:
- Change the initializer of variable oct in INTCON
- Compile INTCON2

```
main()
{
    int dec = 16;
    int oct = 028;          /* Octal constants begin with 0 */
    int hex = 0x10;         /* Hex constants begin with 0x */
```

```
     printf("\nValues printed in decimal format = %d %d %d",
          dec, oct, hex);
     printf("\nValues printed in octal format = %o %o %o",
          dec, oct, hex);
     printf("\nValues printed in hexadecimal format = %X %X %X",
          dec, oct, hex);
}
```

RESULT:

```
C:\>PC/C/E INTCON2
Power C - Version 2.1.3
(C) Copyright 1989-1991 by Mix Software
Compiling ...
INTCON2.C(4):     int oct = 028;          /* Octal constants begin with 0 */
************             ^ 21, 14
      21: Invalid octal digit
      14: ';' expected
-----------------------------------------------------------------------
INTCON2.C(5):     int hex = 0x10;         /* Hex constants begin with 0x */
************      ^ 9
       9: Right braces expected
-----------------------------------------------------------------------
INTCON2.C(7):     printf("\nValues printed in decimal format = %d %d %d",
************           ^ 4
       4: ')' expected
-----------------------------------------------------------------------
INTCON2.C(8):         dec, oct, hex);
************                   ^ 31
      31: Left braces expected or semi-colon missing on function declaration
-----------------------------------------------------------------------
INTCON2.C(9):     printf("\nValues printed in octal format = %o %o %o",
************           ^ 4
       4: ')' expected
-----------------------------------------------------------------------
INTCON2.C(10):        dec, oct, hex);
*************                   ^ 31
      31: Left braces expected or semi-colon missing on function declaration
-----------------------------------------------------------------------
INTCON2.C(11):    printf("\nValues printed in hexadecimal format = %X %X %X",
*************           ^ 4
       4: ')' expected
-----------------------------------------------------------------------
INTCON2.C(12):        dec, oct, hex);
*************                   ^ 31
      31: Left braces expected or semi-colon missing on function declaration
-----------------------------------------------------------------------
INTCON2.C(13):}
************* ^  3
       3: Variable or function declaration expected
```

```
---------------------------------------------------------------------
   13 lines compiled
   10 Compile errors
```

ANALYSIS:

1. The first compiler error tells you exactly what is wrong with the change: you have used an invalid octal digit.
2. The remaining barrage of errors is the result of the first error—a dramatic illustration of how one error can have side effects.

Long integer constants

When using a constant with a long integer, you must specify that it is a long constant by adding an *L* after the value. This ensures that the constant is the same size (the same number of bytes) as the long variable. The next program illustrates the proper use of long constants with variables of the data type *long*.

Listing 3.12 INTCON3.C Long integer constants

DO:
- Modify the previous program to use type long
- Compile and run INTCON3

```
main()
{
      long dec;
      long oct;
      long hex;

      dec = 16L;                /* Long decimal constant */
      oct = 020L;               /* Long octal constant */
      hex = 0x10L;              /* Long hexadecimal constant */

      printf("\nLong decimal print format = %ld", dec);
      printf("\nLong octal print format = %lo", oct);
      printf("\nLong hexadecimal print format = %lX", hex);
}
```

RESULT:

```
C:\>INTCON3
```

```
Long decimal print format = 16
Long octal print format = 20
Long hexadecimal print format = 10
```

ANALYSIS:

1. Program INTCON3 assigns the same value to the long integers *dec, oct,* and *hex*: it assigns a long decimal constant to *dec*, a long octal constant to *oct*, and a long hexadecimal constant to *hex*.
2. The three printf() statements illustrate how the same value can be displayed with different output formats. The printf() statements also show how you change the display formats to work with long integers by adding the long modifier (*l*) after the percent sign (%) in the format specification.

CHARACTERS

Character data types hold text information in the form of character codes. The *char* keyword always allocates 1 byte (8 bits) of storage, regardless of the computer model. Character codes are a set of integer numbers that correspond to letters of the alphabet, to punctuation, and to other special symbols. One byte can have 256 different code values, so it can represent 256 different text characters. Appendix G lists the character codes used for PCs; these are ASCII (American Standard Code for Information Interchange) codes. For example, the ASCII code for character A is 65 and the ASCII code for a space character is 32. Some other computer systems use different character codes. For example, IBM mainframe computers use EBCDIC (Extended Binary Coded Decimal Interchange Code). However, all PC software, including Power C, works with ASCII codes.

CHARACTER VARIABLES USED FOR NUMBERS

Unlike some other programming languages, C allows you to perform integer arithmetic with character data types. This has two benefits: (1) you can use *char* instead of *int* to save space when working with large arrays of small integers, and (2) you can produce letters of the alphabet with arithmetic. Variables of type *char* are treated as 8-bit integers by the compiler, and it can choose either a signed or an unsigned representation. Power C defaults to an unsigned form, but you can control this with the modifying keyword *signed*. This program demonstrates the limits of a signed character.

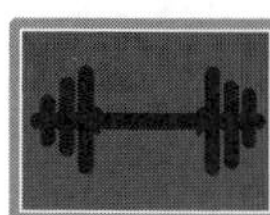

Listing 3.13 CHARMAX.C Minimum and maximum values for signed character

DO: Enter, compile, and run CHARMAX

```
#define MINCHAR -128 /* Minimum value for char data type */
#define MAXCHAR  127 /* Maximum value for char data type */
main()
{
      signed char int_char;

      int_char = MINCHAR;
      printf("\nMinimum integer for a signed char is %d", int_char);
      int_char = MAXCHAR;
      printf("\nMaximum integer for a signed char is %d", int_char);
}
```

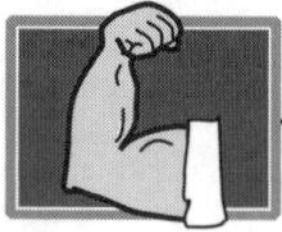

RESULT:

```
C:\>CHARMAX

Minimum integer for a signed char is -128
Maximum integer for a signed char is 127
```

ANALYSIS:

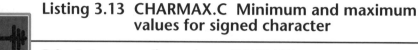

1. The symbolic constants in the first two lines are equivalent to the minimum and maximum limits of an 8-bit integer.

2. The program declares the variable *int_char* to be of the data type *signed char*. Notice that you can use the keyword *char* (and the keyword *int*) as **part** of the identifier even though it would be illegal to use either as the **whole** identifier.

3. This program first assigns the minimum value to the variable and displays it, then assigns the maximum value and displays it.

You can also declare characters to be *unsigned* to allow larger positive integer values. Modify the previous program and look at the value limits of an unsigned character. Negative numbers are not allowed and the maximum value is twice that of a *signed char*, plus one.

Listing 3.14 CHARMAX2.C Unsigned character integers

DO: • Modify the limits and data type in program CHARMAX
• Compile and run CHARMAX2

```
#define MINCHAR 0              /* Minimum value for unsigned char  /* 1*/
#define MAXCHAR 255            /* Maximum value for unsigned char  /* 2*/
main()
{
      unsigned char int_char;                                      /*3*/

      int_char = MINCHAR;
      printf("\nMinimum integer for an unsigned char is %d", int_char);
      int_char = MAXCHAR;
      printf("\nMaximum integer for an unsigned char is %d", int_char);
}
```

RESULT:

```
C:\>CHARMAX2

Minimum integer for an unsigned char is 0
Maximum integer for an unsigned char is 255
```

ANALYSIS:

1. The *unsigned* prefix on the definition of variable *int_char* modifies the use of a *char* variable in the same way as for an *int*.
2. This program displays the numeric limits of an *unsigned* character.

Character codes are numbers, and C allows you to perform arithmetic with variables that are character data types (*char*). The next short example proves this.

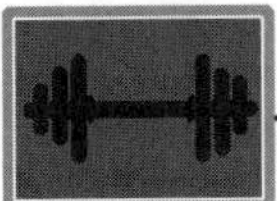

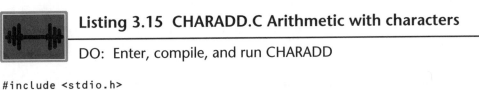

Listing 3.15 CHARADD.C Arithmetic with characters

DO: Enter, compile, and run CHARADD

```
#include <stdio.h>
main()
{
      char letter = 'A';
```

```
    printf("\nThe ASCII code for %c is %d", letter, letter);
}
```

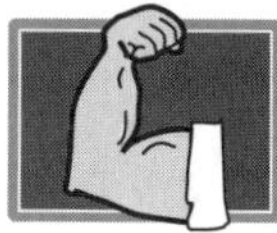

RESULT:

```
C:\>CHARADD

The ASCII code for A is 65
```

ANALYSIS:

1. The printf() statement displays the value of *letter* first as a character (with the %c conversion specifier), then as a decimal integer (with the %d conversion specifier). Therefore, C allows a variable of type *char* to be treated as either a character or an integer.

The next program uses character arithmetic to produce letters of the alphabet in a way that comes in handy. It is not usually good programming practice to use "tricks" because unorthodox coding techniques obscure the meaning of the code, making it more difficult for others to work with a program. However this "trick" is useful and is not uncommon in C programs.

Listing 3.16 CHARADD2.C Arithmetic with characters

DO: Enter, compile, and run CHARADD2

```
main()
{
    char letter = 'A';
    char digit  = '0';

    printf("\nAdd one to A and you get %c", letter+1);
    printf("\nAdd five to A and you get %c", letter+5);
    printf("\nAdd ten to A and you get %c", letter+10);

    printf("\n\nAdd one to 0 and you get %c", digit+1);
    printf("\nAdd five to 0 and you get %c", digit+5);
    printf("\nAdd ten to 0 and you get %c", digit+10);
}
```

RESULT:

```
C:\>CHARADD2

Add one to A and you get B
Add five to A and you get F
Add ten to A and you get K

Add one to 0 and you get 1
Add five to 0 and you get 5
Add ten to 0 and you get :
```

ANALYSIS:

1. Since the letters of the alphabet are contiguous in the table of ASCII codes (see Appendix G), and since C allows you to do arithmetic with character data, you can generate other letters by adding integers to 'A' as in the first three printf() statements.

2. Character codes for the numbers 0 through 9 are also contiguous in the table of ASCII codes, so you can produce displayable characters for these digits with character arithmetic as shown in the last three printf() statements. Two of the last three lines of output may look like trivial arithmetic, and indeed the process is quite simple, but the point is that you are generating displayable character codes, not numbers. The last line of output illustrates this; it generates a colon (:) by adding ten to the character zero ('0').

FLOATING-POINT AND LARGE FLOATING-POINT NUMBERS

Floating-point data types are real numbers that have an integer part and a fractional part, like 3.14159, 10.5, and 0.0001. Floating-point numbers can be very large or very small (much larger or smaller than integers), so they can be used for applications where integers cannot be used. The amount of memory storage allocated for a *float* variable depends on the computer model, but it is usually 4 bytes, as for Power C on an IBM PC. The keyword *double* also designates a floating-point data type, and according to the C specification it must be at least as large as *float*. Usually *double* occupies twice as much memory as *float* (as in Power C), but another compiler might make it the same size as *float*.

Before getting into the details of floating-point limits, we must introduce the basics of floating-point notation. If you are already familiar with fixed-point and exponential representations, you might want to skip the next section.

Floating-point notation

You can write floating-point constants two ways: as a decimal number with a decimal point and a fractional part (fixed-point notation), or with a base number and an exponent (exponential notation). Exponential notation is similar to scientific notation, in which the placement of the decimal point for very large or very small numbers is determined by a power of ten exponent. The exponent determines how many zeros precede or follow the base number, or *mantissa*. Table 3-5 shows several examples of fixed-point and exponential notation.

Fixed-point notation	Scientific notation	Exponential notation
1000000000	1.0×10^{9}	1.0e9
123000	1.23×10^{5}	1.23e5
322.56	3.2256×10^{2}	3.2256e2
0.000056	5.6×10^{-5}	5.6e-5

Table 3-5 Fixed-point and exponential notation

You can assign values to both *float* and *double* variables with either notation (fixed-point or exponential). Also, when you use the printf() function, you can choose either the %e (exponential) or %f (fixed) format specifier to display either data type. The following program uses both forms of notation:

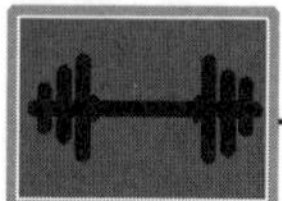

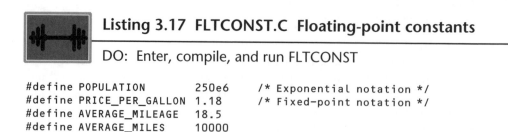

Listing 3.17 FLTCONST.C Floating-point constants

DO: Enter, compile, and run FLTCONST

```
#define POPULATION        250e6     /* Exponential notation */
#define PRICE_PER_GALLON 1.18       /* Fixed-point notation */
#define AVERAGE_MILEAGE  18.5
#define AVERAGE_MILES    10000
main()
{
     float total_miles;             /* Total US miles per year */
```

```
    float total_cost;              /* Total U.S. gasoline cost */

    total_miles = POPULATION * AVERAGE_MILES;
    total_cost  = PRICE_PER_GALLON * total_miles / AVERAGE_MILEAGE;
    printf("A guess at the total annual cost of gasoline"
           "in the U.S. is $%.2e or $%.2f", total_cost, total_cost);
}
```

RESULT:

```
C:\>FLTCONST
A guess at the total annual cost of gasoline in the U.S. is $1.59e+011 or
$159459459072.00
```

ANALYSIS:

1. You can use symbolic constants for floating-point numbers just as easily as you can use them for integers. The first two preprocessor statements define numbers using two forms of notation, exponential and fixed-point.
2. You can use either form of floating-point constant with any *float* or *double* variable, as in the calculation of *total_miles*, where *POPULATION* is in exponential notation and *AVERAGE_MILES* is in fixed-point notation.
3. The printf() statement displays the total cost of gasoline both using an exponential format (%.2e) and using a fixed-point format (%.2f). Notice that the exponential format is more compact, but the fixed-point display is more accurate. Actually, these aspects of a floating-point display are controllable with format modifiers, as you will learn in Chapter 4.
4. The printf() statement is too long to fit on one line, so you must break it in half. The break occurs in the middle of the format string, so you should use double quotes to make two string constants out of it. The compiler puts the strings back together—when it encounters two string constants, it merges or *concatenates* them into one.

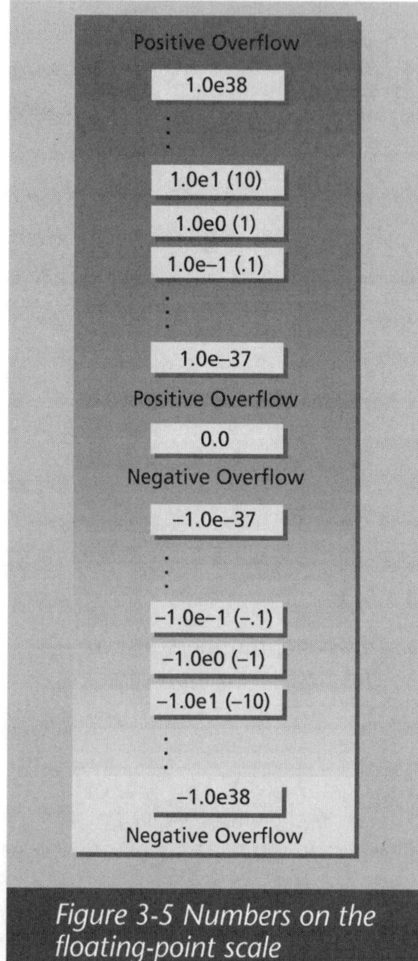

Figure 3-5 Numbers on the floating-point scale

Floating-point limits

Even though floating-point variables can represent extremely large and small numbers, there are limits with them just as there are with integers. The minimum positive value that a *float* variable can have is 1.0e-37, or a 1 preceded by a decimal point and 36 zeros (a pretty small number). The maximum value is 1.0e38, or a 1 followed by 38 zeros (an extremely large number). Type *double* extends the upper and lower limits to even larger astronomical and smaller microscopic limits that depend on the computer system in use.

Floating-point numbers can also overflow and underflow. However, unlike integers, an overflow from a maximum value does not result in the minimum possible value; nor does an underflow result in the maximum possible value. Figure 3-5 illustrates the noncircular nature of floating-point values and the dead-end overflow at each limit.

You can think of integers as living on a round world where they can travel without reaching an end, while floating-point numbers live on a flat earth where they fall off when they reach the end. Floating-point numbers yield erroneous values when they overflow and underflow, as the next program will illustrate.

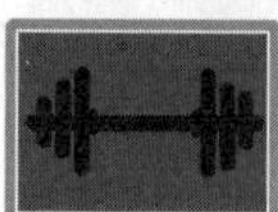

Listing 3.18 FLTMAX.C Minimum and maximum floating-point values

DO: Enter, compile, and run FLTMAX

```
#define FLT_MIN 1.e-37
#define FLT_MAX 1.e38
main()
{
     float f_min = FLT_MIN;
     float f_max = FLT_MAX;
```

```
    printf("\nMinimum floating-point value is %e", f_min);
    printf("\nMaximum floating-point value is %e", f_max);

    f_min = f_min / 10.;
    printf("\nFloating-point underflow is %e", f_min);
    f_max = f_max * 10.;
    printf("\nFloating-point overflow is %e", f_max);
}
```

RESULT:

```
C:\>FLTMAX

Minimum floating-point value is 1.000000e-037
Maximum floating-point value is 1.000000e+038
Floating-point underflow is 0.000000e-001
Floating-point overflow is 1.382400e+005
```

ANALYSIS:

1. In the first two lines, the program defines symbolic constants for the minimum and maximum values of *float*. Then it assigns the values to variables *f_min* and *f_max* and displays them.
2. The last two printf() statements show what happens when you make the minimum value underflow by dividing by 10, and when you make the maximum value overflow by multiplying by 10. The program performs the arithmetic without complaining, but the results are not valid. The way a program responds to floating-point overflow will vary depending on the compiler and computer system.

Floating-point precision

Precision is the accuracy of a number. You measure the precision of a floating-point number by the number of digits available to represent the number. The number of digits determines how small the smallest part of a number can be. The ratio of the circumference to the diameter of a circle is known as *pi*, which can be written with hundreds of digits and still not be represented exactly. Let's see how precisely you can represent the value of *pi* with your computer.

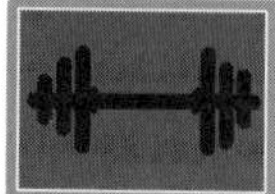

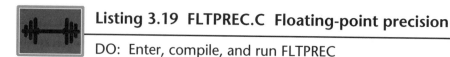

Listing 3.19 FLTPREC.C Floating-point precision

DO: Enter, compile, and run FLTPREC

```
#define PI 3.1415926535897896
main()
{
     float  float_pi  = PI;
     double double_pi = PI;

     printf("\n  Type float has a precision of 7, pi = %20.16f",
          float_pi);
     printf("\nType double has a precision of 15, pi = %20.16f",
          double_pi);
}
```

RESULT:

```
C:\>FLTPREC

Type float has a precision of 7, pi = 3.1415927410125730
Type double has a precision of 15, pi = 3.1415926535897900
```

ANALYSIS:

1. The program defines the symbolic constant *PI* as the value of pi to a precision of 17 places. There is no limit to the precision of a symbolic constant, but there is a limit to the precision of a variable.
2. The printf() statements illustrate that the precision of *double* (15) is more than twice that of *float* (7). The format specifier (%20.16f) causes the number to print out with 16 digits after the decimal point. Notice that the *double* value displays correctly out to 15 digits while the *float* value is correct only to the first 7 digits.

FLOATING-POINT NUMBERS VERSUS INTEGERS

Whenever you write a program that works with numbers, you have to decide which data type to use. First you have to determine how big the numbers will be, then you must use a data type that will hold the largest. Why not just always use *double,* which will handle the smallest and largest numbers? One answer is that you are interested in holding down the amount of memory required, and *double* uses the most memory. You should usually select the smallest data type that will work with the largest expected number. Another criterion is speed of execution; computations based on floating-point numbers are slower than those based on integers.

The next program compares the amount of time it takes to do floating-point arithmetic versus integer arithmetic—this is a procedure known as *benchmarking*, or testing two programs for relative performance.

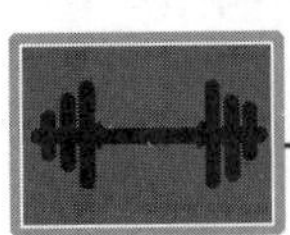

Listing 3.20 BENCHINT.C Benchmark for integer arithmetic

DO:
- Enter and compile BENCHINT
- Run BENCHINT and note the time it takes to run

```
main()
{
      int sum;
      long count;

      printf("\nStarting");
      for (count=1; count<=1000000L; ++count)
           sum = 2 + 2;
      printf("\nFinished");
}
```

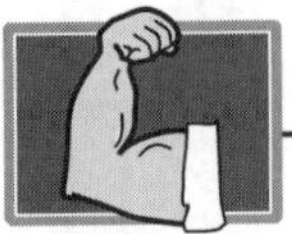

RESULT:

```
C:\>BENCHINT
Starting
(time the delay)
Finished
```

ANALYSIS:

1. This program allows you to establish the time required to add 2 and 2 one million times using integer arithmetic. You should use a clock or count the seconds between the display of **Starting** and **Finished**. On a 20MHz 386 PC system, we timed the program at approximately 8 seconds.

2. We had to introduce a *for* statement (a topic discussed in Chapter 6) to generate this benchmark. For now, let's gloss over the details of the *for* statement and suffice it to say that it causes the sum of 2 plus 2 to be repeated one million times.

3. You must use a *long* data type for the variable **count** because it must count up to a value of one million and this would overflow type *int*.

Now repeat the benchmark, except this time use floating-point arithmetic.

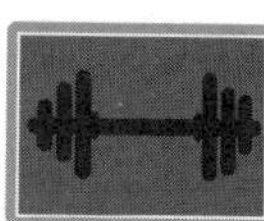

Listing 3.21 BENCHFLT.C Benchmark for floating-point arithmetic

DO:
- Modify BENCHMRK to calculate a floating-point sum (change **sum** to type float and add a decimal point to the constants)
- Compile BENCHFLT
- Run BENCHFLT and note the time it takes to run

```
main()
{
      float sum;                                              /*1*/
      long count;

      printf("\nStarting");
      for(count=1; count<=1000000L; ++count )
           sum = 2. + 2.;                                     /*2*/
      printf("\nFinished");
}
```

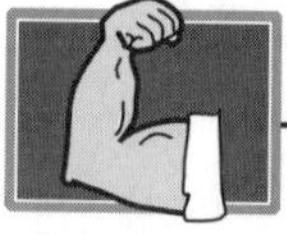

RESULT:

```
C:\>BENCHFLT
Starting
(time the delay)
Finished
```

ANALYSIS:

1. A 20MHz 386 PC system (without a 80387 floating-point coprocessor) took about 37 seconds to complete the one million floating-point additions. Therefore, we conclude that integer addition is about 4.5 times faster than floating-point addition on this machine.

Your results may be different, especially if you have a floating-point coprocessor hardware chip installed, but in general there is a big difference between the time it takes to do integer and the time it takes to do floating-point arithmetic.

In conclusion, because of the size and speed penalty, floating-point data types should be used only when dealing with fractions or numbers that won't fit in an integer.

DATA TYPE *void*

The data type *void* is a generic data type that has no specified size or range of values associated with it. A *void* value is nonexistent; you cannot store any values in a variable of the data type *void*. Data type *void* is like the black hole shown in Figure 3-6; anything you put into it disappears, and you can never get anything out of it.

If you attempt to assign a value to a *void* variable, as in the next program, the compiler will issue an error message.

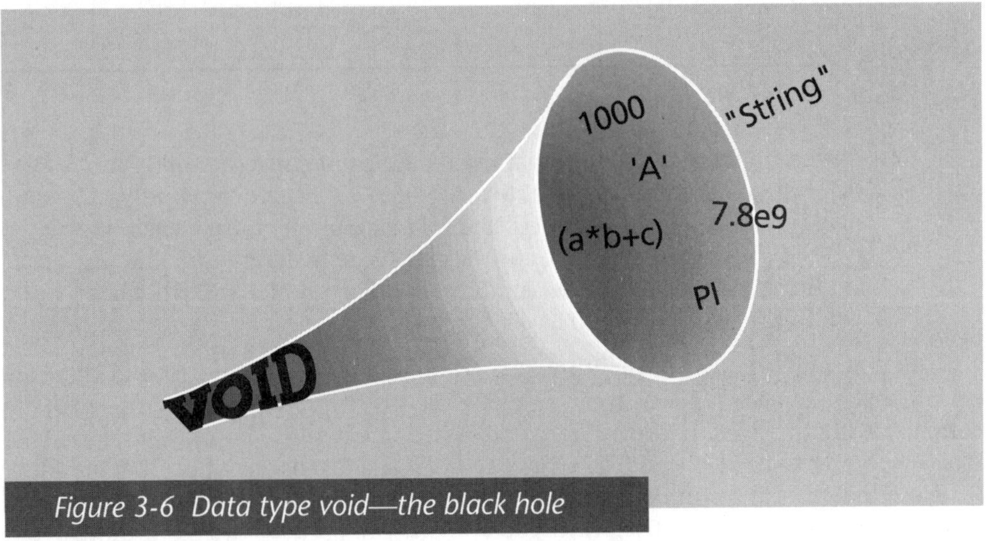

Figure 3-6 Data type void—the black hole

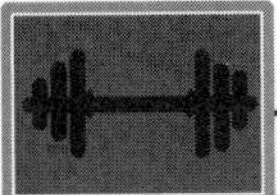

Listing 3.22 NOVALUE.C Void values

DO: Enter and compile NOVALUE

```
main()
{
      void black_hole = 1000;
}
```

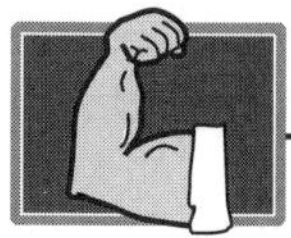

RESULTS:

```
C:\>pc/c/e NOVALUE

Power C - Version 2.1.3
(C) Copyright 1989-1991 by Mix Software
NOVALUE.C(3):     void black_hole = 1000;
************                          ^ 30
      30: Invalid type in assignment
------------------------------------------------
Compiling ...
   4 lines compiled
   1 Compile error
```

ANALYSIS:

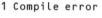

1. The compiler message says that the data type of constant 1000 is not valid for assignment to variable *black_hole*. In fact, there is no valid data type that can be assigned to a *void* variable. You can select any type of constant or variable for the right-side assignment value, including type *void*, with the same result: the compiler will not allow you to assign anything to a *void* variable.

You may find it a little difficult to see a use for data type *void* at first, but there are several valuable reasons for using it, one of which is to signal to the compiler that a function will not have a return value (as discussed in Chapter 8). Another reason is to allow a pointer to hold the address of any type of data (as discussed in Chapter 10).

Now that you know about the different types of data in computer memory and have some experience with the printf() statement, you are ready to learn more about how to read data from the keyboard and write it to the screen. In the next chapter, you will delve into the details of how to convert data during input and output operations to suit the needs of your programs.

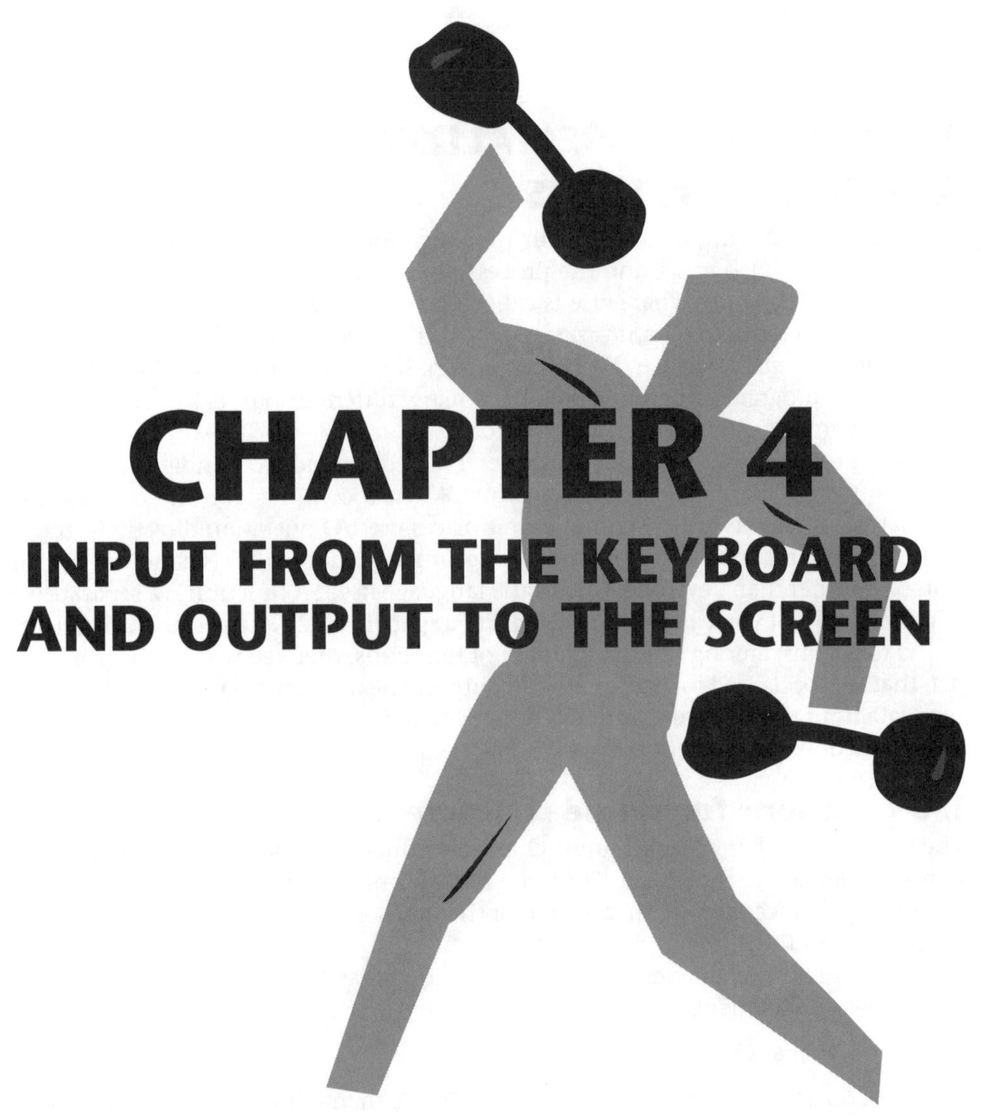

CHAPTER 4

INPUT FROM THE KEYBOARD AND OUTPUT TO THE SCREEN

In this chapter you will learn how to read data into a program from the keyboard and how to display it on the screen. This is an important part of programming because the keyboard and screen are where the interaction between human and computer occurs. You will learn to control how the computer reads data from the keyboard, and you will practice different ways to format data for presentation on the screen. You will also learn about differences between internally stored data and external representations of data.

TEXT I/O WITH SPECIALIZED GET AND PUT FUNCTIONS

The process of moving data into your program from the keyboard, disk files, or any other source is called *input*, and the process of moving data from your program to the screen, disk files, or anywhere else is called *output*. In general, C deals with input and output (I/O) in terms of data *streams*. A stream is the sequence of data items transferred to or from an outside device (keyboard, screen, file, or other device). By dealing with streams, a C program can handle data from many different sources in a consistent way without worrying about where it came from.

Most programming languages have reserved commands to handle input and output_commands like read, write, and print. When a compiler for one of these other languages encounters an I/O command, it places the I/O operation directly in the program. C is different from other programming languages in that I/O is handled with function calls rather than keywords within the language itself. A function is a separate piece of a program that you can call on to perform a specific task. C has a standard collection of I/O functions; among them is a family of functions, prefixed with the words *get* and *put*, that are specialized for text input and output. The functions getchar() and gets() read text data from the keyboard, and functions putchar() and puts() write text to the screen. These functions are efficient and easy to use because they are built for a single purpose.

I/O functions for single characters

The function getchar() reads a single character from the keyboard and putchar() writes a single character to the screen. These are not the only functions that can handle character I/O, but since they are specialized for that purpose, they have a compact form and are faster than the others.

You can read a character from the keyboard and assign it to the variable *key* with the following statement:

```
key = getchar();
```

Function getchar() waits for you to press ENTER, then returns the ASCII code for the last key pressed before ENTER, so to input the character X you would press X ENTER. Most keyboards are *buffered*, which means that when you type a character, it goes into a holding area called a *buffer* (a special memory in the keyboard). The keyboard buffer is a fixed size, so it will hold only so much data. When the buffer fills up, most computers will sound an alarm in the form of a beep. If you hold down a key, the keyboard will repeatedly put the key code in the buffer and it will shortly fill up. Try it: hold down the X key (or any other key) until the alarm sounds. When the alarm goes off, you can find out how big your keyboard buffer is by counting the number of Xs on your screen. When you press ENTER, the buffer empties out and you can start filling it again. The contents of the keyboard buffer are not available to your program until the buffer receives a newline character (ASCII code 10), which happens when you press ENTER.

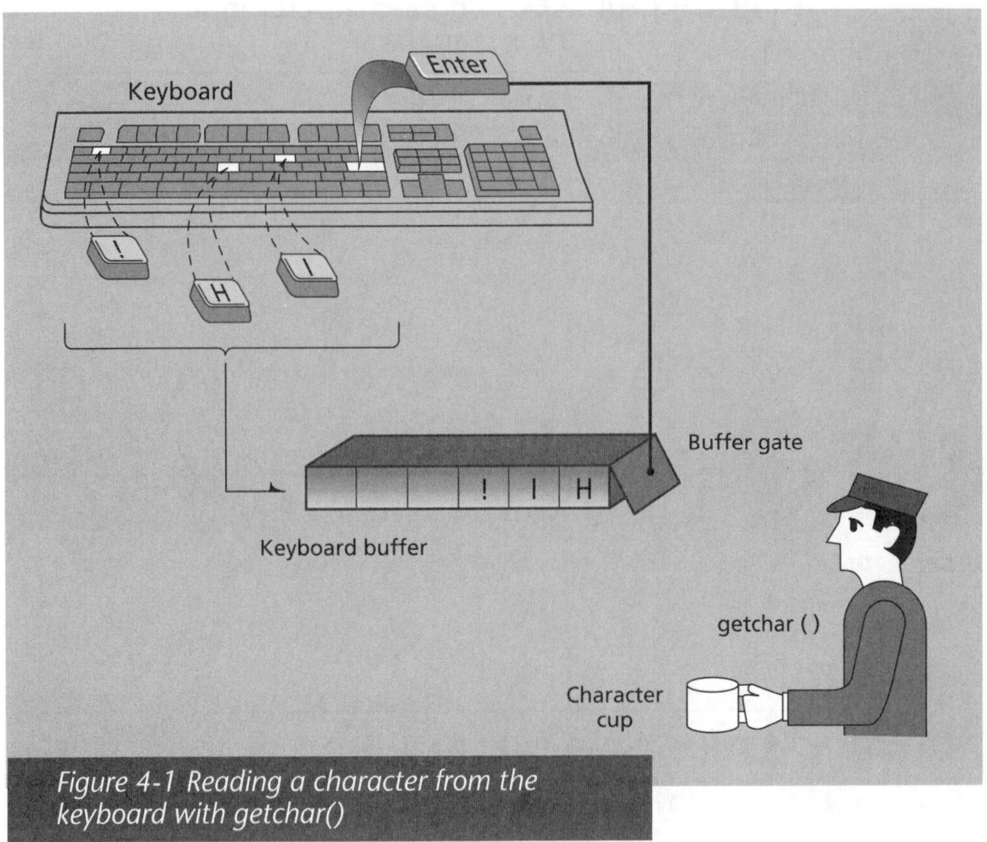

Figure 4-1 Reading a character from the keyboard with getchar()

Figure 4-1 illustrates the process of reading a character from a buffered keyboard with getchar().

Function getchar() is like a messenger whose sole duty is to pick up one character at a time from the keyboard buffer and deliver it to your program. If you press several keys, the character codes for the keys will queue up in the keyboard buffer. Then when you press ENTER, the newline character opens the gate to the keyboard buffer, allowing getchar() to retrieve a character.

You can display a character corresponding to the ASCII code in the variable *key* with the following statement:

```
putchar(key);
```

In the next program, you will see how easy it is to use getchar() and putchar().

Listing 4.1 CHARIO.C Single-character input from the keyboard

DO:
- Enter and compile CHARIO
- Run CHARIO, then press (A) (ENTER)

```
#include <stdio.h>
main()
{
      char key;

      key = getchar();
      putchar(key);
}
```

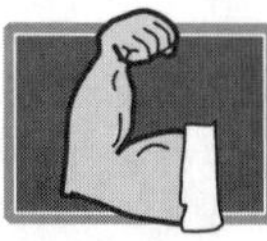

RESULT:

```
C:\>CHARIO
A
A
```

ANALYSIS:

1. Program CHARIO reads one character from the keyboard and stores it in memory using function getchar(), then takes the character from memory and writes it to the screen with function putchar().
2. The program defines the character variable *key* to hold the ASCII code.
3. Line 1 contains a command that you will use in almost every program you will ever write in C. This is the *#include <stdio.h>* preprocessor statement. It causes one of the standard header files (stdio.h) provided with the compiler to be inserted into your program so that I/O functions are properly defined for the compiler. The brackets that enclose the file name (< >) tell the compiler to look for the file in the "usual place"; this usual place depends on the compiler and operating system. With Power C and DOS, the usual place is the directory specified by the PATH environment variable (see Installing Power C in Chapter 1); other compilers and operating systems have different

methods for specifying the "usual place" for header files. Notice that the compiler has reported that it compiled 115 lines even though your program only contains eight lines—the rest were in file stdio.h. Many C compilers (including Power C) will operate just fine if you don't include stdio.h, but some compilers will issue warning statements. You should get in the habit of always including stdio.h.

You can transfer any character from the keyboard to the screen with CHARIO, but you will only see *displayable* characters. The term displayable refers to the normal characters of the alphabet, plus numbers and punctuation that can be displayed in readable form. Some character codes are used for control purposes and are not intended to be displayed (codes 0–31). For example, when you press ENTER, the keyboard generates a *newline* character (code 10) that is not displayed but causes the cursor to move to the next line.

DO: Run CHARIO and just press ENTER

```
C:\>CHARIO

(cursor is now here on the third line)
```

ANALYSIS:

1. You don't see any characters displayed on your screen, but if you look closely, you will see that the cursor has moved an extra line to the third line below the CHARIO run command.

2. The cursor moves to the first line when you press ENTER after CHARIO. It moves to the second line when you press ENTER the second time, and it moves to the third line when putchar() writes the newline character to the screen.

Some of the other nondisplayable characters are: Bell (code 7, which sounds a beep), Backspace (code 8, which moves the cursor back), Tab (code 9, which jumps the cursor forward), and Formfeed (code 12, which causes the printer to eject a page). There are 32 such characters with ASCII codes ranging from 0 through 31. Nondisplayable characters are like the subatomic particles that scientists study; they cause all sorts of things to happen, but you never see them directly. You can indirectly see nondisplayable characters by displaying their character codes; do this by using the next program.

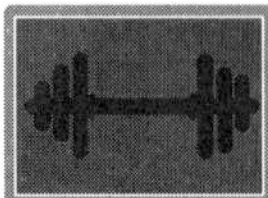

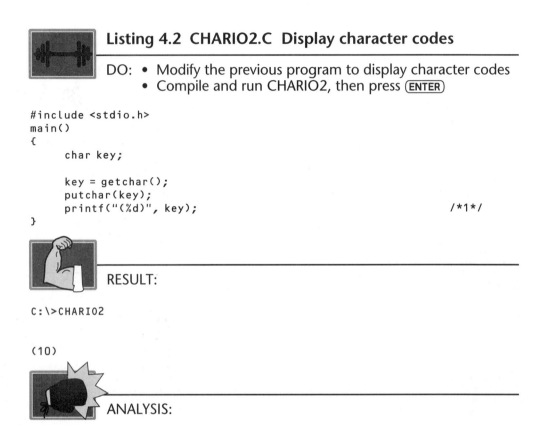

Listing 4.2 CHARIO2.C Display character codes

DO:
- Modify the previous program to display character codes
- Compile and run CHARIO2, then press ENTER

```
#include <stdio.h>
main()
{
      char key;

      key = getchar();
      putchar(key);
      printf("(%d)", key);                                    /*1*/
}
```

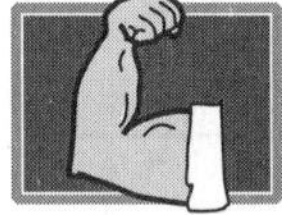

RESULT:

```
C:\>CHARIO2


(10)
```

ANALYSIS:

1. Line /*1*/ adds a printf() statement to display the decimal integer value of the character code. The *"(%d)"* format string causes an integer to be displayed enclosed in parentheses. The printf() function responds to the characters *%d* by displaying a decimal integer and literally displays all other characters inside the double quotes (the parentheses).
2. Now you can have a look at the newline character; its code appears just after putchar() sends the newline to the screen.

Experiment with ASCII codes by repeatedly running CHARIO2 and entering different key sequences. Enter some letters in alphabetic sequence and you will see the serial nature of ASCII codes for the alphabet. Enter both lowercase and uppercase characters and compare your results with the codes in Appendix G. Enter some numeric digits (0, 1, ...) and notice that these ASCII codes are also in sequence. You can enter the nondisplayable characters by holding down the ALT key while you press the numeric keys corresponding to the ASCII code. For example, if you enter ALT-7 (the Bell character), a beep will sound.

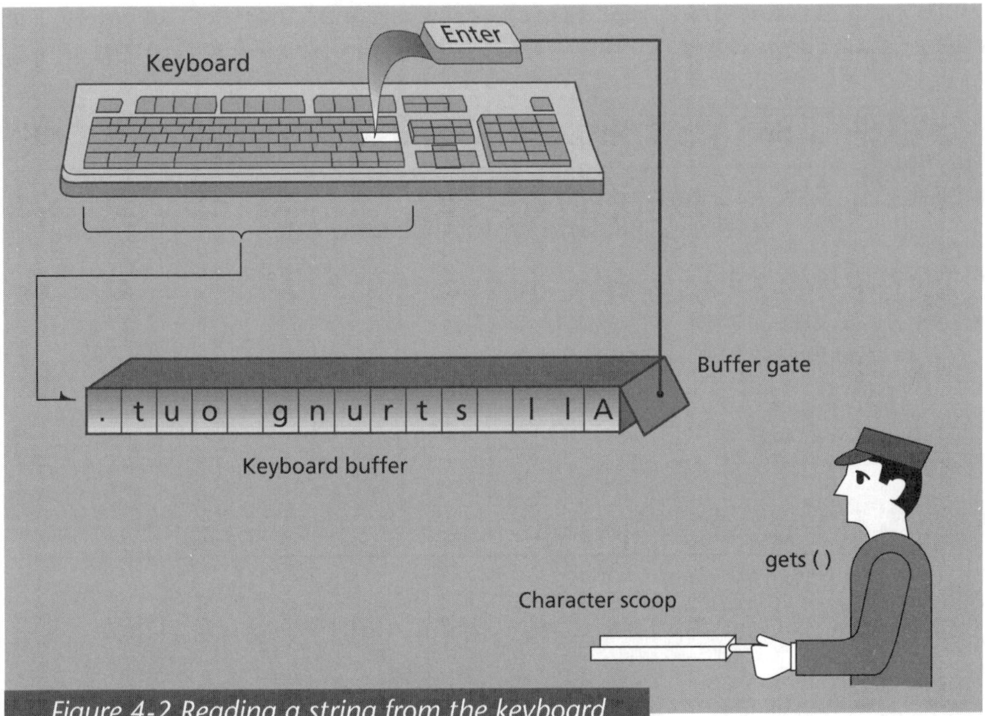

Figure 4-2 Reading a string from the keyboard with gets()

I/O functions for character strings

The function gets() reads a character *string* from the keyboard, and puts() writes a string to the screen. Figure 4-2 shows gets() retrieving character data from the keyboard buffer.

Function gets() is like a messenger whose only task is to scoop up character strings from the keyboard buffer and deliver them to your program. A character string is a connected sequence of characters ending with a null value (a zero). Figure 4-3 illustrates the layout of a string in computer memory. The last entry, '\0', is notation for a character constant having zero value. This is one of the control codes—ASCII code 0 for the null character; do not confuse it with the code for the character zero, which is ASCII 48.

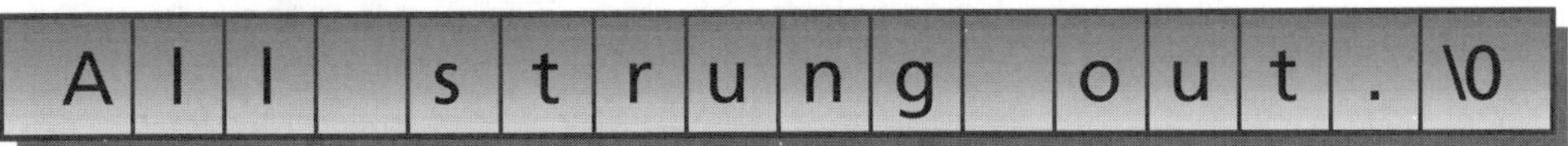

Figure 4-3 A character string

To read and write strings you must allocate several connected bytes in memory. The next program shows how to do this.

Listing 4.3 STRIO.C Read and write a string

DO: • Enter and compile STRIO
• Run STRIO and enter **All strung out.**

```
#include <stdio.h>
main()
{
      char phrase[16];

      gets(phrase);
      puts(phrase);
}
```

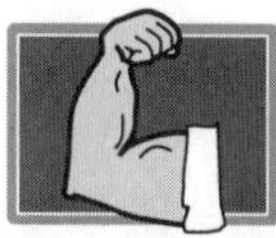

RESULT:

```
C:\>STRIO
All strung out.
All strung out.
```

ANALYSIS:

1. With one statement, this program allocates 16 bytes of contiguous storage to hold a string of characters. The program defines an *array* of characters and gives them a single identifier, *phrase*. We will discuss arrays more in Chapter 9—right now it is sufficient to know how to allocate space for one.

2. Strings always end with an extra byte having a null (or zero) value, so the array *phrase* can hold a string of no more than 15 characters.

3. The gets() function reads a string from the keyboard and places it in the array *phrase*. The function will continue to take input until it receives a newline character (when you press ENTER); gets() then discards the newline and adds a terminating null character to the string.

4. The next line calls function puts(), which writes the string to the screen—all except the terminating null character. Function puts() replaces it with a newline character to cause the cursor to move to the next line after displaying the string.

5. Notice that gets() will accept spaces within a string of characters—an important feature of this input function.

You must be careful not to enter more characters than the allocated storage will accept, or unpredictable things can happen. Function gets() will blindly keep adding characters to the string as long as you are typing at the keyboard (until you press ENTER). When the designated array is full, gets() will fill other areas of memory with your keystrokes; the result may be serious or harmless depending on where the data goes. You will see some data overflow an array in the next program.

Listing 4.4 STRIO2.C Overrun an array with a string

DO:
- Modify the STRIO lines marked with comments /*n*/
- Compile and run STRIO2
- Enter **All strung out on coffee**

```
#include <stdio.h>
main()
{
      char phrase[16];
      int  cost = 25;                                          /*1*/

      printf("\nCoffee costs %d cents a cup", cost);
      printf("\nEnter a phrase: ");                            /*2*/
      gets(phrase);                                            /*3*/
      printf("\nCoffee now costs %d cents a cup!\n", cost);    /*4*/
      puts(phrase);
}
```

RESULT:

```
C:\>STRIO2
Coffee costs 25 cents a cup.
Enter a phrase: All strung out on coffee.

Coffee now costs 8302 cents a cup!
All strung out on coffee.
```

ANALYSIS:

1. When a compiler allocates storage in response to your definition statements (*char* and *int* in this program), it usually lays out the storage contiguously in the order in which you specify the variables. This

is **not** a C language rule, so the compiler does not have to lay out storage this way, but you can use the likelihood that storage will be ordered in this way to experiment with overrunning strings.

2. In this program, *cost* probably follows *phrase* immediately in memory; therefore, if some string data overruns *phrase*, it will spill over into *cost*.

3. The first printf() statement displays the initial value of cost, then the program asks you to enter a string that is too long to fit into *phrase*. Line /*4*/ shows that bad things have happened to *cost* as a result. The 16 bytes of *phrase* will hold **All strung out o**, then the next two characters, **n** and **space**, fill up the two bytes of *cost*, giving you the integer equivalent of 8302. The next section will give you some insight as to how **n space** can translate into the integer 8302.

FORMATTED I/O WITH scanf() AND printf()

C gives you the ability to customize how you would like to read data into your program, or how you would like it to appear in output—this is called *formatted I/O*. The formatted I/O functions for keyboard input and screen output are scanf() and printf(),

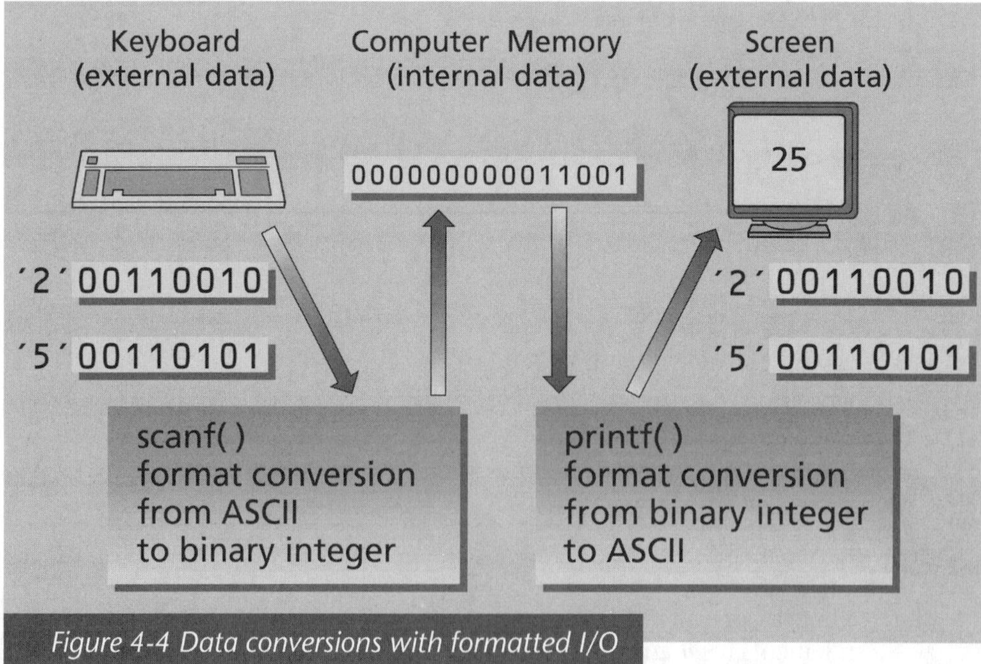

Figure 4-4 Data conversions with formatted I/O

respectively. Function scanf() transfers data from the keyboard to variables in memory while reformatting the data. Function printf() reformats memory data and writes it to the screen. These functions have a similar syntax:

```
scanf(format string, variable list);
printf(format string, variable list);
```

Enclosed in the parentheses of each function call is a *format string,* which specifies the conversion for each variable transferred followed by a *list of variable names* to be transferred; these two *arguments* are separated by a comma (,) and each statement ends with a semicolon (;). The format string enables you to control how data is represented; you place conversion specifiers in the format string, one for each item in the variable list, to instruct scanf() and printf() how to handle the data.

Internal versus external data

Of course you are familiar with the alphabet and the ten decimal digits. These are some of the symbols used to deal with text and numbers outside of computer memory—external data. Internally, this same data is stored as bit patterns, or sequences of ones and zeros that fill up allocated memory areas for your variables. There are methods of moving data in and out of memory unaltered (binary I/O), but usually the data is converted when it is moved to or from memory—this is called formatted I/O. For example, when the last program, STRIO2, displays the value of the integer cost, the printf() function must convert the bit pattern for integer 25 to the character codes for '2' and '5' before it can display them on the screen. Figure 4-4 outlines the process of reading character data from the keyboard and formatting it for internal storage with scanf(), and then reformatting the data and writing it to the screen with printf().

Formatted I/O for single characters

You specify single-character transfers in scanf() and printf() by using a character *conversion specifier* in the format string. The format string "%c" tells scanf() to expect the input to be a character representation. The characters % and *c* together constitute a *conversion specifier* within the format string. You can use this same format string to tell printf() to display output in character form. With the %c conversion specifier, scanf() operates very much like getchar(), and printf() operates much like putchar(), as in the next program.

Listing 4.5 FMTIO.C Formatted input and output

DO: Enter and compile FMTIO, then enter (A) (ENTER)

```
#include <stdio.h>
main()
{
    char ch1;
```

```
    scanf("%c", &ch1);
    printf("%c", ch1);
}
```

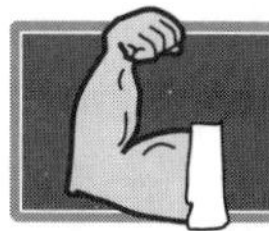

RESULT:

```
C:\>FMTIO
A
A
```

ANALYSIS:

1. The call to function scanf() transfers a single character from the keyboard to variable *ch1*. Function scanf() transfers the data to the variable named *ch1*; the ampersand (&) in front of *ch1* is an operator that designates the address of *ch1* as the destination for the data. The combination *&ch1* tells scanf() where in memory to store the incoming data.

2. The printf() function formats the data in variable *ch1* as a single character and writes it to the screen.

Notice that this program does exactly the same thing as program CHARIO, except that it uses scanf() and printf() instead of getchar() and putchar(). Why does C supply getchar() when scanf() can do the same thing and more? Because getchar() is much smaller and faster; scanf() is able to handle a lot of data types in different ways, but this costs in terms of size and speed. Take a look at the difference in size between CHARIO.EXE and FMTIO.EXE.

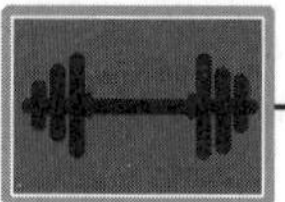

DO: Display the directory containing CHARIO.EXE and FMTIO.EXE

```
C:\>DIR *.EXE

 Volume in drive C has no label
 Directory of  C:\WC04

CHARIO   EXE     3440  11-18-91    1:56p
CHARIO2  EXE    15712  11-18-91    1:57p
```

```
STRIO2   EXE    16112  11-18-91    1:57p
STRIO    EXE     4192  11-18-91    1:57p
FMTIO    EXE    22448  11-18-91    1:57p
      5 File(s)   4476928 bytes free
```

ANALYSIS:

The executable code for FMTIO is over 22,000 bytes in size whereas CHARIO takes only about 3000 bytes! The considerable difference is the extra code devoted to the power and flexibility of scanf() and printf().

You can enter data into more than one variable with a single scanf() statement by having several conversion specifiers and an equal number of identifiers in the variable list. Each conversion specifier should match up with its intended variable in both position and data type. You can read and write two characters in this fashion with the next program.

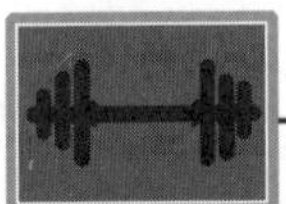

Listing 4.6 FMTIO2.C Read multiple characters

DO:
- Modify FMTIO to read and write two characters
- Compile FMTIO2

```
#include <stdio.h>
main()
{
     char ch1, ch2;                                          /*1*/

     scanf("%c%c", &ch1, &ch2);                              /*2*/
     printf("%c%c", ch1, ch2);                               /*3*/
}
```

ANALYSIS:

1. The scanf() statement on line /*2*/ will not end until it receives two characters from the keyboard because there are two conversion specifiers and two variables.

2. The printf() on line /*3*/ formats the data and writes it to the screen This statement also contains two conversion specifiers in the format string and two identifiers in the variable list.

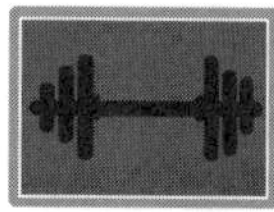

DO: Run FMTIO2 and press (A) (B)(ENTER)

```
C:\>FMTIO2

AB
AB
```

DO: Run FMTIO2 and press (SPACE) (A) (ENTER)

```
C:\>FMTIO2

 A
 A
```

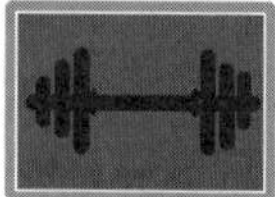

DO: Run FMTIO2 and press (A) (ENTER)

```
C:\>FMTIO2

A
A
```

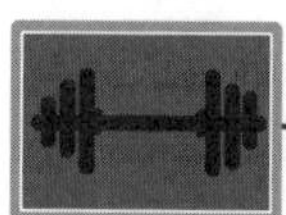

DO: Run FMTIO2 and press (A) (B) (C) (ENTER)

```
C:\>FMTIO2

ABC
AB
```

ANALYSIS:

1. The point of the above exercises is that two characters plus (ENTER) are required to satisfy the scanf() on line /*2*/ and that **any** character from the keyboard works with the %c format, including (SPACE) and (ENTER).

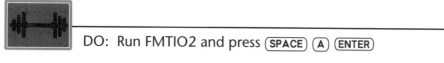

2. During the first two runs, you entered two displayable characters and ended with (ENTER) (notice that (SPACE) is considered to be a displayable

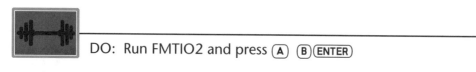

character)—all with the expected result that printf() echoed your input on the next line. But what happened during the third run when you entered (A)-(ENTER)? Why did only one input character work, and why did an extra space appear below the last A? The answer is that (ENTER) serves as the second character; more specifically, the newline character that (ENTER) generates serves as the second character. In the last run, you entered too many characters, but the program only needed two, and so it accepted the first two from the keyboard buffer.

Let's add a display of the character codes to the program and repeat the series of entries to see exactly what is occurring.

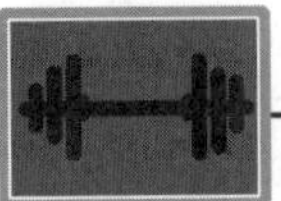

Listing 4.7 FMTIO3.C Display character codes

DO:
- Add display of character codes to FMTIO2
- Compile FMTIO3

```
#include <stdio.h>
main()
{
      char ch1, ch2;

      scanf("%c%c", &ch1, &ch2);
      printf("%c(%d)%c(%d)", ch1, ch1, ch2, ch2);                    /*1*/
}
```

ANALYSIS:

On line /*1*/ you should add the necessary format control to display each ASCII character code after the character itself. You should enclose the decimal conversion specifier in parentheses (%d) and repeat *ch1* and *ch2* in the variable list.

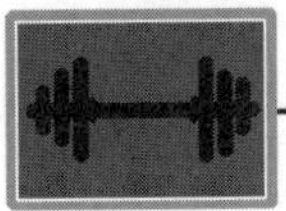

DO: Run FMTIO3 and press (A) (B) (ENTER)

```
C:\>FMTIO3

AB
A(65)B(66)
```

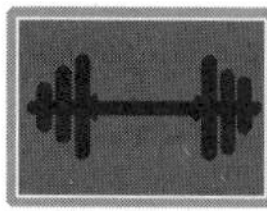

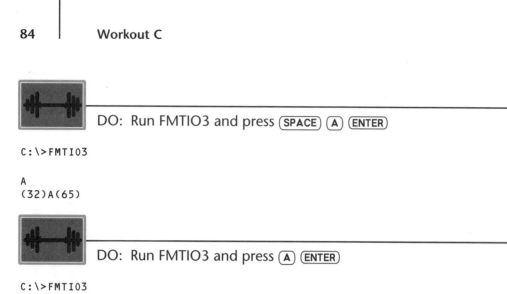

DO: Run FMTIO3 and press SPACE A ENTER

```
C:\>FMTIO3

A
(32)A(65)
```

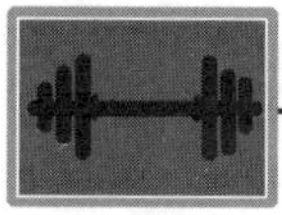

DO: Run FMTIO3 and press A ENTER

```
C:\>FMTIO3

A
A(65)
(10)
```

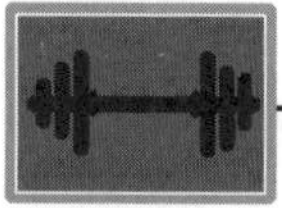

DO: Run FMTIO3 and press A B C ENTER

```
C:\>FMTIO3

ABC
A(65)B(66)
```

ANALYSIS:

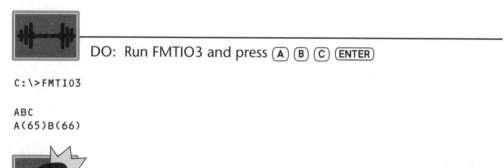

1. Now it is clear what is happening. In the first two runs, the cursor moves off the entry line when you press ENTER, then the program displays both characters, followed by their respective character codes.

2. In the third run you can see the character code for A displayed (65). Then, when the program writes the newline character to the display, it causes the cursor to move to the next line; newline is a nondisplayable character, so it just changes the cursor position. Finally, the program displays the ASCII code for a newline (10).

You should always have as many variables in the variable list of a printf() or scanf() as there are conversion specifiers—no more and no less. If they don't match up, nothing drastic happens; your program will compile and execute, but you may be a bit puzzled about its behavior until you figure out what is wrong. Modify the last program to produce this kind of error.

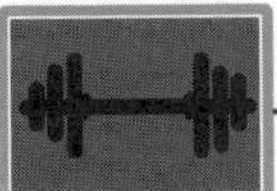

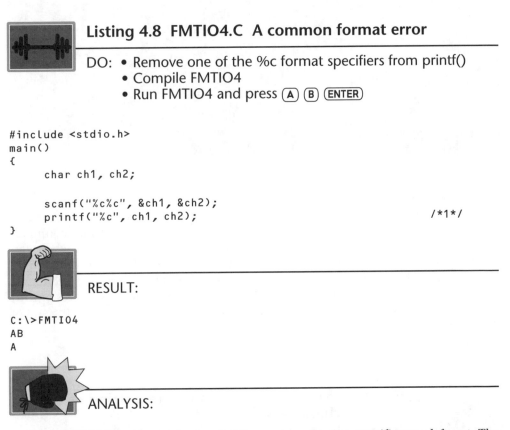

Listing 4.8 FMTIO4.C A common format error

DO:
- Remove one of the %c format specifiers from printf()
- Compile FMTIO4
- Run FMTIO4 and press (A) (B) (ENTER)

```
#include <stdio.h>
main()
{
      char ch1, ch2;

      scanf("%c%c", &ch1, &ch2);
      printf("%c", ch1, ch2);                                    /*1*/
}
```

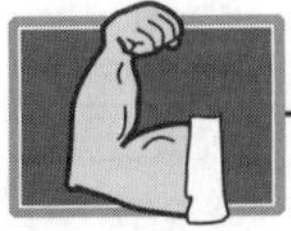

RESULT:

```
C:\>FMTIO4
AB
A
```

ANALYSIS:

Line /*1*/ illustrates a common mistake: one conversion specifier was left out. The program compiles and runs without telling you anything is wrong, except that it only displays one variable.

The scanf() and printf() examples that you have worked with so far have used the conversion character c. There are many other conversion characters and format modifiers that you can insert after the percent sign (%) when working with other data types. Table 4-1 summarizes the available conversion characters, some of which you will experiment with in the remaining sections of this chapter.

Conversion specifier	Use
%c	Single character
%d or %i	Signed decimal integer
%e or %E or %f	Floating-point number
%g or %G	Floating-point number
%o	Octal number
%p	Pointer
%s	Character string
%u	Unsigned decimal integer
%x or %X	Hexadecimal integer

Table 4-1 Format conversion specifiers

Formatted I/O for strings

You use the %s conversion specifier in scanf() to read character strings and in printf() to display them. The string conversion specifier (%s) makes the scanf() function perform just like gets() with one very important difference: the string ends when you enter a *white space* character. A white space character is a newline (issued by ENTER), SPACE or TAB); therefore you cannot include spaces in a string with scanf()—you must use gets() when spaces are needed. The string conversion specifier (%s) makes printf() perform just like puts(), except printf() does not add a newline character at the end of the string. Here is a simple program used to read and write a string.

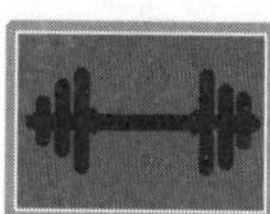

Listing 4.9 FMTIO5.C Read and write a string of characters

DO:
- Enter and compile FMTIO5
- Run FMTIO5 and enter **Proficient Programmer**

```
#include <stdio.h>
main()
{
      char name[15];

      scanf("%s", name);
      printf("%s", name);
}
```

RESULT:

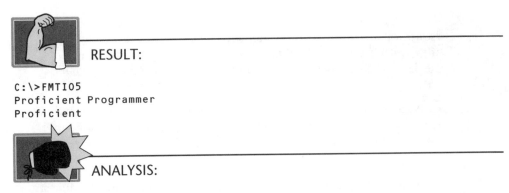

```
C:\>FMTIO5
Proficient Programmer
Proficient
```

ANALYSIS:

1. This program reads a string of characters from the keyboard and writes it to the screen.
2. Caution—just as with gets(), you must be sure to allocate enough space to hold the maximum length string that will be entered. This program has space for 14 characters plus a terminating null in the array *name*.

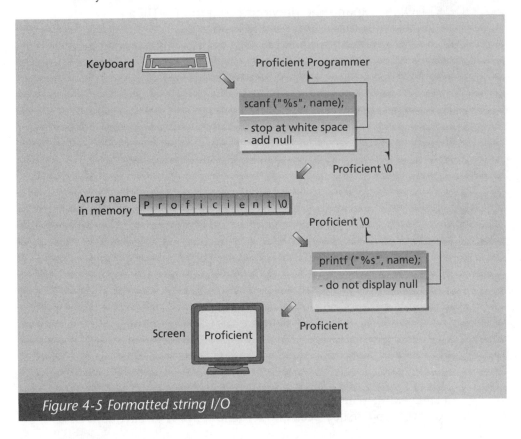

Figure 4-5 Formatted string I/O

3. Notice that the program does not have an ampersand (&) in front of the array *name* in the scanf() statement. This is because an array identifier by itself, without the dimension brackets, refers to the address of the data, so the ampersand is not necessary. Thus the identifier *name* is the address of the array.

4. The space between **Proficient** and **Programmer** is a white space character that determines the end of the input string, so the program only reads and displays **Proficient**.

Figure 4-5 illustrates the formatting operations associated with %s.

We have pointed out the similarities between gets() and scanf() when reading strings and also between puts() and printf() when displaying strings. Now you can do an exercise that highlights the differences, which are: the reaction of scanf() to white space characters on input, and the need for explicit newline characters in printf() for output.

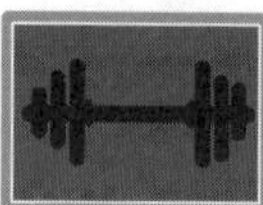

Listing 4.10 FMTIO6.C Print more than one string

DO:
- Expand the previous program, FMTIO5
- Compile and run FMTIO6
- Enter your first and last name with a space between

```
#include <stdio.h>
main()
{
      char first_name[15], last_name[20];                    /*1*/

      scanf("%s%s", first_name, last_name);                  /*2*/
      printf("%s", first_name);                              /*3*/
      printf("%s", last_name);                               /*4*/
}
```

RESULT:

```
C:\>FMTI06
Proficient Programmer
ProficientProgrammer
```

ANALYSIS:

1. The scanf() on line /*2*/ reads two strings separated by one or more blanks (white space characters). This can be advantageous when you want the input to be placed into separate arrays as we have done here.

2. Caution! If your first name is longer than 14 characters, this program will not handle it correctly because the definition for *first_name* specifies 15 bytes of storage. Can you predict what will happen if more than 14 characters are entered for a first name? Try it.

3. Each printf() statement on lines /*3–4*/ writes a string to the screen **at the current cursor location**, so the last name follows immediately after the first name.

Formatted I/O gives you explicit control over how the display appears, so printf() does not automatically insert newline characters or anything else. You can alter the appearance of the output by inserting additional text and nondisplay control characters in the format string.

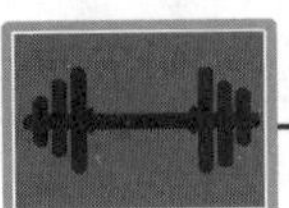

Listing 4.11 FMTIO7.C Text in a format string

DO:
- Add display text to program FMTIO6
- Compile and run FMTIO7
- Enter your first and last name separated by a space

```
#include <stdio.h>
main()
{
      char first_name[15], last_name[20];

      scanf("%s%s", first_name, last_name);
      printf("\nSo your LAST NAME is: %s, \                    /*1*/
\n and your FIRST NAME is: %s; \                              /*2*/
\nWe've got a job for you, %s %s.",                          /*3*/
last_name, first_name, first_name, last_name);               /*4*/
}
```

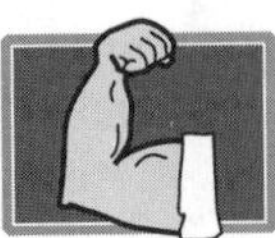

RESULT:

```
C:\>FMTIO7
Proficient Programmer
So your LAST NAME is: Programmer,
and your FIRST NAME is: Proficient;
We've got a job for you, Proficient Programmer.
```

ANALYSIS:

1. You can insert text anywhere in the format string except between % and the conversion character. This example includes text that pre-

cedes and explains what is being displayed, and it also includes punctuation that makes a complete sentence of the output (notice the comma, semicolon, and period).

2. The backslash (\) and n are interpreted by the compiler as a single nondisplay control character that causes a line feed to occur—this is the new*line* character. The effect of newline here is that the cursor moves to the next line before each of the name strings and associated text is displayed.

3. Lines /*1–4*/ combine the conversion characters and string names from the previous program so that only one printf() is necessary. The printf() statement extends over four lines, so you must use *line splicing* to hold the format string together. If you end a line with a backslash (\), the compiler splices the next line (by deleting the backslash) and the following newline before it processes the line. To correctly represent a string constant (characters in double quotes) longer than will fit on one line, you must use line splicing. Line /*3*/ ends outside of the format string, so splicing is not required there.

You can also use multiple sets of double quotes to break long character strings into multiple lines. Using this method, you would write the printf() statement in program FMTIO7 as:

```
printf("\nSo your LAST NAME is: %s, "
       "\n and your FIRST NAME is: %s; "
       "\nWe've got a job for you, %s %s.",
       last_name, first_name, first_name, last_name);
```

The compiler will concatenate adjacent character string constants into a single string constant, so the result is one format string. This approach to splicing is valid only for character strings, but it allows you to create a neater statement. Line splicing with the backslash (\) is a more general approach that will work with any kind of source line; it is often used with long macros (see Chapter 15).

Escape sequences

The backslash (\) is a special character that causes the compiler to interpret both it and the character that follows it as a single control code. These dual characters are called escape sequences, and Table 4-2 lists the escape sequences that can be used in printf() format strings.

The next program illustrates how your computer screen reacts to several of the escape characters from Table 4-2.

Escape sequence	Meaning
\a	Alert or bell
\b	Backspace
\f	Formfeed
\n	Newline
\r	Carriage return
\t	Horizontal tab
\v	Vertical tab
\\	Backslash
\?	Question mark
\'	Single quote
\"	Double quote
\<octal digits>	Octal number
\x<hex digits>	Hexadecimal number

<octal digits> and <hex digits> represent a sequence of digits.

Table 4-2 Escape sequences

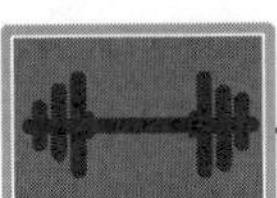

Listing 4.12 ESCAPE.C Escape sequences

DO: Enter, compile, and run ESCAPE

```
#include <stdio.h>
main()
{
     printf("\n\\n causes\na line feed to occur");
     printf("\n\\\" causes a double quote (\") to be printed");
     printf("\n\\a causes the BELL, or beep, to sound\a");
     printf("\n\\t can be used to align some numbers to tab \
columns\n\t1\t2\t3\n\t4\t5\t6");
     printf("\nYou use two %% characters together to display \
the percent sign");
}
```

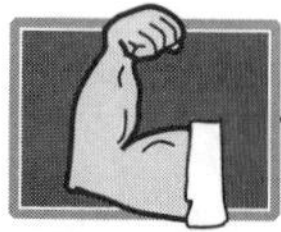

RESULT:

```
C:\>ESCAPE

\n causes
a line feed to occur
\" causes a double quote (") to be printed
\a causes the BELL, or beep, to sound
\t can be used to align some numbers to tab columns
        1       2       3
        4       5       6
You use two % characters together to display the percent sign
```

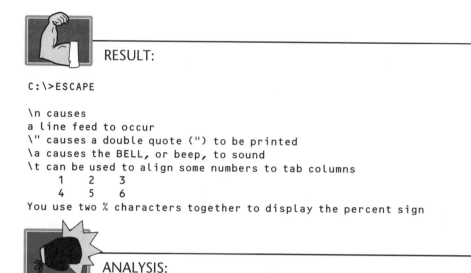

ANALYSIS:

1. The first printf() contains a newline character just after the word **causes**, so the line splits at that point. Notice also that you must insert two backslashes (\\) at the beginning of the format string to display a single backslash.
2. To prevent a double quote intended for the display from prematurely ending the format string, you must use the escape sequence (\"), as in the second printf().
3. If you listen as this program executes, you will hear a short tone as the alert escape sequence (\a) in the third printf() causes the bell to sound.
4. The fourth printf() statement shows how you can use the tab escape sequence (\t) to output columns of data.
5. The last printf() does not involve an escape sequence; it simply illustrates how to display a percent sign (%) by using two percent characters. This is necessary because otherwise the compiler would interpret the percent as a conversion specifier.
6. Notice that the last two printf() statements use line splicing because the format strings are especially long.

Formatted I/O for integers

You can read numeric data from the keyboard and convert it to internal, binary form with an integer conversion specifier (%d or %i). Conversely, you can reformat internal

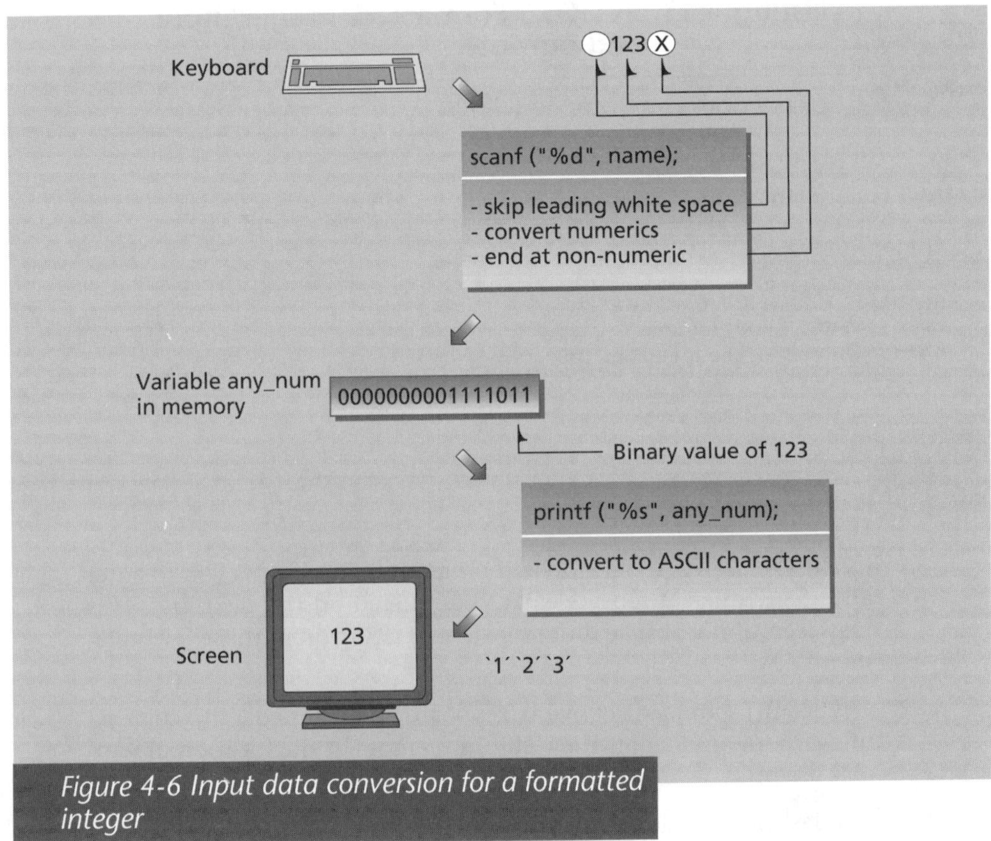

Figure 4-6 Input data conversion for a formatted integer

integer data into displayable, ASCII characters with the same conversion specifier. An integer conversion specifier regulates input from a scanf() function according to the following rules:

1. Skip leading white space characters.
2. Accept one plus or minus character preceding any number of numeric characters (0–9).
3. End when any non-numeric character is entered and leave that character in the input buffer.

Figure 4-6 illustrates the rules for formatted integer conversions.

The next program allows you to experiment with formatted integer input.

Listing 4.13 INTIO.C Formatted integer input and output

DO: Enter and compile INTIO

```
#include <stdio.h>
main()
{
   int any_num;

   printf("\nEnter a number: ");
   scanf("%d", &any_num);
   printf("Here's the result: %d", any_num);
}
```

ANALYSIS:

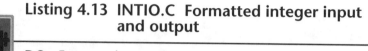

1. INTIO is a pretty straightforward program that prompts you to enter an integer; then it repeats what you entered on the next line. This may seem almost trivial, but there is a lot going on in those few statements.
2. The scanf() statement converts keyboard character codes to internal integer form and stores the result in memory at the location of variable *any_num*.
3. The last printf() statement displays the three words of text on the screen, then it fetches the internal integer from memory, reformats it to a series of external character digits, and displays these digits on the screen.

DO: Run INTIO and enter (SPACE) (SPACE) **123** (ENTER)

```
C:\>INTIO
Enter a number:   123
Here's the result: 123
```

ANALYSIS:

This example illustrates Rule 1: "Skip leading white space characters."

DO: Run INTIO and enter **-123-4**

```
C:\>INTIO
Enter a number: -123-4
Here's the result: -123
```

ANALYSIS:

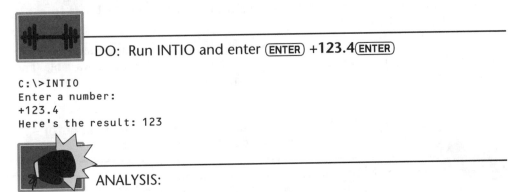

This illustrates Rule 2: "Accept a leading minus sign," and Rule 3: "End on any non-numeric after receiving numeric characters."

DO: Run INTIO and enter (ENTER) **+123.4**(ENTER)

```
C:\>INTIO
Enter a number:
+123.4
Here's the result: 123
```

ANALYSIS:

This illustrates all three rules: The (ENTER) key generates a newline, which scanf() ignores because it is a leading white space character, it accepts the three numeric characters that follow the +, and input terminates at the decimal point.

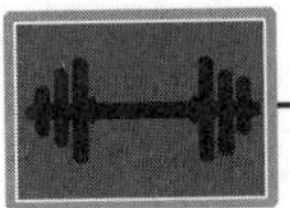

DO: Run INTIO and enter **0012300x** (ENTER)

```
C:\>INTIO
Enter a number: 0012300x
Here's the result: 12300
```

ANALYSIS:

This illustrates the correct conversion of an integer with leading zeros, trailing zeros, and termination with the input of an alphabetic (non-numeric) character.

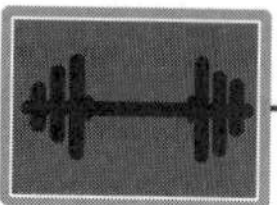

DO: Run INTIO and enter **1234567890** (ENTER)

```
C:\>INTIO
Enter a number: 1234567890
Here's the result: 722
```

ANALYSIS:

1. In this example, you have entered a number too large for a 2-byte integer, with the incorrect result of 722. This is the part of the larger number that is left over if you chop it in half and keep the lower 16 bits (two bytes).

Rule 3 for reading integers says that scanf() leaves the terminating character in the input buffer. You can read that character from the buffer with another variable (and associated conversion specifier) in the same scanf() statement.

Listing 4.14 INTIO2.C Capture the ending character of integer entry

DO:
- Modify INTIO to read an extra character
- Compile and run INTIO2, then enter **123x** (ENTER)

```
#include <stdio.h>
main()
{
      int any_num;
      char ch_end;                                               /*1*/

      printf("\nEnter a number and a letter: ");                 /*2*/
      scanf("%d%c", &any_num, &ch_end);                          /*3*/
      printf("The result is %d, \nand the terminating "          /*4*/
            "character is %c", any_num, ch_end);                 /*5*/
}
```

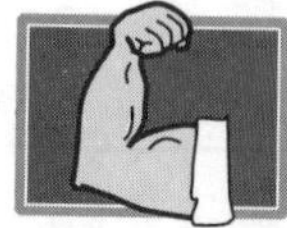

RESULT:

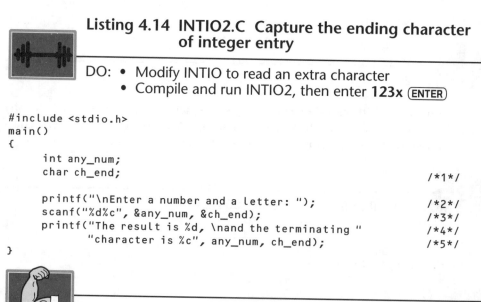

```
C:\>INTIO2
Enter a number and a letter: 123x
The result is 123,
and the terminating character is x
```

ANALYSIS:

1. The scanf() on line /*3*/ has a variable and corresponding conversion character to accept the terminating character for the integer, which in this case is **x**. Try some other non-numeric characters at the end of the integer (including ENTER).
2. Notice that both the scanf() on line /*3*/ and printf() on line /*4*/ have two conversion specifiers and two matching variables.

You have to be careful to precede each integer variable with an ampersand (&) in scanf() statements. This very important operator returns the address of a variable so that scanf() knows where to store the incoming data. Leave the ampersand off just once to see what happens.

Listing 4.15 INTIO3.C A scanf() syntax error

DO:
- Modify INTIO to leave off the address operator (&)
- Compile and run INTIO3, then enter 123 ENTER

```
#include <stdio.h>
main()
{
   int any_num;

   printf("\nEnter a number: ");
   scanf("%d", any_num);                                         /*1*/
   printf("This is NOT the number you entered: %d",              /*2*/
       any_num);
}
```

RESULT:

```
C:\>INTIO3
Enter a number: 123
This is NOT the number you entered: 0
```

ANALYSIS:

This example includes a very common programming error—it leaves the address operator (&) off the input variable *any_num*. This error causes scanf() to place the converted integer data in some unknown location of memory, not in *any_num* where you want it to go. The variable *any_num*, has not been given any value; it just contains whatever happens to be in that location in memory, so you can't predict what value will be displayed by line /*2*/.

Formatted I/O for long integers requires that you add a *conversion modifier*, lowercase ell (*l*), to the integer conversion specifier. This modifier tells scanf() and printf() that the associated variable is of data type *long*, and that the internal data occupies the memory space allocated to a long integer. You will learn more about conversion modifiers later in this chapter.

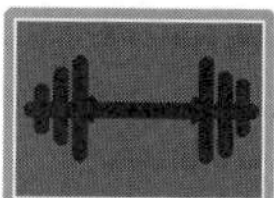

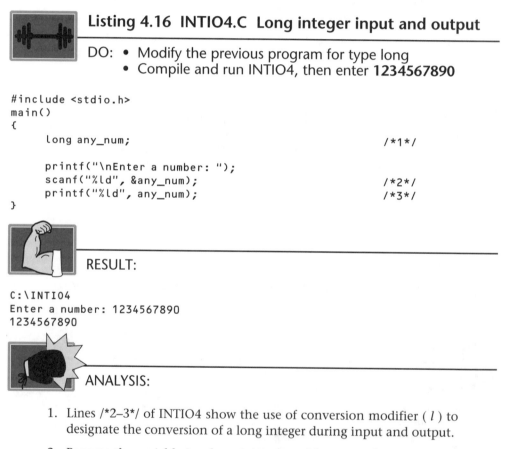

Listing 4.16 INTIO4.C Long integer input and output

DO:
- Modify the previous program for type long
- Compile and run INTIO4, then enter **1234567890**

```
#include <stdio.h>
main()
{
      long any_num;                                    /*1*/

      printf("\nEnter a number: ");
      scanf("%ld", &any_num);                          /*2*/
      printf("%ld", any_num);                          /*3*/
}
```

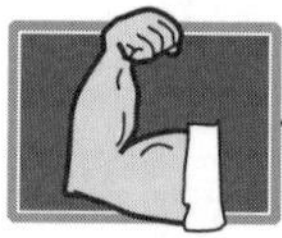

RESULT:

```
C:\INTIO4
Enter a number: 1234567890
1234567890
```

ANALYSIS:

1. Lines /*2–3*/ of INTIO4 show the use of conversion modifier (*l*) to designate the conversion of a long integer during input and output.
2. Because the variable is a long integer, and because a long integer is four bytes on this machine, scanf() will accept the larger number that was not valid for INTIO in Program 4.13.

When using a compiler that allocates different sizes for *int* and *long* variables, you should be precise in using the conversion modifier (*l*) for formatted I/O, and you should also be careful to add *L* to long integer constants. Here's what happens if you don't pay proper attention to these modifiers.

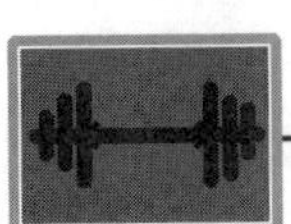

Listing 4.17 INTIO5.C Common errors with long integer I/O

DO:
- Take the long modifier (*l*) out of INTIO4
- Compile and run INTIO5, then enter **1234567890** twice

```
#include <stdio.h>
main()
{
      long any_num;

      printf("\nEnter a number: ");
      scanf("%d", &any_num);                                  /*1*/
      printf("Error: %ldÑscanf() modifier l is missing\n",    /*2*/
            any_num);
      printf("\nEnter a number: ");                           /*3*/
      scanf("%ld", &any_num);
      printf("This is the real value: ", any_num);            /*4*/
      printf("\nError: %dÑprintf() modifier l is missing",    /*5*/
           any_num);
}
```

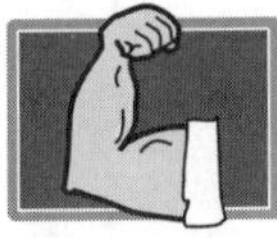

RESULT:

```
C:\INTIO5
Enter a number: 1234567890
Error: 722--scanf() modifier is missing
Enter a number: 1234567890
This is the real value: 1234567890
Error: 722--printf() modifier is missing
```

ANALYSIS:

1. On line /*1*/, the conversion modifier (*l*) is missing, causing scanf() to incorrectly convert the input to a 2-byte integer instead of a 4-byte long integer.
2. The printf() on line /*3*/ is missing the modifier (*l*), causing the output conversion to be wrong—again, a 2-byte instead of a 4-byte integer.

3. Omitting the long modifier (*l*) when working with long variables is an easy mistake—be aware!

Formatted I/O for floating-point numbers

The rules for reading a floating-point number are the same as those for reading an integer, except that a single decimal point is allowed within the sequence of numeric characters. The rules are:

1. Skip leading white space characters.
2. Accept an optional plus (+) or minus (-), then any number of numeric characters (0–9) with an optional decimal point (.).
3. End when any non-numeric character is encountered.

Compile the next program to see floating-point conversion in action.

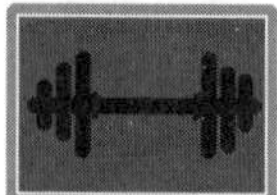

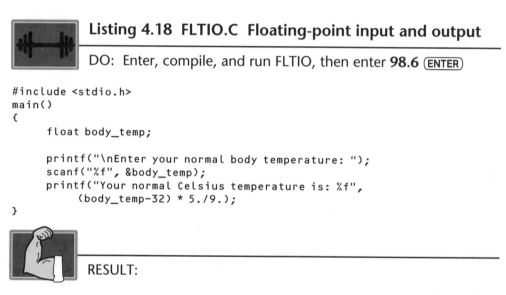

Listing 4.18 FLTIO.C Floating-point input and output

DO: Enter, compile, and run FLTIO, then enter **98.6** (ENTER)

```
#include <stdio.h>
main()
{
      float body_temp;

      printf("\nEnter your normal body temperature: ");
      scanf("%f", &body_temp);
      printf("Your normal Celsius temperature is: %f",
           (body_temp-32) * 5./9.);
}
```

RESULT:

```
C:\>FLTIO
Enter your normal body temperature: 98.6
Your normal Celsius temperature is: 36.999999
```

ANALYSIS:

1. The program prompts you to enter your temperature, which it converts to internal form according to the rules for reading floating-point numbers with conversion specifier %f.

2. This program introduces something new in the last printf() statement. Instead of listing a simple variable name after the format string, the statement includes a calculation involving the variable *body_temp*. This is called an *expression*, and printf() will display the result of the expression. In fact, previous examples have also used expressions because an identifier by itself is the simplest form of an expression—a *primary expression*. However, in general, an expression is a group of operands (variables and constants) connected by operators.
3. Notice also that the last printf() is split into two lines without line splicing (without a backslash at the end). The split can occur after the comma separator because it is not in the middle of a string constant. You should compare this with the last line of program INTIO2 (Program 4.14), in which the split is in the middle of the format string and line splicing is necessary.

For very large or small floating-point numbers (larger than 1.e38 or smaller than 1.e-37) and for numbers requiring more than seven digits of precision, you must use double precision data types. If you substitute type *double* for *float* in the definition of variable *body_temp* in FLTIO, the program will work the same way. You could also substitute conversion specifier %e for %f in the scanf() and printf() statements. You must add the conversion modifier (*l*) to the conversion specifier for formatted reading of data type double with scanf(), but you don't need it to output data type double in printf(). If the compiler you are using follows the ANSI standard (as Power C does), you can enter either exponential or decimal forms with either conversion specifier (%e or %f).

Conversion modifiers

You can place certain characters, called *conversion modifiers*, between the percent sign (%) and its conversion character. These modifiers serve to specify in greater detail how you want the input or output conversion to occur. You have already used the long conversion modifier to notify printf() and scanf() of a long integer conversion. We will discuss other conversion modifiers in two categories: those for scanf() and those for printf().

Conversion modifiers for scanf()

Table 4-3 lists conversion modifiers for the scanf() function.

Modifier	Effect
*	Suppression—skip the field
Integer	Specifies the maximum field width
h	Specifies a short integer
l	Specifies a long integer or double floating point
L	Specifies a long double floating point

Table 4-3 scanf() conversion modifiers

If you include a suppression modifier (*) in a format specifier, scanf() will throw away any data that you enter into that format specifier. Because scanf() does not assign the data to a variable, you do not have to add a name to the list of variables for that format specifier. For example, the following scanf() statement has two format specifiers, but only one variable:

```
scanf("%*d %d", &value);
```

You will enter two numbers, and this scanf() will read both of them, but it will discard the first and place the second one into *value*. Suppression is especially useful for reading formatted data from files when you need to skip over certain fields to get to the data you are interested in. In Chapter 12, you will learn how to use fscanf() (scanf()'s cousin) to read data from files. Function fscanf() uses the same conversion specifiers and modifiers that scanf() does, so you can use the suppression modifier (*) there to skip data in a file.

If you place an integer constant in a format specifier, the integer limits the number of characters that scanf() will read. For example, the following statement will read integers with only two digits:

```
scanf("%2d", &value);
```

The next example gives you a chance to use the first two modifiers from Table 4-3 to accomplish field suppression and field width control.

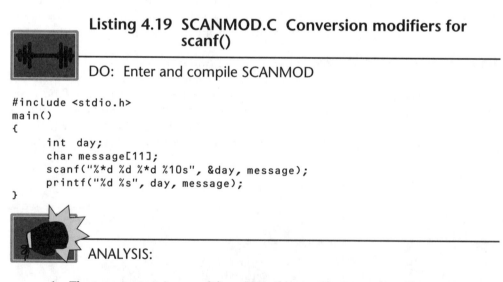

Listing 4.19 SCANMOD.C Conversion modifiers for scanf()

DO: Enter and compile SCANMOD

```
#include <stdio.h>
main()
{
      int day;
      char message[11];
      scanf("%*d %d %*d %10s", &day, message);
      printf("%d %s", day, message);
}
```

ANALYSIS:

1. The two suppression modifiers (*) in the scanf() statement will cause it to discard the first and third numbers. The scanf() will follow the usual rules in reading three integers from the input stream; however, it will not assign the first and third integers to any variable—they are skipped.

2. The string conversion modifier, 10, limits the number of input characters for the string to ten.

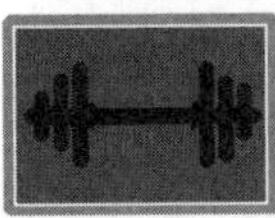

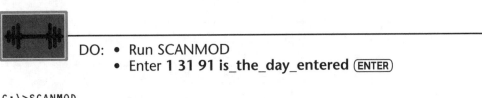

DO: • Run SCANMOD
• Enter **1 31 91 is_the_day_entered** (ENTER)

```
C:\>SCANMOD
1 31 91 is_the_day_entered
31 is_the_day
```

ANALYSIS:

The conversion modifiers extract the day from the date and limit the length of the character string.

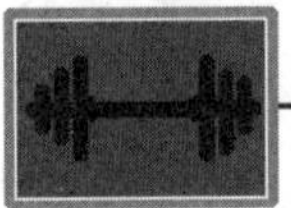

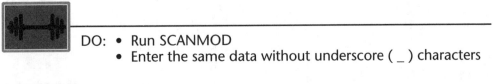

DO: • Run SCANMOD
• Enter the same data without underscore (_) characters

```
C:\>SCANMOD
1 31 91 is the day entered
31 is
```

ANALYSIS:

1. Now the first white space after **is** terminates the string, even before you enter ten characters. So the %10s format specifier makes the program stop reading after 10 characters or the first white space character, whichever comes first.

Conversion modifiers for printf()

Modifiers for printf() are any of the following five items appearing in the order shown:

```
<flag><width><.><precision><length>
```

You can use some of the items and omit others, but you must preserve the order. Table 4-4 lists conversion modifiers for the printf() function categorized under these five item names.

Flag modifier	Effect
-	Left justify the item.
+	Show the sign of a number (+ or -).
space	Show the sign of a number (- if negative), show space if the number is positive.
0	Pad numbers with leading zeros.
#	Use an alternate form of numeric output.
	Add prefix 0 for octal (%o), add prefix 0x for hexadecimal (%x), and force a decimal point for floating-point numbers (%e, %f, %g) even if there is no fractional part.
Width modifier	**Effect**
Integer	Specifies the minimum field width.
*	Width is given by next listed variable.
Precision modifier	**Effect**
Integer	Specifies the number of digits after the decimal point for floating-point numbers (%e, %f, %g), the minimum number of digits to display for an integer (%d), or the maximum number of characters to display for a string (%s).
*	Precision is given by next listed variable.
Length modifier	**Effect**
h	Specifies a short integer.
l	Specifies a long integer or double floating-point number.
L	Specifies a long double floating-point.

Table 4-4 Function printf() conversion modifiers

There are five allowed flags and any or all can be used in any order at the beginning of a modification.

The next program shows you how to use some of these modifiers for printf().

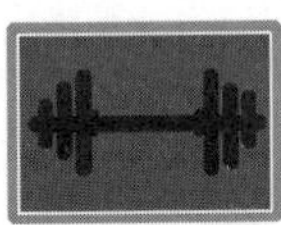

Listing 4.20 PRINTMOD.C Conversion modifiers for printf()

DO: Enter, compile, and run PRINTMOD

```
#include <stdio.h>
main()
{
      int   i   = 123;
      char  s[] = "abcdef";
      float f   = -45.6;

      printf("\n\nMinimum width:/%10s/%10d/%10f/",       s, i, f);
      printf("\n\n    Precision:/%10.5s/%10.5d/%10.5f/", s, i, f);
      printf("\n\n Left justify:/%-10s/%-10d/%-10f/",    s, i, f);

      printf("\n\n Space prefix:/% 10d/% 10.5f/", i, f);
      printf("\n\n  Zero prefix:/%010d/%010.5f/", i, f);
      printf("\n\n  Sign prefix:/%+d/%+e/%+f/", i, f, f);

      f = i;
      printf("\n\n   Alternates:/%#o/%#x/%#f/", i, i, f);
}
```

RESULT:

```
C:\>PRINTMOD
Minimum width:/    abcdef/       123/-45.599998/

    P recision:/     abcde/     00123/ -45.60000/

 Left justify:/abcdef    /123       /-45.599998/

 Space prefix:/       123/ -45.60000/

  Zero prefix:/0000000123/-045.60000/

  Sign prefix:/+123/-45.599998/

   Alternates:/0173/0x7b/123.000000/
```

ANALYSIS:

1. On each line, this program illustrates the effect of one of the conversion modifiers on several data types. It places a slash character (/) at the beginning and end of each field to mark the absolute limits of the display item.

2. The first printf() shows the effect of a minimum width flag modifier of 10. The format modifiers cause both the string and integer displays to be padded on the left with spaces to fill out the 10 characters specified. The floating-point number displays as a negative sign and decimal point plus eight significant digits. Eight digits are one more than type *float* will support, so the display appears not to be exactly -45.6 unless you mentally round it off to seven digits.

3. The second printf() shows the effect of a precision modifier of 5. It displays only the first five characters of the string, it pads the integer out to five digits with zeros, and it displays the floating-point number with five digits to the right of the decimal point. Notice that the number is exact (-45.6), now that the number of significant digits is seven.

4. The third printf() shows the effect of left justification; it moves all fields to the extreme left and pads with spaces on the right.

5. The next three printf() statements show the use of flag modifiers to affix different prefixes to numeric displays: spaces, zeros, and a sign.

6. The last printf() shows how the alternate flag (#) prefixes octal integers with zero and hexadecimal integers with zero-ex. The program assigns an integer with no fractional part to variable *f* so that the last printf() can illustrate how the # flag forces the display of a decimal point.

Any character that appears between conversion specifiers in the format string of a scanf() statement requires you to use that character as a separator in the entered input stream. The next program requires you to separate entered numbers with a hyphen.

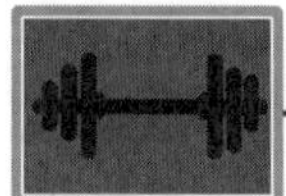

Listing 4.21 SEPARATE.C Separator characters for input data

DO: Enter and compile SEPARATE

```
#include <stdio.h>
main()
{
      int mm, dd, yy;

      scanf("%d-%d-%d", &mm, &dd, &yy);
      printf("Tax day is %d/%d/%d", mm, dd, yy);
}
```

ANALYSIS:

1. Here you use the hyphen (-) to separate the month, day, and year; the program does not confuse the hyphen with a left justify flag because that modifier is always used **after** the %. You can use any character that you like for a separator, it doesn't have to be a hyphen.

DO: Run SEPARATE and enter **4-15-91** (ENTER)

```
C:\>SEPARATE
4-15-91
Tax day is 4-15-91
```

ANALYSIS:

1. The hyphens correctly separate three integers in the input data.
2. Notice that the output string uses the slash (/) as a separator; there is no reason for the output separator (if any) to be the same as the input separator.

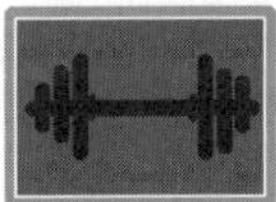

DO: Run SEPARATE and enter **4/15/91** (ENTER)

```
C:\>SEPARATE
4/15/91
Tax day is 4/0/0
```

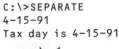

ANALYSIS:

A slash in the input stream is the wrong separator, so input terminates at the first slash.

FORMATTED OUTPUT TO A STRING

A very useful function that is a close relative to printf() is sprintf(). This function sends converted output to a string array instead of to the display. The result of sprintf() is always a null terminated string stored in the specified character array. You will find sprintf() very useful in preparing a string for display by formatting values from different data types. The next program does this.

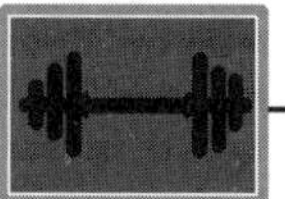

Listing 4.22 FMTSTR.C Format an output string

DO: Enter, compile, and run FMTSTR

```
#include <stdio.h>
main()
{
      char buffer[24];
      char *month = "April";
      int  number = 4;

      sprintf(buffer, "%s is the %dth month", month, number);
      printf("\n%s", buffer);
}
```

RESULT:

```
C:\>FMTSTR

April is the 4th month
```

ANALYSIS:

1. The sprintf() function formats a phrase containing literal characters ("is the th month"), a string (*month*), and a converted integer (*number*), then copies it into an array **buffer** to produce a single string. The conversion specifiers *%s* and *%d* regulate the formatting of the two variables *month* and *number*, respectively.
2. The printf() function shows you the result of the previous line.

Figure 4-7 shows how sprintf() builds the string in program FMTSTR.

The sprintf() function also has a role in representing data in different ways. You can convert values to any desired format by properly selecting of the conversion specifier. For example, you can represent an address in hexadecimal form by using the %p conversion specifier, as in the next program.

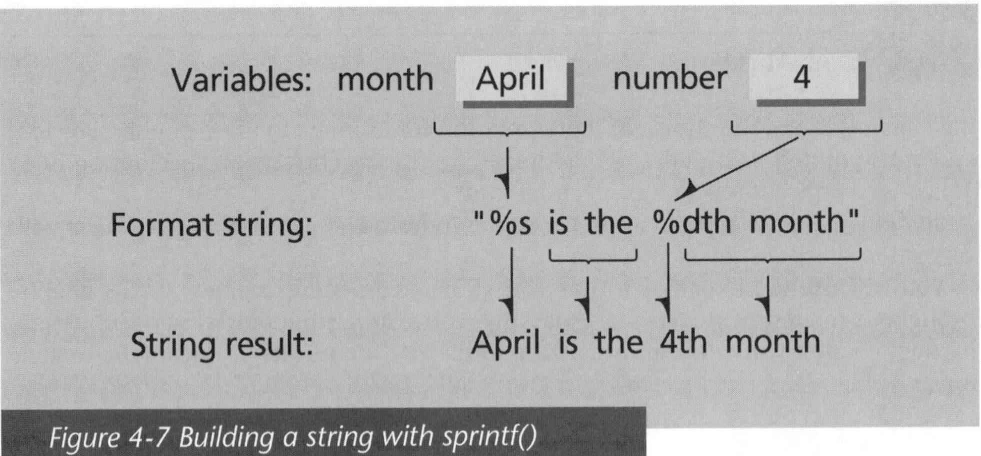

Figure 4-7 Building a string with sprintf()

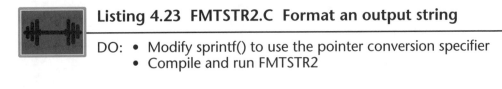

Listing 4.23 FMTSTR2.C Format an output string

DO:
- Modify sprintf() to use the pointer conversion specifier
- Compile and run FMTSTR2

```
#include <stdio.h>
main()
{
      char buffer[24];
      char *month = "April";
      int  number = 4;

      sprintf(buffer, "The address of number is %p",      /*1*/
            &number);                                     /*2*/
      printf("\n%s", buffer);
}
```

RESULT:

```
C:\>FMTSTR2

The address of number is 829C
```

ANALYSIS:

In general, C leaves the choice of representation for pointers to the compiler. Power C represents pointers as hexadecimal addresses, so the *%p* conversion specifier on line /*1*/ converts the address to hexadecimal form.

Similarly, you can represent integer values in hexadecimal form or octal form with conversion specifiers *%x* or *%o*.

You will use the experience that you gathered in the examples of this chapter throughout the rest of *Workout C*, especially while formatting output with printf(). In the next chapter you will use formatting to display the results of arithmetic calculations.

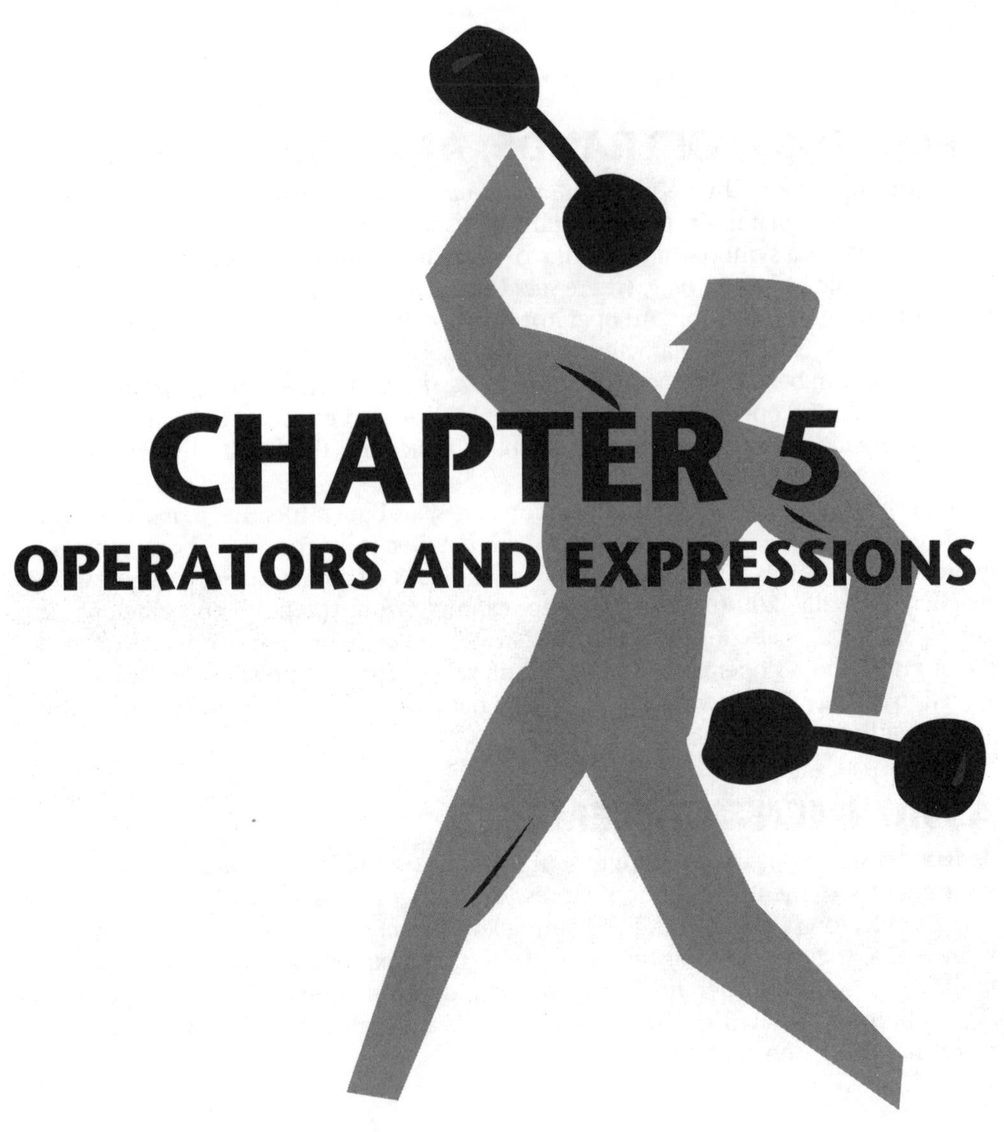

CHAPTER 5
OPERATORS AND EXPRESSIONS

In this chapter you will get down to business and start changing data values with operators and expressions. You will learn about moving data to and from variables with assignment statements and you will learn about using operators to perform arithmetic. You will also learn the rules of precedence for operators—rules that determine which things get done first. There are other rules that determine how and when programs change the data types of variables during assignments and calculations, and you will learn about them in this chapter.

OPERATORS, OPERANDS, AND EXPRESSIONS

We begin this chapter by defining the terms *operators, operands,* and *expressions* to be sure that you understand these important items in C language.

An *operator* is a symbol that uses one or more *operands* to produce a single result. A simple example is: *speed * time,* where *speed* and *time* are operands and * is an operator that performs multiplication. An operator can be a single character (like * or /) or it may consist of more than one character (like ++ or *sizeof()*).

Operands can be variables, constants, or *expressions*. In this example, *distance = speed * 2,* the multiplier operator (*) has the variable *speed* and constant *2* as operands, and the assignment operator (=) has the variable *distance* and the result of the expression *speed * 2* as operands.

An *expression* is a group of variables, constants, and operators that a program evaluates to yield a single result. The example *speed * time* from the above paragraph is an expression. If *speed* is 50 (miles per hour) and *time* is 4 (hours), the expression *speed * time* has the value 200 (miles). The other example from the previous paragraph, *distance = speed * 2,* is also an expression because * and = are both operators and *distance, speed,* and *2* are all operands. The resultant value of this expression is the value assigned to *distance.* To reiterate, an expression has three elements: **operands, operators,** and a **result.**

ASSIGNMENT STATEMENTS

Assignment statements use the assignment operator (=) to set the value of a variable. An assignment statement is really an expression that contains the assignment operator plus a semicolon (;) at the end. For example, *time = hours* is an expression that sets the value of *time* to be the same as the value of *hours.* The expression has a left-side operand (*time*) and a right-side operand (*hours*). If you add a semicolon at the end of the expression, it becomes a statement: *time = hours.* Here's a program with an assignment statement that uses a constant operand.

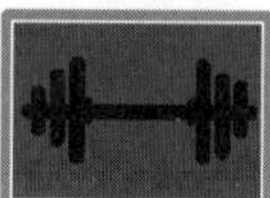

Listing 5.1 ASSIGN.C Assignment statement

DO: Enter, compile, and run ASSIGN

```
#include <stdio.h>
#define SEVEN 7
main()
{
     int dwarfs;

     dwarfs = SEVEN;
     printf("There are %d dwarfs", dwarfs);
}
```

RESULT:

```
C:\>ASSIGN
There are 7 dwarfs
```

ANALYSIS:

1. The equal sign (=) is the assignment operator. Its purpose is to set the value of the variable on the left to be the same as the variable, constant, or expression on the right. In this case, it assigns *dwarfs* the value of an integer constant, 7.
2. The preprocessor directive *#define SEVEN 7* reinforces our recommendation in Chapter 3 that you use symbolic constants whenever possible.

An assignment expression (like all expressions) returns a value, which is the value assigned to the left-side operand. This returned value can be used as an operand by other C operators in very useful ways, one of which is shown in the next program.

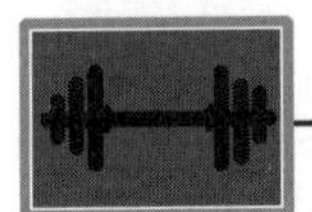

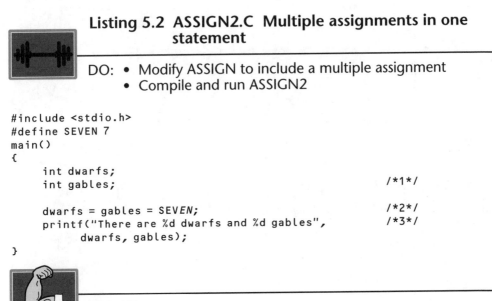

Listing 5.2 ASSIGN2.C Multiple assignments in one statement

DO:
- Modify ASSIGN to include a multiple assignment
- Compile and run ASSIGN2

```
#include <stdio.h>
#define SEVEN 7
main()
{
     int dwarfs;
     int gables;                                          /*1*/

     dwarfs = gables = SEVEN;                             /*2*/
     printf("There are %d dwarfs and %d gables",          /*3*/
            dwarfs, gables);
}
```

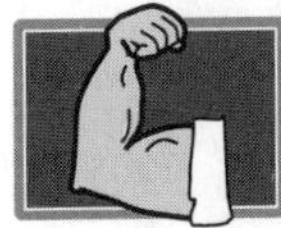

RESULT:

```
C:\>ASSIGN2
There are 7 dwarfs and 7 gables
```

ANALYSIS:

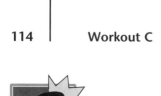

1. You can make more than one assignment in a single statement as shown in line /*2*/, which assigns the value 7 to the variables *dwarfs* and *gables*.

This construction is particularly suitable when you need to set the initial value of two or more related variables. For instance, suppose you use the variables *donkey* and *elephant* to count votes in a political race between a Democrat and a Republican. You might then initialize the two counters to zero with the following statement:

```
donkey = elephant = 0;
```

Using variables in a single statement implies a logical connection between them, so if two variables are not related in some way (by meaning or usage), it is best to assign values with separate statements, like:

dwarfs = gables = (constant); (expression result)

7

dwarfs = gables = (constant); (expression result)

7 7 7

Assignment 1

dwarfs = gables = (constant); (expression result)

7 7 7 7

Assignment 2

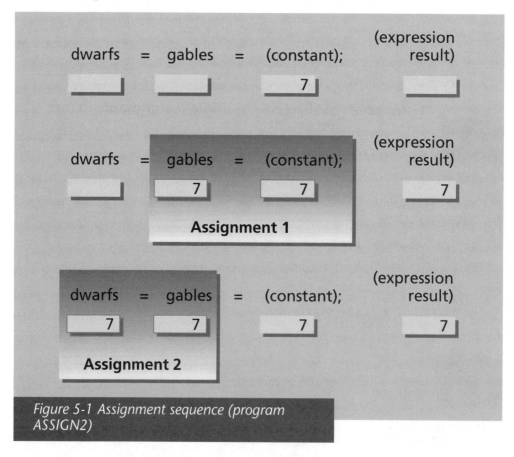

Figure 5-1 Assignment sequence (program ASSIGN2)

```
donkey    = 0;
elephant  = 0;
```

The compiler will not favor one form over the other—your program will be no smaller or faster if you combine the assignments into one statement.

In a multiple assignment statement, the assignments occur in a particular order, moving from right to left. This is the first instance of *precedence* and *associativity*—the properties of operators that determine the order of evaluation. *Precedence* is the rule that says which operator your program applies first, and *associativity* determines whether your program evaluates an expression moving from left to right or right to left when operators of equal precedence are present. Because the two assignment operators in the last example have the same precedence, associativity determines the order. First, the program assigns constant (7) to *gables*, then it assigns the returned value of the first expression (7) to *dwarfs*. Figure 5-1 shows the sequence of events as program ASSIGN2 stores values in memory. After each assignment, the program also returns the result of the expression to a temporary memory location, shown at the right of Figure 5-1.

The quantities in parentheses in Figure 5-1 represent memory areas inaccessible to you, the programmer. These are memory locations reserved by the compiler to hold constants or temporary values needed by the program. The symbolic constant, *SEVEN*, and the result of each expression are examples of these reserved memory locations.

There are wrong or illegal assignments in C; for instance you cannot assign a value to a constant, as the next program tries to do.

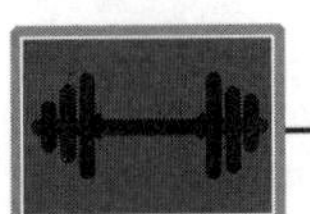

Listing 5.3 ASSIGN3.C Incorrect order of multiple assignments

DO:
- Modify the order of assignment in ASSIGN2
- Compile ASSIGN3

```
#include <stdio.h>
#define SEVEN 7
main()
{
    int dwarfs;
    int gables;

    dwarfs = SEVEN = gables;                    /*1*/
    printf("There are %d dwarfs and %d gables",
        dwarfs, gables);
}
```

RESULT:

```
PC/C/E ASSIGN3
Power C - Version 2.1.3
```

```
(C) Copyright 1989-1991 by Mix Software
Compiling ...
ASSIGN3(9):   dwarfs = SEVEN = gables;              /*1*/
*************                   ^ 27
27: Lvalue expected (invalid expression on left-hand side of assignment)
---------------------------------------
    118 lines compiled
    1 Compile errors
```

ANALYSIS:

1. In line /*1*/, the order of assignment is wrong: You cannot change the value of a constant—the compiler knows this and generates an error because the statement is trying to assign the value of gables to *SEVEN*.
2. The error statement above says that the compiler expected an *lvalue*; this is another new term. An lvalue refers to a named area of storage, or an area of memory that can accept a value. One form of lvalue is any identifier, such as the name of a variable, that can legally appear on the left side of an assignment operator (the *l* in lvalue is for left). In the above expression, *SEVEN* appears on the left of an assignment operator (=), but it is not an lvalue, so it leads to an error.

You should not assign the value of a variable to another variable if you have not previously given the first variable a value. The next program makes this mistake.

Listing 5.4 ASSIGN4.C Incorrect order of multiple assignments

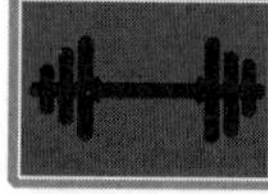

DO:
- Remove the initialization constant in ASSIGN3
- Compile and run ASSIGN4

```
#include <stdio.h>
#define SEVEN 7
main()
{
     int dwarfs;
     int gables;

     dwarfs = gables;                                /*1*/
     printf("There are %d dwarfs and %d gables",
          dwarfs, gables);
}
```

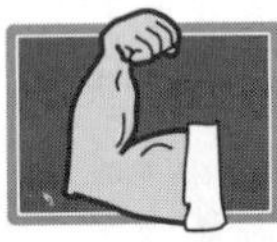

RESULT:

```
C:\>ASSIGN4
There are 0 dwarfs and 0 gables
```

ANALYSIS:

1. If you are lucky, you will get the result shown above—a zero value for both variables. Otherwise, the program will display some "garbage" value. Any value is possible because you have not instructed the program to move any data at all into the memory location allocated for *gables*.

Some compilers will give a warning when you attempt to use the value of a variable that has not been initialized, but the program will still execute, as this one did. In C a compiler is not required to automatically initialize allocated memory space to zero or any other value—that is left up to you, the programmer.

ARITHMETIC OPERATORS

You can perform calculations on numbers with *arithmetic operators*. There are seven arithmetic operators in C; they fall into two categories: *unary* and binary. The seven operators are listed here.

Unary Arithmetic Operators	Binary Arithmetic Operators
+ (positive sign)	+ (addition)
– (negation)	– (subtraction)
	* (multiplication)
	/ (division)
	% (modulus or remainder)

Unary arithmetic operators

Unary operators are those having only one operand. The result of applying a unary minus (–) operator is the negative of the operand value, and the result of applying a unary plus (+) operator is the same as the operand value. The unary plus is almost a "do nothing" operator; the ANSI C specification added it for symmetry with the unary minus. The next program illustrates how they both work.

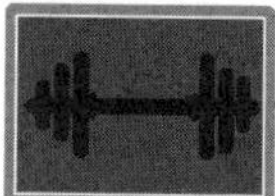

Listing 5.5 UNARY.C Unary operators

DO: Enter, compile, and run UNARY

```
#include <stdio.h>
#define HUNDRED 100
main()
{
     int credit = HUNDRED;
     int debit;
     int same;

     debit = -credit;                 /* Unary minus */
     same  = +debit;                  /* Unary plus */
     printf("\ncredit = %d\ndebit = %d\nsame = %d",
          credit, debit, same);
}
```

RESULT:

```
C:\>UNARY

credit = 100
debit = -100
same = -100
```

ANALYSIS:

1. The unary minus in the first statement reverses the sign of the value of *credit* and the statement assigns the result to *debit*. The unary minus is the equivalent of multiplying the operand by –1: *-credit* is the same as *–1 * credit*. The unary expression is more compact, but it is probably not more efficient—a good compiler will generate the same machine code for either expression.

2. The unary plus takes the value of *debit* as is (it is already negative), then the statement assigns the result to the variable *same*. The unary plus really has no effect; you would get the same result if you left it out.

Binary arithmetic operators

Binary arithmetic operators have two operands—one preceding and one following the operator. The operator processes the two operands to produce a single result. Associativity (remember that term?) tells you how the two operands relate, or associate, with the operator. All of the binary arithmetic operators associate from left to right. That is, an operator uses the left operand first, then applies the right operand. With the expression, 3 – 2, left to right associativity tells you to subtract 2 from 3 rather than 3 from 2 (which would be right to left associativity). Associativity determines which of the two operands will be subtracted from the other, or which is divided by the other.

The next program uses four of the five binary arithmetic operators. You can use these operators (+, –, *, /) with any of the numeric data types (*int, float, double,* and *char* with numeric values). These are all the data types that we have discussed so far, but later on you will learn about other data types that the arithmetic operators cannot use.

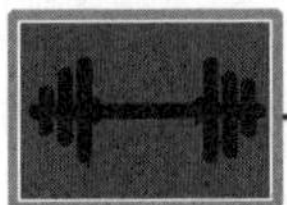

Listing 5.6 ARITH.C Add, subtract, multiply, and divide

DO: Enter, compile, and run ARITH

```
#include <stdio.h>
main()
{
     float x = 100.8;          /* Operand */
     float y = 25.2;           /* Operand */
     float sum;                /* Add result */
     float difference;         /* Subtract result */
     float product;            /* Multiply result */
     float dividend;           /* Divide result */

     sum = x + y;
     difference = x - y;
     product = x * -y;
     dividend = x / y;

     printf("\n%f plus %f is %f", x, y, sum);
     printf("\n%f minus %f is %f", x, y, difference);
     printf("\n%f times -%f is %f", x, y, product);
     printf("\n%f divided by %f is %f", x, y, dividend);
}
```

RESULT:

```
C:\>ARITH

100.800003 plus 25.200001 is 126.000008
100.800003 minus 25.200001 is 75.600006
```

```
100.800003 times -25.200001 is -2540.160156
100.800003 divided by 25.200001 is 4.000000
```

ANALYSIS:

1. Each of the four assignment statements has an expression on the right side of the equal sign that uses a binary operator. The program assigns the result of each of these expressions to the variable on the left side of the assignment operator (=).

2. Sometimes the distinction between the unary plus and minus operators and their binary counterparts is contextual—a unary plus or minus has no operand immediately to the left of the operator. Look closely at the statement

   ```
   product = x * -y;
   ```

   The minus sign is a unary operator because there is another operator just to the left of it instead of another operand. However, if you look at the preceding statement:

   ```
   difference = x - y;
   ```

   The compiler knows that the minus is a binary operator because it is surrounded by two operands.

3. You should take notice of the last few digits of the displayed numbers. Why are the last digits after the decimal point not zero? The answer is that data type *float* has a precision of seven digits and the unmodified floating-point format specifier (%f) displays six places after the decimal point plus however many are required on the left. The result is that printf() displays more digits than the internal precision allows. Only the first seven displayed digits are meaningful. To avoid displaying the extraneous digits, you can add a modifier to the conversion specifier, such as %.2f, which will display only two digits after the decimal point.

The fifth binary arithmetic operator is the modulus (%) operator, which results in the remainder of the first operand after division by the second. As an example, the result of 5 % 3 is 2 because if you divide five by three you get a dividend of 1 with a remainder of 2. Figure 5-2 shows how the result of a modulus corresponds to the remainder of a division.

In grammar school, you probably learned the above technique for performing long division. The last nondivisible number at the bottom of the operation is the remainder, which is the same result that the modulus operator returns.

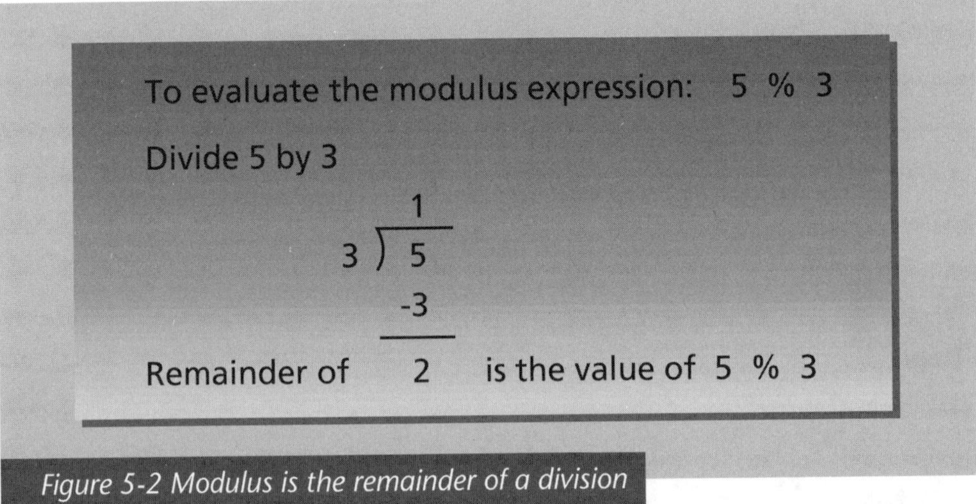

To evaluate the modulus expression: 5 % 3
Divide 5 by 3
1
3) 5
-3
Remainder of 2 is the value of 5 % 3

Figure 5-2 Modulus is the remainder of a division

Table 5-1 lists several instances of modulus arithmetic.

You can use the modulus operator in a program to tell if a given year is a leap year with the next program.

Modulus expression	Result
1492 % 10	2
1492 % 100	92
1492 % 2	0
13 % 5	3
13 % 7	6
5 % 100	5

Table 5-1 Modulus arithmetic

Listing 5.7 LEAPYEAR.C Calculate leap years using modulus operator

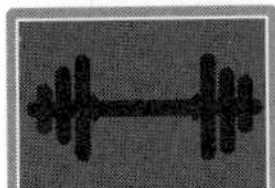

DO:
- Enter and compile LEAPYEAR
- Run LEAPYEAR and enter 1980

```
#include <stdio.h>
main()
{
```

```
    int year;
    int leap_year;

    printf("Enter any year: ");
    scanf("%d", &year);
    leap_year = year % 4;
    printf("%d is a leap year if the remainder (%d) is zero",
        year, leap_year);
}
```

RESULT:

```
C:\>LEAPYEAR
Enter any year: 1980
1980 is a leap year if the remainder (0) is zero
```

ANALYSIS:

1. The statement *leap_year = year % 4;* divides *year* by 4 and assigns the result to variable *leap_year*. As the printf() statement shows, if the result is zero, then the year is evenly divisible by 4 and it is a leap year.

The modulus operator works with any integer data type or integer constant (including type *char* and integers qualified by *long, short, signed, unsigned*), but not with other data types. Try using modulus with some different data types.

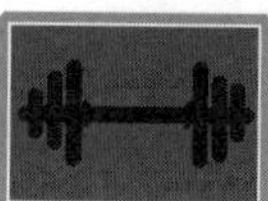

Listing 5.8 MODERR.C Some modulus errors

DO: Enter and compile MODERR

```
main()
{
    float f_op = 13.;
    long l_op = 4L;
    char c_op = 4;
    unsigned u_op = 13;
    int remainder;

    remainder = f_op % 4;          /* Illegal float variable */
    remainder = u_op % 4.;         /* Illegal float constant */

    remainder = u_op % c_op;       /* unsigned and char ok */
    remainder = u_op % l_op;       /* unsigned and long ok */
```

```
    remainder = 12 % 4;             /* integer constants ok */
    remainder = remainder % 2;      /* int and constant ok */
}
```

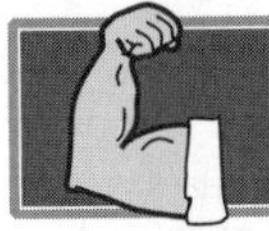

RESULT:

```
PC/C/E MODERR
Power C - Version 2.1.3
(C) Copyright 1989-1991 by Mix Software
Compiling ...
MODERR.C(9):    remainder = f_op % 4;       /* Illegal float variable */
***********                        ^134
     134: Illegal type of operands
-------------------------------
MODERR.C(10):    remainder = u_op % 4.;      /* Illegal float constant */
************                          ^134
     134: Illegal type of operands
-------------------------------
   16 lines compiled
   2 Compile errors
```

ANALYSIS:

1. The program repeatedly uses the variable *remainder* to hold the result of each right-side expression involving the modulus operator.
2. The compiler will not accept a noninteger operand with the modulus operator. The first two modulus expressions result in compile errors because of floating-point operands: variable f_*op* in the first expression and constant *4.* in the second (the decimal point makes it floating-point 4). Notice that the compiler astutely reports that there is an "Illegal float variable" on line 9 and an "Illegal float constant" on line 10 even though it can't point directly to each error.
3. The rest of the modulus expressions are legal because they use various forms of integers.

Remove the illegal lines of code from MODERR and recompile.

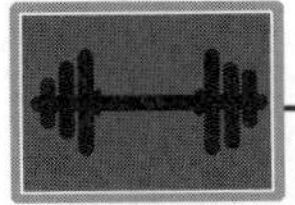

Listing 5.9 MODERR2.C Correct the modulus errors

DO:
- Delete two lines and add printf()s in MODERR
- Compile and run MODERR2

```
#include <stdio.h>
```

```
main()
{
     float f_op = 13.;
     long l_op = 4L;
     char c_op = 4;
     unsigned u_op = 13;
     int remainder;

     remainder = u_op % c_op;                    /* unsigned and char ok */
     printf("\nRemainder = %d", remainder);                        /*1*/

     remainder = u_op % l_op;                    /* unsigned and long ok */
     printf("\nRemainder = %d", remainder);                        /*2*/

     remainder = 13 % 5;                         /* integer constants ok */
     printf("\nRemainder = %d", remainder);                        /*3*/

     remainder = remainder % 2;                  /* int and constant ok */
     printf("\nRemainder = %d", remainder);                        /*4*/
}
```

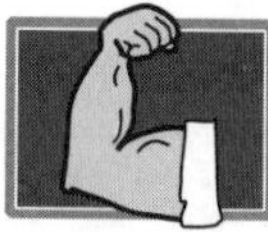

RESULT:

```
C:\>MODERR2
Remainder = 1
Remainder = 1
Remainder = 3
Remainder = 1
```

ANALYSIS:

1. From these results it should be clear that you can mix any type of integer with any other type as the two operands of the modulus operator.

The sign of the result of modulus applied to a negative number depends on the computer being used—you cannot be sure whether it will be positive or negative.

DO: Run program LEAPYEAR and enter -1982

RESULT:

```
C:\>LEAPYEAR
```

```
Enter any year: -1982
1982 is a leap year if the remainder (-2) is zero
```

ANALYSIS:

1. LEAPYEAR shows the sign of the result for the machine you are presently using, but the sign may be different if you run this program on another computer.

INCREMENT AND DECREMENT OPERATORS

The increment (++) operator adds one to the value of an operand, and the decrement (--) operator subtracts one. These unary operators exemplify why the C language is fast and efficient. The syntax is simple, making source statements more compact and making compilation more efficient. The operators correspond to hardware instructions inherent in the central processing unit (CPU) of any computer, so execution is very fast. The ++ operator is undoubtedly the most famous C operator, and it is part of the name of C++, an advanced, object-oriented language that extends the use of C. The increment and decrement operators change the value of an operand without the use of a separate assignment operator—in this respect they are different from other arithmetic operators. You can use increment and decrement operators with any numeric operand, including floating-point numbers. Your next program changes both integer and floating-point numbers with these operators.

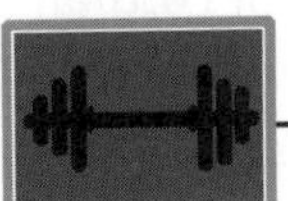

Listing 5.10 INCDEC.C Increment and decrement operators

DO: Enter, compile, and run INCDEC

```
#include <stdio.h>
#define BEGIN              1990
#define BASE_PRODUCTION    1000.5
main()
{
     int   year        = BEGIN;
     float factory1    = BASE_PRODUCTION;

     printf("\nProduction at factory1 in %d was %.1f widgets.",
          year, factory1);

     ++year;
     ++factory1;
     printf("\nProduction at factory1 in %d was %.1f widgets.",
          year, factory1);
```

```
    ++year;
    -factory1;
    printf("\nProduction at factory1 in %d was %.1f widgets.",
         year, factory1);
}
```

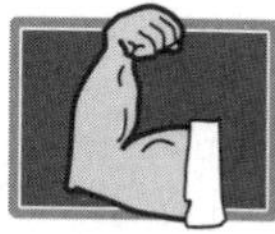

RESULT:

```
C:\>INCDEC

Production at factory1 in 1990 was 1000.5 widgets.
Production at factory1 in 1991 was 1001.5 widgets.
Production at factory1 in 1992 was 1000.5 widgets.
```

ANALYSIS:

1. This program displays the values of two variables (*year* and *factory1*) after initializing them with constants.
2. Next, the program displays the value of both variables (one integer and one floating-point) after it increments them.
3. Finally, the program increments the integer *year* again and decrements the floating-point *factory1*. After one increment and one decrement, f*actory1* is the same as it was when originally initialized.

Increment and decrement operators are for use with variables only, not constants or expressions. If you try to increment a constant or expression, you will encounter compile errors, as in the following program.

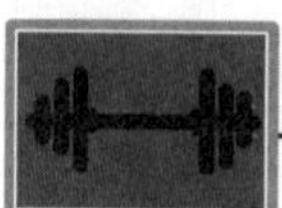

Listing 5.11 INCDEC2.C Errors incrementing a constant or expression

DO:
- Modify the indicated lines in INCDEC
- Compile INCDEC2

```
#include <stdio.h>
#define BEGIN              1990
#define BASE_PRODUCTION    1000.5
main()
{
     int   year      = BEGIN;
     float factory1  = BASE_PRODUCTION;
     float factory2;
```

```
    printf("\nProduction at factory1 in %d was %.1f widgets.",
         year, factory1);

    year = ++BEGIN;                                      /*1*/
    ++factory1;
    printf("\nProduction at factory1 in %d was %.1f widgets.",
         year, factory1);

    factory2 = ++(factory1 + BASE_PRODUCTION);           /*2*/
    printf("\nProduction at factory2 in %d was %.1f widgets.",
         year, factory2);                                /*3*/
}
```

RESULT:

```
PC/C/E INCDEC2
Power C - Version 2.1.3
(C) Copyright 1989-1991 by Mix Software
Compiling ...
INCDEC2.C(13):     year = ++1990 ;                       /*1*/
*************                ^ 29
      29: Variable required for ++ and --
-------------------------------
INCDEC2.C(18):     factory2 = ++(factory1 + 1000.5 );    /*2*/
*************                              ^ 29
      29: Variable required for ++ and --
-------------------------------
   128 lines compiled
   2 Compile errors
```

ANALYSIS:

1. The compile error on line 13 shows that it is not legal to attempt to change the value of a constant.

2. The compile error on line 18 shows that it is not legal to apply an increment or decrement operator to the results of an expression. We should hasten to point out a technical exception to this rule: A variable is a special type of expression, a *primary expression*, and you **can** apply an increment or decrement operator to this particular type of expression.

3. In the error message for line 13, you can see the preprocessor in operation. The preprocessor substitutes a value of 1990 for the symbolic constant BEGIN in line 13 before the compiler attempts to evaluate it.

There are two variations on the increment and decrement operators: When the operator is used in front of the operand, it is a *prefix* increment (++x) or decrement (--x), and when the operator follows the operand, it is a *postfix* increment (x++) or decrement (x—). A *prefix* operator changes the operand **before** it is used, whereas a *postfix* operator changes the operand **after** it is used.

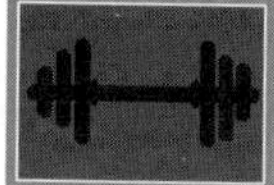

Listing 5.12 INCDEC3.C Prefix and postfix increment and decrement

DO:
- Modify the indicated lines in INCDEC2
- Compile and run INCDEC3

```
#include <stdio.h>
#define BEGIN                   1990
#define BASE_PRODUCTION         1000.5
main()
{
        int   year          = BEGIN;
        float factory1      = BASE_PRODUCTION;
        float factory2;

        printf("\nProduction at factory1 in %d was %.1f widgets.",
                year, factory1);

        ++year;                                         /*1*/
        factory2 = ++factory1;                          /*2*/
        printf("\nProduction at factory2 in %d was %.1f widgets.",
                year, factory2);                        /*3*/

        year++;                                         /*4*/
        factory2 = factory1-;                           /*5*/
        printf("\nProduction at factory2 in %d was %.1f widgets.",
                year, factory2);                        /*6*/
        printf("\nProduction at factory1 in %d was %.1f widgets.",
                year, factory1);                        /*7*/
}
```

RESULT:

```
C:\>INCDEC3

Production at factory1 in 1990 was 1000.5 widgets.
Production at factory2 in 1991 was 1001.5 widgets.
Production at factory2 in 1992 was 1001.5 widgets.
Production at factory1 in 1992 was 1000.5 widgets.
```

ANALYSIS:

1. The program initializes variable *year* to 1990 and *factory1* to 1000.5, then on lines /*1–2*/ it increments both variables. The program assigns *factory1* to *factory2* **after** its prefix increments *factory1*, so the second printf() shows *factory2* to be 1001.5.
2. The statements on lines /*4–5*/ postfix increment and decrement the variables *year* and *factory1*; therefore line /*5*/ assigns *factory1* to *factory2* **before** the decrement takes place. Remember, with postfix you first use the value, then decrement it; therefore, the third printf() displays the same value of 1001.5 as on the previous output line.
3. The fourth printf() verifies that *factory1* was actually decremented to 1000.5 **after** being used in the previous line.

The rules for incrementing are: "**Use** an operand, then change it with a postfix increment," or "Change an operand with a prefix increment, then **use** it." What does "**use**" really mean? "**Use**" means to evaluate the expression in which the operand appears (apply all the C operators). "**Use**" does **not** extend to determining the order of evaluation of function arguments. Here is a case in which it is not easy for you to predict the outcome of incrementing a variable.

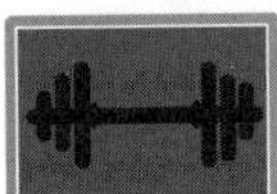

Listing 5.13 INCDEC4.C Caution when incrementing within printf()

DO: Enter, compile, and run INCDEC4

```
#include <stdio.h>
#define BEGIN 1990
main()
{
     int year = BEGIN;

     printf("\nYear (%d) and preincremented year (%d)",
          year, ++year);
}
```

RESULT:

```
C:\>INCDEC4
Year (1991) and preincremented year (1991)
```

ANALYSIS:

1. Since printf() is a function, C does not determine when the increment of *year* will take place in relation to the display of the two values—this is left for the compiler to determine. Your Power C compiler has chosen to preincrement the variable before displaying both values as 1991, but you cannot depend on every compiler to do it this way. Another compiler might display the first value as 1990, then increment year before displaying the second value as 1991.

When you use increment and decrement in normal expressions, you can reliably predict the result based on the rules of prefix and postfix evaluation, but you cannot rely on all compilers treating increment the same way when applied to function arguments. Accordingly, your safest policy should be **don't increment or decrement arguments in a function call.**

C uses some characters to represent more than one operator, relying on context to resolve the meaning. This is a somewhat annoying characteristic of C that is perhaps unavoidable because there are so many operators. You need to use operators such as +, -, ++, --, in a context that is unambiguous to the compiler. Here is an example that is confusing to the compiler.

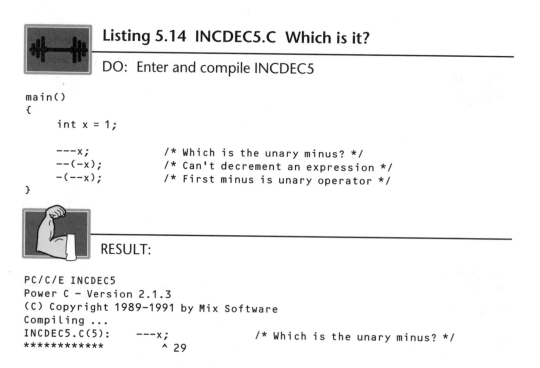

Listing 5.14 INCDEC5.C Which is it?

DO: Enter and compile INCDEC5

```
main()
{
     int x = 1;

     ---x;                 /* Which is the unary minus? */
     --(-x);               /* Can't decrement an expression */
     -(--x);               /* First minus is unary operator */
}
```

RESULT:

```
PC/C/E INCDEC5
Power C - Version 2.1.3
(C) Copyright 1989-1991 by Mix Software
Compiling ...
INCDEC5.C(5):    ---x;               /* Which is the unary minus? */
************        ^ 29
```

```
        29: Variable required for ++ and --
------------------------------------------------------------------
INCDEC5.C(6):    --(-x);          /* Can't decrement an expression */
***********              ^ 29
      29: Variable required for ++ and --
------------------------------------------------------------------
   8 lines compiled
   2 Compile errors
```

ANALYSIS:

1. Line 5 of this program seems to be challenging the compiler to read your mind. Power C assumes the worst: that what you meant was the same as line 6—the erroneous application of the decrement operator to an expression. Note that even a single operator applied to a single operand constitutes an expression.
2. You should always use parentheses to resolve any ambiguity as to the meaning of an expression. The last line does this by making it clear that the compiler should decrement x, then negate it.

Precedence

When a program evaluates an expression, the order in which it applies operators is important to the result. A program needs a traffic cop to decide when each operator should have a turn; in C, the traffic cop takes the form of rules of *precedence* and *associativity*. Without such rules, a program would behave a bit like the Three Stooges, not knowing who is supposed to go through a doorway first. The following example uses two arithmetic operators to illustrate this point.

Listing 5.15 ORDER.C Who goes first?

DO: Enter, compile, and run ORDER

```
#include <stdio.h>
main()
{
     int answer;
     int Mo    = 1;
     int Larry = 2;
     int Curly = 3;

     answer = Mo + Larry * Curly;
     printf("The answer is %d", answer);
}
```

RESULT:

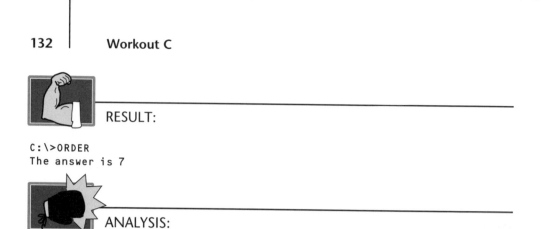

```
C:\>ORDER
The answer is 7
```

ANALYSIS:

1. The result of the arithmetic expression is 7 because the program first multiplied *Larry* and *Curly*, then added *Mo*. But why didn't the program take everything in left to right order, and first add *Mo* and *Larry*, and then multiply by *Curly* to get 9? You can see that the order in which operators are applied is important.

The C rules of *precedence* and *associativity* are properties of operators that determine the order of evaluation of expressions. The rules are very simple: Apply operators with the highest precedence first; if two or more operators are of equal precedence, then associativity determines the order. Table 5-2 shows the precedence and associativity of the operators used in this chapter.

Operators	Associativity
( )	Left to Right
unary +, unary -, sizeof(), ++, --, (type)	Right to Left
*, /, %	Left to Right
binary +, binary -	Left to Right
=, +=, -=, *=, /=, %=	Right to Left

Table 5-2 Precedence and associativity of operators

An operator on any line in the table has higher precedence than operators on lines below it; operators on the same line have the same precedence. Associativity tells you how an operator associates with its operands, and the compiler uses it to "break the tie" between operators having the same precedence. The compiler applies these operators by moving across the expression in either Left to Right or Right to Left order as determined by the associativity.

You should pay particular attention to the parentheses operator on the top line of the table—this operator forces evaluation of an enclosed expression, and because it has the highest precedence, you can use it to force the expression to be evaluated first. The next example shows how you can use parentheses as your "enforcer" to control calculations as you wish instead of accepting the automatic C rules of precedence.

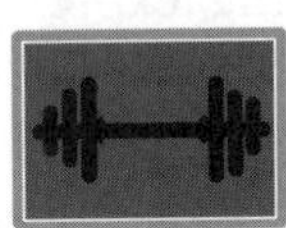

Listing 5.16 PRECEDE.C Apply precedence and associativity

DO: Enter, compile, and run PRECEDE

```
#include <stdio.h>
main()
{
     int a = 5;
     int b = 4;
     int c = 3;
     int d = 2;
     int e = 1;
     int x;

     x = a + b - c * d / e;
     printf("\nResult of automatic ordering: x = %d", x);

     x = (a + (b - ((c * d) / e)));
     printf("\nResult of the same explicit ordering: x = %d", x);

     x = a + (b - c) * d / e;
     printf("\nResult of explicit reordering: x = %d", x);
}
```

RESULT:

```
C:\>PRECEDE

Result of automatic ordering: x = 3
Result of the same explicit ordering: x = 3
Result of explicit reordering: x = 7
```

ANALYSIS:

1. The second calculation gives the same result as the first. By inserting parentheses, you have explicitly imposed the same ordering as called for by the rules of precedence and associativity.
2. In the third calculation, you have changed the order of evaluation with parentheses that cause the subtraction to be performed first.
3. Note that in all cases, the assignment occurs last because this operator is on the last line of the precedence table.

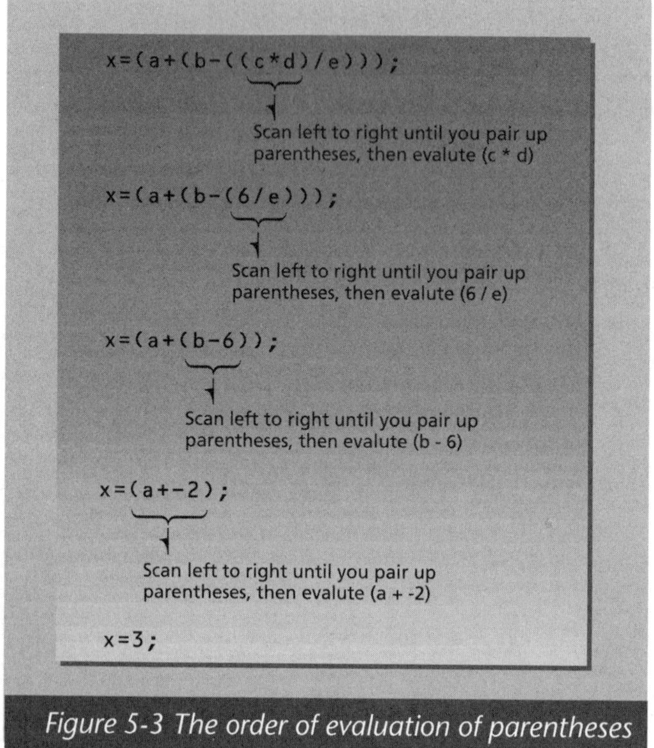

x=(a+(b-((c*d)/e)));
Scan left to right until you pair up parentheses, then evalute (c * d)
x=(a+(b-(6/e)));
Scan left to right until you pair up parentheses, then evalute (6 / e)
x=(a+(b-6));
Scan left to right until you pair up parentheses, then evalute (b - 6)
x=(a+-2);
Scan left to right until you pair up parentheses, then evalute (a + -2)
x=3;

Figure 5-3 The order of evaluation of parentheses

In evaluating expressions with nested parentheses, the compiler always evaluates expressions within the innermost parentheses first, then proceeds to the next innermost parentheses, and so on until it evaluates the last expression. This occurs because of the Left to Right associativity of parentheses; the compiler evaluates an expression in parentheses when it encounters the closing (or right) parenthesis of a pair. When the compiler scans from left to right through some nested parentheses, it will pair up the innermost parentheses first. Figure 5-3 shows the order of evaluation of the expressions within the second calculation of the above example.

TYPE CONVERSION

You have no doubt heard the phrase "mixing apples and oranges" when someone tried to compare two different items. Well, C does not like you to mix apples and oranges in expressions by using different types of operands. To avoid this circumstance, a C compiler will automatically change the type of certain variables when it encounters a mixed-type expression. *Type conversion is* a change in the data type of a variable or expression, usually made to match up different data types. Conversion of data types occurs in either of two ways: automatically according to compiler rules, or when you explicitly request it with the *cast* operator.

Automatic conversion

Whenever an expression contains variables or constants of different data types, the compiler converts some of the variables so that the program can consistently evaluate the expression. For instance, a compiler must decide what to do with the result of 3. / 2 (floating-point 3 divided by integer 2). The answer of 1.5 will not fit into an integer, but it will fit into a floating-point number. The safest and best solution for the com-

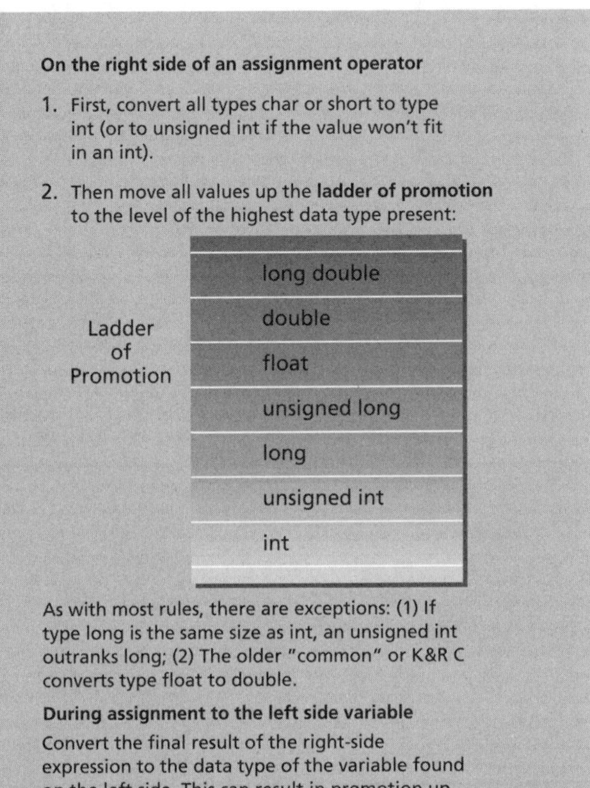

On the right side of an assignment operator
1. First, convert all types char or short to type int (or to unsigned int if the value won't fit in an int).
2. Then move all values up the ladder of promotion to the level of the highest data type present:
Ladder of Promotion
long double
double
float
unsigned long
long
unsigned int
int
As with most rules, there are exceptions: (1) If type long is the same size as int, an unsigned int outranks long; (2) The older "common" or K&R C converts type float to double.
During assignment to the left side variable
Convert the final result of the right-side expression to the data type of the variable found on the left side. This can result in promotion up the ladder, or demotion to a lower ranking type.

Figure 5-4 Automatic conversion rules

piler is to convert the integer to a floating-point number and make the result a floating-point number. Programs do not perform "mixed" arithmetic; that would greatly and unnecessarily complicate things for a compiler, so it converts all data in an expression to a common data type before a calculation is done. The complete rules of automatic conversion are somewhat complex (see Figure 5-4), but the basis for the rules are simple: In a mixed expression, the compiler promotes data types to the largest type present. *Promotion* is the act of expanding a value to fit the size of a larger data type; this can be accomplished without any loss of information or precision. However, the opposite conversion, *demotion*, often requires that some part of a value be discarded. Automatic demotion will occur only when you use an assignment operator, and for obvious reasons you should be aware of when and how the compiler demotes data.

Automatic conversion can be simple, like when a program assigns one variable to another of a different type, or it can involve several conversions in an expression like the one in the next program.

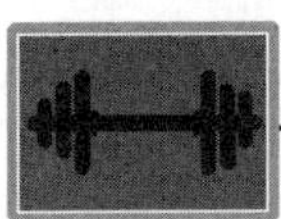

Listing 5.17 AUTOCONV.C Automatic type conversion

DO: Enter, compile, and run AUTOCONV

```
#include <stdio.h>
main()
```

```
{
     int i;
     char c = 2;
     long l = 3L;
     float f = 1.5;

     i = c + l * f - 3;

     printf("\nValue of right-side expression is %f, \
type float", c + l * f - 3);
     printf("\nFinal result after assignment is %d, \
type int", i);
}
```

RESULT:

```
C:\>AUTOCONV

Value of right-side expression is 3.500000, type float
Final result after assignment is 3, type int
```

ANALYSIS:

1. The statement *i = c + l * f - 3;* involves four different data types (*int, char, long,* and *float*) and it forces both promotion and demotion.

2. In the expression on the right side of the assignment, the compiler promotes variables *c* and *l* and constant 3 to type *float,* which is the highest ranking type in the expression. The same thing happens in the printf() statement on the next line, which repeats the expression and displays the result.

3. When the program assigns the result of the right-side evaluation to *i,* it demotes the result to an integer. Demotion of a floating-point number to an integer is accomplished by *truncating,* or dropping, the fractional part.

A very useful application of demotion is the rounding of a floating-point number to the nearest integer. Be aware that truncation of a number is **not** the same as rounding. Truncation always reduces the value of a number to the next lower integer value, whereas rounding can either increase or decrease the value to the nearest integer. The rule for rounding is: If the fractional part of a number is greater than or equal to .5, then round up; otherwise, round down.

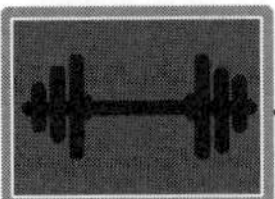

Listing 5.18 ROUNDOFF.C Round off to nearest integer

DO: Enter and compile ROUNDOFF

```
#include <stdio.h>
main()
{
     int rounded;
     float f;

     printf("\nEnter a floating-point number: ");
     scanf("%f", &f);
     rounded = f + .5;
     printf("%f rounded to the nearest integer is %d",
        f, rounded);
}
```

Rounding occurs in the statement *rounded = f + .5;*—this statement adds 0.5 to the floating-point number that you enter and allows automatic demotion of the assignment to truncate the result to an integer.

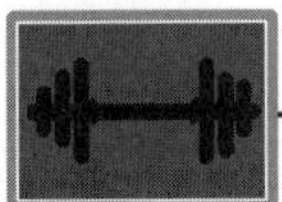

DO: Run ROUNDOFF and enter 6.5

```
C:\>ROUNDOFF
Enter a floating-point number: 6.5
6.500000 rounded to the nearest integer is 7
```

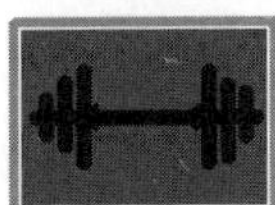

DO: Run ROUNDOFF and enter 6.4999

```
C:\>ROUNDOFF
Enter a floating-point number: 6.4999
6.4999000 rounded to the nearest integer is 6
```

Integer arithmetic

Integer arithmetic occurs when any of the arithmetic operators are applied in an expression with only integer operands. The compiler produces different machine code for integer arithmetic than it does for floating-point arithmetic. Because there are no fractions with integers, the operations are simpler, leading to faster and more compact code. However, in the absence of fractions, the compiler must decide what to do with the fractional part of an integer division. A rule of C tells the compiler to just throw the fraction away, which is what happens in your next program.

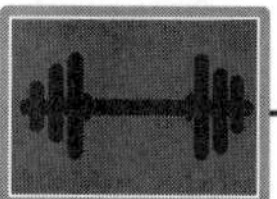

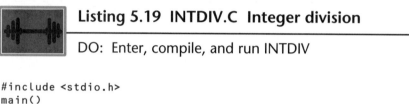

Listing 5.19 INTDIV.C Integer division

DO: Enter, compile, and run INTDIV

```
#include <stdio.h>
main()
{
	int divisor = 10;

	printf("\nResult of pure integer division: 10 / 4 = %d",
		divisor / 4);

	printf("\nResult of division by real: 10 / 4. = %f",
		divisor / 4.);

	printf("\nResult of division by negative integer: \
10 / -4 = %d", divisor / -4);
}
```

RESULT:

```
C:\>INTDIV

Result of pure integer division: 10 / 4 = 2
Result of division by real: 10 / 4. = 2.500000
Result of division by negative integer: 10 / -4 = -2
```

ANALYSIS:

1. When a statement divides an integer by an integer, it truncates the result to an integer. The first printf() illustrates this by showing that dividing an integer variable (with a value of 10) by a constant integer 4 yields 2 (2.5 truncated).

2. If you divide these same numbers, but one or both is a floating-point type, then the result is floating-point and the program retains the fractional part of the answer. The second printf() displays such a floating-point result.

3. If an integer division results in a negative answer, as in the third printf(), the direction of truncation is compiler-dependent. If the displayed answer were floating-point, it would be -2.5, but because both operands are integer, the answer must be truncated. However, does this mean truncating down to -3 or up to -2? The choice is not defined by C, it is determined by the compiler.

The most important thing for you to remember about integer arithmetic is that a C program will truncate the result of integer division to an integer value.

Cast operator

The *cast* operator has the form *(type)*—that is, any data type enclosed in parentheses. The cast operator has the effect of converting a constant, variable, or expression that immediately follows it to the indicated type. For instance, *(int)x*, casts the value of variable *x* to type *int*, regardless of the originally declared data type of *x*. Casting does not affect the original variable, it only returns a result that **temporarily** serves the purpose of the expression in which it appears.

You can use the *cast* operator to ensure correct evaluation of an expression, especially when you need to override the effects of automatic conversion. Suppose you are presented with a temperature in integer form, and your task is to convert it from degrees Fahrenheit to the most accurate Celsius equivalent. The following program illustrates a problem imposed by automatic type conversions and shows how easily you can overcome the problem with a cast operator.

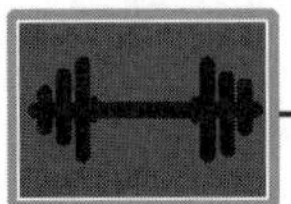

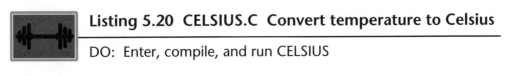

Listing 5.20 CELSIUS.C Convert temperature to Celsius

DO: Enter, compile, and run CELSIUS

```
#include <stdio.h>
main()
{
     float celsius;
     int  fahrenheit;

     printf("\nEnter integer degrees Fahrenheit: ");
     scanf("%d", &fahrenheit);

/* Problem due to integer division */

     celsius = (5 / 9) * (fahrenheit - 32);
     printf("\nThe incorrect Celsius equivalent is %f", celsius);
```

```
/* This is a little better, but still no fractional part */

      celsius = 5 * (fahrenheit - 32) / 9;
      printf("\nThe correct integer Celsius equivalent is %f", \
            celsius);

/* Correct result */

      celsius = ((float)5 / 9) * (fahrenheit - 32);
      printf("\nThe real equivalent Celsius temperature is %f",
            celsius);
}
```

RESULT:

```
C:\>CELSIUS

Enter integer degrees Fahrenheit: 100
The incorrect Celsius equivalent is 0.000000
The correct integer Celsius equivalent is 37.000000
The real equivalent Celsius temperature is 37.777779
```

ANALYSIS:

1. Program CELSIUS calculates the Celsius temperature three times. In the first calculation, the division of integer 5 by integer 9 truncates to zero, causing the result to always be zero.
2. The second calculation partially remedies the problem by first multiplying the temperature by 5 then dividing by 9. Left to right associativity of the multiply (*) and divide (/) operators (Table 5-2) controls the order of these calculations. However, the answer is still limited to an integer value (no fractional part).
3. The third approach casts one of the constants to a floating-point number, which automatically causes the program to perform the entire calculation with floating-point arithmetic, resulting in an accurate answer.

You always need to be alert to how conversions and casting affect the results of calculations. The next program makes a calculation using automatic conversion, then repeats the same calculation with casting. Both results are correct in terms of program execution, but they are different.

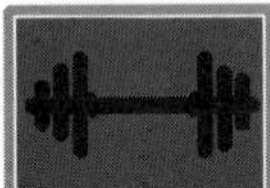

Listing 5.21 CASTINT.C Conversion affects answers

DO: Enter, compile, and run CASTINT

```
#include <stdio.h>
main()
{
     int sum;
     float x = 1.3;
     float y = 1.8;

     sum = (int) x + (int)y;
     printf("\nThe sum using integer cast is %d", sum);

     sum = x + y;
     printf("\nThe sum using automatic conversion is %d", sum);
}
```

RESULT:

```
C:\>CASTINT

The sum using integer cast is 2
The sum using automatic conversion is 3
```

ANALYSIS:

1. The first calculation individually casts the operands to integers, so it converts each operand to 1 before being summed, and the result is 2.

2. Look very carefully at the first cast operator; there is a space between the operator and variable *x*. Whether or not you use a space after the operator is important only for code readability; the compiler ignores such spaces. We recommend that you leave out the space.

3. The second calculation sums two floating-point numbers to yield 3.1, which it truncates to 3 during assignment to the integer *sum*.

4. Casting does not affect the declared type of a variable. If the program refers to the variable elsewhere, its value will reflect the originally declared type. In the calculation of the first sum, the cast operators

affect the values of variables *x* and *y* only in that instance. The other reference to the variables in the second calculation obtains the original floating-point values.

When an expression converts a double-precision number to a regular floating-point number, whether by assignment or casting, precision can be lost. This will not occur, of course, if the size of these two data types is the same, but with Power C operating on a PC, a double is larger than a *float*, so there is a difference, as the next program shows.

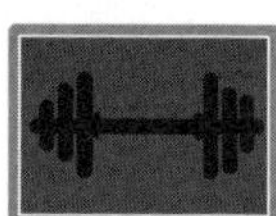

Listing 5.22 CASTERR.C Conversion can lose information

DO: Enter, compile, and run CASTERR

```
#include <stdio.h>
#define PI 3.1415926535897896
main()
{
      double pi = PI;
      double pi_cast;

      pi_cast = (float)pi;
      printf("\nValue of pi before (%17.15f)"
               "\n         and after (%17.15f) cast", pi, pi_cast);
}
```

RESULT:

```
C:\>CASTERR

Value of pi before (3.141592653589790)
         and after (3.141592741012573) cast
```

ANALYSIS:

The program casts the value of pi (type *double*) to *float* before assigning it back to *pi_cast* (also type *double*). The cast operation cuts the precision of *pi* back to seven decimal places, so the resulting value is not as accurate even though *pi_cast* can hold fifteen significant digits. The two values of pi are exactly the same out to seven significant digits, but beyond there the second (cast) value is in error.

When you work with numbers, especially floating-point numbers, you must know the limits of values to expect for your program. Choose data types that are consistent with these limits, then use parentheses and casting when necessary to control the results of your program's arithmetic.

MORE ASSIGNMENT OPERATORS

In addition to =, C has other assignment operators that combine assignment with another operation. These operators constitute a very nice shorthand notation for specifying two operations. For instance, if you wanted to double the value of an investment, you might do it the "old-fashioned way":

```
investment = 2 * investment;
```

However, you could accomplish the same thing just as well with the shorter statement:

```
investment *= 2;
```

Neither statement creates executable code that is faster or more compact than the other; they are different but equivalent ways of writing the same source statement. Given the choice, you should opt for the second method because it is more compact. Just as the *= operator combines assignment with multiplication, other operators combine assignment with other arithmetic operators, as in the next program.

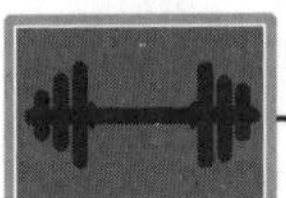

Listing 5.23 COMPOUND.C Two operators in one

DO: Enter, compile, and run COMPOUND

```
#include <stdio.h>
main()
{
     float f1;
     float f2;
     float f3;
     int   i4;
     int   i5;

     f1 = f2 = f3 = i4 = i5 = 1;

     f1 += 2.5;              /* f1 = f1 + 2.5       */
     f2 -= f1;               /* f2 = f2 - f1        */
     f3 *= f2 + 1.;          /* f3 = f3 * (f2 + 1.) */
     i4 /= f3;               /* i4 = i4 / f3        */
     i5 %= 2;                /* i5 = i5 % 2         */
```

```
    printf("\nf1 = %f\nf2 = %f\nf3 = %f\ni4 = %d\ni5 = %d",
         f1, f2, f3, i4, i5);
}
```

RESULT:

```
C:\>COMPOUND

f1 = 3.500000
f2 = -2.500000
f3 = -1.500000
i4 = 0
i5 = 1
```

ANALYSIS:

1. This program begins with an assignment statement that gives all five variables a value of 1.
2. The next five statements illustrate the use of compound assignment operators. A comment to the right of each statement shows an equivalent expression using two operators. The printf() at the end of the program displays the result of each of the preceding five assignment statements.
3. The statement *f1 += 2.5;* adds 2.5 to the value already in *f1*.
4. Statement *f2 -= f1;* subtracts the current value of *f1* (which is 3.5 as a result of the preceding statement) from the initial value of *f2* (which is 1) and assigns the result (-2.5) back to *f2*.
5. The next statement multiplies *f3* by the quantity *f2 + 1*. It performs the addition before the multiplication because of the rules of precedence (*= is on the last line of Table 5-2).
6. Next, the program divides *i4* by *f3* and places the result back in *i4*. The normal rules of conversion apply for these operators, so the program converts the value of *i4* to type *float* for the division (because *f3* is type *float*), then truncates the result during the assignment.

7. The last assignment statement applies the modulus operator (takes the remainder of *i5* divided by 2, which is 1), then replaces *i5* with the result.

You may not feel comfortable using these compound operators at first, preferring to stick with the more familiar, expanded form of expressions. However, with a little practice, you will soon learn to appreciate the efficiency of the shorthand notation as other experienced C programmers have.

In this chapter you have concentrated on the arithmetic operators. C has many other operators, listed in Appendix D, that allow you to test relationships among data, handle bits within variables, and eccess data in different ways. You will have a chance to use all of these operators as you proceed through *Workout C*.

CHAPTER 6
LOOPING CONTROL STATEMENTS

You have written all of the programs in previous chapters so that they flow straight through from top to bottom, executing each statement only once. This is pretty restrictive, and it limits what you can accomplish with a program. Control statements give you a way to vary the flow of a program's statements. C has a small number of very powerful control statements that allow you to change the execution of a program based on values of data. In this chapter, you will learn how to perform repetitive actions by executing some statements more than once—this is called *looping*. There are two principal statements that control looping: *while* and *for*, and there is a variation of *while* called the *do while*. Looping statements contain expressions that control events through the application of operators to operands. In this chapter, you will gain experience with some new operators that are widely used to control looping statements: *logical operators* and *relational operators*.

THE *while* STATEMENT

The *while* keyword allows you to repeat the execution of one or more statements until some predetermined condition occurs (or indefinitely if you wish). The syntax of the *while* statement is:

```
while (control expression)
        statement
```

Control expression is any C expression, and *statement* is any C statement. For clarity, you should always indent the *statement* controlled by the *while*.

Figure 6-1 shows how the *while* statement works: as long as the value of the *control expression* is *true*, the program executes the *statement*, and when the value of the *control expression* becomes *false*, the program moves on to the next statement. The very next section explains the meaning of the terms true and false.

Suppose you wanted to have the computer recite the alphabet; you could write a program to do this without any looping statements by writing 26 printf() statements, one for each letter:

```
printf("A");
printf("B");
printf("C");
    .
    .
    .
printf("Z");
```

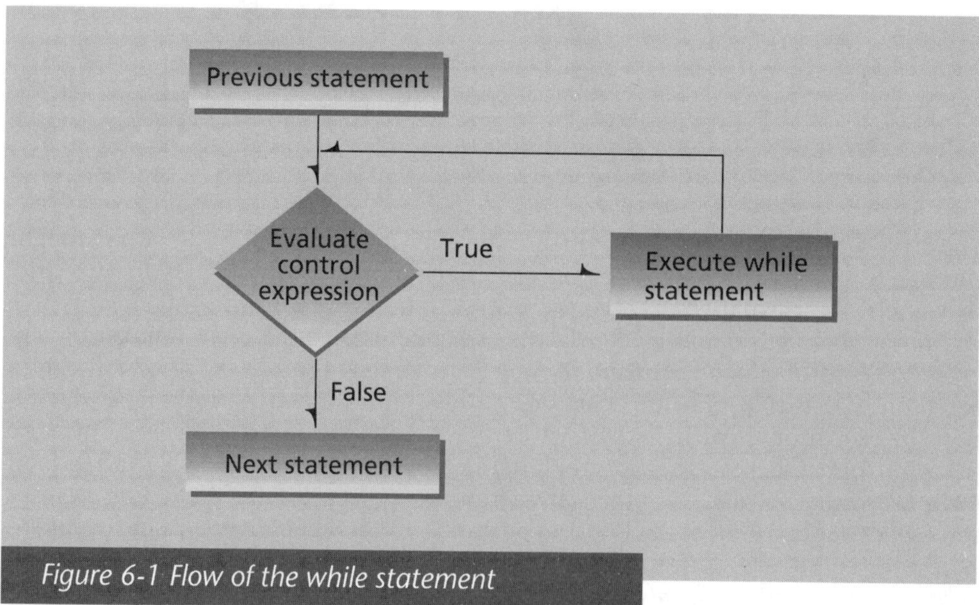

Figure 6-1 Flow of the while statement

This would obviously be a cumbersome program. There has got to be a better way, which is to use a loop. You could write the program with a *while* statement as follows:

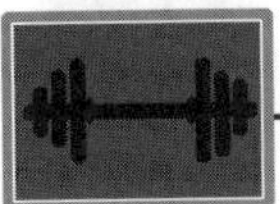

Listing 6.1 RECITE.C Recite the alphabet

DO: Enter, compile, and run RECITE

```
#include <stdio.h>
main()
{
     char alphabet = 'A';

     while (alphabet <= 'Z')
          printf("%c", alphabet++);
}
```

RESULT:

```
C:\>ALPHA
ABCDEFGHIJKLMNOPQRSTUVWXYZ
```

ANALYSIS:

1. The program initializes *alphabet* to 'A', then repeatedly displays and postfix increments the character code so that *alphabet* takes on the value of each letter.

2. The combination of the *while* keyword, the controlling expression *(alphabet <= 'Z')*, and the printf() statement constitutes a **loop** that executes as long as the value of *alphabet* is less than or equal to the ASCII code for 'Z'. The symbol <= is an operator that tests for a less than or equal to condition.

If you substitute parts of the loop from program RECITE into the flow diagram of Figure 6-1, it will look like Figure 6-2.

This is a quick introduction to looping. You will soon go back through the details of the *while* statement, but the above example should give you some notion of how easily you can cause operations to repeat with looping. It is no more difficult for you to repeat an operation one thousand or one million times than it is to repeat it 26 times. The really important parts of a loop are the controlling expressions, because loops continue or end when controlling expressions become true or false.

Previous statement
char alphabet = 'A';

Evaluate control expression
(alphabet <= 'Z')

True

Execute while statement
printf("%c", alphabet++);

False

Next statement
} /* Closing brace of program */

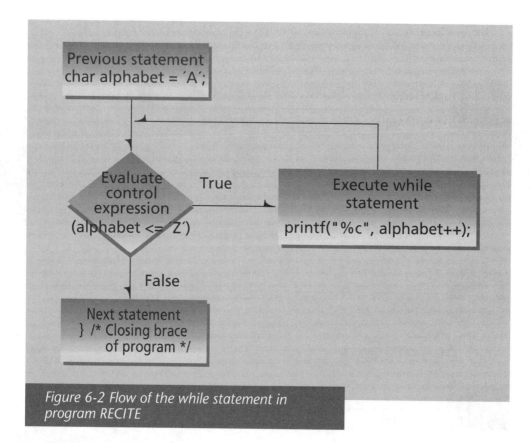

Figure 6-2 Flow of the while statement in program RECITE

True and false

Before working with looping statements, you must become familiar with *true* and *false* values. C defines a value of zero (0) to be *false*; conversely, any nonzero value is *true*. Any constant, variable, or expression can have a true or false value because any of these can have either zero or nonzero values, as evidenced by the following example:

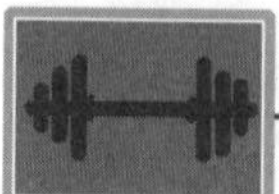

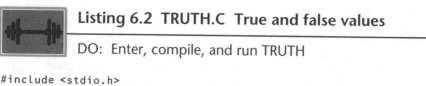

Listing 6.2 TRUTH.C True and false values

DO: Enter, compile, and run TRUTH

```
#include <stdio.h>
#define TRUE  1
#define FALSE 0
#define HALF .5
main()
{
```

```
    int   i = TRUE;
    char  c = FALSE;
    long  l = 0L;
    float f = HALF;

    printf("\nInteger i is %d (TRUE)", i);
    printf("\nCharacter c is %d (FALSE)", c);
    printf("\nLong l is %ld (FALSE)", l);
    printf("\nFloating-point f is %f (TRUE)", f);

    printf("\nExpression c times i is %d (FALSE)", c * i);
    printf("\nExpression f minus 6 is %f (TRUE)", f - 6);
}
```

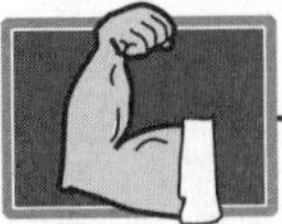

RESULT:

```
Integer i is 1 (TRUE)
Character c is 0 (FALSE)
Long l is 0 (FALSE)
Floating-point f is 0.500000 (TRUE)
Expression c times i is 0 (FALSE)
Expression f minus 6 is -5.500000 (TRUE)
```

ANALYSIS:

1. The symbolic constant *TRUE* (and its value of 1) are true, as is *HALF*, because they are all nonzero values. The symbolic constant *FALSE* and the long constant 0L are false because these values are zero.

2. Any variable that can be evaluated as having either a zero or nonzero value can be interpreted by a C program as being true or false. The four different data types (*i, c, l, f*) defined and initialized at the beginning of TRUTH are interpreted as true or false by the printf() statements that follow. The text in the printf() statements explains whether each value is true or false.

3. Notice that the character variable, *c*, takes on an integer value and displays an integer value.

4. Results of expressions can also be interpreted as true or false, as indicated by the last two printf() statements. One printf() states that the integer result of *c * i* is false, while the next says that the floating-point result of *f - 6* is true.

Suppose you wanted the computer to display the tongue-twister, "Peter Piper picked a peck of pickled peppers," ten times (real fast). If you couldn't use looping, you would have to write ten identical printf() statements, but the *while* statement makes it easy.

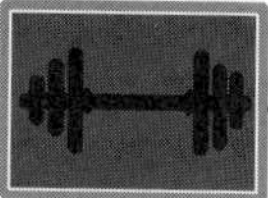

Listing 6.3 PEPPERS.C While statement

DO: Enter, compile, and run PEPPERS

```
#include <stdio.h>
main()
{
      int n = 10;

      while (n--)
            printf( "\n%d Peter Piper picked a peck"
                    " of pickled peppers", n);
}
```

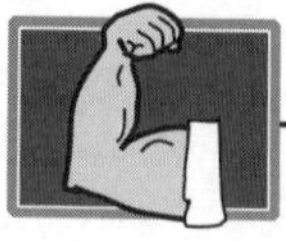

RESULT:

```
C:\>PEPPERS
9 Peter Piper picked a peck of pickled peppers
8 Peter Piper picked a peck of pickled peppers
7 Peter Piper picked a peck of pickled peppers
6 Peter Piper picked a peck of pickled peppers
5 Peter Piper picked a peck of pickled peppers
4 Peter Piper picked a peck of pickled peppers
3 Peter Piper picked a peck of pickled peppers
2 Peter Piper picked a peck of pickled peppers
1 Peter Piper picked a peck of pickled peppers
0 Peter Piper picked a peck of pickled peppers
```

ANALYSIS:

1. Integer *n*, initialized to 10, controls the number of loops that occur.
2. Within the *while* parentheses, the program evaluates the simple expression, n--, and if it yields a nonzero value (true), it executes the printf() statement. Then the program evaluates the expression again, and the looping process continues until the expression yields zero (false) and the *while* statement ends.

3. The program displays *n* so you can easily see how many times it displays the phrase. You can see that *n* counts down from ten and that printf() displays ten values from 9 through 0; when *n* reaches zero, the *while* statement ends and stops executing the printf(). The use of a postfix decrement is vital to getting this exact number of loops—at each iteration, *n* is used, then decremented.

Figure 6-3 makes it clear when the decrement operation occurs in relation to the loop test.

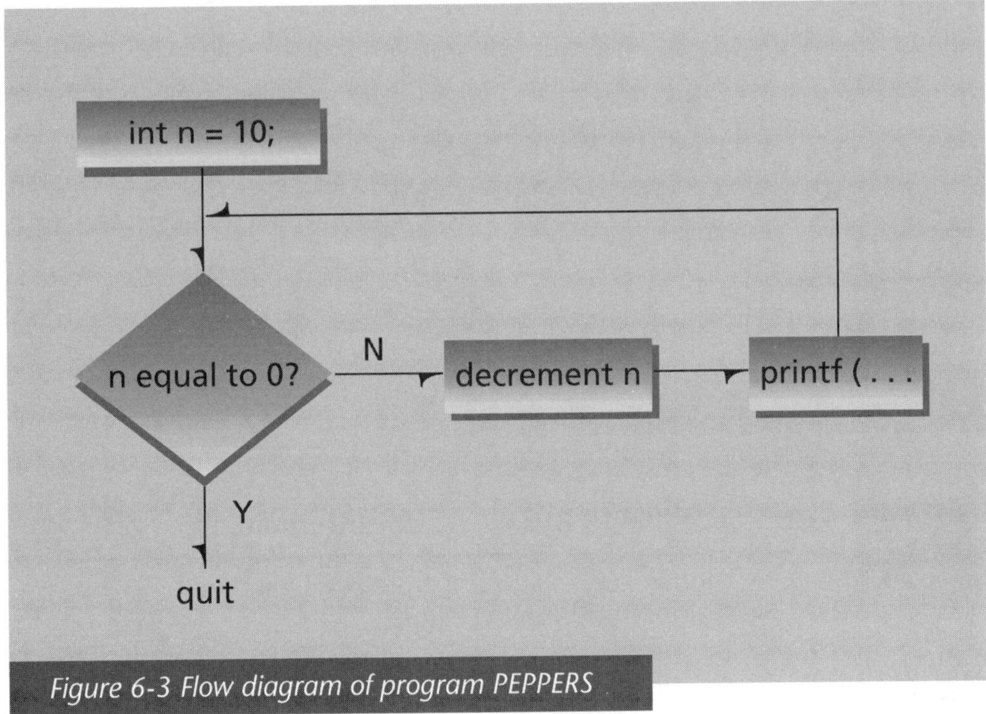

Figure 6-3 Flow diagram of program PEPPERS

The decrement operation is situated **after** the loop test because it is postfix. Yet it plainly occurs before the printf() statement, so the first value that printf() displays is 9, one less than the initial value.

If you change from postfix to prefix, the decrement operation moves **ahead of** the loop test, and the flow diagram will look like Figure 6-4.

Make the change to prefix decrement in the program and run it again to see how many times the loop repeats.

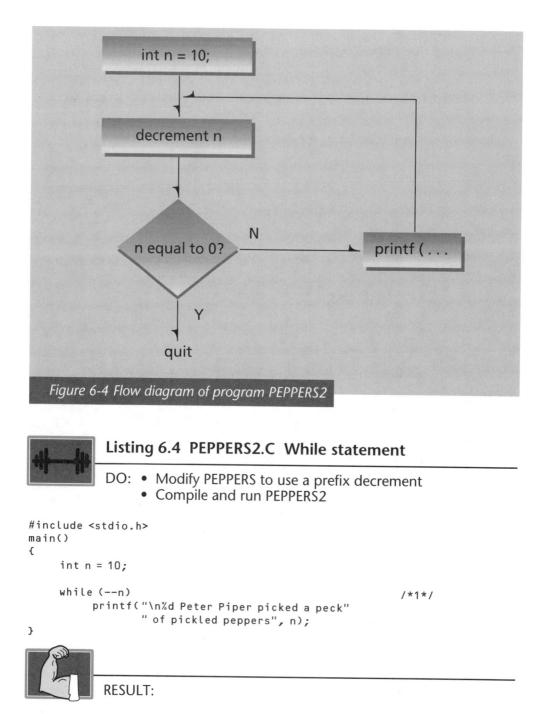

Figure 6-4 Flow diagram of program PEPPERS2

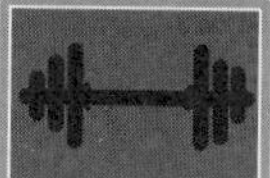

Listing 6.4 PEPPERS2.C While statement

DO:
- Modify PEPPERS to use a prefix decrement
- Compile and run PEPPERS2

```
#include <stdio.h>
main()
{
     int n = 10;

     while (--n)                                          /*1*/
          printf("\n%d Peter Piper picked a peck"
                 " of pickled peppers", n);
}
```

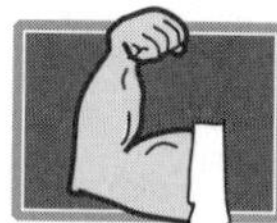

RESULT:

```
C:\>PEPPERS2
```

```
9 Peter Piper picked a peck of pickled peppers
8 Peter Piper picked a peck of pickled peppers
7 Peter Piper picked a peck of pickled peppers
6 Peter Piper picked a peck of pickled peppers
5 Peter Piper picked a peck of pickled peppers
4 Peter Piper picked a peck of pickled peppers
3 Peter Piper picked a peck of pickled peppers
2 Peter Piper picked a peck of pickled peppers
1 Peter Piper picked a peck of pickled peppers
```

ANALYSIS:

1. Now the loop only occurs nine times because the program decrements *n* before testing its value. Therefore when *n* decrements from 1 to 0 in the last cycle, the loop test goes false before printf() has a chance to display the zero value.

Null statement

A semicolon by itself, the *null statement*, is a valid statement that does nothing. However, even though the null statement does not do anything, it serves a valuable purpose, which is particularly evident with the *while* statement. If a *while* control expression performs all of the desired processing with nothing left for the controlled statement to do, then *while* takes the following form:

```
while (control expression)
        ;
```

Note the indented semicolon (;) that occupies a line of its own; this make it clear that the null statement is intentional. You might use this form of *while*, for example, if all you want to do is read some data until a certain value occurs. In that case, you would place an I/O statement in the *while* control expression and follow it with a null statement. Program COMPLEX3 (Program 6.18) does this, but for now we just want to introduce the null statement in order to warn you about the following potential problem.

Caution! Don't make the common programming error of misplacing a semicolon so that the compiler interprets it as a null statement; this will radically alter the flow of your program, as it does in the following example.

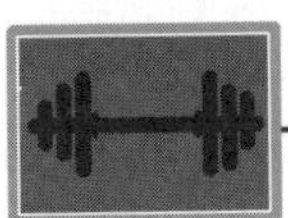

Listing 6.5 PEPPERS3.C The null statement

DO:
- Modify PEPPERS2.C to add a null statement
- Compile and run PEPPERS3

```
#include <stdio.h>
main()
```

```
{
     int n = 10;

     while (--n);                                            /*1*/
          printf("\n%d Peter Piper picked a peck"
                 " of pickled peppers", n);
}
```

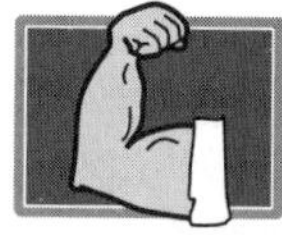

RESULT:

```
C:\>PEPPERS3
0 Peter Piper picked a peck of pickled peppers
```

ANALYSIS:

1. You have inserted an extra, unnecessary semicolon (;) on line /*1*/—a common programming error.
2. Now the *while* statement is complete on one line. The effect of this statement is different from what it was in the previous example: now it just decrements *n* until it becomes zero (false). Previously, the statement also induced the repeated execution of the printf() statement.
3. When the *while* statement ends, the program passes control to the next statement, printf(), which executes once.

The compound statement

A new form of statement that is very useful with *while* is the *compound statement*, consisting of two curly braces enclosing any number of C statements:

```
{
          statement(s)
}
```

With a compound statement, *while* can control as many statements as you desire. The compound statement (also known as a *block*) is fundamental to the structure of C programming, and you will encounter it in many places. A compound statement, or block, is also sometimes called the *body* of a loop. The following program simulates the dealing of cards to a player in the game of 21, or Blackjack, and it uses a compound statement.

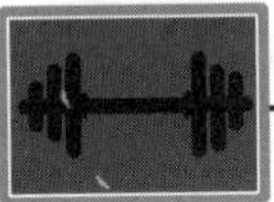

Listing 6.6 CARDS.C A card dealer

DO:
- Enter and compile CARDS
- Run CARDS and enter (8) (ENTER) (6) (ENTER) (0) (ENTER)

```
#include <stdio.h>
main()
{
     int card_total = 0;                /* Running total of cards */
     int hit;                           /* A new card */

     printf("\nDEAL CARDS FOR THE GAME OF 21");
     printf("\nEnter a card (1-13), or 0 to quit: ");
     scanf("%d", &hit);

     while (hit)
     {
          printf("\nYour card total is %d", card_total += hit);
          printf("\nEnter a card (1-13), or 0 to quit: ");
          scanf("%d", &hit);
     }
}
```

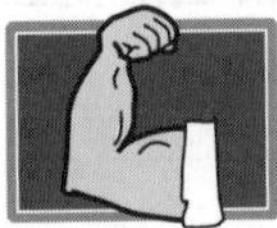

RESULT:

```
C:\>CARDS
DEAL CARDS FOR THE GAME OF 21
Enter a card (1-13), or 0 to quit: 8
Your card total is 8
Enter a card (1-13), or 0 to quit: 6
Your card total is 14
Enter a card (1-13), or 0 to quit: 0
```

ANALYSIS:

1. The program accepts cards in variable *hit* and adds the value of each new card to *card_total*. The program asks for the first card, then enters the *while* loop to repeatedly ask for new cards. If you enter a zero value, the *while* statement detects that *hit* is false and ends.
2. To execute several statements under the control of the *while*, the program uses a compound statement. The compound statement includes the curly braces and the three individual statements enclosed by the braces.

The card dealing simulation is not very sophisticated because you don't yet have all the programming tools needed, but you will make the game more elaborate as you proceed through this chapter and the next.

When you use the curly braces, you should line them up horizontally and indent the enclosed statements, as in the previous program—this is the way we recommend laying out a block, or compound statement. Another commonly used layout places the opening curly brace on the same line as the *while*:

```
while (hit) {
        statement(s)
}
```

This form is also acceptable; you need to make a choice between the two layouts and then use it consistently throughout your programs.

It is easy to forget the curly braces when coding a loop with an intended compound statement. Without the curly braces in the card dealer program, you get an entirely different (and undesirable) result, as the next example illustrates.

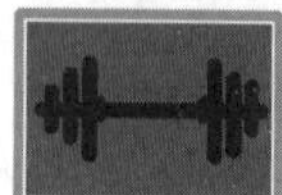

Listing 6.7 CARDS2.C A card dealer

DO: • Modify CARDS to leave out the curly braces
• Compile and run CARDS2, and enter (8) then (CTRL-BREAK)

```
#include <stdio.h>
main()
{
     int card_total = 0;              /* Running total of cards */
     int hit;                         /* A new card */

     printf("\nDEAL CARDS FOR THE GAME OF 21\n");
     printf("\nEnter a card (1-13), or 0 to quit: ");
     scanf("%d", &hit);

     while (hit)
           printf("\nYour card total is %d", card_total += hit);
           printf("\nEnter a card (1-13), or 0 to quit: ");
           scanf("%d", &hit);
}
```

RESULT:

```
C:\>CARDS2
DEAL CARDS FOR THE GAME OF 21

Enter a card (1-13), or 0 to quit: 8
```

```
Your card total is 8
Your card total is 16
Your card total is 24
Your card total is 32
.
.
```

ANALYSIS:

1. In this case, the program enters an "infinite loop" when it executes the *while* statement and you can only stop it by pressing CTRL-BREAK to kill the program (hold down the CTRL key while pressing BREAK).
2. The infinite loop occurs because *while* controls only one statement and the value of *hit* never changes (never becomes false) once the program enters the *while* loop. The compiler ignores indentations, so it does not have a clue that you intended all three statements following the *while* to be included in the loop. The indentations are good for readability, but the compiler relies on the curly braces to combine several statements into one block, or compound statement.

The infinite *while* loop

A special case of the *while* statement occurs if you place a nonzero constant inside the parentheses so that the control expression is always true, like this:

```
while (1)
{
}
```

This form of *while* statement is called an *infinite loop* because it will execute forever, without stopping. This may seem undesirable, and indeed it is if you don't somehow end the process. However, there is a very convenient way of ending a loop—with the *break* command. An infinite loop serves a good purpose in situations in which you need to execute an operation an indefinite number of times. For example, you might need to process some data entered from the keyboard when the amount of data is not known until you start entering. This often occurs when information brought in from the field (survey data, sales figures) is entered into a computer. Similar needs arise in connection with reading data from disk files. You could write a program to handle this kind of situation by including the following code fragment:

```
#define TRUE 1

   while (TRUE)
   {
         /* Enter data, including TRUE or FALSE for end */
```

```
        /* Process the data */

        if (end)
            break;
}
```

You can use either a numeric constant or, as many programmers prefer, a symbolic constant like *TRUE* for the control expression. Either nonzero constant makes the loop execute indefinitely. This infinite loop contains comments that indicate operations that enter and process data, including a flag, *end*, that signals when the program should stop the loop. The last statement takes care of stopping the loop, and it contains two new items: *if* and *break*. The *if* clause executes *break* if the control expression in parentheses (*end*) is true. The *break* command causes the loop to end so that the program goes on to the next statement following the end of the loop. You will learn all about *if* and *break* in the next chapter.

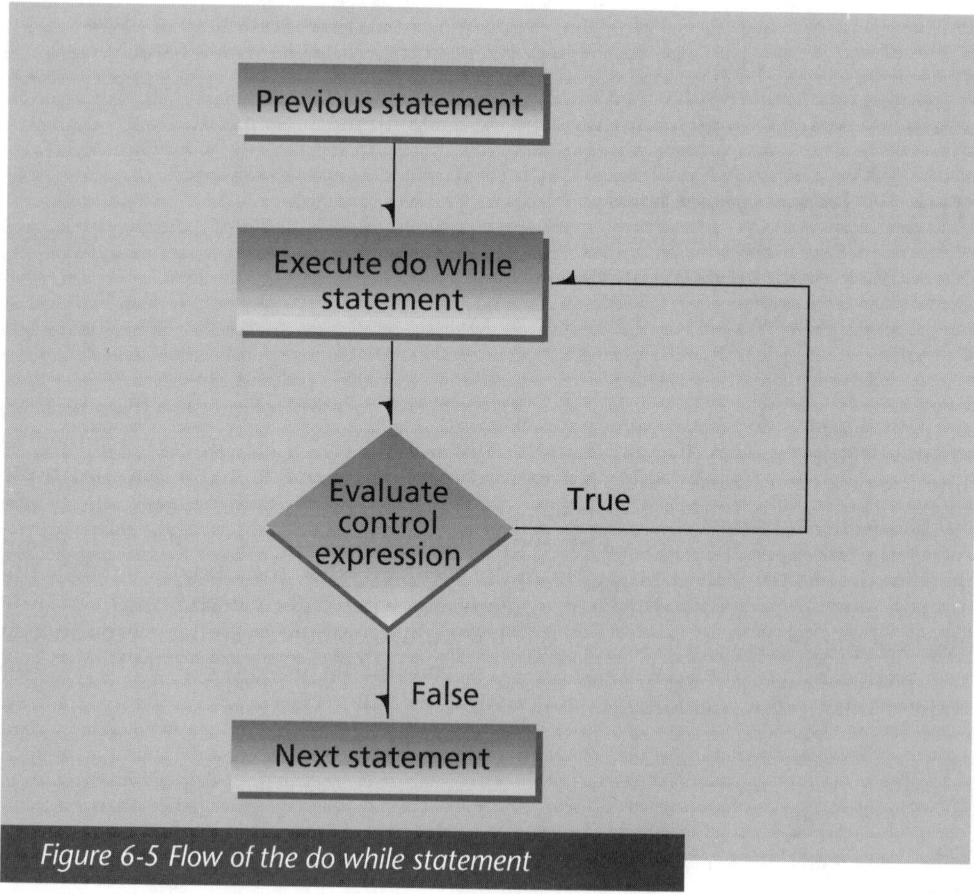

Figure 6-5 Flow of the do while statement

THE *do while* STATEMENT

The *do while* statement is similar to *while*, except that the compiler evaluates the control expression at the end of the loop instead of at the beginning. The syntax of the *do while* statement is:

```
do
        statement
while (control expression);
```

Figure 6-5 shows how the *do while* statement works: First the program executes *statement*, then it evaluates *control expression*, and as long as it is true, the loop continues to execute *statement*. When the value of *control expression* goes false, the program moves on to the next statement. Notice that *statement* always executes at least once because the control expression occurs at the end of the loop.

Now it will be interesting to see the effect of using a *do while* statement in place of *while* in the CARDS program.

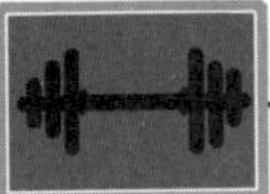

Listing 6.8 CARDS3.C A card dealer

DO:
- Modify CARDS to use *do while*
- Compile and run CARDS3, then enter (8) (6) (0)

```
#include <stdio.h>
main()
{
     int card_total = 0;            /* Running total of cards */
     int hit;                       /* A new card */

     printf("\nDEAL CARDS FOR THE GAME OF 21\n");

     do                             /*1*/
     {                              /*2*/
        printf("\nYour card total is %d", card_total += hit);
        printf("\nEnter a card (1-13), or 0 to quit: ");
        scanf("%d", &hit);
     } while (hit);                 /*3*/
}
```

RESULT:

```
C:\>CARDS3
DEAL CARDS FOR THE GAME OF 21

Your card total is 0
Enter a card (1-13), or 0 to quit: 8
Your card total is 8
```

```
Enter a card (1-13), or 0 to quit: 6
Your card total is 14
Enter a card (1-13), or 0 to quit: 0
```

ANALYSIS:

1. You have simplified the program by using *do while* instead of *while*. You have eliminated one scanf() statement and one printf() statement.
2. Previously, you had to read the first nonzero value into *hit* before the program tested it at the beginning of the loop. Now the program tests *hit* at the end of the loop, so you can eliminate the first scanf().
3. An important effect of the *do while* loop is that the controlled statement always executes at least once. This is evidenced here by the display of a zero card total before you enter the first card value.

To summarize, use *do while* when you want to execute the body of a loop at least once and test for the stopping condition at the end of the loop; use *while* when you want to test at the beginning.

CONTROL EXPRESSIONS

Control expressions serve as the brains for looping statements, in which a program makes decisions about how many times to repeat a loop and when to stop looping.

Control expressions can also accomplish tasks that are not directly related to looping, such as making calculations or reading data. These other tasks are secondary because they can also be accomplished with statements located in the body of the loop. You can only affect control of a loop from within the control expression, so this is the primary purpose. For instance, in the program PEPPERS, you used the control expression (n--) to regulate a *while* loop:

```
while (n--)
        printf(...
```

The mere presence of variable *n* fulfills the primary purpose of this expression; the *while* statement ends when *n* is false, or 0. However, the decrement operation is secondary because you could just as well accomplish this with a separate statement in the body of the loop:

```
while (n)
{
        n--;
        printf(...
```

The central decision of a loop is whether to continue or quit, and a program makes this decision based on whether the value of a control expression is true or false. Therefore, the flow of a loop depends on the combination of operators and operands that you place in a control expression. C has some operators that allow you to compare data values and test the relationship between variables and constants. The next two sections will introduce these new operators that are particularly suited for control expressions.

Logical operators

Programmers often use *logical operators* in the control expressions of looping statements. There are three logical operators in C:

Operator	Meaning
!	NOT
&&	AND
||	OR

The logical operators return true or false values when applied to operands.

NOT is a unary operator that returns false (0) if its operand is true (nonzero) and returns true (1) if the operand is false (0). For instance, if integer variable *x* has a value of 0, then *!x* is 1 (true). If *x* has any other value, say 3, *!x* is 0 (false).

The AND and OR operators are binary, they use two operands. AND returns true (1) if **both** operands are true (nonzero); otherwise it returns false (0). The OR returns true if **either** operand is true (nonzero); otherwise it returns false (0). Here is an example of an OR expression: *x || y*. If either *x* or *y* has a nonzero value, then the expression evaluates to 1 (true). Only when both *x* and *y* are zero is the expression 0 (false). One variable has two possible logical values, true or false, and two variables have four possible combinations. Table 6-1 summarizes the action of the logical operators for all four combinations of two variables.

Operands		— Operator results —			
x	y	!x	!y	x && y	x || y
0	0	1	1	0	0
0	nonzero	1	0	0	1
nonzero	0	0	1	0	1
nonzero	nonzero	0	0	1	1

Table 6-1 Logical operators

A logical operator always returns a value of one (1) for true or zero (0) for false; however, a control expression interprets any nonzero value of an operand as true. The NOT operator (!) has higher precedence than AND (&&), and OR (||) has the lowest precedence of the logical operators. See Appendix B for the precedence of logical operators relative to other operators.

You can apply the NOT operator (!) to any numeric operand, including floating-point types, as the next example shows.

Listing 6.9 LOGICAL.C The NOT operator

DO: Enter, compile, and run LOGICAL

```
#include <stdio.h>
#define TRUE  1
#define FALSE 0
main()
{
   int   mine;
   float yours = 1.23;              /* 1.23 is true */
   char  night = FALSE;
   long  day;

   mine = !yours;
   day  = !night;

   printf("\nMine (%d) is NOT yours (%.2f)", mine, yours);
   printf("\nand day (%ld) is NOT night (%d)", day, night);
```

RESULT:

```
C:\>LOGICAL
Mine (0) is NOT yours (1.23)
and day (1) is NOT night (0)
```

ANALYSIS:

1. The program applies the NOT operator (!) to the floating-point operand *yours*, and also to the character operand *night*.
2. The result of applying NOT to any operand is an integer 1 or 0, and when the result is assigned to a *long* integer, like *day*, the assignment promotes it to type *long*.

You usually find logical operators used only with integer variables. A value of false is zero, but a program cannot reliably calculate an exact value of zero with floating-point arithmetic, so you should avoid floating-point operands with logical operators. The next program uses the AND and OR logical operators with some integer operands.

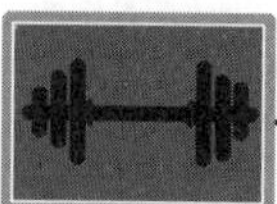

Listing 6.10 LOGICAL2.C The AND and OR operators

DO: Enter, compile, and run LOGICAL2

```
#include <stdio.h>
#define TRUE  1
#define FALSE 0
main()
{
     int heat;
     int oxygen;
     int fuel;
     int fire;

     int   June = TRUE;
     int   July = FALSE;
     int August= FALSE;
     int summer;

/* AND operator */

     heat = oxygen = fuel = TRUE;
   fire = heat && oxygen && fuel;
   printf( "\nFire (%d) requires heat (%d) AND oxygen (%d)"
          " AND fuel (%d)", fire, heat, oxygen, fuel);

/* OR operator */

   summer = June || July || August;
   printf( "\n\nSummer (%d) is June (%d) OR July (%d)"
          " OR August (%d)", summer, June, July, August);
}
```

RESULT:

```
C:\>LOGICAL2
Fire (1) requires heat (1) AND oxygen (1) AND fuel (1)

Summer (1) is June (1) OR July (0) OR August (0)
```

ANALYSIS:

1. The program defines all variables to be of type *int*, the usual data type for logical operators.
2. On the line just after the comment /* AND operator */, the program initializes all three of the variables required for *fire* to be true with a multiple assignment. If any of these variables (*heat*, *oxygen*, or *fuel*) were false, the AND expression on the next line would yield false, and the program would assign 0 to *fire*, but all three are true, and so the statement makes *fire* true.

3. The program initializes the summer months when it defines the variables; it assigns a value of true to only one of the months (June).
4. Summer is true if any of the summer months is true, as determined by the OR expression.

You will make the best use of logical operators in control expressions of branching and looping control statements. Branching control statements are the topic of Chapter 7, but in the next section, you will see logical operators used in connection with relational operators in some looping control expressions.

Relational operators

Relational operators provide the means to compare variables, constants, and expressions so that you can alter the flow of a program based on their values. There are six operators in C that can test relationships between two values:

Operator	Meaning
<	LESS THAN
>	GREATER THAN
==	EQUAL TO
!=	NOT EQUAL TO
<=	LESS THAN OR EQUAL TO
>=	GREATER THAN OR EQUAL TO

The result of an expression involving any of these operators is either true (1) or false (0). If the first operand satisfies the specified relation with respect to the second operand, then the expression returns true (1). For example, if the value of an integer, i, is 3, then the expression i < 4 yields true (1), and i == 2 yields false (0). Appendix D shows the precedence of relational operators. You can expand the card dealer program to include a relational operator.

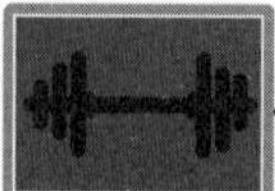

Listing 6.11 CARDS4.C A card dealer

DO: • Add a relational operator to CARDS3
• Compile and run CARDS4, then enter (8) (6) (9)

```
#include <stdio.h>
main()
{
     int card_total = 0;              /* Running total of cards */
     int hit = 0;                     /* A new card */

     printf("\nDEAL CARDS FOR THE GAME OF 21\n");

     do
     {
```

```
        printf("\nYour card total is %d", card_total += hit);
        printf("\nEnter a card (1-13), or 0 to quit: ");
        scanf("%d", &hit);
    } while (hit && card_total <= 21);                              /*1*/
    printf("\nYour final total is %d", card_total);                 /*2*/
}
```

RESULT:

```
C:\>CARDS4
DEAL CARDS FOR THE GAME OF 21

Your card total is 0
Enter a card (1-13), or 0 to quit: 8
Your card total is 8
Enter a card (1-13), or 0 to quit: 6
Your card total is 14
Enter a card (1-13), or 0 to quit: 9
Your final total is 23
```

ANALYSIS:

1. In the game of Blackjack, you lose, or "go bust" if the total of your cards exceeds 21. Line /*1*/ adds a test for this condition which causes the *while* loop to end if it occurs.

2. The <= operator has higher precedence than &&, so the *while* expression first evaluates whether *card_total* is less than or equal to 21. If this result is true AND you have requested a card (*hit* is nonzero) then the compound statement executes again and the *while* loop continues.

You can use relational operators in connection with logical operators to investigate an interesting situation that sometimes occurs. Whenever possible, your C program will take a shortcut in evaluating logical expressions. These shortcuts make your programs run faster, but they can cause problems if you are not aware of them. The shortcut is this: Evaluation of a logical expression will stop when the outcome has been determined. For example, C evaluates the expression x && *y* && *z* from left to right, and if *x* is false, then the expression is known to be false without checking the values of *y* and *z*. You can see the effect of this shortcut in an example—first lay some groundwork by writing a program to count one variable up while simultaneously counting another variable down.

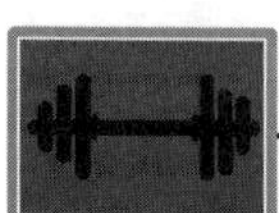

Listing 6.12 SHORT.C Logical expression evaluation shortcut

DO: Enter, compile, and run SHORT, then enter (0) (Space) (10)

```
#include <stdio.h>
main()
{
     int up;
     int down;

     printf("\nEnter two integers: ");
     scanf("%d %d", &up, &down);
     while ((up < 10) || (down > 0))
       printf("\n%d %d", ++up, --down);
}
```

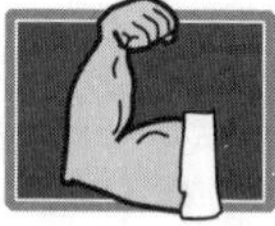

RESULT:

```
C:\>SHORT
Enter two integers: 0 10
1 9
2 8
3 7
4 6
5 5
6 4
7 3
8 2
9 1
```

ANALYSIS:

1. This program reads in two integers and counts one of them (*up*) upwards to 10 and the other (*down*) downwards to zero. The *while* control expression stops this process if either *up* reaches 10 or *down* reaches zero.

2. Both the increment and decrement are prefix operators, so both variables count simultaneously and they both reach their desired limits at the same time.

3. Notice that there are two extra sets of parentheses in the *while* control expression. They are not needed because they do not change the precedence of any of the operators, but it is good programming practice

to make liberal use of parentheses so that there is no confusion about the intended precedence.

It would seem that you could just as well increment and decrement the two variables, *up* and *down*, in the *while* control expression and get the same result. Do this—move the increment and decrement operators from the printf() statement to the *while* expression.

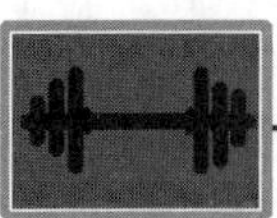

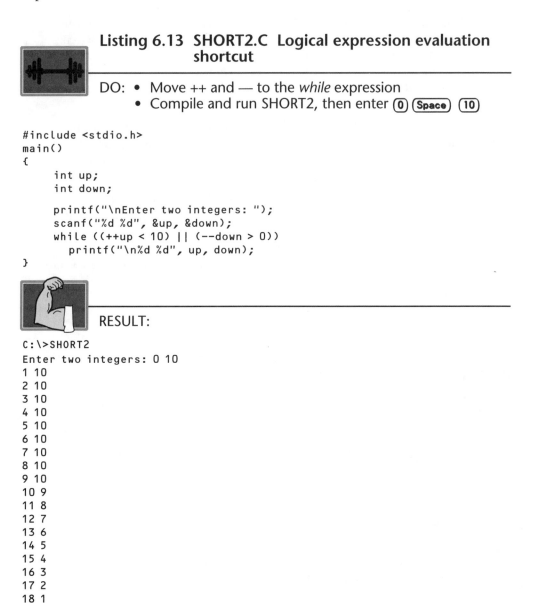

Listing 6.13 SHORT2.C Logical expression evaluation shortcut

DO:
- Move ++ and — to the *while* expression
- Compile and run SHORT2, then enter (0) (Space) (10)

```
#include <stdio.h>
main()
{
      int up;
      int down;

      printf("\nEnter two integers: ");
      scanf("%d %d", &up, &down);
      while ((++up < 10) || (--down > 0))
        printf("\n%d %d", up, down);
}
```

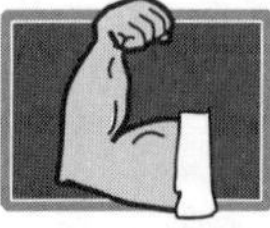

RESULT:

```
C:\>SHORT2
Enter two integers: 0 10
1 10
2 10
3 10
4 10
5 10
6 10
7 10
8 10
9 10
10 9
11 8
12 7
13 6
14 5
15 4
16 3
17 2
18 1
```

ANALYSIS:

1. It still appears that the two operators will count simultaneously, but such is not the case because of the shortcut that occurs within the *while* expression.
2. Because the *while* control expression involves a logical OR, when the program discovers that the first term is true (++up < 10) it knows that the whole expression is true and evaluation stops. Thus as long as *up* is less than 10, the statement never decrements *down*; only when *up* reaches 10 does *down* begin to change (but notice that *up* continues to increment).
3. As long as changes to the variables were confined to the body of the loop in the previous example (in the indented printf() statement of SHORT), any shortcuts in the logical expression did not affect whether or not the decrement was performed.

The moral of this example is that you should avoid the use of operators that change the value of a variable within a logical expression. If you must use such operators (assignment, increment, etc.) in logical expressions, be very aware of program shortcuts.

Operator precedence can also trip you up in a control expression if you are not wary. Suppose you want to prevent program SHORT from counting at all if you enter a zero or negative number for variable *down*. You can do this by ANDing a test *(down > 0)* to the control expression to make sure that *down* is greater than zero before any counting occurs.

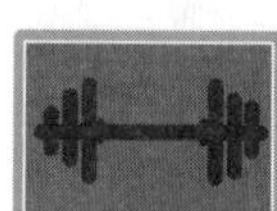

Listing 6.14 SHORT3.C Logical expression evaluation shortcut

DO:
- Add a term to the control expression of SHORT
- Compile and run SHORT, then enter 0 Space 1

```
#include <stdio.h>
main()
{
     int up;
     int down;

     printf("\nEnter two integers: ");
     scanf("%d %d", &up, &down);
     while ((up < 10) || (down > 0) && (down > 0))          /*1*/
        printf("\n%d %d", ++up, ñdown);
}
```

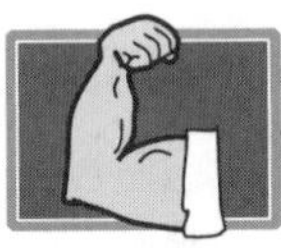

RESULT:

```
C:\>SHORT
Enter two integers: 0 -1
1 -2
2 -3
3 -4
4 -5
5 -6
6 -7
7 -8
8 -9
9 -10
```

ANALYSIS:

1. Hold on, what happened?! The loop was not supposed to cycle even once if *down* was negative.
2. The new relational test did not alter the logic of the control expression at all. Examine the new control expression carefully, especially the terms after the OR operator (||):

   The new subexpression is ANDed only with the last part of the old control expression, *(down > 0)*, not with the whole thing. And the last term of the old expression is the same as the new subexpression, so the added term has no effect.

   ```
   ((up < 10) || (down > 0) && (down > 0))
   ```

Fortunately, there is an easy rule that can save you from this kind of logic error—use lots of parentheses. You should enclose all of the old control expression in an extra set of parentheses, then AND the new subexpression to achieve the desired effect.

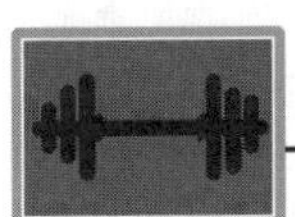

Listing 6.15 SHORT3.C Logical expression evaluation shortcut

DO:
- Add parentheses to the control expression of SHORT2
- Compile and run SHORT, then enter 0 Space -1

```
#include <stdio.h>
main()
{
    int up;
```

```
     int down;

     printf("\nEnter two integers: ");
     scanf("%d %d", &up, &down);
     while (((up < 10) || (down > 0)) && (down > 0))               /*1*/
       printf("\n%d %d", ++up, ñdown);
}
```

RESULT:

```
C:\>SHORT
Enter two integers: 0 -1
```

ANALYSIS:

1. Now the program refuses to count when you enter a negative number for variable *down*, which is exactly what you want.
2. The extra set of parentheses forces the program to evaluate the entire expression. The program properly ANDs the new subexpression *(down > 0)* with the remainder of the control expression, and consequently the whole expression is false when *down* is less than zero.

The lesson here is to be precise in setting up control expressions, and use parentheses to explicitly specify the order of evaluation.

You can use logical and relational operators to form as complex an expression as necessary to control looping and accomplish secondary tasks. The following program illustrates the use of an assignment, an I/O function, and a relational test within a *while* expression.

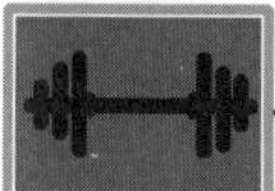

LISTING 6.16 COMPLEX.C A complex while expression

DO: • Enter and compile COMPLEX
• Run COMPLEX and enter (A) (ENTER) (Q) (ENTER)

```
#include <stdio.h>
main()
{
     int key = 0;

     printf("\nEnter any character (Q to quit)");
```

```
     while ((key = getchar()) != 'Q')
       printf("\nYou entered %c, enter another character",
              key);
}
```

RESULT:

```
C:\>COMPLEX
Enter any character (Q to quit): A
You entered A, enter another character:
You entered, enter another character: Q
```

ANALYSIS:

1. This program uses a *while* expression to read keystrokes from the keyboard until you press Q (it must be a capital Q). This is a very useful construct for controlling events from the keyboard within any sort of looping or control statement.
2. When you enter Q, the program ends without displaying what you have entered; this occurs because the *while* expression becomes false at this point, and the *while* ends without executing the controlled printf() statement.
3. Notice that entry of A causes two lines of display to occur. You expect the first line but not the second. The second line displays the newline character ('\n') generated when you pressed ENTER—notice that the line is split by the display of this character. You learned in Chapter 4 (Program 4.2) that getchar() will read any character from the keyboard, including line feed, so the *while* loop picks up all characters until the keyboard buffer is empty.
4. In the *while* expression, you use parentheses to force the assignment of the result of getchar() to *key* before comparing it with 'Q'. Without the parentheses, the != operator would have precedence over =, causing the result of getchar() to be compared to 'Q'. Then the program would assign the result of this comparison (1 or 0) to *key*.

The purpose of the inner parentheses of the control expression will become very clear if you remove them and run the next program.

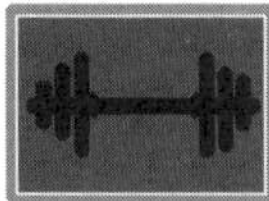

Listing 6.17 COMPLEX2.C A complex while expression

DO:
- Remove the inner parentheses from the while in COMPLEX
- Compile and run COMPLEX2
- Enter (A) (ENTER) (Q) (ENTER)

```
#include <stdio.h>
main()
{
     int key = 0;

     printf("\nEnter any character (Q to quit)");
     while (key = getchar() != 'Q')                              /*1*/
         printf("\nYou entered %c (%d),"
                " enter another character", key, key);
}
```

RESULT:

```
C:\>COMPLEX2
Enter any character (Q to quit): A
You entered  (1), enter another character:
You entered  (1), enter another character: Q
```

ANALYSIS:

1. Without the extra pair of parentheses, the *while* evaluates expression getchar() != 'Q' first and assigns the result to *key*.
2. Your first entry (A) does not equal 'Q'; therefore, the expression is true and the result of 1 is assigned to *key*. Because the result is true, the *while* continues to operate.
3. This program has a numeric display so that the result assigned to *key* is more clear. If you are using an IBM PC, the character display probably shows a little happy face, which is the displayable character equivalent of the integer 1. Once again, the newline character causes a second line of display to occur.
4. Your second entry (Q) causes the w*hile* control expression to be false, which ends the loop.

You can make the loop in program COMPLEX more useful by eliminating printf() from the *while* statement so as not to display all intermediate results. Use a null statement (;) to do nothing while the loop reads the keyboard until Q is entered.

Listing 6.18 COMPLEX3.C A complex while expression

DO:
- Remove printf() from the loop in COMPLEX
- Compile and run COMPLEX3
- Enter A ENTER Q ENTER

```
#include <stdio.h>
main()
{
     int key = 0;

     printf("\nEnter any character (Q to quit)");
     while ((key = getchar()) != 'Q');                          /*
                                                   /*null statement */
     printf("\nThanks for the %c", key);
}
```

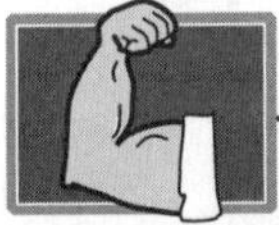

RESULT:

```
C:\>COMPLEX3
Enter any character (Q to quit): A
Q
Thanks for the Q
```

ANALYSIS:

1. Now you have a nice, compact method for reading the keyboard until a certain character is entered.
2. Notice that the null statement occupies a line of its own, with a comment, so that is it easy to see. We recommend this layout because a null statement is so small and easy to overlook.

THE *for* STATEMENT

The *while* statement is particularly useful for controlling indefinite looping, but when you want to loop a fixed number of times, the *for* statement is more suitable. The syntax of the *for* statement is:

```
for (initialize; test; update)
     statement
```

The items *initialize, test,* and *update* are all expressions, and *test* yields a numeric value that the statement can interpret as true or false. The above *for* syntax is equivalent to:

```
initialize;
while (test)
{
       statement
       update;
}
```

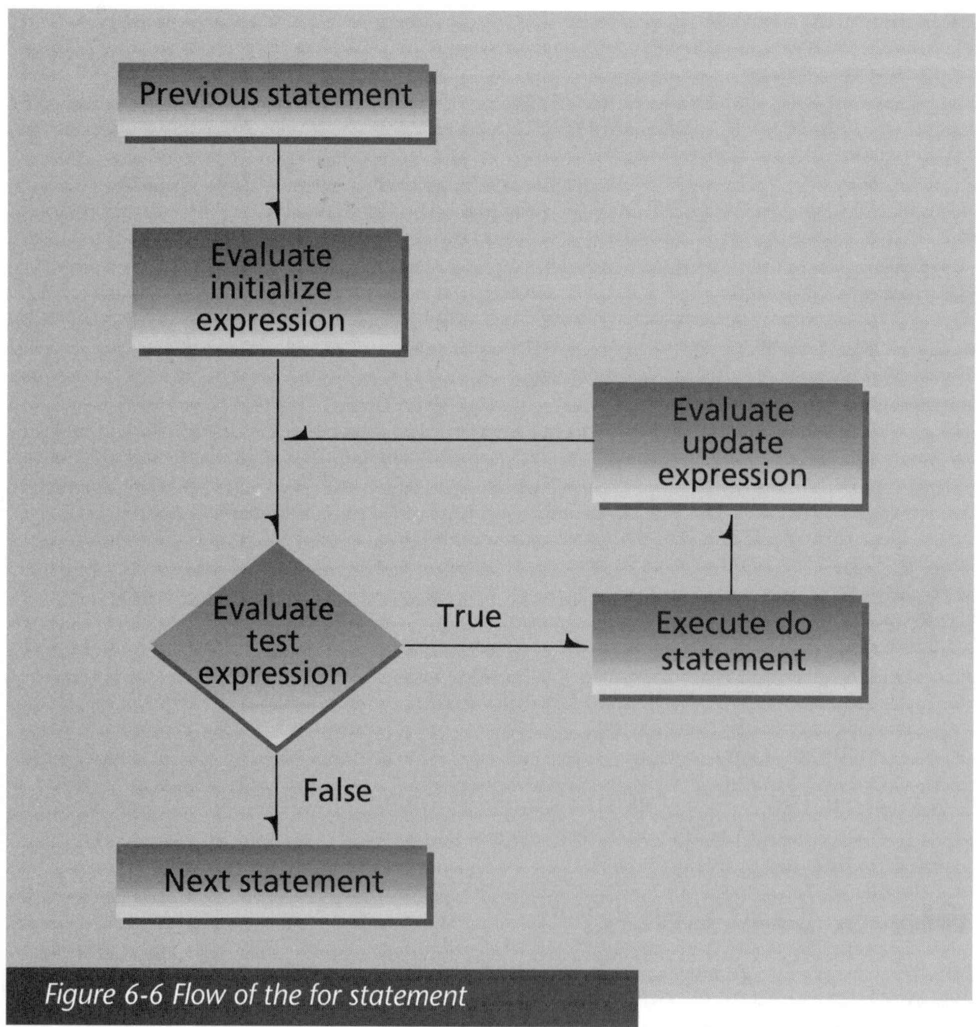

Figure 6-6 Flow of the for statement

Figure 6-6 shows the flow of the *for* statement: A program evaluates the *initialize* expression once (to initialize variables), then it evaluates the *test* expression and quits if the result is false (0). If the result of *test* is true, then the program executes *statement* and evaluates *update* to change the values of controlling variables, then it repeats the sequence.

Perhaps the most common and straightforward use of *for* is to operate a counter to control execution of a loop. The next program counts from zero through nine and displays a tongue twister each time it increments the counter.

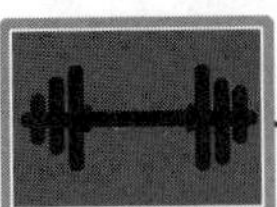

Listing 6.19 COUNTER.C A fixed loop

DO: Enter, compile, and run COUNTER

```
#include <stdio.h>
main()
{
     int up;

     for (up = 0; up < 10; ++up)
          printf("\n%d Peter Piper picked a peck"
                 " of pickled peppers", up);
}
```

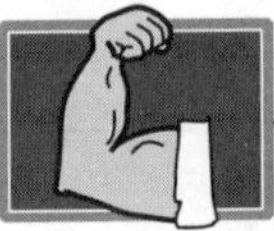

RESULT:

```
C:\>COUNTER
0 Peter Piper picked a peck of pickled peppers
1 Peter Piper picked a peck of pickled peppers
2 Peter Piper picked a peck of pickled peppers
3 Peter Piper picked a peck of pickled peppers
4 Peter Piper picked a peck of pickled peppers
5 Peter Piper picked a peck of pickled peppers
6 Peter Piper picked a peck of pickled peppers
7 Peter Piper picked a peck of pickled peppers
8 Peter Piper picked a peck of pickled peppers
9 Peter Piper picked a peck of pickled peppers
```

ANALYSIS:

Here is an analysis of the workings of the *for* statement: The *initialize* expression is *up=0,* so the statement first sets the variable *up* to zero. The test expression is *up<10,* which is true as long as the value of *up* is less than 10, so the printf() statement executes, then the program evaluates update expression ++*up*. This completes one cycle of the *for* loop. Now the value of *up* is 1, which is less than 10, so the loop continues and makes 10 cycles until *up* reaches a value of 10. The expression *up<10* then returns a value of false and transfers control to the next statement outside the loop. There are no more statements, so the program is finished.

Overall this program does not appear to be simpler than Program 6.3, PEPPERS, which does the same thing using a *while* statement. However, the *for* syntax offers the advantage of localizing all operations associated with looping: initialize, updating, and testing for termination. This becomes important as loop conditions become more complex.

The three expressions within a *for* statement (initialize, test, and update) are optional and you can leave out any or all of them. The minimum *for* statement is:

```
for ( ; ; );
```

which amounts to an *infinite loop* that does nothing. Nothing is initialized, nothing is updated, and the null statement (the last semicolon, outside the parentheses) also does nothing when executed. The loop is infinite (never stops) because when you leave the middle, or test, expression out, *for* assumes that the result is true and always continues executing. To eliminate the test expression you need to use the break statement with an *if* statement to end the *for* loop. These new statements will be introduced in the next chapter, so for now you can leave the test expression in. Modify the previous example to leave out the initialize and update expressions, but leave the test expression alone.

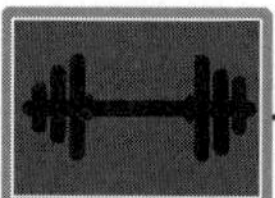

Listing 6.20 COUNTER2.C A fixed loop

DO:
- Modify program COUNTER to eliminate some for expressions
- Compile and run COUNTER2

```
#include <stdio.h>
main()
{
     int up = 0;                                    /*1*/

     for ( ; up<10; )                               /*2*/
     {                                              /*3*/
         printf("\n%d Peter Piper picked a peck"
                 " of pickled peppers", up);
         ++up;                                      /*4*/
     }                                              /*5*/
}
```

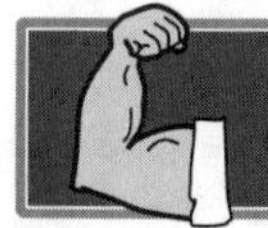

RESULT:

```
C:\>COUNTER2
```

```
0 Peter Piper picked a peck of pickled peppers
1 Peter Piper picked a peck of pickled peppers
2 Peter Piper picked a peck of pickled peppers
3 Peter Piper picked a peck of pickled peppers
4 Peter Piper picked a peck of pickled peppers
5 Peter Piper picked a peck of pickled peppers
6 Peter Piper picked a peck of pickled peppers
7 Peter Piper picked a peck of pickled peppers
8 Peter Piper picked a peck of pickled peppers
9 Peter Piper picked a peck of pickled peppers
```

ANALYSIS:

1. Even though you have eliminated two expressions from the *for* statement, you have not eliminated the requirement for the work that they performed.
2. This program shifts the work of the initialize expression to the definition statement on line /*1*/, where it sets *up* to zero.
3. The work of updating the variable *up* is now done by a separate increment statement on line /*4*/.
4. Notice that you must now use a compound statement (lines /*3–5*/) to include printf() and the statement that updates *up*. You can use compound statements with *for* just as you have with *while*.

A new operator, the comma (,), allows you to use more than one initialize or update expression in a *for* statement. The compiler evaluates a pair of expressions separated by a comma in left-to-right order. Here is a program that uses the comma operator to initialize and update two variables within the *for* expressions.

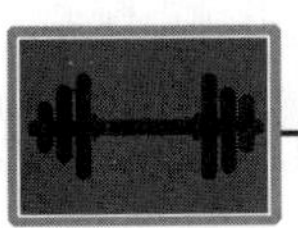

Listing 6.21 COUNTER3.C Count up and down simultaneously

DO: Modify COUNTER, then compile and run COUNTER3

```
#include <stdio.h>
main()
{
     int up;
     int down;                                                /*1*/

     for (up=0, down=10; up<10; ++up, down -= 2)              /*2*/
          printf("\n\n%d %d", up, down);                      /*3*/
}
```

RESULT:

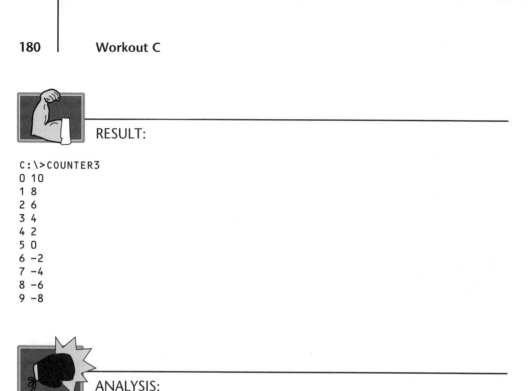

```
C:\>COUNTER3
0 10
1 8
2 6
3 4
4 2
5 0
6 -2
7 -4
8 -6
9 -8
```

ANALYSIS:

1. This program uses a *for* statement to count two integers simultaneously; *up* counts up by 1s and *down* counts down by 2s.
2. COUNTER3 has introduced the comma operator to allow initialization and updating of both *up* and *down* within the *for* statement.
3. Notice that the *for* statement on line /*2*/ uses a tighter grouping of symbols (less spaces) within each expression. This makes the code more readable when there are complex expressions. There is no standard with regard to this; you need to choose a method of spacing that pleases you and use it consistently.

The result of the series of expressions (that is, its value) is the result of the rightmost expression. This latter property is not usually important in the context of *for* because you don't use the comma operator in the test expression, which is the only *for* expression that depends on a result. Using commas, you can initialize and update any number of expressions in a *for* statement.

NESTED LOOPS

You can put a loop within a loop (called *nested* loops) to achieve some very useful and interesting results. You use nested loops when you need to do something several times

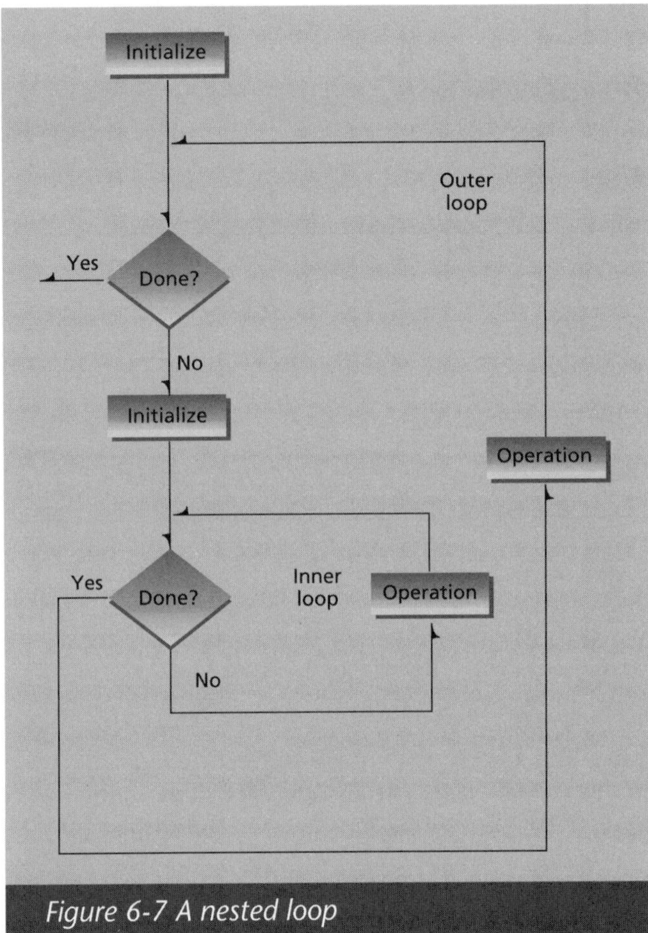

Figure 6-7 A nested loop

for every occurrence of something else. For example, a census program might count the number of children for each family in town, or a text searching program might display every occurrence of a particular word in each file on your hard disk. Figure 6-7 illustrates the basic idea of a nested loop.

An *outer* loop encloses an *inner* loop in the sense that for each cycle of the outer loop, the inner loop runs from beginning to end, completing all of its cycles. The next program uses an outer *for* loop to select letters W through Z, while an inner *while* loop displays the selected letters and all subsequent letters through Z. Nested loops can consist of any combination of *for*, *while*, or *do while* statements.

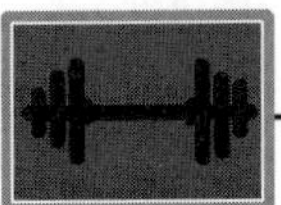

Listing 6.22 NESTED.C A nested loop

DO: Enter, compile, and run NESTED

```
#include <stdio.h>
main()
{
     char outer_char;
     char inner_char;

     for (outer_char = 'W'; outer_char <= 'Z'; ++outer_char)
     {
```

```
        printf("\n%c:", outer_char);
        inner_char = outer_char;          /*            */
        while (inner_char <= 'Z')         /* Inner loop */
            printf("%c", inner_char++);/*               */
        }
}
```

RESULT:

```
C:\>NESTED
W:XYZ
X:YZ
Y:Z
Z:
```

ANALYSIS:

1. Everything encompassed by the *for* statement represents the outer loop, and the three statements with the attached "inner loop" comment represent the inner loop.

2. The outer loop executes four cycles, assigning a different character (W, X, Y, and Z) to the variable *outer_char* at each cycle. The outer loop also moves the cursor to a new line for each cycle and displays the current character (the first printf()).

3. Each time the outer loop enters a cycle, the inner *while* loop executes all of its cycles by initializing the variable *inner_char* to *outer_char* and displaying all subsequent letters up to and including the letter 'Z'.

4. Where does the inner loop really begin? You could argue with some merit that the assignment statement that sets *inner_char* to *outer_char* belongs to the outer loop, but since it involves the controlling variable of the *while* statement, we have included it in the inner loop.

Nested loops are not restricted to two levels; you can have as many loops within loops as are needed for the task at hand. Figure 6-8 graphically depicts a *deeply nested* loop with four levels.

Each iteration (cycle) of one of the outer loops involves all of the cycles of the adjacent inner loop. When the innermost loop ends, it gives control back to the adjacent outer loop, and when that loop ends it passes control outward. Thus, a deeply nested loop is a process of repeatedly spiralling downwards to the innermost loop and then back out again, until the outermost loop has completed all of its cycles. Nested loops with two or three levels are common, but you will rarely encounter deeper loops.

With looping control statements, you have the ability to repeat operations as many times as necessary. The next chapter will expand your repertoire of control tools by introducing statements that change the sequence of operations in a program by branching.

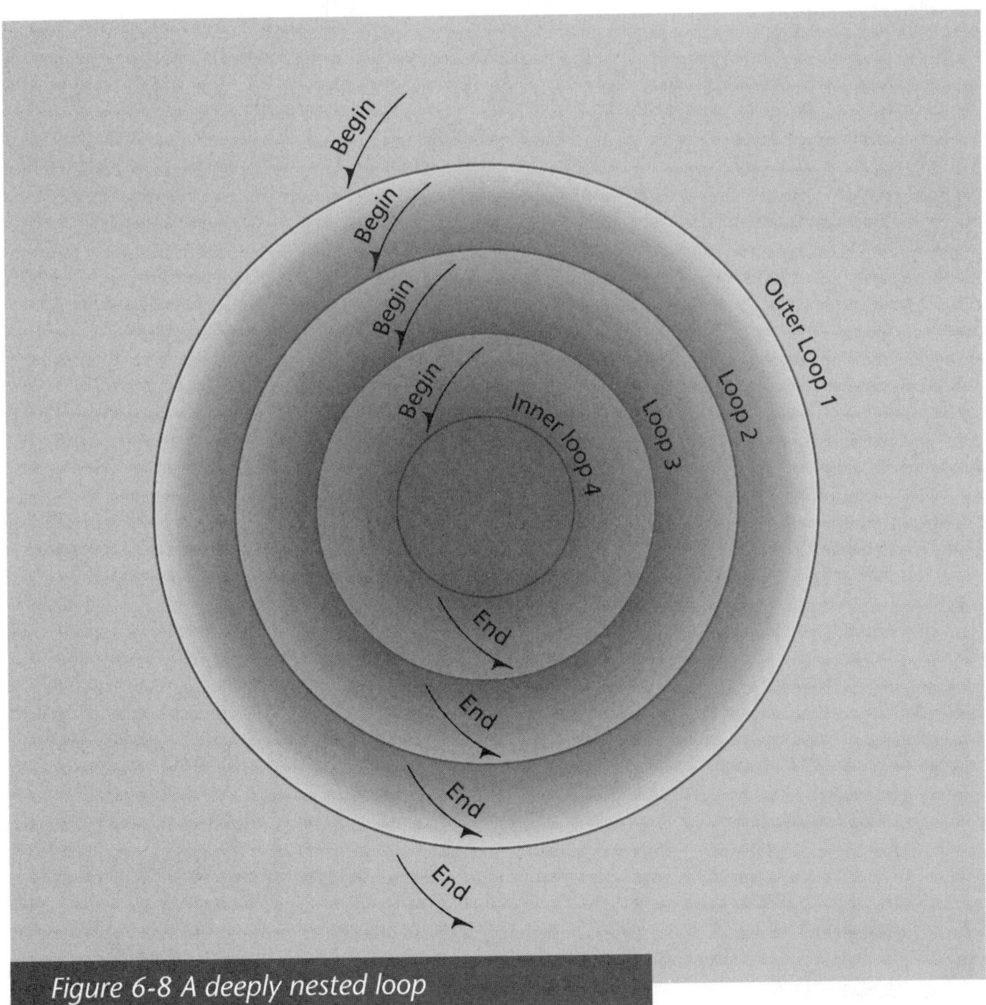

Figure 6-8 A deeply nested loop

CHAPTER 7
BRANCHING CONTROL STATEMENTS

Control statements allow you to use data to alter events in a program. In this chapter, you will learn how to modify the flow of a program with the branching control statements *if*, *if else*, *switch*, *continue*, and *break*. You will use logical and relational operators to test for certain conditions and change the operation of programs based on the results. You will also learn about the *goto* statement and the wisdom of using it sparingly.

PROGRAM BRANCHING

Branching is the process of skipping over certain portions of your program and executing other sections. Program branching can be likened to your progress on a shopping trip through a mall where your path depends on the decisions you make at each store. When you find an item to buy, you will select stores with the next item on your list; if not, you will shop for the needed item in different stores. Suppose you need a pair of dress shoes and a new tennis racquet; a simplified diagram of your shopping trip may look like Figure 7-1.

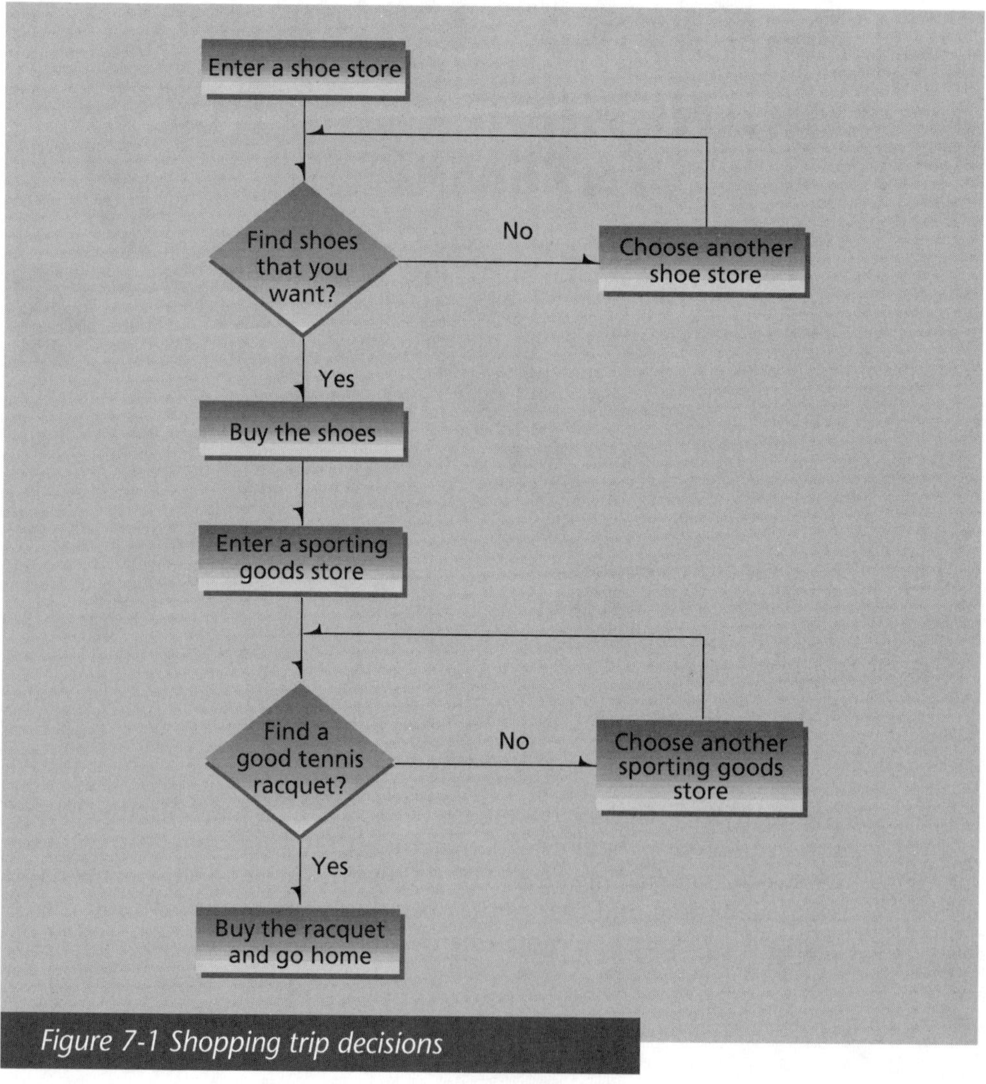

Figure 7-1 Shopping trip decisions

The diamond-shaped boxes are decision points resulting in yes or no answers (no maybes on this shopping trip), and the rectangles represent actions. Yes/no decisions correspond to the true or false results of logical expressions in your programs, and the actions are similar to C statements. Each decision point amounts to a branch where you select one path in favor of another. Let's start the discussion of program branching in C with the *if* statement.

THE *if* STATEMENT

The syntax of the *if* statement is:

```
if (control expression)
        statement
```

A program evaluates the *control expression* and if the result is true, then it executes the *statement*; otherwise, it skips the *statement*. The statement can be either an individual or a compound statement, in which case curly braces enclose several statements. For readability, you should always indent the controlled statement under the controlling *if* expression. With a compound statement, you can choose either of two placements for the curly braces (we prefer the layout on the left):

```
if (control expression)            if (control expression) {
{                                       statement
     statement                                  }
}
```

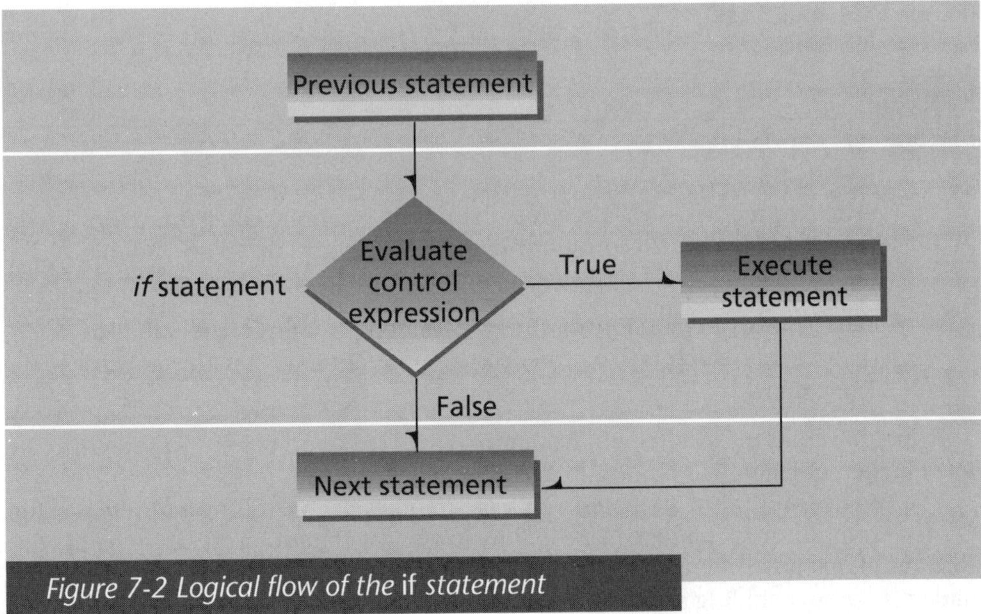

Figure 7-2 Logical flow of the if *statement*

Whichever form you choose, be sure that it is consistent with the way you lay out compound statements with other commands, such as *for* and *while*. Figure 7-2 shows the logical flow of an *if* statement.

You can use the *if* statement to write a program that gives advice on investing in the stock market.

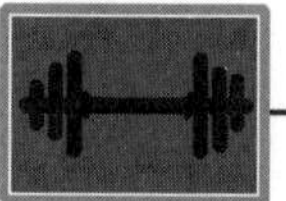

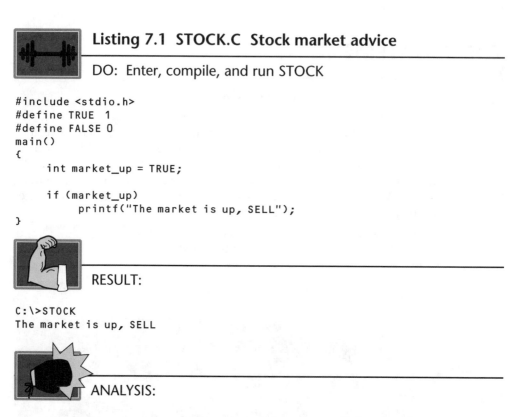

Listing 7.1 STOCK.C Stock market advice

DO: Enter, compile, and run STOCK

```
#include <stdio.h>
#define TRUE  1
#define FALSE 0
main()
{
     int market_up = TRUE;

     if (market_up)
          printf("The market is up, SELL");
}
```

RESULT:

```
C:\>STOCK
The market is up, SELL
```

ANALYSIS:

1. The two preprocessor directives define the symbolic constants *TRUE* and *FALSE*, and the program uses *TRUE* to initialize the variable *market_up* to signify that the current market direction is upward.
2. The control expression of the *if* statement is simply the value of *market_up*, which is 1 or true, so the program executes the printf() statement.

If you pull apart the *if* statement from program STOCK and place the pieces into the flow diagram of Figure 7-2, it looks like Figure 7-3.

You can use multiple *if* statements in a program, each controlling a different statement. A common stock market adage is "buy low and sell high." You can expand your program so that it will advise "buy" when the market is down as well as "sell" when the market is up by including a second *if* statement.

Previous statement

int market_up = TRUE;

if statement

Evaluate control expression (market_up)

True

printf ("the market is up, SELL");

Execute statement

False

Next statement

(closing curly brace of program)

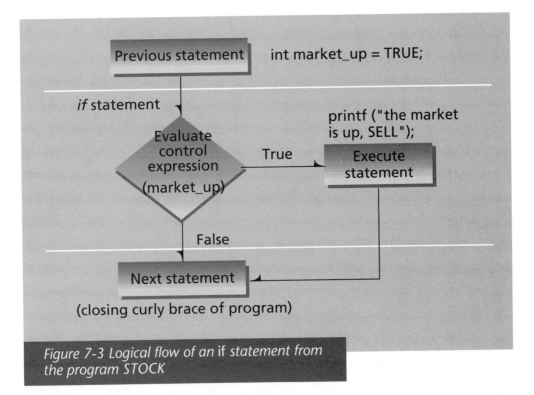

Figure 7-3 Logical flow of an if *statement from the program STOCK*

Listing 7.2 STOCK2.C Stock market advice

DO:
- Add a second *if* statement to STOCK
- Compile STOCK2

```
#include <stdio.h>
#define TRUE  1
#define FALSE 0
main()
{
     int market_up = TRUE;

     printf("Enter the market direction (1=UP, 0=DOWN): ");      /*1*/
     scanf("%d", &market_up);                                     /*2*/

     if (market_up)
          printf("The market is up, SELL");
     if (!market_up)                                              /*3*/
          printf("The market is down, BUY");                      /*4*/
}
```

ANALYSIS:

1. Lines /*1–2*/ give you a chance to select the market direction.
2. If you select an up market direction, the first *if* statement advises "sell" just as it did before, but when you select a down market direction, the new *if* statement on lines /*3–4*/ advises "buy." Notice the logical NOT operator in the control expression of the new *if* statement (*!market_up*). When the first control expression, *market_up*, is true, this control expression is false, and vice versa.

DO: Run STOCK2 and enter **0**

RESULT:

```
C:\>STOCK2
Enter the market direction (1=UP, 0=DOWN): 0
The market is down, BUY
```

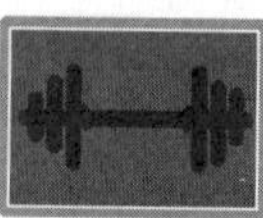

DO: Run STOCK2 and enter **1**

RESULT:

```
C:\>STOCK2
Enter the market direction (1=UP, 0=DOWN): 1
The market is up, SELL
```

DO: Run STOCK2 and enter **2**

RESULT:

```
C:\>STOCK2
Enter the market direction (1=UP, 0=DOWN): 2
The market is up, SELL
```

ANALYSIS:

1. When you enter 0, signifying a down market, the program displays the BUY advice just as you expected, and when you enter 1, signifying an up market, it tells you to SELL.
2. The prompt asks you to enter just 1 or 0, but if you enter any nonzero value (such as 2 in the last exercise), the program responds by displaying advice to SELL. This happens because any nonzero value makes the first control expression true.

THE *if else* STATEMENT

In the previous program, you used two complementary (opposite) *if* statements to display either one line of output or the other. The *if else* statement provides an easier way to accomplish such an either/or selection. The syntax of an *if else* statement is:

```
if (control expression)
     statement1
else
     statement2
```

Either or both of the controlled statements can be compound statements, and you should indent them both for readability as shown. The *if else* will execute statement1 if the controlling expression is true, or statement2 if it is false. Figure 7-4 shows the logical flow of this statement:

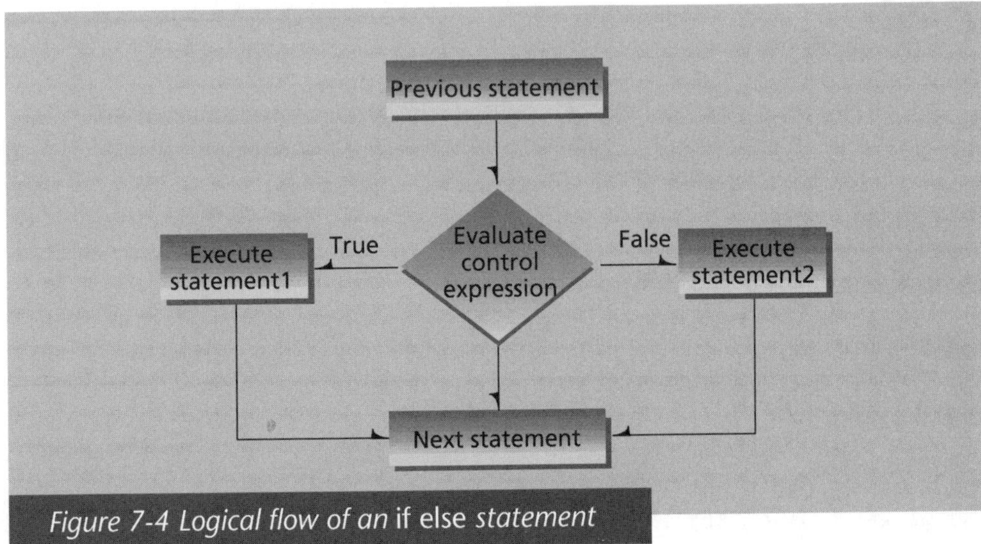

Figure 7-4 Logical flow of an if else *statement*

The source code of an *if else* statement is more compact and easier to read than two complementary *if* statements; however, the executable code is probably not faster or smaller. Most compilers will produce comparable code for both constructions, but the cleaner source layout of *if else* makes it a preferable choice.

You can improve the program STOCK2 by replacing the two complementary *if* statements with an *if else*.

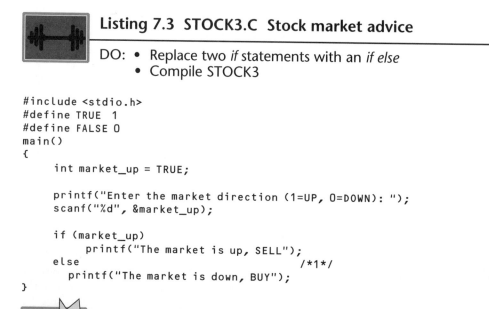

Listing 7.3 STOCK3.C Stock market advice

DO:
- Replace two *if* statements with an *if else*
- Compile STOCK3

```
#include <stdio.h>
#define TRUE  1
#define FALSE 0
main()
{
     int market_up = TRUE;

     printf("Enter the market direction (1=UP, 0=DOWN): ");
     scanf("%d", &market_up);

     if (market_up)
          printf("The market is up, SELL");
     else                                   /*1*/
       printf("The market is down, BUY");
}
```

ANALYSIS:

1. The *else* clause on line /*1*/ replaces the former *if* statement; notice that the second printf() remains indented to make it obvious that it is controlled by the *else*.

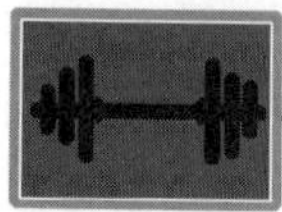

DO: Run STOCK3 and enter **0**

RESULT:

```
C:\>STOCK3
Enter the market direction (1=UP, 0=DOWN): 0
The market is down, BUY
```

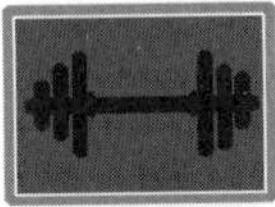

DO: Run STOCK3 and enter **1**

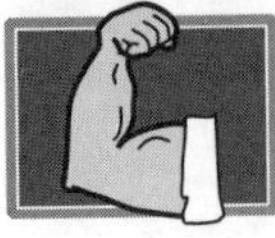

RESULT:

```
C:\>STOCK3
Enter the market direction (1=UP, 0=DOWN): 1
The market is up, SELL
```

ANALYSIS:

1. The program executes exactly as it did before—the *if else* statement controls the program flow in the same way as the two previous *if* statements.

NESTED *if else* STATEMENTS

You can construct nested *if else* statements by placing one *if else* statement within another. It is important that you make the layout of nested *if else* statements reflect the actual operation of these statements. The incorrect use of nesting can lead to confusion at best and programming errors at worst. Indentation can help as much as comments in clarifying nested constructions in a program. There is C language rule and an accompanying programming guideline that go a long way toward keeping nested *if else* statements straight. The rule states:

An else is always paired with the closest previous *if*.

and the programming guideline is:

Indent statements controlled by an *if* or *else*, including other *if else* statements.

Indenting makes no difference in program execution, but this guideline makes the program layout reflect the actual program flow. The following is a very simple program, yet it is a challenge to discern the effect of the nested statements, especially without indentation. Can you (1) state the stock market advice inherent in this program, and (2) predict the displayed result?

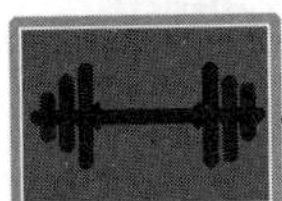

Listing 7.4 STOCK4.C Stock market advice

DO: • Add a nested *if else* statement to STOCK3

- Compile and run STOCK4
- Enter **1**

```
#include <stdio.h>
#define TRUE  1
#define FALSE 0
main()
{
     int market_up = TRUE;
     int own_stock = FALSE;                                /*1*/

     printf("Enter the market direction (1=UP, 0=DOWN): ");
     scanf("%d", &market_up);

     if (market_up)
     if (own_stock)                                        /*2*/
     printf("SELL");                                       /*3*/
     else
     printf("BUY");                                        /*4*/
}
```

RESULT:

```
C:\>STOCK4
Enter the market direction (1=UP, 0=DOWN): 1
BUY
```

ANALYSIS:

1. The *else* is paired with the second *if*, so the advice given here is: "If you own stock, SELL it; otherwise, BUY some, but don't do anything unless the market is up."

2. If you predicted that the program would display "BUY," you were right. You entered a true value for *market_up*, so the program will execute the second *if* statement and display something. The variable *own_stock* is false, so the printf() under the *else* clause executes and displays "BUY."

Now indent the statements to reflect what the program actually does.

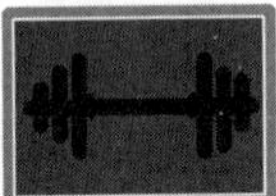

Listing 7.5 STOCK5.C Stock market advice

DO:
- Indent statements in STOCK4
- Compile and run STOCK5
- Enter **1**

```
#include <stdio.h>
#define TRUE  1
#define FALSE 0
main()
{
     int market_up = TRUE;
     int own_stock = FALSE;

     printf("Enter the market direction (1=UP, 0=DOWN): ");
     scanf("%d", &market_up);

     if (market_up)
          if(own_stock)                                    /*1*/
               printf("SELL");                             /*2*/
       else                                                /*3*/
               printf("BUY");                              /*4*/
}
```

RESULT:

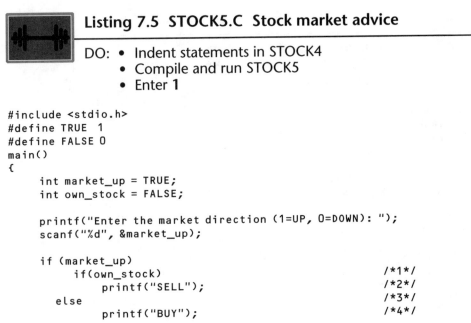

```
C:\>STOCK5
Enter the market direction (1=UP, 0=DOWN): 1
BUY
```

ANALYSIS:

1. Hopefully you agree that both the intent and result of the program are more clear with this indented layout.
2. The executable program, STOCK5.EXE, is exactly the same as STOCK4.EXE; the compiler ignores the indentations, so the code executes exactly as before.

You might not like the advice given by STOCK5 and would rather have it say "If the market is up, SELL stock if you own it; otherwise, if the market is down, BUY stock." The **incorrect** way to attempt this would be to simply indent the statements in a different way, as shown in STOCK6.

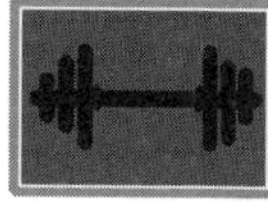

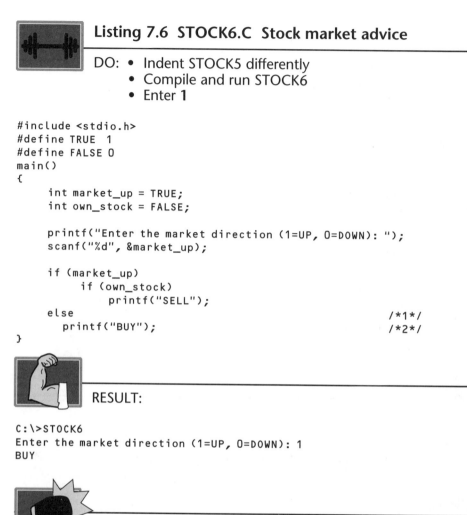

Listing 7.6 STOCK6.C Stock market advice

DO:
- Indent STOCK5 differently
- Compile and run STOCK6
- Enter **1**

```
#include <stdio.h>
#define TRUE  1
#define FALSE 0
main()
{
     int market_up = TRUE;
     int own_stock = FALSE;

     printf("Enter the market direction (1=UP, 0=DOWN): ");
     scanf("%d", &market_up);

     if (market_up)
          if (own_stock)
               printf("SELL");
     else                                                       /*1*/
       printf("BUY");                                           /*2*/
}
```

RESULT:

```
C:\>STOCK6
Enter the market direction (1=UP, 0=DOWN): 1
BUY
```

ANALYSIS:

You have indented as if the *else* goes with the first *if*, but the compiler ignores indentations and still pairs the *else* with the second *if*, so the program repeats the advice to BUY.

You can correctly pair the *else* with the first *if* by using curly braces (a compound statement).

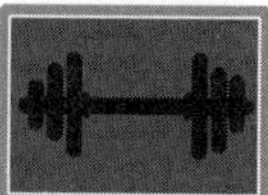

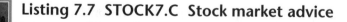

Listing 7.7 STOCK7.C Stock market advice

DO:
- Add curly braces to STOCK6
- Compile STOCK7

```
#include <stdio.h>
#define TRUE  1
#define FALSE 0
main()
{
     int market_up = TRUE;
     int own_stock = FALSE;

     printf("Enter the market direction (1=UP, 0=DOWN): ");
     scanf("%d", &market_up);

     if (market_up)
     {                                                        /*1*/
          if (own_stock)
               printf("SELL");
     }                                                        /*2*/
     else
          printf("BUY");
}
```

ANALYSIS:

The curly braces isolate the second *if* statement so that the closest previous *if* to the *else* is now the first one, as indicated by the indentation.

DO: Run STOCK7 and enter **1**

RESULT:

```
C:\>STOCK7
Enter the market direction (1=UP, 0=DOWN): 1
```

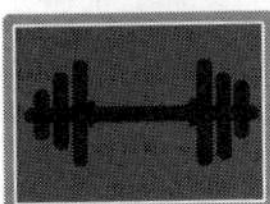

DO: Run STOCK7 and enter **0**

RESULT:

```
C:\>STOCK7
```

```
Enter the market direction (1=UP, 0=DOWN): 0
BUY
```

ANALYSIS:

Now the program is silent and no longer advises you to BUY when the market is up; instead you must select a down market to get the BUY advice.

CONDITIONAL OPERATOR

Sometimes you will use an *if else* statement to evaluate one of two expressions, like this:

```
if (control expression)
        expression1;
else
        expression2;
```

C provides an alternate way of representing this form of *if else* statement. You can use the *conditional operator* (? :) to accomplish the same thing with a shorthand notation called a *conditional expression*:

```
control expression ? expression1 : expression2
```

The conditional operator is a ternary operator, which means that it has three operands. The first operand is the control expression that precedes the question mark (?), the second is expression1 that precedes the colon (:), and the third is expression2 that follows the colon. If the control expression is true, the program evaluates expression1 and returns the result; otherwise, it evaluates expression2 and returns that result. Figure 7-5 shows how a conditional expression works.

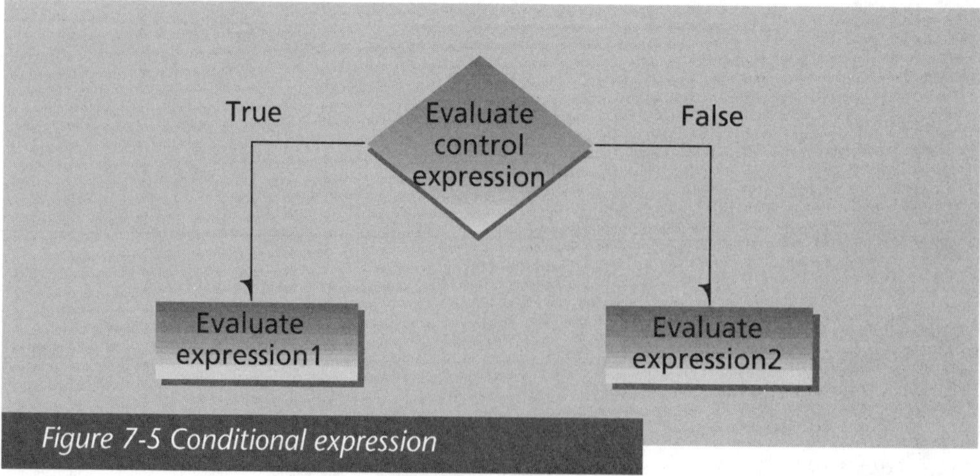

Figure 7-5 Conditional expression

For example, to find the maximum of two numbers, you could write an *if* statement:

```
if (value1 > value2)
    max_value = value1;
else
    max_value = value2;
```

Or you could write an assignment statement with a conditional expression on the right side:

```
max_value = value1 > value2 ? value1 : value2;
```

This statement evaluates the control expression *value1 > value2*, and if it is true (nonzero), it assigns *value1* to *max_value*, otherwise, it assigns *value2* to *max_value*. The spaces around the operators are for clarity only—they are not part of the necessary syntax. You could put parentheses around the control expression, which would help separate it from the rest of the statement, like this:

```
max_value = (value1 > value2) ? value1 : value2;
```

The conditional expression is shorter than the *if* statement—it occupies only one line. However, the *if* statement is easier to read—it makes the operation more explicit. You can use either form, whichever best suits your purpose. A compiler may produce faster code for the conditional expression, but this is not certain. The conditional expression is especially suited for certain *macro* definitions, in which a return value is needed that results from some simple computations. Macros are explained in more detail in Chapter 15, so we won't go into them here except to point out the connection with conditional expressions. For instance, the standard C header file, stdlib.h, contains the macros *max()* and *min()* that return the maximum and minimum values of two numbers. If you look at file stdlib.h in your POWERC directory, you will see conditional expressions in the definitions for *max()* and *min()*.

The next program contains another example of a conditional expression. When you purchase stocks you pay a commission, or sales charge, that depends on the number of shares purchased. If the number of shares is 100 or more, the commission is less than if you purchase an "odd lot" of less than 100 shares.

Listing 7.8 STOCK8.C Stock purchase

DO: Enter and compile STOCK8

```
#include <stdio.h>
main()
{
    int   shares;
    float price = 25.00;
    float commission;
```

```
    printf("Enter the number of shares to purchase: ");
    scanf("%d", &shares);

    commission =
         (shares >= 100) ? .025*price*shares : .05*price*shares;

    printf("The commission on %d shares is $%.2f",
         shares, commission);
}
```

ANALYSIS:

1. The program defines the integer variable *shares* and prompts you to enter the number of shares to purchase into this variable.
2. The program sets the price of a share of stock at $25 by defining the variable price and initializing it to 25.00.
3. The conditional expression (just after the scanf() statement) assigns a value of either 2.5 or 5 percent of the purchase to *commission* depending on the number of shares entered. Notice that *commission* is a floating-point variable, as are the two values that the conditional expression may assign to it; you can use any type of variable, including pointers, in conditional expressions.

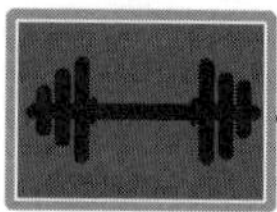

DO: Run STOCK8 and enter **57**

RESULT:

```
C:\>STOCK8
Enter the number of shares to purchase: 57
The commission on 57 shares is $71.25
```

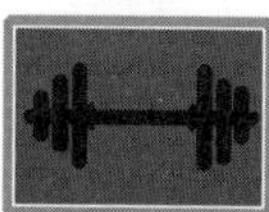

DO: Run STOCK8 and enter **100**

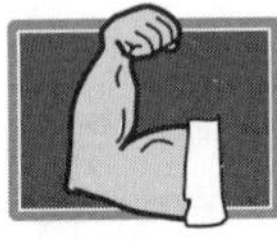

RESULT:

```
C:\>STOCK8
Enter the number of shares to purchase: 100
The commission on 100 shares is $62.50
```

ANALYSIS:

The conditional expression assigns a 5.0 percent commission to any purchase of less than 100 shares, and a 2.5 percent commission to purchases of 100 or more shares. For 100 shares, the conditional expression evaluates *.025*price*shares* to calculate the 2.5 percent commission.

The next couple of programs give you some extra practice in using *if* statements. If you are interested in card games, you will especially enjoy the exercises. In the last chapter, you developed the program CARDS4, which is a rudimentary simulation of the game of '21' or Blackjack. Now you have sufficient skills with branching control statements to enhance this program. There are two principal additions to CARDS4: A batch of new statements preceding the old program allows you to place bets from a bankroll of cash, and a second batch of new statements following the old program reports the results of each hand of cards. Some comments in the new program show you where the two new batches of statements begin and end.

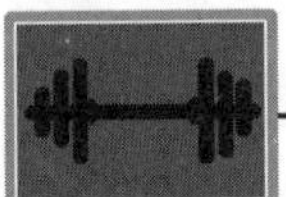

Listing 7.9 CARDS5.C '21' program

DO:
- Enhance the program CARDS4
- Compile and run CARDS5
- Respond to program prompts as shown

```
#include <stdio.h>
main()
{
     int   card_total    = 0;          /* Running total of cards */
     int   hit           = 0;          /* A new card */

/***** Start adding the first batch of statements here *****/

     float cash          = 0.;         /* Betting cash */
     float bet           = 0.;         /* Your bet */

     printf("\nDEAL CARDS FOR THE GAME OF 21\n");

/* Enter a cash total */
```

```
     printf("\nEnter your total cash: ");
     scanf("%f", &cash);

/* Place a bet */

     do
     {
                    printf("\nPlace your bet: ");
                    scanf("%f", &bet);
     } while (bet > cash);

     while ((bet > 0.) && (cash > 0.))
     {
                    card_total = 0;

/***** End of the first batch of added statements *****/

/* Deal cards */

          do
          {
                    printf("\nYour card total is %d",
                    card_total += hit);
                    printf("\nEnter a card (1-13), or 0 to quit: ");
                              scanf("%d", &hit);
          } while (hit && card_total <= 21);

/* Display the results */

          printf("\nYour final total is %d", card_total);

/***** Start adding the second batch of statements here *****/

          if (card_total > 21)
          {
                    printf("--you have gone bust!");
                              cash -= bet;
          }
          else
          {
                    printf("--you win!");
                    cash += bet;
                    }
                    printf("\nYour cash is now $%.2f\n", cash);

          do
          {
                    printf("\nPlace your bet: ");
                    scanf("%f", &bet);
          } while (bet > cash);
}
```

```
/***** End of the second batch of added statements *****/

}
```

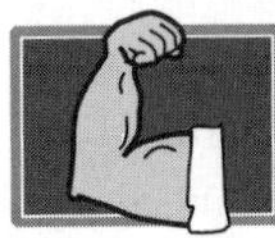

RESULT:

```
C:\>CARDS5

DEAL CARDS FOR THE GAME OF 21

Enter your total cash: 100

Place your bet: 25

Your card total is 0
Enter a card (1-13), or 0 to quit: 13

Your card total is 13
Enter a card (1-13), or 0 to quit: 11

Your card total is 24
Enter a card (1-13), or 0 to quit: 0

Your final total is 24--you have gone bust!
Your cash is now $75.00

Place your bet: 100

Place your bet: 75

Your card total is 0
Enter a card (1-13), or 0 to quit: 11

Your card total is 11
Enter a card (1-13), or 0 to quit: 11

Your card total is 22
Enter a card (1-13), or 0 to quit: 0

Your final total is 22--you have gone bust!
Your cash is now $0.00

Place your bet: 0
```

ANALYSIS:

1. The first batch of changes begins by defining the variables *cash* and

bet so that you can enter a cash amount to begin playing the game of 21, and so that you can place an amount to bet on each hand that is played.

2. After you have entered a cash total, the program enters a *do while* loop to prompt you for a bet and make sure that you don't bet more cash than you have. This loop insistently continues to ask for a bet as long as the amount entered is more than the cash available.

3. Once you have entered an initial cash amount and placed the first bet, the program enters a *while* loop that repeats the process of dealing a hand of cards as long as you enter a bet and as long as your cash total is greater than zero. The beginning of this loop is near the end of the first batch of new statements:

   ```
   while ((bet > 0.) && (cash > 0.))
   ```

4. The first statement in the *while* loop sets your card total to zero at the beginning of each cycle of the *while* loop, before the statements that deal a new hand of cards.

5. The second batch of new statements begins with an *if else* that controls two mutually exclusive compound statements. The compound statements display the result of the hand and either increase or decrease the cash amount. The controlling if expression compares your card total with 21, and if the total is greater, it displays "—you have gone bust!" and the program reduces your cash by the amount of the bet. Otherwise, it congratulates you by displaying "—you win!" and increases your cash by the amount of the bet.

6. Following the *if else* statement, a printf() displays the current cash amount.

7. The last operation in the main *while* loop is a nested *do while* that asks for another bet; this loop is identical to the *do while* that prompted for an initial bet at the beginning of the program.

8. The next to the last line of the program is the closing brace of the main *while* loop for continuing card play. The main loop (and the program) ends if you enter a zero amount for the next *bet*, or if your *cash* amount is zero; otherwise, play continues.

The game of cards is becoming a little more interesting, but it is still a very strange game because you determine your own cards; you will have to wait for a later chapter to correct this deficiency.

At this point it makes sense to introduce a rule that says you should not use an *if* expression (or any other expression) to test floating-point variables for equal status. Because of their limited precision, floating-point variables are not exact, and you should not test them for equality. Only integer numbers can be reliably tested for exact values.

The main *while* loop in CARDS5 allows you to continue play as long as your cash is greater than zero. You could install the following *if* statement after the end of the loop to display a message when you run out of money.

```
if (cash < .01)
      printf("\nSorry, you are broke!");
```

The new statement checks to see if you have any money left just before the program ends; if not, a message informs you that you are broke. Notice that the *if* expression does not test for a zero value of *cash*—the statement does **not** use the expression (cash == 0.). Instead, it checks if the value is less than one penny (.01).

This illustrates an important rule: You should never use exact equal (==) or not equal (!=) relational operators with floating-point variables. Floating-point variables are accurate only within the **precision** of the data type used (7 digits for data type *float*). A floating-point calculation that should yield a result of zero could actually result in a value of .0000001, and a subsequent test for exactly zero would not work as expected.

Now use the *if else* statement to further enhance the program by giving the dealer a hand of cards. The dealer takes "hits" as long as his card total is less than 17. Instead of selecting his cards, you can use the expediency of repeatedly dealing him the last card given to the player. This is impossible with a real deck of cards—a strange twist to the game that you will correct in a later chapter when you have the necessary programming tools. With the addition of a competing player (the dealer) in the next program, you need to use a more complex, nested if *else* statement to determine whether you win or lose.

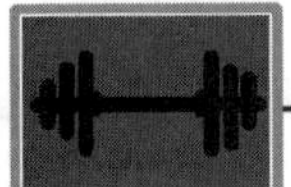

Listing 7.10 CARDS6.C '21' program

DO:
- Add a dealer hand to CARDS5
- Compile and run CARDS6
- Respond to prompts as shown

```
#include <stdio.h>
main()
{
      int   card_total    = 0;      /* Running total of cards */
      int   hit            = 0;     /* A new card */
      int   dealer_total;           /* Total of dealer's cards */     /*1*/
      int   last_hit      = 1;      /* Last player card */            /*2*/
      float cash          = 0.;     /* Betting cash */
      float bet           = 0.;     /* Your bet */

      printf("\nDEAL CARDS FOR THE GAME OF 21\n");

/* Enter a cash total */
```

```
     printf("\nEnter your total cash: ");
     scanf("%f", &cash);

/* Place a bet */

     do
     {
                    printf("\nPlace your bet: ");
                    scanf("%f", &bet);
     } while (bet > cash);

     while ((bet > 0.) && (cash > 0.))
   {

/* Deal cards */

         card_total = 0;
         dealer_total = 0;                                              /*3*/
         do
         {
                printf("\nYour card total is %d",
                card_total += hit);
                printf("\nEnter a card (1-13), or 0 to quit: ");
                scanf("%d", &hit);
                if (hit > 0) last_hit = hit;                            /*4*/
         } while (hit && card_total <= 21);

/* Display the results */

         printf("\nYour final total is %d", card_total);
         if (card_total > 21)
         {
                printf("--you have gone bust!");
                cash -= bet;
         }
         else

/* Dealer cards */

         {                                                              /*5*/
                while ((dealer_total < 17) && (last_hit > 0))           /*6*/
                    dealer_total += last_hit;                           /*7*/

                printf("\nDealer's total is %d",                        /*8*/
                    dealer_total);                                      /*9*/
                if ((dealer_total > 21) ||                              /*10*/
                   (card_total > dealer_total))                         /*11*/
                {
                    printf("--you win!");
                    cash += bet;
                }
                else                                                    /*12*/
                {                                                       /*13*/
```

```
                printf("--you lose!");                          /*14*/
                cash -= bet;                                    /*15*/
            }                                                   /*16*/
        }
        printf("\nYour cash is now $%.2f\n", cash);
        do
        {
            printf("\nPlace your bet: ");
            scanf("%f", &bet);
        } while (bet > cash);
    }

    if (cash < .01)                                             /*17*/
        printf("\nSorry, you are broke!");                      /*18*/
}
```

RESULT:

```
C:\>CARDS6

DEAL CARDS FOR THE GAME OF 21

Enter your total cash: 25

Place your bet: 12

Your card total is 0
Enter a card (1-13), or 0 to quit: 4

Your card total is 4
Enter a card (1-13), or 0 to quit: 10

Your card total is 14
Enter a card (1-13), or 0 to quit: 0

Your final total is 14
Dealer's total is 20--you lose!
Your cash is now $13.00

Place your bet: 0
```

ANALYSIS:

1. Added lines /*1–7*/ give the dealer a hand of cards. Line /*4*/ saves the last player's card so that it can be added to the dealer's total by the *while* loop on lines /*6–7*/.

2. Lines /*8–16*/ expand the test that determines whether you win or lose. Both your and the dealer's card total are now compared against each other and the limit of 21 to make the determination. These lines constitute a nested *if* because they fall under the *else* clause of the prior *if* statement.

3. On lines /*17–18*/ at the end of the program is an *if* statement that informs you when your cash level reaches zero.

THE *break, continue,* AND *goto* STATEMENTS

You now know how to set up loops to repeat a sequence of program steps, and you know how to test for certain conditions and execute different statements depending on the test results. Armed with these skills, you are ready to end a loop prematurely with the *break* statement or to skip part of a loop with the *continue* statement. You can use these new statements with a looping program to calculate some average ages. First, develop the basic program.

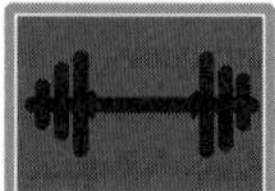

Listing 7.11 AGE.C Calculate some average ages

DO:
- Enter, compile, and run AGE
- Enter four ages as shown

```
#include <stdio.h>
main()
{
      int i;              /* Loop index */
      int age;            /* Individual age */
      int male_sum;       /* Sum of male ages */
      int female_sum;     /* Sum of female ages */
      int num_males;      /* Number of males */
      int num_females;    /* Number of females */
      char sex;           /* Individual's sex */

/* Enter ages */

      male_sum = female_sum = num_males = num_females = 0;
      for (i=0; i<4; ++i)
      {
              printf("\nEnter age and sex (M/F): ");
              scanf("%d %c", &age, &sex);

/* Accumulate ages */

          if (sex == 'M')
          {
```

```
            male_sum += age;
            ++num_males;
        }
        else if (sex == 'F')
        {
            female_sum += age;
            ++num_females;
        }
        else
            printf("Enter only <M>ale or <F>emale");
        }

/* Report the average age */

   printf("\nAverage age for %d males is %d",
        num_males, male_sum/num_males);
   printf("\nAverage age for %d females is %d\n",
        num_females, female_sum/num_females);
}
```

RESULT:

```
C:\>AGE

Enter age and sex (M/F): 41 M

Enter age and sex (M/F): 6 F

Enter age and sex (M/F): 15F

Enter age and sex (M/F): 29M

Average age for 2 males is 35
Average age for 2 females is 10
```

ANALYSIS:

1. The *for* loop processes the age and sex of four people, which you enter from the keyboard. Note that you don't have to include a space between the age and sex entries; the alphabetic entry for the sex is sufficient to end the numeric age entry.

2. The *if else* statement within the loop determines whether you entered M (for male) or F (for female), then accumulates the number of individuals and the ages accordingly. The final *else* makes sure that you enter only capital M or F for the sex.

3. When the loop ends (after four entries) the program displays the average ages, then it ends.

The *break* statement

It is not very realistic to expect a fixed number of individuals (like four) to be involved in a census data accumulation. The program needs to be modified so that you can enter data for any number of individuals. This can be done by replacing the *for* statement with a *while* loop that goes on indefinitely (an infinite loop). However, this creates a problem in that you must find a way to end the loop besides killing the program with CTRL-BREAK, which is unacceptable because the average ages would not be displayed—the whole purpose of the program. The *break* statement can solve this problem very nicely.

A *break* statement is simply the keyword *break* followed by a semicolon (;), and it causes any single loop (*for*, *while*, or *do while*) in which it appears to end right then. When a loop ends as a result of *break*, the program continues execution with the next statement following the loop. Figure 7-6 shows the action of a *break* statement.

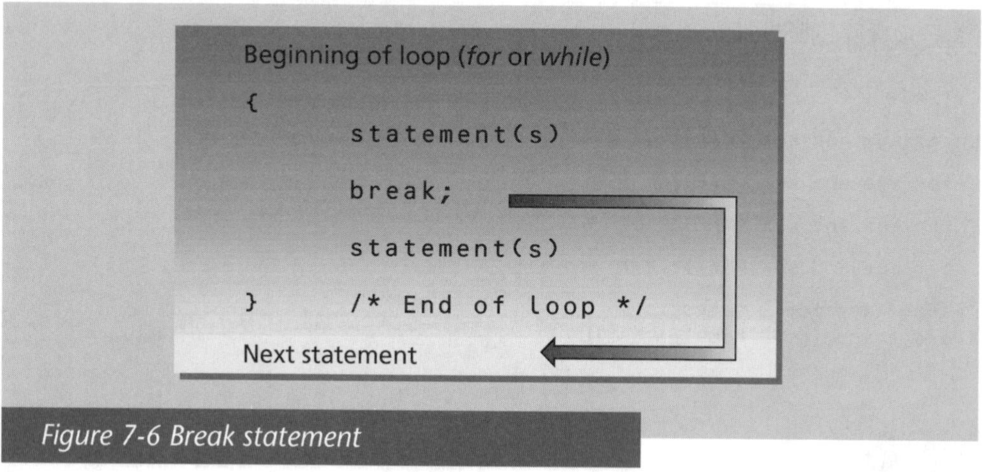
Beginning of loop (*for* or *while*)
{
statement(s)
break;
statement(s)
} /* End of loop */
Next statement

Figure 7-6 Break statement

Now modify program AGE to allow an indefinite number of entries, and use a *break* statement to quit when the letter Q is entered.

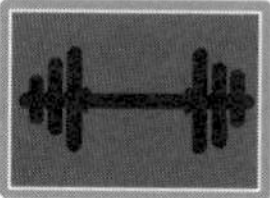

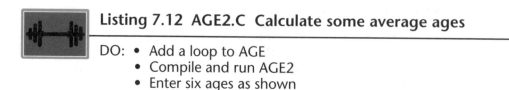

Listing 7.12 AGE2.C Calculate some average ages

DO:
- Add a loop to AGE
- Compile and run AGE2
- Enter six ages as shown

```
#include <stdio.h>
#define TRUE 1                                                          /*1*/
main()
{
    int age;                /* Individual age */
    int male_sum;           /* Sum of male ages */
    int female_sum;         /* Sum of female ages */
    int num_males;          /* Number of males */
    int num_females;        /* Number of females */
    char sex;               /* Individual's sex */

/* Enter ages */

    male_sum = female_sum = num_males = num_females = 0;
    while (TRUE)                                                        /*2*/
    {
        printf("\nEnter age and sex (M/F/Q): ");                        /*3*/
        scanf("%d %c", &age, &sex);

/* Accumulate ages */

        if (sex == 'M')
        {
            male_sum += age;
            ++num_males;
        }
        else if (sex == 'F')
        {
            female_sum += age;
            ++num_females;
        }
        else if (sex == 'Q')                                            /*4*/
            break;      /* while */                                     /*5*/
        else
            printf("Enter only <M>ale, <F>emale,"
                         " or <Q>uit");                                 /*6*/
    }

/* Report the average age */

    printf("\nAverage age for %d males is %d",
        num_males, male_sum/num_males);
    printf("\nAverage age for %d females is %d\n",
        num_females, female_sum/num_females);
}
```

RESULT:

```
C:\>AGE2
```

```
Enter age and sex (M/F/Q): 41 M

Enter age and sex (M/F/Q): 6 F

Enter age and sex (M/F/Q): 15 F

Enter age and sex (M/F/Q): 29 M

Enter age and sex (M/F/Q): 23 F

Enter age and sex (M/F/Q): 56 F

Enter age and sex (M/F/Q): 0 Q

Average age for 2 males is 35
Average age for 4 females is 25
```

ANALYSIS:

1 Changes /*1–2*/ replace the *for* loop with an infinite *while* loop. The *while* expression is the constant *TRUE,* which causes the controlled compound statement to execute repeatedly and indefinitely.

2. Changes /*3*/ and /*6*/ give some extra prompts to allow (Q) to be entered in addition to (M) and (F).

3. Lines /*4–5*/ detect when you enter (Q), and end the *while* loop with a *break* statement when that happens.

4. On line /*5*/ a comment appears after the *break* to identify the affected looping statement. This is just another of the ways that comments can clarify a program.

Here is a good place to illustrate an error that is easy to make and sometimes very difficult to discover—this error occurs when you inadvertently use the assignment operator (=) in place of the equality operator (==). It is easy to make this typographic error, but the error is particularly devilish because it usually results in a perfectly valid C statement that the compiler accepts. It only shows up as a logic error in the program execution. By deleting one character from program AGE2, you can induce this error and see its effect.

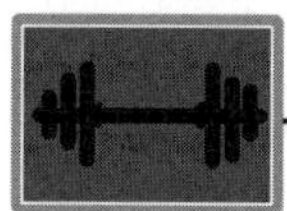

Listing 7.13 AGE3.C Calculate some average ages

DO:
- Induce an error in AGE2
- Compile and run AGE3
- Enter two ages as shown

```
#include <stdio.h>
#define TRUE 1
main()
{
     int age;             /* Individual age */
     int male_sum;        /* Sum of male ages */
     int female_sum;      /* Sum of female ages */
     int num_males;       /* Number of males */
     int num_females;     /* Number of females */
     char sex;            /* Individual's sex */

/* Enter ages */

     male_sum = female_sum = num_males = num_females = 0;
     while (TRUE)
     {
          printf("\nEnter age and sex (M/F/Q): ");
          scanf("%d %c", &age, &sex);

/* Accumulate ages */

          if (sex = 'M')                                      /*1*/
          {
               male_sum += age;
               ++num_males;
          }
          else if (sex == 'F')
          {
               female_sum += age;
               ++num_females;
          }
          else if (sex == 'Q')
               break; /* while */
          else
               printf("Enter only <M>ale, <F>emale, or <Q>uit");
      }

/* Report the average age */

      printf("\nAverage age for %d males is %d",
            num_males, male_sum/num_males);
      printf("\nAverage age for %d females is %d\n",
            num_females, female_sum/num_females);
}
```

RESULT:

```
C:\>AGE3

Enter age and sex (M/F/Q): 41 M
```

```
Enter age and sex (M/F/Q): 6 F

Enter age and sex (M/F/Q): 0 Q

Enter age and sex (M/F/Q): CTRL-BREAK
```

ANALYSIS:

1. The *if* expression on line /*1*/ now amounts to an assignment of the letter 'M' to variable *sex*. Because the result of this assignment is nonzero, the *if* test is always true and the program accumulates all data in the male category, including your command to quit! Because the program is ignoring your quit entry, you must stop the program with CTRL-BREAK (hold down the CTRL key while pressing BREAK).

If you experience errors in a program that uses the equality operator (==), you should remember to check for this error. Some programmers avoid using the symbol == directly by defining a symbolic constant *EQ* to take its place in the source code. That is, you could do the following in program AGE3:

```
#define EQ ==

/* Intervening program lines */

if (sex EQ 'M')
```

By letting the preprocessor substitute == for all occurrences of *EQ*, you can avoid typing the equality operator except for the one time in the define statement.

In Chapter 6 you wrote a program (COUNTER2) that used a *for* statement with only one expression. By adding a *break*, you can now write a version of that program without any control expressions in the *for* statement.

Listing 7.14 COUNTER4.C A fixed loop

DO:
- Modify program COUNTER2 to eliminate all *for* expressions
- Compile and run COUNTER4

```
#include <stdio.h>
main()
{
    int up = 0;

    for ( ; ; )                                   /*1*/
    {
```

```
        if (up >= 10)                                    /*2*/
             break; /* for */                            /*3*/

        printf("\n%d Peter Piper picked a peck"
               " of pickled peppers", up);
        ++up;
    }
}
```

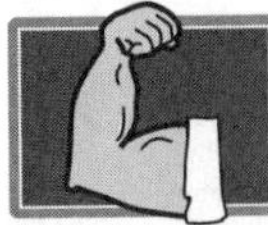

RESULT:

```
0 Peter Piper picked a peck of pickled peppers
1 Peter Piper picked a peck of pickled peppers
2 Peter Piper picked a peck of pickled peppers
3 Peter Piper picked a peck of pickled peppers
4 Peter Piper picked a peck of pickled peppers
5 Peter Piper picked a peck of pickled peppers
6 Peter Piper picked a peck of pickled peppers
7 Peter Piper picked a peck of pickled peppers
8 Peter Piper picked a peck of pickled peppers
9 Peter Piper picked a peck of pickled peppers
```

ANALYSIS:

1. The *for* statement is now equivalent to an infinite loop (the same as a *while (TRUE)* statement) because the compiler assumes that a missing *for* test expression is true.
2. The *if* statement takes care of ending the loop by executing the *break* when *up* reaches a value of 10.

A *break* placed inside nested loops ends only the innermost loop in which it appears. You can use one of the previous programs from Chapter 6 to see this; in case you haven't already entered the program NESTED, here is a repeat of the source code.

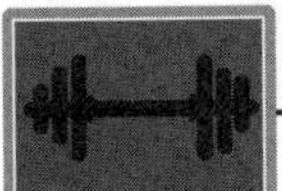

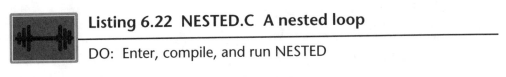

Listing 6.22 NESTED.C A nested loop

DO: Enter, compile, and run NESTED

```
#include <stdio.h>
main()
{
    char outer_char;
```

```
    char inner_char;

    for (outer_char = 'W'; outer_char <= 'Z'; ++outer_char)
    {
        printf("\n%c:", outer_char);
        inner_char = outer_char;          /*            */
        while (inner_char <= 'Z')         /* Inner loop */
            printf("%c", inner_char++);   /*            */
    }
}
```

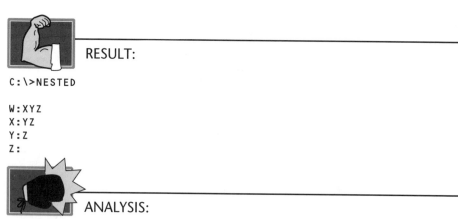

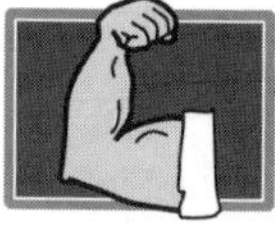

RESULT:

```
C:\>NESTED

W:XYZ
X:YZ
Y:Z
Z:
```

ANALYSIS:

Now, add a *break* to the inner loop of this program.

Listing 7.15 NESTED2.C Nested loops

DO: Add a *break* to NESTED, then compile and run NESTED2

```
#include <stdio.h>
main()
{
    char outer_char;
    char inner_char;

    for (outer_char='W'; outer_char<='Z'; ++outer_char)
    {
        printf("\n%c:", outer_char);
        inner_char = outer_char;
        while (inner_char <= 'Z')
        {                                              /*1*/
            if (inner_char == 'Z')                     /*2*/
                break;    /* while */                  /*3*/
            printf("%c", inner_char++);
        }                                              /*4*/
    }
}
```

RESULT:

```
C:\>NESTED2

W:WXY
X:XY
Y:Y
Z:
```

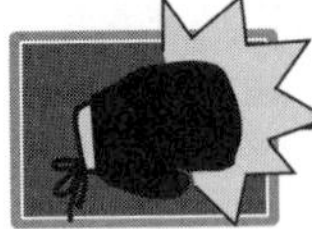

ANALYSIS:

1. Changes /*2–3*/ end the inner *while* loop so that Z no longer appears in the output. It is evident that the *break* does not affect the outer loop because all four outer displays are still present.
2. Lines /*1*/ and /*4*/ are needed to make the controlled statement a compound statement.

The *continue* statement

A *continue* statement consists of the keyword *continue* followed by a semicolon (;), and it is used within loops in a similar way to the *break* statement. However, the effect is different: All statements between the *continue* and the end of the loop are skipped and the loop continues to operate. Figure 7-7 illustrates the operation of *continue*.

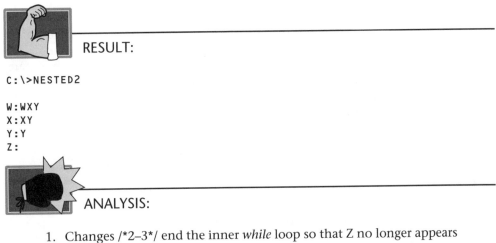

Beginning of loop (*for* or *while*)

```
{
        statement(s)

        continue;

        statement(s)

}       /* End of loop */
```

Next statement

Figure 7-7 The operation of continue

Unlike *break*, the *continue* statement does not transfer program control out of the loop, it only skips the second set of statements and takes you to the end of the loop so that it can continue operating at the beginning of the next cycle. If you were to use *continue* by itself, without an *if* test as shown in Figure 7-7, the second group of statements would never be executed; *continue* is normally used in conjunction with a conditional test. Now let's return to the AGE program and use a *continue* statement to process only retirement-age individuals.

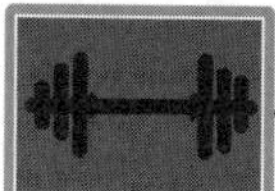

Listing 7.16 AGE4.C Calculate some average ages

DO:
- Add a *continue* to AGE3 to accept only ages 65 or over
- Compile and run AGE4
- Enter four ages as shown

```
#include <stdio.h>
#define TRUE 1
main()
{
     int age;             /* Individual age */
     int male_sum;        /* Sum of male ages */
     int female_sum;      /* Sum of female ages */
     int num_males;       /* Number of males */
     int num_females;     /* Number of females */
     char sex;            /* Individual's sex */

/* Enter ages */

     male_sum = female_sum = num_males = num_females = 0;
     while (TRUE)
     {
          printf("\nEnter age and sex (M/F/Q): ");
          scanf("%d %c", &age, &sex);

/* Accumulate ages */

          if (sex == 'M')
          {
               if (age < 65)                                       /*1*/
                       continue;                                   /*2*/
               male_sum += age;
               ++num_males;
          }
          else if (sex == 'F')
          {
               if (age < 65)                                       /*3*/
                       continue;                                   /*4*/
               female_sum += age;
               ++num_females;
          }
```

```
        else if (sex == 'Q')
            break; /* while */
        else
            printf("Enter only <M>ale, <F>emale, or <Q>uit");
    }

/* Report the average age */

    printf("\nAverage age for %d males is %d",
        num_males, male_sum/num_males);
    printf("\nAverage age for %d females is %d\n",
        num_females, female_sum/num_females);
}
```

RESULT:

```
C:\>AGE4

Enter age and sex (M/F/Q): 41 M

Enter age and sex (M/F/Q): 6 F

Enter age and sex (M/F/Q): 65 F

Enter age and sex (M/F/Q): 79 M

Enter age and sex (M/F/Q): 23 F

Enter age and sex (M/F/Q): 66 M

Enter age and sex (M/F/Q): 0 Q

Average age for 2 males is 72
Average age for 1 females is 65
```

ANALYSIS:

1. The addition of lines /*1–4*/ causes the program to skip the accumulation of any ages under 65; otherwise, operation of the program is the same as before.

2. You need to nest the *if* test for age 65 under both the male and female test, rather than ahead of the *if* tests, so that the other operations (for Q and invalid entries) are not affected.

The *goto* statement

The *goto* statement is unique in that it should be the least used statement in your C programs. A *goto* statement unconditionally and immediately transfers control to another part of the program. The operation and syntax of *goto* are shown in Figure 7-8.

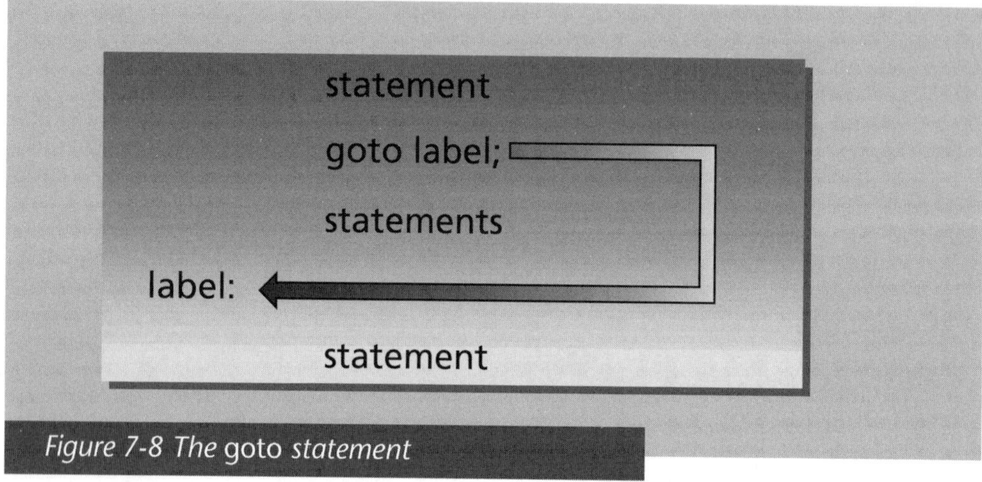

Figure 7-8 The goto *statement*

A *goto* is always associated with a label to identify where the program should transfer control. A label is any name formed with the same rules as for a variable identifier (any letter or underscore followed by letters, numbers, or underscores). In Figure 7-8 we have used the identifier **label**, but you can choose any name as long as it follows the rules for an identifier. You attach a colon (:) to the end of the label when you use it to identify a transfer location, which can be anywhere in the program. You can place the label either before or after a matching *goto*, that is, you can make a program jump either backward or forward. You cannot repeat a label, or the transfer location will not be unique; however, any number of *goto*s can use one label.

The *goto* is not recommended because it leads to confused code and is easily abused. Theoretically, there is no need ever to use the *goto*, and as a practical matter you can almost always write better, more efficient, and more readable code without it. Any transfer of control that is needed can also be accomplished by using variations of looping statements (*for, while*) and other branching statements (*if, else, break, continue*). There is only one situation in which the *goto* is sometimes preferred—exiting from deeply nested loops. The next two programs will illustrate two methods for dealing with this, one with and one without *goto*; you can decide which is best when faced with a similar circumstance. First, modify the program NESTED2 to escape from both nested loops at once with a *goto*.

Listing 7.17 NESTED3.C Escape from nested loops

DO: Modify NESTED2 with a *goto*, then compile and run NESTED3

```
#include <stdio.h>
main()
{
     char outer_char;
     char inner_char;

     for (outer_char='W'; outer_char<='Z'; ++outer_char)
     {
          printf("\n%c:", outer_char);
          inner_char = outer_char;
          while (inner_char <= 'Z')
          {
               if (inner_char == 'Z')
                       goto quit;                          /*1*/
               printf("%c", inner_char++);
          }
     }
quit:                                                      /*2*/
}
```

RESULT:

```
C:\>NESTED3

W:WXY
```

ANALYSIS:

1. By adding a label on line /*2*/ and replacing the *break* with a *goto* on line /*1*/, you can jump out of both loops to the end of the program. The program has produced only one line of output because of the *goto* statement.

Now do the same thing without using a *goto*. In the second method of escaping loops, the following program tests the status of a variable within each loop and executes a *break* for each loop when the test becomes *TRUE*.

Listing 7.18 NESTED4.C Escape from nested loops

DO: Modify NESTED3 to eliminate *goto*, then compile and run NESTED4

```
#include <stdio.h>
#define TRUE  1                                                 /*1*/
#define FALSE 0                                                 /*2*/
main()
{
    char outer_char;
    char inner_char;
    int  done = FALSE;                                          /*3*/

    for (outer_char='W'; outer_char<='Z'; ++outer_char)
    {
        printf("\n%c:", outer_char);
        inner_char = outer_char;
        while (inner_char <= 'Z')
        {
              if (inner_char == 'Z')
              {                                                 /*4*/
                  done = TRUE;                                  /*5*/
                  break;
              }                                                 /*6*/
              printf("%c", inner_char++);
        }
        if (done)                                               /*7*/
            break;                                              /*8*/
    }
}
```

RESULT:

```
C:\>NESTED4

W:WXY
```

ANALYSIS:

1. Lines /*1–3*/ define the *TRUE/FALSE* constants and initialize the variable *done* to *FALSE.*
2. Line /*5*/ sets *done* to *TRUE* just before the *break* statement stops the inner loop.

3. On lines /*7–8*/, the program also exits the outer loop when *done* becomes *TRUE*.

It takes more lines of code (8 versus 2 in the previous example) to escape nested loops without a *goto* than with it, and the number of lines required increases with more loops. Even so, many professional programmers prefer to completely avoid the *goto*.

THE *switch* STATEMENT

The *switch* statement is an alternative to the *if else* statement for creating multiple branches. You can use it when you need to control statements by comparing an expression with several discrete values. For instance, if you want to take some action in your program depending on which key was pressed on the keyboard, you could test for the keys of interest (ignoring the rest) and branch with the *switch* statement. The result of the expression to be tested must be an integer, so you cannot use *switch* to branch on floating-point values. But you **can** use characters, because character expressions result in integer values. The syntax of the *switch* statement is:

```
switch (expression)
{
        case constant1:
             statement(s)
             break;
        case constant2:
             statement(s)
             break;
                                    .
                                    .
                                    .
        default:
             statement(s)
             break;
        }
```

You place the expression to be tested inside parentheses following the *switch* keyword and then enclose the rest of the statement in the curly braces of a compound statement. For clarity, you should indent the case specifications under the *switch*, and under each case you should also indent a *break* and all associated statements. Some programmers prefer to place the opening curly brace on the same line as the *switch*:

```
switch (expression) {
     .
     .
     .
}
```

You should make your placement of the curly brace consistent with how you use it with other statements (*for, while, if*).

Each *case* keyword within the curly braces represents a branch associated with the constant that follows it. If the value of the expression is equal to the constant, then the program executes all statements after the *case*, down to the next *break*. The final *default* keyword handles all values of the expression that are not covered by other *case* specifications. An equivalent *if else* statement would be:

```
if (expression == constant1)
{
        statement(s)
}
        else if (expression == constant2)
{
        statement(s)
}

.
.
.

else                        /* This is the default */
{
        statement(s)
}
```

A four-function calculator can easily fit into the branching scheme of the above *if else* logic.

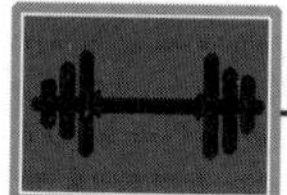

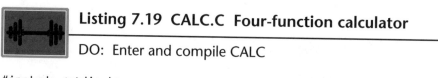

Listing 7.19 CALC.C Four-function calculator

DO: Enter and compile CALC

```
#include <stdio.h>
main()
{
     char operator;          /* Arithmetic operator  */
     float op1;              /* First operand        */
     float op2;              /* Second operand       */
     float answer;           /* Result of arithmetic */

/* Enter data */

     printf("Enter a calculation: ");
     scanf("%f %c %f", &op1, &operator, &op2);

/* Perform calculation */

     if (operator == '+')                  /* Addition */
          answer = op1 + op2;
     else if (operator == '-')             /* Subtraction */
          answer = op1 - op2;
```

```
    else if (operator == '*')                /* Multiplication */
        answer = op1 * op2;
    else if (operator == '/')                /* Division */
        answer = op1 / op2;
    else                    /* Bad operator */
        printf("Illegal operator  ");

/* Display results */

    printf("%.1f %c %.1f = %.1f\n\n",
        op1, operator, op2, answer);
}
```

ANALYSIS:

1. This calculator reads floating-point operands with a floating-point format specifier (%f) in the scanf() statement, so you can enter numbers either with or without a decimal fraction. Because the scanf() format string includes a space between each of the conversion specifiers, you should also include SPACE after each of your entries (after the first operand and after the operator). However, due to the fact that a non-numeric operator will automatically terminate the input conversion of a number, this line of input will work even if you forget the spaces. Interestingly, the input will not work if you take the spaces out of the format specifier and enter SPACE after the first operand, because the character operand will then accept the space. Try it.

2. The five-part *if* statement (with four *else* clauses) selects the correct calculation based on the value of the variable *operator*. If the statement does not recognize one of the four allowed operators, the last *else* sees that an error message is displayed.

3. The final printf() displays the calculation result in the form of an equation by repeating the input operands and including *answer*; it displays each value to an accuracy of one decimal place.

DO: Run CALC and enter **2 + 2**

```
C:\>CALC
Enter a calculation: 2 + 2
2.0 + 2.0 = 4.0
```

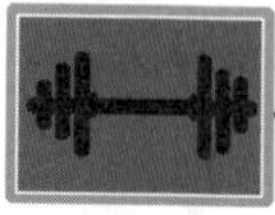

DO: Run CALC and enter **2+2**

```
C:\>CALC
Enter a calculation: 2+2
2.0 + 2.0 = 4.0
```

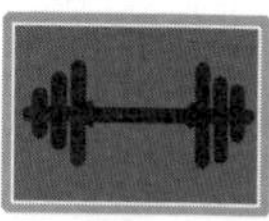

DO: Run CALC and enter **2#2**

```
C:\>CALC
Enter a calculation: 2#2
Illegal operator 2.0 # 2.0 = 0.0
```

ANALYSIS:

You can handle multi-way branching with either an *if* or a *switch* statement; substitute *switch* for the *if* in the calculator program.

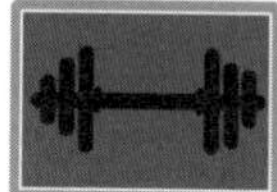

Listing 7.20 CALC2.C Four-function calculator

DO:
- Replace the *if* statement in CALC with a *switch* statement
- Compile CALC2

```
#include <stdio.h>
main()
{
     char operator;            /* Arithmetic operator  */
     float op1;                /* First operand        */
     float op2;                /* Second operand       */
     float answer;             /* Result of arithmetic */

/* Enter data */

     printf("Enter a calculation: ");
     scanf("%f %c %f", &op1, &operator, &op2);

/* Perform calculations */

     switch (operator)
     {
          case '+':            /* Addition */
               answer = op1 + op2;
               break;
```

```
        case '-':           /* Subtraction */
             answer = op1 - op2;
             break;
        case '*':           /* Multiplication */
             answer = op1 * op2;
             break;
        case '/':           /* Division */
             answer = op1 / op2;
             break;
        default:            /* Bad operator */
             printf("Illegal operator  ");
             break;
    }

/* Display results */

    printf("%.1f %c %.1f = %.1f\n\n",
        op1, operator, op2, answer);
}
```

ANALYSIS:

1. The *switch* control expression is the variable *operator* (a primary expression). *Switch* expressions must result in integers; *operator* is type *char*, which is OK because characters evaluate to integers in an expression.
2. The *switch* statement causes the program to jump to whichever *case* has a constant that matches the value of *operator*, or to *default* if no match occurs.
3. After *switch* selects an operator, it performs the appropriate calculation, then encounters a *break* which directs your program to the next statement after the closing curly brace of the *switch* statement (the final printf()).

DO: Run CALC2 and enter **2 + 2**

```
C:\>CALC2
Enter a calculation: 2 + 2
2.0 + 2.0 = 4.0
```

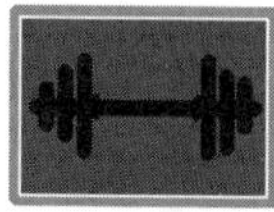

DO: Run CALC2 and enter **2+2**

```
C:\>CALC2
Enter a calculation: 2+2
2.0 + 2.0 = 4.0
```

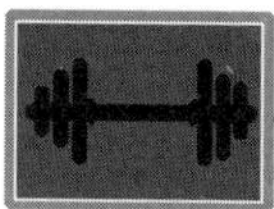

DO: Run CALC2 and enter **2#2**

```
C:\>CALC2
Enter a calculation: 2#2
Illegal operator 2.0 # 2.0 = 0.0
```

ANALYSIS:

It took 18 lines of source code in the *switch* statement to replace 10 lines occupied by the *if* code. So what have you gained? You have gained several things that are not directly evident from the source code, namely, speed and expandability.

First of all, the number of source code lines is not of primary importance. In spite of the slightly expanded source requirement, the compiler will usually produce smaller, faster executable code for a *switch* statement than for an *if* statement because *switch* is specialized for multi-way branching on discrete integer values.

With *switch*, you have also gained the ability to expand the multi-way branch without having to repeat an *if* test expression—you simply add a *case* clause.

Another advantage of *switch* is that you do not need the curly braces to imply a compound statement under each *case*—all statements are executed down to the next *break*. This advantage is not evident in the CALC2 program, because there is only one controlled statement for each *case*; however, if several controlled statements were needed, the *if* version of the program (CALC) would require curly braces for each occurrence of a compound statement.

Often there is very little difference between the speed, expandability, and source code size of a *switch* and that of an *if* statement. Generally, you should use a *switch* for multi-way branching on discrete integer values, whereas you **must** use an *if* when branching is based on tests of floating-point variables or tests involving ranges of values.

The order in which *case* clauses appear makes no difference; you should place the *default* last, but even this is not necessary. Each *case* constant must be unique; you should not repeat any of these constants or your branching will be ambiguous and a compiler error may occur, as shown in the next example.

Listing 7.21 CALC3.C Four-function calculator

DO: • Add a duplicate *case* constant to CALC2
• Compile CALC3

```
#include <stdio.h>
main()
{
    char operator;        /* Arithmetic operator   */
    float op1;            /* First operand         */
    float op2;            /* Second operand        */
    float answer;         /* Result of arithmetic  */

/* Enter data */

    printf("Enter a calculation: ");
    scanf("%f %c %f", &op1, &operator, &op2);

/* Perform calculations */

    switch (operator)
    {
        case '+':           /* Addition */
            answer = op1 + op2;
            break;
        case '-':           /* Subtraction */
            answer = op1 - op2;
            break;
        case '*':           /* Multiplication */
            answer = op1 * op2;
            break;
        case '/':           /* Division */
            answer = op1 / op2;
            break;
        default:            /* Bad operator */
            printf("Illegal operator  ");
            break;
        case 43:            /* ASCII code for '+' */      /*1*/
            printf("ASCII code for +\n");                 /*2*/
            break;                                        /*3*/
    }

/* Display results */

    printf("%.1f %c %.1f = %.1f\n\n",
        op1, operator, op2, answer);
}
```

RESULT:

```
C:\>pc/c/e CALC3
```

```
Power C - Version 2.1.3
(C) Copyright 1989-1991 by Mix Software
Compiling ...
CALC3.C(33):          case 43:             /*ASCII code for '+' */
/*1*/
***********                  ^184
       184: Duplicate case in switch statement
------------------------------------------------------------------
   149 lines compiled
     1 Compile error
```

ANALYSIS:

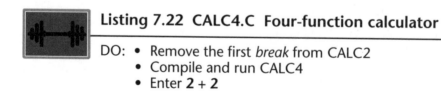

1. Line /*1*/ uses integer 43 for a *case* constant, which is the ASCII code for the plus character (+). This is an indirect way of repeating the plus constant already used to select addition.
2. Line /*2*/ displays a message to show you when the program branches to this new *case*.
3. The new *case* is added last, after the *default*, but this is perfectly ok. What is not ok is that there are two branches having the same test constant, and the C compiler has no way of knowing which one to use. Power C signals an error, but another compiler could choose one or the other branches. There is nothing in the C language specification that tells a compiler how to set up the ordering of *case* tests, so this program is a bit unpredictable in its behavior.

You should use a *break* after each *case* or *default*, including the last one, even though it has no effect (the last statement will just fall through to the end of the *switch*). You may want to come back to the program later and add another *case* at the end, and having a *break* there may prevent a bug from creeping in at that time. Try leaving the first *break* (after the '+') out of the CALC2 program to see what happens when you make this kind of error.

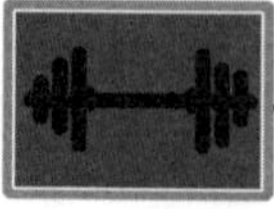

Listing 7.22 CALC4.C Four-function calculator

DO:
- Remove the first *break* from CALC2
- Compile and run CALC4
- Enter **2 + 2**

```
#include <stdio.h>
main()
```

```
{
     char operator;       /* Arithmetic operator   */
     float op1;           /* First operand         */
     float op2;           /* Second operand        */
     float answer;        /* Result of arithmetic  */


/* Enter data */

     printf("Enter a calculation: ");
     scanf("%f %c %f", &op1, &operator, &op2);


/* Perform calculations */

     switch (operator)
     {
          case '+':            /* Addition */
               answer = op1 + op2;

          case '-':            /* Subtraction */
               answer = op1 - op2;
               break;
          case '*':            /* Multiplication */
               answer = op1 * op2;
               break;
          case '/':            /* Division */
               answer = op1 / op2;
               break;
          default:             /* Bad operator */
               printf("Illegal operator  ");
               break;
     }


/* Display results */

     printf("%.1f %c %.1f = %.1f\n\n",
          op1, operator, op2, answer);
}
```

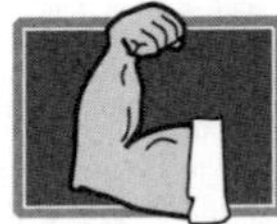

RESULT:

```
C:\>CALC4
Enter a calculation: 2 + 2
2.0 + 2.0 = 0.0
```

ANALYSIS:

Whenever you attempt to add two numbers, the program subtracts them instead. Actually the program does both, but it performs the subtraction last. First the program performs a normal addition, then because there is no *break*, it continues on through the next case clause (*case '-':*) to perform subtraction and assigns this result to *answer*.

There are situations in which you can intentionally leave out a *break* to good advantage. Letting a program go directly into one *case* after completing another is known as a "fall-through" construction, and you accomplish this by simply omitting *break* from the first *case*. You can modify the CALC2 program to implement a different form of subtraction with this technique.

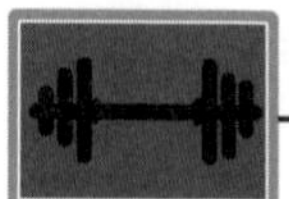

Listing 7.23 CALC5.C Four-function calculator

DO:
- Modify CALC2 to implement a "fall-through" case for subtraction
- Compile and run CALC5
- Enter **2.3 - 1.1**

```
#include <stdio.h>
main()
{
     char operator;          /* Arithmetic operator  */
     float op1;              /* First operand        */
     float op2;              /* Second operand       */
     float answer;           /* Result of arithmetic */
     float op3;                                                /*1*/

/* Enter data */

     printf("Enter a calculation: ");
     scanf("%f %c %f", &op1, &operator, &op2);
     op3 = op2;                                                /*2*/

/* Perform calculations */

     switch (operator)
     {
          case '-':     /* Subtraction */                      /*3*/
               op2 = -op2;                                     /*4*/
          case '+':     /* Addition Ñ fall through */          /*5*/
               answer = op1 + op2;
               break;
          case '*':     /* Multiplication */
               answer = op1 * op2;
```

```
            break;
        case '/':       /* Division */
            answer = op1 / op2;
            break;
        default:        /* Bad operator */
            printf("Illegal operator  ");
            break;
    }

/* Display results */

    printf("%.1f %c %.1f = %.1f\n\n",
        op1, operator, op3, answer);                /*6*/
}
```

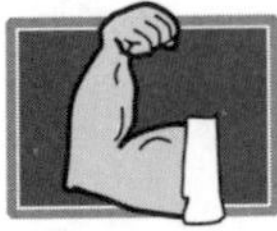

RESULT:

```
C:\>CALC5
Enter a calculation: 2.3 - 1.1
2.3 - 1.1 = 1.2
```

ANALYSIS:

1. The *case* clause for the minus operator now appears above the plus operator with no *break* in between.
2. Subtraction now proceeds as follows: The *switch* directs program control to lines /*3–5*/, where the sign of variable *op2* is reversed by a unary minus operator. Then the program just "falls-through" to execute the statement following line /*5*/, adding *op1* to *op2* before finally encountering a *break* to end the *switch* statement.
3. The statement, *answer = op1 + op2;* does double duty; it performs the arithmetic for both addition and subtraction.
4. Notice the expanded comment on line /*5*/, where the phrase **fall through** appears. It is good programming practice to make a comment about the occurrence of a fall-through construction so that it is plainly intentional.
5. The new variable, *op3*, is necessary on lines /*1–2*/ and /*6*/ so that the program can display the original value of the second operand instead of its modified value from line /*4*/.

You may be curious about why the *case '+':* did not intercept the fall-through sequence in the above example and prevent further processing—after all, the value of the *operator* was '-'. A *switch* statement accepts only one match with a *case* constant. Once that occurs, further *case* testing stops for the current pass through the *switch* statement. This is why fall-through works; after the first match, any other *case* is ignored.

There are a couple of things that the calculator program could use to make it more useful: (1) continuous operation, and (2) protection against division by zero. You can achieve continuous operation by wrapping most of the program in a *while* loop, and you can use an *if* test to implement the protection.

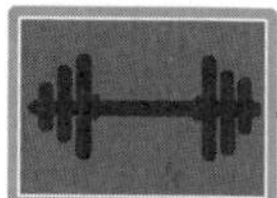

Listing 7.24 CALC6.C Four-function calculator

DO:
- Add looping and a zero check CALC4
- Compile and run CALC6
- Enter **2 / 0**

```
#include <stdio.h>
#define TRUE  1
#define FALSE 0
main()
{
     int  done = FALSE;          /* Finished flag          */
     char operator;              /* Arithmetic operator */
     float op1;                  /* First operand          */
     float op2;                  /* Second operand         */
     float answer;               /* Result of arithmetic */

     while (!done)                                              /*1*/
     {                                                          /*2*/

/* Enter data */

          printf("Enter a calculation (or 0 Q 0 to quit): ");
          scanf("%f %c %f", &op1, &operator, &op2);

/* Perform calculations */

          switch (operator)
          {
               case '+':            /* Addition */
                    answer = op1 + op2;
                    break;
               case '-':            /* Subtraction */
                    answer = op1 - op2;
                    break;
               case '*':            /* Multiplication */
                    answer = op1 * op2;
                    break;
               case '/': /* Division */
                    if ((op2 > 1.e-6) || (op2 < -1.e-6))        /*3*/
                         answer = op1 / op2;
```

```
                else /* Illegal zero divisor */                 /*4*/
                     printf("Can't divide by zero  ");          /*5*/
                break;
           case 'q':            /* Quit */                      /*6*/
           case 'Q':            /* fall through */              /*7*/
                done = TRUE;                                    /*8*/
                break;                                          /*9*/
           default:             /* Unknown operator */
                printf("Illegal operator  ");
                break;
      }

/* Display results */

      printf("%.1f %c %.1f = %.1f\n\n",
          op1, operator, op2, answer);
   }
                                                                /*10*/
}
```

RESULT:

```
C:\>CALC6
Enter a calculation (or 0 Q 0 to quit): 2 / 0
Can't divide by zero  2.0 / 0.0 = 0.0

Enter a calculation (or 0 Q 0 to quit): 0 q 0
0.0 q 0.0 = 0.0
```

ANALYSIS:

1. Lines /*1–2*/ and /*10*/ constitute the new *while* loop that makes the calculator operate continuously until you enter Q. When you enter 'Q' or 'q' in place of an operator, lines /*6–9*/ cause the program to quit by assigning *TRUE* to the variable *done*. The next cycle of the *while* loop will find the control expression *!done* to be *FALSE*, thus, the loop, and the program, will end. Note that all of the *break* statements in this program are devoted to ending the *case* clauses of the *switch* statement; they have no effect on the *while* loop.

2. Lines /*6–7*/ illustrate how you can use fall-through to select either a lowercase or uppercase letter to perform the same operation in a *switch* statement.

3. Before performing division, it is always a good idea to check the divisor for zero, because this will always result in an error. However, this program uses floating-point variables, and a test for exactly zero is not dependable for floating-point variables. Line /*3*/ does the next best thing—it tests the value of *op2* for a very narrow range of values that includes zero. Actually, in this program, if you enter a zero divisor, it **will** be exactly zero, but in general it is not a good idea to test floating-point variables for exactly zero.

Using the CALC6 program to take numbers from the keyboard and display calculated results presents an opportunity to illustrate an easy way to work with hexadecimal numbers. With a very few changes, you can adapt CALC6 to work with hexadecimal integers instead of floating-point decimal numbers. All that is required is to accept operand values from the keyboard in hexadecimal form (and convert them to internal representation), then convert the answer and display it in hexadecimal form. Chapter 4 discusses how to use formatted I/O to accomplish these conversions via scanf() and printf(), which you can now use to set up the hex calculator.

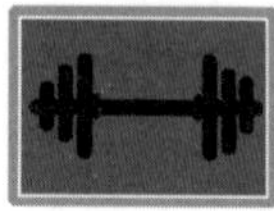

Listing 7.25 CALC7.C Hex calculator

DO:
- Modify CALC6 to take hexadecimal input and output
- Compile and run CALC7
- Enter **B + 4**

```
#include <stdio.h>
#define TRUE  1
#define FALSE 0
main()
{
     int  done = FALSE;          /* Finished flag         */
     char operator;              /* Arithmetic operator   */
     int op1;                    /* First operand         */    /*1*/
     int op2;                    /* Second operand        */    /*2*/
     int answer;                 /* Result of arithmetic  */    /*3*/

/* Enter data */

     while (!done)
     {
          printf("Enter a calculation (or 0 Q 0 to quit): ");
          scanf("%X %c %X", &op1, &operator, &op2);            /*4*/

/* Perform calculations */

          switch (operator)
          {
               case '-':              /* Subtraction */
```

```
                op2 = -op2;
          case '+':            /* Addition */
                answer = op1 + op2;
                break;
          case '*':            /* Multiplication */
                answer = op1 * op2;
                break;
          case '/':            /* Division */
                if (op2 != 0)                               /*5*/
                     answer = op1 / op2;
                else           /* Illegal zero divisor */
                     printf("Can't divide by zero  ");
                break;
          case 'q':            /* Quit */
          case 'Q':            /* fall through */
                done = TRUE;
                break;
          default:             /* Operator not recognized */
                printf("Illegal operator  ");
                break;
     }

/* Display results */

     printf("%X %c %X = %X\n\n",
         op1, operator, op2, answer);                       /*6*/
   }
}
```

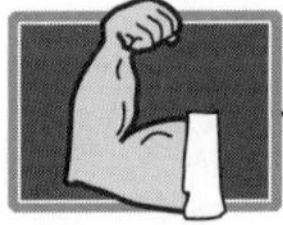

RESULT:

```
C:\>CALC7

Enter a calculation (or 0 Q 0 to quit): B + 4
B + 4 = F

Enter a calculation (or 0 Q 0 to quit): 0 q 0
0 q 0 = F
```

ANALYSIS:

1. Hexadecimal numbers are integers, so you change all numeric variables from floating-point to integer data types on lines /*1–3*/.
2. The use of integers allows you to test a divisor for exactly zero, as on line /*5*/.

3. The most important change that you make is to replace decimal format conversion specifiers in the formatted I/O statements with hexadecimal specifiers (lines /*4*/ and /*6*/). The rest of the calculator program works just as before.

A capital X in the hexadecimal conversion specifier is allowed by the ANSI specification; older, common C compilers will recognize only a lowercase x. A printf() conversion specifier of %X will display uppercase letters for hexadecimal digits A through F, whereas %x will display lowercase a through f. With input, either conversion specifier will cause scanf() to accept either uppercase or lowercase.

You can use a *switch* statement to make the card totals in program CARDS7 more realistic. As configured, the program scores face cards with values of 11, 12, and 13 instead of 10 as in a real game of 21. Also, the ace always counts as 1, whereas in a real game it can be scored as 1 or 11 at the option of the player. Add a *switch* statement to realistically score aces and face cards.

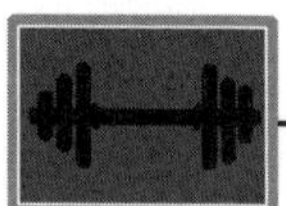

Listing 7.26 CARDS7.C '21' program

DO: • Add improved scoring to CARDS6
• Compile and run CARDS7
• Respond to program prompts as shown

```
#include <stdio.h>
#define ACE    1                                      /*1*/
#define JACK  11                                      /*2*/
#define QUEEN 12                                      /*3*/
#define KING  13                                      /*4*/
main()
{
     int   card_total = 0;                  /* Running total of cards */
     int   hit        = 0;                  /* A new card */
     int   dealer_total;                    /* Total of dealer's cards */
     int   last_hit   = 1;                  /* Last player card */
     float cash       = 0.;                 /* Betting cash */
     float bet        = 0.;                 /* Your bet */

     printf("\nDEAL CARDS FOR THE GAME OF 21\n");

/* Enter a cash total */

     printf("\nEnter your total cash: ");
     scanf("%f", &cash);

/* Place a bet */

     do
     {
          printf("\nPlace your bet: ");
```

```
        scanf("%f", &bet);
    } while (bet > cash);

    while ((bet > 0.) && (cash > 0.))
    {

/* Deal cards */

        card_total = 0;
        dealer_total = 0;
        do
        {

        printf("\nYour card total is %d",
             card_total += hit);
        printf("\nEnter a card (1-13), or 0 to quit: ");
        scanf("%d", &hit);

/***** Begin the new switch statement *****/

             switch (hit)
             {
                 case JACK:
                 case QUEEN:
                 case KING:               /* Fall through */
                     hit = 10;
                     break;
                 case ACE:
                     if ((card_total + 11) <= 21)
                        hit = 11;
                     break;
                 default:
                     break;
                 }

/***** End of the new switch statement *****/

         if (hit > 0) last_hit = hit;
         } while (hit && card_total <= 21);

/* Display the results */

         printf("\nYour final total is %d", card_total);
         if (card_total > 21)
         {
                  printf("--you have gone bust!");
                  cash -= bet;
         }
         else

/* Dealer cards */

         {
```

```
            dealer_total = last_hit;
            while ((dealer_total < 17) && (last_hit > 0))
                dealer_total += last_hit;

            printf("\nDealer's total is %d", dealer_total);
            if ((dealer_total > 21) ||
                (card_total > dealer_total))
    {
                printf("--you win!");
                cash += bet;
    }
    else
    {
                printf("--you lose!");
                cash -= bet;
    }
    }
    printf("\nYour cash is now $%.2f\n", cash);
    do
    {
                printf("\nPlace your bet: ");
                scanf("%f", &bet);
    } while (bet > cash);

    }

    if (cash < .01)
        printf("\nSorry, you are broke!");
}
```

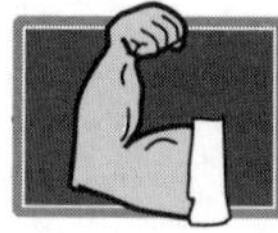

RESULT:

```
C:\>CARDS7

DEAL CARDS FOR THE GAME OF 21

Enter your total cash: 33

Place your bet: 18

Your card total is 0
Enter a card (1-13), or 0 to quit: 8

Your card total is 8
Enter a card (1-13), or 0 to quit: 11

Your card total is 18
Enter a card (1-13), or 0 to quit: 0
```

```
Your final total is 18
Dealer's total is 20--you lose!
Your cash is now $15.00

Place your bet: 0
```

ANALYSIS:

1. You enhance readability of the program by defining the symbolic constants *ACE, JACK, QUEEN, KING* on lines /*1–4*/. Each symbolic gets a value that identifies the card (1, 11, 12, 13).
2. The new *switch* statement reassigns the value of the variable *hit* depending on its original value. A fall-through construction assigns a value of 10 for the face cards, and it changes the value of an *ACE* to 11 if this will not put the total over 21. The most common use of the fall-through feature is to invoke a single action with any of several case values, just as is done here with *JACK, QUEEN,* and *KING*. Notice that the program added a value of 10 to the player's card total when it received 11 (or *JACK*) from the keyboard.
3. The program totals all other cards at their face value because they pass through the *default* branch and the original value of *hit* remains unchanged.

In this chapter you have rounded out your skills in using control statements; you have learned how to execute different sequences of statements based on relationships of data values. Functions augment your ability to control programs in C by making it easy for you to organize groups of statements that represent an identifiable operation. You will begin using functions in the next chapter.

CHAPTER 8
FUNCTIONS

Functions are the basic building blocks of C programs. In this chapter, you will learn why, when, and how to use functions in your programs. You will practice writing functions, and you will learn how to pass values into, and return results from, functions. You will also use some standard library functions supplied with your compiler.

THE WHAT, WHY, AND WHEN OF FUNCTIONS

The C language was designed for modularity to allow you to build large programs by tying together many smaller pieces, or functions. A good C program is composed of several functions, and each function performs a distinct task when that function is invoked (or called).

What is a function?

The source code for a function is a separate, isolated section of code that has the form of a name followed by curly braces that enclose function statements:

```
function_name()
{
     statement(s)
}
```

This should look familiar to you; it closely resembles the form of a main program. You call a function by referring to its name within a main program or another function. For example, a program that calls a function to say hello looks like this:

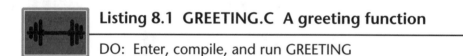

Listing 8.1 GREETING.C A greeting function

DO: Enter, compile, and run GREETING

```
#include <stdio.h>
main()
{
     greeting();
}

greeting()
{
     printf("\nHello");
}
```

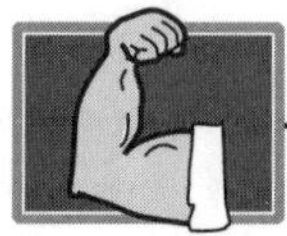

RESULTS:

```
C:\>GREETING

Hello
```

ANALYSIS:

1. The main program calls the greeting function by referencing the name, *greeting*, with a pair of parentheses attached. A semicolon after the parentheses makes the call a complete C statement.

2. You place the source code for the greeting function completely outside of the main program; it consists of the name, *greeting*, with a pair of parentheses, followed by the curly braces and the single printf() statement.

In C, even the main program is a function; the main program is formed by using *main* as the name of the primary function. The name *main* identifies the beginning of the main program to the compiler, to the linker, and eventually to the operating system. The operating system transfers control to the function identified by *main* after it loads the program into memory for execution.

Why use functions?

Functions provide the following advantages:

- ☐ Function code is reusable. You can write a function once and call it many times from many different places instead of rewriting the same code over and over.

- ☐ Functions make program smaller. Lines of code are eliminated by calling functions instead of replicating source lines; this also makes compiling faster.

- ☐ Functions make program easier to write. Functions allow you to break the programming problem down into smaller, more manageable pieces.

- ☐ Functions lead to improved commenting and readability. They provide a logical and understandable structure for a program, suggesting natural divisions where you can add comments. Well-chosen function names are themselves descriptive of the underlying process.

- ☐ Functions make program easier to maintain. It is always easier to understand and modify programs that are well-documented, smaller, and more logical.

There is one possible disadvantage to using functions: program execution **can** be slower. Calling a function takes some additional time that would not be necessary if the code were *in-line* with the program—that is, repeated wherever needed. Programs that use functions are not always slower, and they are usually not even noticeably slower. However, there are instances in which a function is called a great many times (like from within a loop), and then the associated overhead can make an important difference in the execution time.

When to use a function

There are five situations in which you should seriously consider making an operation a function. The following is a list of them along with a specific example for each:

1. You should use a function if an operation is used in two or more separate places in a program.

Example:
You write a program that displays a company name and address several times during different processing steps, so you should consolidate repeated printf() statements into a single function.

```
main
{
    /* Processing statements */

    company_name();

    /* More processing statements */

    company_name();
}

company_name()
{
    /* printf() statements to display company name & address */
}
```

2. You should use a function when an operation needs to serve more than one program. Later in the chapter you will learn how to enable different programs to share functions (see the LIBRARIES topic).

Example:
You write two programs, each of which displays the same company name and address, so you should use the same function in different programs.

```
/* First program in a file of its own */
main()
{
    /* Processing statements */

    company_name();
}

/* Second program in another file of its own */
main()
```

```
{
    /* Processing statements */

    company_name();
}

/* Display function in yet a third file of its own */
company_name()
{
    /* printf() statements to display company name & address */
}
```

3. You should use a function when an operation returns a single value. When an operation yields a single result and a program uses it repeatedly, it is a natural candidate for a function even though it may be a very simple calculation.

Example:
You write a program that calculates the total cost, including sales tax, of selected items, so you should use a function to calculate this total cost.

```
#define TAX_RATE .08   /* 8 percent sales tax */
main()
{
    /* Looping statements to select items and prices */

          total_cost(price);
}

total_cost(price)
{
    return( price + TAX_RATE * price );
}
```

4. You should use a function when an operation can be described concisely as a distinct task. An operation may deserve function status if it is a separate or unique task, even if a program only uses it once.

Example:
You write a program that performs a lot of processing, then summarizes all items with a total cost in excess of a certain ceiling, so you call a function once at the end of the program to produce the summary.

```
main()
{
    /* Processing steps to calculate costs */

    summarize(ceiling_cost);
}

summarize(ceiling_cost)
```

```
{
    /* Statements to produce the desired summary */
}
```

5. You should use a function when a program is too long and can be broken into separate operations. "Too long" is a relative term; some programming projects prohibit programs or functions longer than a single page, whereas others allow programs to be hundreds of lines long. If a program reaches your limit of tolerance for the number of pages or the time required for a compile, then you should look for logical functional divisions.

A function becomes especially attractive when more than one of the above guidelines applies.

MODULAR PROGRAM DESIGN

Before you write a program you should take time to design it. Just as an architect makes sketches of ideas for a building, then refines the sketches into finished drawings, you should sketch out the architecture of your program before programming the details. A flow diagram can really help you visualize the operation of a program during the design stage. A flow diagram is a series of boxes that segregate and describe distinct program operations; the boxes are linked together by arrows showing the direction of flow of the program. In its simplest form, a flow diagram uses rectangles to show operations and diamonds to signify decision points. You derive a flow diagram from a description of the program requirements, which could be merely a list of desired features. The process of listing requirements and creating a flow diagram makes you think about what is needed for a program and how it will operate. The process may cause you to realize that something has been left out, or it may force you to think about the programming techniques required to accomplish certain steps.

In Chapters 6 and 7, you gradually expanded a card playing program, which partially simulates the card game of "21" or Blackjack. The following is a list of requirements for an improved version of this program:

1. Enter a total cash amount for player betting.
2. Place bets up to the cash amount.
3. Deal cards at random and identify (ID) the cards as 1 through 13, allowing repeats without restriction and ignoring suits. Assign a value of 10 to face cards (card IDs 11, 12, 13) and assign a value of either 1 or 11 to an Ace (card ID 1)—whichever will give the maximum total of 21 or less.
4. Deal two cards each to the player and the dealer.
5. Deal "hits" to the player first.
6. Deal "hits" to the dealer as long as the dealer total is under 17.

7. The player or dealer automatically loses if the card total exceeds 21.
8. The highest total under 22 wins, and the dealer wins any ties.
9. Add the amount of the bet to the player's cash amount if he wins or subtract it if he loses.
10. Quit when a zero bet is placed or the cash total is zero.

Figure 8-1 is a flow diagram based on the above requirements. The flow diagram does not contain all of the details of the requirements list—the main purpose is to outline the sequence of operations of the program.

A flow diagram will show the major components of a program, components that could become functions. The flow diagram in Figure 8-1 makes it clear that there are two operations that are candidates for functions. Three of the operations ("Deal 2 cards to each player," "Player hit," and "Dealer hit") involve dealing cards, and three others involve checking scores. Figure 8-2 shows a slightly expanded flow diagram that includes calling these new functions.

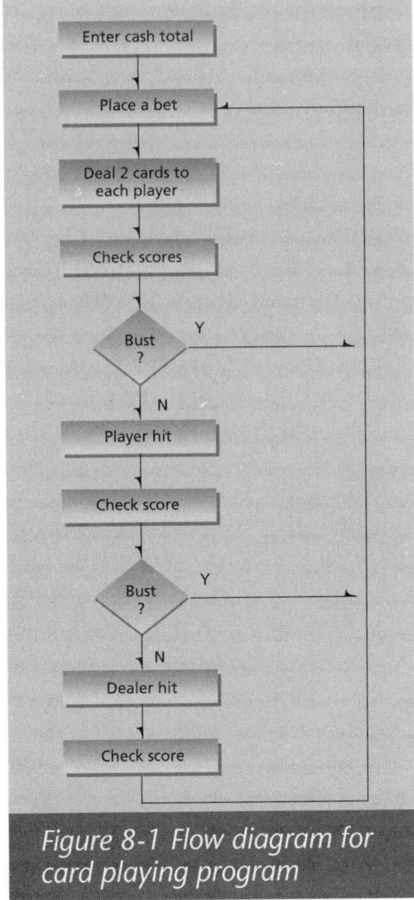

Figure 8-1 Flow diagram for card playing program

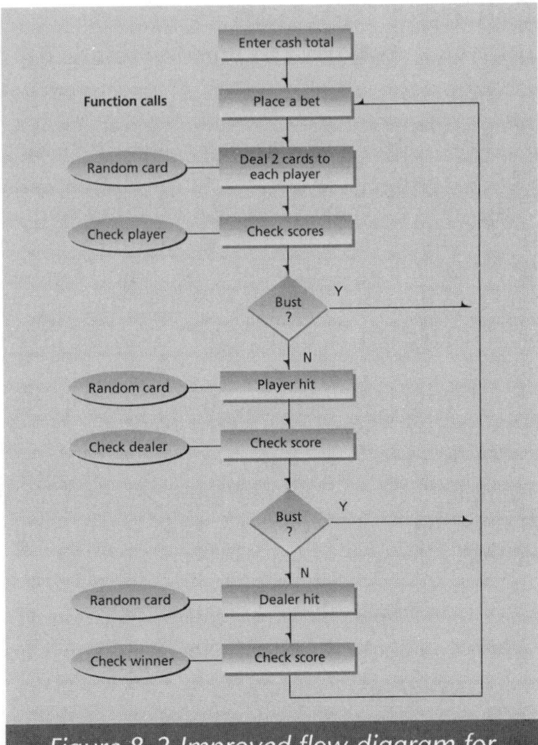

Figure 8-2 Improved flow diagram for card playing program

The three "dealing" operations are not entirely identical, so they cannot be covered by writing a single, common function. However, each does require that a random card be dealt, so a function that will randomly pick a single card and return it to the caller is required. The three "check scores" operations differ only in which scores are checked, the player's, the dealer's, or both. Therefore, you will need to write this function so that it can work with either card total and report the appropriate result. You will develop these two functions gradually as you work the examples in this chapter.

USING FUNCTIONS

When you want to use a new function in a program, you *define* it and *call* it. You define a function by writing it as a separate segment of source code, and you call it by referencing the name within other functions.

Many useful functions are available to you as part of a standard library that comes with the compiler. You have already used some of the standard I/O functions, such as printf() and scanf(), and in later chapters, you will learn about other categories of standard functions, like those used for string handling. Library functions have already been written, compiled, and tested, so all you need to do is call them.

Calling a function

The complete syntax of a function call is:

```
function_name(arg1, arg2,...)
```

A function name can be any identifier that obeys the same rules as those for variable identifiers. That is, any name that begins with a letter and contains only letters, digits, or underscores can be a function name. The parentheses attached to the function name contain arguments. Arguments are references to values passed into a function; they are separated by commas and can be constants, variables, or expressions. If a function does not expect any values, the arguments can be omitted, but the parentheses must remain. Arguments in function calls will be discussed more a little later in this chapter.

A function calls another function simply by referring to the called function name with attached parentheses. Two things are accomplished by a function call: (1) the function is executed, and (2) a value is returned in place of the function reference. For example, if you had written a function day_of_month(), which returns the integer day of the month, then you could call the function and assign the day to a variable with the following statement:

```
day = day_of_month();
```

Or, you could display the day with this statement:

```
printf("%d", day_of_month());
```

Here, the return value of function day_of_month() provides the value displayed by printf(). In general, you can call a function anywhere in a C program that a return value can be used. You can call a function that has no return value (or call a function and ignore its return value) by using the function reference as a statement all by itself. For example, if the function day_of_month() displayed the day directly to the screen without returning a value, then you would call it with the following statement:

```
day_of_month();
```

Defining a function

The complete syntax for defining a function is:

```
return_type function_name(parameter list)
{
        statement(s)
}
```

There are four elements in the syntax of a function: (1) a return type, (2) a function name, (3) a parameter list, and (4) the body of the function. Figure 8-3 identifies these four elements for the function in the next example, the RANDOM program.

The function *return type*

The first element in this definition is the *return type*. Because a function can return a value when it ends, you must specify the data type of this returned value. This is done in the same way as for a variable—by preceding the function name with a type declaration. For example, to define the day_of_month() function with an unsigned integer return value, you would write:

```
unsigned int day_of_month()
{
        /* Statements to obtain the day of the month */
}
```

This declares that day_of_month() will return an *unsigned int* value to the function that called it. If you do not specify a return type, the compiler will assume type *int*. For instance, the function greeting() in the GREETING program (Program 8.1) is really type *int* even though the program did not declare a type. However, the proper way to write C functions is to explicitly declare function types, rather than to depend on the compiler default. You should make it standard practice to declare the type of all functions. If you do not want the function to return anything, you should declare it to be type *void*. This is a way of telling the compiler that the function will not return a value.

Function name

The second element in a function definition is the function name, which is an identifier beginning with a letter and containing only letters, digits, and underscores. You should avoid beginning function names with an underscore because this normally signifies a special library function. The maximum length of a function name in C is 31 characters. Actually, a function name can be longer, but only the first 31 characters are guaranteed to be used by the compiler, so you should avoid longer names.

Function parameter list

The third element in a function definition is the parentheses, which can optionally include a parameter list. The parentheses are a necessary part of the definition even without parameters. The parameter list includes the names and types of variables that will accept values passed into the function from the calling function. The topic of passing values to a function deserves an extensive and detailed explanation, and we defer this discussion to a separate section of this chapter—transferring values to a function.

The function body

The body of a function is the fourth element, and you enclose the body in the curly braces of a compound statement. You should always align the curly braces with the left edge of the function type and name.

In the flow diagram of Figure 8-3, you previously identified the need for a function to deal a random card, and your task is now to define (write) that function. But how do you write a function that randomly picks a card? The answer is readily at hand—there is a function that will generate a random number, and that function is supplied in the standard C library that accompanies your compiler. You can gain some experience in generating random numbers with the next program, which calls the function deal().

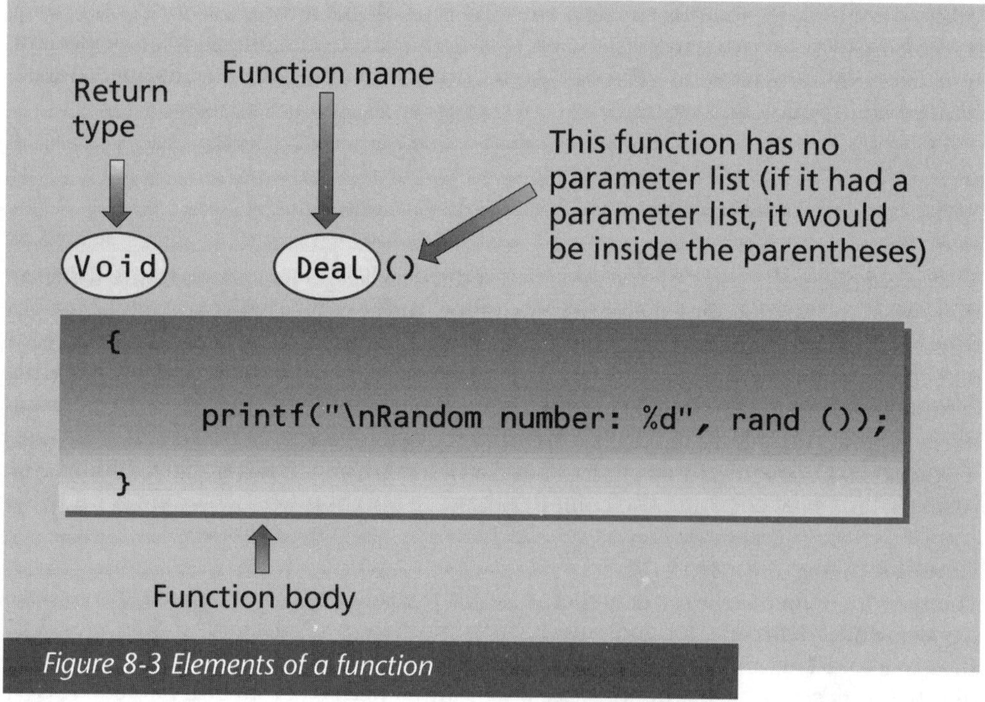

Figure 8-3 Elements of a function

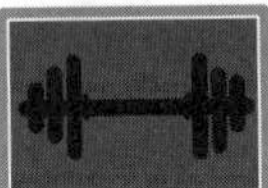

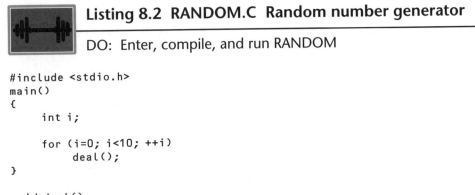

Listing 8.2 RANDOM.C Random number generator

DO: Enter, compile, and run RANDOM

```
#include <stdio.h>
main()
{
     int i;

     for (i=0; i<10; ++i)
          deal();
}

void deal()
{
     printf("\nRandom number: %d", rand());
}
```

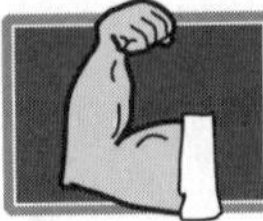

RESULTS:

```
C:\>RANDOM

Random number: 0
Random number: 4310
Random number: 24759
Random number: 15029
Random number: 17457
Random number: 7174
Random number: 1541
Random number: 22245
Random number: 22259
Random number: 30628
```

ANALYSIS:

1. The *for* statement in the main function calls the function deal() ten times.
2. The printf() statement displays a random integer, which is the result of a call to function rand(). Notice that the program declares function deal() to be type *void* because there is no return value.

3. With this program, you are already having functions call other functions. The main function calls your function, *deal()*, which in turn calls the standard library function, *rand()*.

4. Function *rand()* returns a random integer with a value that can be anything in the valid range for type *int* (0-32767 for the IBM PC). By running the RANDOM program, you can display ten numbers in this range.

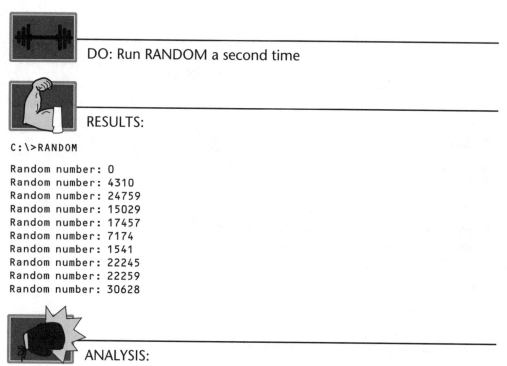

DO: Run RANDOM a second time

RESULTS:

```
C:\>RANDOM

Random number: 0
Random number: 4310
Random number: 24759
Random number: 15029
Random number: 17457
Random number: 7174
Random number: 1541
Random number: 22245
Random number: 22259
Random number: 30628
```

ANALYSIS:

1. By running the program a second time, you have displayed the same ten numbers as in the first run.

If the numbers repeat, are they really random? Yes they are—function *rand()* starts with the same number each time the program executes, and progresses through a different random number for each subsequent call until the program ends. The numbers generated **within** each program execution are random, but the random sequence will repeat with each new execution of the program. This is beneficial during the check-out phase, when you want to see the same results each time a program is executed.

Steps in calling a function

The steps that a program takes during a function call are:

1. Identify the return location (the address of the statement following the function).

2. Transfer control to the called function.
3. Execute the body of the called function.
4. Transfer control back to the calling function at location 1.

Figure 8-4 illustrates the steps of a function call that passes no values into or out of the function.

You can emulate the workings of a function call by writing a program that performs the same steps as a function, except that you use explicit C statements. You would never do this in an actual program, but this exercise should be interesting, and it will increase your understanding of function calls. You can use the *goto* statement to alter the RANDOM program so that it is has a similar flow and yet works without a function.

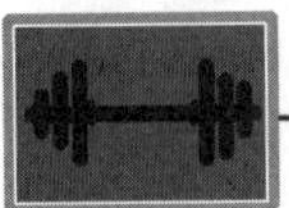

Listing 8.3 RANDOM2.C Emulate a function

DO: • Modify RANDOM to simulate a function call
• Compile and run RANDOM2

```
#include <stdio.h>
main()
{
     int i;

/* Emulate the function call 10 times */

     for (i=0; i<10; ++i)
     {                                                /*1*/
           goto deal;                                 /*2*/
back:                                                 /*3*/
     }                                                /*4*/
     goto quit;                                       /*5*/

/* Emulated function */

deal:                                                 /*6*/
     printf("\nRandom number: %d", rand());
goto back;                                            /*7*/

quit:                                                 /*8*/
}
```

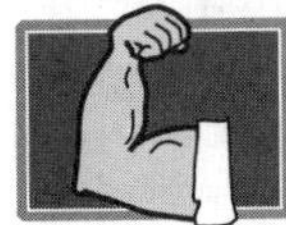

RESULTS:

```
C:\>RANDOM2

Random number: 0
Random number: 4310
Random number: 24759
```

```
Random number: 15029
Random number: 17457
Random number: 7174
Random number: 1541
Random number: 22245
Random number: 22259
Random number: 30628
```

ANALYSIS:

1. This program explicitly shows the four steps for calling a function in terms of individual C statements. On line /*3*/ is a label (*back:*) that identifies the return location—this is step 1. On line /*2*/ *goto deal;* transfers control to the emulated function at the label *deal:*—step 2. The emulated function displays a random number—step 3. Finally, *goto back;* on line /*7*/ in the emulated function transfers control back to the calling location—step 4.
2. The statement *goto deal;* and the label *back:* are both located within the *for* loop, and so the program "calls" the function ten times, displaying the same information as for the RANDOM program.
3. When the *for* loop ends, the *goto quit;* statement on line /*5*/ jumps over the emulated function to reach the ending curly brace of the program following the label on line /*8*/.

The awkwardness of this program should make you appreciate the convenience provided by real function calls. In the RANDOM program, the compiler took care of all of the transfers of control that you had to explicitly provide with *goto* statements in the RANDOM2 program. This program should also impress upon you the reasons to avoid *goto* statements. RANDOM2 has three *goto* statements that jump forward and backward in the program, making even this small program difficult to follow. Code that twists around like this is called "spaghetti code," and you should avoid writing such programs.

The card playing program requires a random number in the range of from 1 to 13 to represent ID values for the 13 cards, ace through king. The next program shows how to accomplish this with the modulus operator with which you became familiar in Chapter 4.

Listing 8.4 RANDOM3.C Random number generator

DO: • Modify RANDOM to restrict numbers to a range of 1–13
• Compile and run RANDOM3

```
#include <stdio.h>
main()
{
```

```
    int i;

    for (i=0; i<10; ++i)
         deal();
}

void deal()
{
    printf("\nRandom card: %d", (rand() % 13) + 1);              /*1*/
}
```

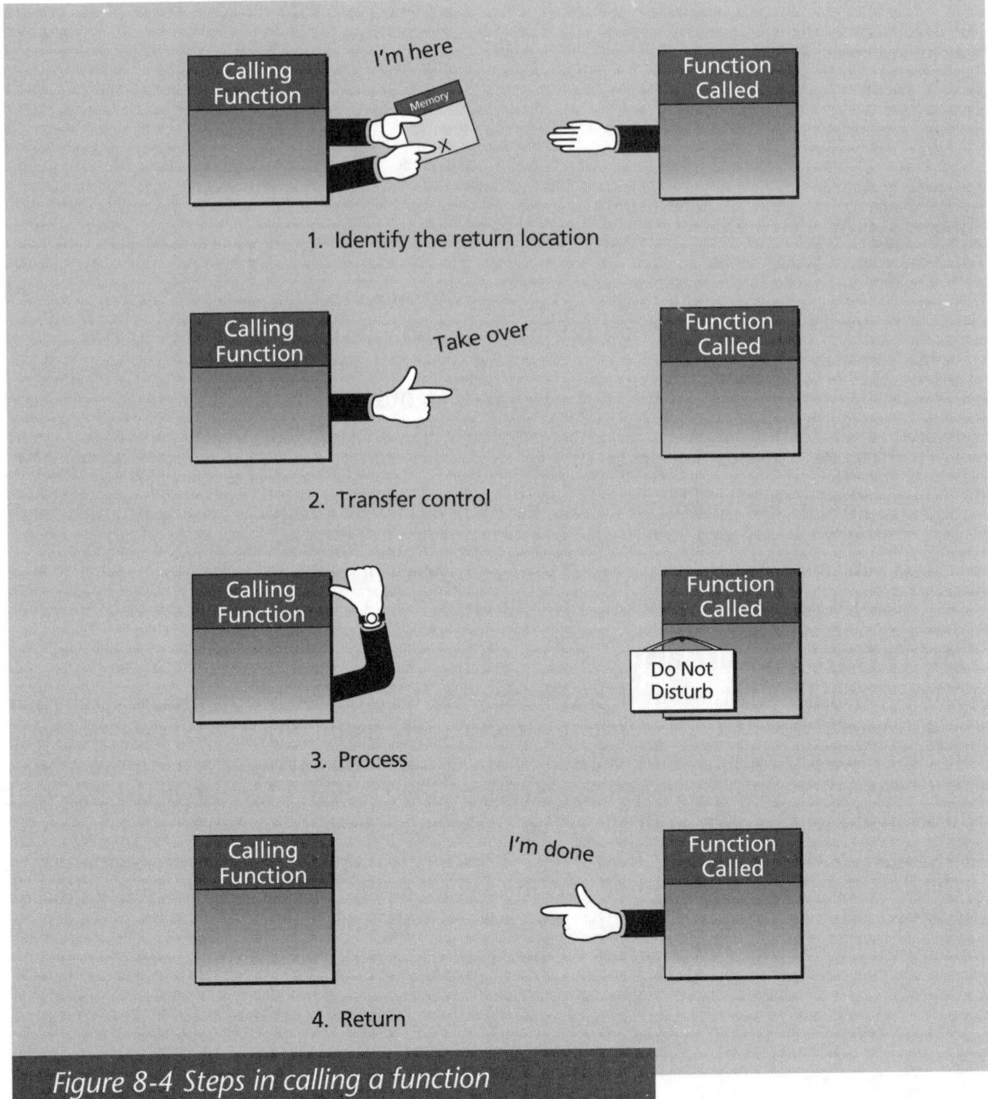

Figure 8-4 Steps in calling a function

RESULTS:

```
C:\>RANDOM3

Random card: 1
Random card: 8
Random card: 8
Random card: 2
Random card: 12
Random card: 12
Random card: 8
Random card: 3
Random card: 4
Random card: 1
```

ANALYSIS:

1. The printf() expression on line /*1*/ now displays the result of the expression *(rand() % 13) + 1*. The modulus operator (%) yields the remainder after dividing the random number by 13. Because this remainder is an integer in the range of from 0 to 12, you must add 1 to get the desired range of 1 to 13.

2. Notice the parentheses that explicitly tell the program to apply the modulus operator before adding 1. This is technically unnecessary, because the modulus operator has precedence over plus anyway, but the parentheses make the intent clear.

The *return* statement

A function ends either when it encounters the last, closing curly brace or when it executes a *return* statement. A *return* is particularly useful when you want to end a function conditionally, usually with an *if* statement. You can use one or more *returns* placed anywhere within a function, and when any of them is executed, the program will immediately transfer control to the curly brace at the end of the function. The next program shows an alternative way to restrict the range of random numbers to 1 through 13, and it makes use of a *return* to end when one of the desired values is displayed. The technique that this program uses to find a random number is not a particularly good one, but it serves to illustrate the *return* statement.

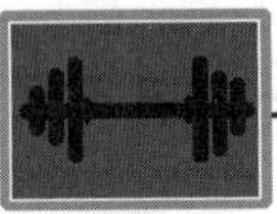

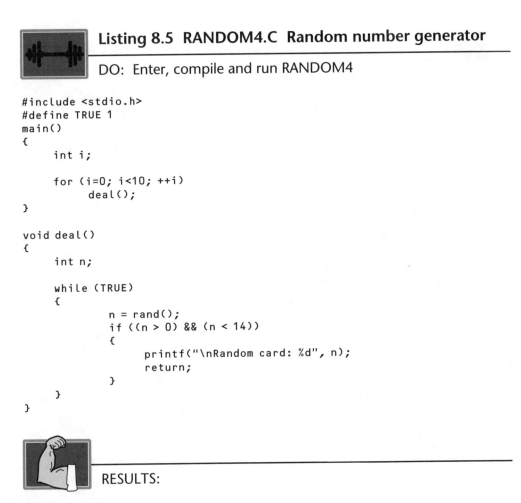

Listing 8.5 RANDOM4.C Random number generator

DO: Enter, compile and run RANDOM4

```
#include <stdio.h>
#define TRUE 1
main()
{
     int i;

     for (i=0; i<10; ++i)
          deal();
}

void deal()
{
     int n;

     while (TRUE)
     {
               n = rand();
               if ((n > 0) && (n < 14))
               {
                    printf("\nRandom card: %d", n);
                    return;
               }
     }
}
```

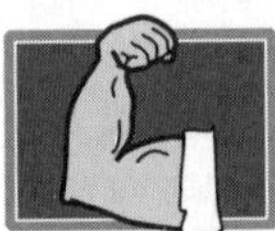

RESULTS:

```
C:\>RANDOM4

Random card: 1
Random card: 9
Random card: 1
Random card: 7
Random card: 3
Random card: 6
Random card: 12
Random card: 13
Random card: 3
Random card: 7
```

ANALYSIS:

1. This function uses the brute force method of throwing out random numbers until it finds one that falls in the acceptable range of from 1 to 13.
2. The *while* statement establishes a loop that executes indefinitely so that the library function *rand()* can generate as many random numbers as needed.
3. The *if* expression becomes true when the program generates a number in the range of from 1 to 13. Then printf() displays the number and the program executes the *return* statement. The *return* transfers control all the way down to the closing curly brace of the function, which is outside of the *while* loop, so the *return* terminates the *while* loop and it ends the function.

This program was useful to illustrate a conditional return from a function, but it is a pretty laborious way of generating the desired random numbers when compared with the previous method. The program is larger and it takes a lot more time to accomplish the task (you probably noticed a slight delay as the program ran), so RANDOM3 will serve as the preferred function for generating random numbers.

Now you have a good way of generating the needed random card ID, but how do you pass it back to the calling function? You can pass it back as the value of the function using a variation of the *return* statement that includes a value.

Returning function values

You can return the value of an expression as the value of a function with either of the following two forms of *return*:

```
return(expression);
```

or

```
return expression;
```

You can enclose the expression in parentheses, or just use a space between *return* and the expression; either form is perfectly acceptable. We prefer to use the parentheses because this isolates the expression, making the statement more readable. The *return* statement evaluates the expression, then assigns the result to the function call in the calling function.

You can make the function RANDOM3 complete by returning the card values generated. All you need to do is declare the function *deal()* to be type *int*, return a random number value, and have the main function display the result.

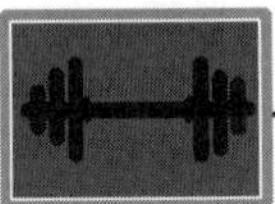

Listing 8.6 RANDOM5.C Random number generator

DO:
- Modify RANDOM3 to return a value
- Compile and run RANDOM5

```
#include <stdio.h>
main()
{
     int i;

     for (i=0; i<10; ++i)
          printf("\nRandom card: %d", deal());                    /*1*/
}

int deal()                                                        /*2*/
{
     return((rand() % 13) + 1);                                   /*3*/
}
```

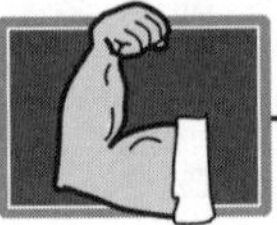

RESULTS:

```
C:\>RANDOM5

Random card: 1
Random card: 8
Random card: 8
Random card: 2
Random card: 12
Random card: 12
Random card: 8
Random card: 3
Random card: 4
Random card: 1
```

ANALYSIS:

1. The display of card IDs has now been moved to line /*1*/ in the main program. The reference to *deal()* in printf() causes this function to be executed, and printf() displays the returned value of *deal()*.
2. Line /*2*/ adds type *int* to the definition of *deal()* so that it can return an integer value.

3. The *return* statement on line /*3*/ causes the value of expression *(rand() % 13) + 1* to be returned when function *deal()* executes.

The return type must match the function type

The data type of the expression in a *return* statement should match the declared type of the function. If it does not, the compiler converts the expression value to the type of the function. Some compilers will issue a warning when this happens, but Power C does not. If the types are different, you should use a cast operator to make the return value match the type of the function so that the conversion will be explicit and you can avoid compiler warnings.

Suppose you require a random number to be a fraction in the range of from 0 to 1. If you were writing programs for video games or for statistical analysis you might need such random numbers. Because the number is a fraction, the function must return a floating-point number. The next program shows how to create fractional random numbers, but it does not correctly return the values. This illustrates one possible error caused by a mismatch between a function data type and a return data type.

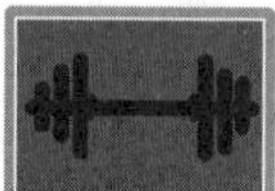

Listing 8.7 RANDOM6.C Random number generator

DO: • Modify RANDOM5 to return a fractional value
• Compile and run RANDOM6

```
#include <stdio.h>
#define MAX_INT 32767                                    /*1*/
main()
{
     int i;

     for (i=0; i<10; ++i)
          printf("\nRandom fraction: %f", deal());       /*2*/
}

int deal()
{
     return((float)rand() / MAX_INT);                    /*3*/
}
```

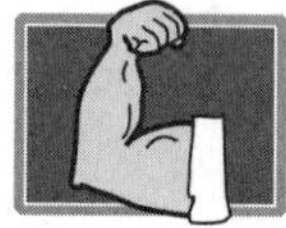

RESULTS:

```
C:\>RANDOM6

Random fraction: -0.000000
```

```
Random fraction: -0.000000
Random fraction: -0.000000
Random fraction: -0.000000
Random fraction: -0.000000
Random fraction: -0.000000
Random fraction: -0.000000
Random fraction: -0.000000
Random fraction: -0.000000
Random fraction: -0.000000
```

ANALYSIS:

1. On line /*2*/ you change the printf() message and conversion specifier because the statement expects a floating-point number.

2. The statement on line /*3*/ creates a fractional random number by casting the integer result of rand() to type *float* and dividing by the maximum possible integer value, given by constant MAX_INT on line /*1*/. This is an expression of mixed types, so the statement converts the integer to type *float*, and the result is a floating-point number.

3. The return value type (*float*) and the type of the function (*int*) are different, so the return causes a conversion to occur. When the program assigns the floating-point fraction to deal(), it truncates the number to zero; consequently, the output of the program is a list of zero values.

You can easily correct this problem by changing the defined data type of function deal(). When you change the data type of deal(), you must also move the function so that the compiler sees the function definition before calling it in main(). When the compiler encounters a function call, it needs to know the data type of the return value in advance; otherwise, the compiler assumes type *int*.

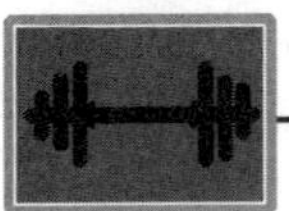

Listing 8.8 RANDOM7.C Random number generator

DO:
- Modify RANDOM6 to correct the function data type
- Compile and run RANDOM7

```
#include <stdio.h>

float deal()
{
      return((float)rand() / 32767);
```

```
}

main()
{
      int i;

      for (i=0; i<10; ++i)
            printf("\nRandom fraction: %f", deal());
}
```

RESULTS:

```
C:\>RANDOM7

Random fraction: 0.000000
Random fraction: 0.131535
Random fraction: 0.755608
Random fraction: 0.458663
Random fraction: 0.532762
Random fraction: 0.218940
Random fraction: 0.047029
Random fraction: 0.678884
Random fraction: 0.679312
Random fraction: 0.934721
```

ANALYSIS:

Now function deal() returns the fractional random numbers without conversion and the program displays the correct values.

If you did not move function deal() in front of main(), the numbers would all be zero because the compiler would assume that deal() returns an integer. There is a better way to tell the compiler about function data types than making sure that all functions occur in the proper order. This better way involves the insertion of function *prototypes* at the top of the file. You will learn about prototypes after a few more exercises.

Different return types

You can return any kind of value from a function as long as it matches the declared type of the function. The expression that you place in the *return* statement determines the data type of the returned value; therefore, you can control the returned data type with the variables that you use in this expression, or by casting the result of the expression. Here is a program that calls several functions, each of which returns a different type of value.

Listing 8.9 TYPES.C Return different data types

DO: Enter, compile, and run TYPES

```
#include <stdio.h>
void void_return()
{
     printf("\n\nExecuting function void_return()");
     return;
}

int int_return()
{
     printf("\n\nExecuting function int_return()");
     return((int)2.4);
}

float float_return()
{
     printf("\n\nExecuting function float_return()");
     return(2.4);
}

void main()
{
     void_return();
     printf("\nThe first function returns no value");
     printf("\nThe second function returns integer %d",
          int_return());
     printf("\nThe third function returns floating-point %.1f",
          float_return());
}
```

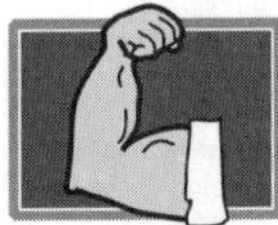

RESULT:

```
C:\>TYPES

Executing function void_return()
The first function returns no value

Executing function int_return()
The second function returns integer 2

Executing function float_return()
The third function returns floating-point 2.4
```

ANALYSIS:

1. The main function calls three other functions and displays the returned values.
2. The three functions are defined above the main function so that the compiler will know the return type of each one before encountering the function calls in main().
3. Function void_return() does not return a value. Its declared type is *void*, and it uses a bare *return* statement, which is optional because the function would return anyway when it encountered the closing curly brace (}).
4. The definition of function int_return() declares it to be type *int*, and the return expression returns an integer by casting the constant 2.4 to an integer value. The compiler would convert the constant to an integer automatically, but the cast operator makes it clear that you intended this to happen and that this is not simply an oversight on your part.
5. Function float_return() returns the floating-point constant, 2.4, which matches the declared type of this function.

Notice that this program declares the main function to be type *void*. This is the first time we have declared a type for main(), but we will do so from now on, and you should do likewise in all your programs. Some compilers will issue a warning if you do not declare a type for main(). You can return a value from the main function to the operating system with the *exit()* statement. If there is no exit value, you should declare it to be type *void*, but you can declare main() to be *int* and return a value that signals the success or failure of the program. The most common use of this capability is in signalling whether a program encountered any errors during execution. The next program shows how you can return a value of either 0 or 1 to the operating system.

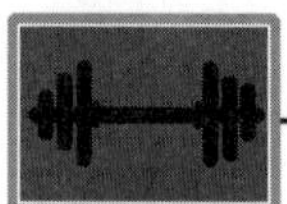

Listing 8.10 EXITCODE.C Return an exit code

DO: Enter and compile EXITCODE

```
#include <stdio.h>
int main()
{
     int status;

     printf("Enter 0 to signal OK or 1 for ERROR: ");
     scanf("%d", &status);

     exit(status);
}
```

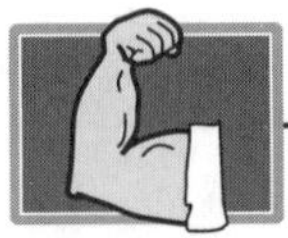

RESULT:

```
C:\>pc/c EXITCODE
```

ANALYSIS:

1. The second line of the program declares main() to be type *int* so that it can return an integer status value.
2. The program prompts you to enter a value of either 0 or 1, then the *exit()* statement returns that value to the operating system as the value of main().

If you are running this program under DOS, you can capture the return code from program EXITCODE by running the program from within a batch command file.

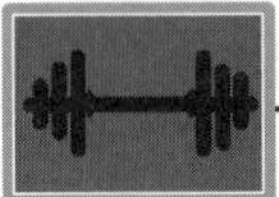

DO: Enter the following commands into file BATCH.BAT

```
echo off
echo RUNNING PROGRAM EXITCODE
exitcode
if errorlevel 1 echo AN ERROR OCCURRED
```

ANALYSIS:

1. These are DOS batch commands. The first *echo* command turns off the display of the commands themselves, and the second *echo* command displays the message, RUNNING PROGRAM EXITCODE.
2. The command *exitcode* executes the program EXITCODE.
3. The last *if* command checks the parameter *errorlevel* and executes the *echo* command if the parameter is equal to or greater than the number 1. The parameter *errorlevel* takes on the return value provided by the program *exit()* statement.

DO: Execute the batch file and enter **0**

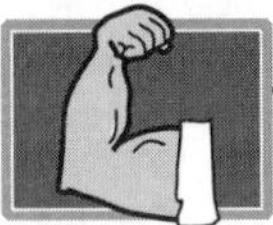

RESULT:

```
C:\>BATCH
echo off
RUNNING PROGRAM EXITCODE
Enter 0 to signal OK or 1 for ERROR: 0
```

DO: Execute the batch file and enter **1**

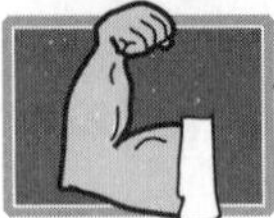

RESULT:

```
C:\>BATCH
echo off
RUNNING PROGRAM EXITCODE
Enter 0 to signal OK or 1 for ERROR: 1
AN ERROR OCCURRED
```

ANALYSIS:

1. An entry of 0 signifies a normal end to the EXITCODE program, so the batch file only displays the RUNNING... message.
2. When you enter a value of 1 to signify an error, the batch file detects it via *errorlevel* and displays an error message.

Transferring values to a function

It is wonderful to be able to isolate sections of code that can be called from different places in a program, but you usually also want to give a function some data and have it return results based on this data. C provides this capability by allowing a list of *arguments* to be included in a function call; this list corresponds to a similar list of *parameters* in the function definition. The terms *argument* and *parameter* refer to the same value in different places: An *argument* is a value in the calling statement that becomes a *parameter* in the function definition. Calling arguments are constants, variables, or expressions that are separated by commas inside the parentheses of the calling statement. Parameters are variables that are separated by commas inside the parentheses of the function definition. Figure 8-5 establishes the correspondence between arguments and parameters (also called *formal parameters*) for the next program example.

Figure 8-6 shows the steps in calling a function in which data values pass into and return from the function.

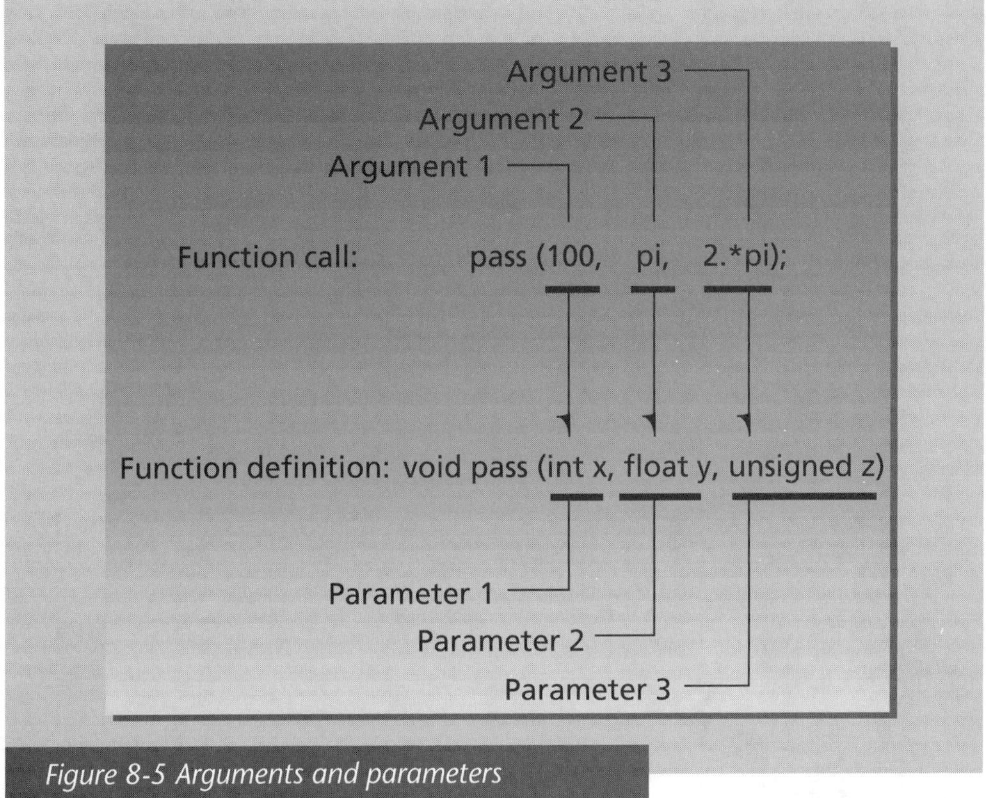

Figure 8-5 Arguments and parameters

Figure 8-6 shows a bucket of data values being passed into a function and some return values being passed back when the function ends. You have already experienced how to return **one** value with a *return* statement, but you haven't yet returned several values. You can do this with the help of a *pointer*, but you need to refer to Chapter 10 to see exactly how this works. In C, arguments are always passed *by value*, which means that each parameter in the function is a **copy** of the value of each calling argument. Therefore, if the function changes the value of a parameter, the original value in the calling function is not affected. Some programming languages allow arguments to be passed *by reference*, making it possible for the function called to directly alter the original value of the argument. C allows you to alter values in the calling function **indirectly** by using pointers, which you will learn about in Chapter 10. Here we will concentrate on passing values into a function. The next program shows how to pass three arguments to a function.

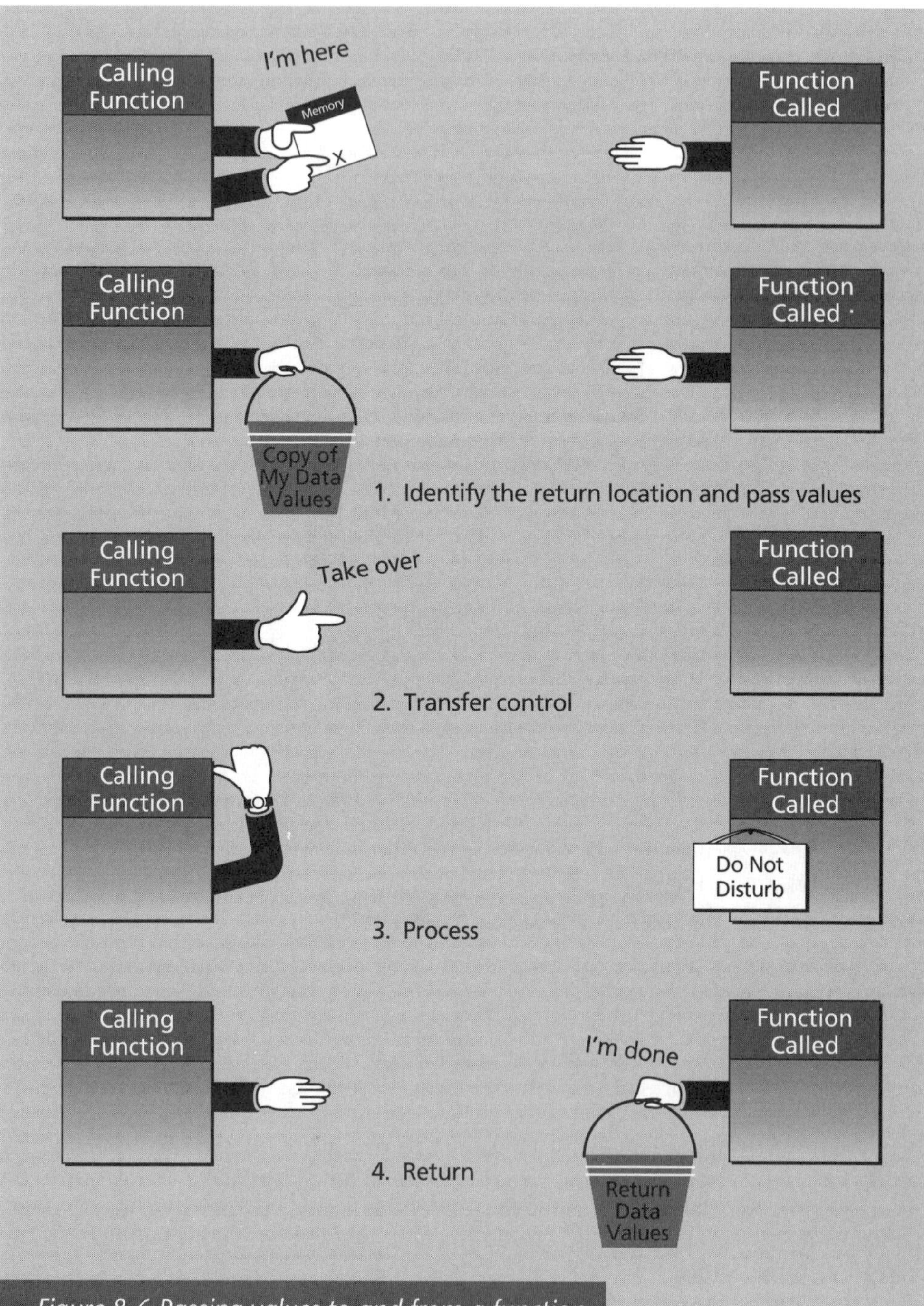

Figure 8-6 Passing values to and from a function

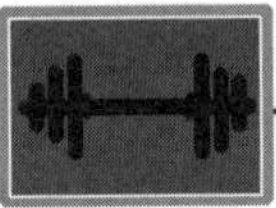

Listing 8.11 ARGUMENT.C Function arguments

DO: Enter, compile, and run ARGUMENT

```
#include <stdio.h>
void pass(int x, float y, unsigned z)
{
     printf("\nThe 1st parameter is %d", x);
     printf("\nThe 2nd parameter is %f", y);
     printf("\nThe 3rd parameter is %u", z);
}

void main()
{
     float pi = 3.1416;

     pass(100, pi, 2.*pi);
}
```

RESULT:

```
C:\>ARGUMENT

The 1st parameter is 100
The 2nd parameter is 3.141600
The 3rd parameter is 6
```

ANALYSIS:

1. Once again, the function is defined before the first appearance of a call in main(). This time it is done so the compiler can know what data types to expect for the calling arguments. We will soon introduce function prototypes, which tell the compiler all about a function. With prototypes, you will not need to place functions ahead of main().

2. When the compiler first encounters the function definition (just below the *#include* statement), it allocates three parameters for function *pass* having data types *int, float,* and *unsigned,* respectively. Then, when the compiler gets to the function call in main(), it knows what to expect in the way of data types for these three parameters. The first two arguments match the function parameter types, so no conversion is necessary. The third argument is a floating-point expression, *2.*pi,* whereas the third parameter calls for an *unsigned* integer, so the compiler knows to truncate the expression result (6.2832) to an integer (6).

A program passes values in a manner that is considerably more organized than implied by the bucket full of data illustrated in Figure 8-5. In reality, it passes the values in the order in which you specify them in the calling argument list, and the mechanism for passing is called a *stack*. As the name implies, the calling function stacks the values in sequential memory locations, then tells the function how many values were stacked and where to find the first value. The function can then fetch the values from the stack in the correct order. Figure 8-7 graphically illustrates the operation of a stack used to pass argument values to a function.

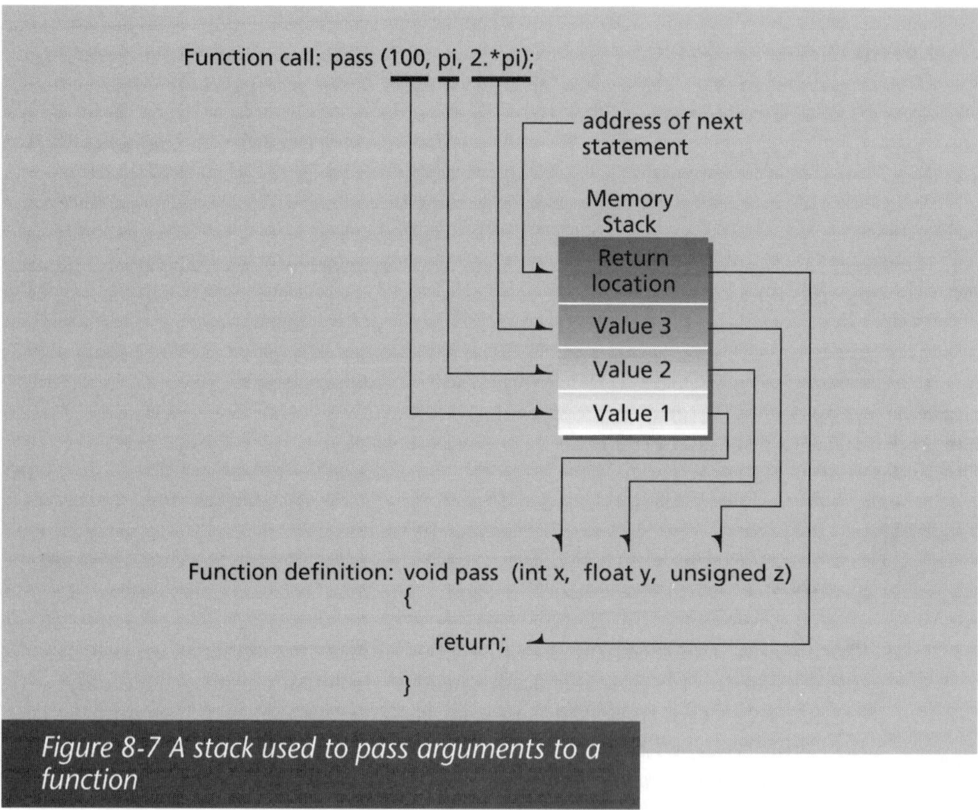

Figure 8-7 A stack used to pass arguments to a function

In addition to argument values, the program passes the return location on the stack—that is, the location in memory where the function will return control when it is finished. This return location is the address of the next statement after the function call. As Figure 8-7 shows, the return location goes on the stack first, before the argument values. A stack is the mechanism for passing argument values to a function, enabling a program to pass **copies** of values to a function and protecting the original values from being changed directly by a function.

Pseudo programs

Now you can resume developing the two new functions, deal() and check(), to enhance the card playing program. Before you dive into the details of writing these new functions, it would be helpful to see how they fit into the program. A good technique for visualizing the structure of a program is to write an abbreviated version of the program with "pseudo code." Pseudo code, as its name implies, is not real. It can look like a real program, but don't try to compile it, because it is incomplete or perhaps even syntactically wrong. Pseudo code allows you to write a program composed only of statements that illustrate the flow and important processing operations of a program while inserting comments to explain the rest. Pseudo code resembles both a flow diagram and a C program; it is a step between the flow diagram and the final program. The pseudo code is a great deal smaller than the C program that it corresponds to, but the essential concepts of the processing steps and sequential flow are there. A pseudo-code representation of the CARDS7 program from Chapter 7 looks like Example 8-1.

```
/* Enter cash */
/* Place an initial bet */
while ((cash > 0.) && (bet > 0.))
{
     do
     {
          /* Enter (deal) player cards */
     } while (hit && player_total > 21);

     if (player_total > 21)
     {
          /* Bust */
     }
     else
     {
          /* Enter dealer's cards */
          /* Determine winner */
          /* Place another bet */
     }
}
```

Example 8-1 Pseudo code for program CARDS7

```
/* Enter cash */
/* Place an initial bet */
while ((cash > 0.) && (bet > 0.))
{
     do
```

```
        {
                /* Enter (deal) player cards */
        } while ( hit && player_total > 21);

        if (player_total > 21)
        {
                /* Bust */
        }
        else
        {
                /* Enter dealer's cards */
                /* Determine winner */
                /* Place another bet */
        }
{
```

The opening comments show where you place the statements used to enter a cash amount and prompt for an initial bet. Then the pseudo code explicitly shows the main *while* loop, which contains indented statements and comments for the body of the loop. The program deals player cards in the *do while* loop, where a comment takes the place of statements to actually enter card values. An *if else* statement outlines the balance of the processing, and once again, comments signify what happens when the *player_total* is greater than 21 (Bust) or not (enter dealer's cards, determine winner, and place another bet).

You have not yet developed the check() function, but it will require a parameter to signify which card total to check, so you might call it with a symbolic constant for an argument. For instance, check (PLAYER) requests that the function check the player's total, and check (DEALER) requests a check of the dealer's total, whereas check (BOTH) determines the winner of the game by checking both totals.

You can insert the new functions, deal() and check(), into the pseudo code as shown in Example 8-2 to indicate where they fit.

```
/* Enter cash */
/* Place an initial bet */
while ((cash > 0.) && (bet > 0.))
{
    do
    {
          /* Enter (deal) player cards */
          deal();
    } while ( hit && player_total > 21);

    if (check (PLAYER) == OK)
    {
          /* Bust */
    }
    else
    {
          /* Dealer's cards */
          deal();
```

```
            check (DEALER);

            /* Determine winner */
            check (BOTH);

            /* Place another bet */
        }
    {
```

```
/* Enter cash */
/* Place an initial bet */
while ((cash > 0.) && (bet > 0.))
{
    do
    {
        /* Enter (deal) player cards */
        deal ();

    } while (hit && card_total > 21);

    if (check (PLAYER) == OK)
    {
        /* Bust */
    }
    else
    {
        /* Dealers cards */
        deal ();
        check (DEALER);

        /* Determine winner */
        check (BOTH);

        /* Place another bet */
    }
}
```

Example 8-2 Pseudo code for CARDS7 with new functions

To finish the function that deals cards you can add one more desirable feature to deal() by passing a value to it. If function deal() can accept an integer parameter that is the total for the hand being dealt, then it has a basis for selecting a value of 1 or 11 for aces. The first line of the new function definition becomes:

```
int deal(int total)
```

where *int total* defines a new parameter of type integer to be passed to the function by each call. Each time you deal to the player, the function call will look like this:

```
player_total += deal(player_total);
```

and each time you deal to the dealer the call will be:

```
dealer_total += deal(dealer_total);
```

Previously, a switch statement in the main program of CARDS7 handled the task of converting a face card (with an ID of 11, 12, or 13) to 10, and an ace (with an ID of 1) to 11. You can move the *switch* statement for setting the value of aces and face cards into the function and gain the benefit of this operation for both the player and dealer cards.

Listing 8.12 RANDOM8.C Random number generator

DO:
- Modify RANDOM5 to select values for face cards and aces (you need to enter new code for function deal())
- Compile and run RANDOM8

```
#include <stdio.h>
#define ACE    1
#define JACK   11
#define QUEEN  12
#define KING   13
void main()
{
     int i;

     for (i=0; i<10; ++i)
          printf("\nFinal value of card: %d", deal(0));  /*1*/
}

int deal(int total)
{
     int card;

/* Deal a random card */

     card = (rand() % 13) + 1;
     printf("\nOriginal random value of card: %d", card);

/* Convert the card identifier into a face value */

     switch (card)
     {
          case JACK:
          case QUEEN:
          case KING:           /* Fall through */
               card = 10;
               break;
          case ACE:
               if ((total + 11) <= 21)
                    card = 11;
```

```
            break;
        default:
            break;
    }

/* Return the value */

    return(card);
}
```

RESULTS:

```
C:\>RANDOM8
Original random value of card: 1
Final value of card: 11
Original random value of card: 8
Final value of card: 8
Original random value of card: 8
Final value of card: 8
Original random value of card: 2
Final value of card: 2
Original random value of card: 12
Final value of card: 10
Original random value of card: 12
Final value of card: 10
Original random value of card: 8
Final value of card: 8
Original random value of card: 3
Final value of card: 3
Original random value of card: 4
Final value of card: 4
Original random value of card: 1
Final value of card: 11
```

ANALYSIS:

1. If you look through the output, you will see the value of aces (with an original card value of 1) altered to a value of 11, and queens (12) altered to a value of 10.
2. The call to function deal() on line /*1*/ now includes the argument 0, which represents a zero card total. The integer parameter *total* in deal() receives a copy of this argument value.
3. To reassign new values to aces and face cards, you must define a new variable, *card,* in function deal(). The function first assigns a random number to *card,* then the *switch* statement alters the value of *card* if it is an ace or face card.

4. The *if* statement under *case ACE:* selects a value of 11 for an ace if adding this value will not make the total exceed 21 and the player or dealer go bust. The fall-through construction substitutes a value of 10 for *JACK, QUEEN,* or *KING.*

This completes the development of function deal(). Now you can proceed to develop function check(). This function should display the card total of either player and check the total against 21 or against the other card total. Then the function must update the cash amount and display an appropriate message. This function will require several values to be passed to it—namely, the card totals, the amount of the bet, and the cash amount. An argument will also be needed to tell the function which total to compare at any given call. The new function call will look like this:

```
check(which, player_total, dealer_total, bet, cash);
```

The following example shows a definition of the proposed new function *check()* that, for now, simply displays the parameters that it receives.

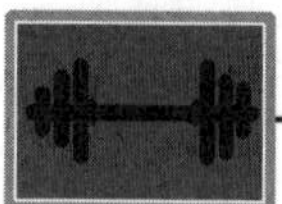

Listing 8.13 CHECK.C Check card totals

DO: Enter, compile, and run CHECK

```
#include <stdio.h>
#define PLAYER 1                    /* Check player's total       */
#define DEALER 2                    /* Check dealer's total       */
#define BOTH   3                    /* Check player versus dealer */
void main()
{
     check(PLAYER, 15, 0, 1.50, 10.00);
}

void check(int   which,             /* Which total to check */
           int   player_total,      /* Player's total       */
           int   dealer_total,      /* Dealer's total       */
           float bet,               /* Player's bet         */
           float cash)              /* Player's cash total  */
{
     printf("\nParameter which is %d", which);
     printf("\nParameter player_total is %d", player_total);
     printf("\nParameter dealer_total is %d", dealer_total);
     printf("\nParameter bet is %.2f", bet);
     printf("\nParameter cash is %.2f", cash);
}
```

RESULTS:

```
C:\>CHECK
```

```
Parameter which is 1
Parameter player_total is 15
Parameter dealer_total is 0
Parameter bet is 1.50
Parameter cash is 10.00
```

ANALYSIS:

1. The main function calls check() with five constants as arguments. The first is a symbolic constant, *PLAYER* (with a value of 1), which will eventually signal the function to check the player's total for a value of over 21. The second argument (*player_total*) is 15, and the third (*dealer_total*) is 0 because this value is not needed when the function checks only the player's total. The fourth and fifth arguments (bet and cash) are the constants 1.50 and 10.00, respectively.

2. The program assigns the values of each of the five arguments to each of the five parameters of the function definition in left-to-right order. By assigning the values to parameter variables, the function call makes a **copy** of the argument values for the function to use.

3. The printf() statements within check() verify that the function received correct copies of all five argument values by displaying the parameter values.

4. Notice that the first line of the function defines parameter data types and names in the parameter list, and notice too that the data types correspond to the argument types. That is, the parameters *which, player_total,* and *dealer_total* are all type *int* and so are the arguments *PLAYER, 15,* and *0.* Also, the parameters *bet* and *cash* are type *float,* as are the corresponding arguments *1.50* and *10.00.*

5. This example shows one way to lay out a list of parameters that is too long to fit on one line. By arranging each parameter on a separate line, you make the type definitions very visible (much like defining variables within a function), and you have an opportunity to add a comment about the purpose of each one. The compiler ignores the intervening blanks and comments.

6. The data type of function *check()* is explicitly defined as an *int* in anticipation of returning an integer value later to indicate the winner of each hand. This requirement became apparent when you inserted check() into the pseudo code of Example 8-2.

The names of the arguments don't have to be the same as the names of corresponding parameters. As a matter of fact, arguments can be expressions of one or more constants and variables, that might bear little or no resemblance to the parameter name. Sometimes it is convenient to use the same names for the corresponding arguments and parameters to help keep them straight and make a program more readable, but this is not necessary.

Using prototypes to check function types and arguments

The compiler associates parameters with calling arguments by position in the list. That is, the compiler assigns the first argument to the first parameter, the second argument to the second parameter, and so on. If you do not match up the calling arguments with their function parameters (in both number and data type), some very troublesome errors can occur. For instance, the following example shows the effect of transposing two of the constants in the function call, the arguments for parameters *dealer_total* and *bet*:

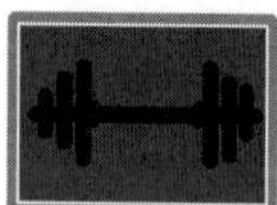

Listing 8.14 CHECK2.C Check card totals

DO:
- Transpose the third and fourth call arguments in CHECK
- Compile and run CHECK2

```
#include <stdio.h>
#define PLAYER 1                  /* Check player's total       */
#define DEALER 2                  /* Check dealer's total       */
#define BOTH   3                  /* Check player versus dealer */
void main()
{
    check(PLAYER, 15, 1.50, 0, 10.00);                      /*1*/
}

void check( int   which,          /* Which total to check */
            int   player_total,   /* Player's total       */
            int   dealer_total,   /* Dealer's total       */
            float bet,            /* Player's bet         */
            float cash)           /* Player's cash total  */
{
   printf("\nParameter which is %d", which);
   printf("\nParameter player_total is %d", player_total);
   printf("\nParameter dealer_total is %d", dealer_total);
   printf("\nParameter bet is %.2f", bet);
   printf("\nParameter cash is %.2f", cash);
}
```

RESULTS:

```
C:\>CHECK2
```

```
Parameter which is 1
Parameter player_total is 15
Parameter dealer_total is 0
Parameter bet is 0.00
Parameter cash is 10.00
```

ANALYSIS:

1. A wrong argument can often be a logic error that goes undetected by the compiler. In this case, the compiler took the first two bytes of the floating-point value, 1.50, and assigned it to the parameter *dealer_total* in function *check()*. Then the compiler converted the remaining two floating-point bytes, plus the 2-byte integer 0, to a floating-point number and assigned it to *bet*. Both of the converted values just happen to be 0.
2. The logic error has serious consequences for the outcome of the program because the player's bet has suddenly been reduced to 0 as far as function *check()* is concerned. However, the player's bet in the calling function is not affected because the function uses a **copy** of the argument.

Similar kinds of errors occur if the number of arguments does not equal the number of parameters in a function. In the next example, try leaving out the last argument and see what happens.

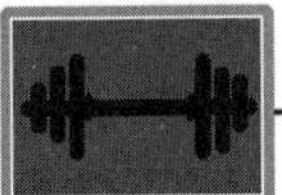

Listing 8.15 CHECK3.C Check card totals

DO: • Take out the last calling argument in CHECK
• Compile and run CHECK3

```
#include <stdio.h>
#define PLAYER 1                    /* Check player's total       */
#define DEALER 2                    /* Check dealer's total       */
#define BOTH   3                    /* Check player versus dealer */
void main()
{
    check(PLAYER, 15, 0, 1.50);                                 /*1*/
}

void check(int   which,             /* Which total to check */
           int   player_total,      /* Player's total       */
           int   dealer_total,      /* Dealer's total       */
           float bet,               /* Player's bet         */
```

```
        float cash)          /* Player's cash total   */
{
    printf("\nParameter which is %d", which);
    printf("\nParameter player_total is %d", player_total);
    printf("\nParameter dealer_total is %d", dealer_total);
    printf("\nParameter bet is %.2f", bet);
    printf("\nParameter cash is %.2f", cash);
}
```

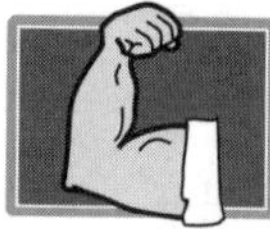

RESULTS:

```
C:\>CHECK3

Parameter which is 1
Parameter player_total is 15
Parameter dealer_total is 0
Parameter bet is 1.50
Parameter cash is 0.00
```

ANALYSIS:

1. There is one less argument than needed, yet the program compiles and runs as if nothing is wrong.

2. The function call does not assign a value to the last parameter, *cash*, so it just retains whatever value was last in its memory location, and the function has some "garbage" data.

Your compiler will make some assumptions and conversions when confronted with mismatched arguments and parameters. The conversion rules, shown in the list that follows, are somewhat complicated because two styles exist for defining functions: an old, pre-ANSI style, and the new, ANSI style.

OLD STYLE (pre-ANSI) RULES

Convert both arguments and parameters as follows:

- ☐ Promote type *char* and *short* to *int*, or to unsigned *int* if the value won't fit in an *int*.
- ☐ Promote type *float* to *double*.

After promotion, if the number and type of arguments does not match the number and type of parameters, the effect is undefined by the C specification; each compiler can handle the situation differently.

NEW STYLE (ANSI) RULES

Convert arguments to parameters as if by assignment. The number of arguments must match the number of parameters.

We have used *new style* (ANSI C-compatible) calls in previous examples by defining parameter data types in the parentheses following the function name. The *old style* (pre-ANSI C) does not recognize the declaration of parameter types within the parentheses; instead, you must define the parameters separately. Example 8-3 is a side-by-side comparison of function check() using either the new style or the old style definitions. For simplicity, we substitute a comment for the body of the function.

The *old style* definition declares data types for function parameters after the function name but before the opening curly brace. This requires repeating the parameter identifiers. ANSI C compilers will accept either form of function definition to retain compatibility with old programs. The *new style* is strongly recommended for new programs, and you should **never** mix the two styles in any program. ANSI adopted the new style definition to allow compilers to check argument types using a new form of statement called a function *prototype*.

New style (ANSI)	Old style

<pre>void check (int   which,
             int   player_total,
             int   dealer_total,
             float bet,
             float cash)
{
     /* statements */
}</pre>
	<pre>void check (which,
	             player_total,
	             dealer_total,
	             bet,
	             cash)
	int which;
	int player_total;
	int dealer_total;
	float bet;
	float cash;
	{
	     /* statements */
	}</pre>

Example 8-3 New style versus old style function definition

Prototype statements

If you are writing new programs with an ANSI C compiler (such as Power C), you do not need to experience any confusion over mismatched parameters. If you use function *prototypes* with the *new style* definition, the compiler will automatically check whether arguments match with parameters. A function prototype is basically a restatement of the first line of the function definition, ended with a semicolon (;). The prototype for function *check()* is:

```
int check(int, int, int, float, float);
```

A prototype contains a type declaration for the function itself, plus one for each parameter of the function. The names of parameters are optional, and they have been left out of the above example. This same prototype with the names included is:

```
int check (int   which,
           int   player_total,
           int   dealer_total,
           float bet,
           float cash);
```

You can choose any name you like because the compiler ignores them anyway; parameter names in a prototype serve only to clarify the purpose of the parameters. In this way, they are like comments.

A prototype is a *declaration*, which does not generate any executable code or allocate any memory. On the other hand, the full function is a *definition*, which does generate code and allocate memory. A prototype provides information about a function to the compiler so that the compiler can verify the correctness of data types in function calls. Repeat the example of transposed arguments, CHECK2, except this time include a function prototype. When you do this, you also need to enable compiler warnings (by including the /w compile option) to get an indication of erroneous calling arguments.

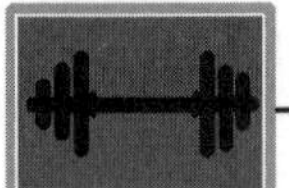

Listing 8.16 CHECK4.C Check card totals

DO:
- Add a function prototype to CHECK2
- Compile CHECK4 with the compiler warning option, /w

```
#include <stdio.h>
void check(int, int, int, float, float);                    /*1*/

#define PLAYER 1                /* Check player's total         */
#define DEALER 2                /* Check dealer's total         */
```

Old style (pre-ANSI) rules

Convert both arguments and parameters as follows:

- Promote type *char* and *short* to *int,* or to *unsigned int* if the value won't fit in an int

- Promote type *float* to *double*

After promotion, if the number and type of arguments does does not match the number and type of parameters, the effect is undefined by the C specification; each compiler can handle the situation differently.

New style (ANSI) rules

Convert arguments to parameters as if by assignment. The number of arguments must match the number of parametes.

List 8-1 Rules for converting argument values to parameters

```
#define BOTH    3                 /* Check player versus dealer */
void main()
{
     check(PLAYER, 15, 1.50, 0, 10.00);
}

void check(int    which,          /* Which total to check  */
           int    player_total,   /* Player's total        */
           int    dealer_total,   /* Dealer's total        */
           float  bet,            /* Player's bet          */
           float  cash)           /* Player's cash total   */
{
     printf("\nParameter which is %d", which);
     printf("\nParameter player_total is %d", player_total);
     printf("\nParameter dealer_total is %d", dealer_total);
     printf("\nParameter bet is %.2f", bet);
     printf("\nParameter cash is %.2f", cash);
}
```

RESULTS:

```
C:\>pc/c/e/w CHECK4
Power C - Version 2.1.3
(C) Copyright 1989-1991 by Mix Software
Compiling ...
CHECK4.C(9):    check(1    , 15, 1.50, 0, 10.00);
*********                          ^229
     229: Warning - Type conversion may cause overflow
------------------------------
  130 lines compiled
    1 Warning
Optimizing ...
   2 functions optimized in 1 file
Linking ...
CHECK4.EXE created
```

ANALYSIS:

The compiler uses information provided by the function prototype on line /*1*/ to determine what data type to expect for each calling argument. Consequently, the Power C compiler converts the floating-point constant, 1.50, to an integer before assigning it to parameter *dealer_total*. With the warning option enabled, the Power C compiler issues a warning that line 9 may produce an overflow during this conversion.

When a compiler issues a warning (as opposed to an error), it completes the processing that produces an object file; therefore, the linker can create an executable program. So, you can run CHECK4 and get the same result as CHECK2.

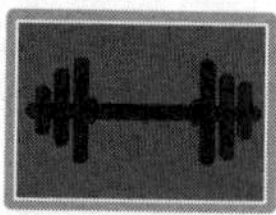

DO: Run CHECK4

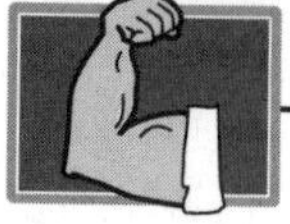

RESULTS:

```
C:\>CHECK4

Parameter which is 1
Parameter player_total is 15
Parameter dealer_total is 1
Parameter bet is 0.00
```

```
Parameter cash is 10.00
```

ANALYSIS:

If you define a function with different parameter types than in the prototype, the compiler will generate a hard error and refuse to produce either an object file or an executable program. Change the third parameter of function check() to type *float* and compile without the warning option.

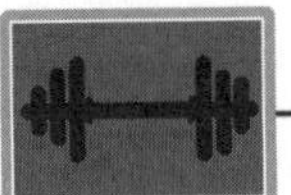

Listing 8.17 CHECK5.C Check card totals

DO:
- Change the type of parameter *dealer_total* in check()
- Compile CHECK5

```
#include <stdio.h>
void check(int, int, int, float, float);

#define PLAYER 1                /* Check player's total      */
#define DEALER 2                /* Check dealer's total      */
#define BOTH   3                /* Check player versus dealer*/
void main()
{
    check(PLAYER, 15, 1.50, 0, 10.00);
}

void check(int   which,         /* Which total to check */
           int   player_total,  /* Player's total       */
           float dealer_total,  /* Dealer's total       */
           float bet,           /* Player's bet         */
           float cash)          /* Player's cash total  */
{
    printf("\nParameter which is %d", which);
    printf("\nParameter player_total is %d", player_total);
    printf("\nParameter dealer_total is %d", dealer_total);
    printf("\nParameter bet is %.2f", bet);
    printf("\nParameter cash is %.2f", cash);
}
```

RESULTS:

```
C:\>pc/c/e CHECK5
Power C - Version 2.1.3
(C) Copyright 1989-1991 by Mix Software
```

```
Compiling ...
CHECK5.C(14):        float dealer_total, /* Dealer's total   */
*********                              ^112
    112: Parameter type does not agree with previous declaration
-----------------------------------------------------------------
 130 lines compiled
   1 compile error
```

ANALYSIS:

The compiler signals an unrecoverable error on line 14, where you declared *dealer_total* to be type *float* rather than *int* as expected by the prototype.

Passing a wrong argument type to a function (as in the CHECK4 program) is a lesser transgression than defining a wrong parameter (as in the CHECK5 program). A wrong argument results in just a compile warning because the program has a chance to operate correctly if the data will fit into the function parameter; for example, an *int* argument value will fit into a parameter of type *long*. C compilers trust you to pay attention to the warnings. They also trust that you want to go ahead with the operation if you ignore the warnings.

If you get in the habit of following these two easy rules, you will eliminate most of the errors that can occur with function arguments.

1. Make calling arguments match the expected parameters (use casting if necessary).

2. Declare function prototypes.

Placement of function prototypes

You should declare prototypes very early in a program so the compiler can know the types and number of arguments to expect for each function call encountered. The prototype in the previous example appears just after the preprocessor *#include* statement, and many programmers prefer this location. Another, very desirable place for prototypes is a *header file*, which you can include in your programs. A header file is a text file, usually with an extension of ".h", that you can bring into your program with the preprocessor *#include* statement. For instance, you could put one or more prototypes into a header file called "proto.h" with the same editor that you use to write programs, then insert them into your program with the statement:

```
#include <proto.h>
```

This technique is most useful for prototypes of utility or library functions that appear repeatedly in many different programs. The *#include* saves you the bother of repeating the prototypes, and it reduces the amount of source code in each file. The file stdio.h that you have been using with each program example is a header file that serves this very purpose. This file contains prototypes of the standard I/O library functions—prototypes for functions such as gets(), puts(), scanf(), and printf(). Example 8-4 is a partial extract from the stdio.h file supplied with your Power C compiler (we added the comments).

```
char    *gets(char *buffer);          /* gets() prototype */
void     perror(char *string);
int      prinf(char *format, ...);   /* prinf() prototype */
int      putc(int c, FILE  *fp);
int      puts(char *string);          /* puts() prototype */
int      remove(char *filename);
int      rename(char *oldname, char *newname);
void     rewind(FILE  *fp);
int      scanf(char *format, ...);   /* scanf() prototype */
```

The prototype for puts() declares that this function will return an integer and that it will expect a single character pointer (a string) as an argument. The asterisk (*) following keyword *char* indicates a pointer; you will learn more about pointers in Chapter 10. The optional name "string" indicates the use of the argument. The prototype for function printf() also declares an integer return value (which will be the number of characters written) and a character pointer argument (which is the expected format string). The ellipsis (...) in the printf() prototype is a special symbol that declares an indefinite number of parameters of unspecified type; this corresponds to the list of values to be displayed. You might find it interesting to browse through stdio.h with your editor; you will see prototypes for a rich assortment of I/O functions that you have not yet learned.

The next example completes function check() by replacing the temporary printf() statements with statements that carry out the specified purpose of this function, which is to look at card totals and report on the outcome of the game of "21".

```
char *gets (char *buffer);          /* gets() prototype */
void  perror(char *string);
int   printf(char *format, ...); /* printf() prototype */
int   putc(int c, FILE *fp);
int   puts(char *string);           /* puts() protype */
int   remove(char *filename);
int   rename(char *oldname, char *newname);
void  rewind (FILE *fp);
int   scanf(char *format, ...);  /* scanf() prototype */
```

Example 8-4 Part of header file stdio.h

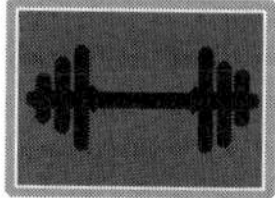

Listing 8.18 CHECK6.C Check card totals

DO:
- Enter function CHECK6 (you will use it later)
- Examine function CHECK6 while reading the explanations

```
#define PLAYER 1
#define DEALER 2
#define BOTH   3
#define OK     0
#define BUST   1
int check(int   which,          /* Which total to check */
          int   player_total,   /* Player's total       */
          int   dealer_total,   /* Dealer's total       */
          float bet,            /* Player's bet         */
          float *cash)          /* Player's cash total  */
{
    switch (which)
    {
        case PLAYER:
            printf("\nYour card total is %d", player_total);
            if (player_total > 21)
            {
                printf("--you are bust!");
                *cash -= bet;
                return(BUST);
            }
            break;

        case DEALER:
            printf("\nDealer's card total is %d",
                dealer_total);
            if (dealer_total > 21)
            {
                printf("--you win!");
                *cash += bet;
                return(BUST);
            }
            break;

        case BOTH:
            if (player_total > dealer_total)
            {
                printf("--you win!");
                *cash += bet;
            }
            else
            {
                printf("--you lose!");
                *cash -= bet;
            }
            break;
```

```
        default:
             printf("\nBad argument value (which=%d)", which);
             break;
    }
    return(OK);
}
```

ANALYSIS:

1. This version of check() includes one small but very important change to parameter *cash*. The function must change the cash amount by the amount of the bet, so it must be able to alter the value of *cash* in the calling function. To do this, the function must declare *cash* to be a pointer by preceding it with an asterisk (*), and it must also precede *cash* with an asterisk whenever a statement assigns it a value. This is how functions use pointers to directly access data in the calling function; Chapter 10 will cover pointers more thoroughly.
2. The *switch* statement uses the parameter *which* to select whether to compare the player's or the dealer's card total against 21, or whether to compare the totals with each other to discover a winner. The *switch* statement uses the symbolic constants *PLAYER, DEALER,* and *BOTH* in this selection; the main program will also use them in the first calling argument to check(). You can use symbolic constants in any of the functions in a source file; they are available from the point where they are defined down to the end of the file.
3. The operations for case *PLAYER* and *DEALER* are similar: First the function displays the card total. If the total is over 21, it displays an additional message informing you that either "you are bust" or "you win," then the function updates the cash total by the amount of the bet and returns a value of *BUST* (1) to tell the main function that the hand is over. If the card total is not over 21, the function encounters a *break* statement that transfers control to the end of the *switch,* and it returns a value of *OK* (0).
4. If the case is *BOTH,* then an *if* statement compares the player's card total, the dealer's total and displays either "you win" or "you lose," and updates the cash total. A *break* after the *if* ends the *switch* statement and the function returns *OK.*
5. The *switch* statement will execute the *default* case only if the calling function passes a bad value to parameter *which,* so this is an error detector.

This completes the development of function check(). Now for the payoff—you can incorporate both deal() and check() into the card playing program and have a respectable simulation of the game of "21". Use the CARDS7 program you developed in Chapter 7 as the basis, add functions deal() from RANDOM8 and check() from CHECK6, then make a few more changes to create CARDS8.

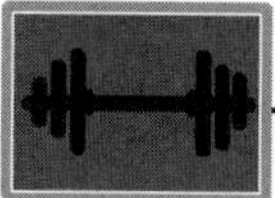

Listing 8.19 CARDS8.C '21' program

DO:
- Add functions deal() and check() to CARDS7
- Compile and run CARDS8
- Play a couple of hands of 21

```
#include <stdio.h>
int deal(int);
int check(int, int, int, float, float *);

/* Card identifiers */

#define ACE     1
#define JACK   11
#define QUEEN  12
#define KING   13

/* Player identifiers */

#define PLAYER 1
#define DEALER 2
#define BOTH   3

/* Check function return codes */

#define OK     0
#define BUST   1

void main()
{
     int  i;                    /* Loop counter          */
     int  player_total;         /* Running total of cards */
     int  dealer_total;         /* Total of dealer's cards */
     float cash;                /* Betting cash          */
     float bet;                 /* Your bet              */
     char  answer;              /* Prompt answer         */

     printf("\nDEAL CARDS FOR THE GAME OF 21\n");

/* Enter a cash total */

     printf("\nEnter your total cash: ");
```

```
    scanf("%f", &cash);

/* Place a bet */

    do
    {
          printf("\nPlace your bet: ");
          scanf("%f", &bet);
    } while (bet > cash);
    getchar();                /* Clear the keyboard */

    while ((bet > 0.) && (cash > 0.))
    {

/* Deal 2 cards to each player */

          player_total = 0;
          dealer_total = 0;
          for (i=0; i<2; ++i)
          {
                player_total += deal(player_total);
                dealer_total += deal(dealer_total);
          }

/* Check card totals */

          if (check(PLAYER, player_total, 0, bet, &cash) == BUST)
               continue;    /* while */
          if (check(DEALER, 0, dealer_total, bet, &cash) == BUST)
               continue;    /* while */
          printf("\n\n");

/* Let the player take "hits" */

          while (player_total <= 21)
          {
               printf("Your card total is %d,"
                       "do you want a hit? (Y/N)", player_total);
               answer = getchar();
               getchar();   /* Clear the keyboard */
               if (answer != 'Y')
                    break;  /* while */
               else
                    player_total += deal(player_total);
          }

/* Hit the dealer if player's total is ok */

          if (check(PLAYER, player_total, 0, bet, &cash) == OK)
          {
               while (dealer_total < 17)
                   dealer_total += deal(dealer_total);
```

```
/* Determine the winner */

                if (check(DEALER, 0, dealer_total, bet, &cash)
                                                      == OK)
                     check(BOTH, player_total, dealer_total,
                            bet, &cash);
          }

          printf("\n\nYour cash is now $%.2f", cash);

          if (cash < .01)
               printf("\nSorry, you are broke!");
          else
          {
               do
               {
                   printf("\nPlace your bet: ");
                   scanf("%f", &bet);
               } while (bet > cash);
               getchar();           /* Clear the keyboard */
               printf("\n");
          }
     }
}

int deal(int total)
{
     int card;

/* Deal a random card */

     card = (rand() % 13) + 1;

/* Convert the card identifier into a face value */

     switch (card)
     {
          case JACK:
          case QUEEN:
          case KING:           /* Fall through */
               card = 10;
               break;
          case ACE:
               if ((total + 11) <= 21)
                      card = 11;
               break;
          default:
               break;
     }

/* Return the value */
```

```
    return(card);
}

int check(int    which,           /* Which total to check */
          int    player_total,    /* Player's total       */
          int    dealer_total,    /* Dealer's total       */
          float  bet,             /* Player's bet         */
          float  *cash)           /* Player's cash total  */
{
    switch (which)
    {
      case PLAYER:
          printf("\nYour card total is %d", player_total);
          if (player_total > 21)
          {
              printf("--you are bust!");
              *cash -= bet;
              return(BUST);
          }
          break;

      case DEALER:
          printf("\nDealer's card total is %d",
               dealer_total);
          if (dealer_total > 21)
          {
               printf("--you win!");
               *cash += bet;
               return(BUST);
          }
          break;

      case BOTH:
          if (player_total > dealer_total)
          {
              printf("--you win!");
              *cash += bet;
          }
          else
          {
              printf("--you lose!");
              *cash -= bet;
          }
          break;

      default:
          printf("\nBad argument value (which=%d)", which);
          break;
    }
    return(OK);
}
```

RESULTS:

```
DEAL CARDS FOR THE GAME OF 21

Enter your total cash: 100

Place your bet: 25

Your card total is 19
Dealer's card total is 10

Your card total is 19, do you want a hit? (Y/N)N

Your card total is 19
Dealer's card total is 20--you lose!

Your cash is now $75.00
Place your bet: 25

Your card total is 13
Dealer's card total is 12

Your card total is 13, do you want a hit? (Y/N)Y
Your card total is 14, do you want a hit? (Y/N)Y

Your card total is 23--you are bust!

Your cash is now $50.00
Place your bet: 25

Your card total is 6
Dealer's card total is 18

Your card total is 6, do you want a hit? (Y/N)Y
Your card total is 9, do you want a hit? (Y/N)Y
Your card total is 19, do you want a hit? (Y/N)Y

Your card total is 25--you are bust!

Your cash is now $25.00
Place your bet: 0
```

ANALYSIS:

1. The program starts out by declaring prototypes for the functions deal() and check() just after the *#include* directive.

2. The program then defines symbolic constants before the main function so that they are available for use in any of the functions.

3. By adding the function deal(), you are able to eliminate some lines of code and some variables from the main program. You no longer have to enter cards; they are obtained by calling deal(), so the variable *hit* can be eliminated. The dealer can also get cards from the function deal(), so you can get rid of the phoney way of dealing cards to the dealer and the variable *last_hit* along with it. The new variable *i* will count up to two while dealing cards to both players, and the new variable *answer* will accept your reply to a prompt as to whether you want to accept a hit.

4. You place an initial bet and enter the main *while* loop just as before, then you enter a new *for* loop that counts with *i* and calls deal() to realistically deal two cards to each player. The *switch* statement that previously reassigned values for aces and face cards in main() is now out of the way in function deal().

5. Following the initial deal, you use the new function check() to see if either player has a total that exceeds 21. If so, function check() displays an appropriate message and updates *cash*, then a *continue* statement in main() skips to the end of the *while* loop to begin another hand.

6. If both card totals are under 22, you are ready to take "hits." You install the *while* loop in favor of the old *do while* because you must now check for an "over 21" card total at the beginning of the loop before asking if the player wants a hit. Previously, the *do while* loop started before the player had any cards, so you needed the check at the end.

7. The player can take "hits" by choosing to accept a random card from the new function rather than entering his own card. The input function getchar() reads a single-character reply to the prompt, "Do you want a hit?" If the reply is not an uppercase Y, the *break* statement controlled by the following *if* causes the *while* loop to end; otherwise, the program calls deal() and accumulates hits in *player_total*. An extra getchar() reads the newline character from the keyboard buffer so that it is not there for the next call to getchar(). After each input call (scanf() or getchar()), an extra getchar() clears the keyboard by reading the newline character created each time you press ENTER. You will see this in three places in the program next to the comment /* Clear the keyboard */.

8. After the player takes hits, the program calls check() to see if the player's total exceeds 21. If the function returns the value *OK*, then

the dealer can accept hits. A *while* loop calls deal() and accumulates cards as long as the *dealer_total* is less than 17.

9. The program calls check() to see if the dealer went over 21 while taking hits. If the dealer did not go bust, a final call to check(), with the first argument set to *BOTH*, determines the winner of the hand.

By including functions in the CARDS program, you have enhanced the capability of the program, and at the same time you have made it more readable and easier to maintain. The program is modular; it is composed of a group of smaller functions that hold up well under pressure for change and expansion. These characteristics become even more important when you write larger, more complex programs.

LIBRARIES

A *library* is a file containing previously compiled object modules that you can link with a program. Typically, you will place functions into a library if you use them repeatedly, if they are "tools" or "utilities," or if they constitute the lower level calls of a particular application. Some examples of "tools" are functions that handle date conversions, file I/O, or keyboard control. Once such functions are complete, you can get them out of the way by placing them in a library, and you can easily link them into your programs by referencing the single library name during the link step.

Separate object modules

All of the functions used by a program do not have to be in the same file (either source file or object file). For instance, you could place the three functions for program CARDS8 (main(), deal(), and check()) in three separate source files, then compile them separately and link them together into one final program. If the three source files were CARDS.C, DEAL.C, and CHECK.C, then you would compile each source file with the commands:

```
C:\>pc/c CARDS
C:\>pc/c DEAL
C:\>pc/c CHECK
```

As a result, the compiler creates three object files, CARDS.MIX, DEAL.MIX, and CHECK.MIX. You can then link the files to form the executable file CARDS.EXE with the command:

```
C:\>pcl CARDS, DEAL, CHECK
```

If these object modules are useful with other programs, you can link them without having to write new source code and without repeating the compile steps. For instance, if you were also creating a program to play gin rummy, you could link the object file DEAL.MIX and reuse the function deal() without any additional effort.

Creating a library with the MIX utility

As an alternative, you could place the object files DEAL.MIX and CHECK.MIX in a library called CARDSLIB.MIX and create the final executable file with the following command:

```
C:\>pcl CARDS; CARDSLIB
```

The semicolon instructs the Power C linker to treat CARDSLIB as a library and search for only the functions needed. If you use a comma in place of the semicolon, the linker will include **all** of the object modules in your program whether they are needed or not.

Libraries are not a part of the C language specification; the methods for building and using them are different from one linker and operating system to the next. You normally use a library utility supplied with your compiler to build a library—the Power C utility is the program MERGE.EXE. You build a library by entering a command to run MERGE, followed by the name of a library file and the names of one or more object files:

```
merge <library> <object1>, <object2> ...
```

You separate the library name from the first object name with a space, and separate the object names from each other with commas (,). For example, you can build a library named CARDSLIB.MIX containing the object modules for the functions deal() and check() as follows:

```
merge CARDSLIB DEAL, CHECK
```

Notice that you don't need to specify the .MIX file extensions; MERGE automatically attaches this extension if you leave it off. To link the functions deal() and check() with a program, all you need to do is list CARDSLIB in the link command.

Standard Power C libraries

Power C handles the standard C libraries (which contain important functions like printf() and scanf()) differently from your libraries. These library files have names beginning with PC (PCLIB.MIX, PCAUTO.MIX, etc.), and you do not need to list them in the link command. The Power C linker automatically searches for them and links the necessary object modules from them when needed.

RECURSION

C allows a function to call itself. The process of a function repeatedly calling itself is called recursion. You will probably not often use recursion, but sometimes it is very useful and it is always very interesting. You begin recursion by calling a function within itself; the following function is recursive:

```
again()
{
    again();
}
```

This function will call itself endlessly and will not stop until your computer runs out of memory (each call uses some memory called *stack space*). As with an avalanche, an important part of recursion is getting it to stop. You must do this with a conditional statement that causes the function to return at some point. The above example can be made to stop with a conditional test similar to that shown below.

```
again()
{
      if (finished)
               return;
      else
               again();
}
```

Here is a puzzler: How can you repeat an operation without using a looping control statement (*for*, *while*, or *do while*) and without using a *goto* statement? You could use the unthinkable approach of repeating source lines the required number of times, or you could use a recursive function. The following program begins with any character that you enter and uses a recursive function to get the next character in the alphabet until it reaches the character Z.

Listing 8.20 RECURSE.C A recursive function

DO: Enter and compile RECURSE

```
#include <stdio.h>
unsigned char nextchar(unsigned char);

void main()
{
          unsigned char start;

          printf("Enter a starting character: ");
          start = getchar();
          printf("\nThe final character is %c", nextchar(start));
}

unsigned char nextchar(unsigned char x)
{
          printf("\nCalling parameter is %c", x);
          if (++x != 'Z')
               x = nextchar(x);
          printf("\nReturned value is %c", x);
          return(x);
}
```

ANALYSIS:

1. The main function prompts for, and reads, a starting character from the keyboard. Then it calls the recursive function from within a printf() statement that displays the final, returned character value.
2. The first print() statement within function *nextchar()* displays the value of the calling parameter as received by the function, and the

other printf() displays the value about to be returned from the function. These printf() statements help clarify the sequence of calls while the program executes.

3. The heart of this function is the *if* statement that causes and ends recursion:

```
if (++x != 'Z')
        x = nextchar(x);
```

The expression prefix increments the value of parameter *x*, then compares it with the constant 'Z'. If *x* is not equal to 'Z,' the statement calls nextchar() again. None of the function calls can be completed (by returning) until the value of 'Z' occurs, which stops the recursive calls.

Figure 8-8 is a diagram of the RECURSE program in execution.

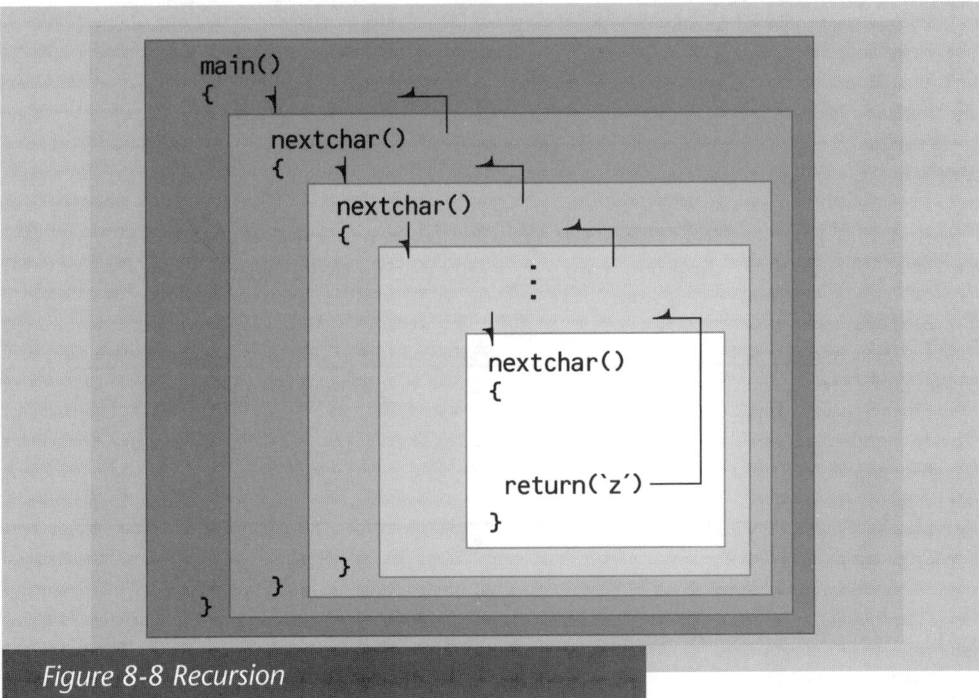

Figure 8-8 Recursion

The shrinking boxes represent successive calls of the recursive function. The innermost box is reached when the value of parameter *x* is 'Z'. At this point, the program stops repeated calls and begins to unwind back through each instance of the function. The unwinding consists of the sequence of returns, which occur in rapid succession. From there, the value 'Z' is assigned to parameter *x* each time a *return* occurs, all the way back to the original call to nextchar() in the main function.

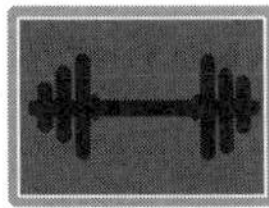

DO: Run RECURSE and enter (W)

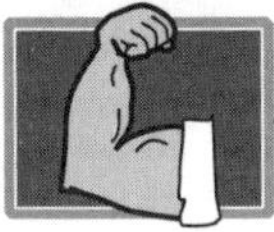

RESULT:

```
C:\>RECURSE
Enter a starting character: W

Calling parameter is W
Calling parameter is X
Calling parameter is Y
Returned value is Z
Returned value is Z
Returned value is Z
The final character is Z
```

ANALYSIS:

The first half of the display lines (W, X, and Y) occurs while the recursive calls are happening and the last half (the four Zs) occurs during the unwinding phase.

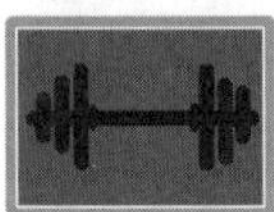

DO: Run RECURSE and enter (a), then stop the program with (CTRL-BREAK)

RESULTS:

```
C:\>RECURSE
Enter a starting character: a

Calling parameter is a
Calling parameter is b
Calling parameter is c
Calling parameter is d
Calling parameter is e
Calling parameter is f
Calling parameter is g
Calling parameter is h
Calling parameter is i
Calling parameter is j
```

```
Calling parameter is k
Calling parameter is l
Calling parameter is m
Calling parameter is n
Calling parameter is o
Calling parameter is p
Calling parameter is q
Calling parameter is r
Calling parameter is s
Calling parameter is t
Calling parameter is u
Calling parameter is v
Calling parameter is w
Calling parameter is x
Calling parameter is y
Calling parameter is z
Calling parameter is {
Calling parameter is |
Calling parameter is }
Calling parameter is ~
Calling parameter is --
Calling par^C
```

ANALYSIS:

1. The program does not stop on its own; somehow the *if* expression fails to become false to stop the recursive calls.

2. If you let the program run, you will see that the entire sequence of ASCII codes is displayed over and over again. Notice that the computer beep, or bell, sounds each time ASCII code 7 is written to the display. Don't let it run too long though, or the program will run out of memory and possibly lock up your system and you will have to reboot.

3. The starting character, 'a', has an ASCII value (97) that is **higher** than the value of 'Z' (90). Therefore, the value of *x* must count up to the maximum value of an unsigned character (255), then overflow to zero and begin counting back up to 90. However, *x* is no longer an *unsigned char* because it has been automatically converted to an *int* by the C *integral promotion* rule. The integral promotion rule states that "If type *char* or *short* is used in an expression, it is converted to type *int.*" The expression ++x is sufficient to cause *x* to be promoted to *unsigned int*; therefore, its maximum value is 65535, not 255. This is why the value of *x* does not overflow and count back up to 90 immediately—it must count up to 65535 before overflowing. The printf() conversion specifier (%c) displays only the first eight bits of *x*, so it

only **looks** like it equals 'Z' on its way to 65535. Figure 8-9 illustrates the circle of values for an *unsigned int* and shows the distance the program must travel from the starting point at 97 (a) to overflow at 0 and count back up to 90 (Z).

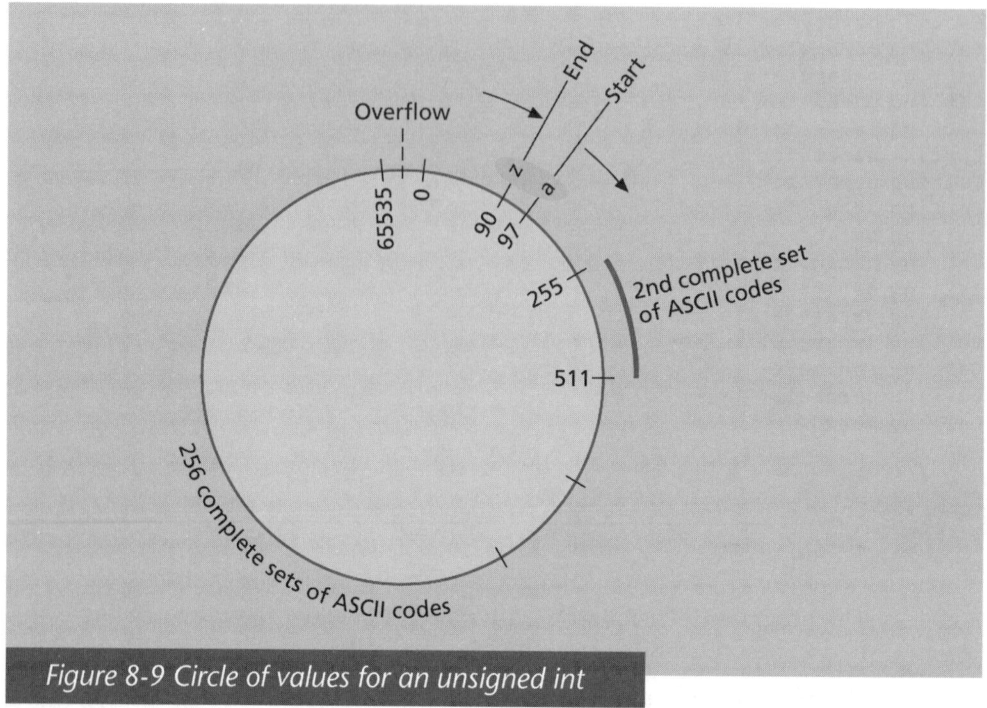

Figure 8-9 Circle of values for an unsigned int

You can correct the problem of the repeating alphabet by casting *x* to be type *unsigned char* as it is incremented.

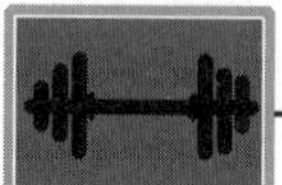

Listing 8.21 RECURSE2.C A recursive function

DO:
- Add a cast operator to RECURSE
- Compile and run RECURSE2, then enter (a)

```
#include <stdio.h>
unsigned char nextchar(unsigned char);

main()
{
     unsigned char start;
```

```
    printf("Enter a starting character: ");
    start = getchar();
    printf("\nThe final character is %c", nextchar(start));
}

unsigned char nextchar(unsigned char x)
{
    printf("\nCalling parameter is %c", x);
    if ((unsigned char)++x != 'Z')                         /*1*/
        x = nextchar(x);
    printf("\nReturned value is %c", x);
    return(x);
}
```

RESULTS:

```
C:\>RECURSE2

Calling parameter is a
Calling parameter is b
Calling parameter is c
.
.
.
Calling parameter is x
Calling parameter is y
Calling parameter is z
Calling parameter is {
.
.
.
Calling parameter is ?
Calling parameter is @
Calling parameter is A
Calling parameter is B
Calling parameter is C
.
.
.
Calling parameter is X
Calling parameter is Y
Returned value is Z
Returned value is Z
Returned value is Z
.
.
.
The final character is Z
```

ANALYSIS:

The *unsigned char* cast on line /*1*/ demotes variable *x* to an 8-bit integer with a maximum value of 255. Therefore, *x* quickly becomes equal to Z, then the expression goes false and stops the recursive calls.

Figure 8-10 shows the smaller circle of values for an *unsigned char* value that is being incremented by this program.

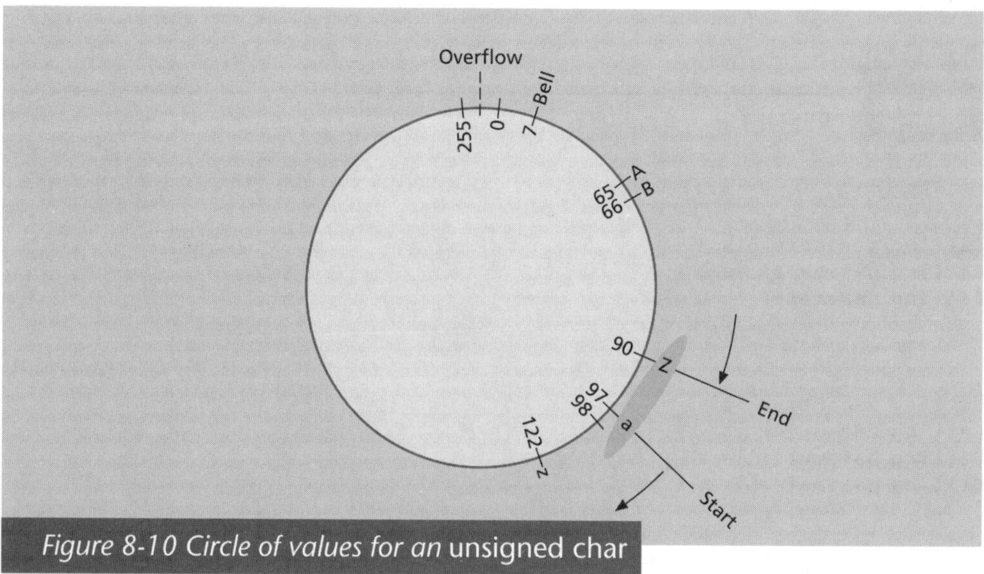

Figure 8-10 Circle of values for an unsigned char

EFFICIENCY OF FUNCTIONS

Functions offer many benefits, but they suffer from one disadvantage: They are slower than in-line code. Whenever your program calls a function, it takes a certain amount of overhead, or time, to pass argument values to the function, to transfer control to the function, to return a value, and to transfer back to the calling function. The compiler generates the extra code required to handle all this overhead, so all of these operations are invisible to you. Usually, the extra memory space required for function calls is not significant, but occasionally, the extra time can become important. If you are working on a program that must execute fast, you should carefully choose when and where to use functions. You should first identify sections of your program that are time critical and concentrate on them. For instance, functions that handle data coming from the keyboard are not time critical—the computer can easily keep up with keyboard activity, so you should feel free to use functions there. However, writing graphic data to the screen can be time critical because large amounts of data must be moved to the screen as fast as possible, so you should carefully design functions involved with this kind of operation. In Chapter 4 you used a technique called *benchmarking* to measure the difference in performance between integer arithmetic and floating-point arithmetic. Benchmarking is just as effective in measuring the relative performance of function calls versus in-line code. You can do a benchmark comparison between in-line code that performs some simple counting and a function call that does the same thing with the next two programs.

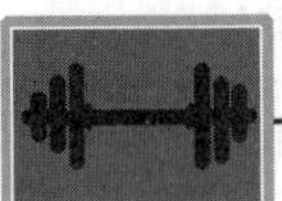

Listing 8.22 BENCHMK3.C Function call benchmark

DO:
- Enter and compile BENCHMK3
- Run BENCHMK3 and measure the time from start to end

```
#include <stdio.h>
main()
{
     long count = 0L;

     while ((count = ++count) < 1000000L)
        ;
     printf("\n%ld", count);
}
```

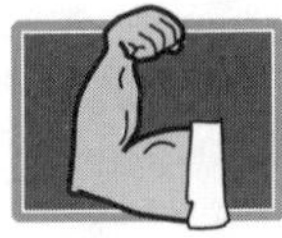

RESULT:

```
C:\>BENCHMK3
(measure the run time)
1000000
```

ANALYSIS:

1. You must define the variable *count* to be type *long* to hold a count of one million. The increment operator (++) counts very fast, and you want enough time to elapse to make it convenient to measure.
2. The *while* uses a null statement (;) to do nothing while the counting occurs within the control expression. The assignment *count* = ++*count* seems unnecessary (wouldn't just ++*count* do?), but a similar assignment will be needed when you introduce a function to do the same thing. The assignment is there to make it a fair race.

3. You should use a watch or count the seconds between the time that you press ENTER after the run command and the time when the program displays the final count on the screen.
4. Using a 20MHz 386 IBM PC system, we measured approximately 9 seconds as the run time for this program.

Now modify the program to use a function to do the same thing, then time the operation.

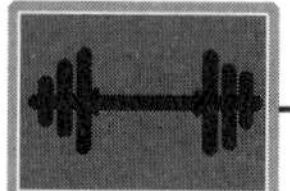

Listing 8.23 BENCHMK4.C Function call benchmark

DO:
- Modify BENCHMK3 to use a function and compile BENCHMK4
- Run BENCHMK4 and measure the time from start to end

```
#include <stdio.h>
long increment(long);                                          /*1*/

main()
{
     long count = 0L;

     while ((count = increment(count)) < 1000000L)             /*2*/
             ;
     printf("\n%ld", count);
}

long increment(long x)                                         /*3*/
{                                                              /*4*/
     return(++x);                                              /*5*/
}                                                              /*6*/
```

RESULT:

```
C:\>BENCHMK3
(measure the run time)
1000000
```

ANALYSIS:

1. Line /*1*/ is a prototype for the counting function, which expects an argument of type *long* and returns a *long* value.

2. The *while* statement is the same as in the previous program except that the function *increment()* takes the place of the increment operator (++).

3. The function (lines /*3–6*/) has only one statement that increments the value of the parameter passed to the function, then it returns that value. Notice that the parameter has a different name (*x*) than the argument (*count*) in the calling statement.

4. It took approximately 14 seconds for this version of the counting program to execute. From this benchmark, you could conclude that a function call with one parameter and a return value adds over 50% to the time that it takes to do an assignment and a relational compare.

Your decision whether to use a function should be based on the time required for a function call as a percentage of the total operational time. If the overhead is a very small percentage, then the function imposes no real penalty. In the above benchmark, the percentage is high (> 50%), and you should not use the function if optimum speed is important.

An interesting situation arises if you use a postfix increment instead of a prefix increment in this example. What do you think the effect will be if you move the increment operator in the *return* statement behind variable *x* instead of in front? Remember, the rule for a postfix operator is to use the value, then increment.

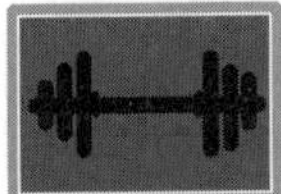

Listing 8.24 BENCHMK5.C Function call benchmark

DO:
- Modify BENCHMK4 to use postfix incrementing
- Compile and run BENCHMK5

```
#include <stdio.h>
long increment(long);

main()
{
      long count = 0L;

      while ((count = increment(count)) < 1000000L)
            ;
      printf("\n%ld", count);
}

      long increment(long x)
{
            printf("\n%ld", x);                              /*1*/
            return(x++);                                     /*2*/
}
```

RESULT:

```
C:\>BENCHMK5

0
0
0
0
.
.
.
<Ctrl-Break>
```

ANALYSIS:

1. The printf() statement on line /*1*/ displays what is happening to parameter *x* within the function.
2. The program passes a **copy** of the value of *count* (initially zero) into the function, and the printf() statement displays it. Then function increment() returns the value, and the main function assigns it back to variable *count*. Only then does the return statement increment the value of *x* (a **copy** of *count*). Therefore, the value of *count* in the main function never changes, and the program remains in an infinite loop.

Functions are perhaps the most central element in C. The focus of your thinking while designing a C program should be on functions—how many functions to write, which operations to isolate into functions, and how to pass data into and out of functions. The structure and performance of your programs depends heavily on your decisions about functions.

CHAPTER 9
ARRAYS

Most of the time, C programs receive data in large quantities. Whether the data are insurance estimates from a field office, temperature readings from a weather balloon, or player statistics for a baseball team, it often amounts to a lot of information that is organized in some sort of tabular fashion. How are you supposed to deal with such data? You cannot declare a separate variable for every piece of information—that could require thousands of declarations. What you **can** do is declare *arrays*, which allow you to define large amounts of memory storage at one time. In this chapter, you will learn how to declare arrays, how to initialize arrays, and how to access data in arrays. You will pass array data into and out of functions, and use a pointer to modify array values in another function. You will also use arrays to hold character strings.

DECLARING ARRAYS

You should use arrays when you need to store and access a number of associated data values of the same type. You can think of an array as many variables, all of the same data type, that can be accessed under the same name. An array definition consists of a data type, an identifier, and square brackets that hold the array size:

```
array_type array_name[array_size]
```

The following statement defines an array of integers called *population* that you could use to hold census data for five cities.

```
int population[5];
```

Each member of the array, called an *element*, is a variable of the same data type as the array, and there are five elements in the array *population*. When the compiler allocates storage for an array in memory, it places the elements of the array right next to each other so that the entire array is one contiguous block of storage. Figure 9-1 shows the layout of the array *population*.

You use only integers to specify the size of an array, not floating-point numbers. You can use constants, symbolic constants, or constant expressions to declare the size of an array, but they must result in an integer value. The first program example for Chapter 9 shows several ways to declare the size of an array, including one way that is not valid.

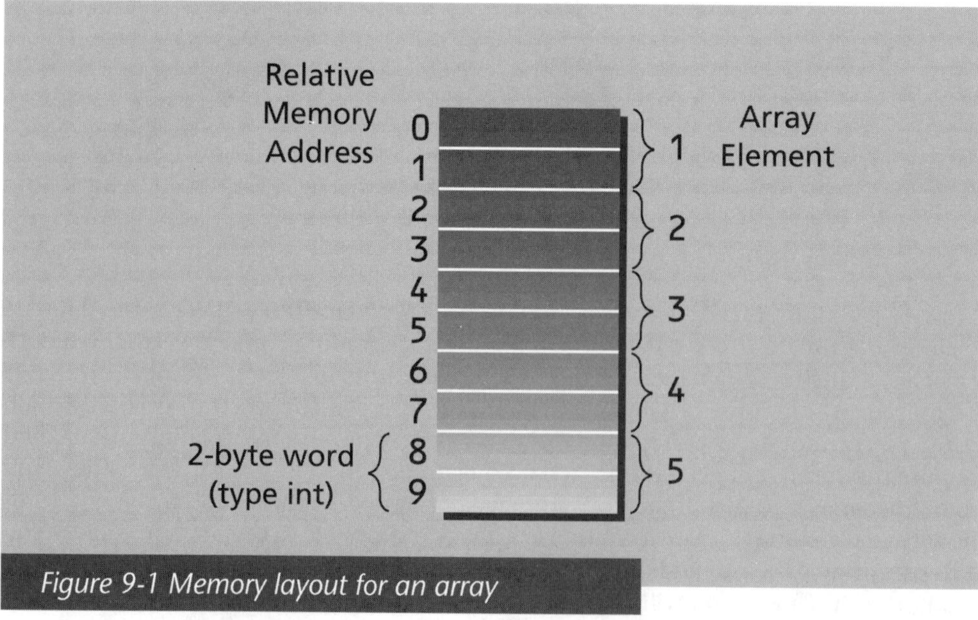

Figure 9-1 Memory layout for an array

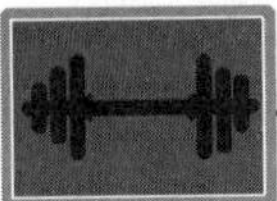

Listing 9.1 ARRAY.C Array definitions

DO: Enter and compile ARRAY

```
#include <stdio.h>
#define TEN 10
void main()
{
   int    array[10];         /* Integer constant is ok        */
   char   array2[TEN];       /* Integer symbolic constant ok */
   double array3[4 * TEN];   /* Constant expression is ok    */
   float  array4[10L];       /* Long integer constant is ok  */
   int    array5[15.5];      /* Floating-point size not ok   */
}
```

RESULT:

```
C:\>pc/c ARRAY.C
Power C - Version 2.1.3
(C) Copyright 1989-1991 by Mix Software
Compiling ...
ARRAY.C(11):          int array6[15.5];          /* Floating-point size
not ok   */
***********                        ^187
     187: Array subscript must be int
------------------------------------------------------------------
  126 lines compiled
    1 Compile error
```

ANALYSIS:

1. The first array definition allocates storage for ten integer elements (20 bytes for Power C on an IBM PC).
2. The second array (*array2*) can hold 10 bytes of character data.
3. An integer constant expression determines the size of *array3*, which is type *double*. The compiler will evaluate the expression and use the result (40) to set the number of elements.
4. There is no connection between the declared type of an array and the type of integer used to declare its size. The program declares *array5* to be type *float*, while a *long* integer declares its size.

5. A floating-point number declares the number of elements for the sixth array (*array6*). This is not legal, so the compiler generates an error; it makes no sense to declare a fractional part of an array element.

ARRAY INDEXING

You refer to elements in arrays by placing an integer *index* between the square brackets following the array name. For instance, *population[2]* refers to the third element in the array *population*. Why does an index of 2 refer to the third element rather than the second? Because in C array indexing always starts with 0, this is called *zero-based* indexing. Some programming languages, like FORTRAN, use *one-based* indexing that follows the convention of starting with 1 to identify the first array element. The zero-based indexes used in C number elements in an array beginning with 0 for the first element and count up for subsequent elements. Thus, an index of 0 refers to the first element in an array, an index of 1 refers to the second element, and so on. Therefore, the index of the last element of an array of size x is x-1. Indexes for the array *population* are shown in Figure 9-2.

The next program assigns a value to an array element and displays the value.

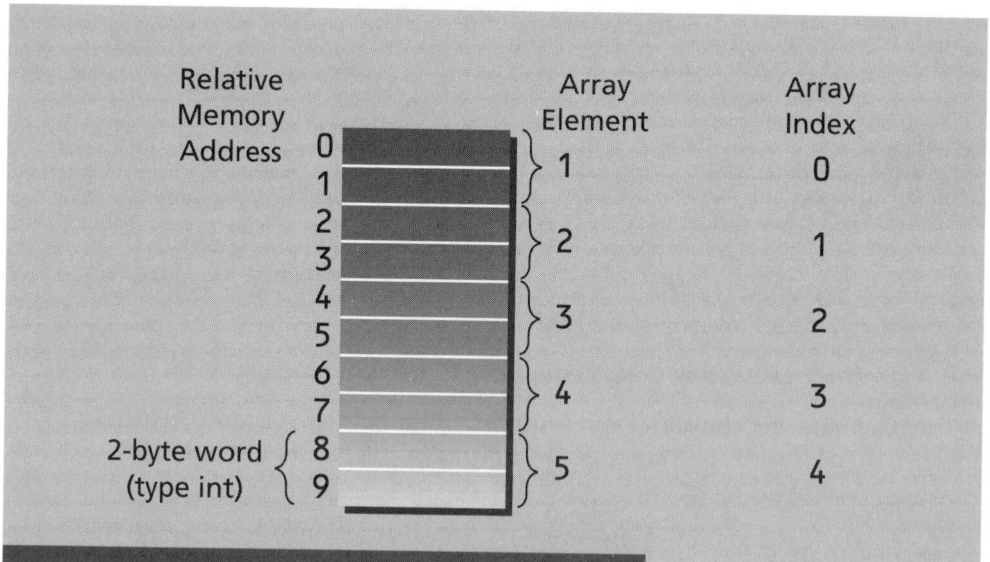

Figure 9-2 Array indexes

Listing 9.2 ARRAY2.C Deck of cards

DO: Enter, compile, and run ARRAY2

```
#include <stdio.h>
void main()
{
   int deck[52];

   deck[0] = 100;
   printf("\nThe first element of deck is %d", deck[0]);
}
```

RESULT:

```
C:\>ARRAY2.C

The first element of deck is 100
```

ANALYSIS:

1. The program defines an array named *deck* that can store 52 integer values. The total memory required for this array is 104 bytes because each integer element occupies 2 bytes (for Power C).
2. The assignment statement assigns a value of 100 to the first element of the array. The statement references the first element with an index value of 0.
3. The printf() statement displays the value of the first element of the array. Notice that you use array elements in a program the same way you use single variables.

Looping control statements are particularly suitable for dealing with data in arrays. You can initialize the entire array by adding a *for* loop in ARRAY3.

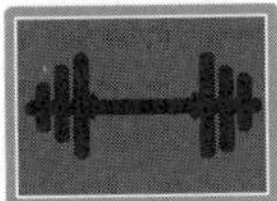

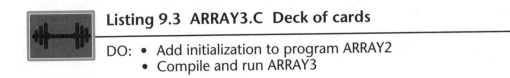

Listing 9.3 ARRAY3.C Deck of cards

DO: • Add initialization to program ARRAY2
• Compile and run ARRAY3

```
#include <stdio.h>
void main()
{
   int index;                                                  /*1*/
   int deck[52];

   for (index=0; index<52; ++index)                           /*2*/
       deck[index] = index;                                    /*3*/
   printf("\nThe tenth element of deck is %d", deck[9]); /*4*/
}
```

RESULT:

```
C:\>ARRAY3.C

The tenth element of deck is 9
```

ANALYSIS:

1. The *for* loop of lines /*2–3*/ initializes each element in the array to a value equal to its index. The loop causes the variable *index* to count up from 0 to 51, which are the exact lower and upper limits of the array indexes.

2. The printf() statement shows that the value (and the index) of the tenth element is 9.

One of the most common and troublesome errors in C programming occurs when an index value goes out of range for an array—that is, when an index value is less than zero or greater than the size of the array minus one. This is sometimes known as "blowing a subscript"; another name for index is *subscript*, because in mathematics, array elements are identified by subscripts. Programmers are more prone to blow a subscript when calculating an index, because the index value is not explicitly visible in that case. Most C compilers do not check for valid index values, because this can be a very complex task, so these errors only show up during program execution. This is also one of those areas in which the C language grants you freedom so as not to restrict your programming power. In the next program, you purposely use an index that overruns an array; in doing so, you can see that the compiler does your bidding without complaint.

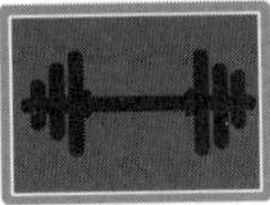

Listing 9.4 ARRAY4.C Deck of cards

DO: • Install wrong index limits
• Compile and run ARRAY4

```
#include <stdio.h>
void main()
{
   int index;
   int deck[52];
   int extra = 99;                                              /*1*/

   printf("\nThe initial value of extra is %d", extra);  /*2*/
   for (index=1; index<=52; ++index)                          /*3*/
       deck[index] = index;
   printf("\nThe tenth element of deck is %d", deck[9]);
   printf("\nThe value of extra (%d) is the same"
       " as deck[52] (%d)", extra, deck[52]);                 /*4*/
}
```

RESULT:

```
C:\>ARRAY4

The initial value of extra is 99
The tenth element of deck is 9
The value of extra (52) is the same as deck[52] (52)
```

ANALYSIS:

1. Line /*1*/ defines a variable named *extra* immediately **after** the array and initializes it to a value of 99. The placement of this variable will allow you to see the effect of indexing past the end of the array *deck*. The compiler will allocate the variables in the order of their occurrence in the program, so it will allocate memory for *extra* just beyond the end of the array *deck*.
2. Line /*2*/ erroneously shifts the limits of the *for* loop upward by one so that the program attempts (successfully) to assign the value of 52 to memory beyond the end of the array.
3. The loop does not assign a value to the first element in the array, because indexing begins with 1, but the second printf() statement

shows that other elements (the tenth included) receive values equal to their indexes.

4. The third printf() statement shows what has happened to the value of the variable *extra*—a blown subscript in the last assignment of the loop changes its value. The printf() statement uses the blown subscript, 52, once again to display the fictitious 53 element of *deck*.

In the above example, you have only moved the index out of bounds by one in a relatively safe manner. In general, this phenomenon can have disastrous effects on the execution of a program, especially when an index goes way out of bounds. If you have a program that is doing weird things with arrays, check the values of the array indexes. You can do this in three ways: (1) examine your code carefully, looking for invalid index values—you may have to manually calculate the extreme limits of index values to do this, (2) insert printf() statements to display index values just before the program uses them in an array, and (3) if you have a debugging utility available, use it to examine index values as the program runs.

In situations where you need to fill an array with a single value, the standard library function, memset(), is particularly effective. This function offers the advantage of being terse as well as fast. You can use memset() in the next program.

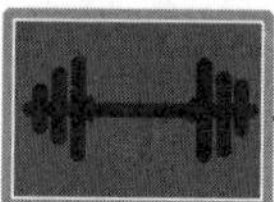

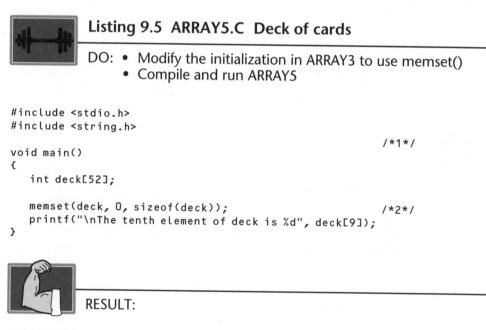

Listing 9.5 ARRAY5.C Deck of cards

DO:
- Modify the initialization in ARRAY3 to use memset()
- Compile and run ARRAY5

```
#include <stdio.h>
#include <string.h>
                                                    /*1*/
void main()
{
   int deck[52];

   memset(deck, 0, sizeof(deck));                   /*2*/
   printf("\nThe tenth element of deck is %d", deck[9]);
}
```

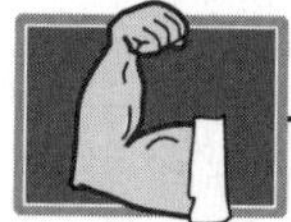

RESULT:

```
C:\>ARRAY5

The tenth element of deck is 0
```

ANALYSIS:

1. The result is correct but rather unspectacular: memset() just fills the array with zeros. The main purpose of memset() is to efficiently perform this kind of initialization chore.
2. The prototype for the function memset() is in the header file string.h, so it is included on line /*1*/.
3. The first argument for memset() is a *pointer* to the array, which is the address of the starting memory location. The name of an array, without square brackets, is a pointer to the array. On line /*2*/, the name *deck* is a pointer to (or the address of) the array to be initialized.
4. The second argument for memset() is the value that will fill the array—0 in this case. The function memset() fills memory on a byte basis, so it will use only the first 8 bits of the data value; a character constant such as ' ' (space) is often used to initialize character arrays.
5. The third argument for memset() is the number of bytes to be initialized. The sizeof() operator serves very nicely for this argument; not only does sizeof() return the needed number, but it also automatically adjusts the number if you change the declared array size.

As with a variable, you can initialize an array at the time it is defined. The initialization takes the form of a list of values, or *initializers*, separated by commas and enclosed in curly braces:

```
array_type array_name[array_size] = { value1, value2, ... };
```

Each value must be a constant expression—that is, a constant or an expression that evaluates to a constant. The next example initializes each element of an array to a different value in the definition statement.

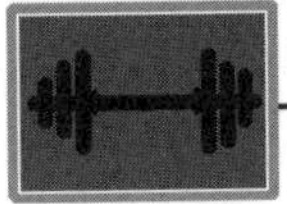

Listing 9.6 ARRAY6.C Deck of cards

DO:
- Modify ARRAY3 to initialize in the definition statement
- Compile and run ARRAY6

```
#include <stdio.h>
void main()
{
/*1*/int deck[52] =
/*2*/  { 1, 2, 3, 4, 5, 6, 7, 8, 9, 10, 11, 12, 13,
```

```
/*3*/   14, 15, 16, 17, 18, 19, 20, 21, 22, 23, 24, 25, 26,
/*4*/   27, 28, 29, 30, 31, 32, 33, 34, 35, 36, 37, 38, 39,
/*5*/   40, 41, 42, 43, 44, 45, 46, 47, 48, 49, 50, 51, 52};

   printf("\nThe tenth element of deck is %d", deck[9]);
}
```

RESULT:

```
C:\>ARRAY6

The tenth element of deck is 10
```

ANALYSIS:

1. Lines /*1–5*/ define and initialize the array *deck* to values 1–52. Each of the initializer values uniquely represents one card (value and suit) in a full deck of cards. Values 1–13 represent the heart suit, 14–26 are diamonds, 27–39 are clubs, and 40–52 are spades.
2. In general, any of the initializer constants could also be a constant expression, for instance, the value 12 could also be listed as 8 + 4, or 3 * 4.

With this form of initialization, you set the values as early as possible, but the source statement can be lengthy. You do not have to specify initializers for all elements in an array; the compiler will set any unspecified elements to 0. You can take advantage of this rule if you need to initialize only the first few elements of an array, as in the next example.

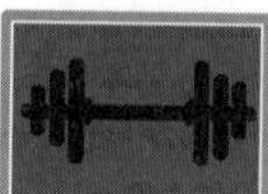

Listing 9.7 ARRAY7.C Deck of cards

DO:
- Modify ARRAY6 to initialize part of an array
- Compile and run ARRAY7

```
#include <stdio.h>
void main()
{
   int deck[52] =
/*1*/  { 1, 2, 3, 4, 5, 6, 7, 8, 9};

   printf("\nThe tenth element of deck is %d", deck[9]);
}
```

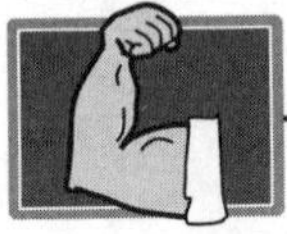

RESULT:

```
C:\>ARRAY7

The tenth element of deck is 0
```

ANALYSIS:

1. Line /*1*/ lists only nine initializer values, so the statement sets the first nine elements of *deck* to these values, and it sets the remaining elements to 0.
2. The printf() statement shows that the tenth element is 0 because of the implied initialization.

If you do not initialize any elements of an array, the compiler will **not** implicitly set all elements to 0. C does not specify that the compiler automatically initialize all variables and arrays. The values of an array are undetermined unless you initialize it either in the definition statement or by explicit assignment.

What happens if you specify too many initializers in the definition? The compiler generates an error, as in the following program:

Listing 9.8 ARRAY8.C Deck of cards

DO:
- Modify ARRAY6 to have too many initializers
- Compile ARRAY8

```
#include <stdio.h>
void main()
{
   int deck[52] =
       { 1,  2,  3,  4,  5,  6,  7,  8,  9, 10, 11, 12, 13,
        14, 15, 16, 17, 18, 19, 20, 21, 22, 23, 24, 25, 26,
        27, 28, 29, 30, 31, 32, 33, 34, 35, 36, 37, 38, 39,
        40, 41, 42, 43, 44, 45, 46, 47, 48, 49, 50, 51, 52,
/*1*/   53};

   printf("\nThe tenth element of deck is %d", deck[9]);
}
```

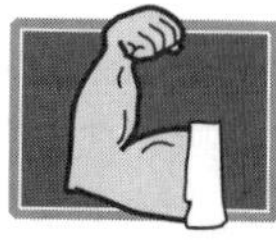

RESULT:

```
C:\>pc/c ARRAY8
Power C - Version 2.1.3
(C) Copyright 1989-1991 by Mix Software
Compiling ...
ARRAY8.C(9):/*1*/     53};
***********           ^170
     170: Too many items in initializer
-----------------------------------------------------------------
  119 lines compiled
    1 Compile error
```

ANALYSIS:

1. On line /*1*/ you have added an initializer constant that has no corresponding array element, so the compiler displays an error message.

You can use a list of initializers to determine the number of elements in an array by leaving the array size out of the square brackets. The following program shows how to do this:

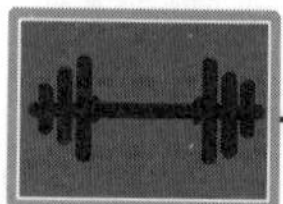

Listing 9.9 ARRAY9.C Deck of cards

DO:
- Modify ARRAY8 to let initializers set the array size
- Compile and run ARRAY9

```
#include <stdio.h>
void main()
{
/*1*/   int deck[] =
        { 1, 2,  3, 4, 5,  6, 7, 8, 9, 10, 11, 12, 13,
         14, 15, 16, 17, 18, 19, 20, 21, 22, 23, 24, 25, 26,
         27, 28, 29, 30, 31, 32, 33, 34, 35, 36, 37, 38, 39,
         40, 41, 42, 43, 44, 45, 46, 47, 48, 49, 50, 51, 52,
         53};

   printf("\nThe tenth element of deck is %d", deck[9]);
}
```

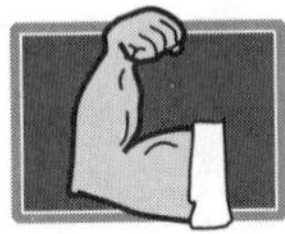

RESULT:

```
C:\>ARRAY9

The tenth element of deck is 10
```

ANALYSIS:

The array definition statement contains the same 53 initializers as did the previous program, except now there is no compile error. An explicit array size is absent, so the compiler determines that the array size is 53 based on the number of initializing constants.

USING ARRAYS AS FUNCTION ARGUMENTS

You often use functions to work with arrays, and you often need to access arrays defined in other functions. There are two methods for communicating array values between functions: The first method is good for transferring individual element values, and the second method allows access to the entire array.

Array elements used as arguments and return values

You can pass individual array element values into and out of a function in much the same way as you pass variable values. Soon you are going to simulate another card game, so you need a function to shuffle the deck. The next program accomplishes a crude form of shuffling by passing array element values into and out of a function.

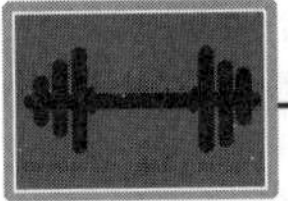

Listing 9.10 ARRAY10.C Deck of cards

DO:
- Modify ARRAY7 to share array values with a function
- Compile and run ARRAY10

```
#include <stdio.h>
int shuffle(int);                                        /*1*/
void main()
{
   int deck[52] =
       { 1, 2, 3, 4, 5, 6, 7, 8, 9};

   deck[9] = shuffle(deck[0]);                           /*2*/
   printf("\nThe tenth element of deck is %d", deck[9]);
}
```

```
int shuffle(int card)                                /*3*/
{                                                    /*4*/
   return(card);                                     /*5*/
}                                                    /*6*/
```

RESULT:

```
C:\>ARRAY10

The tenth element of deck is 1
```

ANALYSIS:

1. The prototype on line /*1*/ declares a new function named *shuffle* as type *int* with one argument that is also type *int*.
2. The assignment statement on line /*2*/ calls the function *shuffle* with the value of the first element of the array *deck* as the argument, then assigns the return value to the tenth element.
3. Lines /*3–6*/ define the function *shuffle*; all it does is return the value of the parameter received. Therefore, line /*2*/ in the main function assigns the value of deck[0] to deck[9].

The above program nicely illustrates how to pass array element values into and out of a function, but the shuffling method is deficient in a couple of ways. You could accomplish the same thing by directly assigning deck[0] to deck[9] in the main function, and you have only copied the value of one card to another position in the array, when what you really need to do is **exchange** the values. If you have access to the entire array, you can easily exchange values in the array; the next section explains how this is done.

Accessing arrays between functions

In C, pointers are addresses of data. An array name by itself (without square brackets) is a pointer to the array—that is, it represents the address of the first element of the array. A pointer can be used as a function argument, and as such, it represents a way to access the entire array. Figure 9-3 illustrates the relationship between an array and the pointer to the array.

In general, pointers can be constants or variables; an array name is a pointer constant. Figure 9-3 shows that the array name *deck* is a constant that holds the address of

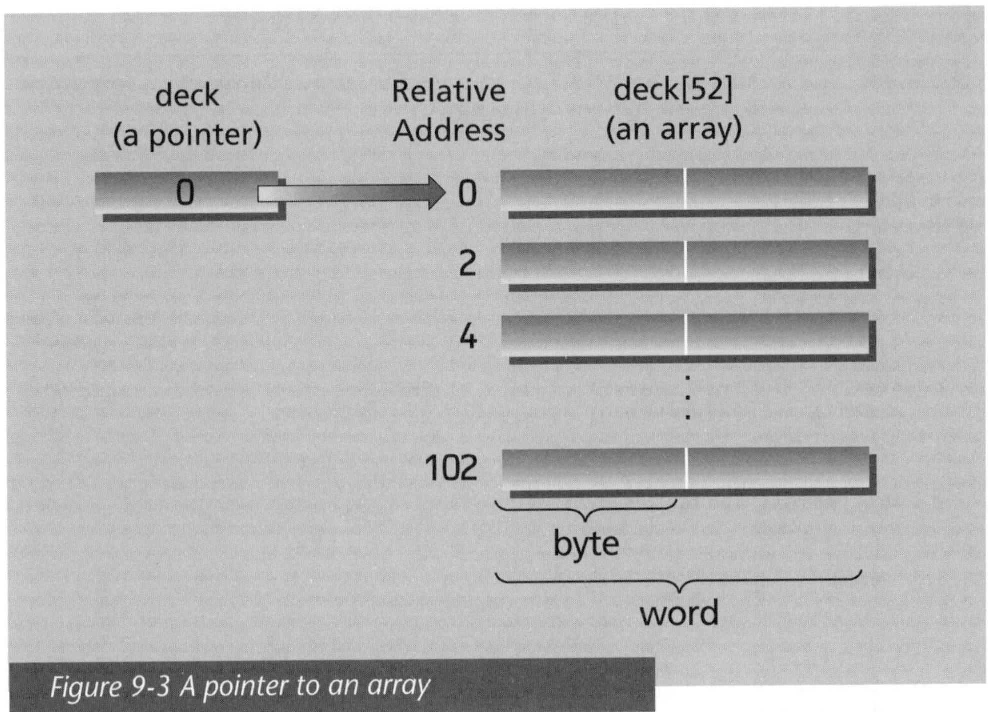

Figure 9-3 A pointer to an array

the first element in the array *deck*. Chapter 11 explains pointers thoroughly, but a brief introduction is necessary here so that you can see how they are used as a function argument. A pointer can be a variable, so you can declare it an argument in a function prototype and a parameter in the function definition just as you would any other variable. The declaration of a pointer is unique in that you include an asterisk (*) after the data type. The data type for a pointer is the same as the type of the data that it will point to. That is, if a pointer is to be used with an integer array, it is declared as *int* *; if it is going to point to character data, it must be declared *char* *. For instance, you could declare an integer pointer as follows:

```
int *cards = deck;
```

This statement declares a pointer to integer data (an integer pointer named *cards*) and initializes its value to the address of the array *deck*. The space between the data type and the asterisk is optional (the compiler will ignore it), but this is the standard form for declaring pointers.

The next program improves the shuffling operation by passing a pointer to the array *deck* into the function.

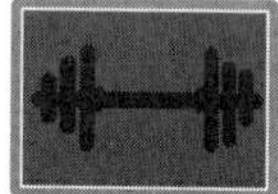

Listing 9.11 ARRAY11.C Deck of cards

DO:
- Modify ARRAY10 to pass the array pointer to a function
- Compile and run ARRAY11

```
#include <stdio.h>
void shuffle(int *);                                           /*1*/
void main()
{
   int deck[52] =
    { 1, 2, 3, 4, 5, 6, 7, 8, 9, 10, 11, 12, 13};              /*2*/

   shuffle(deck);                                              /*3*/
   printf("\nThe first element of deck is %d", deck[0]);      /*4*/
   printf("\nThe tenth element of deck is %d", deck[9]);
}

void shuffle(int *cards)
                                                               /*5*/
{
   int temp;
                                                               /*6*/

   temp = cards[9];                                            /*7*/
   cards[9] = cards[0];                                        /*8*/
   cards[0] = temp;                                            /*9*/
}
```

RESULT:

```
C:\>ARRAY11

The first element of deck is 10
The tenth element of deck is 1
```

ANALYSIS:

1. The prototype on line /*1*/ declares a function named *shuffle* with one argument that is an integer pointer. The function has no return value, so the prototype declares it to be of data type *void*.
2. The statement on line /*3*/ calls shuffle() with the array name *deck* (which is a pointer, or address, to the beginning of the array) as the argument.

3. The definition of the function shuffle() begins on line /*5*/ and includes the same type declarations as in the prototype; notice the use of a space between *int* and * for the pointer. The name of the pointer parameter is *cards*—it does not have to be the same as the argument name *deck*. When main() calls shuffle(), it assigns a copy of the *deck* address to the parameter *cards*.
4. Line /*6*/ in the body of the function defines an integer variable *temp* that the function will use for temporary storage during the exchange of data values.
5. Lines /*7–9*/ exchange the values of the first and tenth elements of the array using three assignment statements.
6. You can use a pointer to an array just as you use the name of an array; therefore, on lines /*7–9*/ inside the function shuffle(), you can use indexing with the pointer *cards* to access elements of the array.

Before this example, you were unable to directly alter data in the calling function because parameter values are always a copy of calling arguments. The pointer parameter *cards* in this example is also a copy of the pointer argument *deck*, but because it is a pointer, you are able to directly alter values in the original array through the power of pointer indexing. Passing the address of *deck* tells shuffle() where to find the original array, allowing shuffle() to access and alter the elements.

Now you have all the techniques necessary to do a complete shuffle of the deck of cards. If you use the standard function rand() to randomly select which cards to exchange and add a loop to repeat the exchange process a large number of times, you will have accomplished a real shuffle of the deck of cards.

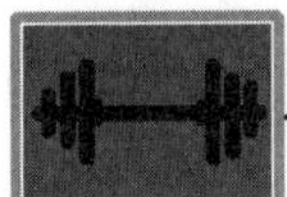

Listing 9.12 ARRAY12.C Deck of cards

DO: Enter, compile, and run ARRAY12

```
#include <stdio.h>
void shuffle(int *);
void main()
{
   int i;
   int deck[52];

/* Initialize the deck */

   for (i=1; i<=52; ++i)
       deck[i-1] = i;

/* Shuffle the deck */
```

```
   shuffle(deck);

/* Display results */

   printf("\nBefore  After   Before  After    ");
   printf("Before  After   Before  After");
   for (i=0; i<52; i+=4)
     printf("\n%6d %6d   %6d %6d   %6d %6d   %6d %6d",
i+1, deck[i], i+2, deck[i+1], i+3, deck[i+2], i+4, deck[i+3]);
}

void shuffle(int *cards)
{
   int i;                       /* Repeat index */
   int i1, i2;                  /* Random card index */
   int temp;                    /* Temporary card value */

/* Shuffle 1000 times */

   for (i=0; i<1000; ++i)
   {

/* Randomly select two cards */

      i1 = rand() % 52;
      i2 = rand() % 52;

/* Swap the cards */

      temp = cards[i1];
      cards[i1] = cards[i2];
      cards[i2] = temp;
   }
}
```

RESULT:

```
C:\>ARRAY12

 Before  After   Before   After   Before   After   Before   After
   1      44       2       36       3       31       4       25
   5      30       6       52       7        4       8       38
   9      48      10       27      11       16      12        7
  13      26      14       22      15       49      16       23
  17      35      18       10      19       45      20       19
  21       8      22       42      23       28      24       46
  25      51      26       11      27       50      28       12
  29      17      30       43      31        6      32        1
  33      13      34        5      35       21      36       47
```

```
37      2     38     18     39     32     40     29
41     37     42     14     43     20     44     39
45      9     46      3     47     15     48     33
49     34     50     40     51     24     52     41
```

ANALYSIS:

1. The main function first initializes the array *deck* to integer values that represent each of the 52 cards. The program uses a *for* loop because it is more compact than a list of initializer constants.
2. Next the program shuffles the deck and displays the array of card values before and after shuffling. Actually, printf() displays the **before** value as the index of each element plus one because this is the initialized value of each element. Notice how the *for* loop displays four cards per line by incrementing the counter (*i*) by 4 each time.
3. The first two lines in the function shuffle() define some new integer variables: one (*i*) will control a loop, and two others (*i1* and *i2*) will hold indexes for elements of the array to be exchanged. The variable *i* in the main function is different from the variable *i* in shuffle(), even though they have the same name, because they are separately defined inside the functions.
4. The *for* loop in shuffle() causes 1000 card exchanges to occur.
5. Inside the loop, two assignment statements randomly select indexes of two array elements (cards) to be exchanged. The standard function rand() returns a random integer, then the modulus operator (%) takes the remainder after division by 52, and the final result is an index in the range of from 0 to 51. This is similar to the technique that you previously used in the RANDOM8 program (Program 8.12 in Chapter 8) to randomly select a card value.
6. The function exchanges the selected cards (array element values) with the same three-statement construct that you used in the previous example.

Now you have finished the function shuffle(), and you'll be using it in some upcoming programs in this chapter, so you can simplify future programming chores if you put it in a library. By doing this you will not have to deal with the source code for shuffle() while developing other functions, and future compile times will be shorter. The steps are:

1. Compile the source code for SHUFFLE:

```
C:\>pc/c SHUFFLE
```

2. Put the object file in the library CARDSLIB with the merge utility:

   ```
   C:\>merge CARDSLIB SHUFFLE
   ```

3. Link future programs that use shuffle() with the following command:

   ```
   pcl PROGRAM; CARDSLIB
   ```

Before you put shuffle() in the library, it is imperative that you create documentation about how to use the function for future reference. The generally accepted method of recording information about a function is to attach a *header box* of comments at the top of the function. A header box can be written any time during the development of a function, and programmers often compose the header first. A header box is a comment or series of comments that describes, minimally, the name of the function, the author, the date programming was started, an abstract or purpose of the function, the function prototype, and a description of all arguments and return values. You should also provide a place to record information about future changes to the function. You can make up the details of your own header, but you should use the same form of header consistently on any given programming project. The following header box is a format that has proven useful.

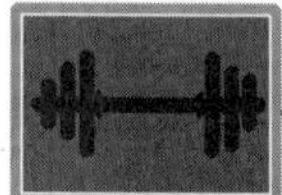

Listing 9.13 HEADER.C Program documentation

DO:
- Add a header to SHUFFLE
- Compile SHUFFLE
- Add SHUFFLE to library CARDSLIB

```
/****************************************************************
         Function: shuffle
       Programmed: Your name, The current date

          Purpose: Shuffle a deck of cards.

        Prototype: void shuffle(char *deck);

   Input Argument: Pointer to a 52-element array of card
                   identifiers (values 1-52).
     Return value: None.

        Revisions: Name, Date, Description
****************************************************************/
void shuffle(int *deck)
{
   int i;                     /* Repeat index */
   int i1, i2;                /* Random card index */
   int temp;                  /* Temporary card value */

/* Shuffle 1000 times */
```

```
   for (i=0; i<1000; ++i)
   {

/* Randomly select two cards */

        i1 = rand() % 52;
        i2 = rand() % 52;

/* Swap the cards */

        temp = deck[i1];
        deck[i1] = deck[i2];
        deck[i2] = temp;
   }
}
```

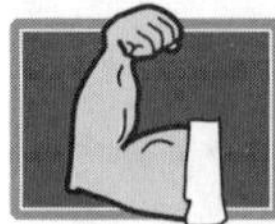

RESULT:

```
C:\>pc/c SHUFFLE

C:\>merge CARDSLIB SHUFFLE
```

ANALYSIS:

The header box contains the minimum information necessary to document the function.

MULTIDIMENSIONAL ARRAYS

You can declare arrays of more than one dimension so that data can be stored and accessed in more complex and useful ways. Two- and three-dimensional arrays are commonly used, and a program can declare any number of dimensions. Two-dimensional arrays are the simplest, so they are a good starting point.

Two-dimensional arrays

You declare a two-dimensional array by adding a second pair of square brackets to a one-dimensional array. Suppose you wanted to simulate a game of gin rummy; you might want to define an array to hold a hand of seven cards like this:

```
int hand[7];
```

You could just as well make this a two-dimensional array to accommodate four hands of seven cards:

```
int hand[4][7];
```

This is an array of 28 integer elements, which takes up the same memory area as an array declared:

```
int hand[28];
```

In both cases, the compiler allocates 56 bytes of memory (28 times 2 bytes for each element), as illustrated in Figure 9-4.

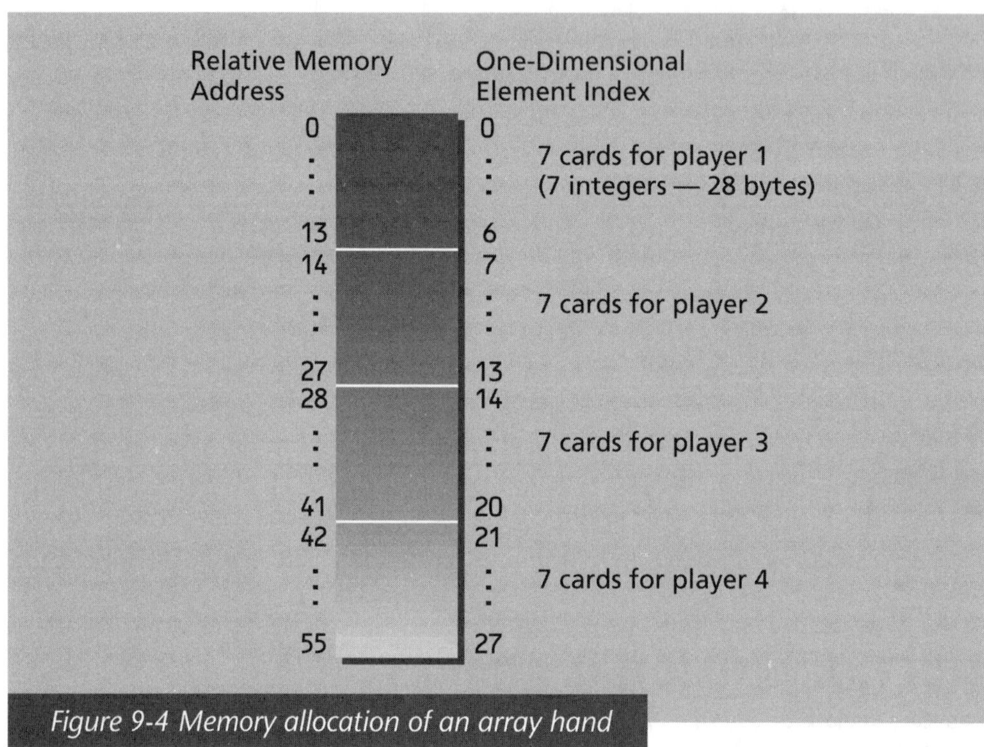

Figure 9-4 Memory allocation of an array hand

The difference between a one-dimensional declaration and a two-dimensional declaration is the way you access the data. With a one-dimensional declaration, you access a card with a single index calculated from the desired player number and card number. The calculation for a one-dimensional index is:

```
7 * player_number + card_number
```

The assumption here is that both *player_number* and *card_number* are zero-based—that is, the first player is player number 0, and the first card is card number 0. Therefore, the first card for the first player of the one-dimensional array is hand[0], and the first card for the second player is hand[7]. You can select any card from any player with the next program.

Listing 9.14 PICK.C Pick a card

DO: Enter and compile PICK

```
#include <stdio.h>
void main()
{
   int player_index;
   int card_index;
   int hand[28] = {  0,  1,  2,  3,  4,  5,  6,
                    10, 11, 12, 13, 14, 15, 16,
                    20, 21, 22, 23, 24, 25, 26,
                    30, 31, 32, 33, 34, 35, 36 };

   printf("Pick a player (0-3): ");
   scanf("%d", &player_index);
   printf("Pick a card (0-6): ");
   scanf("%d", &card_index);

   printf("Card %d for player %d is: %d",
        card_index, player_index,
        hand[player_index * 7 + card_index]);
}
```

ANALYSIS:

1. The program defines the one-dimensional array *hand* and initializes it with 28 integers in four groups of sequential identifiers, so that the breaks between players are obvious. The identifiers are chosen so that the two digits in the value of each element match the player/card selection for the element. For instance, the array value for player 1, card 2 is 12.

2. You are prompted to pick a player and a card by entering an index for each.

3. The final printf() statement displays the selected card. The index to the one-dimensional array, *hand,* is the result of the calculation: *7 * player_index + card_index.*

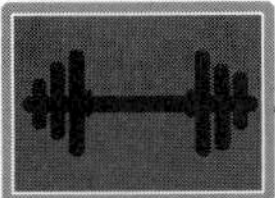

DO: Run PICK and enter **2** then **3**

RESULT:

```
C:\>PICK
Pick a player (0-3): 2
Pick a card (0-6): 3
Card 3 for player 2 is: 23
```

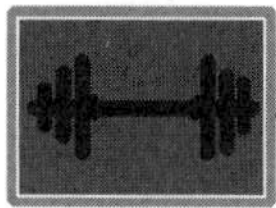

DO: Run PICK and enter **1** then **4**

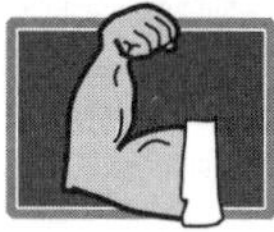

RESULT:

```
C:\>PICK
Pick a player (0-3): 1
Pick a card (0-6): 4
Card 4 for player 1 is: 14
```

ANALYSIS:

1. In the first run, you have selected the fourth card for the third player, with a value of 23. In the second run, you selected the fifth card for the second player, with a value of 14.

With a two-dimensional array, the compiler provides a separate index for each dimension (in the next example the first dimension is the player, and the second dimension is the card). So the first card for the first player is hand[0][0], and the first card for the second player is hand[1][0]. With a two-dimensional array, the compiler performs the indexing calculations for you. You can select a card from a two-dimensional array if you modify PICK to create the next program.

Listing 9.15 PICK2.C Pick a card

DO:
- Modify PICK to use a two-dimensional array
- Compile PICK2

```
#include <stdio.h>
void main()
{
```

```
    int player_index;
    int card_index;
    int hand[4][7] = { 0,  1,   2,   3,   4,   5,   6,       /*1*/
                      10, 11,  12,  13,  14,  15,  16,
                      20, 21,  22,  23,  24,  25,  26,
                      30, 31,  32,  33,  34,  35,  36 };

    printf("Pick a player (0-3): ");
    scanf("%d", &player_index);
    printf("Pick a card (0-6): ");
    scanf("%d", &card_index);

    printf("The %d card for player %d is: %d",
        card_index, player_index,
        hand[player_index][card_index]);                    /*2*/
}
```

ANALYSIS:

1. Line /*1*/ changes the declaration of *hand* to a two-dimensional array.
2. The program uses the index values that you enter to directly access the card value on line /*2*/ without any kind of calculation.

DO: Run PICK2 and enter **2** then **3**

RESULT:

```
C:\>PICK2
Pick a player (0-3): 2
Pick a card (0-6): 3
Card 3 for player 2 is: 23
```

DO: Run PICK2 and enter **1** then **4**

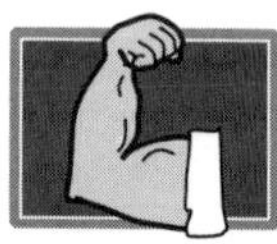

RESULT:

```
C:\>PICK2
Pick a player (0-3): 1
Pick a card (0-6): 4
Card 4 for player 1 is: 14
```

ANALYSIS:

1. PICK2 gives the same result as the original PICK program. The only difference is how the source code specifies indexing.

Computer memory is one-dimensional, so to translate the two-dimensional indexing into one-dimensional memory access, the compiler must make a very similar calculation to the one that you performed in program PICK. It is likely that the compiler will not even generate faster executable code for the two-dimensional array than the calculation that you specified. Even so, you should prefer two-dimensional arrays, because the source code is easier to deal with, and the compiler will usually optimize the indexing calculations, saving you the bother.

Dimension ordering

Memory is one-dimensional; memory addresses progress in a linear, low-to-high fashion, so the compiler must lay out elements of a two-dimensional array in sections within memory. The first dimension of a two-dimensional array is commonly referred to as a row, and the second dimension as a column. The compiler places elements of the first dimension of a two-dimensional array contiguously in sections (or rows) as shown in Figure 9-5. Thus, all of the cards for the first player are together on the first row, all of the cards for the second player are on the second row, and so on. The size of the first (or row) dimension of a two-dimensional array is declared in square brackets closer to the array name, and the size of the second (or column) dimension is declared farther away from the name.

Look back at the two previous programs and notice that the initialization list in PICK2 is the same as in PICK; the order in which you have specified the two dimensions in PICK2, [4][7], correctly matches the sequential order of the initialization constants. That is, the seven cards for each player match up with the seven array elements of each row. If you were to reverse the order of the dimensions (to [7][4]), then you would also have to reorder the initialization list. To see this, first reverse the declared dimension order without changing the initialization list.

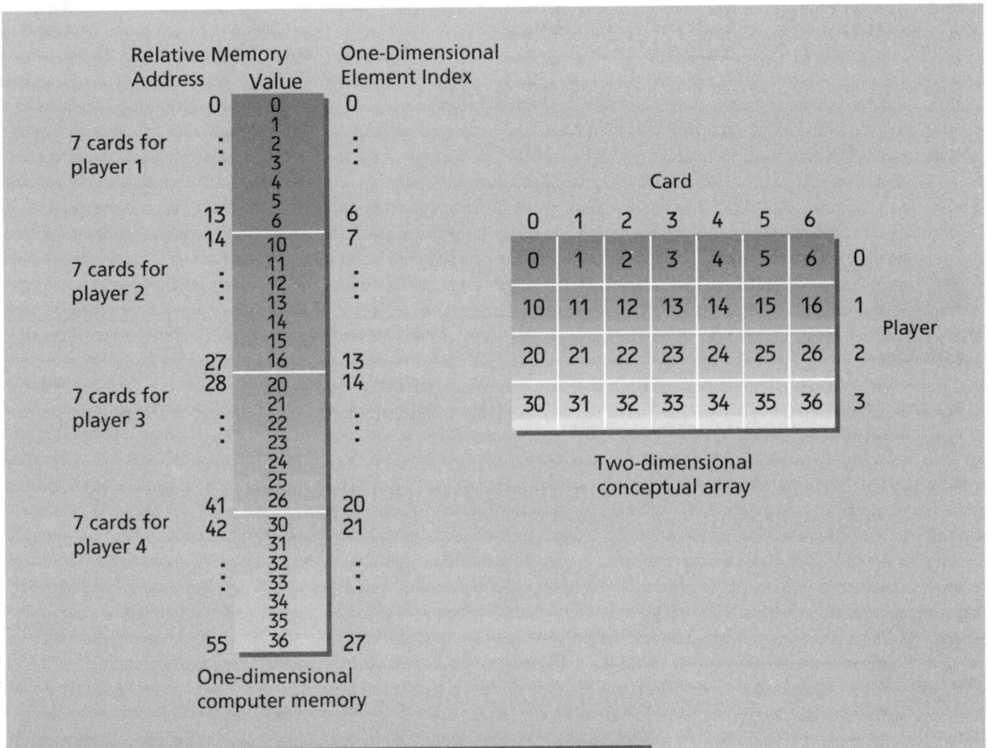

Relative Memory Address	Value	One-Dimensional Element Index
0	0	0
	1	
7 cards for player 1 ⋮	2	⋮
	3	
	4	
	5	
13	6	6
14	10	7
	11	
7 cards for player 2 ⋮	12	⋮
	13	
	14	
	15	
27	16	13
28	20	14
7 cards for player 3	21	
⋮	22	⋮
	23	
	24	
	25	
41	26	20
7 cards for player 4 42	30	21
	31	
⋮	32	⋮
	33	
	34	
	35	
55	36	27

One-dimensional computer memory

Card

	0	1	2	3	4	5	6	Player
0	0	1	2	3	4	5	6	0
1	10	11	12	13	14	15	16	1
2	20	21	22	23	24	25	26	2
3	30	31	32	33	34	35	36	3

Two-dimensional conceptual array

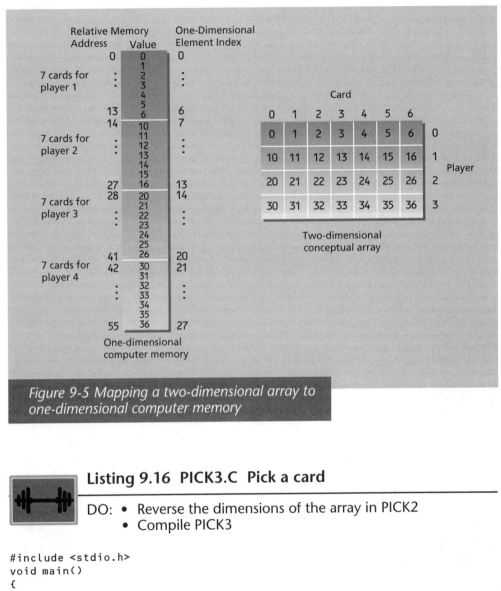

Figure 9-5 Mapping a two-dimensional array to one-dimensional computer memory

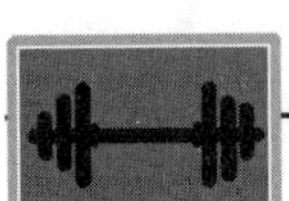

Listing 9.16 PICK3.C Pick a card

DO:
- Reverse the dimensions of the array in PICK2
- Compile PICK3

```
#include <stdio.h>
void main()
{
   int player_index;
   int card_index;
   int hand[7][4] = { 0,   1,   2,   3,   4,   5,   6,       /*1*/
                     10,  11,  12,  13,  14,  15,  16,
                     20,  21,  22,  23,  24,  25,  26,
                     30,  31,  32,  33,  34,  35,  36 };

   printf("Pick a player (0-3): ");
   scanf("%d", &player_index);
```

```
    printf("Pick a card (0-6): ");
    scanf("%d", &card_index);

    printf("The %d card for player %d is: %d",
        card_index, player_index,
        hand[card_index][player_index]);                    /*2*/
}
```

ANALYSIS:

1. On line /*1*/ you have reversed the dimensions of the array, from [4][7] to [7][4].
2. On line /*2*/ you have also reversed the corresponding indexes, from [player_index][card_index] to [card_index][player_index].

DO: Run PICK3 and enter **2** then **3**

RESULT:

```
C:\>PICK3
Pick a player (0-3): 2
Pick a card (0-6): 3
Card 3 for player 2 is: 20
```

DO: Run PICK3 and enter **1** then

RESULT:

```
C:\>PICK3
Pick a player (0-3): 1
Pick a card (0-6): 4
Card 4 for player 1 is: 23
```

ANALYSIS:

Now the program selects different values than before, because the array layout is different.

Figure 9-6 shows the correspondence between memory locations and the new two-dimensional array. The first card in each hand is on the first row, the second card is on the second row, and so on. As the figure shows, the initialization sequence has not changed, but the order of access is different because of the new indexing scheme. Therefore, the data values in memory are in the same place as before, but the indexes direct the program to different locations.

Finally, change the initialization order to match the new indexing scheme, and the program will work as originally designed.

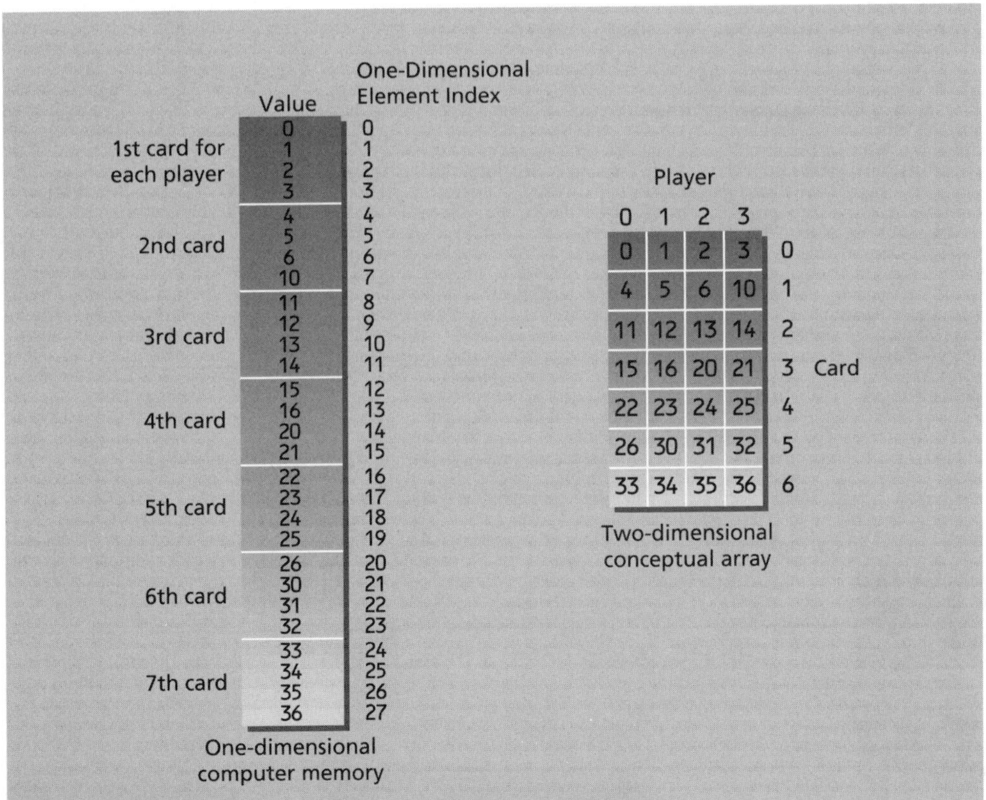

One-dimensional computer memory

	Value	One-Dimensional Element Index
1st card for each player	0	0
	1	1
	2	2
	3	3
2nd card	4	4
	5	5
	6	6
	10	7
3rd card	11	8
	12	9
	13	10
	14	11
4th card	15	12
	16	13
	20	14
	21	15
5th card	22	16
	23	17
	24	18
	25	19
6th card	26	20
	30	21
	31	22
	32	23
7th card	33	24
	34	25
	35	26
	36	27

Two-dimensional conceptual array

Card \ Player	0	1	2	3
0	0	1	2	3
1	4	5	6	10
2	11	12	13	14
3	15	16	20	21
4	22	23	24	25
5	26	30	31	32
6	33	34	35	36

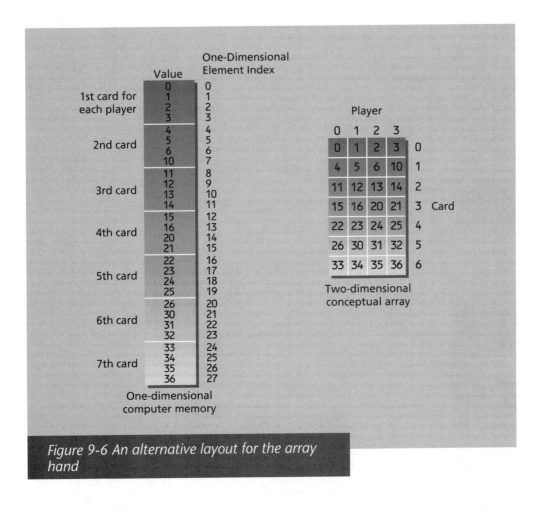

Figure 9-6 An alternative layout for the array hand

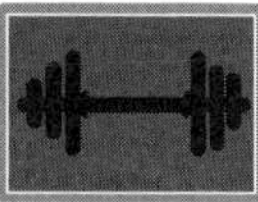

Listing 9.17 PICK4.C Pick a card

DO:
- Reorder the initialization list in PICK3
- Compile PICK4

```
#include <stdio.h>
void main()
{
   int player_index;
   int card_index;
   int hand[7][4] = { 0,  10,  20,  30,                 /*1*/
                      1,  11,  21,  31,                 /*2*/
                      2,  12,  22,  32,                 /*3*/
                      3,  13,  23,  33,                 /*4*/
                      4,  14,  24,  34,                 /*5*/
                      5,  15,  25,  35,                 /*6*/
                      6,  16,  26,  36 };               /*7*/

   printf("Pick a player (0-3): ");
   scanf("%d", &player_index);
   printf("Pick a card (0-6): ");
   scanf("%d", &card_index);

   printf("The %d card for player %d is: %d",
       card_index, player_index,
       hand[card_index][player_index]);
}
```

ANALYSIS:

1. Line /*1*/ assigns the first card to all four players, line /*2*/ assigns the second card to all four players, and so on, until line /*7*/ assigns the seventh card.

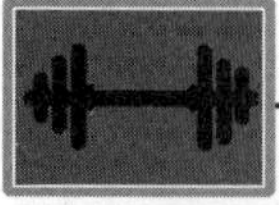

DO: Run PICK4 and enter **2** then **3**

RESULT:

```
C:\>PICK4
Pick a player (0-3): 2
```

```
Pick a card (0-6): 3
Card 3 for player 2 is: 23
```

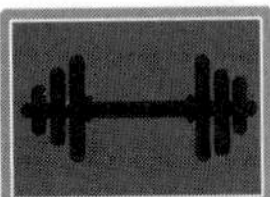

DO: Run PICK4 and enter **1** then **4**

RESULT:

```
C:\>PICK4
Pick a player (0-3): 1
Pick a card (0-6): 4
Card 4 for player 1 is: 14
```

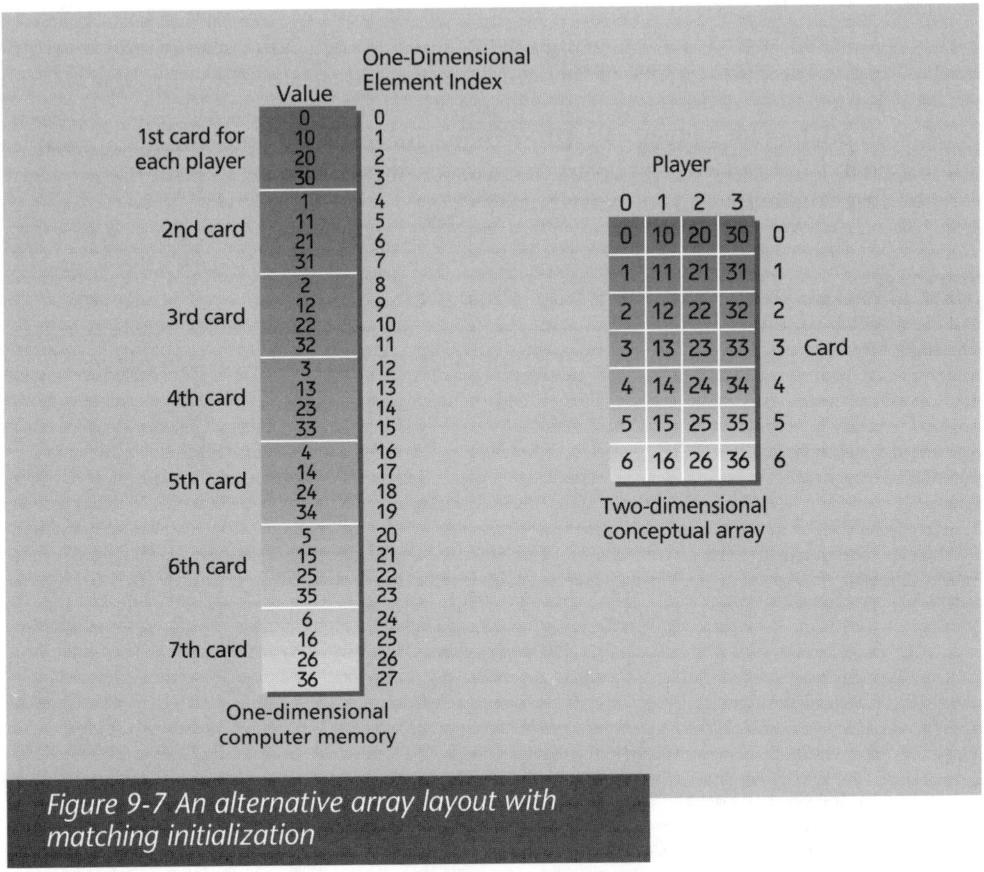

One-dimensional computer memory

	Value	One-Dimensional Element Index
1st card for each player	0	0
	10	1
	20	2
	30	3
2nd card	1	4
	11	5
	21	6
	31	7
3rd card	2	8
	12	9
	22	10
	32	11
4th card	3	12
	13	13
	23	14
	33	15
5th card	4	16
	14	17
	24	18
	34	19
6th card	5	20
	15	21
	25	22
	35	23
7th card	6	24
	16	25
	26	26
	36	27

Two-dimensional conceptual array

Player 0	Player 1	Player 2	Player 3	Card
0	10	20	30	0
1	11	21	31	1
2	12	22	32	2
3	13	23	33	3
4	14	24	34	4
5	15	25	35	5
6	16	26	36	6

Figure 9-7 An alternative array layout with matching initialization

ANALYSIS:

This version of the program responds in the same way as the original program, PICK.

Figure 9-7 shows the alternative array layout with an initialization sequence that matches the new dimension order.

With programs PICK and PICK4, you have two equivalent ways of configuring array data. Either layout is OK, and neither one is better than the other—they are just two different ways of looking at the data. If you understand how the changes in these last four programs affected memory data access and why PICK3 selected different cards than the other programs did, you have a good grasp of the relationship between indexing and memory allocation for multidimensional arrays.

Initialization lists for multidimensional arrays

An initialization list assigns values to an array in sequential order until the list is exhausted. With a list enclosed by a single set of curly braces, you can omit values from the end of the list (and the end of the array), as you did in the ARRAY7 program. You can also omit values from the end of any dimension of a multidimensional array by using additional sets of curly braces. For example, in the PICK4 program, if you want to initialize hands for only three players, you can omit the last card in each row of array *hand* by inserting extra pairs of curly braces.

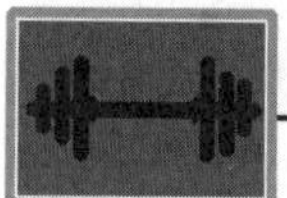

Listing 9.18 PICK5.C Pick a card

DO:
- Modify PICK4 to initialize cards for only three players
- Compile PICK5

```
#include <stdio.h>
void main()
{
   int player_index;
   int card_index;
   int hand[7][4] = { { 0, 10, 20 },                  /*1*/
                      { 1, 11, 21 },                  /*2*/
                      { 2, 12, 22 },                  /*3*/
                      { 3, 13, 23 },                  /*4*/
                      { 4, 14, 24 },                  /*5*/
                      { 5, 15, 25 },                  /*6*/
                      { 6, 16, 26 } };                /*7*/

   printf("Pick a player (0-2): ");                   /*8*/
   scanf("%d", &player_index);
   printf("Pick a card (0-6): ");
```

```
    scanf("%d", &card_index);

    printf("The %d card for player %d is: %d",
        card_index, player_index,
        hand[card_index][player_index]);
}
```

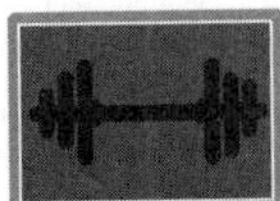

DO: Run PICK5 and enter **2** then **3**

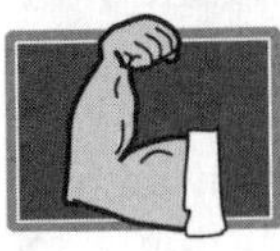

RESULT:

```
C:\>PICK5
Pick a player (0-2): 2
Pick a card (0-6): 3
Card 3 for player 2 is: 23
```

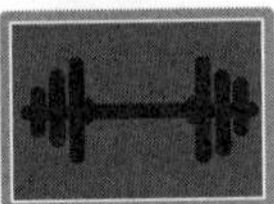

DO: Run PICK5 and enter **1** then **4**

RESULT:

```
C:\>PICK5
Pick a player (0-2): 1
Pick a card (0-6): 4
Card 4 for player 1 is: 14
```

ANALYSIS:

1. On each of the lines /*1–7*/, the row of initializer values are enclosed by an extra set of parentheses. The row dimension of the array is still four, but there are only three initializer values. The extra curly braces tell the compiler to stop assigning values from your list after the third one, and to assign the fourth element a default value of 0.

2. The first prompt on line /*8*/ asks you to select one of only three players (0–2).

For multidimensional arrays, you can use one set of curly braces in an initialization list, or more, up to the number of dimensions in the array. With the curly braces, you can control how the compiler assigns initializer values to the elements of each dimension of the array.

CHARACTER ARRAYS USED FOR STRINGS

You can store a *string* in a character array. A string is a sequence of characters that ends with a null value. The null value that terminates a string is a null byte, which is the same as the character '\0', 8 zero bits, or an 8-bit integer zero. The length of a string is the number of bytes required to hold the string, not counting the terminating null. Therefore, the maximum-length string that you can store in an array of size x is x-1. Figure 9-8 shows a string of length 5 stored in an array of size 6.

To avoid a potential point of confusion, the terms *string* and *character array* are not synonymous. A string is a special kind of character array, an array containing a sequence of character values that ends with a null. On the other hand, a character array does not have to contain a string, it can just be an array of character values, none of which is null.

One way that you can create a string is to initialize an array with a *string constant*, as shown in the following program. A string constant is a sequence of characters enclosed by double quotes (" "); the memory size of a string constant is one more than the number of characters between the quotes because it includes the terminating null. When the compiler encounters a string constant, it allocates memory to hold all the characters enclosed by the quotes plus one more byte for the terminating null. Thus, the double quote (" ") operators have the effect of appending '\0' to the characters they enclose.

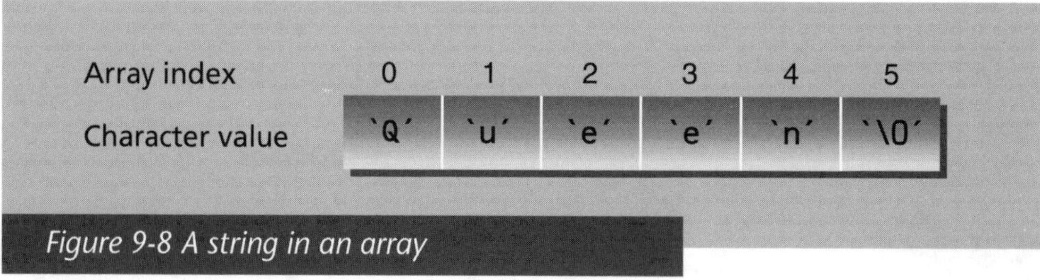

Figure 9-8 A string in an array

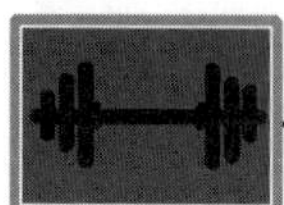

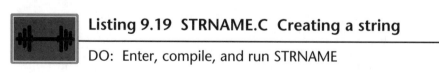

Listing 9.19 STRNAME.C Creating a string

DO: Enter, compile, and run STRNAME

```
#include <stdio.h>
void main()
{
   char card_name[8] = "Queen";
```

```
    printf("The string in card_name is %s", card_name);
}
```

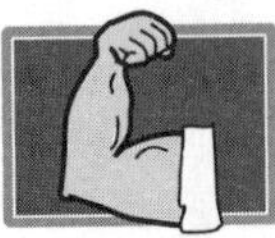

RESULT:

```
C:\>STRNAME
The string in card_name is Queen
```

ANALYSIS:

1. The program defines the character array *card_name* and initializes it to the string constant, "Queen," with one statement. The size of the array is larger than that required to hold the initial string; the array must be at least as large as the string length plus one, but it can be larger.

2. The printf() statement displays the string using the bare name of the array (*card_name*) to specify the data address. The array contains zero values in the last two elements, but the display stops at the first terminating null, so you do not see these other values.

In previous exercises, you used integer values to represent each of the 52 cards in a deck by assigning a range of identifying values to each of the four suits in the following way:

```
 1-13 are Hearts
14-26 are Diamonds
27-39 are Clubs
40-52 are Spades
```

Under this coding scheme, the identifier 30 represents the four of Clubs. It would be very useful to have a function that translates the integer identifier of a card into a displayable description of the card value and suit. You could easily write a function like this using a two-dimensional array.

The declaration *card_names[13][8]* specifies a two-dimensional array of 13 names, each being eight characters long; this array can hold 13 strings of length 7. You can initialize a two-dimensional array with a list of string constants in the following manner:

```
char card_names[13][8] =
    {"H Ace  ", "H 2    ", "H 3    ", "H 4    ", "H 5    ",
     "H 6    ", "H 7    ", "H 8    ", "H 9    ", "H 10   ",
    "H Jack ", "H Queen", "H King "};
```

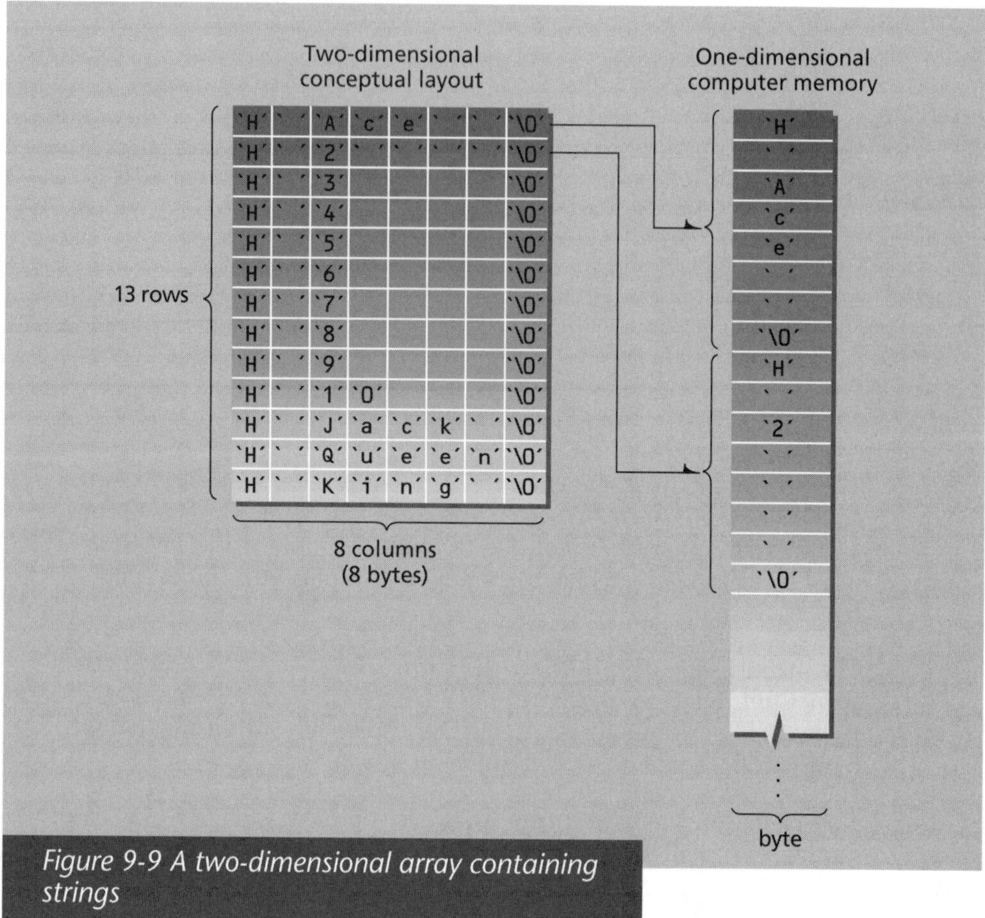

Figure 9-9 A two-dimensional array containing strings

Now you can see why we have been using an array size of 8; we have been planning to include a character to designate the card suit (the H designates Hearts). Figure 9-9 shows how this array is laid out in memory.

Accessing two-dimensional strings

You access individual elements of a two-dimensional array by specifying two indexes inside the square brackets, with the row index first and the column index last. You would place row and column indexes in the *card_names* array in this order:

```
card_names[row][col].
```

Thus, all of the characters of the first string are together on the first row, then all of the second string is on the second row, and so on. Figure 9-10 shows some specific array indexes.

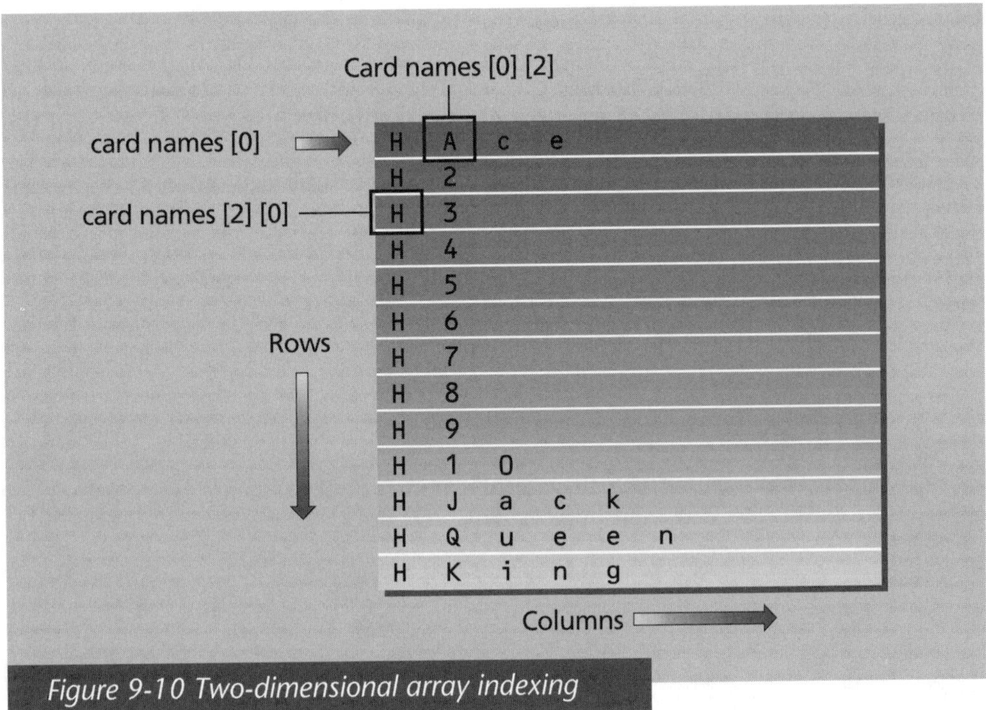

Figure 9-10 Two-dimensional array indexing

If you specify card_names[0][2], you have accessed the third element in the first row, or the A in Ace, and if you specify card_names[2][0], you have accessed the first element in the third row, or H for card 3. You can specify the address of the beginning of one of the strings with the array name and just the row number in square brackets, thus card_names[0] is the address of string "H Ace." You can think of *card_names* as an array of strings, you can think of *card_names[0], card_names[1]*, etc., as individual strings, and you can think of *card_names[0][2], card_names[1][1]*, etc., as individual characters in the strings.

The array *card_names* is the basis for a function used to translate card identifiers to displayable descriptions with a *table lookup* operation. Table lookup is a much-used technique in computing that is a fast and convenient way to convert one form of data into another. You can use a lookup table if you have a fixed amount of data to be translated. You first initialize an array (the table) with the translation results, placing the data in a predetermined order so that they can be retrieved with a known set of index values. A table lookup procedure amounts to accessing the data (looking them up) with the proper index values. Suppose you were writing a program that added sales tax to the prices of thousands of items. You could calculate the sales tax for each item with a formula like: tax = rate * price. Or you could store precalculated tax values in a table and look them up when needed. While shopping, you may have seen the printed tax tables used by store clerks to "look up" the amount of tax—a computer tax look-up table would be similar. You could build one table to store the tax amount on dollar amounts, and another with 99 entries to hold the tax on amounts less than one dollar. Table 9-1 contains a look-up table for the tax on dollar amounts from 1 to 10. To find the tax on $7, you would use 7 as the index and extract the seventh item from the table, or $0.56.

A look-up table can take a little effort to set up, but it runs faster than most calculations (including multiply) and is often the only way to implement certain conversions. The card translation shown in the following program amounts to a very straight-forward look-up table wherein each of the 52 card identifiers (the integers 1–52) is an index to a description in the array *card_names*. That is, the program converts an identifier (like 1) to the corresponding card name ("H Ace").

Amount	Tax
$1.00	$ .08
$2.00	$ .16
$3.00	$ .24
$4.00	$ .32
$5.00	$ .40
$6.00	$ .48
$7.00	$ .56
$8.00	$ .64
$9.00	$ .72
$10.00	$ .80

Table 9-1 A tax look-up table

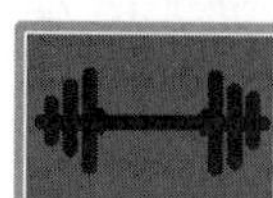

Listing 9.20 CONVERT.C Translate a card ID to a description

DO: Enter, compile, and run CONVERT

```
#include <stdio.h>
char *cardname(int);
void main()
{
   int card;
```

```
    printf("Pick a card (any card from 1 to 52): ");
    scanf("%d", &card);
    printf("You have selected: %s", cardname(card));
}

char *cardname(int card_id)
{
    static char card_names[14][8] =
        {"H Ace ", "H 2    ", "H 3    ", "H 4    ", "H 5    ",
         "H 6    ", "H 7    ", "H 8    ", "H 9    ", "H 10   ",
         "H Jack ", "H Queen", "H King ", "       "};

    char suit[4] = {'H', 'D', 'C', 'S'};

    if ((card_id < 1) || (card_id > 52))
        return(card_names[13]);

    --card_id;
    card_names[card_id % 13][0] = suit[card_id / 13];
    return(card_names[card_id % 13]);
}
```

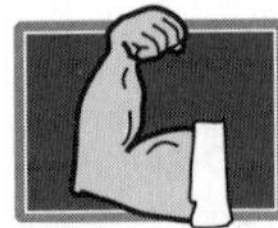

RESULT:

```
C:\>CONVERT
Pick a card (any card from 1 to 52): 26
You have selected: D King
```

ANALYSIS:

1. The main function prompts you to enter an integer card identifier, then displays the equivalent card description.
2. The function cardname() will return a pointer to a null-terminated string (an array), so both the prototype and the first line of the definition declare the function data type to be a character pointer (*char* *). The function declares its single argument (card identifier) to be of data type *int*.
3. The first item in the body of cardname() is the look-up table (array *card_names*). The declaration of *card_names* has a new qualifier, *static*—this ensures that the function does not throw away the array after returning to the main function. Ordinarily, a variable declared

within a function is created when the function begins, and it ceases to exist when the function ends. If you declare a variable or array to be *static*, it remains until the main program quits.

4. The simplest form of look-up table for a deck of cards would contain 52 entries—one for each card of each suit. This example uses a look-up table with only 13 name entries (and one blank) because it looks up the card, then replaces the first character of the selected string with the appropriate suit.

5. The four-element array *suit* holds identifiers for the four card suits—'H' for Hearts, 'D' for Diamonds, 'C' for Clubs, and 'S' for Spades.

6. The first *if* statement in cardname() checks to see if the parameter received is in the range of from 1 to 52; if not, the function returns a blank string by returning a pointer to the fourteenth row of the array *cardnames*.

7. The function decrements *card_id* so as to convert it into a zero-based index—that is, so that an identifier of 1 becomes 0, or the index to the first element in *card_names*.

8. The next line assigns the suit to the appropriate card description string. On the right side of the assignment operator (=), the statement selects the suit with an index that is the *card_id* divided by 13. The resulting index value is 0 if *card_id* is in the range of from 0 to 12 (Hearts), 1 for the range 13–25 (Diamonds), 2 for the range 26–38 (Clubs), or 3 for the range 39–51 (Spades). The statement assigns the single-character suit to the first character in the appropriate description string. The program chooses the appropriate string by computing the row index as the *card_id* modulus 13, which selects one of the 13 card values.

9. On the last line, the function returns a pointer to the selected description string. The calling function will display the string data residing in the function cardname(); this is the reason the array *card_names* is declared to be *static*—so that it will not disappear when the function returns.

If you are working on an IBM PC with a screen that will display the standard IBM PC graphic character set, you can change the initializers for the array *suit* from the character constants 'H', 'D', 'C', and 'S' to the integers 3, 4, 5, and 6, respectively—use integer constants without quotes, **not** character constants ('3', '4', '5', '6'). The integer constants are the ASCII codes for symbols that will graphically display a heart, a diamond, a club, and a spade. You don't have to change the declared type of the array to do this, type *char* is fine because it can accept integer values.

Now that you have this nice little translation function working, it would be a good idea to put it in the library, CARDSLIB. It is also good programming practice to attach an information header of comments before doing so.

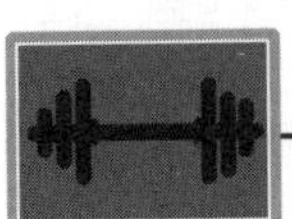

Listing 9.21 CONVERT2.C Document function cardname()

DO:
- Add a header to CONVERT
- Compile CONVERT2
- Add CONVERT2 to library CARDSLIB

```
/*****************************************************************
   Function: cardname
   Programmed: Your name, The current date

   Purpose: Translate an integer card identifier into a
            null-terminated description string.

   Prototype: char *cardname(int card_id);

   Input Argument: card identifier (1-52).
   Return value: Pointer to null-terminated description string.

   Revisions: Name, Date, Description
*****************************************************************/
char *cardname(int card_id)
{
   static char card_names[14][8] =
{"H Ace  ", "H 2    ", "H 3    ", "H 4    ", "H 5    ",
 "H 6    ", "H 7    ", "H 8    ", "H 9    ", "H 10   ",
 "H Jack ", "H Queen", "H King ", "       "};

   char suit[4] = {'H', 'D', 'C', 'S'};

   if ((card_id < 1) || (card_id > 52))
      return(card_names[13]);

   --card_id;
   card_names[card_id % 13][0] = suit[card_id / 13];
   return(card_names[card_id % 13]);
}
```

RESULT:

```
C:\>pc/c CARDNAME

C:\>merge CARDSLIB shuffle, convert2
```

ANALYSIS:

1. The header box contains the minimum information necessary to document the function.
2. You now have the function cardname() in the library CARDSLIB along with shuffle().

Declaring arrays of three or more dimensions

You can declare greater-than-two-dimensional arrays with multiple square brackets:

```
array_type array_name[size1][size2][size3]...
```

There is no limit to the number of dimensions that you can declare; three or four dimensions are not uncommon. For instance, if you needed to declare an array to hold census data on the number of males and females in each of the ten largest cities in each state; you could define the array as:

```
int census[50][10][2];
```

Figure 9-11 shows a three-dimensional memory layout of this array.

No matter how many dimensions you declare for an array, the compiler will always assign array elements to memory in a one-dimensional layout because physical memory is one-dimensional. However, you will find it convenient to visualize multidimensional arrays as geometric figures to clarify indexing. In a geometric drawing, the first two dimensions are rows and columns and the third dimension is a series of planes. Be-

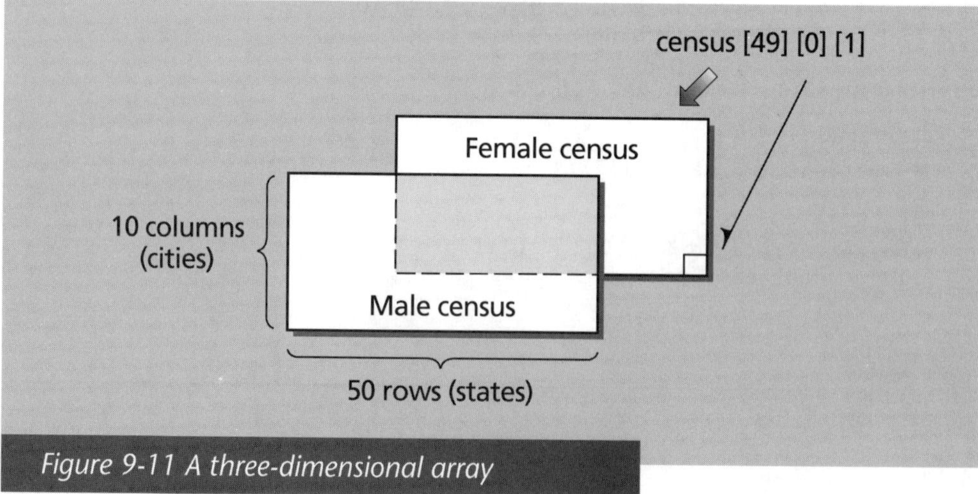

Figure 9-11 A three-dimensional array

yond three dimensions, it becomes harder to visualize the dimensions with a geometric description. However, the memory layout progresses in the same fashion, with all the memory elements of smaller dimensions contained within each larger dimension. You need *n* indexes to access an individual element of an *n*-dimensional array. For example, in the census array, the number of females in the first city of the 50th state would be referenced with three indexes:

```
census[49][0][1].
```

PUT IT ALL TOGETHER AND PLAY SOLITAIRE

Now for the payoff of your hard-earned groundwork in this chapter—you can put arrays and the library functions, shuffle() and cardname(), to use in a simulation of the game of solitaire. In the interest of keeping the program shorter, you will simulate a modified version of solitaire with the following rules:

1. Deal seven piles of cards with one card in the first pile, two in the second, and so on. All cards are face down except for the top card.
2. You can play a card onto a pile if the card is of the opposite color from and its value is one less than the top card in the pile. Face-up cards will accumulate on the piles; your opportunities for play from a pile are determined by the bottom (oldest) face-up card on the pile.
3. When you play by moving from one pile to another, you move all of the face-up cards from the first pile and turn over the newly exposed face-down card. If your play brings the number of cards in a pile to zero, you may play any King there.
4. If you have no play, either from the piles or the deck, then you examine the next card in the deck.
5. You win if the deck becomes empty, and you lose if you examine the entire deck without a play.

Play proceeds within the large loop. You control the game by selecting one of four actions for each cycle of the loop: (1) move face-up cards from one pile to another, (2) play the top deck card to a pile, (3) get the next deck card, or (4) quit. The simplest way to show the board is to redisplay everything at the beginning of each loop cycle. With a few more programming tools to control the screen, you could just update cards that change after each play, but this is not feasible in this chapter. You will use the functions, shuffle() and cardname(), that you have already developed and placed in the library, CARDSLIB, when you shuffle the deck and display the board. You can develop this program in parts; begin by defining variables and writing the code to deal the seven piles.

Shuffle
Initialize the deck and shuffle
Deal out 7 piles
Convert
Display the board
Enter an action
(M)ove ?
Y
Select the 'from' and 'to' piles
Move the cards
Update pile variables
(P)lay ?
Y
Select the 'to' pile
Place top deck card on pile
Update deck and pile variables
(N)ext ?
Y
Get the next deck card
(Q)uit ?
N
Y

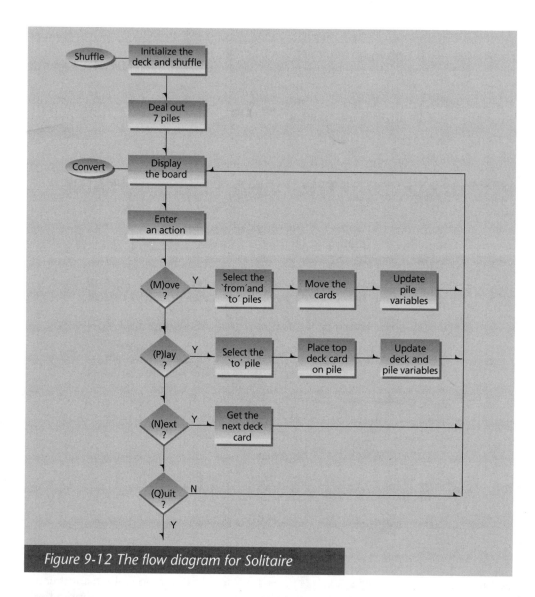

Figure 9-12 The flow diagram for Solitaire

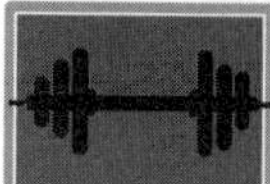

Listing 9.22 SOLO.C Solitaire

DO:
- Enter and compile SOLO
- Link SOLO with library CARDSLIB
- Run SOLO

```
#include <stdio.h>
void shuffle(int *);
```

```
char *cardname(int);
void main()
{
   int i;                     /* Re-useable counter      */
   int deck[52];              /* Deck of cards           */
   int deck_index;            /* Index for array deck    */
   int num_deck;              /* # of active deck cards  */
   int pile[13][7];           /* Playing piles           */
   int row, col;              /* Indexes for array pile  */
   int num_cards[7];          /* Total # of cards        */
   int num_down[7];           /* # of face-down cards    */

/* Initialize and shuffle the deck */

   num_deck = 52;
   for (i=1; i<=52; ++i)
       deck[i-1] = i;
   shuffle(deck);

/* Lay out the piles */

   deck_index = 0;
   for (col=0; col<7; ++col)                /* 7 piles            */
   {
       printf("\nPile %d:", col + 1);
       for (row=0; row<=col; ++row)         /* Up to 7 cards      */
       {
              pile[row][col] = deck[deck_index];
              deck[deck_index++] = 0;       /* Mark as gone       */
              --num_deck;
              printf(" %s", cardname(pile[row][col]));
       }
       num_down[col] = col;                 /* # face-down cards */
       num_cards[col] = col + 1;            /* Total # of cards   */
   }
}
```

RESULT:

```
C:\>pc/c SOLO
C:\>pcl SOLO;CARDSLIB
C:\>SOLO

Pile 1: S 5
Pile 2: C 10    C 5
Pile 3: D Queen C 4     S King
Pile 4: H 4     C Queen S 9     C Ace
Pile 5: D 3     H 7     D King  D 9     S 10
Pile 6: D 10    C 9     H 10    S 6     D 6     H 8
Pile 7: S 3     C 2     S 7     S Queen H Jack  S Jack  H Queen
```

ANALYSIS:

1. This program contains lots of comments to explain the purpose of each variable and array that it defines. You should find this very helpful in understanding the operation of the program and be encouraged to use the same technique in your own programs. Notice how the comments are neatly lined up for readability.

2. The program needs a general-purpose integer counter for looping (as do many C programs), so it defines the reusable variable *i* for this purpose. The program defines array *deck* to hold a full deck of 52 card identifiers, the variable *deck_index* to access cards in the deck, and the variable *num_deck* to keep track of the number of unused cards left in the deck. Each of the 7 piles needs space to hold up to 13 cards, so you can declare a two-dimensional, 13-row by 7-column array for this purpose. You can use the variables *row* and *col* to access values in the array *pile*. Finally, the array *num_cards* will keep track of the total number of cards in each pile and *num_down* will keep track of the number of face-down cards.

3. The comment, "Initialize and shuffle the deck," heads the first program section. Here a *for* loop assigns identifiers 1–52 to each card in the deck, then the program calls the function shuffle() to shuffle the deck.

4. The next section is titled, "Lay out the piles." In this section, the program deals cards from the deck to each of the seven piles. Actually, the program assigns values from elements in the array *deck* to elements in the array *pile*. Each of the seven piles has space for 13 cards (the row dimension of the array) because that is the maximum number of cards that a pile can hold during a game. The first *for* loop increments the column index, *col*, across all of the seven piles, and the second, nested *for* loop, determines the number of cards assigned to each pile. The number of cards assigned to each pile increases in step with the pile index. Figure 9-13 illustrates the operation of this nested *for* loop.

   After dealing each card, the program sets the value of the card in the deck to 0 to signify that the card has been used, then updates the number of remaining cards in the deck by decrementing *num_deck*. The program initializes the number of face-down cards in each pile, *num_down*, as equal to the pile column index, and the total number of cards, *num_cards*, is just one more than that.

5. You can use the library function cardname() to good advantage to watch the program deal cards to the seven piles. The first printf() statement moves the cursor to the beginning of the next line and displays the pile number. The second printf() statement displays a description of each card as it is dealt to the pile.

The first version of the solitaire program reveals all of the cards, but in a real game, only the top card in each pile is face up. Now you can proceed to develop the next part of the program, which displays the board with face-down cards shown as a string of asterisks (*******). This new version of the solitaire program also wraps a *do while* loop around the display section to prepare for continuous play. For now, the loop performs only one cycle, but the program after the following one will continue playing through an entire game.

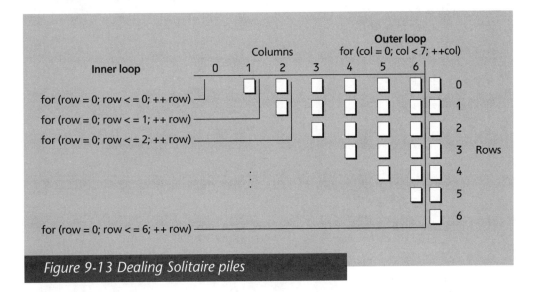

Outer loop
for (col = 0; col < 7; ++col)
Columns
Inner loop
0 1 2 3 4 5 6
for (row = 0; row < = 0; ++ row)
for (row = 0; row < = 1; ++ row)
for (row = 0; row < = 2; ++ row)
for (row = 0; row < = 6; ++ row)
0 1 2 3 4 5 6 Rows

Figure 9-13 Dealing Solitaire piles

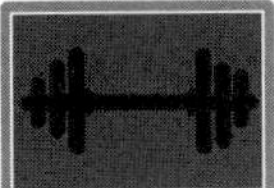

Listing 9.23 SOLO2.C Solitaire

DO:
- Add display capability to SOLO and compile SOLO2 (declare variable *done* and add the section titled "Play solitaire")
- Link SOLO2 with library CARDSLIB
- Run SOLO2

```
#include <stdio.h>
void shuffle(int *);
char *cardname(int);
```

```
#define TRUE  1
#define FALSE 0
void main()
{
   int i;                     /* Re-useable counter    */
   int deck[52];              /* Deck of cards         */
   int deck_index;            /* Index for array deck  */
   int num_deck;              /* # of active deck cards*/
   int pile[13][7];           /* Playing piles         */
   int row, col;              /* Indexes for array pile*/
   int num_cards[7];          /* Total # of cards      */
   int num_down[7];           /* # face-down cards     */
   int done = TRUE;           /* TRUE = game is over   */

/* Initialize and shuffle the deck */

   num_deck = 52;
   for (i=1; i<=52; ++i)
       deck[i-1] = i;
   shuffle(deck);

/* Lay out the piles */

   deck_index = 0;
   for (col=0; col<7; ++col)                 /* 7 piles */
   {
       for (row=0; row<=col; ++row)          /* Up to 7 cards */
       {
              pile[row][col] = deck[deck_index];
              deck[deck_index++] = 0;        /* Mark as gone */
              --num_deck;
       }
       num_down[col] = col;           /* # face-down cards */
       num_cards[col] = col + 1;      /* Total # of cards  */
   }

/* Play solitaire */

   do
   {

/* Display the board */

       printf("\n\n        1       2       3   \
   4       5       6       7");
       printf("\n       ------  ------  ------  \
------  ------  ------  ------");

       for (row=0; row<13; ++row)
       {
              printf("\n    ");
              for (col=0; col<7; ++col)
```

```
                    if (row < num_down[col])
                          printf("  *******");
                    else
                          printf("  %s",
                                cardname(pile[row][col]));
        }

        printf("\n\n       Deck  ");
        printf("\n     ------");
        printf("\n     %s", cardname(deck[deck_index]));

    } while (!done);
}
```

RESULT:

```
C:\>pc/c SOLO2

C:\pcl SOLO2;CARDSLIB


C:\>SOLO2


  1        2        3        4        5        6        7
------   ------   ------   ------   ------   ------   -------
S 5      *******  *******  *******  *******  *******  *******
         C 5      *******  *******  *******  *******  *******
                  S King   *******  *******  *******  *******
                           C Ace    *******  *******  *******
                                    S 10     *******  *******
                                             H 8      *******
                                                      H Queen






 Deck
------
D 4
```

ANALYSIS:

1. The new *do while* loop makes play continue until the variable *done* becomes true. At this stage the program will just display the board

and quit, so it initializes *done* to *TRUE*, and only one cycle of the loop occurs.

2. The section of code inside the main *do while* loop is titled "Display the board," and here the program displays the cards on each pile plus the top card of the deck. To do this, the program calls the library function cardname() in two places.

3. The first two printf() statements create column headers for the card piles. Notice how blank lines in the source code group associated display statements and make the program more readable.

4. The first *for* loop increments the index *row* through all 13 possible row positions for cards in each pile. Statements inside the curly braces will display the cards in each row; the first printf() statement begins the row on a new line and spaces over to the first column.

5. The inner, nested *for* loop increments the column index *col* across all seven piles. This loop contains one *if* statement that displays the card identifier of any face-up card, or it displays a string of asterisks for each face-down card. The *if* expression (row < num_down[col]) determines which string to display; any row that is less than the number of face-down cards for that column (pile) contains a face-down card, so the *if* expression is true and asterisks are displayed. When it encounters a face-up card, the *if* statement calls the function cardname() with the value of pile[row][col] as the argument and displays the returned string.

6. The board display concludes by showing the top card of the deck. Two printf() statements display a heading, then the final printf() fetches and displays the top card description by calling cardname().

The rows and columns of the array *pile* correspond nicely to how you want to display the data, with the piles oriented as columns on the screen. However, the way that you define a two-dimensional array does not dictate how you must display it. If you had defined *pile* to have 7 rows and 13 columns, you could display the same layout by reversing the indexes.

You can complete the simulation program by developing the code for moving cards.

Listing 9.24 SOLO3.C Solitaire

DO:
- Add to SOLO2 and compile SOLO3 (declare variables *to*, *from*, and *j*, and add the section titled "Carry out your selection")
- Link SOLO3 with library CARDSLIB
- Run SOLO3 and play a game of Solitaire

```
#include <stdio.h>
void shuffle(int *);
char *cardname(int);
#define TRUE  1
#define FALSE 0
void main()
{
   int i, j;                    /* Re-useable counters    */
   int deck[52];                /* Deck of cards          */
   int deck_index;              /* Index for array deck   */
   int num_deck;                /* # of active deck cards */
   int pile[13][7];             /* Playing piles          */
   int row, col;                /* Indexes for array pile */
   int num_cards[7];            /* Total # of cards       */
   int num_down[7];             /* # face-down cards      */
   int done = FALSE;            /* TRUE = game is over    */
   int from;                    /* Play from this pile    */
   int to;                      /* Play to this pile      */

/* Initialize and shuffle the deck */

   num_deck = 52;
   for (i=1; i<=52; ++i)
       deck[i] = i;
   shuffle(deck);

/* Lay out the piles */

   deck_index = 0;
   for (col=0; col<7; ++col)                 /* 7 piles */
   {
       for (row=0; row<=col; ++row)          /* Up to 7 cards */
       {
              pile[row][col] = deck[deck_index];
              deck[deck_index++] = 0;        /* Mark as gone */
              --num_deck;
       }
       num_down[col] = col;          /* # face-down cards */
       num_cards[col] = col + 1;     /* Total # of cards  */
   }

/* Play solitaire */

   do
   {

/* Display the board */

       printf("\n\n        1       2       3   \
  4       5       6       7");
       printf("\n      -------  -------  -------  \
-------  -------  -------  -------");
```

```
        for (row=0; row<13; ++row)
        {
                printf("\n    ");
                for (col=0; col<7; ++col)
                        if (row < num_down[col])
                                printf("  *******");
                        else
                                printf("  %s",
                                        cardname(pile[row][col]));
        }

        printf("\n\n      Deck  ");
        printf("\n     -------");
        printf("\n     %s", cardname(deck[deck_index]));

/* Carry out your selection */

        printf("\n\n     (N)ext deck card, (P)lay deck card,"
                 " (M)ove a pile, or (Q)uit: ");

        switch (getchar())
        {
                case 'M':               /* Move cards from a pile */
                case 'm':
                        printf("\nMove which pile? (1-7) ");
                        scanf("%d", &from);
                        --from;
                        printf("\nTo which pile? (1-7) ");
                        scanf("%d", &to);
                        --to;
                        for (i=num_down[from],j=num_cards[to];
                                i<num_cards[from];
                                ++i,++j)
                        {
                                pile[j][to] = pile[i][from];
                                pile[i][from] = 0;
                                --num_cards[from];
                                ++num_cards[to];
                        }
                        --num_down[from];    /* New face-up card */
                        break;

                case 'P':               /* Play from the deck */
                case 'p':
                        printf("\nPlay to which pile? (1-7) ");
                        scanf("%d", &to);
                        --to;
                        pile[num_cards[to]++][to] = deck[deck_index];
                        deck[deck_index] = 0;       /* Mark as gone   */
                        if (--num_deck == 0)
                        {
                                printf("\n\nCongratulations you win!");
```

```
                                done = TRUE;
                                break;
                        }
                                                /* Fall through */
                case 'N':                       /* Examine next deck card */
                case 'n':
                        do
                        {
                                if (++deck_index > 51)
                                        deck_index = 0;
                        } while (deck[deck_index] == 0);
                        break;

                case 'Q':                       /* Quit */
                case 'q':
                        done = TRUE;
                        break;

                default:                        /* Invalid command */
                        break;
        }
        getchar();
   } while (!done);
}
```

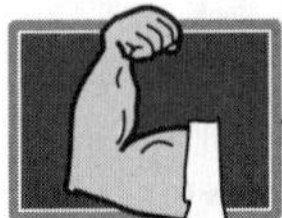

RESULT:

```
C:\>pc/c SOLO3

C:\pcl SOLO3;CARDSLIB


C:\>SOLO3


   1        2        3        4        5        6        7
-------  -------  -------  -------  -------  -------  -------
S 4      *******  *******  *******  *******  *******  *******
         C 4      *******  *******  *******  *******  *******
                  S Queen  *******  *******  *******  *******
                           D King   *******  *******  *******
                                    S 9      *******  *******
                                             H 7      *******
                                                      H Jack



 Deck
------
```

```
D 3

(N)ext deck card, (P)lay deck card, (M)ove a pile, or (Q)uit:
```

ANALYSIS:

1. At any given time, you have four options for play: (1) play a card from the deck, (2) move cards from one pile to another, (3) examine the next deck card, or (4) quit playing. After displaying the board at the beginning of each cycle of the *do while* loop, the program prompts you to select an option. The *getchar()* statement within the *switch* parentheses reads your keyboard selection; this is a typical C efficiency, in which the return value of an I/O statement provides data for a conditional statement.

2. The *switch* statement transfers program control to the appropriate *case* to carry out your command or to *default* if you enter any character other than M, N, P, or Q (uppercase or lowercase). We'll discuss the options in reverse order, from the bottom of the *switch* statement to the top. The default does absolutely nothing except allow another cycle of the main loop to occur. The quit option, Q, assigns *TRUE* to the controlling variable *done*, causing the *do while* loop to end.

3. If you select, N, the program enters a *do while* loop to find the next available card in the deck. Used cards have a 0 identifier, so the loop searches the deck until it finds a nonzero identifier. An *if* statement increments the index *deck_index* and resets it back to 0 when it exceeds the maximum value of 51.

4. If you choose to play a card from the deck with P, you receive a prompt to select the pile where you want to play the card. The scanf() statement reads the selected pile number (1–7) into the variable named *to*, which is immediately decremented so that it can be used as a zero-based index. The program plays the card to a pile with a very interesting assignment statement:

   ```
   pile[num_cards[to]++][to] = deck[deck_index];
   ```

Figure 9-14 illustrates the operation of this statement:

The right-side variable is the top deck card, and the statement assigns it to the pile location that you selected—in the two-dimensional array element on the left side of the assignment. The pile column index (the second dimension) is the variable *to* that you just entered. The next card location in the pile (the first dimension, or row index) is in the array that holds the total number of cards in each column, *num_cards*. Thus, you have used an element from one array as an index to access a value in another array. After the statement uses the value from array *num_cards* (the row index), it postfix increments the value because a card has just been added to this column. The increment operator (++) affects the array **element** because it is attached to the element reference, *num_cards[to]++*; if it were inside the brackets, *num_cards[to++]*, it would increment the **index** instead. So, with this one C statement, you can assign an element from one array to another and increment the value of a third array. After playing the card from the deck, the program checks *num_deck* to see if the deck is empty; if so, it displays a congratulations message including that you have won. If not, the program falls through to the next *case* to find the next active card in the deck (there is no *break* at the end of case 'P').

5. If you choose to move cards from one pile to another with (M), the program prompts you to select the *from* and *to* piles, then decrements these variables to serve as zero-based indexes. A compound statement controlled by a *for* loop transfers the cards. Expressions within the *for*

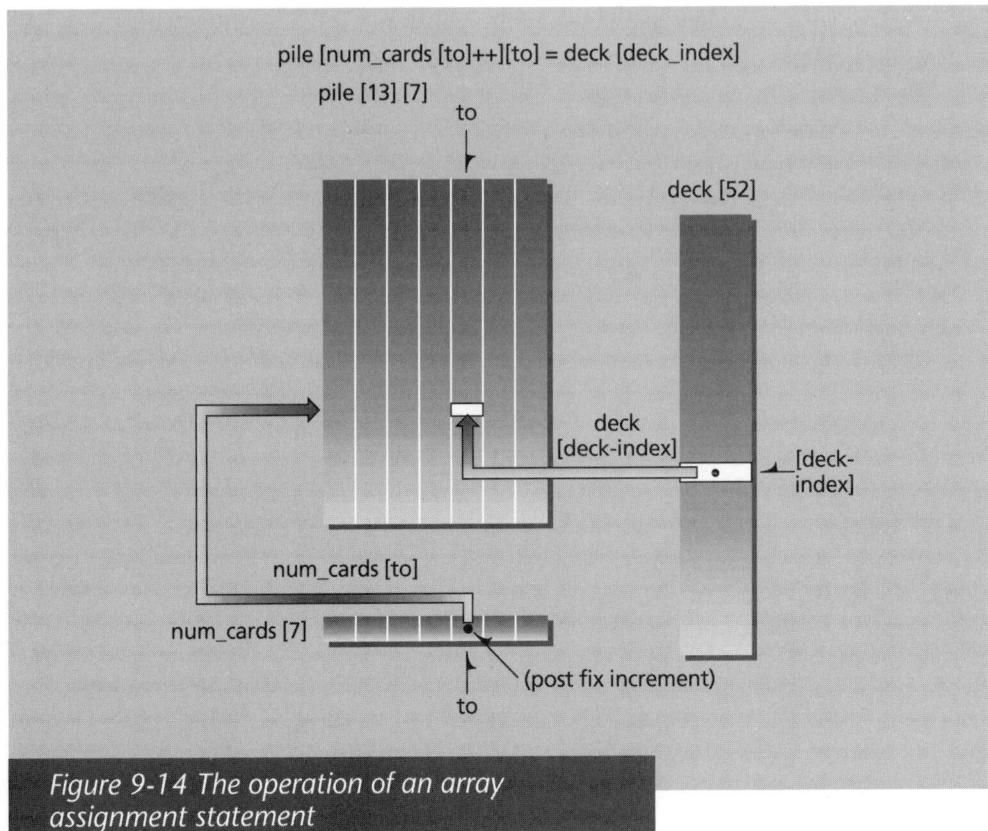

Figure 9-14 The operation of an array assignment statement

parentheses initialize and increment the controlling indexes *i* and *j*. Notice that the *for* expressions are on separate lines because they are too long for one line. Index *i* selects face-up cards on the *from* pile; the number of face-down cards represents the index of the first face-up card, so the program initializes *i* to this value, then increments it until *i* reaches the total number of cards, *num_cards*. Index *j* selects the card destination on the *to* pile, and the program initializes it to the current total number of cards on this pile, then increments *j* in step with *i*. The first statement within the loop assigns cards from one pile to the other, and the second statement sets the *from* card to 0 to remove it. The next two statements decrement the number of cards on the *from* pile and increment the number on the *to* pile. After transferring all cards, the program turns over a new face-up card on the *from* pile by decrementing the number of face-down cards.

In general you can declare arrays to hold any type of data, including floating-point numbers. In this chapter, you have used arrays chiefly to hold integer and character data. You have also stored character strings in arrays, which is a particular use of character arrays. The next chapter details some additional ways to work with strings in arrays.

CHAPTER 10

STRINGS

The topic of strings appropriately follows the chapter on arrays because strings are stored in arrays and because the last chapter gave you a brief introduction to strings. The best way to work with text data in C is to use strings and string functions. Previously, you learned how to read and write strings (in Chapter 4), and you have experienced some ways to initialize and access string data in arrays (in Chapter 9). In this chapter, you will review and expand these skills, then you will learn how to operate on strings with library functions. The standard C library contains a rich set of functions that allow you to read, write, search, copy, merge, and convert string data; you will practice using these functions. You will also learn how to pass string data to a program from the command line that starts the program.

STRINGS AND ARRAYS

A string is a contiguous sequence of character data ending with a *null character* ('\0'). Strings come in two flavors: *string constants* and *string arrays*.

String constants

In previous chapters, you have already seen most of the important uses of string constants. Starting with Chapter 1, you used string constants for printf() format specifiers and as prompts for data entry. As you saw in Chapter 9, they are important for initializing table looke-up information. You can also use string constants to initialize arrays that will be used as internal data for searching and comparison with text data.

A string constant is a sequence of characters enclosed by double quotes (" "), such as "This is a string constant." The ending null character is implied in a string constant. When you define (write) a string constant in your program, the compiler allocates memory space for the string, and it stores a null in an extra byte at the end. In the following experiment, you can see the effect that defining string constants has on the amount of memory required for a program.

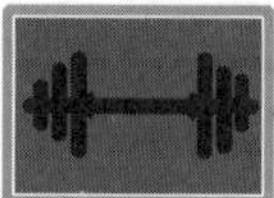

Listing 10.1 STRMEM.C String memory requirements

DO:
- Enter and compile STRMEM
- Note the size of STRMEM.EXE

```
#include <stdio.h>
main()
{
   printf("E");
}
```

RESULT:

```
C:\>pc/c/e STRMEM

C:\>dir STRMEM.EXE

 Directory of  C:

STRMEM   EXE    3136   8-21-91   8:04p
      1 File(s)  8525824 bytes free
```

ANALYSIS:

1. The printf() format specifier is the string constant "E", which takes two bytes of storage. This statement causes the character E to be displayed.

2. The size of STRMEM.EXE is 3136 bytes when compiled and linked on an IBM PC with Power C. The size of your program may be different if you have a different version of Power C than the one we used to produce this result.

Now make the format string 16 characters longer and repeat the experiment.

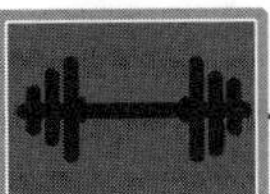

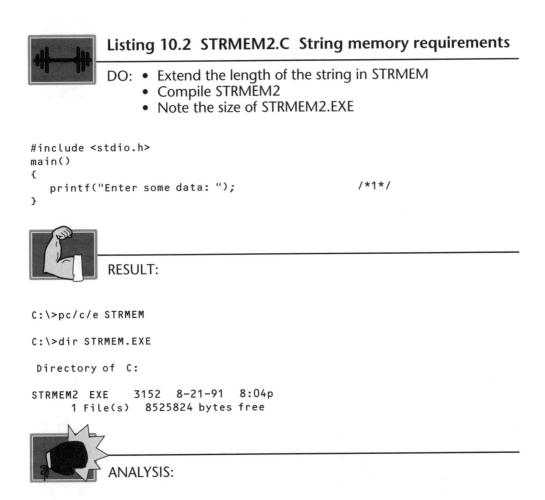

Listing 10.2 STRMEM2.C String memory requirements

DO:
- Extend the length of the string in STRMEM
- Compile STRMEM2
- Note the size of STRMEM2.EXE

```
#include <stdio.h>
main()
{
   printf("Enter some data: ");                    /*1*/
}
```

RESULT:

```
C:\>pc/c/e STRMEM

C:\>dir STRMEM.EXE

 Directory of  C:

STRMEM2  EXE    3152   8-21-91   8:04p
      1 File(s)   8525824 bytes free
```

ANALYSIS:

The size of STRMEM2.EXE is larger than STRMEM.EXE by 16 bytes, enough to hold the added characters.

In the preceding programs, you do not have access to the string constants; the programs use them only for the printf() statements in which they appear. You did not define storage for the string—the compiler did. That is, you did not define a variable in the usual manner to hold values of the string, and as a consequence, there is no identifier that you can refer to.

The point of this exercise is that string constants take up memory; they are a useful and necessary part of C programs, but be mindful of the space that they use. You should not repeat string constants in a program; if you need a string more than once, put it in an array.

String arrays

A string array is an ordinary character array that contains string data. You can define an array and initialize it with a string constant in one statement.

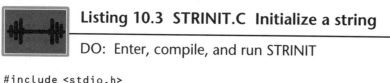

Listing 10.3 STRINIT.C Initialize a string

DO: Enter, compile, and run STRINIT

```
#include <stdio.h>
main()
{
   char prompt[18] = "Enter some data: ";

   printf(prompt);
}
```

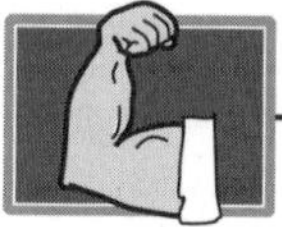

RESULT:

```
C:\>STRINIT
Enter some data:
```

ANALYSIS:

1. The program defines the character array *prompt* and initializes it with the string constant, “Enter some data: ”. The size of 18 bytes is exactly enough to hold the 17 characters of data plus a terminating null ('\0').
2. The printf() statement uses *prompt* as the format string. The format string contains no conversion specifiers and needs none, because there are no variables to be displayed.

Figure 10-1 shows how array *prompt* appears in memory.

The next program shows several ways to initialize a string array, two of which are not recommended because they are awkward and inefficient.

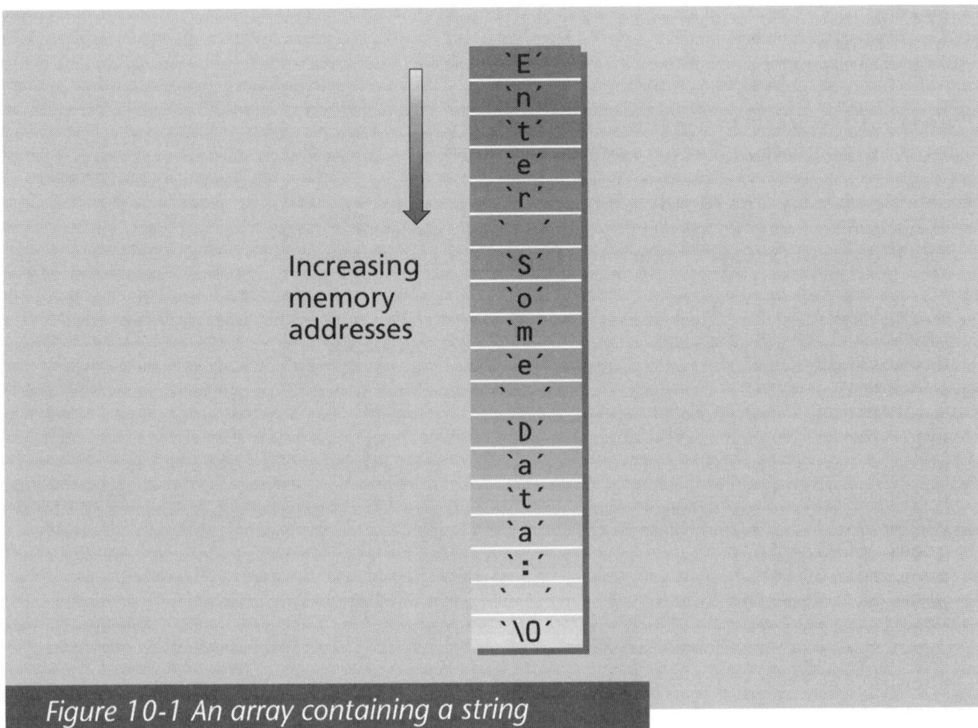

Figure 10-1 An array containing a string

Listing 10.4 STRINIT2.C Initialize strings

DO: Enter and compile STRINIT2

```
#include <stdio.h>
#include <string.h>
main()
{
/* Initialize with a string */
   char prompt1[18] = "Enter some data: ";

/* Let the initializer set the array size */
   char prompt2[] = "Enter some data: ";

/* Array is larger than the string */
   char prompt3[25] = "Enter some data: ";

/* Initialize with character constants--awkward */
   char prompt4[18] = 'E', 'n', 't', 'e', 'r', ' ',
                      's', 'o', 'm', 'e', ' ',
                      'd', 'a', 't', 'a', ':', ' ', '\0';
```

```
/* Define unitialized arrays */
   char prompt5[18];
   char prompt6[18];

/* Initialize with standard library function */
   strcpy(prompt5, "Enter some data: ");

/* Initialize by assigning character constants */
/* (you don't have to actually do this because it is really
   tedious and is the wrong way to initialize arrays) */

   prompt6[0] = 'E';
   prompt6[1] = 'n';
   prompt6[2] = 't';
   prompt6[3] = 'e';
   prompt6[4] = 'r';
   prompt6[5] = ' ';
   prompt6[6] = 'S';
   prompt6[7] = 'o';
   prompt6[8] = 'm';
   prompt6[9] = 'e';
   prompt6[10] = ' ';
   prompt6[11] = 'D';
   prompt6[12] = 'a';
   prompt6[13] = 't';
   prompt6[14] = 'a';
   prompt6[15] = ':';
   prompt6[16] = ' ';
   prompt6[17] = '\0';
}
```

1. The program defines and initializes *prompt1* in the same manner as the previous program does.

2. When you include initialization, you can leave out the declared size of an array and allow the compiler to determine the size from the number of initializer elements. The program defines the second array *prompt2* without specifying its size. The compiler examines the number of characters in the string (17) and adds one for the terminating null, then allocates 18 bytes for the array.

3. You can specify an array size larger than that required for an initializer. The program defines *prompt3* to be size 25 even though only 18 elements are needed to hold the string constant. When you initialize an array with less than the total number of elements, the compiler assigns null (zero) values to the remaining elements.

4. You can initialize a string one character at a time. The program initializes the array *prompt4* with a list of character constants, the last of

which is the terminating null character ('\0'). This statement has the same effect as the statements that define *prompt1* and *prompt2*. This form of initialization is not recommended, because it is more lengthy than using a string constant.

5. Often you need to initialize an array later in a program, **after** it is defined. You may need to initialize an array more than once, using different data, or you may want to initialize closer to where the data will be used. The standard library function, *strcpy()* (string copy), provides an excellent means for initializing a character array anywhere in a program. The prototype for this function is located in the header file, string.h, so the second statement of the program includes this header file. Function strcpy() has two arguments: it copies the second string argument into the first. The program initializes the array *prompt5* with a string constant using strcpy().

6. If you want to use the most awkward form of initialization that you can devise, you should emulate the method used for *prompt6*. The program first defines *prompt6* without initialization, then uses a separate statement to assign a character constant to each element of the array. This method works, but it is not recommended, for obvious reasons.

The beginning C programmer is understandably tempted to assign a string to a character array like this:

```
prompt5 = "Enter some data: ";    /* NOT ALLOWED */
```

Outside of the definition of an array, this is not a valid assignment—thus the need for the library function, strcpy(), that fulfills this purpose. If you look into file string.h, you will see that the prototype for strcpy() is:

```
char   *strcpy(char *str1, char *str2);
```

The prototype specifies that the function return a character pointer (char *), and it declares the two arguments to be character pointers as well. This function copies the string pointed to by str2 (the source string) into the location pointed to by str1 (the destination string). The source string can be either a string array or a string constant, but the destination string can only be a string array (you cannot change the value of a constant). You are responsible for ensuring that the destination is large enough to hold the source data. The C compiler does not check the size of the destination, and strcpy() will copy the data (including the teminating null) regardless of how much data there is or where it is going.

Function strcpy() returns a pointer to the destination string, so you can copy a string to two arrays in the following fashion:

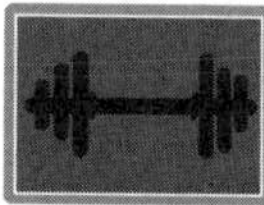

Listing 10.5 STRINIT3.C Initialize strings

DO: Enter, compile, and run STRINIT3

```
#include <stdio.h>
#include <string.h>
main()
{
   char prompt1[18];
   char prompt2[18];

   strcpy(prompt1, strcpy(prompt2, "Enter some data: "));
   printf("\n%s \n%s", prompt1, prompt2);
}
```

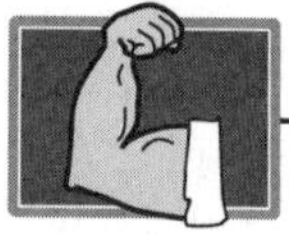

RESULT:

```
C:\>STRINIT3

Enter some data:
Enter some data:
```

ANALYSIS:

1. The prototype for function strcpy() is in string.h, so the program includes this header file.
2. The first (inner) strcpy() function copies a constant string into *prompt2*, then the second strcpy() uses the returned result (a character pointer) as the second argument. Therefore, the new string in *prompt2* is copied to *prompt1*.
3. As the printf() statement proves, both arrays end up with the same string contents.

In stdio.h, the prototype for printf() declares the format argument to be a character pointer (char *); you can use either a string constant or the name of a string array for this argument. The next program shows various combinations of string constants and arrays used with printf().

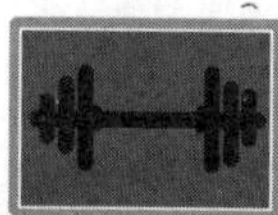

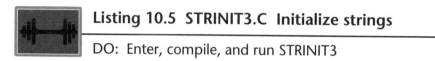

Listing 10.6 STRDISP.C Display a string

DO: Enter, compile, and run STRDISP

```
#include <stdio.h>
main()
{
   char format[] = "\nFormat is a string array %s";
   char data[] = "Data is a string array";

   printf(format, data);
   printf("\nFormat is a string constant %s", data);
   printf("\nFormat is a string constant %s",
       "Data is a string constant");
   printf(format, "Data is a string constant");
}
```

RESULT:

```
C:\>STRDISP

Format is a string array Data is a string array
Format is a string constant Data is a string array
Format is a string constant Data is a string constant
Format is a string array Data is a string constant
```

ANALYSIS:

1. The program defines and initializes an array to be used as a format string, plus an array of string data.
2. The program uses the arrays in different combinations with string constants in a printf() statement to show that either form of string will work for the format or for the data.

The next program shows the manipulation of a string array used for a format string. This example customizes output text to be singular or plural, depending on the data being displayed.

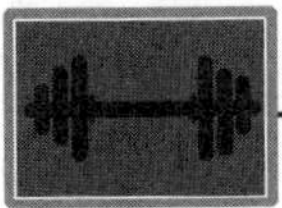

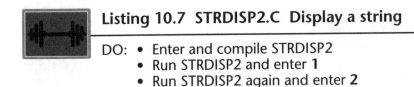

Listing 10.7 STRDISP2.C Display a string

DO:
- Enter and compile STRDISP2
- Run STRDISP2 and enter **1**
- Run STRDISP2 again and enter **2**

```
#include <stdio.h>
```

```
main()
{
   int dollars;
   char format[40];

   printf("Enter the number of dollars in your pocket: ");
   scanf("%d", &dollars);

   if (dollars == 1)
       strcpy(format, "There is %d dollar in my pocket");
   else
       strcpy(format, "There are %d dollars in my pocket");

   printf(format, dollars);
}
```

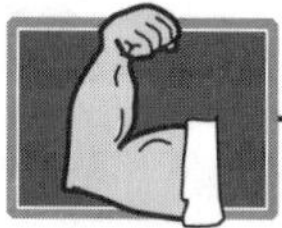

RESULT:

```
C:\>STRDISP2
Enter the number of dollars in your pocket: 1
There is 1 dollar in my pocket


C:\>STRDISP2
Enter the number of dollars in your pocket: 2
There are 2 dollars in my pocket
```

ANALYSIS:

1. The last statement in the program displays the number of dollars in your pocket, using an array to control the format.
2. The program copies one of two string constants to the array *format* depending on whether you have one dollar or more than one. By using a string array for the format, you are free to change the display as needed to fit the desired output.

STRING POINTERS

A pointer is a memory location that can hold the address of another memory location. Pointers can be constants, or they can be variables that you explicitly declare. A string pointer is a separate item from the string that it points to, and it occupies a separate memory location. The value of a string pointer is the address of a string. Figure 10-2 shows the relationship of a string pointer to string data.

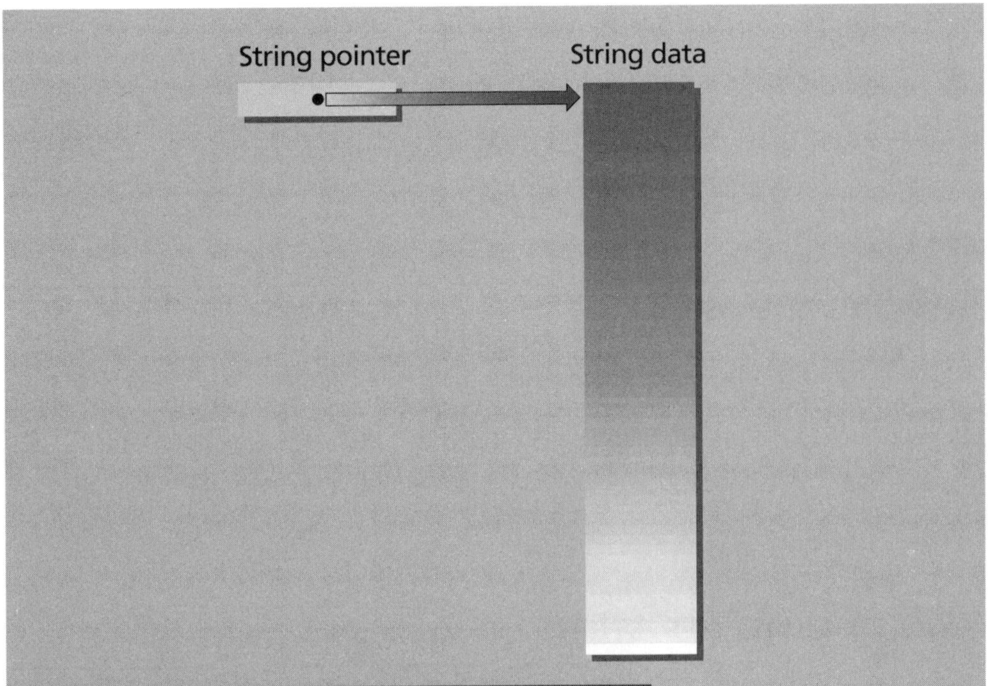

Figure 10-2 String pointer

You need string pointers primarily for arguments in functions like printf(), scanf(), strcpy(), and others. There are two ways to specify string pointers for function arguments. You can explicitly declare a character pointer variable, then initialize it, or you can refer directly to the location of a string. You have previously referred directly to the address of string constants in statements like printf("%s", "Enter some data: "), or to the address of arrays in statements like printf(prompt). The next program shows how to define a character pointer and use it as an argument in printf().

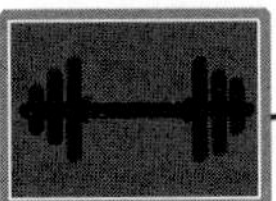

Listing 10.8 STRPTR.C String pointers

DO: Enter, compile, and run STRPTR

```
#include <stdio.h>
main()
{
   char *str_ptr = "Enter some data: ";

   printf(str_ptr);
}
```

RESULT:

```
C:\>STRPTR
Enter some data:
```

ANALYSIS:

The program defines and initializes the pointer, *str_ptr*, to the address of a string constant. The string is not in an array even though it is stored in memory. The compiler allocates space for the string constant, and you can access it through the pointer.

You can also initialize a character pointer so that it points to an array, as in the next program. Remember that the bare name of an array is the address of the beginning, or first element, of the array.

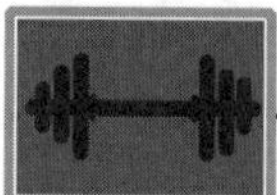

Listing 10.9 STRPTR2.C String pointers

DO:
- Change the string pointer initialization
- Compile and run STRPTR2

```
#include <stdio.h>
main()
{
   char prompt[18] = "Enter some data: ";
   char *str_ptr   = prompt;

   printf(str_ptr);
}
```

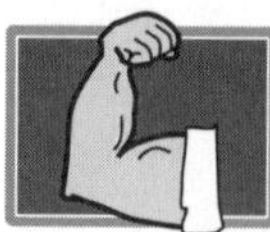

RESULT:

```
C:\>STRPTR2
Enter some data:
```

ANALYSIS:

1. This program defines a character array *prompt* and initializes it with a string constant.

2. The program then defines a pointer variable *str_ptr*, which will be used as a string pointer. The pointer is of the same data type (char) as the data it will point to. The program initializes the pointer by referring to the name *prompt*, which is the address of the array.
3. The initialized pointer serves as the format string argument for the printf() statement.

The value of a pointer is an address, and an address is a number that represents one of the locations in your computer memory. You can display the value of a pointer with the %p conversion specifier in a printf() statement.

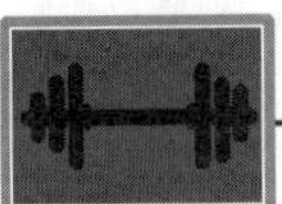

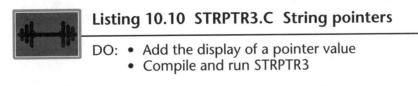

Listing 10.10 STRPTR3.C String pointers

DO:
- Add the display of a pointer value
- Compile and run STRPTR3

```
#include <stdio.h>
main()
{
   char *str_ptr = "Enter some data: ";

   printf(str_ptr);
   printf("\nThis is the value of str_ptr displayed as a \
pointer: %p", str_ptr);
}
```

RESULT:

```
C:\>STRPTR3
Enter some data:
This is the value of str_ptr displayed as a pointer: 0004
```

ANALYSIS:

The pointer value is the memory address where the compiler stores the string constant; the address is the number of bytes from the beginning of the memory where the string is located.

Each compiler determines how to display pointer values with %p—C does not specify the format. Power C displays pointer values as hexadecimal numbers, which is the most popular way for computer scientists to represent memory addresses.

So far you have learned several ways to point to the beginning of a string. You can point to any element in a string by using the *address* operator (&) in conjunction with an array index. For example, &prompt[0] is the address of (or pointer to) the beginning of *prompt*, and &prompt[1] is the address of the second element of the string. The next program shows how the *address* operator (&) can specify the value of the pointer argument for printf().

Listing 10.11 STRPTR4.C String pointers

DO:
- Enter, compile, and run STRPTR4
- Enter **Have a good day**

```
#include <stdio.h>
main()
{
   char sentence[80];

/* Enter a string */

   printf("Enter a sentence: ");
   gets(sentence);

/* Display the beginning of a string */

   printf("\nThis is sentence displayed as a string: %s",
       sentence);
   printf("\nThis is sentence displayed as a pointer: %p",
       sentence);

/* Display another part of the string */

   printf("\nThis is &sentence[5] displayed as a string: %s",
       &sentence[5]);
   printf("\nThis is &sentence[5] displayed as a pointer: %p",
       &sentence[5]);
}
```

RESULT:

```
C:\>STRPTR4
Enter a sentence: Have a good day

This is sentence displayed as a string: Have a good day
This is sentence displayed as a pointer: 833E
This is &sentence[5] displayed as a string: a good day
This is &sentence[5] displayed as a pointer: 8343
```

ANALYSIS:

1. After the program reads some data into the array *sentence*, it displays the data (the whole sentence) and the pointer to the data.
2. The last two printf() statements display the data and a pointer to the data, beginning at the sixth element of the string array. Notice that the value of this pointer is five (bytes) greater than the previous pointer value (you must subtract the two hexadecimal address values to see this).

When printf() displays a string (using conversion specifier %s), it starts at the address given in the variable list and displays consecutive characters until it reaches a null ('\0'). Thus, you can display the whole string by listing the beginning address, or you can display the last part of a string by listing an intermediate address. You can use a variable index value to select any part of the string in the next program.

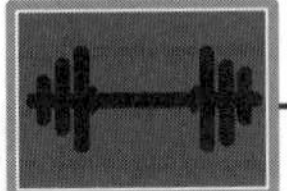

Listing 10.12 STRPTR5.C String pointers

DO:
- Modify STRPTR4 to use a variable index
- Compile SRPTR5

```
#include <stdio.h>
main()
{
   char sentence[80];
   int index;                                          /*1*/

/* Enter a string */

   printf("Enter a sentence: ");
   gets(sentence);

   index = -1;                                         /*2*/
   while (index)                                       /*3*/
   {                                                   /*4*/

/* Select an index to the string */

      printf("\nEnter an index (0 to quit): ");
      scanf("%d", &index);

/* Display the selected part of the string */

      printf("\nThis is &sentence[index] displayed"
```

```
                    " as a string: %s", &sentence[index]);
        printf("\nThis is &sentence[index] displayed"
                    " as a pointer: %p", &sentence[index]);
    }                                                       /*5*/
}
```

The *while* loop allows you repeatedly to enter an index and see a selected part of the string and the value of the string pointer.

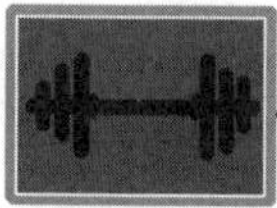

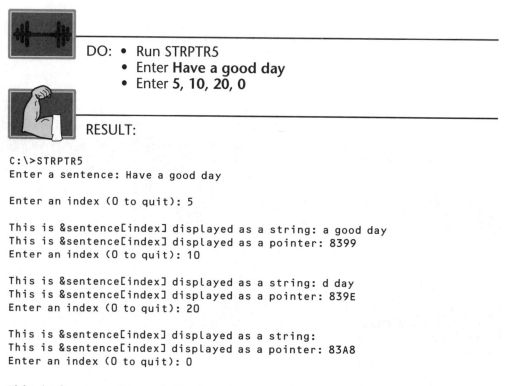

DO: • Run STRPTR5
• Enter **Have a good day**
• Enter **5, 10, 20, 0**

RESULT:

```
C:\>STRPTR5
Enter a sentence: Have a good day

Enter an index (0 to quit): 5

This is &sentence[index] displayed as a string: a good day
This is &sentence[index] displayed as a pointer: 8399
Enter an index (0 to quit): 10

This is &sentence[index] displayed as a string: d day
This is &sentence[index] displayed as a pointer: 839E
Enter an index (0 to quit): 20

This is &sentence[index] displayed as a string:
This is &sentence[index] displayed as a pointer: 83A8
Enter an index (0 to quit): 0

This is &sentence[index] displayed as a string: Have a good day
This is &sentence[index] displayed as a pointer: 8394
```

ANALYSIS:

1. The first display is the same result as for the previous program, STRPTR4.
2. By entering 10 as the second response, you have selected the 11th character of the string as the starting point. Notice that the pointer value is 5 more than the last one.

3. With the third selection, you will get some unpredictable garbage displayed because an index of 20 is beyond the end of the string. The printf() statement goes right ahead, however, and displays the character data until it encounters a null value in memory. Our program displayed nothing because the first unpredictable value happened to be a null. Notice that the beginning pointer value is correct; it is 10 bytes greater than the last value.
4. When you enter 0 to end the program, it displays the string one more time before quitting. This is because you enter the zero value for *index* **inside** the loop, and the control expression only becomes false at the **beginning** of the next cycle of the *while* statement.

STANDARD LIBRARY STRING FUNCTIONS

In this section, you will use more of the standard library functions to manipulate strings. It will be useful to have a program to serve as a focal point for developing skills in working with strings. Figure 10-3 is a flow diagram of a program that analyzes words in a sentence.

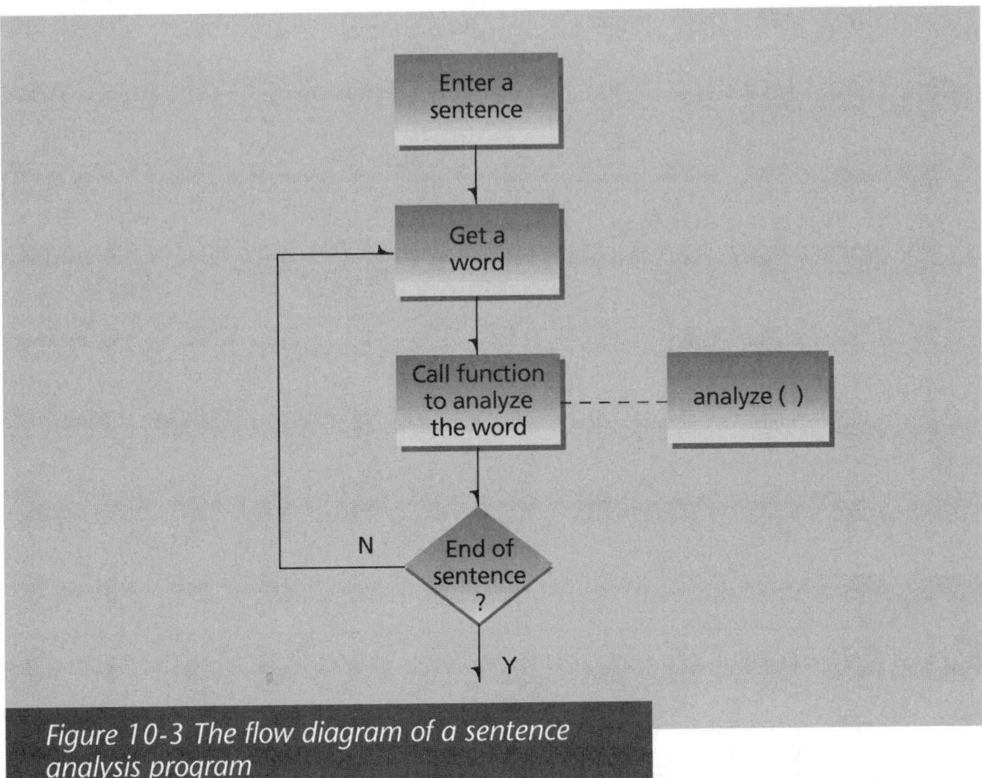

Figure 10-3 The flow diagram of a sentence analysis program

The main function will prompt you to enter a sentence. It will then separate (parse) the individual words of the sentence and then call a function to analyze the words. The term *parse* may be new to you. Parse is defined in Webster's dictionary as: "To break (a sentence) down into its component parts...." We will use this program to illustrate several different analysis operations, so we have designed the analysis function to be replaceable in a sort of "plug and play" fashion—an advantage provided by modular programming.

Your first task is to develop the main function for sentence analysis; begin by installing the code to enter a sentence and call the analysis function. This initial program establishes the framework for processing a sentence; you can leave the task of parsing the sentence into separate words for Program 10.14.

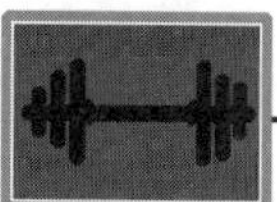

Listing 10.13 ANALYZE.C Analyze a sentence

DO:
- Enter, compile, and run ANALYZE
- Enter **Have a good day**

```
#include <stdio.h>
#include <string.h>
void analyze(char *);
main()
{
   char sentence[80];          /* Original sentence */
   char word[80];              /* Word parsed from sentence */

/* Enter a sentence */

   printf("Enter a sentence: ");
   gets(sentence);
   strcpy(word, sentence);

/* Analyze a word */

   analyze(word);
}

void analyze(char *word)
{
   printf("\nThe sentence is: %s", word);
}
```

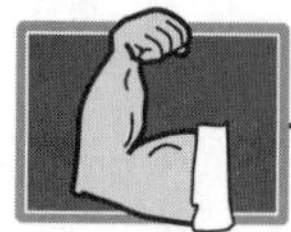

RESULT:

```
C:\>ANALYZE
Enter a sentence: Have a good day
The sentence is: Have a good day
```

ANALYSIS:

1. The program defines two character arrays of length 80: *Sentence* will hold the entered string, which can be as long as 79 characters (one is reserved for the ending null). The array *word* will hold words parsed from the sentence; it is the same size as *sentence* to allow for the longest possible word.

2. The printf() and gets() statements under the section titled "Enter a sentence" should be familiar to you. The strcpy() function copies the entered *sentence* to *word* so that, for now, analyze() will work with the whole sentence string.

3. Function analyze() will not return any value, so both the prototype and the function definition declare it to be of data type void. The single argument of analyze() is declared as a pointer to a string (type char *) in both places.

4. For the time being, analyze() just displays the string referred to by the pointer parameter.

5. Header file string.h contains prototype declarations for the standard library string functions. You should include file string.h so that the compiler can check for the correct function return type and argument type.

Your next task will be to add sentence parsing to the program. Figure 10-4 is a flow diagram of the parsing algorithm.

The term *algorithm* may also be new to you. An algorithm is a procedure that has a definite outcome or result. The parsing algorithm in Figure 10-4 is a series of steps that finds blank spaces between words in a sentence and copies each word to a separate string. To add parsing to the program, you need a good way to find the length of each word, because part of the parsing algorithm requires skipping past each word. The next program expands the function analyze() to find the length of the parsed string.

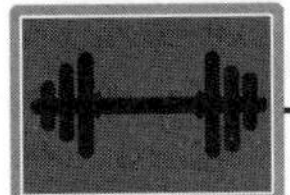

Listing 10.14 ANALYZE2.C Analyze a sentence

DO:
- Add some processing to function analyze()
- Compile and run ANALYZE2
- Enter **Have a good day**

```
#include <stdio.h>
#include <string.h>
```

```
void analyze(char *);
main()
{
   char sentence[80];
   char word[80];

/* Enter a sentence */

   printf("Enter a sentence: ");
   gets(sentence);
   strcpy(word, sentence);

/* Analyze a word */

   analyze(word);
}
```

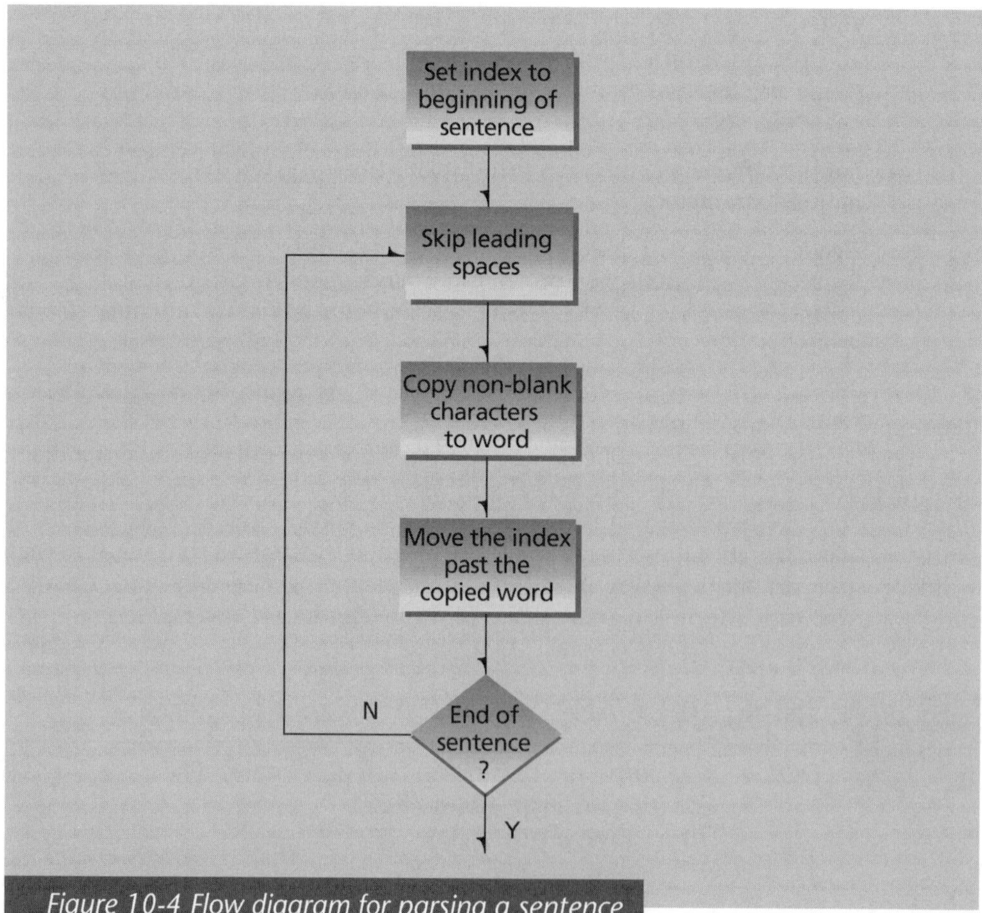

Figure 10-4 Flow diagram for parsing a sentence

```
void analyze(char *word)
{
   int index = 0;                                     /*1*/

   while (word[index++] != '\0')                      /*2*/
       ;                                              /*3*/
   printf("\nThe length of \"%s\" is %d",             /*4*/
       word, index - 1);                              /*5*/
}
```

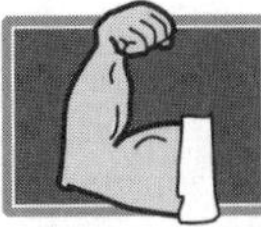

RESULT:

```
C:\>ANALYZE2
Enter a sentence:
The length of Have a good day is 15
```

ANALYSIS:

1. Function analyze() uses two statements to find the length of the word. Statement /*1*/ defines *index* and initializes it to zero (the beginning of the word string).
2. The *while* loop in statement /*2*/ postfix increments *index* and examines each element in the string array until it finds a null element. When the *while* loop ends, the value of *index* is one greater than the length of the string *word*.
3. Notice that the printf() format string uses an escape sequence \" to insert double quotes in the display line.

Finding the length of a string—function strlen()

As easy as it was to find the length of a string with two statements, there is a better way. There is a standard library function that returns the length of a string, called strlen(). If you insert strlen(), the function is even simpler.

Listing 10.15 ANALYZE3.C Analyze a sentence

DO:
- Simplify function analyze() with strlen()
- Compile and run ANALYZE3
- Enter **Have a good day**

```
#include <stdio.h>
```

```
#include <string.h>
void analyze(char *);
main()
{
   char sentence[80];
   char word[80];

/* Enter a sentence */

   printf("Enter a sentence: ");
   gets(sentence);
   strcpy(word, sentence);

/* Analyze a word */

   analyze(word);
}

void analyze(char *word)
{
   printf("\nThe length of \"%s\" is %d",
       word, strlen(word));                              /*1*/
}
```

RESULT:

```
C:\>ANALYZE3
Enter a sentence: Have a good day
The length of "Have a good day" is 15
```

ANALYSIS:

The function strlen() counts the number of characters in a string, excluding the terminating null, so in this example it reports the total number of characters that you entered, 15.

The function strlen() does not check the received pointer parameter; it assumes that you have given it a pointer to a valid, null-terminated string. It will start at the beginning of the string and search memory until it finds a null, much the same way as you did in the previous version of analyze(). If the character array does not contain a null, strlen() will continue stepping through memory until it eventually finds one, but the returned length will be a bogus number.

The library function will execute faster than your own version because it was written with efficiency in mind. This is generally true of standard library functions, and it is one reason that you should use them instead of "reinventing the wheel" with your own code.

Next, you can develop the algorithm to parse the sentence with the help of the strlen() function and a new standard I/O function, sscanf(). This function works much like scanf(), but it takes input from a string instead of the keyboard. The general form of a call to sscanf() is:

```
sscanf(string, format, list)
```

The first argument is a pointer to the input string; the second and third arguments are the same format specifier and variable list with which you are familiar from scanf(). You will use sscanf() to extract (parse) individual words from a sentence in the next version of analyze().

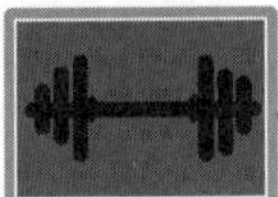

Listing 10.16 ANALYZE4.C Analyze a sentence

DO:
- Add parsing to ANALYZE3
- Compile and run ANALYZE4
- Enter **Have a good day**

```
#include <stdio.h>
#include <string.h>
void analyze(char *);
main()
{
   char sentence[80];
   char word[80];
   int index = 0;                                              /*1*/

/* Enter a sentence */

   printf("Enter a sentence: ");
   gets(sentence);

/* Parse the sentence */

   while (index < strlen(sentence))                            /*2*/
   {
                                                               /*3*/
      sscanf(&sentence[index], "%s", word);                    /*4*/
      index += strlen(word) + 1;                               /*5*/
      while (sentence[index] == ' ')                           /*6*/
            ++index;                                           /*7*/

/* Analyze a word */

      analyze(word);
   }
```

```
}

void analyze(char *word)
{
   printf("\nThe length of %s is %d", word, strlen(word));
}
```

RESULT:

```
C:\>ANALYZE4
Enter a sentence: Have a good day

The length of Have is 4
The length of a is 1
The length of good is 4
The length of day is 3
```

ANALYSIS:

1. Line /*1*/ defines *index* and initializes it to zero (the beginning of the array *sentence*); *index* will step to the beginning of each word in the sentence.
2. Parsing occurs within the *while* loop that spans lines /*2–8*/, and it continues as long as *index* is less than the length of the *sentence* string (that is, until *index* has stepped past the last word).
3. The sscanf() statement on line /*4*/ copies each word from the sentence. Function sscanf() works just like scanf() except that the input stream comes from a character array (*sentence*) instead of from the keyboard. You will recall that the string conversion specifier (%s) skips leading spaces, then causes characters to be read from the input stream until a **white space** character is encountered. Thus, sscanf() begins at location *&sentence[index]* and copies characters from this array to *word* until it encounters a SPACE in *sentence* (at the end of a word). It then adds a terminating null character to the output array *word*.
4. On line /*5*/ the program gets ready to parse the next word by moving *index* to the SPACE character at the end of the current word. Line /*5*/ adds the length of a word, plus one, to *index*—the extra one accomodates only a single space character. To make the program work with additional spaces, lines /*6–7*/ move the *index* past multiple space characters between each word.

5. After the program parses a word from the sentence, it calls analyze(), which displays the word and its length.

Comparing strings, function strcmp()

There is a standard library function, called strcmp(), that compares two strings. You call strcmp() this way:

```
strcmp(str1, str2);
```

where *str1* and *str2* are string pointers. Strcmp() returns the integer 0 if the strings are equal. Two strings are equal if they are the same length and have the same characters in the same positions. You can easily count the occurrences of a particular word in a sentence with function strcmp(). The main function for reading and parsing a sentence will not change for the rest of this chapter, so it is not listed even though it is part of each ANALYZE program. You should carry the code for main() from program ANALYZE4 through to each new example.

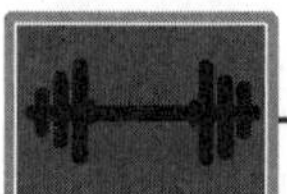

Listing 10.17 ANALYZE5.C Analyze a sentence

DO:
- Change analyze() to search for a particular word
- Compile and run ANALYZE5
- Enter **That was the week that was**

```
void analyze(char *word)
{
   static int num_occurrence = 0;                              /*1*/
   static int num_words = 0;                                   /*2*/
   if (strcmp(word, "that") == 0)                              /*3*/
        ++num_occurrence;                                      /*4*/
   printf("\n%d words analyzed with %d occurrences \           /*5*/
of \"that\"", ++num_words, num_occurrence);                    /*6*/
}
```

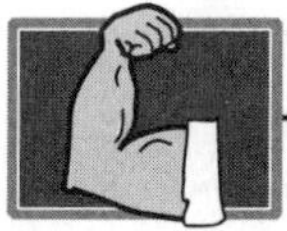

RESULT:

```
C:\>ANALYZE5
Enter a sentence: That was the week that was

1 words analyzed with 0 occurrences of "that"
2 words analyzed with 0 occurrences of "that"
3 words analyzed with 0 occurrences of "that"
4 words analyzed with 0 occurrences of "that"
5 words analyzed with 1 occurrences of "that"
6 words analyzed with 1 occurrences of "that"
```

ANALYSIS:

1. The function declares variables *num_occurrence* and *num_words* to be *static* on lines /*1–2*/ so that the accumulated values will not change between calls to analyze(). When a function declares a variable *static*, the program initializes the variable only once, at the first call to the function.
2. Line /*3*/ calls function strcmp(), which returns a value of zero if the string pointed to by *word* equals "that"; if so, variable *num_occurrence* increments.
3. The printf() statement on lines /*5–6*/ increments the total number of words analyzed along with the accumulated number of occurrences of "that."
4. Notice that strcmp() is sensitive to case because the program does not count the first occurrence of "That" (with uppercase T). You could make the test case-insensitive by converting all characters in the word to uppercase and comparing them with "THAT." You can do this with the library function toupper(), as shown in the following version of analyze().

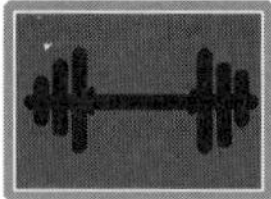

Listing 10.18 ANALYZE6.C Analyze a sentence

DO:
- Modify function analyze() for case insensitivity
- Compile and run ANALYZE6
- Enter **That was the week that was**

```
#include <ctype.h>                                              /*1*/
void analyze(char *word)
{
   int i;                                                       /*2*/
   static int num_occurrence = 0;
   static int num_words = 0;

   for (i=0; i<strlen(word); ++i)                               /*3*/
        word[i] = toupper(word[i]);                             /*4*/
   if (strcmp(word, "THAT") == 0)
        ++num_occurrence;
   printf("\n%d words analyzed with %d occurrences \
of \"that\"", ++num_words, num_occurrence);
}
```

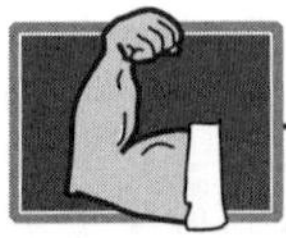

RESULT:

```
C:\>ANALYZE6
Enter a sentence: That was the week that was

1 words analyzed with 1 occurrences of "that"
2 words analyzed with 1 occurrences of "that"
3 words analyzed with 1 occurrences of "that"
4 words analyzed with 1 occurrences of "that"
5 words analyzed with 2 occurrences of "that"
6 words analyzed with 2 occurrences of "that"
```

ANALYSIS:

1. The prototype for function toupper() is in header file ctype.h, included on line /*1*/ so that the compiler can check data types and arguments. You should position this *#include* directive above the main function, along with the *#include* for stdio.h.
2. Lines /*3–4*/ scan the length of the input string and call function toupper() for each character in *word*. If the argument is in the range 'a' to 'z' (lowercase), function toupper() returns the corresponding uppercase equivalent; otherwise, it returns the argument value unchanged.
3. As a result of your change to a case-insensitive comparison, analyze() now finds two occurrences of the word **that**.

The standard C library has a companion function, tolower(), that returns the lowercase equivalent of the letters 'A' through 'Z'.

Power C offers you an easier way to accomplish a case-insensitive string comparison—with function strcmpi(). This function is not included in the standard ANSI C library, so it will not be available with all C compilers, but it is very useful.

Listing 10.19 ANALYZE7.C Analyze a sentence

DO:
- Use strcmpi() in place of strcmp() in ANALYZE5
- Compile and run ANALYZE7
- Enter **That was the week that was**

```
void analyze(char *word)
{
```

```
   static int num_occurrence = 0;
   static int num_words = 0;

   if (strcmpi(word, "that") == 0)                              /*1*/
        ++num_occurrence;
   printf("\n%d words analyzed with %d occurrences \
of \"that\"", ++num_words, num_occurrence);
}
```

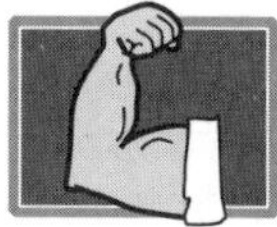

RESULT:

```
C:\>ANALYZE7
Enter a sentence: That was the week that was

1 words analyzed with 1 occurrences of "that"
2 words analyzed with 1 occurrences of "that"
3 words analyzed with 1 occurrences of "that"
4 words analyzed with 1 occurrences of "that"
5 words analyzed with 2 occurrences of "that"
6 words analyzed with 2 occurrences of "that"
```

ANALYSIS:

This simpler change achieves the same result as before; it counts all occurrences of **that** regardless of case.

Programmers often need to sort character data in alphabetic order. In the next example, you will alter the function analyze() to produce a list of words from the sentence in alphabetic order. To do this, you can use additional information from the call to function strcmp(str1, str2), which returns a negative value if *str1* is less than *str2*, and a positive value if *str1* is greater than *str2*. The function compares strings *lexicographically*—that is, it compares the numeric codes for characters in corresponding positions. Figure 10-5 shows how strcmp() compares two strings.

Beginning with the first character of each string, strcmp() compares the numeric codes; if they are equal, it proceeds to the next character position. If they are not equal, or the end of one of the strings occurs, the comparison ends. If *str2* ends first, or if the nonmatching character code in *str1* is greater than the corresponding code in *str2*, then the first string *str1* is greater than the second and strcmp() returns a positive integer. For instance, "ABC" is greater than either "AB" or "ABA." Function strcmp() returns a negative integer if *str1* is less than *str2*. You can use strcmp() to sort some words alphabetically. Figure 10-6 is a flow diagram of the sorting algorithm embodied in the analyze() function of the next program.

For each new word that analyze() receives, it either places the word on the bottom of a list, or it inserts the new word in its proper place among other words already on the list.

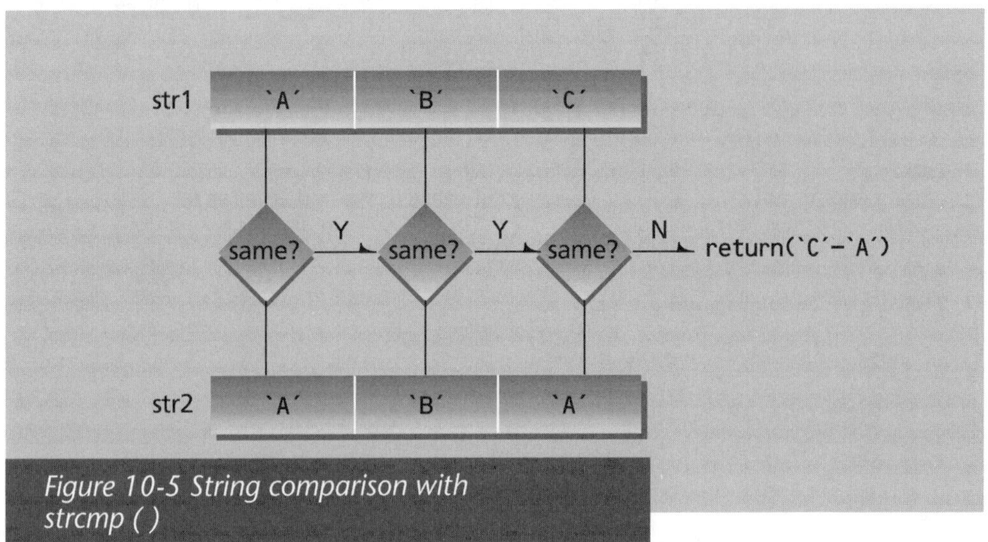

Figure 10-5 String comparison with strcmp ( )

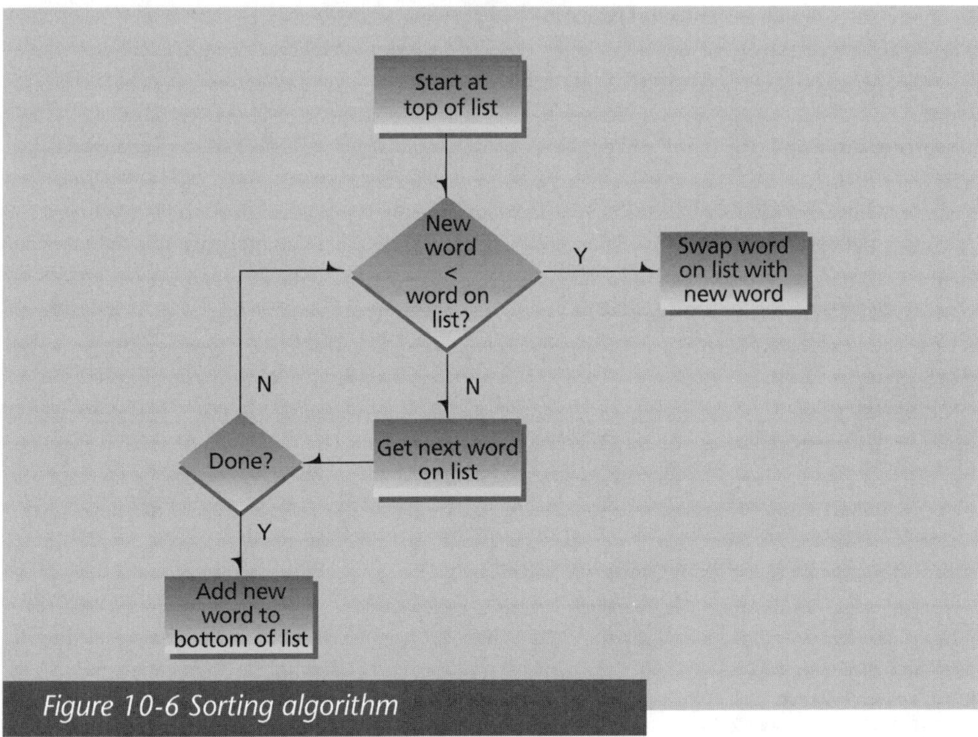

Figure 10-6 Sorting algorithm

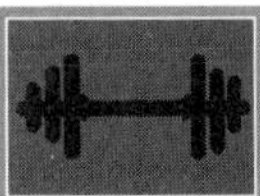

Listing 10.20 ANALYZE8.C Analyze a sentence

DO:
- Enter a new function to sort words alphabetically
- Compile and run ANALYZE8
- Enter **Have a very good day**

```
void analyze(char *word)
{
   int n;                            /* Loop counter */
   char temp_word[80];               /* Temporary word storage */
   static int num_words = 0;         /* Number of words received */
   static char words[40][80];        /* Words received */

/* Store the incoming word */

   strcpy(words[num_words], word);

/* Sort the words */

   for (n=0; n<num_words; ++n)
        if (strcmp(words[num_words], words[n]) < 0)
        {
                strcpy(temp_word, words[n]);
                strcpy(words[n], words[num_words]);
                strcpy(words[num_words], temp_word);
        }

/* Set the index to the next available word storage */

   ++num_words;

/* Display the sorted sentence */

   printf("\n");
   for (n=0; n<num_words; ++n)
        printf("%s ", words[n]);
}
```

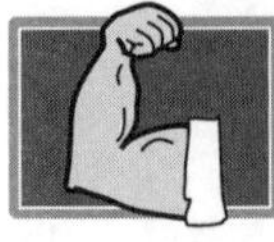

RESULT:

```
C:\>ANALYZE8
Enter a sentence: Have a very good day

Have
Have a
Have a very
Have a good very
Have a day good very
```

ANALYSIS:

1. The first thing that the function must do is store the incoming words so that there will be a place to sort them. The two-dimensional array *words* serves this purpose; the function declares it to be *static* so that the program will not discard the array and its contents each time the function ends; you do not want to lose previous words that are stored there. The array has 40 rows because there can be up to 40 words in a sentence of 80 characters. The array *words* has 80 columns to accommodate the longest word possible. The array can store 40 x 80 = 3200 characters, and there are, at most, 80 characters in the sentence, so there is a lot of wasted space in *words*. C provides ways to dynamically allocate variable amounts of memory space to make maximum use of memory, but an explanation of this technique will have to wait until the next chapter (see "Dynamic memory allocation" in Chapter 11).

2. The integer *num_words* keeps a count of the total number of words received; the function also declares it to be *static* so that the program retains its value between function calls. It serves as an index to the next available location in the array *words*.

3. You store the incoming word with function strcpy(); the destination argument is a pointer to the next available row in array *words*, *words[num_words]* (the index to the second array dimension is not present, making this a pointer reference to the row).

4. The function places each new word in its correct alphabetic order in the list. The *for* loop scans down the list from top to bottom and compares the new word (at location *num_words*) with each word in the list. When it finds that the new word is less than a word in the list, it swaps the two words. The word swapped out of the list then serves as the new word for the next comparison. When the loop finishes, the list is in alphabetic order. All uppercase characters precede all lowercase characters in the table of ASCII codes, so 'H' is ahead of 'a' in alphabetic order and the word "Have" goes ahead of "a."

5. A final *for* loop displays the words in the order in which they occur in the list, then the function increments *num_words* to get ready for the next word.

Figure 10-7 shows what happens to each word in the example as the function compares it with words already on the sentence list.

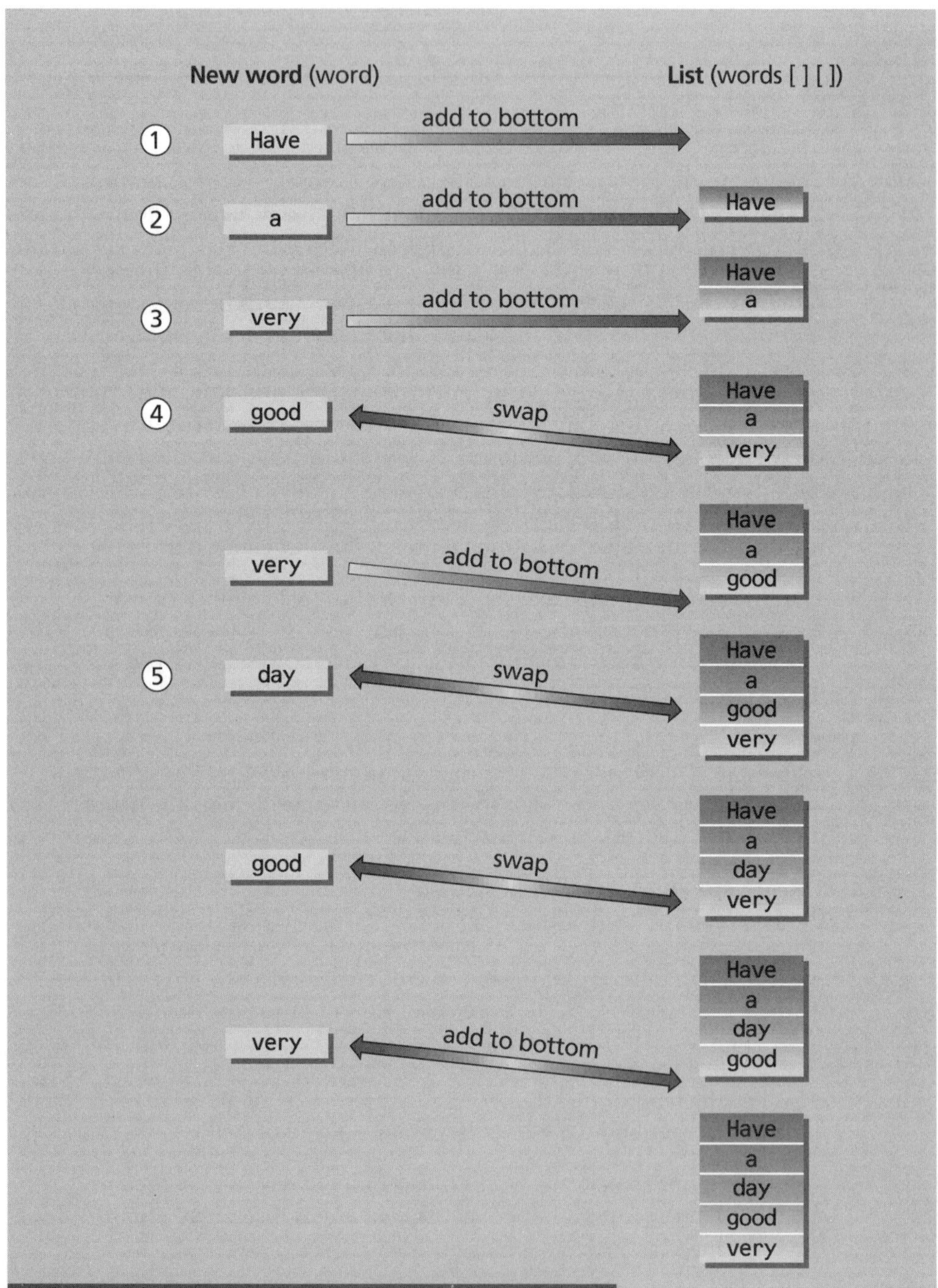

Figure 10-7 A sorting operation

The first three words are already in alphabetical order, so analyze() adds them to the bottom of the list. The fourth word, "good," is alphabetically below both "Have" and "a," but above "very," so the program swaps these two words, then it adds "very" to the bottom of the list. The last word, "day," belongs above "good," so analyze() swaps these words, and "good" becomes the new word. The function then compares "good" with "very" and again makes a swap so that "very" moves off the list to become the new word for the second time. Finally, the function adds "very" at the bottom of the list, and the sorted sentence is complete.

Putting strings together—function strcat()

Function strcat() allows you to concatenate two strings to form a single string. The call: strcat(str1, str2) adds *str2* to the end of *str1* and returns a pointer to *str1*. You must be certain that the destination string *str1* is large enough to hold both strings, because strcat() does not do any size checking. Figure 10-8 shows how strcat() works.

Function strcat() copies all of the characters of the second string (including the ending null) to the first string, beginning at the location of the ending null of the first

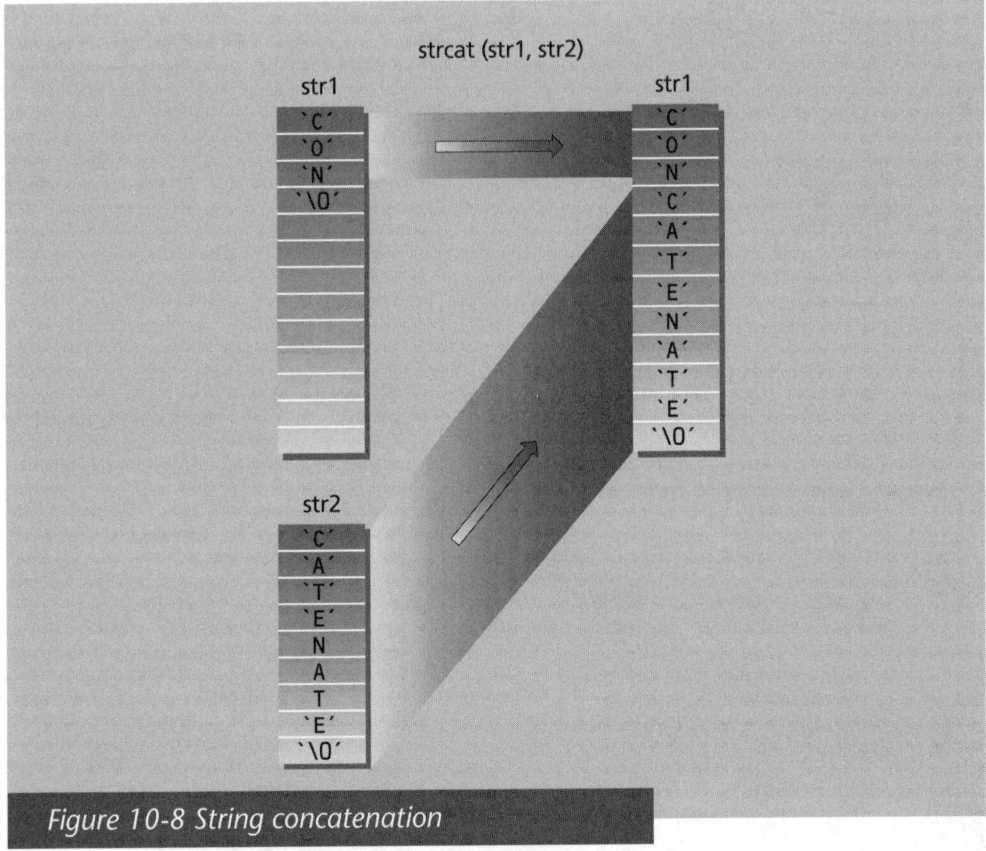

Figure 10-8 String concatenation

string. Thus, the first character of the second string replaces the ending null of the first string. The resulting string has one terminating null character, and its length is the sum of the lengths of the original strings; the following expression is TRUE:

```
strlen(str1) + strlen(str2) == strlen(strcat(str1, str2))
```

You can arrange the sorted words of a sentence back into sentence form with strcat().

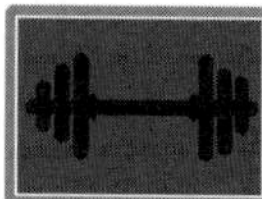

Listing 10.21 ANALYZE9.C Analyze a sentence

DO:
- Change analyze() to display the sorted sentence
- Compile and run ANALYZE9
- Enter **Have a good day**

```
void analyze(char *word)
{
   int n;                             /* Loop counter */              /*1*/
   char output[80];                   /* Output string */
   char temp_word[80];                /* Temporary word storage */
   static int num_words = 0;          /* Number of words received */
   static char words[40][80];         /* Words received */

/* Store the incoming word */

   strcpy(words[num_words], word);

/* Sort the words */

   for (n=0; n<num_words; ++n)
       if (strcmp(words[num_words], words[n]) < 0)
       {
              strcpy(temp_word, words[n]);
              strcpy(words[n], words[num_words]);
              strcpy(words[num_words], temp_word);
       }

/* Set the index to the next available word storage */

   ++num_words;

/* Display the sorted sentence */

strcpy(output, "");                   /* Init. with null string */ /*2*/
for (n=0; n<num_words; ++n)           /* Form the output string */ /*3*/
{                                                                  /*4*/
   strcat(output, words[n]);                                       /*5*/
   strcat(output, " ");                                            /*6*/
}                                                                  /*7*/
printf("\nSorted sentence: %s", output);/* Display */              /*8*/
}
```

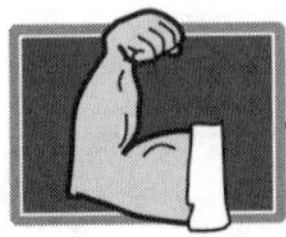

RESULT:

```
C:\>ANALYZE9
Enter a sentence: Have a good day

Sorted sentence: Have
Sorted sentence: Have a
Sorted sentence: Have a good
Sorted sentence: Have a day good
```

ANALYSIS:

1. Line /*1*/ defines a new character array for the output string, and line /*2*/ initializes it to a *null string*. Double quotes with no intervening character data are the null string constant. A null string has only one null character ('\0') and its length is zero. The initial null string, copied to *output* by the statement on line /*2*/, makes it possible for the first call to strcat() to concatenate the first word.

2. Lines /*3–7*/ concatenate each of the sorted words in the array *words* to *output*; *words[n]* is a pointer to row *n* of the two-dimensional array *words*.

3. Line /*8*/ displays the resulting sorted sentence.

Locating characters within strings—function strchr()

The standard library contains a function thet searches for any single character value within a string. You call strchr() as follows:

```
strchr(str, chr)
```

where *str* is a pointer to a string and *chr* is a character constant or variable. The function returns a pointer to the first occurrence of the character in the string, or *NULL* if the character is not in the string. The symbolic constant *NULL* is defined in string.h as a null pointer:

```
#define NULL ((void *)0)
```

This directive defines *NULL* as the constant 0, cast to a void pointer so that the size of *NULL* is the proper size for a pointer.

The next function discovers the first instance of the letter 't' in any word.

Listing 10.22 ANALYZ10.C Analyze a sentence

DO:
- Enter a new analyze() to detect the letter ‘t’
- Compile and run ANALYZ10
- Enter **Don’t be facetious**

```
void analyze(char *word)
{
   if (strchr(word, 't') != NULL)
       printf("\n\"%s\" contains the letter 't'", word);
}
```

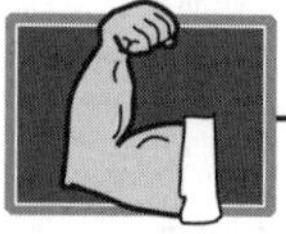

RESULT:

```
C:\>ANALYZ10
Enter a sentence: Don't be facetious

"Don't" contains the letter 't'
"facetious" contains the letter 't'
```

ANALYSIS:

The single call to strchr() searches the incoming word for the character ‘t’. If strchr() finds a ‘t’, it returns a pointer to its location; therefore, the *if* control expression is true and printf() displays a line of output.

You can use strchr() to locate any desired combination of characters; the next version of analyze() identifies all words that have the five vowels in alphabetic order (a, e, i, o, u).

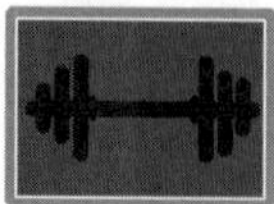

Listing 10.23 ANALYZ11.C Analyze a sentence

DO:
- Change analyze() to detect 5 vowels in order
- Compile and run ANALYZ11
- Enter **Don’t be facetious**

```
void analyze(char *word)
{
   char *ptr;

   if ((ptr = strchr(word, 'a')) != NULL)
       if ((ptr = strchr(ptr, 'e')) != NULL)
```

```
            if ((ptr = strchr(ptr, 'i')) != NULL)
                if ((ptr = strchr(ptr, 'o')) != NULL)
                    if ((ptr = strchr(ptr, 'u')) != NULL)
                        printf("\n\"%s\" has the vowels"
                            " in order!", word);
}
```

RESULT:

```
C:\>ANALYZ11
Enter a sentence: Don't be facetious

"facetious" has the vowels in order!
```

ANALYSIS:

1. This function consists of five nested *if* statements; each one calls strchr() to search for a different vowel.
2. The first *if* calls strchr() to search the string *word* for 'a' and assigns the result to *ptr*. If the word doesn't contain an 'a', the result is *NULL*, the *if* expression is false, and function analyze() ends with no action. On the other hand, if an 'a' exists, the program proceeds to the next level of nested *if*, and *ptr* points to the 'a'.
3. The second *if* calls strchr() to search for 'e' beginning at the location of 'a'. If 'e' doesn't exist between the 'a' and the end of the string, the second *if* expression is false and analyze() ends.
4. The last three nested *if* statements repeat the search procedure, progressing steadily toward the end of the string as each *if* locates a vowel.
5. If all five *if* statements are successful, the printf() statement displays a message to announce success.

Because strchr() returns *NULL* when it fails to find the specified character, and because *NULL* is zero, you could simplify each of the *if* statements to:

```
if (ptr = strchr(word, 'a'))
```

However, the original form is better because it explicitly shows that the statements expect a non-*NULL* result. You could simplify even further by replacing the nested *if* statements with one *if* containing nested calls to strchr():

```
if (strchr(strchr(strchr(strchr(strchr(word, 'a'), 'e'), 'i'), 'o'), 'u'))
```

In this expression, the result of each call is the first argument of the next call to strchr(). If any of the searches fails to find the specified character, the first argument for the next call is a *NULL* pointer, and the subsequent search also fails. This construction seems to work, but it is not recommended, because C does not specify the reaction of strchr() to a *NULL* pointer argument. Power C reacts gracefully to the situation, but another compiler could produce unpredictable results.

Converting strings to numbers—functions atoi(), atol(), and atof()

You can convert numeric strings to integers or floating-point numbers with the standard library functions atoi(), atol(), and atof(). The header file stdlib.h contains the prototypes for these functions:

```
int atoi(char *string);
long atol(char *string);
double atof(char *string);
```

The functions all have one argument, a character pointer to a string with numeric characters. The function atoi() returns an integer value that is the converted equivalent of the string, atol() returns a long integer, and atof() returns the double-precision floating-point equivalent of the string. For example, atoi("123") returns the integer value 123, atol("456L") returns a *long* value of 456, and atof("7.89") returns the floating-point number 7.89.

These functions are particularly good in situations in which using scanf() is awkward or impossible. One of these situations occurs if you need to input an indefinite number of values, and the values are integers and floating-point numbers mixed in an unpredictable order. You can't use scanf() because you don't know how many variables and conversion specifiers to use, nor do you know the order in which to specify the two data types. A solution to this problem is to read the input as one long string of numeric values (with gets()), then parse the individual values and convert them. The following program implements this solution. With strchr(), you can easily detect whether or not a value contains a decimal point.

Listing 10.24 ANALYZ12.C Analyze a sentence

DO: • Enter a new analyze() to convert numbers from a string
• Compile ANALYZ12

```
#include <stdlib.h>                                            /*1*/
void analyze(char *word)
{
   static int    int_sum   = 0;              /* Sum of int values   */
   static double float_sum = 0.;             /* Sum of float values */
```

```
    if (strchr(word, '.') != NULL)          /* Float or int?      */
        printf("\nFloating-point entry: %.1f, and sum: %.1f",
               atof(word), float_sum += atof(word));
    else
        printf("\nInteger entry: %d, and sum: %d",
               atoi(word), int_sum += atoi(word));
}
```

ANALYSIS:

1. For this program, the input "sentence" will be numbers separated by spaces, so the main function parses each number and passes it to analyze() as the argument *word*.
2. Prototypes for the conversion functions are located in the header file stdlib.h, so you should add line /*1*/ at the top of the file, above the main function. You could also include stdlib.h just before analyze(), but the usual place is at the beginning of the file.
3. This version of analyze() will separately accumulate integers and floating-point numbers found in the input string, so it defines *static* variables to hold the two sums—*static* so the program will retain the values between function calls.
4. An *if* test checks to see whether the number is an integer or a floating-point number by calling strchr() to search for a decimal point ('.'). If the number contains a decimal point, strchr() returns the address (a nonzero pointer value) and the *if* expression is true. If there is no decimal point, strchr() returns *NULL* and the printf() under the *else* branch is executed.
5. Both of the printf() statements display two values: The value of the number received is the result of a call to atof() or atoi(), and the accumulated value for either data type is the result of an assignment expression within printf(). For instance, the result of int_sum += atoi(word) is the value displayed for the accumulated integer sum.

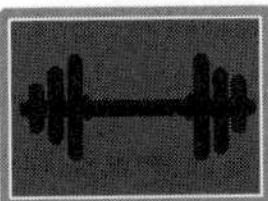

DO:
- Run ANALYZ12
- Enter **1 2.2 3 4.4 5.5 6 7 8.8 9**

RESULT:

```
C:\>ANALYZ12
```

```
Enter a sentence: 1 2.2 3 4.4 5.5 6 7 8.8 9

Integer entry: 1, and sum: 1
Floating-point entry: 2.2, and sum: 2.2
Integer entry: 3, and sum: 4
Floating-point entry: 4.4, and sum: 6.6
Floating-point entry: 5.5, and sum: 12.1
Integer entry: 6, and sum: 10
Integer entry: 7, and sum: 17
Floating-point entry: 8.8, and sum: 20.9
Integer entry: 9, and sum: 26
```

DO:
- Run ANALYZ12
- Enter **1 2 3 4 5 6.6 7.7 8.8**

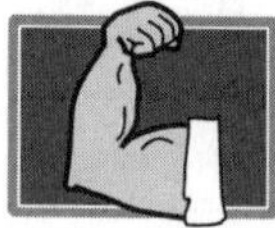

RESULT:

```
C:\>ANALYZ12
Enter a sentence: 1 2 3 4 5 6.6 7.7 8.8

Integer entry: 1, and sum: 1
Integer entry: 2, and sum: 3
Integer entry: 3, and sum: 6
Integer entry: 4, and sum: 10
Integer entry: 5, and sum: 15
Floating-point entry: 6.6, and sum: 6.6
Floating-point entry: 7.7, and sum: 14.3
Floating-point entry: 8.8, and sum: 23.1
```

ANALYSIS:

As these runs indicate, you can change the number, order, and mix between integers and floating-point values, and the program will operate correctly.

The first non-numeric character encountered by a conversion function causes the conversion to end at that point (as if a terminating null occurred).

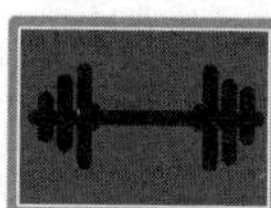

DO:
- Run ANALYZ12
- Enter **1x1 2.2* -3END45**

RESULT:

```
C:\>ANALYZ12
Enter a sentence: 1x1 2.2* -3END45

Integer entry: 1, and sum: 1
Floating-point entry: 2.2, and sum: 2.2
Integer entry: -3, and sum: -2
```

ANALYSIS:

The converted values reflect only digits found before the function encounters a non-numeric character. Notice that a negative sign ('-') and decimal point ('.') are acceptable numeric characters.

Another situation in which scanf() is inadequate occurs when you need to enter numbers in combination with character data. In Chapter 7, the AGE2 program (Listing 7.12) reads a person's age and sex as an integer followed by a character with the statement: scanf("%d %c", &age, &sex); 1 This works fine for entering the data, but to quit you have to enter **0 Q**. It would be preferable to enter just **Q** to quit. The CALC5 program (Listing 7.23) has a similar but even more serious problem; you have to enter **0 Q 0** to quit. You can accomplish a much more relaxed and intuitive keyboard interaction by parsing string input and interpreting the data instead of using a formatted scanf(). The next program shows a method for doing this.

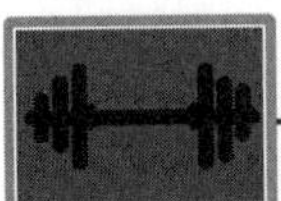

Listing 10.25 ANALYZ13.C Analyze a sentence

DO:
- Enter a new analyze() to interpret data in a string
- Compile ANALYZ13

```
#include <stdlib.h>
void analyze(char *word)
{
   static int age;

/* Test for numeric digits */

   if ((word[0] >= '0') && (word[0] <= '9'))
        age = atoi(word);

/* Process non-numeric data */

   else
```

```
        switch (word[0])
        {
                case 'M':
                        printf("\nAge of male is %d", age);
                        break;
                case 'F':
                        printf("\nAge of female is %d", age);
                        break;
                case 'Q':
                        printf("\nQuit command received");
                        break;
                default:
                        printf("\nEnter only (F)emale, (M)ale,"
                                " or (Q)uit");
        }
}
```

ANALYSIS:

1. This version of analyze() will not plug directly into the original program AGE2, but it illustrates how you might modify AGE2 or CALC5 to read data from the keyboard and quit more gracefully. The form of input for this program is a person's age followed by either (F) for female or (M) for male, then (ENTER).
2. The function checks the first character to see if it is a numeric digit in the range of '0' to '9'. If so, a call to atoi() converts the string and assigns the result to the integer *age*. Variable *age* is *static* so that the program will hold its value until the function can analyze the next *word* and include *age* in the subsequent display.
3. If the incoming *word* contains non-numeric information, the *switch* statement selects one of four printf() statements to execute, depending on the value of the first character. In its present form, analyze() does not return a value, but it could be modified to return a code to signal the main function to quit when (Q) is received.

DO:
- Run ANALYZ13
- Enter **41 M 6 F Q**

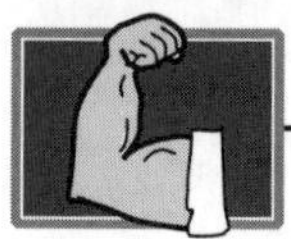

RESULT:

```
C:\>ANALYZ13
```

```
Enter a sentence: 41 M 6 F Q

Age of female is 41
Age of male is 6
Quit command received
```

ANALYSIS:

The benefit of this method over using scanf() for input occurs when you enter ªQº instead of numeric data at the beginning of the string; the program interprets this correctly as a command to end.

You may find that there are many situations in which it is difficult to make scanf() react to input data in the desired way. By reading character data into a string, you establish full control over how it is parsed and interpreted, thereby allowing yourself freedom of design for interaction with input data.

Copying partial strings—function strncpy()

You can perform other types of interpretations of string information using additional standard library functions such as strncpy(). The prototype for this function (from string.h) is:

```
char *strncpy(char *str1, char *str2, size_t n);
```

The function copies *n* characters from *str2* to *str1* and returns a pointer to *str1*. Function strncpy() does NOT copy an ending null into *str1* unless the length of *str2* is less than *n* characters. Then strncpy() copies all of the characters of *str2* and substitues nulls ('\0') for the rest. The data type size_t is a synonym for an *unsigned int;* a *typedef* statement within string.h declares it to be the same as an *unsigned int* data type. Chapter 16 explains more about typedefs. You can use strncpy() to extract embedded string information, as in the next example, which finds an integer quantity and a floating-point dollar amount in a sentence no matter where the numbers are or what surrounds them.

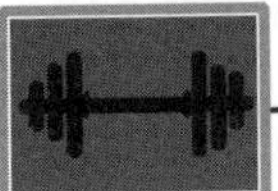

Listing 10.26 ANALYZ14.C Analyze a sentence

DO:
- Enter a new version of analyze() to extract numbers embedded in a string
- Compile ANALYZ14

```
void analyze(char *word)
{
   int index = 0;              /* Index to string data */
   int start = 0;              /* Index of start of number */
```

```
   char temp[20];              /* Extracted number */

/* Find the beginning of a number */

   while (((word[index] < '0') || (word[index] > '9')) &&
          (index < strlen(word)))
        ++index;

   if (index < strlen(word))
   {
        start = index;

/* Find the end of the number */

        while (((word[index] >= '0') && (word[index] <= '9'))
               || (word[index] == '.') && (index < strlen(word)))
               ++index;

/* Extract the number */

        strncpy(temp, word[start], index - start);
        temp[index - start] = '\0';

/* Display the data */

        if (strchr(temp, '.'))
               printf("\nThe cost is: %s", temp);
        else
               printf("\nThe quantity is: %s", temp);
   }
}
```

ANALYSIS:

1. This version of function analyze() scans each word to find and extract any number that is there, even if it is surrounded by other characters.

2. The first *while* loop finds the beginning digit of a number (if it exists). As long as the character is outside the range of zero through nine (< '0' or > '9'), the loop continues to increment *index*. When the loop ends, if the value of *index* is beyond the end of the string, then *word* doesn't contain a number and analyze() returns.

3. If the value of *index* is within the string length, the function assigns it to *start* to mark the beginning of a number. Then a second *while* loop searches for the end of the number. This loop continues to increment *index* as long as the characters are numeric digits in the range of from 0 through 9, or a decimal point ('.'). When the loop ends, *index* refers

to the next character beyond the end of the number (which may be the terminating null for the string).

4. Function strncpy() extracts the number from the string *word* and copies it to the array *temp*; copying starts at the character *word[start]* and continues for *index - start* characters.
5. At this point in the program, *temp* is an array of character data; the next statement makes it a string by assigning a terminating null ('\0') to the element following the last copied digit.
6. The final *if* test calls strchr() to see if the number in *temp* contains a decimal point. If so, the number is displayed in the context of a cost message; otherwise, it is displayed as a quantity.

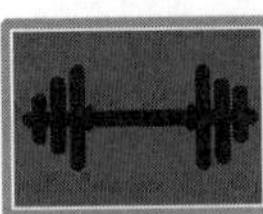

DO: • Run ANALYZ14
• Enter **A dozen (12) apples costs $2.76.**

RESULT:

```
C:\>ANALYZ14
Enter a sentence: A dozen (12) apples costs $2.76.

The quantity is: 12
The cost is: 2.76.
```

ANALYSIS:

Notice that the period at the end of the sentence accompanies the extracted cost number because the program doesn't know how many decimal points are allowed. You could correct this anomaly by making the second *while* loop end if it encounters a second decimal point.

DO: • Run ANALYZ14
• Enter **I paid $37600.00 for 1 Mercedes.**

RESULT:

```
C:\>ANALYZ14
```

```
Enter a sentence: I paid $37600.00 for 1 Mercedes.

The quantity is: 1
The cost is: 37600.00
```

The program can extract numbers from a wide variety of sentences.

You can also use strncpy() instead of strcpy() to ensure that you don't copy too many characters from a longer string and overrun the length of a target string. You would accomplish this by making the third argument equal to the length of the destination string:

```
strncpy(destination, source, strlen(destination));
```

Similar functions exist for comparing (strncmp()) and concatenating (strncat()) partial strings—for details, refer to Appendix C, "Power C library functions."

Finding substrings within strings—function strstr()

You can search for a substring within a string with the standard library function strstr(), which has the prototype:

```
char *strstr(char *str1, char *str2);
```

This function will return a pointer to the beginning of substring *str2* where it first appears in *str1*, or *NULL* if *str2* is not in *str1*. The following version of analyze() is an example of how strstr() can be used to search some genealogical text for the occurrence of a surname that could take on any of three spellings.

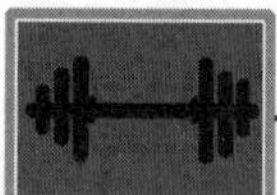

Listing 10.27 ANALYZ15.C Analyze a sentence

DO:
- Enter a version of analyze() that searches for a substring
- Compile and run ANALYZ15
- Enter **In 1857 the Schmidt family emigrated to New York.**

```
void analyze(char *word)
{
   int i;
   static char *spellings[] = {"Schmid", "Schmit", "Smid"};

   for (i=0; i<3; ++i)
        if (strstr(word, spellings[i]) != NULL)
             printf("\n%s contains %s", word, spellings[i]);
}
```

RESULT:

```
C:\>ANALYZ14
```

```
Enter a sentence: In 1857 the Schmidt family moved to New York.

Schmidt contains Schmid
```

ANALYSIS:

1. The program first initializes an array of character pointers (*spellings*) to point to the three spelling variations of the name "Schmidt."
2. The task of this version of analyze() is to search each word parsed from the sentence to see if it contains any of the variations of "Schmidt." The *for* loop indexes to each of the three string constants, spellings[i], which serves as the substring argument for strstr(). Whenever a call to strstr() returns a non-*NULL* value (indicating that the substring was located), printf() displays the *word* and substring.

Ragged arrays

An array of pointers initialized to point to a group of string constants, like *spellings* in the above program, is called a *ragged array*. Figure 10-9 shows the layout of a ragged array in memory.

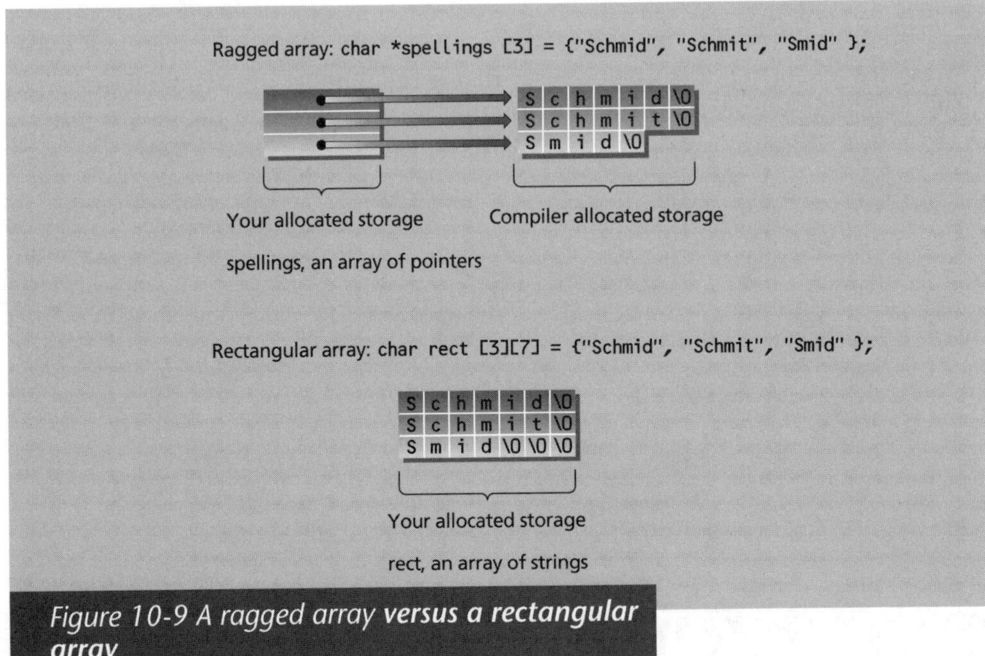

Figure 10-9 A ragged array **versus a rectangular** *array*

The name **ragged** stems from the fact that the array is not rectangular; if the strings are listed with the left sides lined up, then the right edge of the array is not straight—it is **ragged**. A ragged array is an array of pointers, each of which refers to a string constant that the compiler stores somewhere in memory. Contrast this with a regular character array in which you specify the amount of storage to be allocated. You can use a ragged array when the string entries are constant. You cannot use ragged arrays when you need to alter the strings. The advantage of a ragged array is that no space is wasted on unused elements

COMMAND LINE ARGUMENTS

You can pass data to a program from a command line that executes the program. When you type the name of the program, you can insert data that conveys instructions or information to the program. The DOS command to format a system disk is:

```
C:\>FORMAT A: /S E
```

This command executes the FORMAT program and passes two arguments to it. The first argument, **A:**, tells the program which drive contains the disk to be formatted, and the second argument, **/S**, instructs it to place the system files on the disk. There can be any number of arguments on a command line, separated by spaces. C provides a mechanism for the main function of a program to accept command line arguments. Like any other function, main() declares a list of parameters within parentheses; by convention, the following form is used to list the command line parameters:

```
void main(int argc, char *argv[])
```

The first parameter, *argc*, is an integer that is the number of command line arguments received. The second parameter is an array of pointers to the command line

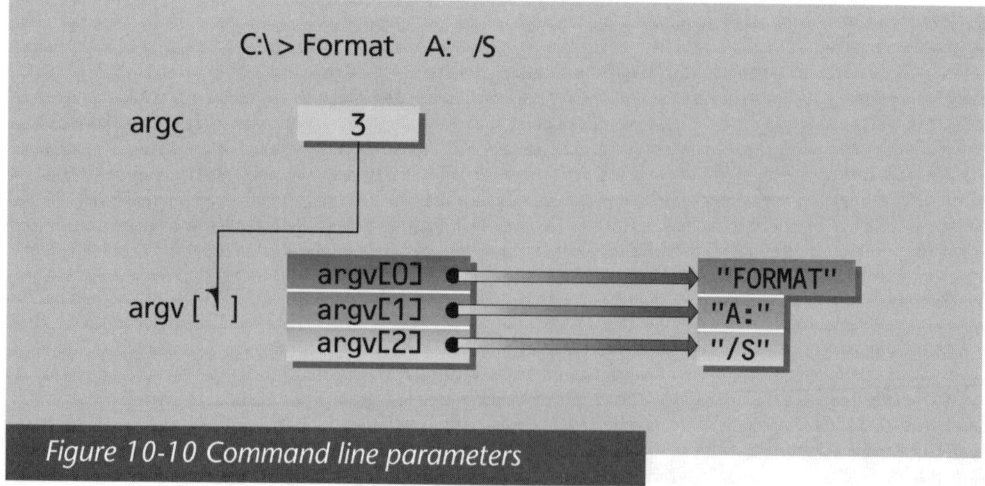

Figure 10-10 Command line parameters

arguments. The operating system (DOS) passes the starting command line to the program, and as a part of the startup operation, the program parses the command line into a sequence of string pointers. The character array *argv[]* receives the pointers and the value of *argc* is the size of the array. For DOS 3.0 or later versions, the first parameter is the program name; earlier versions of DOS set the first parameter to null ('\0'). Figure 10-10 shows the parameters of main() for disk formatting:

You do not need a prototype for the main function—C does not require it. The arguments for main() are always either none or the two shown here. The next example shows how to accept command line arguments and redisplay them within a program.

Listing 10.28 CMDLINE.C Command line arguments

DO:
- Enter and compile CMDLINE
- Run CMDLINE with the arguments shown

```
#include <stdio.h>
main(int argc, char *argv[])
{
   int i;

   printf("\nProgram: %s", argv[0]);
   for (i=1; i<argc; ++i)
       printf("\nCommand line argument %d: %s", i, argv[i]);
}
```

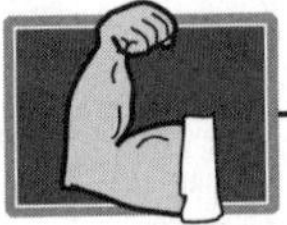

RESULT:

```
C:\>CMDLINE This is a test

Program: C:\CMDLINE.EXE
Command line argument 1: This
Command line argument 2: is
Command line argument 3: a
Command line argument 4: test
```

ANALYSIS:

1. Following the normal convention, the program declares the main() parameters to be an integer *argc* and an array of character pointers *argv[]*.

2. The first element in *argv* is a pointer to the name of the program, which the first printf() displays.
3. The *for* loop displays the rest of the command line arguments (from 1 to *argc-1*); printf() pairs the pointer to each argument string *argv[i]* with a string conversion specifier (%s) to display each one.

Command line parameters are commonly used to specify options for a program. The accepted form is to start each argument with a hyphen (-) or slash (/), then follow with a simple one- or two-character code. For example you could install an option to display a program banner with the command -B, and you could double-space all program output with the command -D. The following program implements these commands:

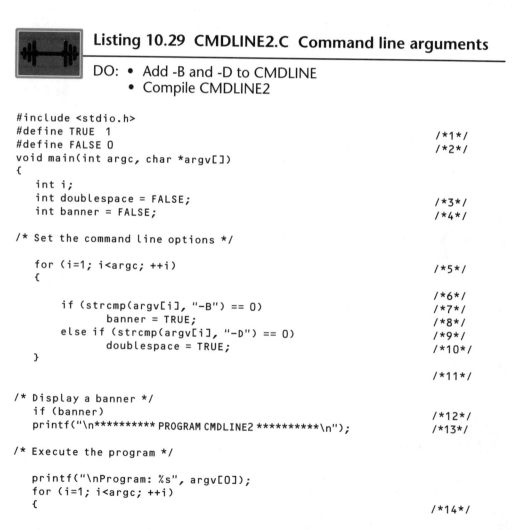

Listing 10.29 CMDLINE2.C Command line arguments

DO:
- Add -B and -D to CMDLINE
- Compile CMDLINE2

```
#include <stdio.h>
#define TRUE  1                                              /*1*/
#define FALSE 0                                              /*2*/
void main(int argc, char *argv[])
{
   int i;
   int doublespace = FALSE;                                  /*3*/
   int banner = FALSE;                                       /*4*/

/* Set the command line options */

   for (i=1; i<argc; ++i)                                    /*5*/
   {
                                                             /*6*/
       if (strcmp(argv[i], "-B") == 0)                       /*7*/
              banner = TRUE;                                 /*8*/
       else if (strcmp(argv[i], "-D") == 0)                  /*9*/
              doublespace = TRUE;                            /*10*/
   }
                                                             /*11*/

/* Display a banner */
   if (banner)                                               /*12*/
   printf("\n********** PROGRAM CMDLINE2 **********\n");     /*13*/

/* Execute the program */

   printf("\nProgram: %s", argv[0]);
   for (i=1; i<argc; ++i)
   {                                                         /*14*/
```

```
        if (doublespace) printf("\n");                                /*15*/
        printf("\nCommand line argument %d: %s",
              i, argv[i]);
    }                                                                 /*16*/
}
```

ANALYSIS:

1. Lines /*1–4*/ define and initialize the variables *banner* and *doublespace*; these integers will be set to *TRUE* or *FALSE* to signal whether the options are in effect or not.
2. Lines /*5–11*/ scan the command line arguments to see which options were requested. The *for* loop indexes from the second to the last argument (the first argument is the program name). If the command line contained no options, the value of *argv* will be 1 and the loop will not execute.
3. For each possible option, an *if* statement within the loop checks to see if the current command line string matches that option. If you executed the program with the double space option (-D), then the second strcmp() would match one of the argument strings with the string constant "-D" and set *doublespace* to *TRUE*. Since the loop compares each option with each incoming argument, you can specify options in any order.
4. Lines /*12–13*/ display the program banner if *banner* is *TRUE*, and lines /*14–16*/ add an extra newline between display lines if *doublespace* is *TRUE*.

DO: Run CMDLINE2 with the doublespace option

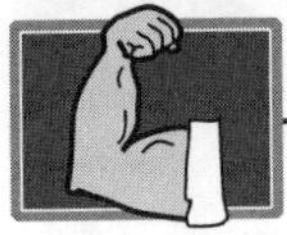

RESULT:

```
C:/>CMDLINE2 -D This is a test

Program: C:\CMDLINE2.EXE

Command line argument 1: -D

Command line argument 2: This
```

```
Command line argument 3: is

Command line argument 4: a

Command line argument 5: test
```

DO: Run CMDLINE2 with both options

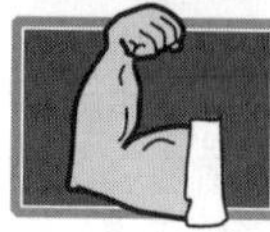

RESULT:

```
C:/>CMDLINE2 -D -B This is a test

********** PROGRAM CMDLINE2 **********

Program: C:\CMDLINE2.EXE

Command line argument 1: -D

Command line argument 2: -B

Command line argument 3: This

Command line argument 4: is

Command line argument 5: a

Command line argument 6: test
```

DO: Run CMDLINE2 with no options

RESULT:

```
C:/>CMDLINE2 This is a test

Program: C:\CMDLINE2.EXE
Command line argument 1: This
Command line argument 2: is
Command line argument 3: a
Command line argument 4: test
```

ANALYSIS:

1. You can use as many command line options as desired, and you can use them in any order.

Sometimes it is useful to modify the meaning of a command by having more than one character per argument. In other words, you might want commands that are several characters long, in which each character means something different. For instance, -B1 could signify one style of banner, whereas -B2 could call for another. In that case, you would need to examine each character to interpret the command. You can gain access to each element in an argument string as shown in the next example.

Listing 10.30 CMDLINE3.C Command line arguments

DO:
- Modify CMDLINE to display command string elements
- Compile CMDLINE3
- Run CMDLINE3 with the arguments shown

```
#include <stdio.h>
main(int argc, char *argv[])
{
   int i;
   int j;                                                  /*1*/
   char *ptr;                                              /*2*/

   printf("\nProgram: %s", argv[0]);
   for (i=1; i<argc; ++i)
   {                                                       /*3*/
       ptr = argv[i];                                      /*4*/
       printf("\n");                                       /*5*/
       for (j=0; j<strlen(ptr); ++j)                       /*6*/
             printf("\nElement %d of argument %d: %c",     /*7*/
                   j, i, ptr[j]);                          /*8*/
   }                                                       /*9*/
}
```

RESULT:

```
C:\>CMDLINE3 -aBc -XY

Program: C:\POWERC\CMDLINE3.EXE

Element 0 of argument 1: -
```

```
Element 1 of argument 1: a
Element 2 of argument 1: B
Element 3 of argument 1: c

Element 0 of argument 2: -
Element 1 of argument 2: X
Element 2 of argument 2: Y
```

ANALYSIS:

1. If you assign the value of an element in *argv* (which is a pointer to the argument string) to a character pointer as in line /*4*/, then you can index the pointer to get any element of the command line argument.
2. The *for* loop on lines /*6–8*/ displays each character in the argument string; printf() accesses each character as *ptr[j]*, and the loop increments index *j* for the entire string length.

When working with strings, you should use standard library functions as much as possible. The library functions are small and fast, and by using them you don't have to spend the time to develop additional code. Appendix C lists the string functions that accompany your Power C compiler, many of which we have not covered in this chapter. You should browse through Appendix C to become familiar with the string functions, which are prefixed with the characters, *str*.

CHAPTER 11

POINTERS

Pointers head the list of features that contribute to the power and efficiency of C. In previous chapters, you used pointers with strings and arrays. In this chapter, you will build on that experience and expand your knowledge about how to use pointers. You will learn the relationship of pointers to arrays and experience additional ways to access data in arrays. You will also look at new ways to pass data between functions using pointers. You will learn how to dynamically allocate memory and access it with pointers, and you will even learn how to call functions using pointers.

POINTERS ARE ADDRESSES

Pointers are addresses of memory locations. Figure 11-1 makes an analogy between a letter addressed to a post office box and a pointer to data in computer memory.

You can liken an address to a pointer value, and a letter in a post office box to the contents of computer memory. Just as an address tells a mailman where to deliver a letter, a pointer tells your program where to go to find data.

Each byte in computer memory is numbered, starting at zero for the first byte and counting up by one for each additional byte until the end of memory is reached. These numbers are the addresses used by a program to store and retrieve data in specific locations; the value of a pointer is one of these addresses.

Pointers are data, similar to other kinds of integer data that you have used. However, pointer data is special because you can use them to access other data. Like other data, a pointer can take the form of a constant or variable in computer memory. You can readily define and initialize pointer variables. You can also change the values of pointer variables and perform arithmetic with them. On the other hand, the compiler allocates pointer constants, and you can only refer to them without changing their

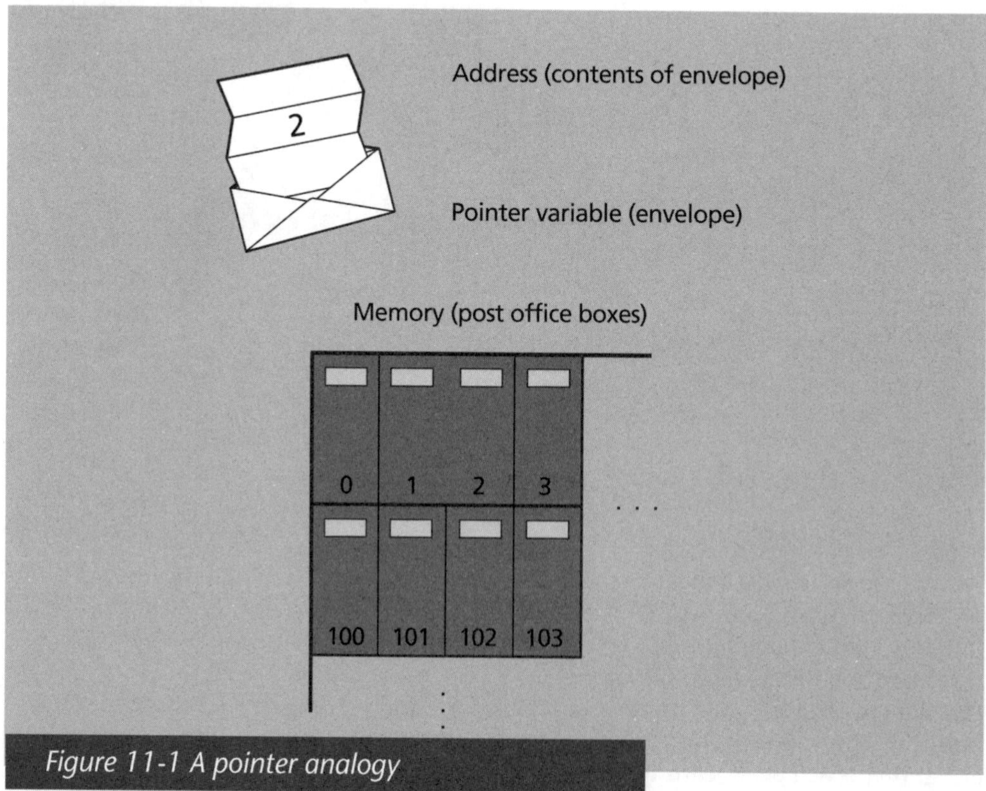

Figure 11-1 A pointer analogy

values. A pointer variable is like the envelope in Figure 11-1 that contains an address where data is to be delivered or picked up. The address on the envelope can be changed, and likewise, the address on a pointer variable can be changed. A constant pointer is like an envelope with an address written on the outside with indelible ink that cannot be changed.

WHY USE POINTERS?

Here is a list of things you can do with pointers:

1. Use pointers instead of indexes to access array elements.
2. Alter data in other functions by passing pointers as function arguments.
3. Use arrays of pointers to refer to other blocks of data.
4. Dynamically allocate memory.
5. Dynamically call functions.

There are two important advantages to using pointers: They are sometimes faster than alternate methods of accessing data, and some operations are possible only by using pointers (see items 2–5 above).

There are also two disadvantages to using pointers: They can sometimes be confusing for an inexperienced C programmer, and they can be dangerous if misused by any programmer.

DEFINING A POINTER

The statement to define a pointer variable has the following form:

```
type *ptr_id;
```

where *type* is any data type used for declaring data variables, and *ptr_id* is any C identifier (a letter or underscore, followed by any letters, numbers, or underscores). The type of a pointer must be consistent with the type of data that it will access because the compiler needs to know the size of the data elements being addressed. The reason the compiler needs this information will become evident when you learn *pointer arithmetic* a little later in this chapter. For instance, if you need a pointer for character data, you should declare the pointer to be *char *ptr_id*, which makes *ptr_id* a pointer to type char. The asterisk (*) is the *indirection* operator that modifies the meaning of *type* and makes *ptr_id* a pointer. The asterisk must be placed between *type* and *ptr_id*. You could add spaces anywhere in the declaration, such as: *type * ptr_id* or *type* ptr_id*, because the compiler doesn't care about intervening spaces. But you should use the conventional representation and put the asterisk after a space and next to the identifier (*type *ptr_id*).

The amount of memory that a compiler allocates for pointers depends on the computer and memory model in use, typically it is either two or four bytes. The following program will show how much memory your compiler allocates for pointers.

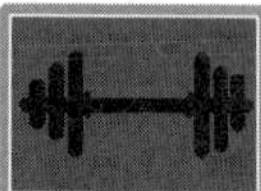

Listing 11.1 POINT.C Pointers

DO: Enter, compile, and run POINT

```
#include <stdio.h>
void main()
{
   char *cptr;

   printf("\nThe size of a pointer is %d bytes.",
       sizeof(cptr));
}
```

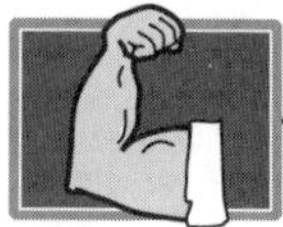

RESULT:

```
C:\>POINT
```


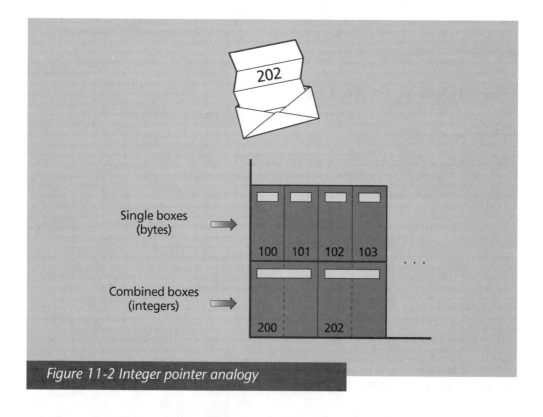

Figure 11-2 Integer pointer analogy

ANALYSIS:

```
The size of a pointer is 2 bytes.
```

1. The first line of this program defines a pointer of type *char*; it is intended for use with character data.
2. The printf() statement uses the *sizeof()* operator to find and display the number of memory bytes that the pointer will occupy, 2 in the case of Power C.

It will not make any difference if you change the data type of the pointer—its size will remain the same. Try it; change the data type to *int* or *double* and look at the size. This is because addresses are all the same size regardless of what data the pointer refers to. A pointer has a size large enough to refer to the location of a byte of data anywhere that data is allowed in memory. For data that is larger than one byte, a pointer refers to the first byte of the data element. Figure 11-2 returns to the analogy between pointers and post office boxes to show how pointers work with two-byte integers.

A 2-byte integer is like two combined post office boxes in which the pointer is the address of the first of the two boxes. The address of the next combined box is two larger than the first address. Likewise, a pointer to a 2-byte integer points to the first of the 2 bytes, and the next integer element would have an address 2 greater than the first.

You can use the pointer conversion specifier (%p) in a printf() statement to see memory addresses.

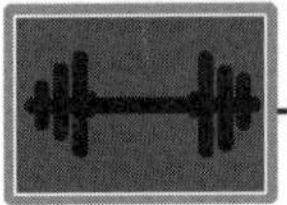

Listing 11.2 POINT2.C Pointers

DO:
- Modify POINT to initialize and display a pointer
- Compile and run POINT2

```
#include <stdio.h>
void main()
{
   char greeting[] = "Hello";                              /*1*/
   char *cptr = greeting;                                  /*2*/

   printf("\nThe value of cptr is %p", cptr);              /*3*/
}
```

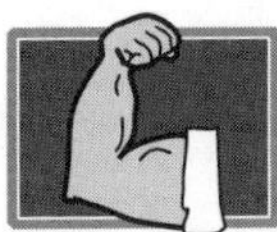

RESULT:

```
C:\>POINT2
```

```
The value of cptr is 8332
```

ANALYSIS:

1. Line /*1*/ defines and initializes a character array *greeting* with a string just as you learned in Chapter 10.

2. Line /*2*/ initializes pointer *cptr* to the address of the first byte of the array *greeting*. Remember, the isolated name of an array refers to its address.

3. The printf() on line /*3*/ displays the value of *cptr*, which is the address of *greeting*. The pointer conversion specifier (%p) converts the address to a hexadecimal representation. The address that you get may very well be different from our result, because the operating system (DOS) can place the program in a different part of memory.

C does not dictate how a compiler must convert pointers for formatted display. The hexadecimal format used by Power C is a very good choice, because memory sizes come in powers of two, and programmers are accustomed to interpreting memory locations in terms of hexadecimal addresses.

The bare array name *greeting* in the POINT2 program is an example of a pointer constant. The compiler determines the value of the pointer constant and uses it to initialize the pointer variable *cptr* on line /*2*/.

Once you initialize a pointer, you can use it in the same way as you can use an array name. You can use the pointer in the last program to display a string.

Listing 11.3 POINT3.C Pointers

DO:
- Modify POINT2 to display a string with the pointer
- Compile and run POINT3

```
#include <stdio.h>
void main()
{
   char greeting[] = "Hello";
   char *cptr = greeting;

   printf("\nThe value of cptr is %p", cptr);
   printf("\nThe string is %s", cptr);                          /*1*/
}
```

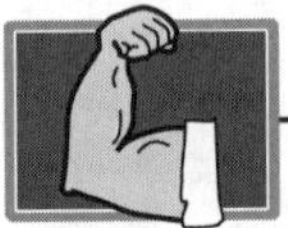

RESULT:

```
C:\>POINT3

The value of cptr is 833C
The string is Hello
```

ANALYSIS:

1. The conversion specifier on line /*1*/ is %s, which expects an address of a string to appear in the variable list, and the pointer variable *cptr* supplies the expected address.

2. In this example, you can see the difference that a conversion specifier makes in formatted display. Both printf() statements display the same variable *cptr*; the first printf() converts the value to a hexadecimal pointer address, and the second printf() uses the address to display the character string.

Now you can make things a little more interesting by entering a few addresses of your own and seeing what part of the string the program displays.

Listing 11.4 POINT4.C Pointers

DO:
- Modify POINT3 to read a pointer from the keyboard
- Compile POINT4

```
#include <stdio.h>
void main()
{
   char greeting[] = "Hello";
   char *cptr = greeting;

   printf("\nThe value of cptr is %p", cptr);
   printf("\nThe string is %s", cptr);
   printf("\nEnter a new pointer value: ");              /*1*/
   scanf("%p", &cptr);                                   /*2*/
   printf("\nThe string is %s", cptr);                   /*3*/
}
```

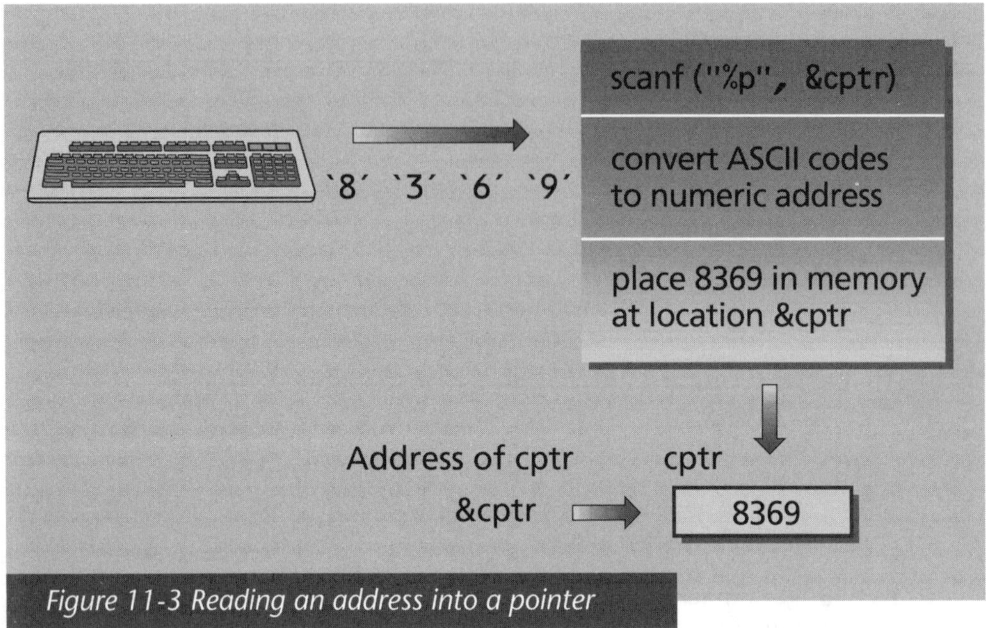

Figure 11-3 Reading an address into a pointer

ANALYSIS:

1. Line /*1*/ prompts you to enter a pointer value to replace the one in *cptr*.
2. The scanf() on line /*2*/ reads a hexadecimal value (because of the conversion specifier %p) and places it in *cptr*. Here is something interesting—the ampersand specifies the address of variable *cptr*. This makes sense, because scanf() needs to read a value from the keyboard, convert it, and place it into the variable at the specified address. Figure 11-3 illustrates the operation of scanf() as it reads an address and assigns it to the pointer.
3. The new pointer value is the beginning of a string to be displayed on line /*3*/.

DO:
- Run POINT4
- Add 1 to the first address displayed and enter it

RESULT:

```
C:\>POINT4

The value of cptr is 8368
The string is Hello
Enter a new pointer value: 8369
The string is ello
```

DO: • Run POINT4
• Add 4 to the first address displayed and enter it

RESULT:

```
C:\>POINT4

The value of cptr is 8368
The string is Hello
Enter a new pointer value: 836C
The string is o
```

ANALYSIS:

1. You are initializing the pointer with some pointer constants of your own.

2. By entering new addresses, you change the location where printf() begins displaying the string.

You will need to enter the new addresses in hexadecimal form, and you must also mentally add the offsets in hexadecimal form. If you aren't accustomed to hexadecimal arithmetic, there are two easy ways to add the numbers. The easiest way, if you have saved programs from previous chapters, is to use the hexadecimal calculator from Chapter 7 (Program 7.24, CALC6.C) to perform the addition. Otherwise, because the numbers to be added are small, you can simply count in hexadecimal arithmetic. To add five to the original displayed address, just add one five times. Remember that a hexadecimal digit can increase to F (decimal 15) before it rolls over to zero and you carry one to the next place. For example, if the original address is 14AE, then you add five by counting in the sequence: 14AF, 14B0, 14B1, 14B2, 14B3. In all of the examples, the memory addresses that you see will probably be different from the ones in the book because the operating system (DOS) will load programs into different places in memory depending on the computer configuration.

DO: • Run POINT4
• Add 5 to the first address displayed and enter it

RESULT:

```
The value of cptr is 8368
The string is Hello
Enter a new pointer value: 836D
The string is
```

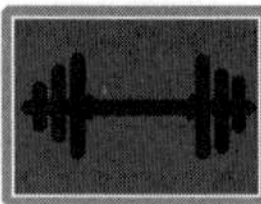

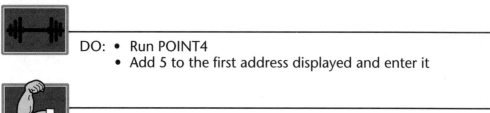

DO: • Run POINT4
• Add 10 to the first address displayed and enter it

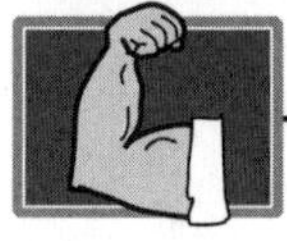

RESULT:

```
The value of cptr is 8368
The string is Hello
Enter a new pointer value: 8372
The string is
```

ANALYSIS:

1. If you add 5 to the original starting address, you point to the ending null for the string, so printf() displays a null string, or nothing.
2. If you add 10, the resulting address is beyond the end of the string. You have no idea what is in this area of memory, so don't be surprised if printf() shows you some garbage or if it shows you nothing because a null is there.

The worst that can happen while **reading** data from strange parts of memory is that printf() might display some garbage on the screen. Trouble can really begin if you misuse pointers and write or assign values to strange parts of memory. This illustrates one of the dangers of pointers: You can access areas of memory totally outside of your own program. Through pointers, C grants you great freedom and power, but it is your responsibility to use it wisely. Pointers are like sticks of dynamite—you can do wonderful, constructive things with them or you can blow up your own program and everything around it with them.

In spite of the dire warnings about the misuse of pointers, don't be deterred from experimenting with them. With a single-user PC system, the very worst thing that can happen is that you will have to reboot the computer. Certain exercises in this chapter will give you the chance to abuse pointers in a controlled manner.

You will rarely, if ever, deal directly with absolute memory addresses as you did in the above exercises. This manner of assigning pointer values was used only to illustrate what pointers really are: absolute memory addresses are much too difficult to use in actual programming practice. There are better ways, which you will see next.

ADDRESS (&) AND INDIRECTION (*) OPERATORS

There are two operators that are often used with pointers: the *address operator* (&) allows you to obtain addresses, and the *indirection operator* (*) allows you to fetch values at address locations. These operators are complementary—that is, they perform opposite operations. If you place one immediately after the other, *& or &*, they cancel each other. For example, *&x is the same as x. When you want to assign an address to a pointer, you will often use the address operator (&), and when you want to access data using the pointer, you will use the indirection operator (*).

Address operator (&)

You have already had occasion to use the unary address operator (&), which returns the address of a variable or array element. The address operator precedes its operand, and it is customary to place it immediately in front of the variable or array identifier:

```
&variable          /* Pointer to a variable */
&greeting[1]       /* Pointer to element 2 of an array */
```

As usual, C allows intervening spaces:

```
& greeting[1]
```

but we do **not** recommend it. You can use & to get the address of any type of variable or any element in an array, but you cannot use it with constants or expressions. The address operator enjoys very high precedence—just below parentheses in the table of priorities (see Appendix D).

The next program illustrates some ways to use the address operator and some ways not to use it. When you compile this program, turn on the warning option, /w, to get all of the compiler messages about incorrect pointer usage.

Listing 11.5 POINT5.C Pointers

DO: • Modify POINT2 to initialize pointers in different ways
• Compile POINT5 with the warning option, /w
• Examine the source lines while reading the explanations

RESULT:

```
#include <stdio.h>
void main()
{
   char greeting[] = "Hello";/* Character array  */
   char goodbye[2][8] = {"Bon", "Voyage"};                    /*1*/
   char *cptr = greeting;    /* Character pointer */
   int  number;              /* Integer variable  */           /*2*/
   int  *iptr = &number;     /* Integer pointer   */           /*3*/

/* Correct usage of address operator (&) */

   cptr = &greeting[0];      /* Address of the first element     4*/
   cptr = greeting;          /* Same as above                    5*/
   cptr = &greeting;         /* Same as above--& is redundant    6*/
   cptr = &greeting[3];      /* Address of the fourth element    7*/
   cptr = &goodbye[1][2];    /* Address of the 'y'               8*/
   cptr = &goodbye[1];       /* Address of "Voyage"              9*/
   iptr = &number;           /* Address of integer variable     10*/

/* Incorrect usage of address operator (&) */

   cptr = &'H';              /* Wrong--address of constant      11*/
   iptr = &(number + 1);     /* Wrong--address of expression    12*/
   iptr = &greeting[0];      /* Wrong--mixed data types         13*/
}
```

RESULT:

```
C:\>pc/c/e/w POINT5
Power C - Version 2.1.3
(C) Copyright 1989-1991 by Mix Software
Compiling...
POINT5.C(29):/*11*/cptr = &'H';          /* Wrong--address of constant
**********              ^ 36
     36: Variable required for & and * unary operators
----------------------------------------------------------------
POINT5.C(31):/*12*/iptr = &(number + 1);  /* Wrong--address of constant
**********                   ^ 36
     36: Variable required for & and * unary operators
```

```
-----------------------------------------------------------------
POINT5.C(33):/*13*/iptr = &greeting[0];    /* Wrong--mixed data types
**********                     ^221
     221: Warning - Pointers to different types
-----------------------------------------------------------------
  149 lines compiled
    1 Warning
    2 Compile errors
```

ANALYSIS:

1. Line /*3*/ defines a pointer to an integer, *iptr*, and initializes it to the address of the variable *number*.
2. Lines /*4–10*/ show legal ways to get an address and assign it to a pointer. Lines /*4–6*/ are three ways to derive the same pointer. Notice that lines /*4–9*/ assign a character address to a character pointer, and line /*10*/ assigns an integer address to an integer pointer.
3. You cannot take the address of a constant, so the compiler flags an error on line /*11*/.
4. You also cannot take the address of an expression, so the compiler generates an error on line /*12*/.
5. The statement on line /*13*/ attempts to assign the address of a character element to an integer pointer; the compiler will allow the assignment to happen after issuing a warning. Ignore the warning at your own peril. There are times when you will need to assign mixed pointer types, but you should use a cast operator to avoid compiler warnings and assure correct program execution. You could eliminate the warning by changing line /*13*/ to:

   ```
   iptr = (int *)&greeting[0];
   ```

   The topic of pointer casting will be discussed more thoroughly later in this chapter.

In the POINT4 program, you changed the value of a pointer by directly entering a new address. The next program also changes a pointer, but it does so with the address operator (&) and an index.

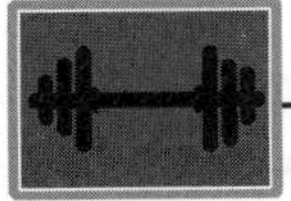

Listing 11.6 POINT6.C Pointers

DO:
- Modify POINT4 to change a pointer via an index
- Compile POINT6

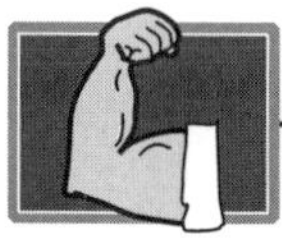

RESULT:

```
#include <stdio.h>
void main()
{
   char greeting[] = "Hello";
   char *cptr = greeting;
   int  index;                                          /*1*/

   printf("\nThe string is %s", cptr);
   printf("\nEnter an array index: ");                  /*2*/
   scanf("%d", &index);                                 /*3*/
   cptr = &greeting[index];                             /*4*/
   printf("\nThe string is %s", cptr);                  /*5*/
}
```

ANALYSIS:

1. Lines /*1–3*/ allow you to select any element in the string array by entering an index.
2. Line /*4*/ assigns a selected pointer value to *cptr*. The statement applies the address operator (&) to element *greeting[index]*, and this returns the starting address of the string that printf() displays.
3. The printf() statement on line /*5*/ displays the string, beginning with the selected element.

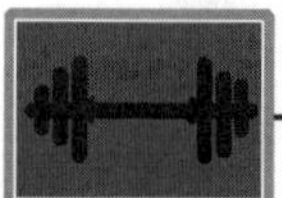

DO: Run POINT6 and enter **0**

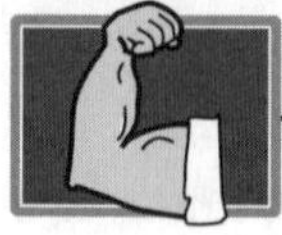

RESULT:

```
C:\>POINT6

The string is Hello
Enter an array index: 0
The string is Hello
```

DO: Run POINT6 and enter **3**

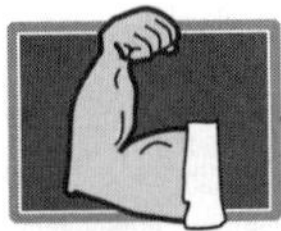

RESULT:

```
C:\>POINT6

The string is Hello
Enter an array index: 3
The string is lo
```

ANALYSIS:

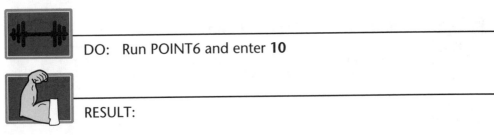

You can display different parts of the string by entering index values in the range of from 0 to 5.

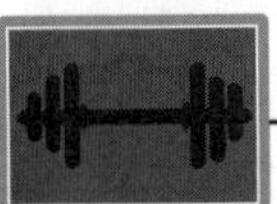

DO: Run POINT6 and enter **10**

RESULT:

```
The string is Hello
Enter an array index: 10
The string is
```

ANALYSIS:

1. C allows you to create pointers to memory outside of your program area. By entering an index of 10, you have gone beyond the end of the array *greeting* and are displaying an unknown string. Our example displayed a null string, but yours could display something different.

Indirection operator (*)

When the unary indirection operator (*) is applied to a pointer, it returns the value of the data to which it points. This operator precedes its pointer operand, and you usually place it immediately in front of the pointer identifier with no intervening spaces, like: *ptr. The name of this operator arises because the operator **indirectly** retrieves a value. A **direct** reference is like handing someone a book from the library, whereas an **indi-**

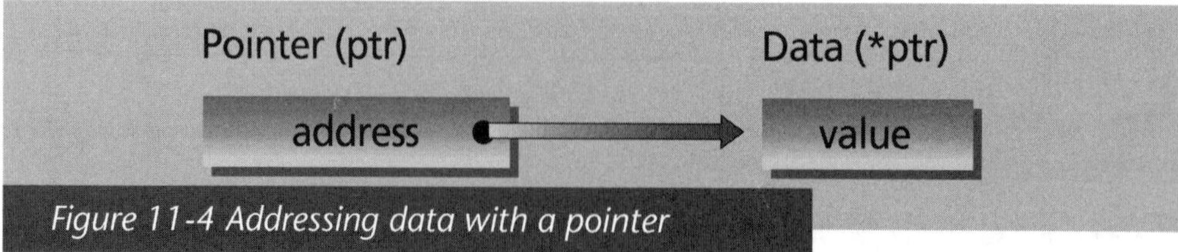

Figure 11-4 Addressing data with a pointer

rect reference is like handing them a card from the card catalog that tells them where the book can be found. If you attach an asterisk to a pointer, you **indirectly** get the value of the data pointed to. Figure 11-4 illustrates how you refer to data by applying the indirection operator to a pointer.

The indirection operator has the same high precedence as the address operator.

You can drop back to the POINT2 program and make a minor modification to see the indirection operator in action.

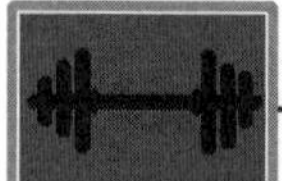

Listing 11.7 POINT7.C Pointers

DO:
- Modify POINT2 to use the indirection operator
- Compile and run POINT7

```
#include <stdio.h>
void main()
{
   char greeting[] = "Hello";
   char *cptr = greeting;                           /*1*/

   printf("\nThe data pointed to is %c", *cptr);   /*2*/
}
```

RESULT:

```
C:\>POINT7

The data pointed to is H
```

ANALYSIS:

The printf() statement displays the character value returned by the indirection operator applied to pointer *cptr*.

It may bother you that the asterisk appears to be used for two different purposes in this program: On line /*1*/ it declares *cptr* to be a pointer, and on line /*2*/ it is the indirection operator. Actually the asterisk is an indirection operator in both cases. When the asterisk appears between a type declaration and an identifier (like *char *cptr*) it declares a pointer. You can think of this as indirection because first, the declaration tells the compiler the data type, and then, the asterisk tells the compiler that this identifier is a pointer to that data type. When the asterisk appears in front of a pointer identifier outside a declaration (like **cptr*), it returns the value at the pointer location. You can think of this as indirection because first, the pointer tells the compiler where to look, and then, the asterisk tells it to retrieve the data value.

Unfortunately, some symbols serve more than one purpose in C, and the asterisk is one of these symbols—it is the multiplication operator and also the indirection operator. When an asterisk appears in front of a pointer, it is the indirection operator, and when it appears between two numeric values, it is the multiplication operator. If you use the asterisk out of proper context, the compiler will signal an error. For example, you cannot apply the indirection operator to a nonpointer operand.

Listing 11.8 POINT8.C Pointers

DO:
- Modify POINT7 to use an asterisk out of context
- Compile and run POINT8

```
#include <stdio.h>
void main()
{
   char greeting[] = "Hello";
   char *cptr = greeting;

   printf("\nThe data pointed to is %c", *greeting[0]);  /*1*/
}
```

RESULT:

```
C:\>pc/c/e POINT8
Power C - Version 2.1.3
(C) Copyright 1989-1991 by Mix Software
Compiling...
POINT8.C(7):/*1*/printf("\nThe data pointed to is %c", *greeting[0]);
***********
^141
     141: Type of variable is not pointer
-------------------------------------------------------------
  115 lines compiled
    1 Compile error
```

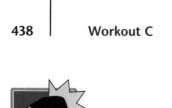

ANALYSIS:

On line /*1*/, the reference *greeting[0]* is a data value (character 'H'), and you cannot use a data value as an operand for the indirection operator (*), so the compiler generates an error.

The next program demonstrates the complementary relationship between the address operator (&) and the indirection operator (*). If you apply either of these operators to the result of the other, it reverses the effect of the first operator. The associativity of both of these operators is right-to-left, so the operator closest to the operand is executed first.

Listing 11.9 POINT9.C Pointers

DO:
- Modify POINT8 to use complementary operators
- Compile and run POINT9

```
#include <stdio.h>
void main()
{
   char greeting[] = "Hello";
   char *cptr = greeting;

   printf("\nPointer address %p is the same as %p",          /*1*/
        &*cptr, cptr);
   printf("\nData value %c is the same as %c",               /*2*/
        *&greeting[0], greeting[0]);
}
```

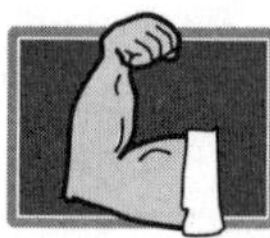

RESULT:

```
C:\>POINT9

Pointer address 8344 is the same as 8344
Data value H is the same as H
```

ANALYSIS:

1. The first display item in the printf() on line /*1*/ is *&*cptr*, which contains two operators. Following right-to-left associativity, the indi-

rection operator (*) first gets the value pointed to by *cptr*, then the address operator (&) returns the address of the value. The end result is the address originally in *cptr*.

2. The first display item in the printf() on line /*2*/ is **&greeting[0]*, which has the operators in another order. First, the address operator (&) finds the address of the element *greeting[0]*, then, the indirection operator (*) returns the value stored at this address. The final value displayed is the same as the original value in *greeting[0]*.

The above program is useless, and there is no reason to use the operators in this way, but it is a good illustration of how the operators work. Table 11-1 summarizes pointer notation for the address and value of an integer variable.

```
int data;
int *ptr = &data;
```

Address	Value
ptr &data	*ptr data

Table 11-1 Pointer notation

You can apply the indirection operator to a pointer of any type, and it will return the value stored at the pointer address. The type of the returned data value will be the same as the declared type of the pointer, as the next program illustrates. This program defines and initializes pointers to variables of different types, then assigns values to the variables and accesses the values in different ways using the pointers.

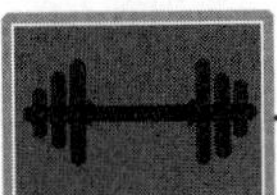

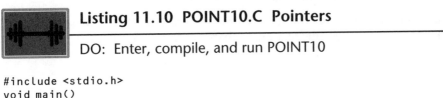

Listing 11.10 POINT10.C Pointers

DO: Enter, compile, and run POINT10

```
#include <stdio.h>
void main()
{
   char c_val = 'A';
   int  i_val;
   float f_val;
   char  *cptr = &c_val;
```

```
    int   *iptr = &i_val;
    float *fptr = &f_val;

    *iptr = *cptr;
    printf("\nThe integer value is: %d", i_val);
    f_val = *iptr / 2.;
    printf("\nThe float value is: %f", *fptr);
}
```

RESULT:

```
C:\>POINT10
The integer value is: 65
The float value is: 32.500000
```

ANALYSIS:

1. The program first defines three variables of data type *char, int,* and *float* and initializes the character variable to 'A'.
2. Next, the program defines three pointers and initializes each one to the address of the variable that matches the declared type.
3. The first assignment statement assigns the value of the character variable, *c_val,* to the integer variable, *i_val.* It does this by applying the indirection operator (*) to the respective pointers to these two variables. The printf() statement proves that the assignment was correct (the ASCII code for 'A' is 65).
4. The next assignment statement accesses the integer value with the indirection operator (*) applied to the pointer *iptr,* divides the value by two, and assigns the result to *f_val.* The printf() statement displays the result by using a pointer to retrieve the value of *f_val.*

An interesting place to put the indirection operator is with command line arguments. You can retrieve the value of a single character from a command line argument as shown in the next program.

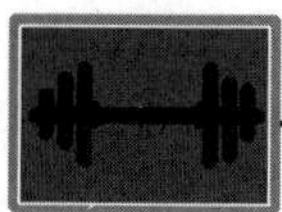

Listing 11.11 POINT11.C Pointers

DO:
- Enter and compile POINT11
- Run POINT11 with a command line argument

```
#include <stdio.h>
void main(int argc, char *argv[])
{
   printf("The first character of the command line argument "
        "is: %c", *argv[1]);
}
```

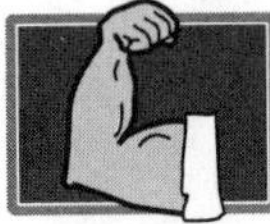

RESULT:

```
C:\>POINT11 -H
The first character of the command line argument is: -
```

ANALYSIS:

The second argument to main() is an array of pointers *argv[ ]*, and the second element in the array points to the first command line argument. Therefore, the indirection operator applied in the printf() statement **argv[1]* will return the first character of the command line string.

POINTER ARITHMETIC

The term *pointer arithmetic* refers to the process of altering pointer values (addresses) with arithmetic operators. You can increment and decrement pointers, subtract two pointers, and add and subtract integers from them. All other arithmetic operations are illegal, including multiplication, division, and all floating-point operations.

Pointer arithmetic is not the same as normal integer arithmetic; before a program adds or subtracts an integer from a pointer, it multiplies the integer by the size (in bytes) of the data type. This moves the pointer to the first byte of another storage element. For instance, if you add 1 to a pointer for 2-byte integers, the address (or pointer value) increases by 2. Start using pointer arithmetic by incrementing a character pointer in the next program.

Listing 11.12 POINT12.C Pointers

DO:
- Modify POINT10 to use pointer arithmetic
- Compile and run POINT12

```
#include <stdio.h>
void main()
{
   char greeting[] = "Hello";
   char *cptr = greeting;
```

```
   printf("\nData at address %p is %c", cptr, *cptr);    /*1*/
   ++cptr;                                                /*2*/
   printf("\nData at address %p is %c", cptr, *cptr);    /*3*/
}
```

RESULT:

```
C:\>POINT12

Data at address 833E is H
Data at address 833F is e
```

ANALYSIS:

1. The first printf() statement gives you a reference address and value that *cptr* points to.
2. Line /*2*/ increments the character pointer by 1.
3. Line /*3*/ displays the address and value after the pointer is incremented. The address is larger by 1 because that is the size of the data elements (a character is 1 byte).

Now do some pointer arithmetic with other types of pointers.

Listing 11.13 POINT13.C Pointers

DO:
- Add integer and floating-point types to POINT12
- Compile and run POINT13

```
#include <stdio.h>
void main()
{
   char greeting[] = "Hello";
   char *cptr = greeting;
   int  i_array[] = {1, 2, 3, 4, 5};                            /*1*/
   int  *iptr = i_array;                                        /*2*/
   float f_array[] = {6., 7., 8., 9., 10.};                     /*3*/
   float *fptr = &f_array[4];                                   /*4*/

/* Character data (1-byte elements) */

   printf("\n\nCHARACTER POINTER ARITHMETIC");                  /*5*/
```

```
   printf("\nData at address %p is %c", cptr, *cptr);
   ++cptr;
   printf("\nData at address %p is %c", cptr, *cptr);

/* Integer data (2-byte elements) */

   printf("\n\nINTEGER POINTER ARITHMETIC");                     /*6*/
   printf("\nData at address %p is %d", iptr, *iptr);            /*7*/
   ++iptr;                                                       /*8*/
   printf("\nData at address %p is %d", iptr, *iptr);            /*9*/

/* Floating-point data (4-byte elements) */

   printf("\n\nFLOATING-POINT POINTER ARITHMETIC");              /*10*/
   printf("\nData at address %p is %f", fptr, *fptr);            /*11*/
   fptr -= 2;                                                    /*12*/
   printf("\nData at address %p is %f", fptr, *fptr);            /*13*/

   printf("\nDifference between the last and first"
          " address of the array is: %p elements"
          " or %ld bytes",
        &f_array[4] - &f_array[0],                               /*14*/
       (long)&f_array[4] - (long)&f_array[0]);                   /*15*/
}
```

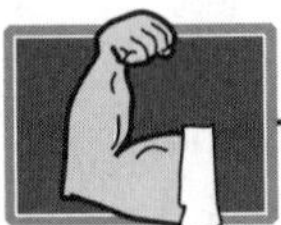

RESULT:

```
C:\>POINT13

CHARACTER POINTER ARITHMETIC
Data at address 83C0 is H
Data at address 83C1 is e

INTEGER POINTER ARITHMETIC
Data at address 83C8 is 1
Data at address 83CA is 2

FLOATING-POINT POINTER ARITHMETIC
Data at address 83E4 is 10.000000
Data at address 83DC is 8.000000
Difference between the last and first address of the array is: 0004 ele-
ments or 16 bytes
```

ANALYSIS:

1. Lines /*1–4*/ define and initialize an integer, a floating-point array, and corresponding pointers. Notice that line /*4*/ initializes *fptr* so that it points to the **end** of *f_array*.

2. Line /*7*/ displays the first integer pointer value, which is the address of the beginning of *i_array*.
3. Line /*8*/ increments the integer pointer, then line /*9*/ displays the incremented address and the new value. The new address is greater than the first address by 2 (bytes) because this is the size of the data elements.
4. Line /*11*/ displays a first address for the floating-point pointer, which is the address of the last element in *f_array*.
5. The statement on line /*12*/ subtracts 2 from *f_ptr*. This has the effect of reducing the address by 8 (2 * 4 bytes), because the size of each floating-point element is 4 bytes.
6. The printf() on line /*13*/ confirms that *f*_ptr has been decreased by 8 (subtract the two hexadecimal addresses).
7. Lines /*14–15*/ contain an example of subtracting two pointers; the difference between the address at the end and the address at the beginning of the floating-point array is 16 bytes (four elements times 4 bytes per element). This printf() statement shows the result of the subtraction both in terms of array elements and address bytes. If you subtract two pointers as on line /*14*/ and display the result with %p, it will be presented in terms of array elements (4 in this instance). If you want to see the result of pointer arithmetic in terms of bytes, you must cast each pointer to an integer value—type *long* is used on line /*15*/. In this case, the operands are not two declared pointer variables—they are the result of applying the address operator (&).

The real value of pointer arithmetic occurs when you use it in conjunction with the indirection operator (*) to assign values to or from an array, as in the statement:

```
x = *(ptr + 1);
```

This statement assigns the value of the second element of an array, at the address given by *ptr*, to variable *x*. The expression inside the parentheses evaluates to the address in *ptr* plus one element, and the indirection operator (*) returns the data value stored at this location. When you do this, you should use parentheses so that pointer arithmetic will occur first; otherwise, the indirection operator will take precedence. The next program shows the difference that parentheses make.

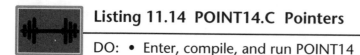

Listing 11.14 POINT14.C Pointers

DO: • Enter, compile, and run POINT14

```
#include <stdio.h>
void main()
```

```
{
   int i_array[] = {10, 20, 30, 40, 50};
   int *iptr = i_array;
   int result;

   result = *iptr + 2;              /* Add 2 to value at iptr */
   printf("\nWithout parentheses the value is %d", result);

   result = *(iptr + 2);            /* Value at iptr plus 2 */
   printf("\nWith parentheses the value is %d", result);
}
```

RESULT:

```
C:\>POINT14

Without parentheses the value is 12
With parentheses the value is 30
```

ANALYSIS:

1. The first assignment statement (without parentheses) actually does not use pointer arithmetic at all; it gets the first value in the array (10), adds 2 to it, and assigns 12 to *result.*

2. The parentheses in the second assignment statement forces the pointer addition to occur first, so that the statement retrieves the value of the third array element (30) and assigns this to *result.* In other words, the first assignment statement adds 2 to a value, while the second adds 2 to an address.

POINTER ASSIGNMENT

C does not allow you to legally assign pointers of one type to another type; for instance, you should not assign a character pointer to an integer pointer. The compiler may issue a warning, but it will probably allow the assignment to happen. An assignment between different pointer types constitutes a potential logic error. You may be thinking that an integer pointer can be used to access a character array, but if the program performs pointer arithmetic, it will access incorrect data. This logic error is illustrated in the next program.

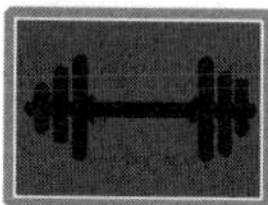

Listing 11.15 POINT15.C Pointers

DO: • Modify POINT12 to use an integer pointer
• Compile and run POINT15

```
#include <stdio.h>
void main()
{
   char greeting[] = "Hello";
   int  *cptr = greeting;                                      /*1*/

   printf("\nData at address %p is %c", cptr, *cptr);
   ++cptr;
   printf("\nData at address %p is %c", cptr, *cptr);
}
```

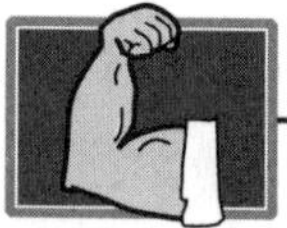

RESULT:

```
C:\>POINT15

Data at address 833E is H
Data at address 8340 is l
```

ANALYSIS:

1. This program compiles and executes with no error messages even though it assigns the address of a character array to an integer pointer on line /*1*/.

2. The pointer *cptr* is now an integer type, so when incremented, it increases by 2 bytes—the size of an integer element. The pointer address changes according to the type of the pointer, not the type of the data.

3. This is a logic error, because the original intent of the program was to display the first and second characters in the array. Now the program displays the first and third characters.

You can avoid logic errors of this sort by making pointers match the type of data that they access. This becomes even more important when the data involved is a *derived* data type. A derived type is a "custom" data type that you declare as some combination of other data types. Derived types are discussed in Chapter 16.

Void pointers

You can declare a pointer to be of data type void. The void pointer type deserves special mention at this time, because in C it is legal to assign any type of pointer to a void pointer, and conversely, you can assign a void pointer to any other type. This property allows you to legally exchange addresses between pointer types, but you should restrict your use of void pointers to the direct assignment of addresses and data values. Do not index or do arithmetic with void pointers! You cannot perform pointer arithmetic with a void pointer, because the size of the element is unknown. The output of the next program will not be correct, because it is based on incrementing a pointer to data type void.

Listing 11.16 POINT16.C Pointers

DO: • Enter, compile, and run POINT16

```
#include <stdio.h>
void main()
{
   int array[] = {1, 2, 3, 4};
   int  *iptr;
   void *vptr;

   vptr = array;
   iptr = vptr;
   printf("\nFirst value at %p is: %d", vptr, *iptr);

   ++vptr;
   iptr = vptr;
   printf("\nNext value at %p is: %d", vptr, *iptr);
}
```

RESULT:

```
C:\>POINT16

First value at 8338 is: 1
Next value at 8338 is: 1
```

ANALYSIS:

1. All statements in this program are perfectly legal down to and including the first printf(). The program defines an integer pointer and a

void pointer, then assigns the address of *array* to the void pointer *vptr* and immediately reassigns this to *iptr*. These two assignments are legal because one of the pointers is type void in both cases.

2. Notice that the printf() statement displays the address by using *vptr*, but it uses **iptr* to display the data value. You cannot use the void pointer to reference a value, because it does not carry any information about the type or size of the data.
3. The next statement increments the void pointer—a useless operation because the compiler doesn't have an element size for data type *void*. The subsequent display of the new pointer address and data value show that nothing has changed.

Pointer casting

You can temporarily change the type of a pointer with the cast operator. The form of the cast operator for pointers is (type *). You cast a character pointer *cptr* to an integer pointer with the expression *(int *)cptr*. The next program shows how to use casting to accomplish pointer arithmetic and data access with a void pointer.

Listing 11.17 POINT17.C Pointers

DO:
- Modify POINT16 to cast the void pointer
- Compile and run POINT17

```
#include <stdio.h>
void main()
{
    int array[] = {1, 2, 3, 4};
    int  *iptr;
    void *vptr;

    vptr = array;
    printf("\nFirst value at %p is: %d",
        vptr, *(int *)vptr);                          /*1*/

    ++(int *)vptr;                                    /*2*/
    printf("\nNext value at %p is: %d",
        vptr, *(int *)vptr);                          /*3*/
}
```

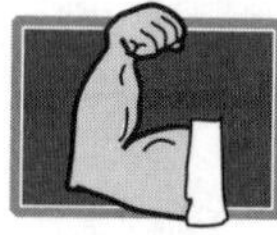

RESULT:

```
C:\>POINT17
```

```
First value at 8338 is: 1
Next value at 833A is: 2
```

ANALYSIS:

1. In POINT16, the printf() statements had to rely on the integer pointer *iptr* to access the data value. In this program, **(int *)vptr* replaces **iptr*, temporarily declaring type *int* for the pointer. Both operators in this expression (indirection and cast) have the same precedence, and both have right-to-left associativity, so the program first casts the pointer to type *int*, then returns the data value at that address.
2. Line /*2*/ correctly increments the pointer as a result of casting. Again, both operators (increment and cast) have the same precedence and right-to-left associativity, so the program applies cast first, and the increment knows to add 2 bytes (the size of an *int*) to the address.

POINTERS AND ARRAYS

Pointers have a very close relationship with arrays. You can use array names in many of the same ways as you can see pointers and vice versa. The next two sections discuss the similarities and the differences between pointers and arrays.

Similarities between pointers and array names

Here is a list of the ways that pointers and arrays are alike (*ptr* is a pointer and *array* is an array name):

1. The value of both *array* and *ptr* is an address.
2. You can index either one: *array[index]* or *ptr[index]*.
3. You can use indirection with either **array* or **ptr*.
4. You can perform pointer addition and subtraction with either **(array + index)* or **(ptr + index)*.

You can use pointer arithmetic anywhere that array indexing is used in a program by substituting **(array_ptr + index)* in place of *array[index]* or *array_ptr + index* in place of *&array[index]*. The next example shows two methods of accessing a string.

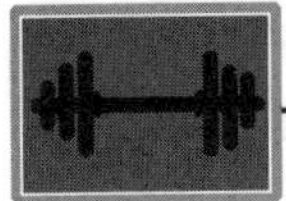

Listing 11.18 POINT18.C Pointers

DO:
- Add array access via pointer arithmetic to POINT6
- Compile and run POINT18
- Enter **2**

```
#include <stdio.h>
void main()
{
   char greeting[] = "Hello";
   char *cptr = greeting;
   int  index;

   printf("\nThe string is: %s", cptr);
   printf("\nEnter an array index: ");
   scanf("%d", &index);
   printf("\nUsing indexing: %s", &greeting[index]);      /*1*/
   printf("\nUsing pointer access: %s", cptr + index);    /*2*/
}
```

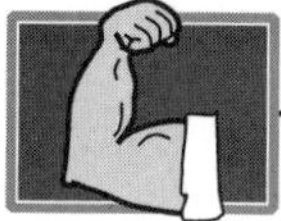

RESULT:

```
C:\>POINT18

The string is: Hello
Enter an array index: 2
Using indexing: llo
Using pointer access: llo
```

ANALYSIS:

1. Line /*1*/ is the original method used in POINT6, in which the address operator (&) returned the beginning string address.
2. Line /*2*/ adds *index* to the pointer to get the same address.

Differences between pointers and array names

An array name is different from a pointer in one very important way. An array name is a constant pointer, so it cannot be changed. You cannot assign a new address to an array name, and you cannot apply the increment (++) or decrement (—) operator to it. The next program shows how the compiler reacts to attempts to modify an array name.

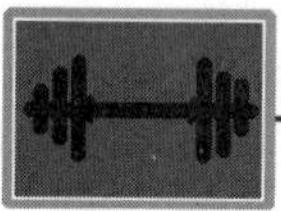

Listing 11.19 POINT19.C Pointers

DO: Enter and compile POINT19

```
#include <stdio.h>
void main()
```

```
{
   int array1[10];
   int array2[10];
   int *iptr = array2;

/* Can't assign to an array name */

   array1 = array2;
   array1 = iptr;
   array2 = &array1[1];

/* Can add to an array name without changing it */

   iptr = array2 + 1;

/* Can't increment an array name */

   ++array1;
   array2 += 2;
   array1 = array2 + 1;
}
```

RESULT:

```
C:\>pc/c/e POINT19
Power C - Version 2.1.3
(C) Copyright 1989-1991 by Mix Software
Compiling...
POINT19.C(10):    array1 = array2;
*************                 ^ 30
     30: Invalid type in assignment
-----------------------------------------------------------------
POINT19.C(11):    array1 = iptr;
*************               ^ 30
     30: Invalid type in assignment
-----------------------------------------------------------------
POINT19.C(12):    array2 = &array1[1];
*************                    ^ 30
     30: Invalid type in assignment
-----------------------------------------------------------------
POINT19.C(20):    ++array1;
*************             ^ 30
     30: Invalid type in assignment
-----------------------------------------------------------------
POINT19.C(21):    array2 += 2;
*************               ^ 30
     30: Invalid type in assignment
-----------------------------------------------------------------
POINT19.C(22):    array1 = array2 + 1;
*************                    ^ 30
```

```
     30: Invalid type in assignment
-----------------------------------------------------------------------
  130 lines compiled
    6 Compile errors
```

ANALYSIS:

1. The first three compiler errors make it clear that no matter how you may try, you cannot assign a new value to an array name.
2. You **can** perform pointer addition and subtraction with an array name, as shown by the statement that assigns an address to *iptr*, but you cannot put the result back into the array name, as the next three statements attempt to do.

The merits of pointers versus indexing

The notation for array indexing is usually cleaner and more readable than pointer arithmetic is, but pointers are always at least as fast as, and are sometimes faster than, indexing. You should use indexing when processing a small-to-medium amount of array data, when speed is not paramount, or when program readability is important. If your program needs to efficiently process large amounts of array data, and this is the central purpose of the program, then you may want to use pointer arithmetic. Pointer arithmetic is also recommended for utility functions, in which you need to maximize program efficiency because you do not know where the function will be applied in the future.

Pointer arithmetic is closer to the way that a compiler ends up accessing array data than indexing is. The compiler will interpret a reference to a two-dimensional array element such as *array[row][col]* and make it the equivalent of **(array + 100 * row + col)*. As an aside, notice that the asterisk becomes two different operators (indirection and multiplication) in this expression, determined by operand context. An optimizing compiler, like Power C, will generate the most efficient executable code for either index or pointer access to arrays. However, not all compilers will do this, and if you want to retain full control over programming techniques, you can do so with pointers.

POINTERS AS FUNCTION ARGUMENTS

Like other variables, pointers can serve as arguments to a function. Pointer arguments are especially important because they allow you to access original data in the calling function. When you pass a pointer to a function, you pass an address; it can be the address of an array of data to be used as input by the function, or it can be the address of a variable that is to receive a result. The next program shows both these uses of a pointer argument.

Listing 11.20 TOTAL.C Total an array of values

DO: Enter, compile, and run TOTAL

```
#include <stdio.h>
void sum(int *, int *);
void main()
{
   int i_array[] = {1, 2, 3, 4};
   int total;

   sum(i_array, &total);
   printf("The total is %d", total);
}

void sum(int *pi_array, int *p_total)
{
   int i;

   *p_total = 0;
   for (i=0; i<4; ++i)
       *p_total += pi_array[i];
}
```

RESULT:

```
C:\>TOTAL
The total is 10
```

ANALYSIS:

1. This program calls a function to add numbers from an array and return the sum. The prototype for the summation function, sum(), declares two integer pointers—one for the input array and one for the returned answer.
2. The main function defines an array initialized with integer values and the integer *total* to accept the sum of the array values.
3. The first argument in the call to function sum() is a pointer to the input array, *i_array*, and the second argument is a pointer to the location of the answer, *&total*.
4. The definition of function sum() declares the pointer parameters *pi_array* and *p_total* for access to the input and output data locations,

respectively. The identifiers have a prefix of 'p' to emphasize that they are pointers. The function sums the array values by indexing the pointer pi_*array[i]*, and it adds these values into the variable *total* by applying the indirection operator (*) to the pointer *p_total*.

5. Notice that there is no return value for the function sum()—the function places the result directly into variable *total* back in main() via the pointer parameter, *p_total*.

In program TOTAL, you could also declare the function arguments as follows:

```
void sum(int pi_array[], int *pi_total)
```

The notation *int pi_array[]* is equivalent to *int *pi_array* when used to declare a function parameter. The notation with square brackets has the advantage of informing you that the calling argument is expected to be a pointer to an array, as opposed to a pointer to a single variable. You can use either form of declaration; the compiler interprets them both in the same way, and you can use the pointer identifiers in the function in an identical manner.

You could also return the answer as the value of the function; to do this, you would remove the second argument, change the declaration of sum() from type *void* to *int*, and add a *return* statement. However, this doesn't involve a pointer; let's require the answer to be in the form of a string so that the function must return a character pointer. Therefore, you will declare sum() to have a character pointer type and return the total as shown in the following program.

Listing 11.21 TOTAL2.C Total an array of values

DO:
- Modify TOTAL to return a character sum
- Compile and run TOTAL2

```
#include <stdio.h>
char *sum(int *);                                                   /*1*/
void main()
{
   int i_array[] = {1, 2, 3, 4};

   printf("The total is %s", sum(i_array));                         /*2*/
}

char *sum(int *pi_array)                                            /*3*/
{
   int i;
   int i_sum;                /* Integer total */                    /*4*/
   static char s_sum[7];     /* String total */                     /*5*/

   i_sum = 0;                                                       /*6*/
   for (i=0; i<4; ++i)
```

```
        i_sum += pi_array[i];                               /*7*/
    sprintf(s_sum, "%d", i_sum);                            /*8*/
    return(s_sum);                                          /*9*/
}
```

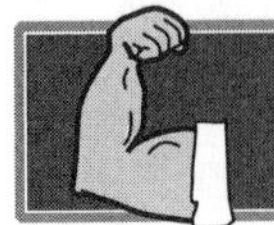

RESULT:

```
C:\>TOTAL2
The total is 10
```

ANALYSIS:

1. The prototype on line /*1*/ and the definition on line /*3*/ both have eliminated the second argument previously used for the return value, and they both change the function type declaration from *void* to *char* *.
2. The function accumulates the sum in the variable *i_sum*, which is local to the function sum() (lines /*4*/, /*6*/, and /*7*/), instead of in the variable *total*, which was previously in the main function.
3. Line /*8*/ converts the integer sum to a string in array *s_sum*, and line /*9*/ returns the array pointer to the calling function. The program declares array s_*sum* to be *static* so the program will not discard it when function sum() ends; the string must be intact for the calling function to display it.

POINTERS TO POINTERS

A pointer is a variable that contains an address, and when that address refers to another pointer, you have a "pointer to a pointer." This is just a catchy phrase that describes the particular use of a pointer; there are no special keywords or declarations in C for handling pointers to pointers. Figure 11-5 illustrates a pointer to a pointer.

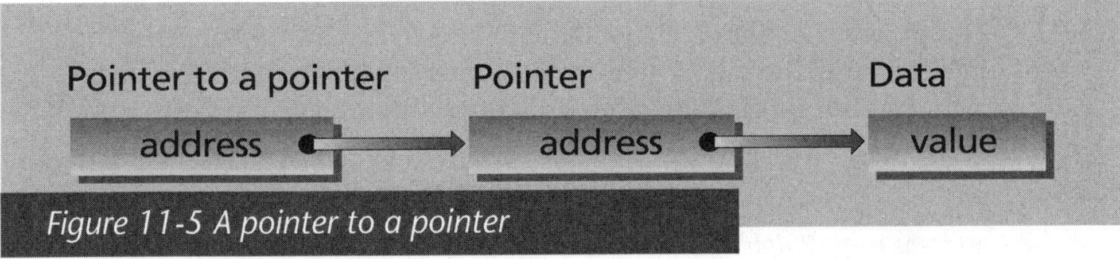

Figure 11-5 A pointer to a pointer

You can declare a variable a pointer to a pointer with two indirection operators in the following way:

```
char **ptr2ptr;
```

You can assign an address of another pointer to this variable, so that the value of *ptr2ptr* would be like the left-most address in Figure 11-5. Here is a program that shows how you would use this pointer to a pointer to access a data value through another pointer.

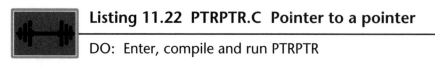

Listing 11.22 PTRPTR.C Pointer to a pointer

DO: Enter, compile and run PTRPTR

```
#include <stdio.h>
void main()
{
   char alpha     = 'A';
   char *ptr2alpha = &alpha;
   char **ptr2ptr  = &ptr2alpha;

   printf("\nptr2ptr is: %p", ptr2ptr);
   printf("\n*ptr2ptr is: %p", *ptr2ptr);
   printf("\n**ptr2ptr is: %c", **ptr2ptr);
}
```

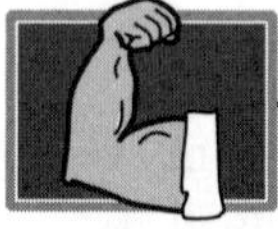

RESULT:

```
C:\>PTRPTR

ptr2ptr is: 839B
*ptr2ptr is: 839A
**ptr2ptr is: A
```

ANALYSIS:

1. The program defines a character variable, *alpha*, and initializes it to 'A'. Then it defines a pointer to a character, *ptr2alpha*, and initializes it to the address of *alpha*. Then it defines a pointer to a pointer to a character, *ptr2ptr*, and initializes it to the address of *ptr2alpha*.

2. The first printf() statement displays the value of *ptr2ptr*, which is the address of *ptr2alpha*.

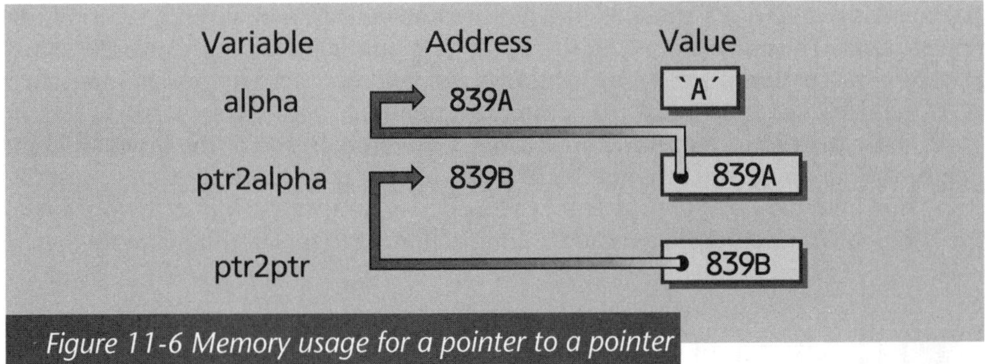

Figure 11-6 Memory usage for a pointer to a pointer

3. The second printf() shows the result of the indirection operator (*) applied to *ptr2ptr*, which is the value of *ptr2alpha*, or the address of *alpha*.

4. The third printf() statement displays the value, A, as a consequence of the double indirection operators. The first indirection returns the value that *ptr2ptr* points to (the value of *ptr2alpha*), then the second indirection returns the value that *ptr2alpha* points to, which is the value of *alpha*, or 'A'.

Figure 11-6 shows the variables in memory for this example.

Another form of a pointer to a pointer can occur with a pointer array. You have previously encountered a couple of instances of pointer arrays: The command line

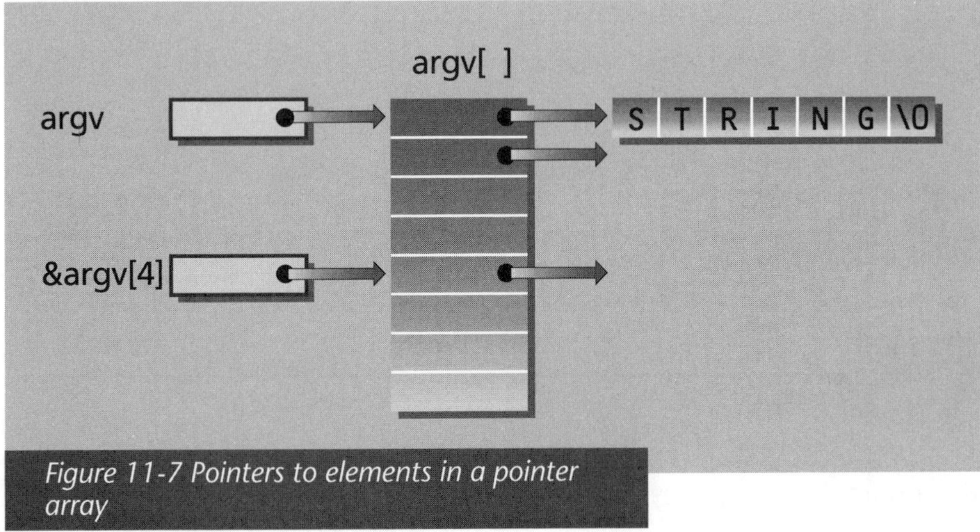

Figure 11-7 Pointers to elements in a pointer array

arguments to main() are stored in the pointer array *argv[]*, and any ragged array is a pointer array. The name *argv* is the address of the pointer array, in other words, *argv* is a "pointer to a pointer," as Figure 11-7 shows. Any address that refers to a pointer, such as *&argv[4]* in Figure 11-7, is also a pointer to a pointer.

When you need to return a pointer from a function as one of the function arguments, the argument will be a pointer to a pointer. Suppose you wanted to return the string sum from the TOTAL2 program via a function argument rather than as the value of the function. You would add a second pointer argument to function sum() as follows:

Listing 11.23 TOTAL3.C Total an array of values

DO:
- Modify TOTAL2 to return the string as an argument
- Compile and run TOTAL3

```
#include <stdio.h>
void sum(int *, char **);                                   /*1*/
void main()
{
   int i_array[] = {1, 2, 3, 4};
   char *total;                                             /*2*/

   sum(i_array, &total);                                    /*3*/
   printf("The total is %s", total);                        /*4*/
}

void sum(int *i_array, char **p_total)                      /*5*/
{
   int i;
   int i_sum;               /* Integer total */
   static char s_sum[7];    /* String total */

   i_sum = 0;
   for (i=0; i<4; ++i)
       i_sum += i_array[i];
   sprintf(s_sum, "%d", i_sum);
   *p_total = s_sum;                                        /*6*/
}
```

RESULT:

```
C:\>TOTAL3
The total is 10
```

ANALYSIS:

1. The function prototype on line /*1*/ and the definition on line /*5*/ are now type *void* because the sum will not be returned as the value of the function. Instead, the function declares a second argument to accept the string result, which is a pointer to a pointer, *char **p_total.*

2. In the main function, line /*2*/ defines the character pointer *total,* and line /*3*/ passes the address of *total* (a pointer to a pointer) to function sum().

3. Line /*6*/ in function sum() assigns the final string pointer to **p_total,* which is the value pointed to by the value of parameter *p_total,* or the value of *total* in the main function.

It is easy to mix up pointers with pointers to pointers, but this is a serious mistake. A common programming error occurs if you use a pointer argument when a pointer to a pointer is needed; a quick modification to the TOTAL3 program illustrates this error.

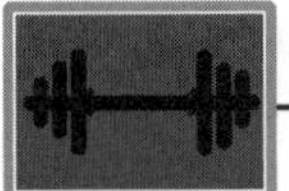

Listing 11.24 TOTAL4.C Total an array of values

DO:
- Modify TOTAL3 to pass the wrong argument
- Compile and run TOTAL4

```
#include <stdio.h>
void sum(int *, char **);
void main()
{
   int i_array[] = {1, 2, 3, 4};
   char *total;

   sum(i_array, total);                                    /*1*/
   printf("The total is %s", total);
}

void sum(int *i_array, char **p_total)
{
   int i;
   int i_sum;                  /* Integer total */
   static char s_sum[7];       /* String total */

   i_sum = 0;
   for (i=0; i<4; ++i)
       i_sum += i_array[i];
   sprintf(s_sum, "%d", i_sum);
   *p_total = s_sum;
}
```

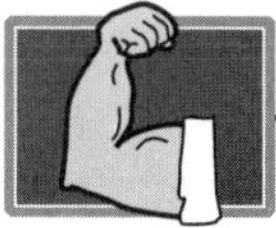

RESULT:

```
C:\>TOTAL4
The total is (null)
```

ANALYSIS:

1. The call on line /*1*/ now passes the value of *total* to the function sum() instead of the address of *total*. Why not—it's a pointer, isn't it? Yes, but it should be a pointer to a pointer.
2. Because the main function does not initialize the value of *total* (it doesn't need to), and because you have passed the address **in** *total* rather than the address **of** *total*, the last line in sum() assigns the string pointer to some unknown memory location. Therefore, the main function never receives the address of the string result. The printf() displays the message (null) to indicate that it received a null pointer instead of a valid string pointer.

A similar error would occur if you assigned the string address, s_*sum*, directly to *p_total* in the function sum() by leaving out the indirection operator (*). The address would replace the address of *total* (as the value of *p_total*) and not the value of *total*, where it should go.

The lesson here is to be thorough when dealing with pointers to pointers; take the time to think until you are clear about what points to what. If a problem occurs, check for the proper level of indirection.

DYNAMIC MEMORY ALLOCATION

There are times when you don't know how much memory a program will need for data that it creates while executing. One of these times occurred back in Chapter 10 (Program 10.20, ANALYZE8.C), where you had to allocate an array much larger than necessary just to be sure to have enough storage for all possible word combinations. C provides a way for you to avoid allocating large amounts of memory just to be prepared for the "worst case." A standard library function, malloc(), allows you to allocate only the amount of memory you need and only when you need it. When you are finished with the memory, you can release it with a call to another standard library function, free(). When you allocate memory by defining variables and arrays, the memory is reserved as long as the function in which it is allocated is executing; dynamic allocation allows you to control the lifetime of the memory usage.

Pointers play an essential role in dynamic memory allocation. You make a call to malloc() as follows:

```
ptr = (char *)malloc(size);
```

where *ptr* is a character pointer and *size* is an integer constant or variable that requests the size of the memory block in bytes. The function malloc() locates a block of contiguous memory of the requested size and returns a void pointer to the first byte in the block. You should cast the result of malloc() to match the type of pointer on the left side of the assignment; thus, you can use the memory any way you wish. If you want to use it as a block of integers, then declare *ptr* to be type *int* and cast the result of malloc() to type *int*:

```
ptr = (int *)malloc(size)
```

If malloc() cannot allocate the requested memory, it returns *NULL* to signify failure, and you should always test the result to be sure that the requested memory was successfully allocated. The header file, stdio.h, defines *NULL* as a null pointer—that is, a pointer with a value of zero that points to type *void*. The DYNAMIC program, which follows shortly, shows how to test the return value of malloc() for a *NULL* value to see if it was successful.

The memory is not initialized by malloc(); you must do this yourself or use another standard library function, calloc(), which does the same thing as malloc() but also clears the memory (sets all bytes to 0).

When you are finished with the memory block, you can release it back to the operating system by calling function free() as follows:

```
free(ptr);
```

This allows the operating system to reuse the memory. When a C program ends, it will automatically free all memory still in use, but it is good programming practice to explicitly free allocated memory when you are done with it.

In Chapter 10, you developed a program called ANALYZE8 (Program 10.20) to sort words alphabetically. This program used a large array to hold a list of words parsed from a sentence. The array was much larger than necessary because each row in the array had to be big enough to hold the largest possible word. Now you can use pointers along with the functions malloc() and free() to replace the large array allocation in the ANALYZE8 program with dynamic memory allocation. In this way, you will allocate only the space needed to handle the words that actually occur.

Listing 11.25 DYNAMIC.C Analyze a sentence

DO:
- Modify ANALYZE8 for dynamic memory allocation
- Compile and run DYNAMIC
- Enter **Have a very good day**

```
#include <stdio.h>
#include <string.h>
#include <stdlib.h>                                                /*1*/
void analyze(char *);

char *word_list[40];        /* List of word pointers */           /*2*/
int num_words = 0;          /* Number of words received */        /*3*/

void main()
{
   char sentence[80];
   char word[80];
   int index = 0;

/* Enter a sentence */

   printf("Enter a sentence: ");
   gets(sentence);

/* Parse the sentence */

   while (index < strlen(sentence))
   {
       sscanf(&sentence[index], "%s", word);
       index += strlen(word) + 1;
       while (sentence[index] == ' ')
             ++index;

/* Analyze a word */

       analyze(word);
   }

/* Free allocated memory */

   for (index=0; index<num_words; ++index)                         /*4*/
       free(word_list[index]);                                     /*5*/
}

void analyze(char *word)
{
   int n;                          /* Loop counter      */
   char *new_word;                 /* Pointer to new word */    /*6*/
   char *temp_ptr;                 /* Temporary word pointer */ /*7*/

/* Store the incoming word */

   new_word = (char *)malloc(strlen(word) + 1);                    /*8*/
   if (new_word == NULL)                                           /*9*/
   {                                                               /*10*/
       printf("\nMemory allocation error");                        /*11*/
       return;                                                     /*12*/
```

```
   }                                                            /*13*/
   strcpy(new_word, word);                                      /*14*/
   word_list[num_words] = new_word;                             /*15*/

/* Sort the words */

   for (n=0; n<num_words; ++n)
     if (strcmp(word_list[num_words], word_list[n]) < 0)        /*16*/
     {
           temp_ptr = word_list[n];                             /*17*/
           word_list[n] = word_list[num_words];                 /*18*/
           word_list[num_words] = temp_ptr;                     /*19*/
     }

/* Set the index to the next available word storage */

   ++num_words;

/* Display the sorted sentence */

   printf("\n");
   for (n=0; n<num_words; ++n)
       printf("%s ", word_list[n]);                             /*20*/
}
```

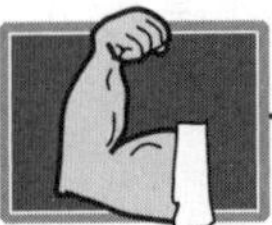

RESULT:

```
C:\>DYNAMIC
Enter a sentence: Have a very good day

Have
Have a
Have a very
Have a good very
Have a day good very
```

ANALYSIS:

1. File STDLIB.H contains prototypes for the dynamic memory allocation functions, and line /*1*/ includes this header file.
2. The program has two global declarations on lines /*2–3*/. Variable *num_words* counts the number of words in the sentence, and *word_list* is an array of pointers to the stored words. This program allocates space to store up to 40 word pointers, and it will rely on dynamic

memory allocation to store the word strings themselves. The size of a character pointer is 2 bytes under Power C, so the total size of *word_list* is 80 bytes. Thus, the total storage required is 80 bytes plus the number of many bytes necessary for the words; contrast this with a fixed 3200 bytes for the previous version of the program.

3. There is a reason that *word_list* and *num_words* are declared to be global: both functions of this program need to access both these items. The function analyze() allocates memory blocks and assigns the allocated memory pointers to *word_list* as it increments *num_words*, and just before ending, the main function uses both these items to free the allocated memory on lines /*4–5*/. Each cycle of the *for* loop releases memory by calling function free() with a pointer to an allocated memory block.

4. Lines /*6–7*/ define two new character pointers: *new_word* will point to dynamically allocated memory for each new word to be analyzed, and *temp_ptr* will be used to swap pointers during the sorting process.

5. On line /*8*/, a call to malloc() allocates exactly enough memory to hold the incoming word plus 1 byte for the terminating null. Lines / *9–13*/ check to see if the allocation succeeded; if malloc() returns a *NULL* value, the function displays an error message and returns without processing the word.

6. The call to strcpy() on line /*14*/ copies the word string into the newly allocated memory space, and line /*15*/ assigns the new pointer to one of the elements in *word_list.*

7. At this point in the processing, the program has placed each word in a separate, allocated memory block, and it has placed a pointer to each memory block in the array *word_list.* Effectively, you have built your own ragged array.

8. The remaining lines of code are devoted to sorting the array of words into alphabetic order as before. The modifications on lines /*16–20*/ accommodate the change from a fixed, two-dimensional array to your new ragged array. These lines are now assignment statements for pointer values instead of calls to strcpy().

Figure 11-8 is a flow diagram of the sorting algorithm.

Compare this diagram with the one in Figure 10-6—the word list is now a list of **pointers** to words instead of the words themselves, so the difference is that the algorithm works with pointers instead of words. The sorting process in the new DYNAMIC program is faster than it was in ANALYZE8 because you are sorting pointers instead of strings. You don't have to move a lot of data around, just pointers to the data.

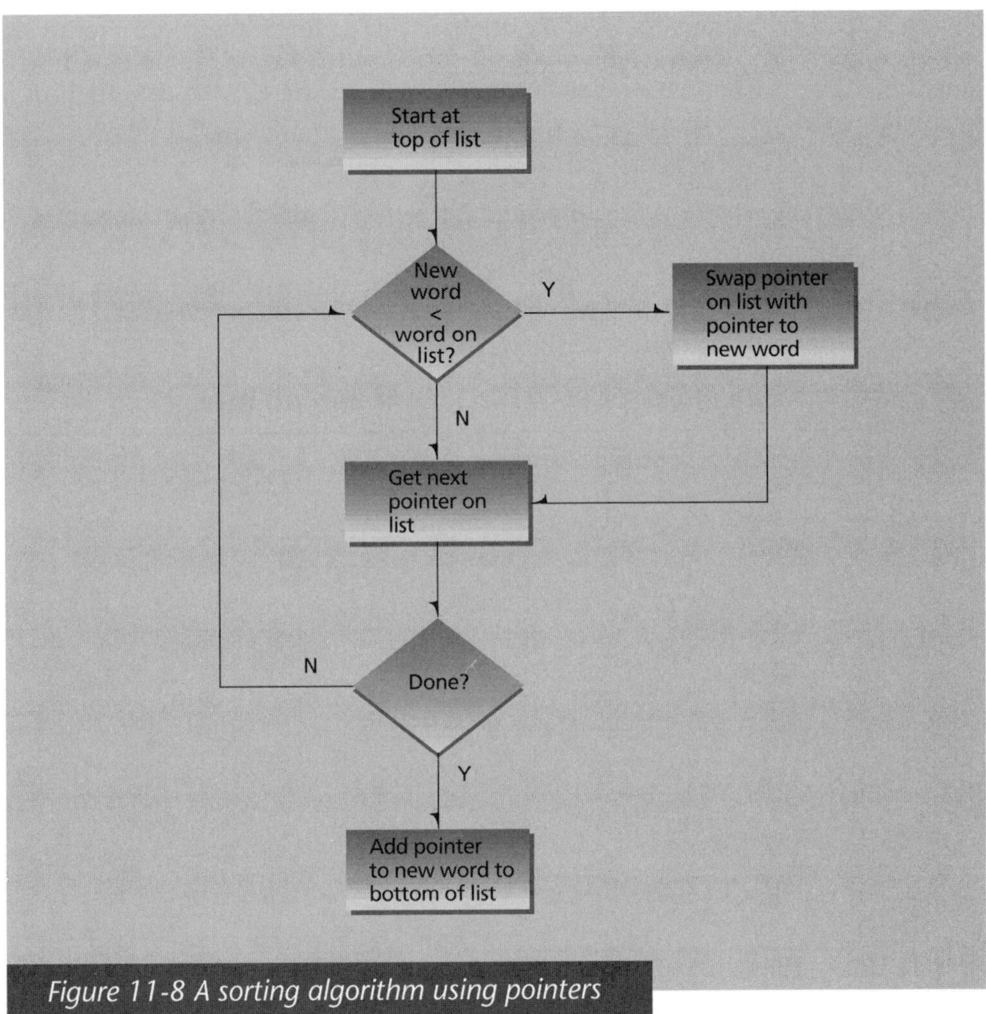

Figure 11-8 A sorting algorithm using pointers

FUNCTION POINTERS

Your use of pointers is not restricted just to data—you can also use them to point to functions. This is a very powerful feature of C that allows you to dynamically change which function is referenced by a calling statement. The executable code for functions resides in memory just as data does, and a pointer to a function is an address to the beginning of the function. The syntax for declaring a function pointer looks very similar to that of a function prototype:

```
type (*identifier)(argument list);
```

The *type, identifier,* and *argument list* are the same as for the function prototype; some additional parentheses and an asterisk surround the *identifier.* Don't confuse a function pointer with a function that returns a pointer. Here is the definition of a function pointer:

```
int (*func_ptr)(void);
```

And here is the prototype for a function that returns a pointer to an integer:

```
int *func(void);
```

The next program shows how to call a function using a function pointer.

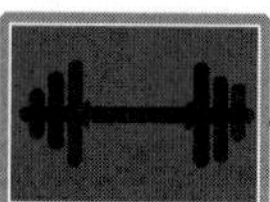

Listing 11.26 FUNCPTR.C Function pointer

DO: Enter, compile, and run FUNCPTR

```
#include <stdio.h>
void english(void);
void main()
{
   void (*func_ptr)(void);

   func_ptr = english;
   (*func_ptr)();
}

void english(void)
{
   printf("\nGood Day");
}
```

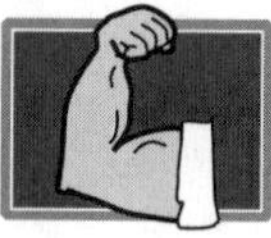

RESULT:

```
C:\>FUNCPTR

Good Day
```

ANALYSIS:

1. This program calls a very simple function, english(), which receives no parameters and returns no value; it just displays a greeting.
2. The first line in the main function declares a function pointer having the identifier *func_ptr*. This is a pointer that can reference functions

that have no arguments and that do not return a value, like function english().

3. The second line of the program assigns the pointer to function english() to the function pointer *func_ptr*. Just as the identifier of an array produces its address, the bare identifier of a function amounts to the address of the function.

4. Finally, the last statement of the main program *(*func_ptr)();* calls the function. You call a function by preceding the pointer with the indirection operator (*) and enclosing this in parentheses; you add the calling arguments in parentheses in the usual way.

Assignment of function pointers

A function pointer really becomes useful when you assign different function addresses to it while a program is running. You can expand the use of the function pointer in the previous program by writing additional functions to display a greeting in different languages.

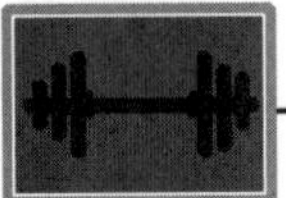

Listing 11.27 FUNCPTR2.C Function pointer

DO:
- Add functions to FUNC_PTR
- Compile and run FUNCPTR
- Enter (E)(ENTER) (F)(ENTER) (G)(ENTER) (ENTER)(Q)(ENTER)

```
#include <stdio.h>
void english(void);
void french(void);
void german(void);
void main()
{
   void (*func_ptr)(void);
   char key;

   func_ptr = english;

   printf("\n\nEnter (E)nglish, (F)rench (G)erman, "
       "or (Q)uit: ");
   while ((key = toupper(getchar())) != 'Q')
   {
       if (key == 'E')
             func_ptr = english;
       else if (key == 'F')
             func_ptr = french;
       else if (key == 'G')
             func_ptr = german;
```

```
        (*func_ptr)();
        if (key != '\n') getchar();
        printf("\n\nEnter (E)nglish, (F)rench (G)erman, "
               "or (Q)uit: ");
    }
}

void english(void)
{
    printf("\nGood Day");
}

void french(void)
{
    printf("\nBon Jour");
}

void german(void)
{
    printf("\nGuten Tag");
}
```

RESULT:

```
C:\>FUNCPTR2


Enter (E)nglish, (F)rench (G)erman, or (Q)uit: E

Good Day

Enter (E)nglish, (F)rench (G)erman, or (Q)uit: F

Bon Jour

Enter (E)nglish, (F)rench (G)erman, or (Q)uit: G

Guten Tag

Enter (E)nglish, (F)rench (G)erman, or (Q)uit:

Guten Tag

Enter (E)nglish, (F)rench (G)erman, or (Q)uit: Q
```

ANALYSIS:

1. This program has two new prototypes, and it has functions, french() and german(), to display a greeting in French and German.

2. The *while* loop in the main function reads a character from the keyboard, and this character determines which language will be displayed.
3. The first *if* statement assigns one of the three function addresses to the function pointer *func_ptr* depending on the keyboard input.
4. The function call *(*func_ptr)();* is the same as before, in the FUNCPTR program.
5. Before prompting for more input, the program calls getchar() to clear the keyboard buffer of the newline character generated when you last pressed ENTER; if you pressed ENTER alone, then the variable *key* would contain the newline ('\n') and the keyboard would not need to be cleared.

To be sure, it would be easier in this program to call the functions in the conventional way, with separate call statements, but this is a program designed to introduce the concept of function pointers.

Arrays of function pointers

You can also declare arrays of function pointers and initialize them with functions to be called under specific circumstances. Modify FUNCPTR2 to use an array of function pointers.

Listing 11.28 FUNCPTR3.C Function pointer

DO:
- Add an array of function pointers to FUNC_PTR2
- Compile and run FUNCPTR3
- Enter E ENTER F ENTER G ENTER ENTER Q ENTER

```
#include <stdio.h>
void english(void);
void french(void);
void german(void);
void main()
{
   void (*func_ptr[])(void) = { english, french, german };      /*1*/
   char key;

   printf("\n\nEnter (E)nglish, (F)rench (G)erman, "
       "or (Q)uit: ");
   while ((key = toupper(getchar())) != 'Q')
   {
       if (key == 'E')
             (*func_ptr[0])();                                  /*2*/
else if (key == 'F')
             (*func_ptr[1])();                                  /*3*/
```

```
        else if (key == 'G')
               (*func_ptr[2])();                                    /*4*/

        if (key != '\n') getchar();
        printf("\n\nEnter (E)nglish, (F)rench (G)erman, "
               "or (Q)uit: ");
    }
}

void english(void)
{
   printf("\nGood Day");
}

void french(void)
{
   printf("\nBon Jour");
}

void german(void)
{
   printf("\nGuten Tag");
}
```

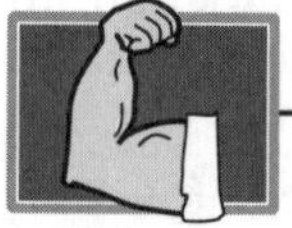

RESULT:

```
C:\>FUNCPTR3


Enter (E)nglish, (F)rench (G)erman, or (Q)uit: E

Good Day

Enter (E)nglish, (F)rench (G)erman, or (Q)uit: F

Bon Jour

Enter (E)nglish, (F)rench (G)erman, or (Q)uit: G

Guten Tag

Enter (E)nglish, (F)rench (G)erman, or (Q)uit: Q
```

ANALYSIS:

1. Line /*1*/ defines an array of function pointers and initializes it with pointers to each of the greeting functions. Notice the placement of

the square brackets—just after the identifier inside the parentheses. The array has three elements because the initializer list contains three values.

2. You call the functions from within the first *if* statement by referring to the appropriate element of the function pointer array.

Figure 11-9 illustrates how the array of function pointers refers to the beginning of each of the greeting functions.

Function pointers as arguments

You can pass a function pointer to another function as an argument. This operation is no different than passing any other type of pointer to a function; you just have to

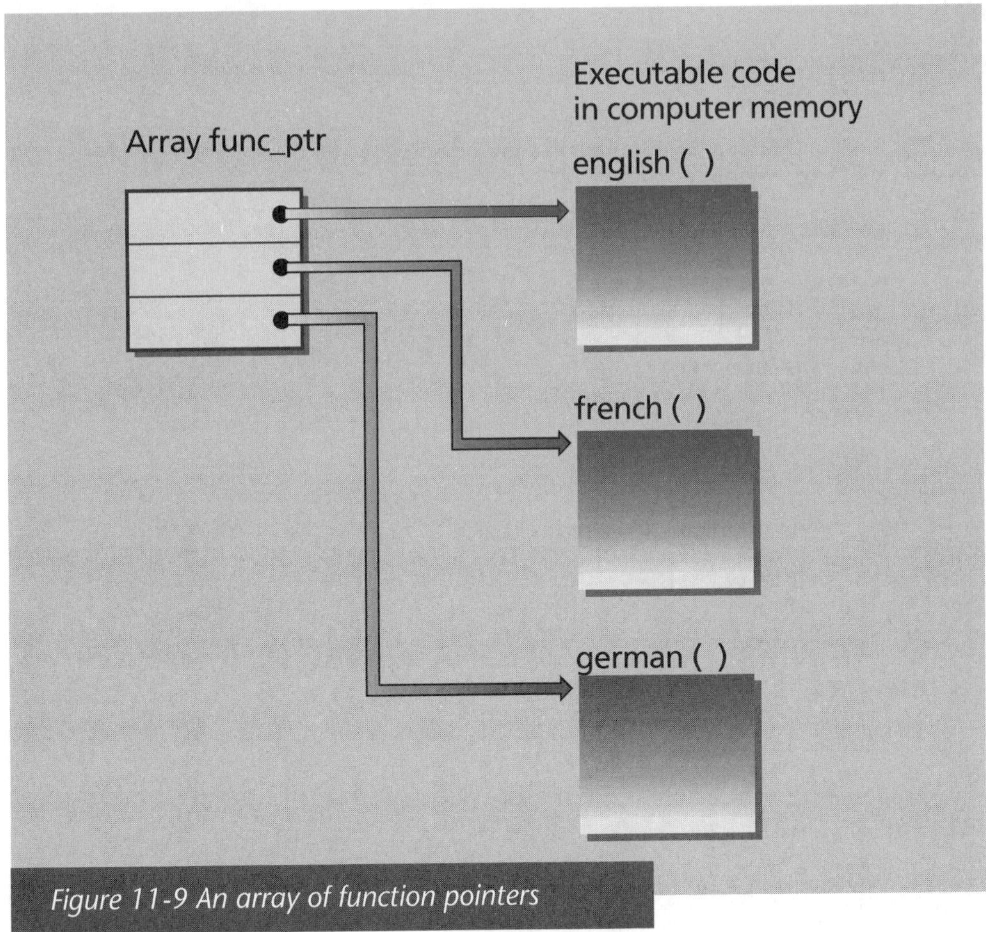

Figure 11-9 An array of function pointers

declare the pointer type properly. You can have the english() function call one of the other functions by passing it the desired function pointer in the next program.

Listing 11.29 FUNCPTR4.C Function pointer

DO:
- Modify FUNC_PTR2 to pass a function pointer
- Compile and run FUNCPTR4
- Enter (F)(ENTER) (G)(ENTER) (ENTER)(Q)(ENTER)

```
#include <stdio.h>
void english(void (*func_ptr)(void));                        /*1*/
void french(void);
void german(void);
void main()
{
   void (*func_ptr)(void);
   char key;

   printf("\n\nEnter (F)rench (G)erman, or (Q)uit: ");  /*2*/
   while ((key = toupper(getchar())) != 'Q')
   {
       if (key == 'F')
              func_ptr = french;
       else if (key == 'G')
              func_ptr = german;

       english(func_ptr);                                     /*3*/
       if (key != '\n') getchar();
       printf("\n\nEnter (F)rench (G)erman, or (Q)uit:");     /*4*/
   }
}

void english(void (*func_ptr)(void))                         /*5*/
{
   printf("\nGood Day");
   (*func_ptr)();                                             /*6*/
}

void french(void)
{
   printf("\nBon Jour");
}

void german(void)
{
   printf("\nGuten Tag");
}
```

RESULT:

```
C:\>FUNCPTR4


Enter (F)rench (G)erman, or (Q)uit: F

Good Day
Bon Jour

Enter (F)rench (G)erman, or (Q)uit: G

Good Day
Guten Tag

Enter (F)rench (G)erman, or (Q)uit: Q
```

ANALYSIS:

1. Line /*1*/ includes the declaration of the new function pointer argument in the prototype for english(), and line /*5*/ includes the parameter declaration in the definition of english(). These declarations have the same form as you previously used to define a variable for the function pointer.
2. The prompts on lines /*2*/ and /*4*/ are shorter because you no longer select the english option.
3. Line /*3*/ calls the function english() with the function pointer as an argument. The preceding *if* statement has already set the value of the pointer to whichever function you selected.
4. After displaying "Good Day" in English, function english() uses the function pointer parameter that it receives to call one of the other greeting functions on line /*6*/.

Function pointers play a key role in the application of advanced software techniques like object-oriented programming and newer languages like C++. This is a topic for further study as you become better acquainted with C. However, we will be content to end this chapter with this brief introduction to function pointers.

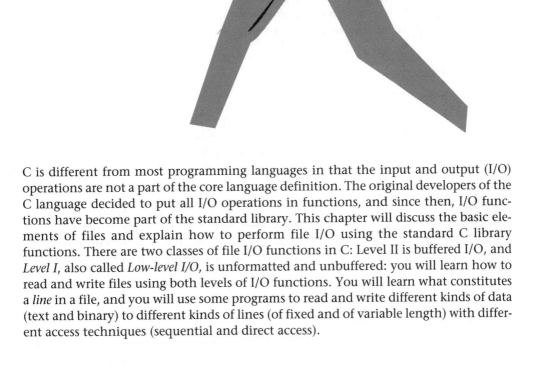

CHAPTER 12
FILE I/O

C is different from most programming languages in that the input and output (I/O) operations are not a part of the core language definition. The original developers of the C language decided to put all I/O operations in functions, and since then, I/O functions have become part of the standard library. This chapter will discuss the basic elements of files and explain how to perform file I/O using the standard C library functions. There are two classes of file I/O functions in C: Level II is buffered I/O, and *Level I*, also called *Low-level I/O*, is unformatted and unbuffered: you will learn how to read and write files using both levels of I/O functions. You will learn what constitutes a *line* in a file, and you will use some programs to read and write different kinds of data (text and binary) to different kinds of lines (of fixed and of variable length) with different access techniques (sequential and direct access).

FILE BASICS

Files are used for all sorts of purposes; some files hold data that programs create and access, and others hold the programs themselves. You have been creating program source files (*.C) that the compiler uses to generate object files (*.MIX), which are then linked to make an executable file (*.EXE). The Power C compiler itself is an executable file named PC.EXE. Another type of file that you use is the header file (*.h), which becomes a part of the source code for a program. Files are usually stored on your disk, but files can also be stored on tape, or even in memory if you have the specialized software to allow it. The operating system (DOS for Power C or perhaps UNIX on another machine) keeps track of the names and locations of files on your disk in a *directory*, which is a special file on the disk. DOS limits the names of files to 8 characters, plus a 3-character extension following a period (NAME.EXT).

In C, a file is a stream of bytes stored on disk. The stream of bytes is separated into lines by control characters. In general, lines in a file are of *variable length*—that is, they don't all have the same number of bytes between the control characters. However, they can be of *fixed length*, which is useful, as you will see when we discuss *direct access* later in the chapter.

C programs go through the operating system to read and write files, so the end-of-line control characters are somewhat dependent on the operating system. With UNIX, a newline ('\n') always signifies the end of a line. DOS has two kinds of files: *binary* and *text*. A DOS binary file is the same as a UNIX file, but a DOS text file uses a carriage return ('\r') and a newline ('\n') to separate lines. A DOS text file sometimes uses a CTRL-Z byte (ASCII code 26) to signal the end of the file. Figure 12-1 shows these two file types for a file with three lines from Shakespeare:

```
To be
or not
to be
```

You can make your own data files, or you may obtain them from another source, but one way or another, files are always created by programs. You can use your editor program to create a file.

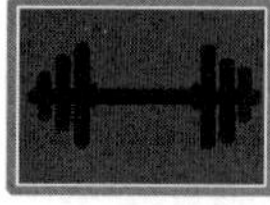

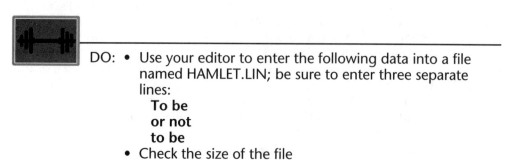

DO: • Use your editor to enter the following data into a file named HAMLET.LIN; be sure to enter three separate lines:

To be
or not
to be

• Check the size of the file

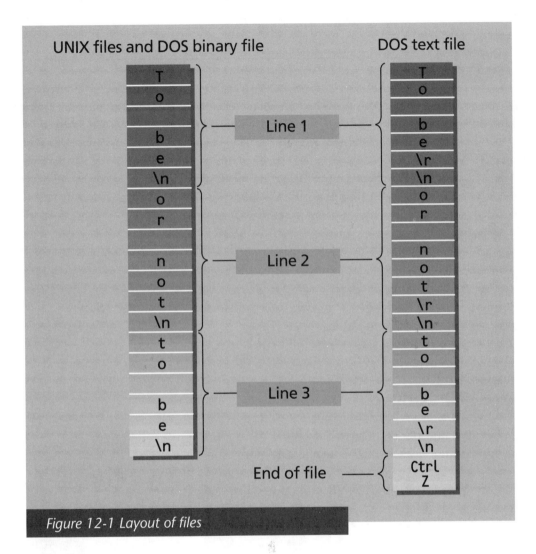

UNIX files and DOS binary file

T
o

b
e
\n
o
r

n
o
t
\n
t
o

b
e
\n

Line 1
Line 2
Line 3
End of file

DOS text file

T
o

b
e
\r
\n
o
r

n
o
t
\r
\n
t
o

b
e
\r
\n
Ctrl
Z

Figure 12-1 Layout of files

RESULT:

```
C:\>dir HAMLET.LIN

 Volume in drive C has no label
 Directory of  C:\

HAMLET   LIN      23   9-08-91   7:08p
      1 File(s)   7440384 bytes free
```

ANALYSIS:

The number of bytes in this file is 16 text characters, plus 6 end-of-line characters, plus 1 end-of-file character—a total of 23 bytes. The total may be 22 bytes if your editor did not add the end-of-file character CTRL-Z.

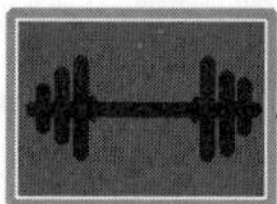

DO: • Display the file HAMLET.LIN

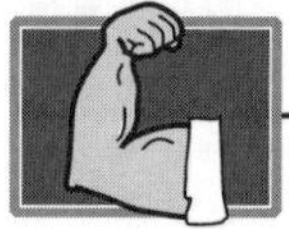

RESULT:

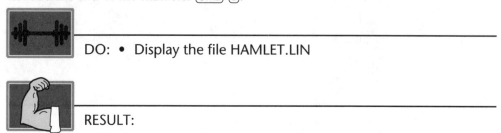

```
C:\>type HAMLET.LIN
To be
or not
to be
```

ANALYSIS:

1. Only the text characters appear on the screen; the end-of-line and end-of-file control characters are not visible.
2. The end-of-line characters ('\r' and '\n') cause the text in each file line to be displayed on a separate screen line.
3. The lines in this file are of variable length.

LEVEL I VERSUS LEVEL II FILE I/O

There are two classes of I/O functions for files: Level I is also called Low-*level* I/O because it interacts directly with, and is dependent on, the operating system; C builds the higher, Level II I/O on top of the Level I functions. The ANSI standard covers only Level II I/O, which is independent of the operating system. You can use either level of I/O, but only Level II is truly portable from one operating system to another.

Level II I/O is buffered and can be either formatted or unformatted; Figure 12-2 illustrates the flow of data for Level II file I/O.

In Chapter 4, you began using formatting in connection with the functions printf() and scanf() to convert between internal and external representations of data. Recall

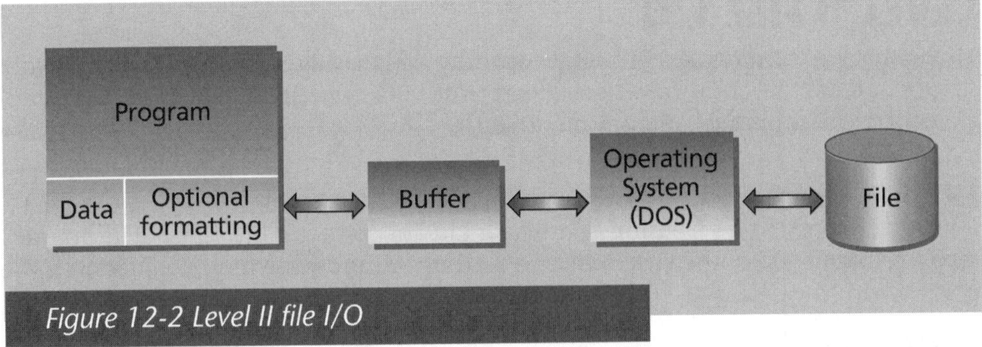

Figure 12-2 Level II file I/O

that you used conversion specifiers in printf() and scanf() to convert ASCII characters, like '1' and '2,' into binary numbers, like 12. You can use the same formatting process to convert data to and from files. For output, a program formats data and sends it to a buffer (a block of storage in memory), as shown in Figure 12-2. Then, when the buffer fills up to a certain level, the program writes the data to the disk file. The buffer makes file I/O more effective by allowing larger amounts of data to be transferred to the disk at one time. Buffering is set up and handled by the compiler and operating system—a process that is totally automatic as far as you are concerned. For input, your program requests data from the file and first reads it into the buffer.Then, it performs any requested formatting before the data is stored into the area designated by your program.

Level I I/O is unformatted and unbuffered, which means that the data goes directly to a file. Figure 12-3 shows the flow of Level I data to and from a file.

Level I I/O **can** be faster than Level II is when used correctly. You have more control than with Level II, and a program does not have to format the data, so you can transfer large blocks of data very quickly. But if you transfer data in small amounts, you can work the disk too hard and end up with a less efficient program overall.

For most of this chapter, you will use the portable Level II I/O functions, but towards the end, you will get a chance to use some of the Level I functions.

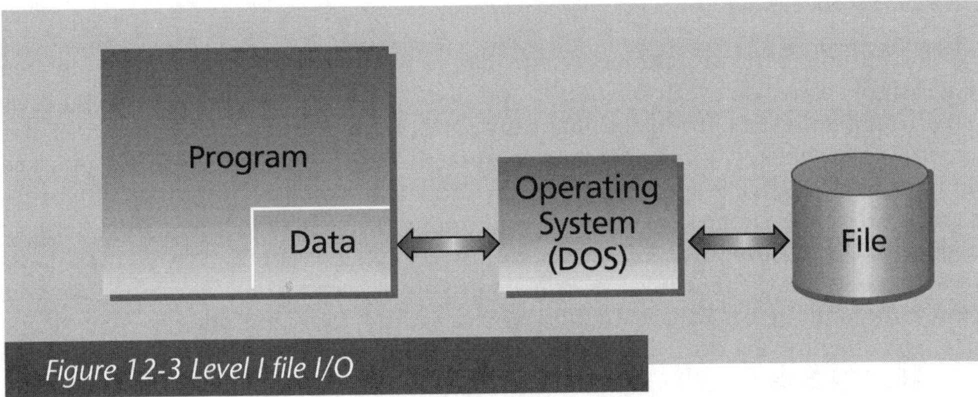

Figure 12-3 Level I file I/O

LEVEL II FILE I/O

You will begin learning Level II I/O by opening and closing files. Then, you will work some examples that show how to read and write data before going on to see the differences between formatted and unformatted I/O.

Level II file open and close

C programs refer to files by using a particular kind of pointer, a file *pointer*. File pointers serve as arguments for the functions that read, write, and close files. You declare a file pointer with the data type *FILE*, defined in the header file stdio.h. For example:

```
FILE *fp;
```

FILE (all uppercase) is a type specifier that is declared in stdio.h, *fp* is an identifier, and the asterisk (*) makes it a pointer. You can designate any identifier for a file pointer; the usual rules apply—begin with a letter or underscore and add any number of letters, numbers, or underscores.

Before you can access any data in a file, you must open the file, and as soon as you are finished with the file, you should close it. The function used to open a file for Level II I/O is fopen(), which returns a file pointer. You call this function as follows:

```
fp = fopen(filename, mode);
```

The argument *filename* is a null terminated string containing the name of the file, and *mode* is a string indicating how you intend to use the file. For instance, to open a file named **BIRDS** to data, you would write the following statement:

```
fp = fopen("BIRDS", "r");
```

If successful, fopen() returns a pointer to the file, and if it cannot open the file for any reason, it returns *NULL*.

The function used to close a file is:

```
fclose(fp);
```

The purpose of fclose() is to write any data remaining in the buffer to the file, free the memory associated with the buffer, and disassociate the file from the file pointer. When a program ends, it will automatically perform these operations on any files that are still open, but it is good programming practice to explicitly close files as soon as you are finished accessing them. Open files consume memory and other system resources, so it is best not to leave them open unnecessarily. The function fclose() returns a value of zero if successful and a nonzero integer otherwise; however, you will have little cause to test the return value. You are usually at the end of a function when you close a file, and there is hardly anything you can do if fclose() indicates an error except perhaps display an error message. The next program opens and closes the HAMLET.LIN file.

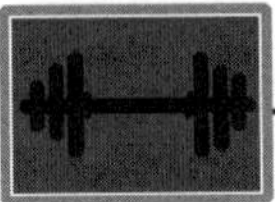

Listing 12.1 FILE.C Open a file

DO: Enter, compile, and run FILE

```
#include <stdio.h>
void main()
{
     FILE *fp;        /* File pointer */

/* Open a file */

     fp = fopen("HAMLET.LIN", "w");

/* Close the file */

     fclose(fp);
}
```

RESULT:

```
C:\>FILE
```

ANALYSIS:

1. The program first defines a file pointer; when only one file is open at a time, C programs often use the identifier *fp*, because it is concise shorthand for "file pointer." However, when a program uses more than one file, it is best to expand the identifier to make it more descriptive of the purpose of the file or the data contained in the file—*fp_hamlet*, for instance.

2. Both arguments for fopen() are string constants in this case. The mode string is "w," which asks that the file be opened for writing only.

3. The last statement in the program closes the file.

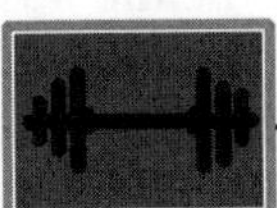

DO: • Display the file HAMLET.LIN

RESULT:

```
C:\>type HAMLET.LIN
```

DO: • Check the size of the file

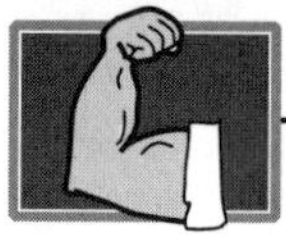

RESULT:

```
C:\>dir HAMLET.LIN

 Volume in drive C has no label
 Directory of  C:\

HAMLET   LIN       0  9-08-91   7:15p
       1 File(s)  7436288 bytes free
```

ANALYSIS:

There is nothing in the file! The FILE program opened the file for writing at the beginning and closed it without writing any data. The lines from Hamlet's soliloquy that you had previously entered are gone. When fopen() opens a file in write mode ("w"), and the file already exists, it discards all the old data in the file. If the file did not already exist, fopen() creates an empty file ready to accept new data.

There are three basic mode strings for fopen():

```
"r" opens the file for reading at the beginning.
"w" opens the file for writing at the beginning.
"a" (append) opens the file for writing at the end.
```

If the named file does not exist, modes "w" and "a" create a new file, while mode "r" fails (returns *NULL*). You can modify each of these modes to allow both reading and writing, and to open the file in *binary* mode; Table 12-1 lists the possibilities.

You will have a chance to use some of these file modes as you work the examples in this chapter.

It is **always** a good idea to check the return value from fopen() to see if the file was successfully opened. Files can be unavailable for many reasons: a file may be in another directory, the name could be misspelled, it could be designated read-only by the operating system when you want to write, or it could possibly not exist at all. Your program may do some very strange things if it tries to use nonexistent data from a file that did not open. You should test for the NULL return value, display a message to indicate an error, and stop processing if a NULL is detected. Here is one way to test for an open error:

Mode string	Meaning
"r"	Read only from beginning of file
"r+"	Read or write from beginning
"r" modes will not create a file.	
"w"	Write from beginning of file
"w+"	Write or read from beginning
"a"	Write from end of file (append)
"a+"	Write or read from end of file
All "w" and "a" modes create a file if it doesn't exist.	
"rb"	b at the end of any mode string
"r+b"	means binary mode with no
"wb"	translation of control characters
"w+b"	
"ab"	
"a+b"	

Table 12-1 File modes

Listing 12.2 FILE2.C Open a file

DO: • Test fopen() for NULL return value
• Compile FILE2

```
#include <stdio.h>
int main()                                                  /*1*/
{
   FILE *fp;            /* File pointer */
   char filename[] = "HAMLET.LIN";                          /*2*/

/* Open a file */

   if ((fp = fopen(filename, "r")) == NULL)                 /*3*/
   {                                                        /*4*/
     printf("\nCould not open file %s", filename);          /*5*/
     exit(1);                                               /*6*/
   }                                                        /*7*/
```

```
/* Close the file */

   fclose(fp);
}
```

ANALYSIS:

1. The file name is now a string array initialized on line /*2*/.
2. The *if* statement on line /*3*/ has three basic roles; it calls fopen(), assigns the result to *fp*, and compares the value of *fp* with *NULL*. The second pair of parentheses, around expression *fp = fopen(filename, "r")*, ensures that the program will call fopen() and assign its result before comparing the value of *fp* with *NULL*.
3. If the comparison is true, then the program executes the compound statement, displays the error message, and exits prematurely. A program normally exits with a return value of zero, so this error exit returns a 1 to signify a problem. Line /*1*/ declares main() to be of data type *int* to return a status value.
4. Notice that the program does not attempt to close the file if the open() was unsuccessful. You should only close files that a previous statement successfully opened. The effect of closing unopened files is unpredictable and depends on the compiler and operating system.

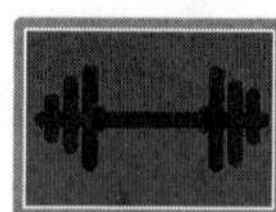

DO: Make sure file HAMLET.LIN exists in the same directory as FILE2.EXE and run the program

RESULT:

```
C:\>FILE2
```

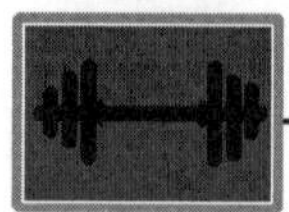

DO: Delete file HAMLET.LIN and run FILE2

RESULT:

```
C:\>del HAMLET.LIN
```

```
C:\>FILE2

Could not open file HAMLET.LIN
```

ANALYSIS:

1. The first run successfully opened and closed the file without displaying any messages.
2. The second run could not open the file because it did not exist, so fopen() returned *NULL* and the program displayed an error message.

Level II file reading and writing

Many Level II file functions are variations of console formatted I/O functions formed by adding a file pointer to the list of arguments. The file functions *fprintf()* and *fscanf()* are similar to the console I/O functions printf() and scanf(). C also has file functions dedicated to string I/O, *fgets()* and *fputs()*, that are similar to gets() and puts().

Standard console files

Actually, you can think of the console I/O functions as special cases of the file I/O functions, because the console is the default file that a program automatically opens so that these functions can operate. Your C program automatically opens the standard input file (the keyboard) and provides the file pointer *stdin*, and it automatically opens the standard output file (the screen) with the file pointer *stdout*. Both *stdin* and *stdout* are pointer constants of type FILE; you can use them as arguments for file functions, but you cannot assign values to them. For instance, the following two statements are equivalent:

```
printf("hello");
fprintf(stdout, "hello");
```

String functions for file I/O: fgets() and fputs()

You will find the prototype for fputs() in header file stdio.h:

```
int fputs(char *string, FILE *fp);
```

This function writes all characters from the *string* to the file referenced by file pointer *fp*. It does **not** write the terminating null to the file, and unlike the console output function puts(), it does **not** write a newline character at the end, so the total number of characters that fputs() writes is strlen(string). Function fputs() returns an integer zero if successful and the nonzero constant *EOF* otherwise. Constant EOF is defined in the header file stdio.h; it serves as the return value for several file I/O functions to indicate when the end of file has been reached.

You can write a file using fopen() and fputs() that will be the same as the one you previously created using an editor.

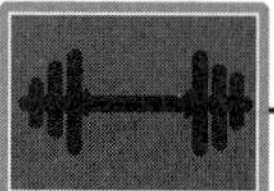

Listing 12.3 FILE3.C Write a file

DO:
- Modify FILE2 to write data to the file
- Compile and run FILE3

```
#include <stdio.h>
int main()
{
    FILE *fp;          /* File pointer */
    char filename[] = "HAMLET.LIN";
    int  i;                                              /*1*/
    char *data[] = {"To be\n", "or not\n", "to be\n"};    /*2*/

/* Open a file */

    if (( fp = fopen(filename, "w")) == NULL)            /*3*/
    {
         printf("\nCould not open file %s", filename);
         exit(1);
    }

/* Write data to the file */

    for ( i=0; i<3; ++i)                                 /*4*/
         fputs(data[i], fp);                             /*5*/

/* Close the file */

    fclose(fp);
}
```

RESULT:

```
C:\>FILE3
```

ANALYSIS:

1. Line /*1*/ defines an integer to serve as an index to the lines being written, and line /*2*/ defines a ragged array initialized with three strings, each of which will become a line in the file. You must explic-

itly attach a newline character ('\n') to the end of each initialization string because puts() does not write a newline to form a file line.

2. You must change the fopen() mode string on line /*3*/ to "w" to write to the file.

3. The *for* loop on lines /*4–5*/ calls function fputs() three times to write the three strings of data to the file.

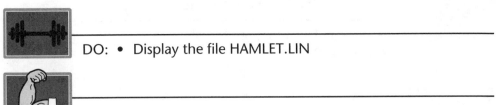

DO: • Display the file HAMLET.LIN

RESULT:

```
C:\>type HAMLET.LIN
To be
or not
to be
```

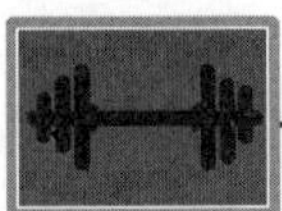

DO: • Check the size of the file.

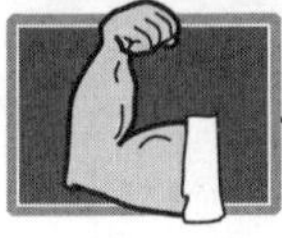

RESULT:

```
C:\>dir HAMLET.LIN

 Volume in drive C has no label
 Directory of  C:\

HAMLET   LIN      22   9-08-91   7:11p
       1 File(s)   7436288 bytes free
```

ANALYSIS:

The new file is the same as the one you created with the editor, except it is only 22 bytes long; FILE3 did not write an end-of-file character at the end.

You will rarely receive an open error in the write mode ("w") because fopen() creates the file if it does not exist. About the only conditions that can cause this error to occur arise when the operating system is out of memory or the maximum number of open files has been reached—these are restrictions imposed by the operating system, not by the C language. The file error that perhaps programmers make most often is opening a file in the wrong mode. Change the last program so that it tries to write to a file opened in read mode.

Listing 12.4 FILE4.C Write a file

DO:
- Modify FILE3 to open the file in read mode
- Compile FILE4

```
#include <stdio.h>
int main()
{
    FILE *fp;           /* File pointer */
    char filename[] = "HAMLET.LIN";
    int i;
    char *data[] = {"Hamlet:\n", "To be\n",                  /*1*/
                    "or not\n", "to be\n"};

/* Open a file */

    if (( fp = fopen(filename, "r")) == NULL)                /*2*/
    {
        printf("\nCould not open file %s", filename);
    }

/* Write data to the file */

    for ( i=0; i<3; ++i)
        printf("\nReturn code = %d", fputs(data[i], fp));    /*3*/

/* Close the file */

    fclose(fp);
}
```

ANALYSIS:

1. Add another string ("Hamlet:\n") to the data on line /*1*/ so you can see a difference in the file if the write is successful. You don't have to write all four of the data strings; just three will be sufficient, because the first new string will show whether or not the program writes to the file.

2. Change the mode of the fopen() to "r" on line /*2*/. Also remove the exit(1) statement so that processing will continue even if an open error occurs.
3. Encapsulate fputs() in a printf() statement on line /*3*/ to display the return code.

DO: • Run FILE4
• Examine the contents of HAMLET.LIN

RESULT:

```
C:\>FILE4

Return code = 0
Return code = 0
Return code = 0

C:\>type HAMLET.LIN
To be
or not
to be
```

ANALYSIS:

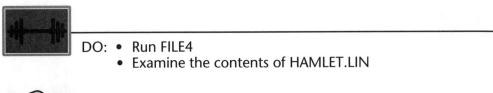

1. Not suprisingly, the file is unchanged because the program cannot write to a file that is open for read operations only.
2. The return code from fputs() gives no indication of an error; the zeros imply that each write was a success.

Watch out for this kind of file I/O error; it is a logic error, so the compiler will not catch it, and you will receive no indication of a problem while the program is running, but the end result will be wrong. You can open a file for both reading and writing by specifying "r+" or "w+" for the mode string; opening a file with "w+" will create a file if it does not exist. These modes are often easier and more desireable, but you should only open a file for the operations that are actually needed—"overkill" can be dangerous.

You can see the return code, *EOF* (or -1), resulting from fputs() by running FILE4 when the data file, HAMLET.LIN, does not exist.

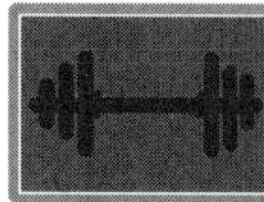

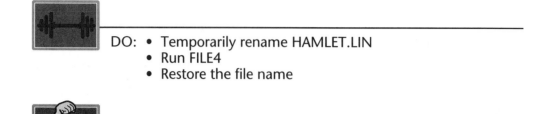

DO:
- Temporarily rename HAMLET.LIN
- Run FILE4
- Restore the file name

RESULT:

```
C:\>rename HAMLET.LIN HAMLET.DAT

C:\>FILE4

Could not open file HAMLET.LIN
Return code = -1
Return code = -1
Return code = -1

C:\>rename HAMLET.DAT HAMLET.LIN
```

ANALYSIS:

The fputs() function returns *EOF* (-1) when it attempts to write to a file that is not open—the file pointer *fp* is *NULL* because you renamed the file and fopen() could not find it.

Now let's see about reading the file with fgets(). Header file stdio.h defines the prototype for fgets():

```
char *fgets(char *buffer, int n, FILE *fp);
```

The first argument is a pointer to a buffer that will receive data; typically, the buffer will be a character array. The second is the size of the buffer in bytes, and the third is a pointer to the file from which data will be read. The function reads data until it encounters a newline ('\n') character or the end of the file, or until it reads *n*-1 characters, whichever comes first. The fgets() function returns *NULL* if it encounters the end of file without reading any data, or if an error occurs (such as when the file is not open); otherwise, it returns a pointer to the buffer. When fgets() has finished reading data, it adds a null character ('\0') to the end of the data to terminate the string; this is why it stops reading after *n*-1 characters.

You can easily modify the FILE3 program to read the file that it wrote by changing the fopen() mode string and replacing fputs() with fgets().

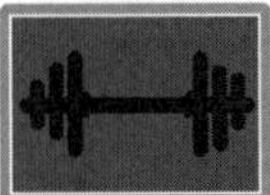

Listing 12.5 FILE5.C Read a file

DO: • Modify FILE3 to read instead of write data
• Compile and run FILE5

```
#include <stdio.h>
int main()
{
    FILE *fp;          /* File pointer */
    char filename[] = "HAMLET.LIN";
    int  i;
    char buffer[81];                                    /*1*/

/* Open a file */

    if (( fp = fopen(filename, "r")) == NULL)          /*2*/
    {
         printf("\nCould not open file %s", filename);
         exit(1);
    }

/* Read data from the file */

    for ( i=0; i<3; ++i)
    {                                                   /*3*/
         fgets(buffer, 81, fp);                         /*4*/
         printf("\n%s", buffer);                        /*5*/
    }                                                   /*6*/

/* Close the file */

    fclose(fp);
}
```

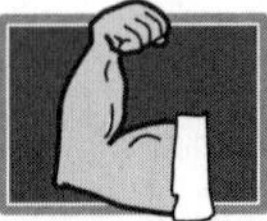

RESULT:

```
C:\>FILE5

To be

or not

to be
```

ANALYSIS:

1. Line /*1*/ supplies a buffer to accept a character string read from the file. The size of the buffer (81 bytes) is much larger than what is

needed for this file, but it can accept strings long enough to fill the screen width (80 characters).

2. On line /*2*/, you change the mode string in fopen() from write ("w") to read ("r").
3. The call to fgets() on line /*4*/ will accept up to 80 characters of data and place them into *buffer*, then attach a terminating null character.
4. The printf() on line /*5*/ displays the string read into *buffer*. Notice that the output is double spaced; the printf() format string contains one newline character ('\n') and fgets() reads another from the file at the end of each line.

When you read from a file, then call a read function again (as in the FILE5 program), the second read will start at a position in the file where the last read ended. Thus, repeated file reads will march through the file in a simple, beginning-to-end sequence. One of the jobs of the file pointer is to keep track of the current position in the file while reading and writing takes place.

A file dump utility

You can generalize the FILE5 program and make it a useful utility function to *dump* text files. The term *dump* means to spill out the contents of a file so that you can see everything that is in there, including nondisplayable control characters. A dump utility can be a very handy tool when you have problems with files. The output from a dump usually displays the data both in hexadecimal and character form.

Listing 12.6 DUMP.C Dump data from a file

DO:
- Modify FILE5 to dump data from any file
- Compile and run DUMP
- Enter **HAMLET.LIN**

```
#include <stdio.h>
int main()
{
    FILE *fp;
    char filename[13];                                          /*1*/
    char buffer[81];
    int  ndx;                                                   /*2*/
    int  i;

/* Prompt for a file name */

    printf("Enter a file name: ");                              /*3*/
    gets(filename);                                             /*4*/
```

```
/* Open the file */

    if ((fp = fopen(filename, "rb")) == NULL)                          /*5*/
    {
         printf("\nCould not open file %s", filename);
         exit(1);
    }

/* Dump data from the file */

    while (fgets(buffer, 81, fp) != NULL)                              /*6*/
{                                                                      /*7*/
           ndx = 0;                                                    /*8*/
           while (ndx < strlen(buffer))                                /*9*/
           {                                                           /*10*/
                  printf("\n");                                        /*11*/
                  for (i=0; i<8; ++i)                                  /*12*/
                      printf("%2X ", buffer[ndx+i]);                   /*13*/
                  printf(" | ");                                       /*14*/
                  for (i=0; i<8; ++i)                                  /*15*/
                      printf("%c ", buffer[ndx+i]);                    /*16*/
                  ndx += 8;                                            /*17*/
           }                                                           /*18*/
           for (i=0; i<81; ++i)                                        /*19*/
               buffer[i] = 0;                                          /*20*/
    }                                                                  /*21*/

/* Close the file */

    fclose(fp);
}
```

RESULT:

```
C:\>DUMP
Enter a file name: HAMLET.LIN

54 6F 20 62 65  D  A  0  | T o  b e

6F 72 20 6E 6F 74  D  A  | o r  n o t

74 6F 20 62 65  D  A  0  | t o  b e

1A  0  0  0  0  0  0  0  |
```

ANALYSIS:

1. To the left of the separation lines in the output, you can see the hexadecimal ASCII code values for each byte in the file; to the right, the program displays each byte in character format.
2. Lines /*3–4*/ allow you to enter a file name of up to 12 characters.
3. You should modify the fopen() mode string on line /*5*/ to open the file in *binary* mode so that control characters will not be stripped or translated (see the explanation below under the heading "Binary versus text mode"). If you use "r" instead of "rb," then gets() will discard (strip) all carriage return ('\r') and end-of-file characters before storing data in the buffer.
4. The first statement of the *while* loop on line /*6*/ reads strings of data of up to 80 characters long from the file until it reaches the end-of-file.
5. For each string that fgets() reads, the inner *while* loop on lines /*9–18*/ formats and displays the data. Lines /*12–13*/ display 8 bytes in hexadecimal format, and lines /*15–16*/ display the same 8 bytes in character format just to the right of the first display.
6. Line /*11*/ starts a new line on the screen for each 8 bytes of display, and line /*14*/ puts a vertical line between the hexadecimal and character displays.
7. Lines /*19–20*/ clear the input buffer so that there is no leftover data from one read operation to the next. The program displays 8 values per line even if the file data ends in the middle of a line, so clearing the buffer ensures that nonexistent data will display as zeros.

The dump program shows the nondisplayable as well as the displayable characters from a file; nondisplayable characters show up in the hexadecimal output. Notice that each time a newline character appears in the hexadecimal output (hex value A), the character format conversion causes the display to start on the next line. The end-of-file character CTRL-Z is visible as the last character of the dump (hex value 1A). You can use this dump utility on any text file; the program reads lines longer than 80 bytes with more than one call to fgets().

Binary versus text mode

You can open files in either of two modes, binary or text; text is the default, and if you need the binary mode, you must explicitly specify it in the mode string of the open statement. Don't be misled into thinking that only character data can be stored in files opened in text mode and that only internal binary data can be stored in files opened in binary mode; either kind of data can be stored in either kind of file. Binary mode allows you to read and write all of the 256 values possible for a byte of data without any side effects. Binary mode also makes it possible for you to write unformatted data to a file, as you will see towards the end of this chapter. The binary mode and unformatted file I/O are often used together because all possible data values can be transferred without a problem. Text mode reading and writing changes a few of the control characters. Under UNIX, there is no difference between binary and text mode—all files are read and written as in binary mode, without changing any data. Under DOS, however, some data translation occurs in text mode, as shown in Figure 12-4.

A DOS text mode write operation changes a single newline character (\n) to a carriage return-newline pair (\r\n). You can see that this translation occurs as the FILE3 program writes lines to HAMLET.LIN because the data strings within the program end with just a newline, yet the dump output of Program 12.6 shows a carriage return (hex D) and a newline (hex A) at the end of each line. A DOS text mode read operation

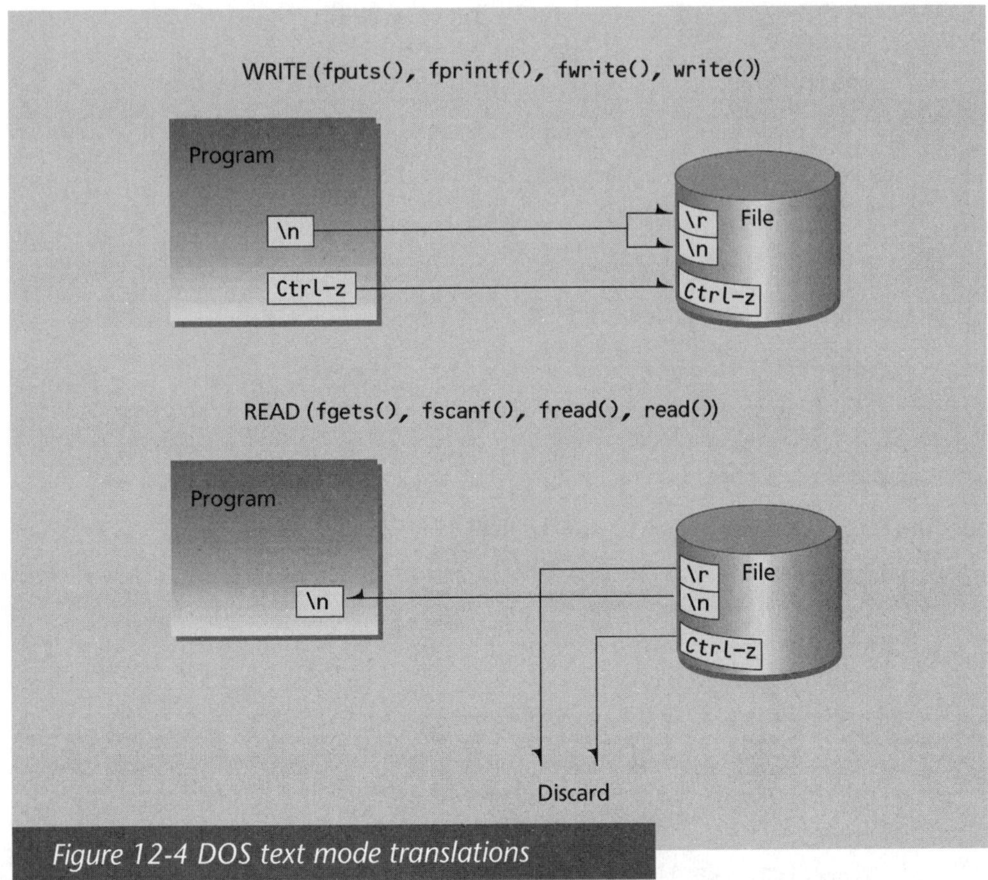

Figure 12-4 DOS text mode translations

makes the opposite translation; it strips the carriage return from any \r\n pair and stores only the newline in memory. In addition, this read strips and ignores the end-of-file character if it is present. If you remove the binary modifier from the mode string for fopen() in the dump program, you will see the effect of read translations.

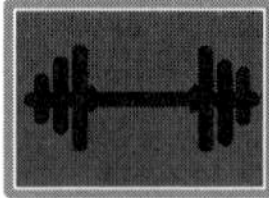

Listing 12.7 DUMP2.C Dump data from a file

DO:
- Modify DUMP to read data in text mode
- Compile and run DUMP2
- Enter HAMLET.LIN

```
#include <stdio.h>
int main()
{
    FILE *fp;                       /* File pointer      */
    char filename[13];              /* File name         */
    char buffer[81];                /* Input buffer      */
    int  ndx;                       /* Buffer index      */
    int  i;                         /* Character counter */

/* Prompt for a file name */

    printf("Enter a file name: ");
    gets(filename);

/* Open the file */

    if ((fp = fopen(filename, "r")) == NULL)                        /*1*/
    {
        printf("\nCould not open file %s", filename);
      exit(1);
    }

/* Dump data from the file */

    while (fgets(buffer, 81, fp) != NULL)
    {
        ndx = 0;
        while (ndx < strlen(buffer))
        {
            printf("\n");
            for (i=0; i<8; ++i)
            printf("%2X ", buffer[ndx+i]);
            printf(" | ");
            for (i=0; i<8; ++i)
            printf("%c ", buffer[ndx+i]);
                        ndx += 8;
        }
        for (i=0; i<81; ++i)
```

```
            buffer[i] = 0;
    }

/* Close the file */

    fclose(fp);
}
```

RESULT:

```
C:\>DUMP2
Enter a file name: HAMLET.LIN

54 6F 20 62 65  A  0  0  | T o  b e

6F 72 20 6E 6F 74  A  0  | o r  n o t

74 6F 20 62 65  A  0  0  | t o  b e
```

ANALYSIS:

1. The fopen() statement on line /*1*/ now defaults to text mode and translations will occur when fgets() reads data.
2. The dump display no longer shows the carriage return (hex D) and end-of-file (hex 1A) characters, because the text-mode translation removes them from the data stream that fgets() reads into *buffer*.

Formatted versus unformatted file I/O

In Chapter 3, you learned about the difference between *internal* and *external* representations of data; usually, internal data values are converted to a stream of ASCII character codes before they are displayed or printed. The same thing happens with formatted disk output; no matter what the original data type (character, integer, floating-point), formatted output converts it to character data (ASCII codes) on the disk. Figure 12-5 shows some internal data with formatted representations.

On the other hand, *unformatted* output takes data just as it is in memory; unformatted values are written unaltered from memory to disk, so that the bytes remain in their original form. Let's first examine formatted file I/O.

Formatted file I/O with fprintf() and fscanf()

Throughout the book, you have been using printf() to format data in many different ways for screen display. You have the same capability for producing formatted file

Data	Internal Representation	Format Specifier	Formatted
int x = 10;	00000000 00001010	"%d"	\`1' \`0'
char y = \`A'';	01000001	"%c"	\`A'
float z = -1.23;	10100100 01110000 10011101 10111111	"%5.2f"	\`-' \`1' \`.' \`2' \`3'

Figure 12-5 Formatted data

output with function fprintf(), which has one additional argument, a file pointer. You call fprintf() as follows:

```
fprintf(fp, format, list);
```

The first argument is the file pointer, the second is a format string, and the third is a list of values for output. With fprintf(), you can format and write any combination of different types of data values to a file. To demonstrate this, suppose you must build a file containing names of employees and a number representing the company where each employee works. You could write the file so that each line contains a name and the corresponding company number with the following program.

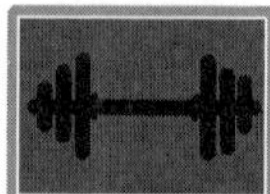

Listing 12.8 EMPLOY.C Make an employee file

DO: Enter and compile EMPLOY

```
#include <stdio.h>
#include <string.h>
#define TRUE 1
int main()
{
     FILE *fp_emp;
     char employee_name[40];
     int  company_number = 0;

/* Open the file */

     if ((fp_emp = fopen("EMPLOYEE.DAT", "w")) == NULL)
     {
            printf("\nCould not open employee file");
            exit(1);
     }

/* Enter employee lines */
```

```
    while (TRUE)
    {
         printf("Enter an employee name: ");
         gets(employee_name);
         if (strlen(employee_name) == 0)
             break;
         ++company_number;
         fprintf(fp_emp, "%d %s\n",
             company_number, employee_name);
    }

/* Close the file */

    fclose(fp_emp);
}
```

ANALYSIS:

1. The program begins by defining a file pointer, *fp_emp*, and storage for the data to be written to the file, string *employee_name* and integer *company_number*.
2. The program then proceeds to open the file named EMPLOYEE.DAT in write mode and checks to make sure that the opening was completed successfully.
3. The *while* loop under the comment /* Enter employee lines */ takes data from the keyboard and writes them to the file. The *while* loop continues as long as you enter name strings into the array *employee_name*. When you press ENTER without entering a name, the gets() statement returns a null string (with length zero), and the next *if* statement breaks out of the *while* loop.
4. The next-to-the-last statement in the *while* loop formats the employee name and company number and writes them to a line in the file. The first argument, *fp_emp*, identifies the file where fprintf() writes the line.

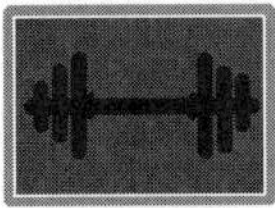

DO: Run EMPLOY and enter the data shown

RESULT:

```
C:\>EMPLOY

Enter an employee name: Paula Programmer (ENTER)
Enter an employee name: Bea Nimble (ENTER)
Enter an employee name: Tom Traveler (ENTER)
Enter an employee name: (ENTER)
```

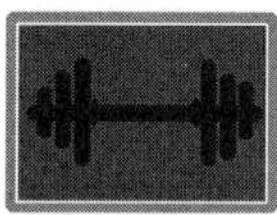

DO: Examine the employee file

RESULT:

```
C:\>type EMPLOYEE.DAT
1 Paula Programmer
2 Bea Nimble
3 Tom Traveler
```

Multiple file pointers

Programs can deal with more than one file at a time. The C language imposes no limit on the number of active files that you can use, but the operating system may. Under DOS, for example, you can set the maximum number of open files allowed with the FILES= command in the CONFIG.SYS file. A limit exists because each open file consumes some memory for data buffering, associating the file name with its disk location, and other overhead items.

With a second file, you can expand the employee information to include company names, and by making the company numbers in the first file correspond to line numbers in the second file, you will have a cross-reference between the two files. This will amount to a small *data base* where you can look up an employee and find his or her employer using the company number as a line *index*. Figure 12-6 shows how this two-file data base works.

You might use this data base to retrieve information in response to requests such as, "Get me the name of Traveler's employer." You would first look up the employee (Traveler) in the employee file, then extract Traveler's company number from the same line, and finally use the company number to access the employer's name in the company file. You can modify the previous program to write the second, company file in addition to the employee file.

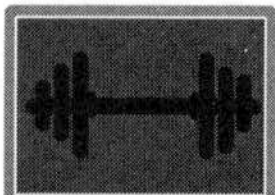

Listing 12.9 EMPLOY2.C Make an employee file

DO:
- Add a company file to EMPLOY
- Compile EMPLOY2

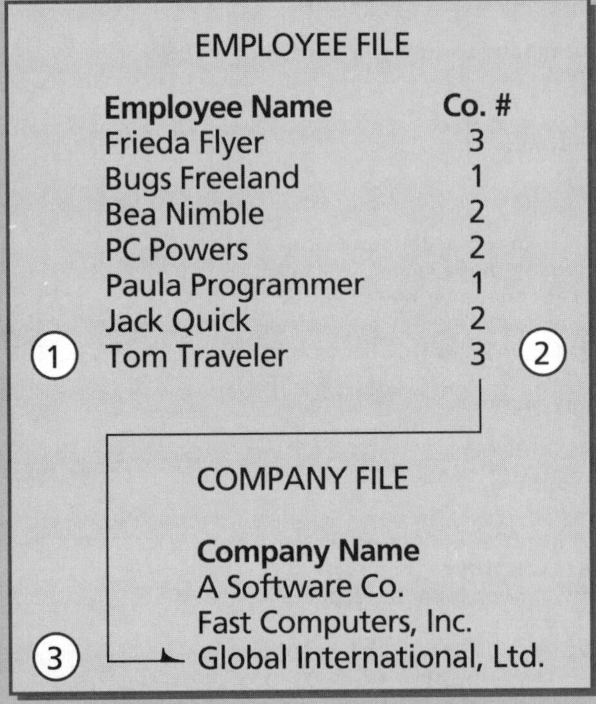

Figure 12-6 The operation of a small data base

```
#include <stdio.h>
#include <string.h>
#define TRUE 1
int main()
{
    FILE *fp_co;                                          /*1*/
    FILE *fp_emp;
```

```
    char company_name[40];                                      /*2*/
    char employee_name[40];
    int  company_number = 0;

/* Open the files */

    if ((fp_co  = fopen("COMPANY.DAT", "w")) == NULL)           /*3*/
    {                                                           /*4*/
        printf("\nCould not open company file");                /*5*/
        exit(1);                                                /*6*/
    }                                                           /*7*/

    if ((fp_emp = fopen("EMPLOYEE.DAT", "w")) == NULL)
    {
        printf("\nCould not open employee file");
        exit(1);
    }

/* Enter company lines */

    while (TRUE)                                                /*8*/
    {                                                           /*9*/
        printf("\nEnter a company name: ");                     /*10*/
        gets(company_name);                                     /*11*/
        if (strlen(company_name) == 0)                          /*12*/
                break;                                          /*13*/
        fprintf(fp_co, "%s\n", company_name);                   /*14*/
        printf("\n");                                           /*15*/
        ++company_number;

/* Enter employee lines */

        while (TRUE)
        {
              printf("Enter an employee name: ");
              gets(employee_name);
              if (strlen(employee_name) == 0)
                  break;
              fprintf(fp_emp, "%d %s\n",
                  company_number, employee_name);
      }
   }                                                            /*16*/

/* Close the files */

   fclose(fp_emp);
   fclose(fp_co);                                               /*17*/
}
```

ANALYSIS:

1. With lines /*1–7*/ this program declares a new file pointer and opens

the second, company file in the same manner as it opens the employee file.

2. Line /*8*/ starts another *while* loop for entering company names, and lines /*9–14*/ accept the names from the keyboard and write them to the new file. The program now has two loops: For each company name written in the outer *while* loop, the inner *while* loop writes a group of employee names to the employee file.
3. The *if* test on line /*12*/ ends the outer *while* loop when you press ENTER without a company name.

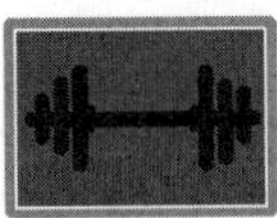

DO: Run EMPLOY2 and enter the data shown

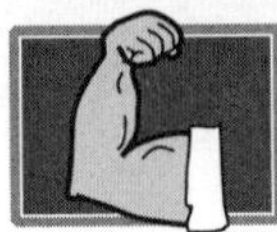

RESULT:

```
C:\>EMPLOY2

Enter a company name: A Software Co. ENTER

Enter an employee name: Paula Programmer ENTER
Enter an employee name: Bugs Freeland ENTER
Enter an employee name: ENTER

Enter a company name: Fast Computers, Inc. ENTER

Enter an employee name: Bea Nimble ENTER
Enter an employee name: Jack Quick ENTER
Enter an employee name: PC Powers ENTER
Enter an employee name: ENTER

Enter a company name: Global International, Ltd. ENTER

Enter an employee name: Tom Traveler ENTER
Enter an employee name: Frieda Flyer ENTER
Enter an employee name: ENTER

Enter a company name: ENTER
```

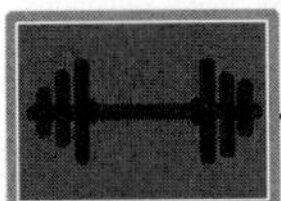

DO: Examine the company file

RESULT:

```
C:\>type COMPANY.DAT
A Software Co.
Fast Computers, Inc.
Global International, Ltd.
```

DO: Examine the employee file

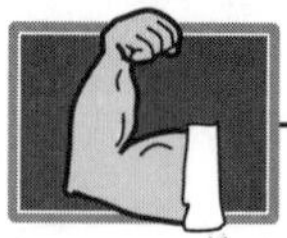

RESULT:

```
C:\>type EMPLOYEE.DAT
1 Paula Programmer
1 Bugs Freeland
2 Bea Nimble
2 Jack Quick
2 PC Powers
3 Tom Traveler
3 Frieda Flyer
```

ANALYSIS:

In the employee file, you can see the name of each employee preceded by the employer number.

Now that you have the data base of employee and company names, you need a program to read the files. You can read the company file with fgets(), but the employee file contains mixed data types that will require the formatting capability of *fscanf()*. This file reading function works just like the familiar keyboard input function scanf(), but it has an additional file pointer argument. You call fscanf() as follows:

```
fscanf(fp, format, list);
```

where *fp* is a pointer to a file opened for reading, *format* is a format string, and *list* is a list of pointers to storage locations. The function fscanf() returns the number of values read from the file, or constant *EOF* if the end of file is reached or an error occurs.

The next program prompts you for a last name, then finds the full name in the employee file and uses the index located there to look up the employer in the company file.

Listing 12.10 EMPLOY3.C Read an employee file

DO:
- Enter EMPLOY3 (you can copy large sections of EMPLOY2)
- Compile EMPLOY3

```
#include <stdio.h>
#include <string.h>
int main()
{
    FILE *fp_co;
    FILE *fp_emp;
    char company_name[40];
    char employee_name[40];
    char first_name[40];
    char last_name[40];
    int  company_number = 0;
    int  i;

/* Open the files */

    if ((fp_co  = fopen("COMPANY.DAT", "r")) == NULL)
    {
         printf("\nCould not open company file");
         exit(1);
    }

    if ((fp_emp = fopen("EMPLOYEE.DAT", "r")) == NULL)
    {
         printf("\nCould not open employee file");
         exit(1);
    }

/* Enter a name */

    printf("\nEnter an employee's last name: ");
    gets(employee_name);

/* Find the name in the employee file */

    while (fscanf(fp_emp, "%d %s %s",
           &company_number, first_name, last_name) > 0)
    {
           if (strcmp(employee_name, last_name) == 0)
           {
                for (i=0; i<company_number; ++i)
                     fgets(company_name, 40, fp_co);
                printf("\nEmployee name: %s %s",
                     first_name, last_name);
                printf("\n Company name: %s", company_name);
                break;       /* while */
           }
    }
```

```
/* Close the files */

     fclose(fp_emp);
     fclose(fp_co);
}
```

ANALYSIS:

1. If you copy lines to open the files from a previous program, be sure to set the mode strings in fopen() to "r."

2. Under the comment, /* Enter a name */, the program prompts you to enter an employee's last name. You must use the exact spelling in the file, observing the same use of uppercase and lowercase letters, or the name will not match. Without too much trouble, you could modify the program to match up the names regardless of case (Hint: use the library function toupper()).

3. The heart of this program is located within the *while* loop under the comment /* Find the name in the employee file */. The expression in the *while* parentheses calls fscanf() to read a line and end the loop if the result is 0 or less, indicating the end of the file. Notice that the format string and list of variables for fscanf() are not quite the same as those for the fprintf() statement in the program, EMPLOY2, that wrote the file. A formatted string conversion ("%s") ends at a white space character, so two strings are required to read the employee's first and last names from the file. This limits the name to two and only two strings—you cannot use only one name, nor can you include a middle name or initial. This is restrictive, and you might be better off reading the entire line with fgets(), which will read through white space characters, and then parsing the company number and employee name separately.

4. After reading each line, the program uses the function strcmp() to compare the *employee_name* string with the *last_name* string.

5. When the program reads a line that contains the *last_name*, it executes the *for* loop to find the employer in the company file. The *company_number* read from the employee file is the line number of the desired company name; therefore, the *for* loop reads this number of lines to obtain the correct company name.

6. Finally, the program displays the employee and company name, then ends the *while* loop with a *break* statement.

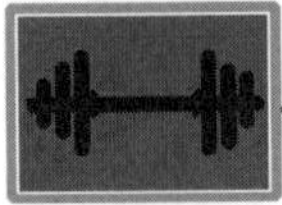

DO: Run EMPLOY3 and enter Traveler

RESULT:

```
C:\>EMPLOY3
Enter an employee's last name: Traveler
Employee name: Tom Traveler
 Company name: Global International, Ltd.
```

ANALYSIS:

1. The program used the employee's name to indirectly access the employer name in the other file. The company name is associated with the employee name via the index number in the employee line.
2. Even if the employee lines were in a different order (perhaps, because of an alphabetic sort), the index numbers would allow you to correctly reference the company name.

DO: Run EMPLOY3 and enter **Jones**

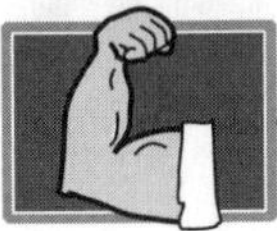

RESULT:

```
C:\>EMPLOY3
Enter an employee's last name: Jones
```

ANALYSIS:

Jones was not in the employee file, so the program did not display anything.

Checking for the end of a file—function feof()

You can improve the program's output by reporting when a name could not be found. This would be easy if, at the end of the program, you could test whether or not the entire employee file had been read (because file reading stops when the name is found). Fortunately, there is a standard library function, feof(), that will tell you whether or not the end of the file has been reached. You call function feof() with the file pointer as the only argument, and it returns a nonzero value (or true) if you are at the end of the file, or zero if you are not. By adding one statement to EMPLOY3, you can indicate when the program did not find a name.

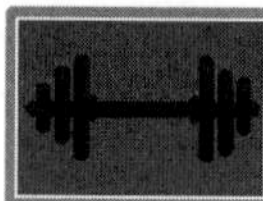

Listing 12.11 EMPLOY4.C Read an employee file

DO:
- Add an end-of-file test to EMPLOY3
- Compile and run EMPLOY4
- Enter **Jones**

```
#include <stdio.h>
#include <string.h>
int main()
{
     FILE *fp_co;
     FILE *fp_emp;
     char company_name[40];
     char employee_name[40];
     char first_name[40];
     char last_name[40];
     int  company_number = 0;
     int  i;

/* Open the files */

     if ((fp_co  = fopen("COMPANY.DAT", "r")) == NULL)
     {
          printf("\nCould not open company file");
          exit(1);
     }

     if ((fp_emp = fopen("EMPLOYEE.DAT", "r")) == NULL)
     {
          printf("\nCould not open employee file");
          exit(1);
     }

/* Enter a name */

     printf("\nEnter an employee's last name: ");
     gets(employee_name);

/* Find the name in the employee file */

     while (fscanf(fp_emp, "%d %s %s",
            &company_number, first_name, last_name) > 0)
```

```
    {
            if (strcmp(employee_name, last_name) == 0)
            {
               for (i=0; i<company_number; ++i)
                    fgets(company_name, 40, fp_co);
               printf("\nEmployee name: %s %s",
                    first_name, last_name);
               printf("\n Company name: %s", company_name);
               break; /* while */
            }
    }

    if (feof(fp_emp))                                                   /*1*/
       printf("\nEmployee %s was not found",                            /*2*/
               employee_name);                                          /*3*/

/* Close the files */

    fclose(fp_emp);
    fclose(fp_co);
}
```

RESULT:

```
C:\>EMPLOY4

Enter an employee's last name: Jones
Employee Jones was not found
```

ANALYSIS:

On line /*1*/, the call to feof() checks to see if the employee file is at the end; if so, the function printf() displays a message to inform you that the program could not find the requested name.

Direct access with fseek()

So far, you have retrieved data by reading lines in the order that they appear in from the beginning of the file; this is called *sequential access*. Given the line number where a particular company name resides, the EMPLOY4 program has to read all the lines from the beginning of COMPANY.DAT down to the desired line to retrieve the information. There is a better, faster, way to get to any desired line, called *direct access*, which makes use of the function fseek(). The prototype for this function is in stdio.h:

```
int fseek(FILE *fp, long offset, int origin);
```

This function sets the current position of the file identified by *fp* to *offset* the number of bytes from the position given by *origin*. The value of the argument *origin* can be one of three constants defined in stdio.h:

```
SEEK_SET is an origin at the beginning of the file.
SEEK_CUR is an origin at the current file location.
SEEK_END is an origin at the end of the file.
```

For example, fseek(fp, 100, SEEK_SET); sets the file position 100 bytes from the beginning, and fseek(fp, -5, SEEK_CUR); sets it 5 bytes back (towards the beginning) from the current position. The function fseek() returns zero if successful and nonzero if an error occurs.

To use fseek() to directly access company lines, you must first make all the lines in COMPANY.DAT a fixed length. You can do this by padding the data strings out to the maximum length with space characters before writing them to the file.

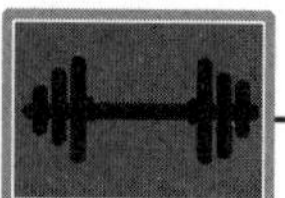

Listing12.12 EMPLOY5.C Make an employee file

DO:
- Alter EMPLOY2 to make the company lines fixed length
- Compile and run EMPLOY5
- Enter the same company and employee data as before

```
#include <stdio.h>
#include <string.h>
#define TRUE 1
int main()
{
    FILE *fp_co;
    FILE *fp_emp;
    char company_name[40];
    char employee_name[40];
    int  company_number = 0;
    int  i;                                                  /*1*/

/* Open the files */

    if ((fp_co  = fopen("COMPANY.DAT", "w")) == NULL)
    {
          printf("\nCould not open company file");
          exit(1);
    }

    if ((fp_emp = fopen("EMPLOYEE.DAT", "w")) == NULL)
    {
          printf("\nCould not open employee file");
          exit(1);
    }

/* Enter company lines */
```

```
    while (TRUE)
    {
          printf("\nEnter a company name: ");
          gets(company_name);
          if (strlen(company_name) == 0)
              break;
          for (i=strlen(company_name); i<39; ++i)          /*2*/
              strcat(company_name, " ");                   /*3*/
          fprintf(fp_co, "%s\n", company_name);
          printf("\n");
          ++company_number;

/* Enter employee lines */

          while (TRUE)
          {
              printf("Enter an employee name: ");
              gets(employee_name);
              if (strlen(employee_name) == 0)
                  break;
              fprintf(fp_emp, "%d %s\n",
                  company_number, employee_name);
          }
    }

/* Close the files */

    fclose(fp_emp);
    fclose(fp_co);
}
```

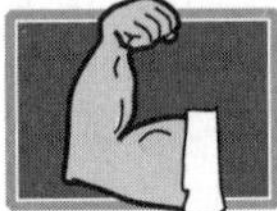

RESULT:

```
C:\>EMPLOY5

Enter a company name: A Software Co. (ENTER)

Enter an employee name: Paula Programmer (ENTER)
Enter an employee name: Bugs Freeland (ENTER)
Enter an employee name: (ENTER)

Enter a company name: Fast Computers, Inc. (ENTER)

Enter an employee name: Bea Nimble (ENTER)
Enter an employee name: Jack Quick (ENTER)
Enter an employee name: PC Powers (ENTER)
Enter an employee name: (ENTER)

Enter a company name: Global International, Ltd. (ENTER)
```

```
Enter an employee name: Tom Traveler (ENTER)
Enter an employee name: Frieda Flyer (ENTER)
Enter an employee name: (ENTER)

Enter a company name: (ENTER)
```

ANALYSIS:

1. The for *loop* on line /*2*/ starts at the first character past the end of the string in *company_name* and ends at the next-to-the-last element in the array. Each cycle of the loop calls strcat() to concatenate a space at the end of the *company_name* string, so that the array will have 39 characters and a terminating null.
2. The resultant file has fixed-length lines of 39 bytes, plus a carriage return ('\r') and a newline ('\n') character.

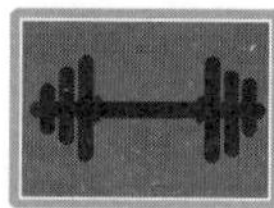

DO: Examine the size of COMPANY.DAT

```
C:\>dir COMPANY.DAT

 Volume in drive C has no label
 Directory of  C:\

COMPANY  DAT     123   9-09-91   7:48a
      1 File(s)   7393280 bytes free
```

ANALYSIS:

There are three 41-byte lines in the file—a total of 123 bytes.

Now you can modify the EMPLOY4 program to get at the company data more quickly using direct access. The speed improvement is not really important in this small example, but for large files, direct access makes an enormous difference in the total processing time. The program reads a selected line from the employee file and extracts a line number for the related company name in the company file. Then, instead of reading multiple lines from the beginning of the file, as in the EMPLOY4 program, it uses fseek() to directly read the one, desired company line.

Listing12.13 EMPLOY6.C Read an employee file

DO: • Change EMPLOY4 to use direct access read for the company file
• Compile and run EMPLOY6
• Enter **Traveler**

```
#include <stdio.h>
#include <string.h>
int main()
{
    FILE *fp_co;
    FILE *fp_emp;
    char company_name[40];
    char employee_name[40];
    char first_name[40];
    char last_name[40];
    int  company_number = 0;
    int  i;

/* Open the files */

    if ((fp_co  = fopen("COMPANY.DAT", "r")) == NULL)
    {
         printf("\nCould not open company file");
         exit(1);
    }

    if ((fp_emp = fopen("EMPLOYEE.DAT", "r")) == NULL)
    {
         printf("\nCould not open employee file");
         exit(1);
    }

/* Enter a name */

    printf("\nEnter an employee's last name: ");
    gets(employee_name);

/* Find the name in the employee file */

    while (fscanf(fp_emp, "%d %s %s",
           &company_number, first_name, last_name) > 0)
    {
           if (strcmp(employee_name, last_name) == 0)
           {
              fseek(fp_co, (long)(41*(company_number-1)),      /*1*/
                    SEEK_SET);
              fgets(company_name, 40, fp_co);
              printf("\nEmployee name: %s %s",
                    first_name, last_name);
```

```
                printf("\n Company name: %s", company_name);
                break; /* while */
            }
    }

    if (feof(fp_emp))
        printf("\nEmployee %s was not found", employee_name);

/* Close the files */

    fclose(fp_emp);
    fclose(fp_co);
}
```

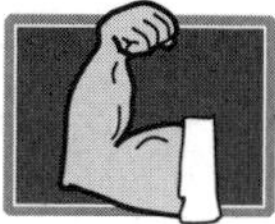

RESULT:

```
C:\>EMPLOY6

Enter an employee's last name: Traveler

Employee name: Tom Traveler
 Company name: Global International, Ltd.
```

ANALYSIS:

1. The fseek() statement on line /*1*/ sets the current file location to the beginning of the desired line. The byte number of the line, from the beginning of the file, is the length of each line (41) times the desired line number. The fseek() statement calculates the line position with the expression:

   ```
   (long)(41 * (company_number-1))
   ```

   Notice that the expression casts the result to type *long* for consistency with the data type of the second parameter of function fseek().

2. After fseek() sets the file position, the program reads the data with a call to fgets() on the next line.

Now it should be obvious why fixed-length lines are necessary: You need to have a constant line length to calculate the byte position of a line from the line number.

You can compare the access times of sequential and direct-access reading by inserting a loop in the EMPLOY4 and EMPLOY6 programs to read the lines 10,000 times. This extends the program run time so that you can easily measure it. First, modify EMPLOY4 to benchmark sequential reading.

Listing12.14 EMPLOY7.C Read an employee file

DO:
- Add a loop to repeat sequential reading in EMPLOY4
- Compile and run EMPLOY7
- Enter **Traveler**
- Measure the run time after entering the name

```
#include <stdio.h>
#include <string.h>
int main()
{
    FILE *fp_co;
    FILE *fp_emp;
    char company_name[40];
    char employee_name[40];
    char first_name[40];
    char last_name[40];
    int  company_number = 0;
    int  i;
    int  count;                                                   /*1*/

/* Open the files */

    if ((fp_co  = fopen("COMPANY.DAT", "r")) == NULL)
    {
        printf("\nCould not open company file");
        exit(1);
    }

    if ((fp_emp = fopen("EMPLOYEE.DAT", "r")) == NULL)
    {
        printf("\nCould not open employee file");
        exit(1);
    }

/* Enter a name */

    printf("\nEnter an employee's last name: ");
    gets(employee_name);

/* Find the name in the employee file */

    while (fscanf(fp_emp, "%d %s %s",
            &company_number, first_name, last_name) > 0)
    {
            if (strcmp(employee_name, last_name) == 0)
            {
               for (count=0; count<10000; ++count)                /*2*/
               {                                                  /*3*/
                    for (i=0; i<company_number; ++i)
                          fgets(company_name, 40, fp_co);
```

```
            fseek(fp_co, 0L, SEEK_SET);                          /*4*/
        }                                                        /*5*/
        printf("\nEmployee name: %s %s",
            first_name, last_name);
        printf("\n Company name: %s", company_name);
        break; /* while */
      }
  }

  if (feof(fp_emp))
      printf("\nEmployee %s was not found", employee_name);

/* Close the files */

  fclose(fp_emp);
  fclose(fp_co);
}
```

RESULT:

```
C:\>EMPLOY7

Enter an employee's last name: Traveler

Employee name: Tom Traveler
 Company name: Global International, Ltd.
```

ANALYSIS:

1. Lines /*1–5*/ make the sequential access repeat 10,000 times.
2. The fseek() on line /*4*/ sets the file position to the beginning of the file before each sequential read; this introduces a distortion into the timing, but it is necessary, and the distortion is a small part of the total time.
3. On a 20MHz 386 PC, the run time was 15 seconds.

Now modify EMPLOY6 to perform direct access reading 10,000 times.

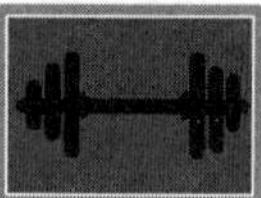

Listing 12.15 EMPLOY8.C Read an employee file

DO: • Add a loop to repeat direct access reading in EMPLOY6

- Compile and run EMPLOY8
- Enter **Traveler**
- Measure the run time after entering the name

```
#include <stdio.h>
#include <string.h>
int main()
{
    FILE *fp_co;
    FILE *fp_emp;
    char company_name[40];
    char employee_name[40];
    char first_name[40];
    char last_name[40];
    int  company_number = 0;
    int  i;
    int  count;                                            /*1*/

/* Open the files */

    if ((fp_co  = fopen("COMPANY.DAT", "r")) == NULL)
    {
         printf("\nCould not open company file");
         exit(1);
    }

    if ((fp_emp = fopen("EMPLOYEE.DAT", "r")) == NULL)
    {
         printf("\nCould not open employee file");
         exit(1);
    }

/* Enter a name */

    printf("\nEnter an employee's last name: ");
    gets(employee_name);

/* Find the name in the employee file */

    while (fscanf(fp_emp, "%d %s %s",
           &company_number, first_name, last_name) > 0)
    {
           if (strcmp(employee_name, last_name) == 0)
           {
           for (count=0; count<10000; ++count)             /*2*/
           {                                               /*3*/
              fseek(fp_co, (long)(41*(company_number-1)),
                    SEEK_SET);
              fgets(company_name, 40, fp_co);
           }                                               /*4*/
           printf("\nEmployee name: %s %s",
              first_name, last_name);
```

```
            printf("\n Company name: %s", company_name);
            break;    /* while */
            }
    }

    if (feof(fp_emp))
        printf("\nEmployee %s was not found", employee_name);

/* Close the files */

    fclose(fp_emp);
    fclose(fp_co);
}
```

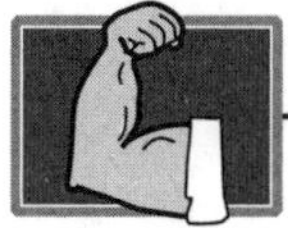

RESULT:

```
C:\>EMPLOY8

Enter an employee's last name: Traveler

Employee name: Tom Traveler
 Company name: Global International, Ltd.
```

ANALYSIS:

The total time is now about 10 seconds, two-thirds of the time required for sequential reading.

The time comparison was made with only three lines in the file; the disparity between sequential and direct file access grows as the number of lines increases. We repeated the test with twelve lines in the company file, retrieving the twelfth line, and found that the sequential access time doubled to 30 seconds, whereas the direct access time remained virtually unchanged at 10 seconds. Imagine the difference for files with thousands of lines!

Unformatted file I/O with fwrite() and fread()

The Level II functions for writing and reading unformatted data are fwrite() and fread(); you call both of these functions with identical arguments:

```
fwrite(ptr, size, num_items, fp);
fread(ptr, size, num_items, fp);
```

The first argument, *ptr,* is the address of a memory location where fwrite() takes data or fread() places data, *size* is an *unsigned int* giving the number of bytes in each item, *num_items* is an *unsigned int* specifying the number of items to transfer, and the fourth argument, *fp*, is a file pointer. The number of bytes transferred is *size * num_items*. Both functions return the number of items actually written or read; thus, if fwrite() or fread() returns less than *num_items*, an error occurred.

With unformatted output, data go to the file unaltered, so that internal memory representations of values are stored on disk. Unformatted data in a file have the same binary representation as do data in internal computer memory; no conversion is necessary to transfer unformatted data between memory and disk files, as indicated in Figure 12-7.

Unformatted file data can produce significant space savings over formatted files, especially with floating-point numbers. Also, you don't need to truncate or round off floating-point values—you can store the numbers on disk with the full accuracy of the internal memory representation. For example, land surveyors often measure positional information to a precision of 12 places. The earth is approximately 40,000,000 meters in circumference, and surveyors can measure distances to an accuracy of 100th of a meter. Therefore, an X or Y coordinate of a point on the earth is: Sxxxxxxxx.hh, where S is the sign of the coordinate, xxxxxxxx is the distance in meters, and hh is the hundredths of meters following a decimal point. You would need to declare variables of type *double* to have enough precision to store such coordinates; double-precision floating-point variables provide 15 places of precision. You could write this number to a file using a formatted fprintf() statement with the format specifier "%12.2f" and the value would consume 12 bytes of storage. Alternatively, you could store the same number in 8 bytes by writing it with an unformatted fwrite() statement. Because each stored coordinate requires two values (X and Y), you would save 8000 bytes of storage for each 1000

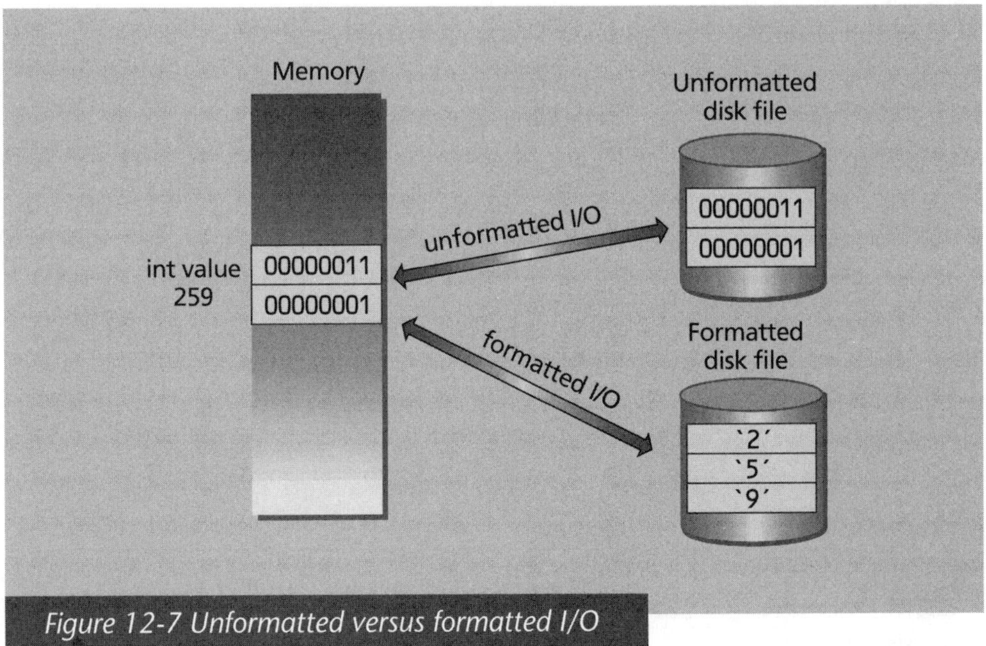

Figure 12-7 Unformatted versus formatted I/O

surveyed points stored using an unformatted fwrite(). You would also realize a speed improvement, because time is not spent formatting the numbers during reading and writing. In the next program, you write and read a few survey coordinates to see how unformatted file I/O works.

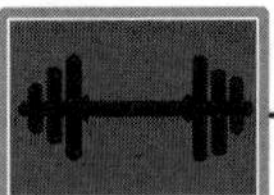

Listing12.16 SURVEY.C Put survey coordinates in a file

DO: Enter, compile, and run SURVEY

```
#include <stdio.h>
void main()
{
     FILE *fp;
     double coordinates[4][2] = { 1000000.00, 200000.00,
                                  1100000.01, 220000.02,
                                  1110000.10, 222000.20,
                                  1111000.11, 222200.22 };
     double read_coord[4][2];
     int i;

/* Open the file for read/write/create */

     fp = fopen("SURVEY.DAT", "w+");

/* Write unformatted coordinates to the file */

     fwrite(coordinates, sizeof(double), 8, fp);

/* Read data back from the beginning of the file */

     fseek(fp, 0L, SEEK_SET);
     fread(read_coord, sizeof(double), 8, fp);

/* Display the data read from the file */

     for (i=0; i<4; ++i)
          printf("\nCoordinate %d  X: %f  Y: %f",
          i+1, read_coord[i][0], read_coord[i][1]);

/* Close the file */

     fclose(fp);
}
```

RESULT:

```
C:\>SURVEY
```

```
Coordinate 1  X:   1000000.00  Y:    200000.00
Coordinate 2  X:   1100000.01  Y:    220000.02
Coordinate 3  X:   1110000.10  Y:    222000.20
Coordinate 4  X:   1111000.11  Y:    222200.22
```

ANALYSIS:

1. The program defines an array of double-precision, floating-point coordinates and initializes all eight values; it also defines a second, similar array, *read_coord*, to hold the values after the program reads the values back from a file.
2. The fopen() statement creates a new file named SURVEY.DAT and opens it for reading and writing.
3. The fwrite() statement writes eight items (the third argument) to the file referred to by *fp*. The statement takes data items from memory starting at the address given by *coordinates*, and the length of each item is sizeof(double), or 8 bytes. In other words, fwrite() transfers 8 values of type *double* from the array *coordinates* to SURVEY.DAT.
4. When fwrite() finishes, the file position is at the end of the last line written, so to read the data back, you must reposition to the beginning of the file with fseek(). The fread() statement then transfers eight values from the file to the array *read_coord*.
5. Lastly, the *for* loop displays the coordinates to show that the data successfully made the round trip into the file and back out again.

You can make the dump program, DUMP, more robust with the unformatted read function, fread(). DUMP uses a string read, fgets(), to read lines from a file, then tests the length of the string to see how many characters were read into the buffer. Because the string length is determined by the first occurrence of a null (0) byte, a null value within a file line will cause DUMP to misinterpret the length of the line. Therefore, function fgets() is inadequate for a general purpose dump utility.

DO: Look at the size of file SURVEY.DAT

RESULT:

```
C:\>dir SURVEY.DAT
```

```
 Volume in drive C has no label
 Directory of  C:\

SURVEY   DAT      65   9-22-91   7:20p
        1 File(s)  4292608 bytes free
```

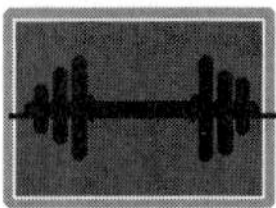

DO: Run program DUMP and enter **SURVEY.DAT**

RESULT:

```
C:\>DUMP
Enter a file name: SURVEY.DAT

41 9A 99 99 19 F0 EF 30  | A Ü Ö Ö Þ p 0
41 9A 99 99 99 81 19  B  | A Ü Ö Ö Ö ü

41 C3 F5 28 1C D8 F3 30  | A Û ¾w  ( Å µ      0
41 29 5C 8F C2 C1 1F  B  | A ) \ Å Ú Ù

41  0  0   0  0  0   0  0 | A
```

ANALYSIS:

1. Look what has happened! SURVEY.DAT is 65 bytes long, but only 33 bytes appear in the dump display—some data is missing because there are null bytes in the file and the program misinterprets the length of one or more fgets() lines.
2. You should ignore the character display portion of the dump (on the right); there is no valid character data in this file.

You can correct this deficiency by replacing fgets() with fread(), which can return the exact number of bytes in each line.

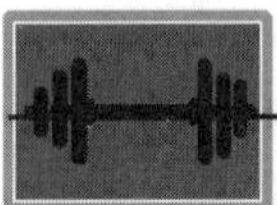

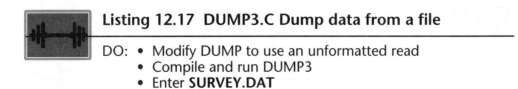

Listing 12.17 DUMP3.C Dump data from a file

DO:
- Modify DUMP to use an unformatted read
- Compile and run DUMP3
- Enter **SURVEY.DAT**

```
#include <stdio.h>
int main()
```

```
{
    FILE *fp;
    char filename[13];
    char buffer[81];
    int ndx;
    int  i;
    int  n;                                                    /*1*/

/* Prompt for a file name */

    printf("Enter a file name: ");
    gets(filename);

/* Open the file */

    if ((fp = fopen(filename, "rb")) == NULL)
    {
        printf("\nCould not open file %s", filename);
        exit(1);
    }

/* Dump data from the file */

    while ((n = fread(buffer, 1, 81, fp)) > 0)                 /*2*/
    {
            ndx = 0;
            while (ndx < n)                                    /*3*/
            {
            printf("\n");
            for (i=0; i<8; ++i)
                printf("%2X ", buffer[ndx+i]);
            printf(" | ");
            for (i=0; i<8; ++i)
                printf("%c ", buffer[ndx+i]);
            ndx += 8;
            }
            for (i=0; i<81; ++i)
                buffer[i] = 0;
    }

/* Close the file */

    fclose(fp);
}
```

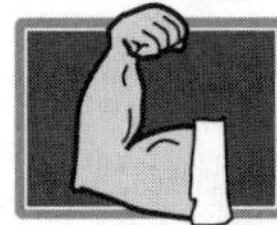

RESULT:

```
C:\>DUMP3
Enter a file name: SURVEY.DAT
```

```
 0   0   0   0  80  84  2E  41  |       Ç ä .   A
 0   0   0   0   0  6A   8  41  |       j A
29  5C  8F   2  E0  C8  30  41  | ) \  Ř Á à 0 A
8F  C2  F5  28   0  DB   D   A  | Ř Ú ¾ ( Ü

41  9A  99  99  19  F0  EF  30  | A Ü Ö Ö p p 0
41  9A  99  99  99  81  19   B  | A Ü Ö Ö Ö Ü

41  C3  F5  28  1C  D8  F3  30  | A Û ¾ ( Ř µ 0
41  29  5C  8F  C2  C1  1F   B  | A ) \  Ř Ú Ù

41   0   0   0   0   0   0   0  | A
```

ANALYSIS:

1. Now all 65 bytes of SURVEY.DAT appear in the dump output.
2. On line /*2*/, you change the file read statement from fgets() to fread().
3. Function fread() returns the number of items read and assigns it to variable *n*. And the *while* loop continues to execute as long as *n* is greater than 0 (as long as the function reads data from the file).
4. The *if* test on line /*3*/ checks the buffer index (*ndx*) against the number of bytes read (*n*)—it used to check against the length of the input string and would erroneously quit when a null (0) byte existed within the string. Now the dump program will accept nulls within the file lines.

Caution—the fread() in DUMP3 poses a potential logic error. You need fread() to return the number of bytes read from the file, and it will if the second argument specifies that each item is 1 byte long and the third argument specifies that 81 items (bytes) be read. If you reversed the values of these arguments (to specify 1 item 81 bytes long), then fread() would return the number of 81-byte lines instead of the number of bytes read.

LEVEL I FILE I/O

Level I file I/O, also known as Low-level I/O, is unformatted and unbuffered. This means that data goes directly from memory through the operating system to the file, without alteration and without stopping in an intermediate buffer, as shown in Figure 12-3. It also means that reading and writing is faster and that files are smaller. Why not always use Level I instead of Level II functions? There are three reasons: (1) Level I functions are not specified by ANSI, so they are not completely portable, (2) there is no formatting, so Level I I/O is less flexible than Level II is, and you sometimes have to do more programming work, and (3) when incorrectly used with too many small transfers, Level I I/O can be less efficient than Level II.

File handles

Instead of using a file pointer, Level I functions use a *file handle* to refer to a file. You will use the handle as an argument for other I/O functions, but you should never be concerned with its value, which is meaningful only to the Level I file functions. A file handle is a variable of data type *int* that you declare in the same way as any other integer; it is assigned a value by the Level I *open()* function.

Level I open() and close()

Before reading or writing a file, you must first obtain a handle to the file by calling the open() function, and you should disconnect the file with a call to close() as soon as you are finished with it. Header file io.h contains prototypes for Level I functions, including open() and close():

```
int open(char *filename, int access, ...);

int close(int fh);
```

Function close() disassociates the file handle from its file and returns a value of zero if successful; otherwise, it returns a nonzero value. The open() function returns a file handle; the first argument is a pointer to a *filename* string, and the second argument is one or more of the access constants from header file fcntl.h, combined with a logical OR. Table 12-2 lists these access constants.

This list contains the mast commonly used constants for opening Level I files; they are defined in fcntl.h and unless otherwise noted, they can be combined with a logical OR ().

Constant	Meaning
O_RDONLY	Read only
O_WDONLY	Write only
O_RDWR	Read or write
The above three constants cannot be combined with each other	
O_CREATE	Create the file if it doesn't exist
O_APPEND	Write from the end of the fil
O_BINARY	Binary mode
O_TEXT	Text mode
The above two constants cannot be combined with each other	

Table 12-2 Level I file access constants

The third argument of open() is a mode specifier that is only required with a file access of O_CREAT—the ellipsis (...) makes this third argument optional. The integer mode is either S_IREAD, S_IWRITE, or the logical OR of both constants, which are defined in file sys\stat.h.

Level I file reading and writing—functions read() and write()

Level I read() and write() functions are almost identical to Level II unformatted fread() and fwrite()—you just have to adjust the arguments slightly and use a file handle instead of a file pointer. Prototypes for Level I unformatted read() and write() declare the same arguments as each other:

```
int read(int fh, char *buffer, int number);

int write(int fh, char *buffer, int number);
```

The first argument is the file handle, the second is the address of the data, and the third is the number of bytes to be transferred. The read() function returns the number of bytes transferred, 0 if the end of file is reached without reading any data, or -1 if a read error occurred. The write() function returns the number of bytes written, or -1 to indicate an error.

With some minor changes, you can substitute Level I functions to write and read the unformatted survey data in the SURVEY program.

Listing 12.18 SURVEY2.C Put survey coordinates in a file

DO: • Change SURVEY to Level I file I/O
• Compile and run SURVEY2

```
#include <io.h>                                                /*1*/
#include <fcntl.h>                                             /*2*/
#include <sys\stat.h>                                          /*3*/
#include <stdio.h>
int main()
{
    int fh;    /* File handle */                               /*4*/
    double coordinates[4][2] = { 1000000.00, 200000.00,
                                 1100000.01, 220000.02,
                                 1110000.10, 222000.20,
                                 1111000.11, 222200.22 };
    double read_coord[4][2];
    int i;

/* Open the file for read/write/create */

    fh = open("SURVEY.DAT", O_RDWR | O_CREAT,                  /*5*/
              S_IREAD | S_IWRITE);
```

```
/* Write unformatted coordinates to the file */

    write(fh, coordinates, sizeof(double)*8);                   /*6*/

/* Read data back from the beginning of the file */

    lseek(fh, 0L, SEEK_SET);                                    /*7*/
    read(fh, read_coord, sizeof(double)*8);                     /*8*/

/* Display the data read from the file */

    for (i=0; i<4; ++i)
        printf("\nCoordinate %d  X: %f  Y: %f",
             i+1, read_coord[i][0], read_coord[i][1]);

/* Close the file */

    close(fh);                                                  /*9*/
}
```

RESULT:

```
C:\>SURVEY2

Coordinate 1  X:   1000000.00  Y:    200000.00
Coordinate 2  X:   1100000.01  Y:    220000.02
Coordinate 3  X:   1110000.10  Y:    222000.20
Coordinate 4  X:   1111000.11  Y:    222200.22
```

ANALYSIS:

1. The first three lines include the three header files that contain constants and function prototypes for Level I I/O.
2. The program declares a file handle by defining integer variable *fh* on line /*4*/.
3. The open() statement on line /*5*/ creates a new file named SURVEY.DAT and assigns the file handle value to *fh*. The second argument specifies that open() should create the file if it does not exist (O_CREATE) and that both reading and writing are allowed (O_RDWR); the two constants are combined into a single value with a logical OR (|). Because the access argument includes O_CREATE, the

third, mode argument is necessary; this argument specifies that the file will be created to permit both reading (S_IREAD) and writing (S_IWRITE).

4. The write() statement on line /*6*/ is very similar to the former fwrite(), and the read() statement on line /*8*/ is likewise similar to the former fread(); the key differences are that you use the file handle to refer to the file instead of a file pointer, and you specify the total number of bytes of data instead of the number and size of items.

5. You use the function lseek() with Level I I/O instead of fseek() on line /*7*/ to reposition the file. You only need to change the first argument to a file handle instead of the file pointer.

6. The final statement of the program closes the file. When the program ends, it automatically closes the file anyway, but you should get in the habit of always explicitly closing files.

In conclusion, you have two classes of file access to choose from: Level I and Level II. Except in special situations requiring the fastest transfers or low-level control over I/O operations, you should stick to Level II I/O functions, because they are portable and easier to use. With Level II functions, you can perform fast I/O of unformatted file data that saves space and preserves the original accuracy of internal memory values. With Level II, you can also work with formatted files, which allows you great flexibility to store data in ASCII form.

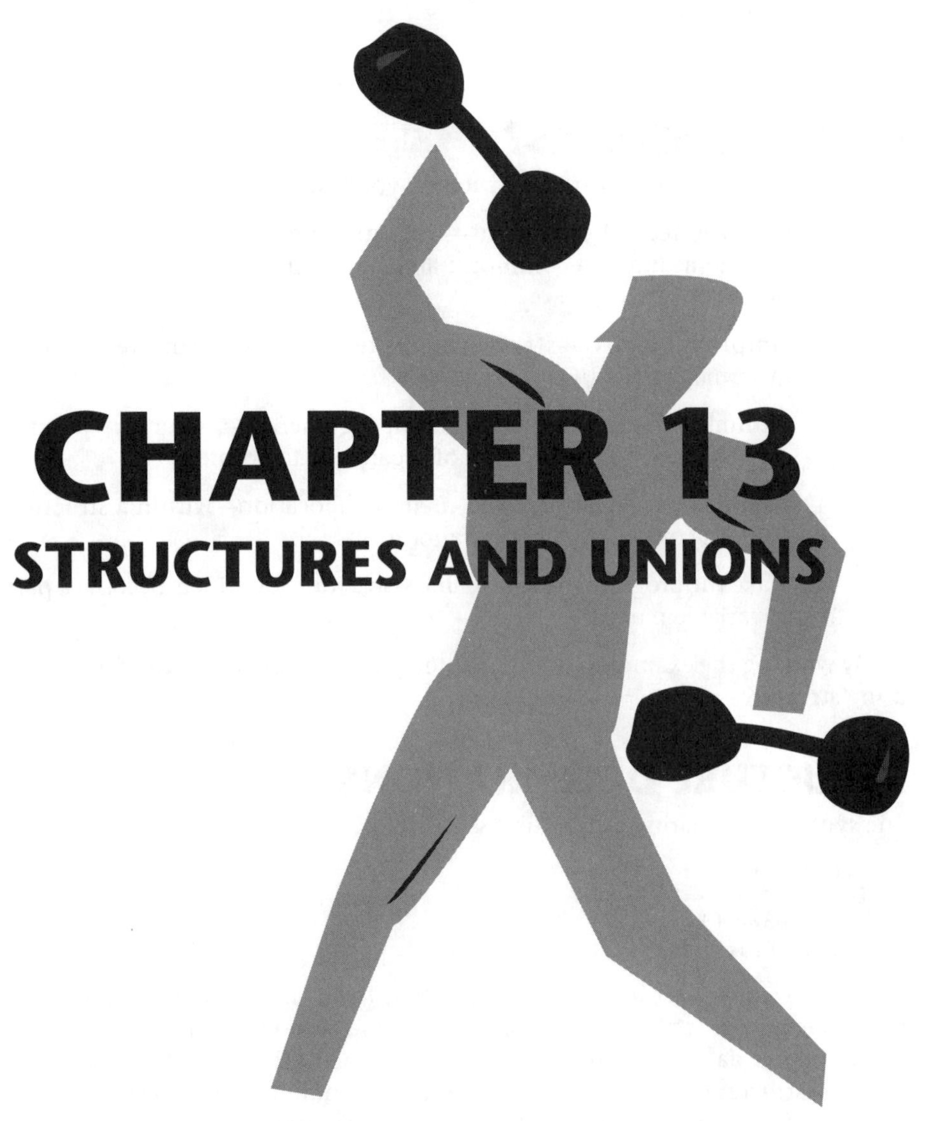

CHAPTER 13
STRUCTURES AND UNIONS

So far in this book, you have defined separate variables, each having its own data type. *Structures* provide a way to group declared items of different types together so that you can handle them as a single entity. *Unions* provide a means to work with different data types in a single storage area.

In this chapter, you will learn how to declare structures, and you will learn how to initialize and access data in structures. You will use arrays of structures to organize large amounts of data, and you will perform file I/O with structures. You will also use structure pointers to pass data to and from functions. The chapter includes a brief introduction to unions, giving an example of assigning different types of data to a single memory location.

WHY STRUCTURES?

By declaring data in the form of a structure, you can:

1. Organize related data items—with structures, you group individual data items under a common name and in a common memory location.
2. Simplify file I/O—structures make for a very simple form of unformatted file I/O.
3. Minimize the number of function arguments—a structure pointer can supplant a large number of separate data pointers.
4. Impose a particular order on memory allocation—within a structure you can control the order of allocation.
5. Make the program more readable—structure identifiers become a part of variable names.

By working the examples in this chapter, you will experience all of these benefits of using structures.

STRUCTURE DECLARATIONS

The syntax for declaring a structure is:

```
struct tag
{
    member list
} name_list;
```

The keyword *struct* tells the compiler that this is a structure declaration, and the curly braces enclose the *members* of the structure. The members are optional declarations of other data types, including other structures. There would be no point in declaring a structure without any members, but the number and type of the members is optional. The *tag* is an identifier for the structure template, and *name_list* is a list of identifiers for structure variables. A structure template describes the layout or design of a structure, while a structure variable represents computer memory allocated according to the template design.

The only parts of this declaration that are always necessary are the keyword *struct* and the terminating semicolon (;). The other optional combinations make the structure declaration a creature that takes on many forms. We will first explain a form that is commonly used and that we recommend, then devote a section to showing other ways that you can use the structure declaration.

You declare structures in two steps: in step one you declare the layout, or template, of the structure, and in step two you declare a variable and allocate memory. These two steps can be separate statements, or you can accomplish both in the same statement. We prefer to use two statements; this first example accomplishes the first step of declaring the template of a structure. The following template, with the tag *vehicle*, declares a structure to hold some data concerning a motor vechicle:

```
struct vehicle
{
     char make[15];
     long miles;
     float operating_costs;
};
```

This form contains all of the elements of a structure declaration except the variable name; it does not identify a variable and it does not allocate any memory—it merely declares the layout of the structure. This particular statement declares a template to hold information about a motor vehicle; the structure has three members, a character array for the vehicle make, an integer variable for the miles driven, and a floating-point variable for the operating costs. The tag *vehicle* identifies the template, and you use the tag to complete the second step and allocate memory:

```
struct vehicle car;
```

This second form of the structure statement contains only the keyword *struct*, the tag, *vehicle*, identifying the template, and a variable identifier, *car*. Figure 13-1 shows the layout of the structure *car* in memory; the compiler allocates each member of the structure in the order in which it appears in the member list.

The combination of keyword *struct* followed by a structure tag has the same role as other data type keywords in C such as *int* and *char*. Thus, the statement *struct vehicle*

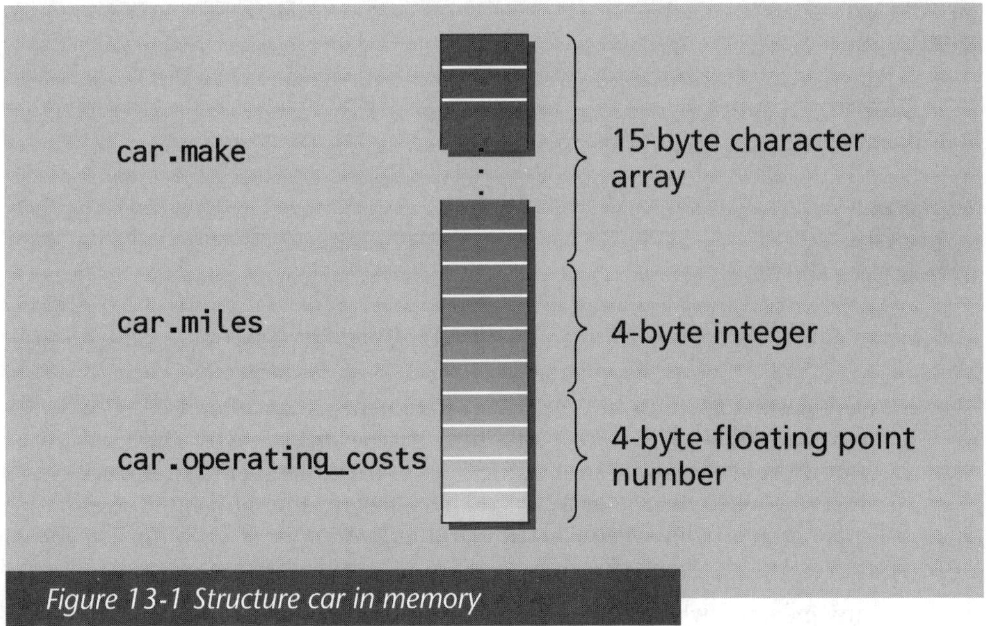

Figure 13-1 Structure car in memory

car; defines the variable *car* as being type *struct vehicle*. The operator sizeof() works with a structure data type just as it does with other data types. In the following program, you can declare a structure and display its size.

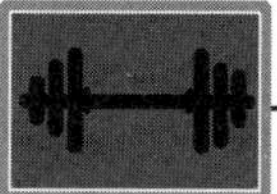

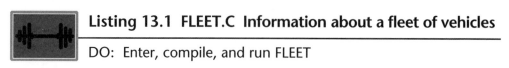

Listing 13.1 FLEET.C Information about a fleet of vehicles

DO: Enter, compile, and run FLEET

```
#include <stdio.h>
void main()
{
/* Declare a structure template */

   struct vehicle
   {
        char  make[15];
        long  miles;
        float operating_costs;
   };

/* Display the size of the structure */

   printf("The size of structure vehicle is %d",
        sizeof(struct vehicle));
}
```

RESULT:

```
C:\>FLEET
The size of structure vehicle is 23
```

ANALYSIS:

1. The *struct* statement declares a structure and identifies it with the tag *vehicle*.
2. The sizeof() operator in the printf() statement returns the number of bytes required to allocate a structure of type *struct vehicle*. The total number of bytes is the sum of the sizes of each member of the structure: 15 bytes for the array *make*, plus 4 bytes for the *long* integer *miles*, plus 4 bytes for the floating-point *operating_costs*.
3. This program only declares a structure template; it does not allocate any memory, which occurs only when a structure variable is defined.

You might want to use the *vehicle* structure if you were charged with keeping track of the cost and usage of your company's vehicles, or maybe if you were writing programs for a rental car agency. You could easily expand the information by adding members to the structure; for instance, you could break down the operating costs into the categories of gasoline, repairs, and insurance. This structure bundles the variables for a vehicle into a neat package; as you work the examples in this chapter, you will see the benefits of organizing the information this way. For certain operations like file I/O or passing arguments to a function, you will deal with the package as a whole, yet you can access each member individually when needed.

You could use the tag *vehicle* to define two more structure variables named *truck* and *van*, which would have similar memory allocations:

```
struct vehicle truck;
struct vehicle van;
```

This points out the advantage of separating the declaration of a structure into two parts—you can use the template to define any number of structure variables.

It is important that you understand the distinction between a tag and the name of a structure variable, so let's reiterate the difference. Both are identifiers, but they identify distinctly separate items; a tag identifies the **template** for a structure, whereas a name identifies a **variable**. Once again, the template just describes what a structure will look like in terms of the names, data types, and sizes of the members. Only when you declare the structure name as a variable does the compiler make the structure a reality by allocating memory for it.

ACCESSING STRUCTURE MEMBERS

When you define a structure variable, you have an identifier for the whole structure, such as the identifer *car* from the statement:

```
struct vehicle car;
```

But you also need a way to refer to the individual elements of the structure. You refer to members of a structure by connecting the structure name to a member with the *structure member operator* (.):

```
structure_name.member_name
```

Thus, the structure name becomes an integral part of every member identifier. For instance, to reference the variable *miles* in the structure *car*, you would write: *car.miles*. This is a variable of type *long* that you can use in the same way as any other type *long* variable.

Member variables in structures

You can use structure member variables within expressions, on both sides of assignment operators, and as arguments, parameters, and function values; in short, you can use them everywhere that you would use nonstructure variables. The FLEET2 program uses structure members in some of these ways.

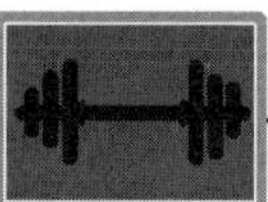

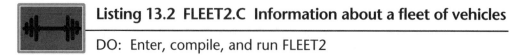

Listing 13.2 FLEET2.C Information about a fleet of vehicles

DO: Enter, compile, and run FLEET2

```
#include <stdio.h>
void main()
{
/* Declare a structure template */

   struct vehicle
   {
       char  make[15];
       long  miles;
       float operating_costs;
   };

/* Define a structure variable */

   struct vehicle car;

/* Initialize some values */

   strcpy(car.make, "Chevrolet");
   car.miles = 10000L;
   car.operating_costs = 3456.78;

/* Display the data */

   printf("MAKE          MILES  OPERATING COSTS");
   printf("\n%-14s %-5ld $%8.2f",
       car.make,
       car.miles,
       car.operating_costs);
}
```

RESULT:

```
C:\>FLEET2
MAKE           MILES  OPERATING COSTS
Chevrolet      10000  $ 3456.78
```

ANALYSIS:

1. The program declares a structure in two steps; the first *struct* statement declares the template as having the tag *vehicle*, and the second

struct statement defines the variable *car* as a structure having the layout of *vehicle*. The second *struct* statement actually allocates memory for the structure.

2. The three statements under /* Initialize some values */ assign data values to the three members of the structure variable *car*. The name of the first member, *car.make*, serves as the destination address for the function strcpy() so that it can copy string "Chevrolet" into the array. The next statement assigns integer 10000 to the second structure member *car.miles*, and the next one assigns the floating-point constant 3456.78 to the third structure member, *car.operating_costs*.
3. The last printf() statement in the program displays the value of each member. Notice that every time the program references a member, the identifier consists of the member name attached to the structure name with the structure member operator (.).

Arrays in structures

Arrays that appear in a structure require no special treatment. You just tack the structure name in front of the array name with the member operator (.) and use it like any other array name. For the structure *car*, *car.make* is the address of the 15-character array, *car.make[1]* is the second element in the array (value 'h'), and *&car.make[1]* is the address of the second element.

ALTERNATIVE FORMS

There are two acceptable placements of the curly braces in a structure declaration:

```
struct tag
{
        member list
};
```

```
struct tag {
    member list
};
```

We prefer to line up the two curly braces as shown on the left, consistent with the way we have used them elsewhere in connection with compound statements. You can choose either placement, but you should make your choice consistent with the way in which you use curly braces for other purposes.

In the previous section we stated a preference for declaring structures in two steps: using one statement to declare the template and one statement to declare each structure variable. This has the advantage of clearly separating the reusable template from the variables. However, there are other ways of using the structure declaration statement.

You can declare one or more structure variables without a tag, as in the following example:

```
struct
{
```

```
        char make[15];
        long  miles;
        float operating_costs;
} car, truck, van;
```

This is a concise way of declaring a fixed, limited number of structure variables. This statement declares the members, so there is a template, but it has no tag and so you cannot reuse the template in a later statement. The statement defines three variables, each having the same structure template: *car*, *truck*, and *van*.

You can also declare both a tag and one or more variables in the same statement as follows:

```
struct vehicle
{
        char  make[15];
        long  miles;
        float operating_costs;
} car, truck;
```

This statement defines two structure variables, *car* and *truck*, but it also identifies the template with the tag *vehicle*. Therefore, you can define another variable having the same structure with a statement like:

```
struct vehicle van;
```

In summary, there are many ways that you can declare structure tags and variables, but we recommend that you stick to the two-step approach of declaring tags first, then defining structure variables with separate statements that refer to the tags.

INITIALIZING STRUCTURES

C provides for initialization structure in much the same way as for arrays. The syntax for initializing a structure during its definition is:

```
struct tag name = { initializer list };
```

The *initializer list* inside the curly braces is a list of comma-separated values for the structure members. Each value must match the data type of its corresponding structure member. For instance, the initializer list for a *vehicle* structure must contain a character string, a long integer, and a floating-point number, in that order. The next program shows how to initialize *car* with the structure definition.

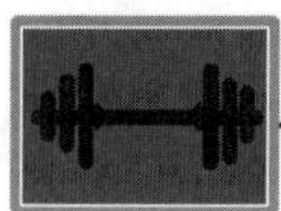

Listing 13.3 FLEET3.C Information about a fleet of vehicles

DO: • Move initialization to the structure definition
• Compile and run FLEET3

```
#include <stdio.h>
```

```
void main()
{
/* Declare a structure template */

   struct vehicle
   {
         char  make[15];
         long  miles;
         float operating_costs;
   };

/* Define and initialize a structure variable */

   struct vehicle car = {"Chevrolet", 10000L, 3456.78};  /*1*/

/* Display the structure members */

   printf("MAKE            MILES  OPERATING COSTS");
   printf("\n%-14s  %-5ld  $%8.2f",
         car.make,
         car.miles,
         car.operating_costs);
}
```

RESULT:

```
C:\>FLEET3
MAKE          MILES  OPERATING COSTS
Chevrolet     10000  $ 3456.78
```

ANALYSIS:

In addition to defining the structure, line /*1*/ also initializes it. The initializer list on line /*1*/ replaces the three statements that formerly were necessary to accomplish the initialization.

This is more compact at the source level than initialization with separate statements; however, it is not any more efficient for the executable program, because the compiler will end up generating practically the same executable code in both cases. The same considerations apply in choosing where to initialize a structure as with any other variable—you may want to initialize as early as possible during the definition, or you may want to initialize with separate assignments closer to where the structure is used in the program.

When you initialize a structure, be sure to place the initializer values in the proper order. The next example shows what happens when a value does not match a structure member.

Listing 13.4 FLEET4.C Information about a fleet of vehicles

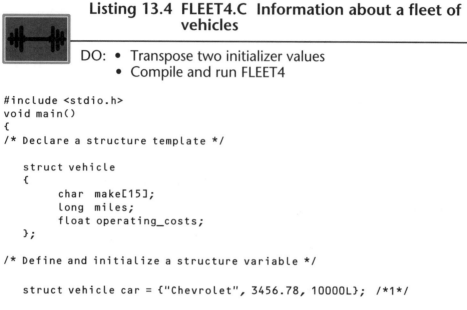

DO: • Transpose two initializer values
• Compile and run FLEET4

```
#include <stdio.h>
void main()
{
/* Declare a structure template */

   struct vehicle
   {
         char  make[15];
         long  miles;
         float operating_costs;
   };

/* Define and initialize a structure variable */

   struct vehicle car = {"Chevrolet", 3456.78, 10000L};  /*1*/

/* Display the structure members */

   printf("MAKE           MILES  OPERATING COSTS");
   printf("\n%-14s  %-5ld  $%8.2f",
         car.make,
         car.miles,
         car.operating_costs);
}
```

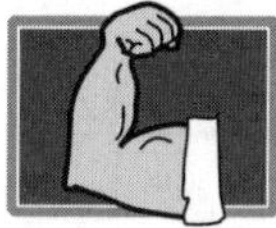

RESULT:

```
C:\>FLEET4
MAKE          MILES  OPERATING COSTS
Chevrolet     3456   $10000.00
```

ANALYSIS:

1. On line /*1*/, the integer and floating-point values are transposed.
2. The compiler accepts the initializer values and converts them to fit the corresponding variables. It truncates the floating-point constant, 3456.78, to fit the integer variable *car.miles*, and it converts the integer constant, 10000, to fit the floating-point *car.operating_costs*.

If there is no initializer list, the compiler does not assign any values to a structure, and you don't know what the memory for the members contains—the values are garbage. However, when you **do** initialize, and the number of values in a structure initializer list is less than the number of members, the compiler sets the remaining members to zero. The next program shows this:

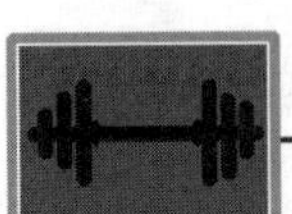

Listing 13.5 FLEET5.C Information about a fleet of vehicles

DO:
- Don't initialize all members of the structure
- Compile and run FLEET5

```
#include <stdio.h>
void main()
{
/* Declare a structure template */

   struct vehicle
   {
         char  make[15];
         long  miles;
         float operating_costs;
   };

/* Define and initialize a structure variable */

   struct vehicle car = {"Chevrolet", 10000L};                    /*1*/

/* Display the structure members */

   printf("MAKE            MILES  OPERATING COSTS");
   printf("\n%-14s  %-5ld  $%8.2f",
         car.make,
         car.miles,
         car.operating_costs);
}
```

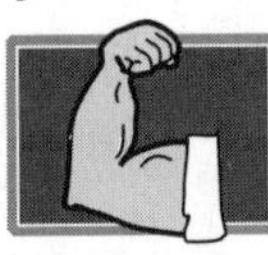

RESULT:

```
C:\>FLEET5
MAKE           MILES   OPERATING COSTS
Chevrolet      10000   $    0.00
```

ANALYSIS:

Line /*1*/ initializes only the first two structure members; the compiler automatically sets the third, *car.operating_costs*, to 0 as shown by the display value.

The compiler will fill an array within a structure with zeros if the initializer does not specify all of its elements. In the example, "Chevrolet" fills only the first 10 bytes of *car.make* (including the terminating null), so the compiler sets the remaining five elements to 0.

ARRAYS OF STRUCTURES

The structure *vehicle* declares room to store information about one vehicle, and you can use the tag to define as many vehicles as needed. But what if you want to allocate storage for a whole fleet, or several fleets? Do you have to declare a separate variable for each vehicle? The answer is no; you can declare an array of structures—an array in which each element is a structure for a different vehicle. You declare an array of structures for a fleet of four vehicles like this:

```
struct vehicle fleet[4];
```

Then you can reference each vehicle by indexing the array. For instance, fleet[0] is the first vehicle and fleet[3] is the fourth. The operating costs for the first vehicle are fleet[0].operating_costs and the miles for the fourth vehicle are fleet[3].miles. Table 13-1 shows this array of structures, including the members of each structure.

The next program defines, initializes, and displays data in an array of structures.

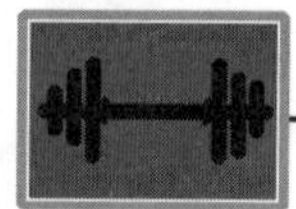

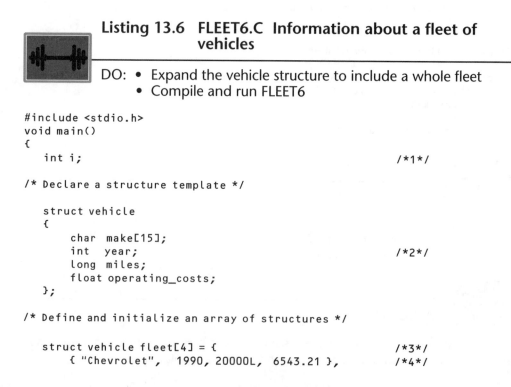

Listing 13.6 FLEET6.C Information about a fleet of vehicles

DO:
- Expand the vehicle structure to include a whole fleet
- Compile and run FLEET6

```
#include <stdio.h>
void main()
{
   int i;                                                    /*1*/

/* Declare a structure template */

   struct vehicle
   {
       char  make[15];
       int   year;                                           /*2*/
       long  miles;
       float operating_costs;
   };

/* Define and initialize an array of structures */

   struct vehicle fleet[4] = {                               /*3*/
       { "Chevrolet",  1990, 20000L,  6543.21 },             /*4*/
```

Member of Structure Array *Fleet*	Relative Memory Location	Size (bytes)
fleet[0].make	0	15
fleet[0].miles	15	4
fleet[0].operating_costs	19	4
fleet[1].make	23	15
fleet[1].miles	38	4
fleet[1].operating_costs	42	4
fleet[2].make	46	15
fleet[2].miles	61	4
fleet[2].operating_costs	65	4
fleet[3].make	69	15
fleet[3].miles	84	4
fleet[3].operating_costs	88	4

Table 13-1 A structure array

```
      { "Ford pickup", 1989, 33000L, 12000.00 },        /*5*/
      { "Ford van",   1985, 99999L, 36000.00 },         /*6*/
      { "Cadillac",    1991,  6666L,  3333.33 } };      /*7*/

/* Display the vehicle information */

   printf("MAKE          YEAR  MILES  OPERATING COSTS");/*8*/
   for (i=0; i<4; ++i)                                  /*9*/
            printf("\n%-14s  %-5d  %-5ld  $%8.2f",      /*10*/
                  fleet[i].make,                        /*11*/
                  fleet[i].year,                        /*12*/
                  fleet[i].miles,                       /*13*/
                  fleet[i].operating_costs);            /*14*/
}
```

RESULT:

```
C:\>FLEET6
```

```
MAKE          YEAR   MILES       OPERATING COSTS
Chevrolet     1990   20000       $ 6543.21
Ford pickup   1989   33000       $12000.00
Ford van      1985   99999       $36000.00
Cadillac      1991    6666       $ 3333.33
```

ANALYSIS:

1. Line /*2*/ expands the structure declaration to include a new member, *year*, which is an integer designed to hold the vehicle's year of manufacture.

2. Line /*3*/ defines the array *fleet* as having four elements; each element is a structure of the type *vehicle*.

3. Lines /*4–7*/ initialize the array with information about each vehicle in the fleet. You initialize multiple elements by listing values for each member of each element in the order in which they appear in the structure. Curly braces delineate the initializer values for each array element on lines /*4–7*/. The extra curly braces are not strictly necessary, because values are present for all structure members, but it is good programming practice to include them. Notice how the statement lines up the fields in the initializer list for readability.

4. Each variable in the printf() statement on lines /*10–14*/ now includes an indexed reference to an element of the structure *fleet*. The *for* loop index, *i*, selects which element of the array to display at each cycle of the loop.

The printf() statement references only the beginning address of each character array *make* in structure *fleet*, so the identifier, *fleet[i].make*, has only one index in one set of square brackets. To get the value of any single element of the character array, you would add a second index; for instance, the first character in the make of the first car is: *fleet[0].make[0]* (which is 'C'), and the last character in the make of the third vehicle is: *fleet[2].make[7]* (value 'n'). When arrays are declared as members of a structure of arrays (as above), there are two kinds of array elements present: a structure array element and a member array element. It is easy to keep the indexing for the two elements straight; you attach the structure index to the structure name and the member index to the member name:

```
structure_name[structure_index].member_name[member_index]
```

Practice referencing some character array values in the array of structures with the next program, which will alter some of the individual character values within each *make* string.

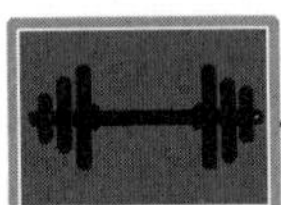

Listing 13.7 FLEET7.C Information about a fleet of vehicles

DO:
- Add extra statements to access character array elements
- Compile and run FLEET7

```
#include <stdio.h>
void main()
{
   int i;

/* Declare a structure template */

   struct vehicle
   {
      char  make[15];
      int   year;
      long  miles;
      float operating_costs;
   };

/* Define and initialize an array of structures */

   struct vehicle fleet[4] = {
      { "Chevrolet",   1990, 20000L,  6543.21 },
      { "Ford pickup", 1989, 33000L, 12000.00 },
      { "Ford van",    1985, 99999L, 36000.00 },
      { "Cadillac",    1991,  6666L,  3333.33 } };

/* Set one character in each make to 'x' */

     for (i=0; i<4; ++i)                                      /*1*/
          fleet[i].make[i] = 'x';                             /*2*/

/* Make last character of make = first character of make */

     for (i=0; i<4; ++i)                                      /*3*/
          fleet[i].make[strlen(fleet[i].make)-1] =            /*4*/
               fleet[i].make[0];                              /*5*/

/* Display the vehicle information */

     printf("MAKE          YEAR  MILES  OPERATING COSTS");
     for (i=0; i<4; ++i)
             printf("\n%-14s %-5d %-5ld $%8.2f",
                    fleet[i].make,
                    fleet[i].year,
                    fleet[i].miles,
                    fleet[i].operating_costs);
}
```

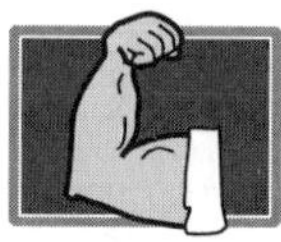

RESULT:

```
C:\>FLEET7
MAKE           YEAR  MILES      OPERATING COSTS
xhevrolex      1990  20000      $ 6543.21
Fxrd pickuF    1989  33000      $12000.00
Foxd vaF       1985  99999      $36000.00
CadxllaC       1991   6666      $ 3333.33
```

ANALYSIS:

1. The *for* loop on lines /*1–2*/ changes one character in the *make* string of each vehicle to 'x'. The same index *(i)* selects the character element and the structure element, so the modified character position keeps in step with the structure element. In other words, the program changes the first character for the first vehicle, the second character for the second vehicle, and so on.

2. The *for* loop on lines /*3–5*/ copies the first character in the *make* string of each vehicle to the last character. The index of the first character of an array is 0, so *fleet[i].make[0]* on the right side of the assignment statement refers to the first character of each make. On the left side of the assignment statement, the index of the last character is *strlen(fleet[i].make)* - 1.

3. The output of program FLEET7 clearly shows that you have successfully accessed elements in the *make* strings to garble them in the prescribed manner. Notice that the last letter for "Chevrolet" is 'x' because it is set after the program changes the first letter in "Chevrolet" to 'x'.

A structure is a natural building block in an important mechanism for connecting related data—a *linked list.* A linked list is an ordered collection of data items that are connected together in a chain. Each item in the chain is linked to two other items, one before and one after. You can place items on a linked list in any order. Figure 13-2 illustrates a linked list.

If each item in the chain is an array element, then the links are indexes referring to other elements. An array of structures is particularly suited for forming linked lists because you can declare structure members for any type of data and you can declare integer members to serve as the link indexes. Here is an example of a linked list structure:

```
struct link                 /* Template for a linked list */
```

```
{
     data members

     int forward_link;     /* Index to next item */
     int backward_link;    /* Index to previous item */
}
```

The index to the next item in the list is known as the *forward* link, and the index connecting to the previous item is called the *backward* link. If you defined an array of the link structures, *struct link linked_list[4]*, you could then fill out the four structure elements with data and link indexes. You can make a linked list of the vehicles in a fleet; modify the FLEET6 program to create this linked list.

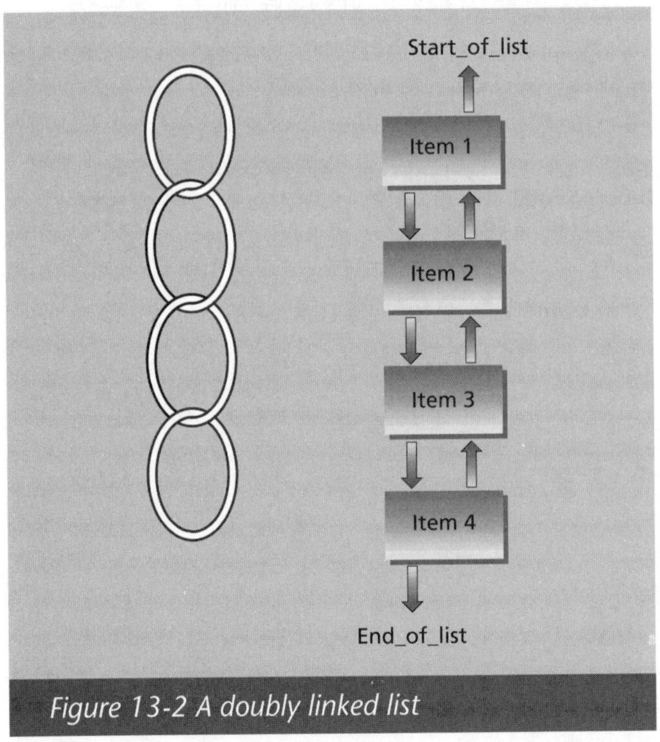

Figure 13-2 A doubly linked list

Listing 13.8 FLEET8.C Information about a fleet of vehicles

DO: • Modify FLEET6 to create a linked list
• Compile and run FLEET8

```
#include <stdio.h>
#define START_OF_LIST -1                                          /*1*/
#define END_OF_LIST   -2                                          /*2*/
```

```
void main()
{
   int i;

/* Declare a structure template */

   struct vehicle
   {
       char  make[15];              /* Vehicle make              */
       int   year;                  /* Vehicle year              */
       long  miles;                 /* Miles driven              */
       float operating_costs;       /* Operating expenditures    */
       int   forward_link;          /* Index to next vehicle     /*3*/
       int   backward_link;         /* Index to prev. vehicle    /*4*/
   };

/* Define and initialize an array of structures */

   struct vehicle fleet[4] = {
{ "Chevrolet",   1990, 20000L,  6543.21, 1, START_OF_LIST },     /*5*/
{ "Ford pickup", 1989, 33000L, 12000.00, 2, 0 },                 /*6*/
{ "Ford van",    1985, 99999L, 36000.00, 3, 1 },                 /*7*/
{ "Cadillac",    1991,  6666L,  3333.33, END_OF_LIST, 2 } };     /*8*/

/* Display the vehicle information */

   printf("MAKE          YEAR  MILES  OPERATING COSTS"
         "  FWD  BACK");                                         /*9*/
   for (i=0; i<4; ++i)
       printf("\n%-14s  %-5d  %-5ld  $%8.2f"
              "        %-3d  %-3d",                              /*10*/
       fleet[i].make,
       fleet[i].year,
       fleet[i].miles,
       fleet[i].operating_costs,
       fleet[i].forward_link,                                    /*11*/
       fleet[i].backward_link);                                  /*12*/
}
```

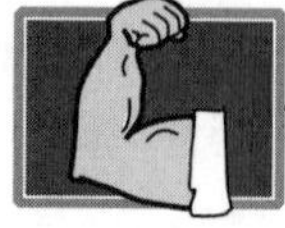

RESULT:

```
C:\>FLEET8
MAKE          YEAR   MILES   OPERATING COSTS  FWD   BACK
Chevrolet     1990   20000   $ 6543.21          1     -1
Ford pickup   1989   33000   $12000.00          2      0
Ford van      1985   99999   $36000.00          3      1
Cadillac      1991   6666    $ 3333.33         -2      2
```

ANALYSIS:

1. Lines /*3–4*/ add the forward and backward link members to the vehicle structure.
2. The initializer list on lines /*5–8*/ is expanded to include index values for the forward and backward links. If you assume that x is the index of the current vehicle, you link each vehicle to its immediate neighbor in the array by placing x+1 in the forward pointer and x-1 in the backward pointer. A value of minus one (*START_OF_LIST*) fills the backward link of the first vehicle because there is no previous vehicle; minus two (*END_OF_LIST*) fills the forward link of the last vehicle because there is no next vehicle. Negative values are invalid indexes; they serve as flags to indicate that no link exists.
3. Lines /*9–12*/ expand the display to show the index values of the link members.

Elements (vehicles) on the linked list don't have to be in the order in which they are initialized. In fact, the whole purpose of a linked list is to easily allow any order. You can change the list order just by changing the links; modify the links in the FLEET8 program to list the fleet of vehicles in the order of their year of manufacture.

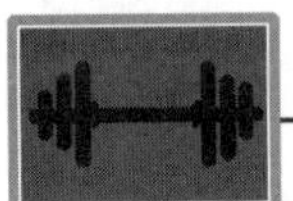

Listing 13.9 FLEET9.C Information about a fleet of vehicles

DO:
- Modify FLEET8 to put the list in year order
- Compile and run FLEET9

```
#include <stdio.h>
#define START_OF_LIST -1
#define END_OF_LIST   -2
void main()
{
   int i;

/* Declare a structure template */

   struct vehicle
   {
       char  make[15];             /* Vehicle make            */
       int   year;                 /* Vehicle year            */
       long  miles;                /* Miles driven            */
       float operating_costs;      /* Operating expenditures  */
```

```
      int  forward_link;          /* Index to next vehicle     */
      int  backward_link;         /* Index to previous vehicle */
   };

/* Define and initialize an array of structures */

   struct vehicle fleet[4] = {
{ "Chevrolet",   1990, 20000L,  6543.21, 3, 1 },                /*1*/
{ "Ford pickup", 1989, 33000L, 12000.00, 0, 2 },                /*2*/
{ "Ford van",    1985, 99999L, 36000.00, 1, START_OF_LIST },    /*3*/
{ "Cadillac",    1991,  6666L,  3333.33, END_OF_LIST, 0 } };    /*4*/

/* Find the start of the list */
   for (i=0; i<4; ++i)                                          /*5*/
      if (fleet[i].backward_link == START_OF_LIST)              /*6*/
           break;                                               /*7*/

/* Display the vehicle information */

   printf("MAKE         YEAR  MILES  OPERATING COSTS  FWD  BACK");
   do                                                           /*8*/
   {                                                            /*9*/
      printf("\n%-14s  %-5d  %-5ld  $%8.2f"
             "         %-3d  %-3d",
           fleet[i].make,
           fleet[i].year,
           fleet[i].miles,
           fleet[i].operating_costs,
           fleet[i].forward_link,
           fleet[i].backward_link);
   } while ((i = fleet[i].forward_link) != END_OF_LIST);        /*10*/
}
```

RESULT:

```
C:\>FLEET9
MAKE          YEAR   MILES   OPERATING COSTS   FWD    BACK
Ford van      1985   99999     $36000.00         1      -1
Ford pickup   1989   33000     $12000.00         0       2
Chevrolet     1990   20000     $ 6543.21         3       1
Cadillac      1991   6666      $ 3333.33        -2       0
```

ANALYSIS:

1. Initializer values for the forward and backward links on lines /*1–4*/ now reorder each vehicle's position in the list to reflect the year. The

list starts with the 1985 "Ford van" and its forward link (1) refers to the 1989 "Ford pickup," which has a forward link (0) that refers to the 1990 "Chevrolet,"and finally, the "Chevrolet" forward link (3) refers to the 1991 "Cadillac" at the end of the list.

2. Lines /*5–10*/ display vehicle information in the order in which vehicles are listed. Lines /*5–7*/ initialize the array index, *i*, to the first item on the list—the loop finds the first item by looking for a *START_OF_LIST* backward link.

3. The *do while* loop on lines /*8–10*/ follows the forward link through the list, displaying each structure element as it is encountered. Line /

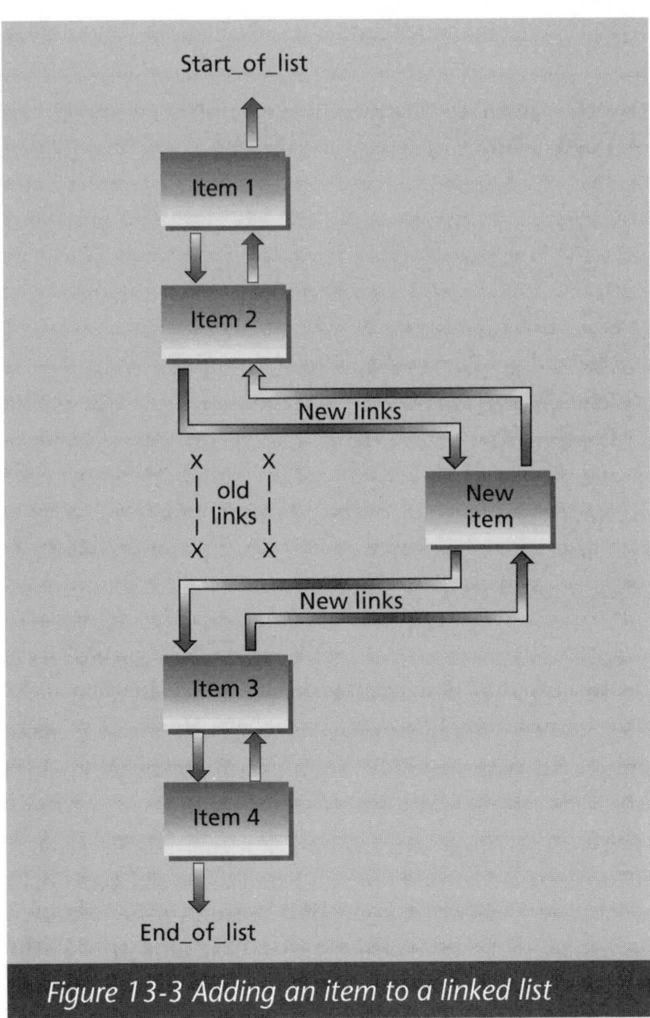

Figure 13-3 Adding an item to a linked list

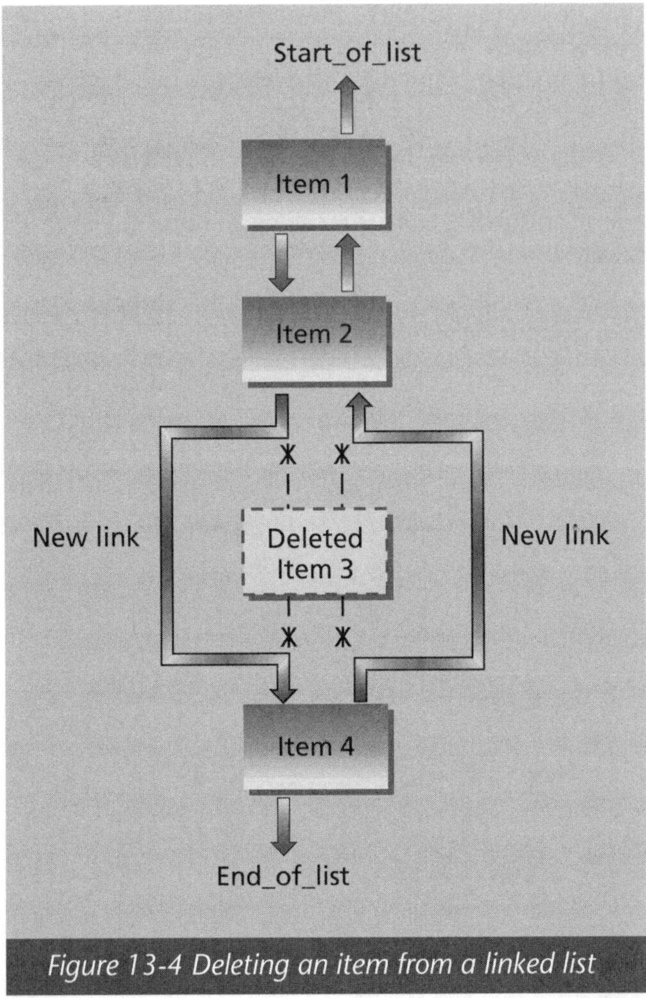

Figure 13-4 Deleting an item from a linked list

10/ assigns each forward link to the structure index, *i*, until the forward link is END_OF_LIST (-2), signalling the end of the list.

4. The output of the program displays the fleet members in year order instead of the order of their array initialization.

The chief advantage of a linked list is that you can add and remove data items anywhere in the list without disturbing other parts of the list. To add an item to an ordinary list, you must move every item below the point of insertion in the list down to make room for the new data. You add an item to a linked list by forging links to the new item, as shown in Figure 13-3, and you delete an item by breaking the links, as shown in Figure 13-4.

You can declare the size of the array for a linked list to be larger than that immediately required so that spare elements are available. These extra elements are collectively known as a *pool* from which individual elements can be filled out and added to the list. The pool also serves as a repository for elements that you delete from the linked list. Some software applications include functions that return deleted structure elements to the pool so they can be reused. With the next program, you can add a vehicle to the fleet by filling out a spare structure element from a pool and inserting it in the linked list.

Listing 13.10 FLEET10.C Information about a fleet of vehicles

DO:
- Add a vehicle to the list
- Compile and run FLEET10

```
#include <stdio.h>
#define START_OF_LIST -1
#define END_OF_LIST   -2
void main()
{
   int i;
   int new;                                                        /*1*/
/* Declare a structure template */

   struct vehicle
   {
       char  make[20];              /* Vehicle make              */
       int   year;                  /* Vehicle year              */
       long  miles;                 /* Miles driven              */
       float operating_costs;       /* Operating expenditures    */
       int   forward_link;          /* Index to next vehicle     */
       int   backward_link;         /* Index to previous vehicle*/
   };

/* Define and initialize an array of structures */

   struct vehicle fleet[15] = {                                    /*2*/
{ "Chevrolet",   1990, 20000L,  6543.21, 3, 1 },
{ "Ford pickup", 1989, 33000L, 12000.00, 0, 2 },
{ "Ford van",    1985, 99999L, 36000.00, 1, START_OF_LIST },
{ "Cadillac",    1991,  6666L,  3333.33, END_OF_LIST, 0 } };

/* Enter a vehicle's make and year */

   new = 4;                                                        /*3*/
   printf("\nEnter the new vehicle's make: ");                     /*4*/
   gets(fleet[new].make);                                          /*5*/
   printf("\nEnter the year: ");                                   /*6*/
   scanf("%d", &fleet[new].year);                                  /*7*/
```

```
/* Find the bottom of list */

   for (i=0; i<4; ++i)                                              /*8*/
       if (fleet[i].forward_link == END_OF_LIST)                    /*9*/
             break;                                                 /*10*/

/* Add the new vehicle to the list */

   fleet[i].forward_link = new;                                     /*11*/
   fleet[new].forward_link = END_OF_LIST;                           /*12*/
   fleet[new].backward_link = i;                                    /*13*/

/* Find the start of the list */

   for (i=0; i<4; ++i)
       if (fleet[i].backward_link == START_OF_LIST)
             break;

/* Display the vehicle information */

   printf("\nMAKE          YEAR  MILES  OPERATING "
        "COSTS  FWD  BACK");                                        /*14*/
   do
   {
       printf("\n%-14s  %-5d  %-5ld  $%8.2f"
               "       %-3d  %-3d",
             fleet[i].make,
             fleet[i].year,
             fleet[i].miles,
             fleet[i].operating_costs,
             fleet[i].forward_link,
             fleet[i].backward_link);
   } while ((i = fleet[i].forward_link) != END_OF_LIST);
}
```

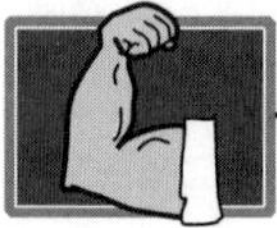

RESULT:

```
C:\>FLEET10

Enter the new vehicle's make: Junker

Enter the year: 1970

MAKE            YEAR    MILES   OPERATING COSTS FWD       BACK
Ford van        1985    99999     $36000.00      1        -1
Ford pickup     1989    33000     $12000.00      0         2
Chevrolet       1990    20000     $ 6543.21      3         1
Cadillac        1991    6666      $ 3333.33      4         0
Junker          1970    0         $     0.00    -2         3
```

ANALYSIS:

1. The program allocates 11 extra structure elements for the *pool* on line /*2*/. The initializer list is large enough to initialize the first four elements, so the compiler initializes members of the last 11 elements to 0.
2. Line /*1*/ defines the index *new*, and line /*3*/ sets it to refer to the first available element in the pool.
3. The statements on lines /*4–7*/ prompt you to enter the new vehicle's make and year.
4. The new vehicle will be added to the end of the list, so on lines /*8–10*/ the program finds the index of the last structure element in the list. The *for* loop looks at the *forward_link* member of each element until it finds the *END_OF_LIST* constant; at that point, the index, *i*, refers to the last element.
5. The last, and most important, task is to modify the forward and backward links. Line /*11*/ changes the forward link of the current last element from *END_OF_LIST* to the index of the new element. Line /*12*/ sets the forward link of the new element to *END_OF_LIST* because this is the new end, and line /*13*/ sets the backward link of the new element to refer to the previous element.

Figure 13-5 illustrates the changes necessary to add this new element to the end of the linked list.

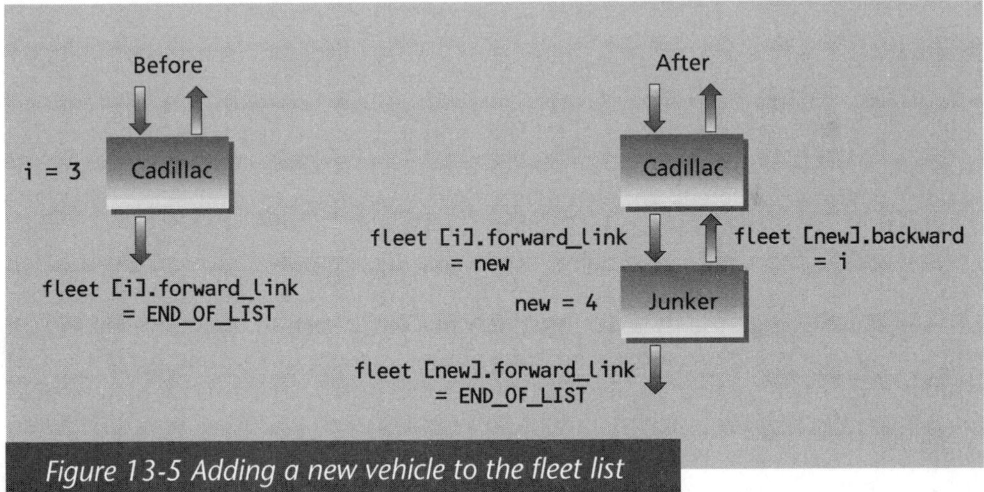

Figure 13-5 Adding a new vehicle to the fleet list

The program placed the new element at the end of the list, which is a little simpler process than inserting it somewhere in the middle. If you were to insert a new vehicle between two existing elements, you would have one more link to change—the backward link of the second existing element.

This example forms a linked list from an array of structure elements, and it links the elements together with indexes that are members of the structure elements. Another way to form a linked list is to allocate single structure items (with the library function malloc()) as they are needed and use pointers to link the items together. Under this scheme, pointers would take the place of indexes as members of the structure, and you would place the memory addresses of allocated items into the pointers. This approach is widely used because it only allocates as much memory as is needed to add items to the list. It also has the advantage that memory can be freed as list items are deleted.

STRUCTURES WITHIN STRUCTURES

It is perfectly legitimate to declare a structure, within a structure and this can be quite a useful thing to do. The template of a structure within a structure looks something like this:

```
struct child_tag
{
    member list1
};

struct parent_tag
{
    member list2
    struct child_tag child_name;
    member list3
};
```

Let's call the main structure the *parent* and the structure within the parent, the *child*. You must declare the template for the child structure ahead of the parent so that the compiler will know what to include in the parent structure. You can declare the child structure anywhere in the member list of the parent; the compiler expands the size of the parent by the size of the child structure.

The *vehicle* structure that you have been using carries some statistical information along with the vehicle's make; the information on miles and operating costs must be lifetime statistics, because there is only one variable for each. If you move these variables to a second structure and use an array of these structures as a member of the first structure, then you can keep miles and cost statistics on a yearly basis for each vehicle. Go back to the FLEET3 program and alter the simple structure for one vehicle to include another structure as a member to hold statistical information.

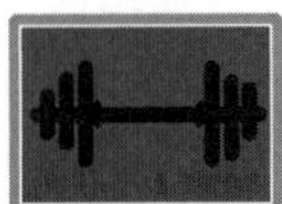

Listing 13.11 FLEET11.C Information about a fleet of vehicles

DO: • Add a second structure to FLEET3
• Compile and run FLEET11

```
#include <stdio.h>
void main()
{
   int i;

/* Declare two structure templates */

   struct info                                                  /*1*/
   {                                                            /*2*/
       int   year;                                              /*3*/
       long  miles;                                             /*4*/
       float operating_costs;                                   /*5*/
   };                                                           /*6*/

   struct vehicle
   {
       char  make[15];
       struct info stats[10];                                   /*7*/
   };

/* Define and initialize a structure variable */

   struct vehicle car = { "Chevrolet",
                          1990, 10000L, 3456.78,                /*8*/
                          1991,  9000L, 3000.00 };              /*9*/

/* Display the structure members */

   printf("MAKE          YEAR  MILES  "
        "OPERATING COSTS");                                     /*10*/
   for (i=0; i<3; ++i)                                          /*11*/
       printf("\n%-14s  %-4d  %-5ld  $%8.2f",                   /*12*/
              car.make,                                         /*13*/
              car.stats[i].year,                                /*14*/
              car.stats[i].miles,                               /*15*/
              car.stats[i].operating_costs);                    /*16*/
}
```

RESULT:

```
C:\>FLEET11
MAKE          YEAR    MILES    OPERATING COSTS
```

```
Chevrolet      1990      10000      $ 3456.78
Chevrolet      1991      9000       $ 3000.00
Chevrolet      0         0          $    0.00
```

ANALYSIS:

1. The program declares the new child structure on lines /*1–6*/; this structure template has the tag *info*, and along with *miles* and *operating_costs*, it includes a new member, *year*, to identify from which year the statistics come.

2. Line /*7*/ defines an array of structures, *stats*, within the parent structure, *vehicle*, based on the new structure tag *info*; there is space for 10 years of statistics.

3. Lines /*8–9*/ initialize the first two elements of the *stats* array with statistics for the years 1990 and 1991; the compiler initializes the remaining eight elements to 0 and makes them available for future use. The program display shows the two initialized elements and the first 0 element.

4. Lines /*14–16*/ within the printf() statement reference values for the members of the elements in the array *stats*. You gain access to an individual member of a child structure within a parent by chaining together the structure names with structure member operators (.). Thus, on line /*16*/, *operating_costs* is a member of the structure *stats[i]*, and *stats[i]* is a member of the structure *car*.

You should always declare structures before they are used. The compiler expects that a child structure template will be declared before it is referenced within the parent structure. With a simple change to FLEET11, you can see the effect of declaring structures in the wrong order when one is a member of the other.

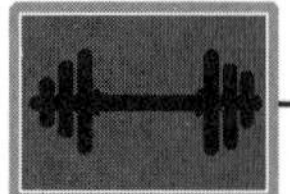

Listing 13.12 FLEET12.C Information about a fleet of vehicles

DO:
- Declare the child structure after the parent
- Compile FLEET12

```
#include <stdio.h>
void main()
{
   int i;
```

```
/* Declare two structure templates */

   struct vehicle
   {
       char  make[15];
       struct info stats[10];
   };

   struct info                                                        /*1*/
   {                                                                  /*2*/
       int   year;                                                    /*3*/
       long  miles;                                                   /*4*/
       float operating_costs;                                         /*5*/
   };                                                                 /*6*/

/* Define and initialize a structure variable */

   struct vehicle car = { "Chevrolet",
                           1990, 10000L, 3456.78,
                           1991,  9000L, 3000.00 };

/* Display the structure members */

   printf("MAKE          YEAR  MILES  OPERATING COSTS");
   for (i=0; i<3; ++i)
       printf("\n%-14s  %-4d  %-5ld  $%8.2f",
              car.make,
              car.stats[i].year,
              car.stats[i].miles,
              car.stats[i].operating_costs);
}
```

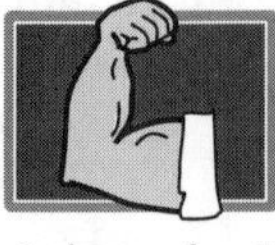

RESULT:

```
C:\>pc/c FLEET12
Power C - Version 2.1.3
(C) Copyright 1989-1991 by Mix Software
Compiling ...
Fleet12.C(11):                struct info stats[10];
*************                              ^105
   105: Struct or Union declaration missing
----------------------------------------------------------------
143 lines compiled
   1 Compile error
[bn]
```

ANALYSIS:

1. Lines /*1–6*/, which were previously **ahead** of the declaration of the structure *vehicle,* are now **behind** it.

2. The compile error indicates that a *struct* declaration is missing because you did not declare the chils tag, *info*, ahead of vehicle.

STRUCTURE POINTERS

You can use pointers to access structures. Pointers to structures play an important role in writing structure data to files and in making structure values accessible to other functions. Also, you can index or modify a pointer to an array of structures with pointer arithmetic to access elements of the array. You can use the address operator (&) to reference the address of the whole structure or any of the members of the structure. The FLEET12 program defines the structure:

```
struct vehicle car;
```

Some addresses for this structure are:

```
&car                    address of beginning of structure
&car.make               address of beginning of character array make
&car.make[1]            address of second character in array make
&car.stats[0]           address of first element of member stats
&car.stats[0].miles     address of member miles of stats[0]
```

Each of these addresses is a constant value that might be assigned to a pointer variable. Notice that the address of the beginning of the structure is *&car*, and **not** just *car*—the parent structure is not an array, so the address operator (&) is needed.

You can also use pointers to access arrays of structures. The name of an array of structures is a constant pointer, and the address operator (&) returns the address of any element of an array of structures, or any member of a structure. The FLEET10 program declares the array of structures:

struct vehicle fleet[15];

Here are some examples of addresses for this array of structures:

```
fleet                 address of beginning of array
&fleet[2]             address of third element
&fleet[2].miles       address of member miles of the third element
```

You declare a structure pointer variable by affixing an asterisk to the pointer name in a declaration statement, like:

```
struct vehicle *vehicle_ptr;
```

This is the same form of statement that you have previously used to declare other pointer types, like:

```
int *iptr.
```

Just as *int* declares the type for pointer *iptr, struct vehicle* declares the type for pointer *vehicle_ ptr*.

There are two syntax conventions for accessing structure data with pointers. The first, older method is seldom used, but we will briefly introduce it here. You could access the member *make* of a *vehicle* structure by writing *(*vehicle_ptr).make;*. The asterisk is the indirection operator, which returns the value at the pointer address (which is the structure itself), and the parentheses force the application of the indirection operator (*) before the structure member operator (.). This original method has proven to be awkward, and structure pointers are so frequently used in C that the authors of the language have supplied another operator that is a little easier to use when referencing members, the *structure pointer operator* (->). We will not dwell on the original method, and just leave it behind in favor of the simpler structure pointer operator. The structure pointer operator is two characters, a hyphen (-) followed by a greater-than (>) character. With a structure pointer, you refer to members by linking the member to the pointer name with the structure pointer operator (->); for example: *vehicle_ptr->make*. So, to summarize the methods for accessing structure members, you can use a structure name with a structure member operator (*car.make*), or you can use a structure pointer with the structure pointer operator (*vehicle_ptr->make*).

Using a structure pointer as a function argument

With a structure pointer, you can pass a whole bunch of values to a function with just one argument. In the next program, you will use a structure pointer to pass values to a function that displays the values in a structure.

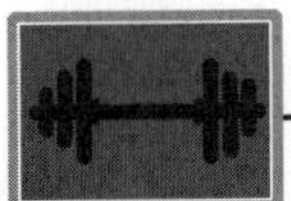

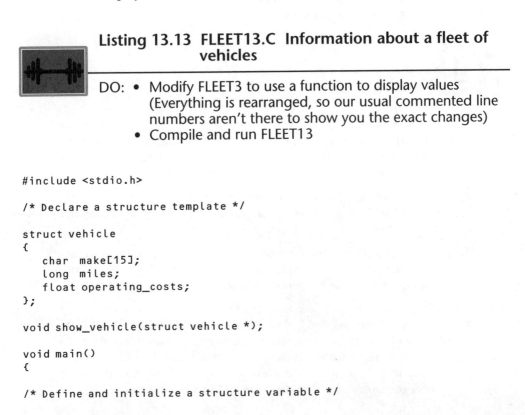

Listing 13.13 FLEET13.C Information about a fleet of vehicles

DO:
- Modify FLEET3 to use a function to display values (Everything is rearranged, so our usual commented line numbers aren't there to show you the exact changes)
- Compile and run FLEET13

```
#include <stdio.h>

/* Declare a structure template */

struct vehicle
{
   char  make[15];
   long  miles;
   float operating_costs;
};

void show_vehicle(struct vehicle *);

void main()
{

/* Define and initialize a structure variable */
```

```
   struct vehicle car = {"Chevrolet", 10000L, 3456.78};

/* Display the structure members */

   show_vehicle(&car);
}

void show_vehicle(struct vehicle *vehicle_ptr)
{
   printf("MAKE          MILES  OPERATING COSTS");
   printf("\n%-14s %-5ld  $%8.2f",
        vehicle_ptr->make,
        vehicle_ptr->miles,
        vehicle_ptr->operating_costs);
}
```

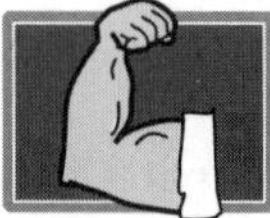

RESULT:

```
C:\>FLEET13
MAKE          MILES      OPERATING COSTS
Chevrolet     10000      $ 3456.78
```

ANALYSIS:

1. The declaration of the structure template (with the tag *vehicle*) must be moved outside the main function so that it can be used by both functions of this program. When you declare a structure inside a function, it can only be used within that function.
2. The prototype for the display function appears after the structure template, because one function argument (*struct vehicle* *) uses the structure tag.
3. The main function consists of only two statements; one used to define the structure *car* and one used to call the new display function. The argument for the function call is the constant structure pointer, *&car*.
4. The display function *show_vehicle()* declares the parameter *vehicle_ ptr*, which will accept the structure address, and it uses this pointer to reference member values in the printf() statement. The function references the three structure members by applying the structure pointer operator (->) to the structure and member names.

Applying pointer arithmetic to structure pointers

You can use pointer arithmetic with structure pointers. If you add one to a structure pointer, the address increases by an amount equal to the number of bytes in the structure. This characteristic is particularly useful with arrays of structures because you can access sequential structure elements in the array simply by incrementing a pointer. Expand the structure in the FLEET13 program into an array of two cars, then use the pointer to display both elements.

Listing 13.14 FLEET14.C Information about a fleet of vehicles

DO:
- Modify FLEET13 to use structure pointer arithmetic
- Compile and run FLEET14

```
#include <stdio.h>

/* Declare a structure template */

struct vehicle
{
   char  make[15];
   long  miles;
   float operating_costs;
};

void show_vehicle(struct vehicle *);

void main()
{

/* Define and initialize a structure variable */

   struct vehicle car[] = {"Chevrolet", 10000L, 3456.78,          /*1*/
                           "Ford",      11000L, 4000.00};

/* Display the data */

   show_vehicle(car);                                              /*2*/
}

void show_vehicle(struct vehicle *vehicle_ptr)
{
   printf("MAKE          MILES  OPERATING COSTS");
   printf("\n%-14s %-5ld $%8.2f",
      vehicle_ptr->make,
      vehicle_ptr->miles,
      vehicle_ptr->operating_costs);

   printf("\n\nPointer value before: %p", vehicle_ptr);           /*3*/
```

```
    ++vehicle_ptr;                                                  /*4*/
    printf(" and after: %p incrementing", vehicle_ptr);            /*5*/

    printf("\n\n%-14s %-5ld $%8.2f",                                /*6*/
        vehicle_ptr->make,
        vehicle_ptr->miles,
        vehicle_ptr->operating_costs);
}
```

RESULT:

```
C:\>FLEET14
MAKE            MILES       OPERATING COSTS
Chevrolet       10000       $ 3456.78

Pointer value before: 82B2 and after: 82C9 incrementing

Ford            11000       $ 4000.00
```

ANALYSIS:

1. The declaration on line /*1*/ makes *car* an array of two structure elements. The statement does not explicitly declare the array size—instead, it lets the compiler imply the array size (2) from the number of structure values in the initializer list. Automatic array sizing applies to arrays of structures just as it does to other types of arrays.

2. Because *car* is now an array, you do not need to apply the address operator (&) to the argument *car* on line /*2*/.

3. Inside the display function, line /*4*/ increments the structure pointer so that a repeat printf() statement on line /*6*/ can display the second structure element.

4. The printf()s on lines /*3*/ and /*5*/ let you see how much the address changes when the structure pointer is incremented; it changes by the size of the structure element (23 bytes). You will have to subtract the two hexadecimal address values and convert to decimal to confirm that the difference is really 23 bytes (see the discussion following Program 11.4, POINT4, Chapter 11, if you are unfamiliar with hexadecimal arithmetic).

STRUCTURE I/O WITH FILES

A structure often consists of related items that correspond to a record in a file; as a matter of fact, programmers often design files and structures so that this is true. In the PASCAL programming language, the equivalent to a C structure is even called a record. A one-to-one relationship between structures and records makes for very simple file I/O, but you must use unformatted I/O statements to take full advantage of the correspondence. With an unformatted I/O statement like fwrite(), you can write the entire record by passing the function a pointer to, and the size of, the structure. The unformatted record will then contain values of all the structure members, no matter what the different types. You are not restricted to unformatted I/O with structures; you can still format the individual members of a structure with a formatted statement like fprintf(), and you may need to do that in certain situations. However, unformatted structure I/O is particularly easy and efficient. The next program expands the display function from FLEET13 to write the structure data to a file as well as display it.

Listing 13.15 FLEET15.C Information about a fleet of vehicles

DO:
- Add file output to the display function of FLEET13
- Compile and run FLEET15

```
#include <stdio.h>

/* Declare a structure template */

struct vehicle
{
   char  make[15];
   long  miles;
   float operating_costs;
};

void show_vehicle(struct vehicle *);

void main()
{

/* Define and initialize a structure variable */

   struct vehicle car = {"Chevrolet", 10000L, 3456.78};

/* Display the data */

   show_vehicle(&car);
}

void show_vehicle(struct vehicle *vehicle_ptr)
```

```
{
   FILE *fp;                                                    /*1*/

   printf("MAKE          MILES  OPERATING COSTS");
   printf("\n%-14s %-5ld $%8.2f",
       vehicle_ptr->make,
       vehicle_ptr->miles,
       vehicle_ptr->operating_costs);

   fp = fopen("AUTO.DAT", "w");                                 /*2*/
   fwrite(vehicle_ptr, sizeof(struct vehicle), 1, fp);          /*3*/
   fclose(fp);                                                  /*4*/
}
```

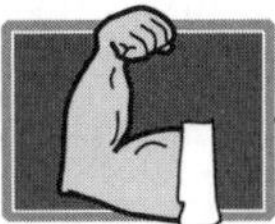

RESULT:

```
C:\>FLEET15
MAKE           MILES  OPERATING COSTS
Chevrolet      10000  $ 3456.78
```

ANALYSIS:

1. Line /*1*/ defines a file pointer that the program uses on line /*2*/ to open the file AUTO.DAT, on line /*3*/ to write to the file, and on line /*4*/ to close the file.
2. On line /*3*/, fwrite() receives the structure pointer *vehicle_ ptr* as its first argument, and it writes data to the file from that address. The second argument is the number of bytes in the structure—the value returned by *sizeof(struct vehicle)*. Being able to derive the size of a structure with the sizeof() operator is a real convenience. The third argument tells fwrite() to output one record to the file.

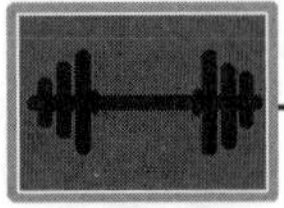

DO: Look at the size of file AUTO.DAT

RESULT:

```
C:\>dir AUTO.DAT
```

```
 Volume in drive C has no label
 Directory of  C:\

AUTO DAT      23   9-21-91   8:59a
      1 File(s)   4300800 bytes free
```

ANALYSIS:

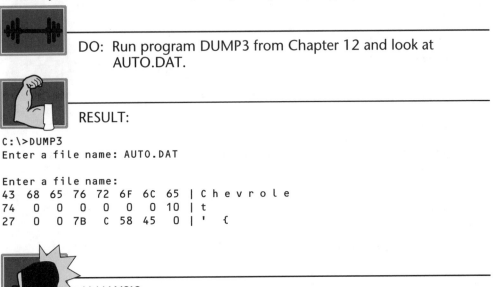

You cannot display or print all the bytes in the file (with a DOS *type* or *print* command) because the data is stored in internal form—it is not formatted. However, you can indirectly look at the data with the dump utility that you programmed in Chapter 12.

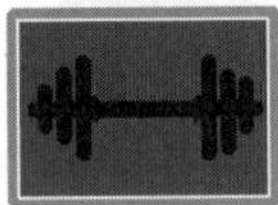

DO: Run program DUMP3 from Chapter 12 and look at AUTO.DAT.

RESULT:

```
C:\>DUMP3
Enter a file name: AUTO.DAT

Enter a file name:
43  68  65  76  72  6F  6C  65  | C h e v r o l e
74   0   0   0   0   0   0  10  | t
27   0   0  7B   C  58  45   0  | '   {
```

ANALYSIS:

You can see all 23 bytes of the record in the hexadecimal display of the dump output. You can readily read the character data, and if you convert the hexadecimal digits 2710 to decimal form (10000), you can make sense out of the integer data, but you cannot decipher the floating-point value, which is the last four nonzero hexadecimal values on the last line. To do this, you must write a program to read the data back into a structure, then reformat and display the floating-point number with a printf() statement.

Listing 13.16 FLEET16.C Information about a fleet of vehicles

DO:
- Modify FLEET15 to read structure data
- Compile and run FLEET16

```
#include <stdio.h>

/* Declare a structure template */

struct vehicle
{
   char  make[15];
   long  miles;
   float operating_costs;
};

void show_vehicle(struct vehicle *);

void main()
{

/* Define and initialize a structure variable */

   struct vehicle car;                                        /*1*/

/* Display the data */

   show_vehicle(&car);
}

void show_vehicle(struct vehicle *vehicle_ptr)
{
   FILE *fp;

   fp = fopen("AUTO.DAT", "r");                               /*2*/
   fread(vehicle_ptr, sizeof(struct vehicle), 1, fp);         /*3*/
   fclose(fp);                                                /*4*/

   printf("MAKE          MILES  OPERATING COSTS");
   printf("\n%-14s %-5ld  $%8.2f",
       vehicle_ptr->make,
       vehicle_ptr->miles,
       vehicle_ptr->operating_costs);
}
```

RESULT:

```
C:\>FLEET16
MAKE          MILES     OPERATING COSTS
Chevrolet     10000     $ 3456.78
```

ANALYSIS:

1. It is really easy to modify FLEET15 to read the AUTO.DAT file instead of write it. All you have to do is move the three lines concerned with

file operations, /*2–4*/, before the printf() statements in show_vehicle(), change the file mode from write ("w") to read ("r") on line /*2*/, and change the function fwrite() to fread() on line /*3*/.

2. You should also remove the initializer list on line /*1*/ in the main function just to ensure that the data comes from the file and not the initialization statement.

This example should prove to you how easy it is to transfer structure data to and from a file. When you design a program, if you have a lot of related information to store in files or to pass between functions, you should always consider using structures.

UNIONS

A *union* is a data type similar to a structure, except that all the members of the union share the same memory space. Unions provide a way for you to declare memory space that can hold values for different data types at different times. You use the same syntax as you do for structures to declare a union, except you use the keyword *union* in place of *struct*:

```
union tag_name
{
     member list
} name_list;
```

The member list can (and usually does) contain members of different types. For example, you could declare:

```
union
{
     int   i_num;
     float f_num;
} both;
```

The value stored in this union could be either an integer or a floating-point number. You can assign a value to any single member at any time; however, your access to the data is restricted to the data type of that member until you assign a new value. It is as if the union put on a different mask each time you assigned a value to a member, and you only knew the union by recognizing the current mask. If you assigned an integer:

```
both.i_num = 123;
```

then you could display the integer value:

```
printf("%d", both.i_num);
```

but not the floating-point value:

```
printf("%f", both.f_num);
```

Then you could switch roles by assigning a floating-point value:

```
both.f_num = 4.56;
```

and display the value as a floating-point number. Figure 13-6 illustrates the identity changing behavior of this union variable.

Unions have the following characteristics in common with structures:

1. You declare them both with the same syntax.
2. You can declare a template separately from the variable.
3. You access members using the same operators: the structure/union member operator (.) and the structure/union pointer operator (->).
4. You can access both types with pointers, using pointer arithmetic or indexing.
5. You can declare arrays of either type, and you access the elements of either type with array indexing.

A couple of differences are worth noting:

1. You can only initialize a union with the data type of the first member declared.

Figure 13-6 The changing faces of a union

2. The size of a union (the value returned by sizeof()) is the size of the largest member, whereas the size of a structure is the sum of the member sizes.

Unions live a kind of Dr. Jeckyll and Mr. Hyde existence, so that is the name of the variable in the following program that displays the size of a union.

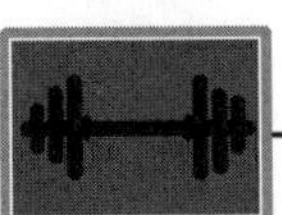

Listing 13.17 SHARE.C Share memory between different data types

DO: Enter, compile, and run SHARE

```
#include <stdio.h>
void main()
{
/* Declare a union template */

   union share
   {
         int  i_face;
         char c_face[8];
   };

/* Define a union variable */

   union share jeckyll_hyde;

/* Display the size of the union */

   printf("\nThe size of the union is %d",
         sizeof(jeckyll_hyde));
}
```

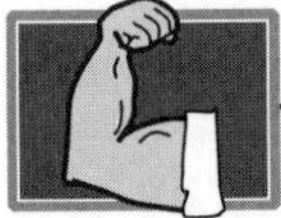

RESULT:

```
C:\>SHARE

The size of the union is 8
```

ANALYSIS:

1. The program declares a union with two members, an integer, *i_face*, and a character array, *c_face*. The first *union* statement declares the

template having the tag, *share*, and the second *union* statement defines the union variable, *jeckyll_hyde*.

2. The printf() statement displays the size of the union, 8 bytes, which is the size of the larger of the members—the character array is 8 bytes, whereas the integer is only 2 bytes. You could have used either the data type, *union share*, or variable *jeckyl/_hyde* as the operand for sizeof().

You can make the union time-share its memory space for different values with the next program.

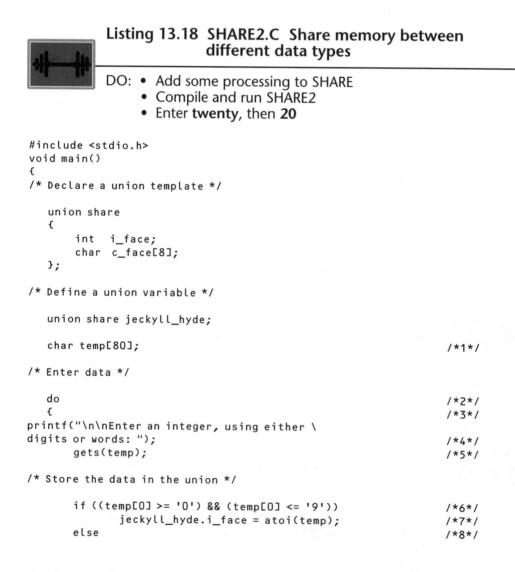

Listing 13.18 SHARE2.C Share memory between different data types

DO:
- Add some processing to SHARE
- Compile and run SHARE2
- Enter **twenty**, then **20**

```
#include <stdio.h>
void main()
{
/* Declare a union template */

   union share
   {
        int   i_face;
        char  c_face[8];
   };

/* Define a union variable */

   union share jeckyll_hyde;

   char temp[80];                                          /*1*/

/* Enter data */

   do                                                      /*2*/
   {                                                       /*3*/
printf("\n\nEnter an integer, using either \
digits or words: ");                                       /*4*/
        gets(temp);                                        /*5*/

/* Store the data in the union */

        if ((temp[0] >= '0') && (temp[0] <= '9'))          /*6*/
                jeckyll_hyde.i_face = atoi(temp);          /*7*/
        else                                               /*8*/
```

```
            strcpy(jeckyll_hyde.c_face, temp);                  /*9*/

/* Display the data in the union */

        printf("\nData displayed as an integer: %d",            /*10*/
               jeckyll_hyde.i_face);                            /*11*/
        printf("\nData displayed as a string: %s",              /*12*/
               jeckyll_hyde.c_face);                            /*13*/
   } while (strlen(temp) > 0);                                  /*14*/
}
```

RESULT:

```
C:\>SHARE2


Enter an integer, using either digits or words: twenty
Data displayed as an integer: 30580
Data displayed as a string: twenty

Enter an integer, using either digits or words: 20
Data displayed as an integer: 20
Data displayed as a string:

Enter an integer, using either digits or words: ENTER
Data displayed as an integer: 0
Data displayed as a string:
```

ANALYSIS:

1. The *do while* loop controlled by lines /*2–3*/ and /*14*/ continues as long as you enter something from the keyboard, and it quits when you just press ENTER.

2. The *if* statement on lines /*6–9*/ tests the first character in the *temp* string to see whether you entered digits or letters. If you entered digits, then the statement calls the standard function atoi() to convert the string to an integer and assigns it to the integer member of the union, *jeckyll_hyde.i_face*; otherwise, it copies the string to the character member of the union, *jeckyll_hyde.c_face*.

3. The program displays the union both as an integer and as a string. When you enter **twenty**, the string display is correct, but the integer display is meaningless. When you enter **20**, the integer display is correct.

This program shows that when you assign a value to a member of a union, then you can retrieve only that same data type until you assign a value to a different member. Basically, you cannot assign data of one type to a union and take it out as another type. However, there is a way to put integer data into a union and extract it differently.

C provides a way to represent unsigned integers in two different forms; you can use these two forms with a union to view the same number in different ways. You can declare an integer as *unsigned* in the usual way:

```
unsigned whole;
```

And you can declare groups of bits within the integer with a structure of bit fields:

```
struct bytes                       /* Bytes of an unsigned int */
{
    unsigned byte1 : 8;            /* First 8 bits  */
    unsigned byte2 : 8;            /* Second 8 bits */
};
```

The 8 and colon (:) after each member in the structure declares that each of these items represents 8, and only 8, bits of the value. You can slice up the bits of an integer in any way you wish with such *structure bit fields*—the next chapter will discuss these structures more thoroughly. If you place the above two declarations into a union, you can assign a value to the whole integer member, then examine the bytes of that number by looking at the other members of the union. In the next example, you can assign a value to a 16-bit *unsigned int* and display the two 8-bit bytes of the value separately with the aid of a union.

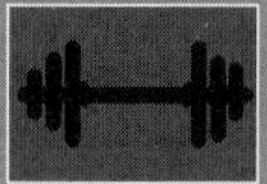

Listing 13.19 SHARE3.C View part of an integer

DO:
- Enter and compile SHARE3
- Run SHARE3 and enter **258**

```
#include <stdio.h>

struct bytes                       /* Bytes of an unsigned int */
{
   unsigned byte1 : 8;             /* First 8 bits  */
   unsigned byte2 : 8;             /* Second 8 bits */
};

union overlap                      /* Overlapping storage */
{
   unsigned whole;                 /* All 16 bits */
   struct bytes part;              /* Two bytes   */
};

void main()
{
```

```
    union overlap number;

    printf("Enter an integer number: ");
    scanf("%d", &number.whole);
    printf("\nThe 1st byte is: %d", number.part.byte1);
    printf("\nThe 2nd byte is: %d", number.part.byte2);
}
```

RESULT:

```
C:\>SHARE3
Enter an integer number: 258

The 1st byte is: 2
The 2nd byte is: 1
```

ANALYSIS:

1. The program declares the structure of two bit fields for the unsigned integer having the tag *bytes*, then it declares a union having the tag *overlap*. The union has two members, one being the 16-bit *unsigned int*, named *whole*, and the other being the structure of two 8-bit bytes, named *part*.

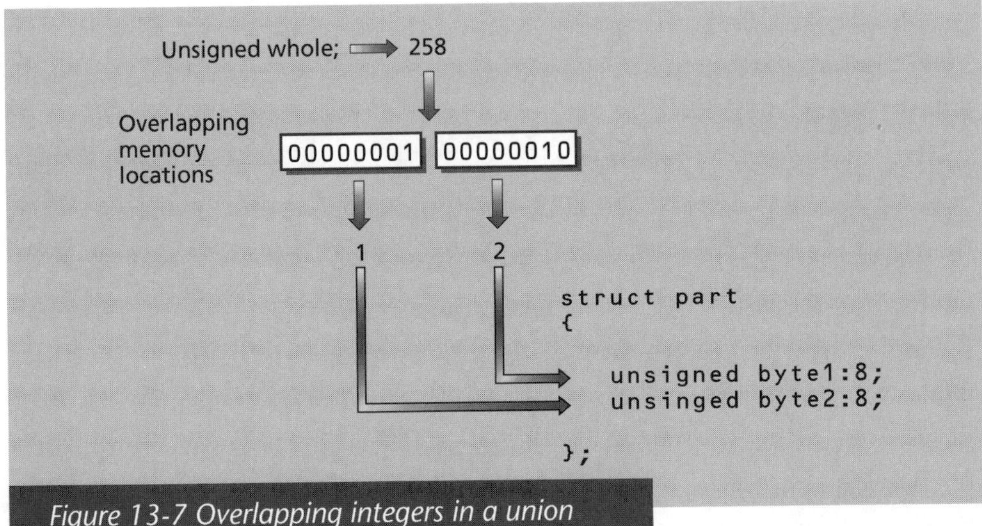

Figure 13-7 Overlapping integers in a union

2. The main function prompts you to enter an integer into *whole*, then displays the number in parts by referring to the members of the structure *part*.

Figure 13-7 illustrates the overlapping nature of this union and how the number, 258, breaks out to the two byte values, 2 and 1.

Extracting integers in a different form than that in which you placed them into a union is a nice trick that is not entirely portable, because not all computer systems put the individual bytes of an integer in the same order. The values that you receive in a structure of bit fields will depend on the byte order used by a particular computer system.

Unions are not widely used in C programs, but they are good for specialized situations, such as outlined in the last three examples. Structures, on the other hand, are widely used because they are such an effective means of organizing data.

CHAPTER 14
BIT MANIPULATION

Some operators deal with variables as a whole, but *bitwise operators* work with the most elemental unit in computing, the *binary digit*, or *bit*. In this chapter, you will probe into the values of integers to alter individual bits with the operators AND (&), OR (|), EXCLUSIVE OR (^), COMPLEMENT (~), LEFT SHIFT (<<), and RIGHT SHIFT (>>). You will use these operators to set and test *flags*, to extract values from integers with *masking* operations, to see how graphic images are stored, and to perform some simple animation. You will also use *structure bit fields* to access bits within integers.

WHY PLAY WITH BITS?

The motivation for bit manipulation is almost always to *compress* data, to make it smaller. Data compression is important when large amounts of data must be stored (on disk or in memory), or when the data has to be moved (to a printer or out over a communication line). Businesses keep massive amounts of data in files that they must frequently transmit between offices, engineering firms use precision drawings and images that they must store, print, and display, and computer bulletin boards must deal with the problem of uploading and downloading large numbers of files. All of these applications benefit from some form of data compression.

As an example of data compression, you could hold single values that range from 0 to 15 in a 2-byte integer, but these values only take up 4 bits of that memory space—the other 12 bits are wasted. You could pack four values into the 2-byte integer and use one-fourth the memory! Figure 14-1 illustrates this instance of data compression.

There are operations other than data compression in which bit manipulation plays an important role. Programs control most hardware devices (printers, displays, etc.) through special memory or I/O locations. These locations have groupings of bits that are meaningful for the status and control of the device. Programs that interact with these devices must set and interpret values in these special locations using bitwise operators.

INTRODUCTION TO BITWISE OPERATORS

Each of the bitwise operators is equivalent to an operation designed into the central processing unit (CPU) of all computers, so they are extremely fast. However, you should not alter bits within a variable unless it is really necessary because it will take

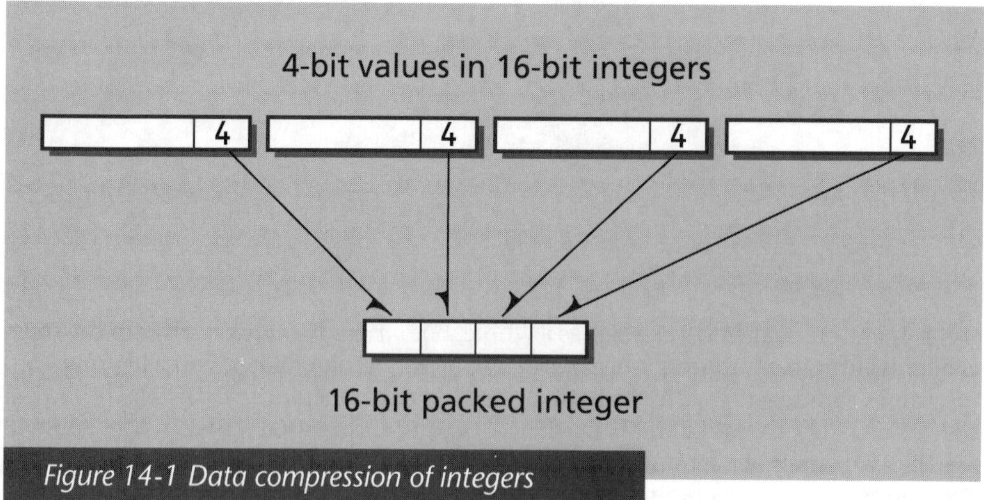

Figure 14-1 Data compression of integers

extra time to do so. If the amount of memory used is critical and/or the amount of data is very large, data compression is the right thing to do. However, if only a few values are involved, you will have unnecessarily complicated your program and slowed it down to boot.

Bitwise operators reuse some of the symbols that represent other operators; here are the similarities and how you tell them apart:

> **Ampersand (&)** The ampersand (&) is the bitwise AND operator. C also uses the ampersand for the address operator and the logical AND (&&). There is no need to be confused though—the logical AND is clearly different because it uses two ampersands, and the address is a unary operator, which is never preceded by an operand. The bitwise AND is a binary operator, which is always preceded and followed by operands.
>
> **Vertical line (|)** The vertical line (|) serves for both the bitwise OR and the logical OR (||). This is not much of a problem though, because the logical OR uses two verticals; you just need to pay particular attention to the proper number of characters for these operators.
>
> **Greater than (>) and less than (<)** The greater-than (>) and less-than (<) characters are relational operators, but they also serve as the shift operators (<< and >>). Once again, the difference between arithmetic and bitwise operators is the number of characters, and you need to be conscious of this when you apply these operators.

Bitwise operators are valid only with integer operands; there is no good reason to want to alter individual bits of floating-point numbers, so C does not allow it. You can apply any of the six bitwise operators to the types *char, int, long, short,* and the *unsigned* variations of each.

Integer values have a fixed number of bits layed out in a linear, left-right fashion. Each bit can have a value of only 0 or 1. A bit is said to be *set* if it has a value of 1, and a bit is said to be *reset* or *cleared* if it has a value of 0. The right-most bit of an integer is called the *least-significant* bit because it represents the smallest possible part of the number, either 0 or 1. Progressing to the left, each bit contributes twice as much to the integer value as the preceding bit. The first (least-significant) bit contributes 1 if it is set, the second bit contributes 2 if it is set, the third contributes 4, and so on. Thus, a bit sequence of 101 has a decimal value of 5. The left-most bit is the *most-significant* bit for unsigned integer, and for a signed integer, it is the sign bit. A sign bit of 1 signifies a negative number and the computer stores negative numbers in *two's complement* form, which is a little different from the usual bit pattern for positive integers. You won't ordinarily have to be concerned about the details of two's complement representations, but a brief explanation is presented under the COMPLEMENT operator section of this chapter. Figure 14-2 shows the bits for an unsigned and a signed 8-bit integer (unsigned char and char).

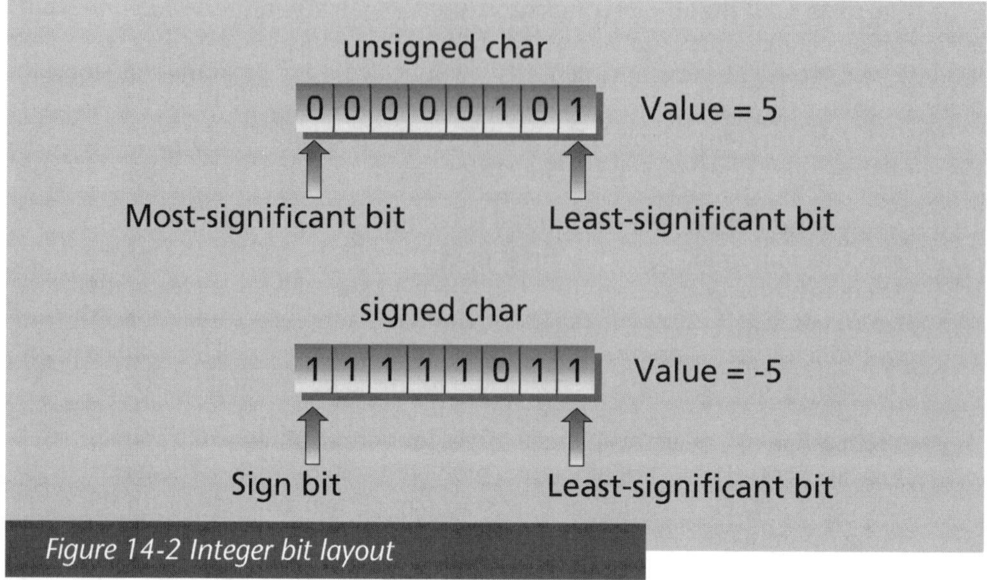

Figure 14-2 Integer bit layout

SHIFTING

The two shift operators, left shift (<<) and right shift (>>), are binary operators; they shift the first operand a distance given by the second operand. These operators use two less-than characters or two greater-than characters. The expression *op1 << amount* copies the value of *op1* to a temporary location and moves all bits to the left (towards the most-significant bit) *amount* places, and *op1 >> amount* moves all bits to the right (toward the least-significant bit) *amount* places. The second operand must be a positive integer—you cannot shift a negative distance. Figure 14-3 shows shifting operations for op1 = 5 and amount = 3.

All bits move in unison so that no values are lost, except at the end of the integer in the direction of the shift. At that end, there is no place for the shifted bits to go, so they simply disappear ("into the bit bucket," as some programmers jokingly say). When you shift left, for each bit lost at the left end of the integer, a new bit appears at the right end; C dictates that each new bit on the right will be 0. A similar rule holds for right shifting of **unsigned** integers: new bits on the left end are filled with 0s. However, C does not dictate the value of new bits when a **signed** integer shifts right; some machines will replicate the original sign bit, and others will set the new values to 0.

LEFT SHIFT OPERATOR

You can see the left shift operator in action in the next program.

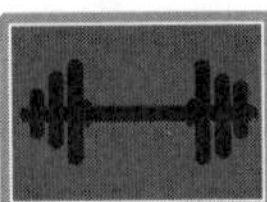

Listing 14.1 BITOP.C Bit operations—left shift

DO: • Enter, compile, and run BITOP
• Enter 3

```
#include <stdio.h>
void main()
{
   int amount;
```


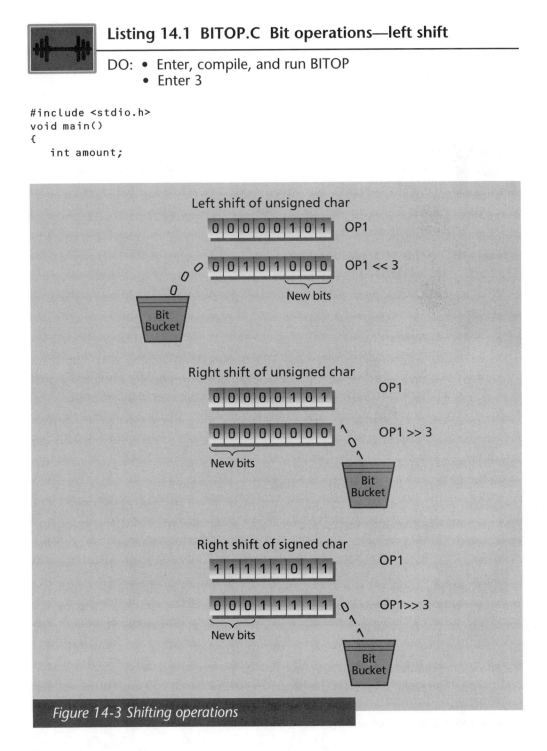

Figure 14-3 Shifting operations

```
    unsigned char operand = 5;

    printf("Enter a shift amount (1-8): ");
    scanf("%d", &amount);

    printf("\n  Result of left shift: %d", operand << amount);
    printf("\nValue of first operand: %d", operand);
}
```

RESULT:

```
C:\>BITOP
Enter a shift amount (1-8): 3

  Result of left shift: 40
Value of first operand: 5
```

ANALYSIS:

1. The program defines an unsigned 8-bit integer *operand* and initializes it to 5, then prompts you to enter the second operand, the shift amount. Notice that the types of the two operands are different—they don't have to be the same for shifting.

2. The printf() statement displays the result of the left shift expression. Note that the value of *operand* does not change during this process, as evidenced by the last display line.

Left shift is the equivalent of multiplying by 2 for every shifted bit position: *operand << 1* multiplies *operand* by 2 and *operand << 3* multiplies it by 8. In the BITOP program, the result of shifting the value 5 to the left 3 places is 40—the same as 5 * 8. This is a much faster method of performing power-of-two multiplication than using the arithmetic operator (*); however, you should always use the arithmetic operator unless speed is really necessary because multiplying by left shifting obscures the purpose of the statements. Another programmer will clearly understand what the expression, *operand * 32,* means, but the intended result of the equivalent expression, *operand << 5,* is not nearly so clear. If left shifting multiplies an integer, then right shifting must divide, so right shifting is a fast way to divide an integer by a power of 2.

The shift operators are nondestructive in that they do not directly change the operand values. If you want to alter the value of the first operand, you must do so with an assignment of the form:

```
operand = operand << amount;
```

Or better yet, use the shorter notation of a compound assignment operator:

```
operand <<= amount;
```

Recall from Chapter 5 that you can combine assignment with any of the arithmetic operators, like +=. You can do the same with all five binary bitwise operators (&=, |=, ^=, <<=, >>=) to produce a shorthand operator notation. Modify the previous program to use this form of assignment operator.

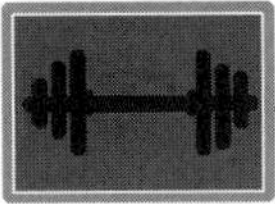

Listing 14.2 BITOP2.C Bit operations—left shift

DO:
- Modify BITOP to assign the result to the first operand
- Compile and run BITOP2
- Enter 3

```
#include <stdio.h>
void main()
{
   int amount;
   unsigned char operand = 5;

   printf("Enter a shift amount (1-8): ");
   scanf("%d", &amount);

   printf("\n   Result of left shift: %d",
       operand <<= amount);                                /*1*/
   printf("\n Value of first operand: %d", operand);
}
```

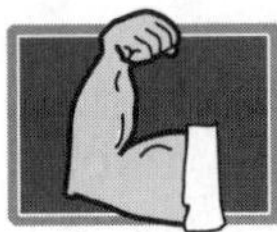

RESULT:

```
C:\>BITOP2
Enter a shift amount (1-8): 3

   Result of left shift: 40
 Value of first operand: 40
```

ANALYSIS:

Now *operand* receives the result, 40, because of the left-shift assignment operator (<<=) on line /*1*/.

AND OPERATOR

The bitwise AND (&) is a binary operator that returns a value based on corresponding bits in the two integer operands. The AND returns a 1 in a bit position if both operand bits are 1; otherwise, it returns 0. Therefore, the result of applying the AND operator to two operands is an integer with bits set only where both operands have bits set. For example, the result of 1100 & 1010 is 1000. The result of an AND expression is the same type as the two operands. Tables of all possible values are called truth tables. Table 14-1 is a *truth table* of all the possible outcomes of an AND between two bits.

One of the best uses for the AND operator is to select particular bits from an integer with a *mask*. A mask is an integer with the desired bit locations set to 1. If you AND the mask with another operand, the result has 0 bits everywhere except where the mask bits are set. That's because **1 & bitvalue** is **bitvalue**, and **0 & bitvalue** is **0**, regardless of whether **bitvalue** is 0 or 1. Figure 14-4 is an example of masking.

The result, *op1 & mask* is the same as *op1* for the bit locations that have 1s in the *mask*, and all other bit locations are 0. If you look at the individual bits in Figure 14-4, you can see bitwise AND results for all the possible combinations of bit operand values. On the left of each operand (*op1* and *mask*), you see four instances of 0 bit values ANDed to a 0 result, then a 0 in *op1* ANDed with a 1 in *mask* to yield 0, then a 1 in *op1* ANDed with a 1 in *mask* to yield 1; then another 0 in *op1* with a 1 in *mask* to yield 0, and finally, on the right end, a 1 in *op1* ANDed with 0 in *mask* to result in a 0.

Bit 1	Bit 2	Bit 1& Bit 2
0	0	0
0	1	0
1	0	0
1	1	1

Table 14-1 Outcomes of bitwise AND

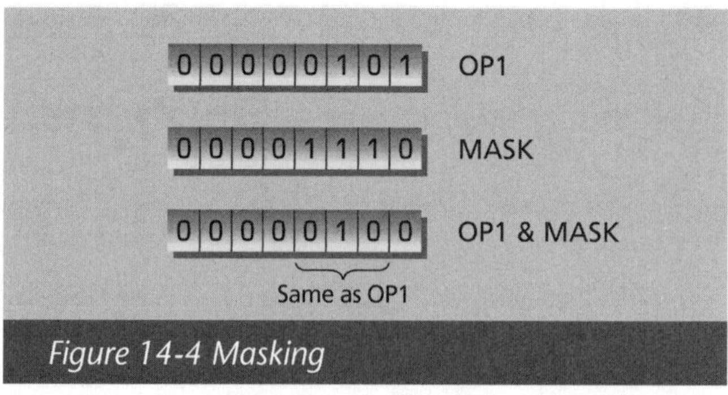

Figure 14-4 Masking

You can use the right-shift operator with the AND to display the individual bits in an integer—this will be useful for observing the effects of other bitwise operators. You can do this with a function to display an integer in binary format, which will be like having a "%b" format specifier for printf(). There is no such specifier in C, but your next program will help make up the deficiency.

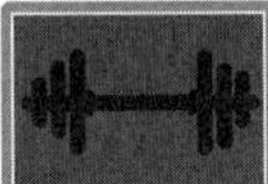

Listing 14.3 BITOP3.C Bit operations—left shift

DO:
- Add a function to show individual bits
- Compile and run BITOP3
- Enter 3

```
#include <stdio.h>
void show_bits(unsigned char);                                    /*1*/
void main()
{
   int amount;
   unsigned char operand = 5;

   printf("Enter a shift amount (1-8): ");
   scanf("%d", &amount);

   printf("\nOperand before: ");                                  /*2*/
   show_bits(operand);                                            /*3*/
   printf("\n    and after: ");                                   /*4*/
   show_bits(operand << amount);                                  /*5*/
   printf("  left shift");                                        /*6*/
}

void show_bits(unsigned char num)                                 /*7*/
{                                                                 /*8*/
   int i;                                                         /*9*/
   unsigned char mask = 0x80;                                     /*10*/

   for (i=0; i<8; ++i)                                            /*11*/
   {                                                              /*12*/
              if (mask & num)                                     /*13*/
                     printf("1");                                 /*14*/
              else                                                /*15*/
                     printf("0");                                 /*16*/
              mask >>= 1;                                         /*17*/
       }                                                          /*18*/
}
                                                                  /*19*/
```

RESULT:

```
C:\>BITOP3
Enter a shift amount (1-8): 3

Operand before: 00000101
     and after: 00101000  left shift
```

ANALYSIS:

1. The output generated by function show_bits() clearly displays the bit pattern before and after shifting.

2. Line /*1*/ declares the prototype for the new show_bits() function; it has one argument, an *unsigned char*, and no return value.
3. Lines /*2–6*/ in the main function call show_bits() from within a new sequence of display statements to show the operand before and after shifting.
4. Lines /*7–19/ define the function show_bits(); the incoming parameter is called *num*.
5. Line /*10*/ defines a *mask* which will be used to pick off the bits from *num* one at a time; the definition statement initializes *mask* to hexadecimal 80, which is the binary number 10000000 (the most significant bit is set).
6. The *for* loop executes 8 times, once for each bit in the unsigned char *num*.
7. On line /*13*/, the *if* expression tests to see if the current bit designated by *mask* is set, and if so, line /*14*/ displays a '1'; otherwise, line /*16*/ displays a '0'. The expression *mask & num* returns a value with bits set in which both *mask* AND *num* have the same bits set. Because *mask* has only one bit set, the expression tests to see whether the corresponding bit is set in *num*.
8. Line /*17*/ shifts the *mask* bit one position to the right to examine the next bit in num.

Figure 14-5 shows the bit pattern in *mask* at each cycle of the loop. Each cycle of the loop positions the mask bit to test a different bit in the character parameter.

Other examples in this chapter will call function show_bits(), but we will not repeat the source code in these programs. You can either carry the source for show_bits() over from example to example, or put it in a separate file, compile it, and use a separate link step. Here are the steps for putting function show_bits() in a separate file named SHOW_BITS.C and linking it with BITOP4:

```
C:\> pc/c SHOW_BITS                /* Compile SHOW_BITS */
C:\> pc/c BITOP4                   /* Compile BITOP4 */
C:\> pcl BITOP4, SHOW_BITS         /* Link */
```

RIGHT SHIFT OPERATOR

The next program performs a right shift on an unsigned integer.

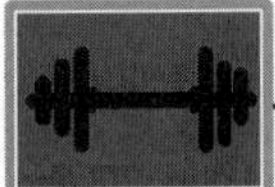

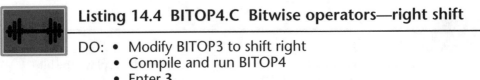

Listing 14.4 BITOP4.C Bitwise operators—right shift

DO:
- Modify BITOP3 to shift right
- Compile and run BITOP4
- Enter **3**

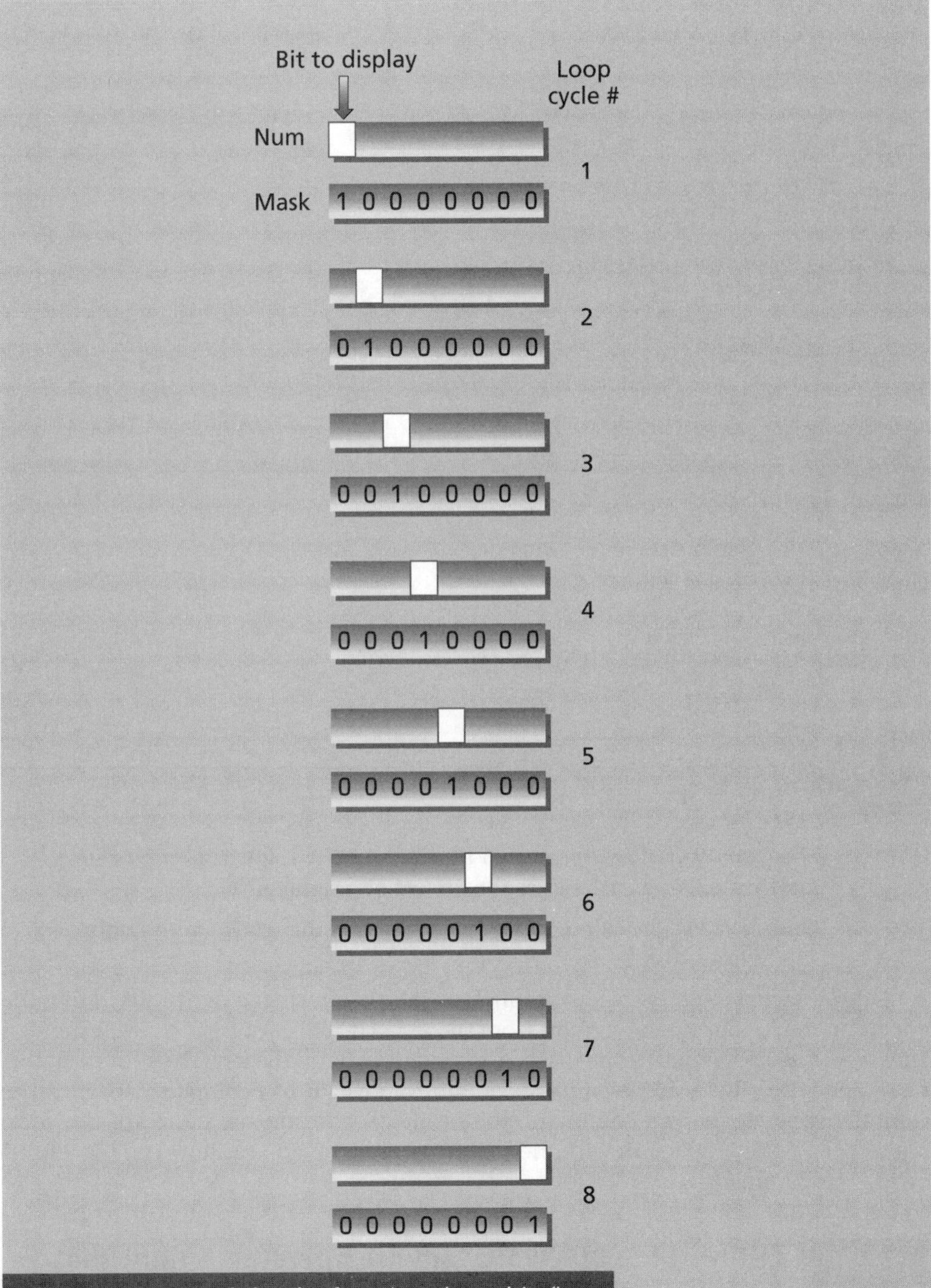

Figure 14-5 Mask for the function show_bits()

```
#include <stdio.h>
void show_bits(unsigned char);
void main()
{
   int amount;
   unsigned char operand = 0xA0;                                  /*1*/

   printf("Enter a shift amount (1-8): ");
   scanf("%d", &amount);

   printf("\nOperand before: ");
   show_bits(operand);
   printf("\n    and after: ");
   show_bits(operand >> amount);                                  /*2*/
   printf(" right shift");                                        /*3*/
}
```

RESULT:

```
C:\>BITOP4
Enter a shift amount (1-8): 3

Operand before: 10100000
     and after: 00010100 right shift
```

ANALYSIS:

1. Line /*1*/ initializes *operand* so that two of the higher-order bits are set; this makes it easier to see the effect of a right shift.
2. On line /*2*/, the call to show_bits() displays the results of the right-shift expression.

A right shift of a signed integer is different from an unsigned right shift in that the operation **may** replicate the sign bit from the left. The effect of right shift on the sign bit is machine-dependent; some machines may fill 0s in on the left. The shift operators correspond directly to shift commands built into the CPU of a computer, so when the compiler generates a shift command, the result depends on the design of the computer. Try a signed right shift with the following program and see how your PC implements this command.

Listing 14.5 BITOP5.C Bitwise operators—right shift

DO: • Modify BITOP4 for right shift of signed operand

- Compile and run BITOP5
- Enter 3

```
#include <stdio.h>
void show_bits(unsigned char);
void main()
{
   int amount;
   signed char operand = -5;                                          /*1*/

   printf("Enter a shift amount (1-8): ");
   scanf("%d", &amount);

   printf("\nOperand before: ");
   show_bits(operand);
   printf("\n    and after: ");
   show_bits(operand >> amount);
   printf(" right shift");
}
```

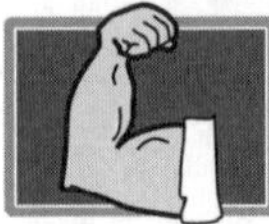

RESULT:

```
C:\>BITOP5
Enter a shift amount (1-8): 3

Operand before: 11111011
     and after: 11111111 right shift
```

ANALYSIS:

1. Line /*1*/ declares *operand* to be a signed 8-bit integer and initializes it to a negative number so the sign bit will be set. The Power C default for type c*har* is *unsigned,* so line /*1*/ uses the qualifier *signed* to make *operand* a signed variable.
2. The program displays 1s after the right shift operation. This result shows that a program running under Power C on an IBM PC replicates the sign bit for a right shift of a signed value.
3. If the **after** result shows three 0s on the left, then your machine does not replicate the sign bit; instead it adds 0s on the left side.

OR AND EXCLUSIVE OR OPERATORS

The bitwise OR (|) is a binary operator that returns a value by combining two integer operands in the following way: Each bit in the returned value is the result of examining

OP1	OP1	OR OP1 OP2	XOR OP1 OP2
0	0	0	0
0	1	1	1
1	0	1	1
1	1	1	0

Table 14-2 Outcomes of Bitwise OR and Exclusive OR

bits in the same locations of the two operands. If either operand bit is 1, the resulting bit is 1; otherwise, it is 0. Therefore, the result of applying the OR operator to two operands is an integer with bits set where either operand has a bit set.

The Exclusive OR (^) is similar, except that each return bit is 0 if both operand bits are 1; the result of applying the Exclusive OR operator to two operands is an integer with bits set wherever one and only one operand has a bit set. Table 14-2 is a *truth table* of all the possible outcomes of an OR and an Exclusive OR.

You may occasionally see the Exclusive OR abbreviated as XOR. The following program displays the bit values after applying an OR and an XOR operator.

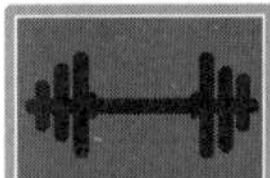

Listing 14.6 BITOP6.C Bitwise operators—OR, and XOR

DO:
- Modify BITOP4 to use OR (|) and XOR (^)
- Compile and run BITOP6
- Enter **3**

```
#include <stdio.h>
void show_bits(unsigned char);
void main()
{
   unsigned char op1 = 0x55;  /* Bit pattern 01010101 */        /*1*/
   unsigned char op2;                                            /*2*/

   printf("Enter an operand (0-255): ");                         /*3*/
   scanf("%d", &op2);

   printf("\nProgram operand: ");                                /*4*/
   show_bits(op1);
   printf("\n  Entered value: ");                               /*5*/
   show_bits(op2);                                               /*6*/
   printf("\n-----------------------");                          /*7*/
   printf("\n    ORed result: ");                                /*8*/
   show_bits(op1 | op2);                                         /*9*/
   printf("\n-----------------------");                          /*10*/
   printf("\n   XORed result: ");                                /*11*/
   show_bits(op1 ^ op2);                                         /*12*/
}
```

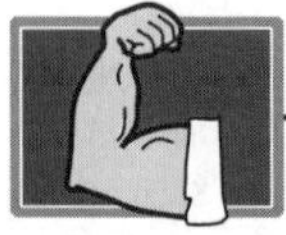

RESULT:

```
C:\>BITOP6
Enter an operand (0-255): 3

Program operand: 01010101
  Entered value: 00000011
---------------------
    ORed result: 01010111
---------------------
   XORed result: 01010110
```

ANALYSIS:

1. Line /*1*/ initializes the first operand with a hexadecimal value that corresponds to an alternating bit pattern, and line /*3*/ prompts you to enter the second operand. Lines /*4–6*/ display the bit patterns of the two operands.
2. Line /*9*/ displays the result of applying the OR operator (|) to the two operands. The four least significant bits present every combination of two binary values—you might recognize the truth table from Table 14–2 in these values.
3. The call to show_bits() on line /*12*/ displays the result of the Exclusive OR operator (^).

The XOR operator has very specialized uses—one important application is animated graphics. Integers in one area of computer memory can hold graphics information for the background of a scene, while integers in another area represent the foreground image. You can make the foreground move across the background by applying repeated XOR operations between selected integers of the foreground and background. For example, suppose a background integer consisted of an alternating pattern of 1s and 0s, 01010101. You could impose a foreground pattern of four 1s in the middle and then erase it by applying the XOR operator twice, as illustrated by Figure 14-6.

In the central zone where the foreground pattern exists, the composite result is a combination of both the background and the foreground patterns. You will use XOR to animate part of a graphics image in the last exercise of this chapter.

PACKING DATA WITH AND/OR OPERATORS

The OR operator is frequently used to compress data before storage or transmission, and the AND operator plays a key role in uncompressing the data while reading it from storage or at the receiving end of a communications line. You can perform some data compression of your own with the next program, which packs two numbers into each byte of storage. A nibble is an element of memory that is 4 bits in size; there are two nibbles per byte. If you have integer values that are all less than 16, they can be stored in a nibble. Of course, they can also be stored in an 8-bit byte, but half of the byte would never be used—wasted space. The next program packs some 4-bit numbers, two to a byte.

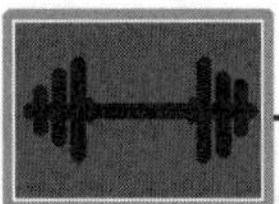

Listing 14.7 NIBBLES.C 4-bit nibbles

DO: • Enter, compile, and run NIBBLES

```
#include <stdio.h>
void show_bits(unsigned char);
void main()
{
   FILE *fp;
   int n;
   int i;
   unsigned char pack[8];

/* Pack 16 integers into 8 bytes */

   for (i=0,n=0; i<8; ++i,n+=2)
   {
        pack[i] = n | ((n + 1) << 4);
        printf("\nByte %d: ", i);
        show_bits(pack[i]);
   }

/* Write the data to a file */

   fp = fopen("NIBBLES.DAT", "wb");
   fwrite(pack, 8, 1, fp);
   fclose(fp);
}
```

RESULT:

```
C:\>NIBBLES

Byte 0: 00010000
Byte 1: 00110010
Byte 2: 01010100
Byte 3: 01110110
Byte 4: 10011000
Byte 5: 10111010
Byte 6: 11011100
Byte 7: 11111110
```

Background 01010101

XOR
with

Foreground 00111100

composite
bit
background|pattern|background
01 1010 01

XOR
with

Foreground 00111100

Background 01010101

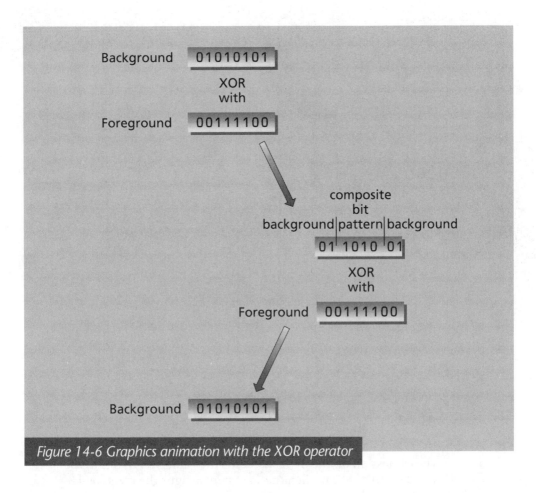

Figure 14-6 Graphics animation with the XOR operator

ANALYSIS:

1. The program declares an *unsigned char* array of 8 bytes, called *pack*, where it will pack the integers.
2. The *for* loop increments the index, *i*, to reference each element in the array *pack*, and at the same time it counts an integer, *n*, up by two for each increment.
3. The first statement in the *for* loop packs two 4-bit integers (two nibbles) into each byte of the variable *nibble*. It puts the value *n* in the right-most (least-significant) 4 bits, and it puts *n+1* in the left-most (most-significant) 4 bits. Figure 14-7 shows the workings of this statement.

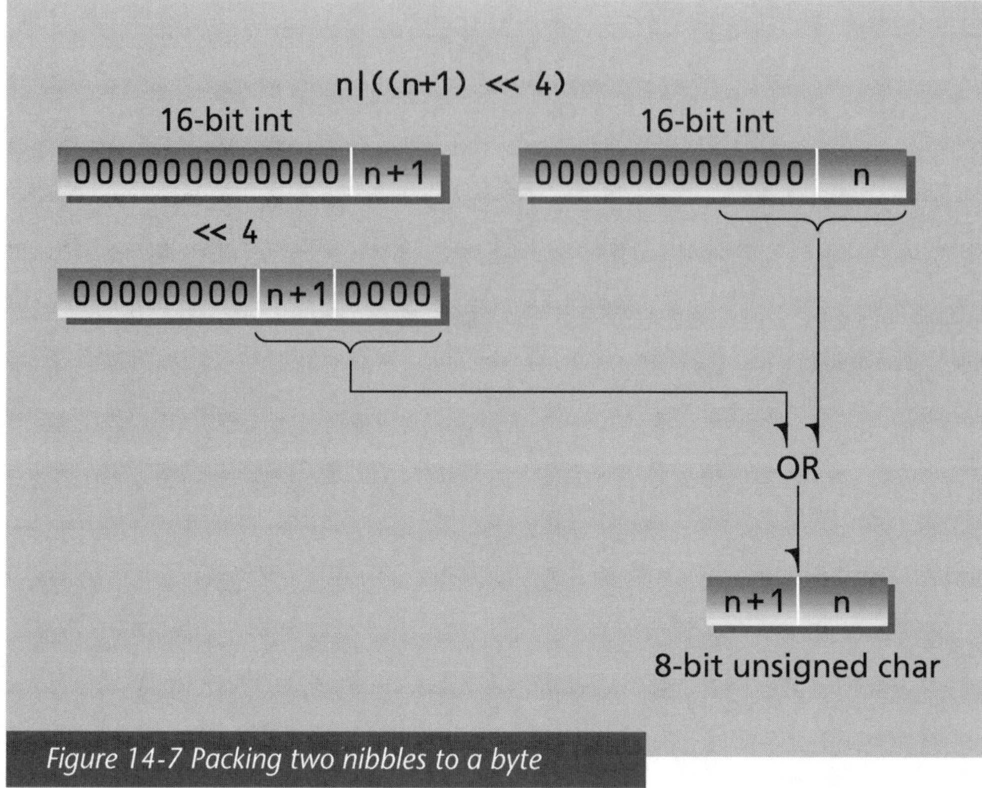

Figure 14-7 Packing two nibbles to a byte

The expression on the right side shifts the value, *n+1*, 4 bits to the left and ORs this with n, then the statement assigns the combined 8-bit result to an element in *pack*. After shifting, the two 4-bit numbers are staggered so that they perfectly dovetail with one another and fit neatly into an 8-bit byte.

4. The call to printf() and show_bits() within the *for* loop displays the contents of each packed element in *pack*.

5. The last three statements at the end of the program create a file that you can read with the next program. Notice that the fopen() statement specifies binary mode "wb" because the data bytes can assume all possible values, and you don't want character translation to occur, such as having fwrite() insert a carriage return character in front of a value of 10 (which happens to correspond to a newline character).

Now write a program to read and unpack the data with an integer mask and the bitwise AND operator.

Listing 14.8 NIBBLES2.C 4-bit nibbles

DO: • Enter, compile, and run NIBBLES2

```
#include <stdio.h>
void show_bits(unsigned char);
#define NIBBLE 0x0F                              /* Bit pattern 00001111*/
void main()
{
   FILE *fp;
   int i;
   unsigned char pack[8];

/* Read the data from the file */

   fp = fopen("NIBBLES.DAT", "rb");
   fread(pack, 8, 1, fp);
   fclose(fp);

/* Unpack 16 integers */

   for (i=0; i<8; ++i)
   {
       printf("\nByte %d: ", i);
       show_bits(pack[i]);
       printf("   Nibble1: %2d, Nibble2: %2d ",
       pack[i] & NIBBLE, pack[i] >> 4);
   }
}
```

RESULT:

```
C:\>NIBBLES2

Byte 0: 00010000   Nibble1:  0, Nibble2:  1
Byte 1: 00110010   Nibble1:  2, Nibble2:  3
Byte 2: 01010100   Nibble1:  4, Nibble2:  5
Byte 3: 01110110   Nibble1:  6, Nibble2:  7
Byte 4: 10011000   Nibble1:  8, Nibble2:  9
Byte 5: 10111010   Nibble1: 10, Nibble2: 11
Byte 6: 11011100   Nibble1: 12, Nibble2: 13
Byte 7: 11111110   Nibble1: 14, Nibble2: 15
```

ANALYSIS:

1. The preprocessor *#define* statement declares a mask constant *NIBBLE* to select the lower 4 bits of a byte. A hexadecimal F is the same as binary 1111, so 0x0F is 00001111.

2. The first three executable statements in the program open the file in binary mode and read 8 bytes of data into the array *pack*.
3. The *for* loop unpacks 16 values from the 8 integers. The show_bits() statement displays the value of each element in *pack* as it is read from the file. The last printf() displays the separate nibbles unpacked from each byte. The most important parts of this statement are the two expressions: (1) *pack[i] & NIBBLE* returns the value of the first (or least-significant) 4 bits, and (2) *pack[i]* >> 4 returns the value of the most-significant 4 bits, shifted right. You don't need a mask here, because the process of shifting the *unsigned char* to the right fills the left 4 bits with 0s.

COMPLEMENT

The *complement* (~) is a unary operator, and it returns a value that is the *one's complement* of the single operand. Stated simply, the complement operator inverts all the bits in the operand—all bits that are 1 in the operand become 0 in the result and vice versa. The one's complement is a **logical** operation, whereas the two's complement is an **arithmetic** operation. Computers use two's complement representations of negative numbers to make addition and subtraction easier. You can derive the bit pattern of a negative number by inverting all the bits of the positive number (taking the one's complement) and adding one. Figure 14-8 shows how to derive a two's complement bit pattern for the value, -5.

You can generate the one's complement of a number with the next program.

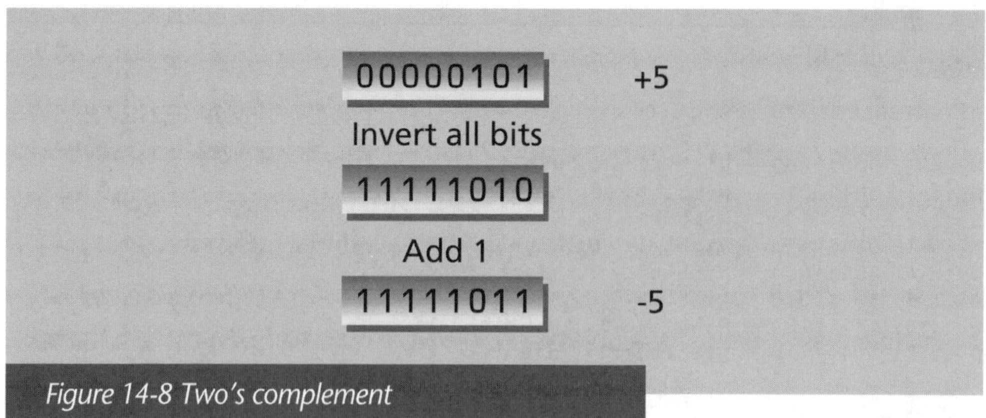

Figure 14-8 Two's complement

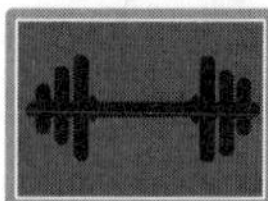

Listing 14.9 BITOP7.C Bitwise operators—complement

DO: • Modify BITOP5 to use COMPLEMENT (~)
• Compile and run BITOP7

```
#include <stdio.h>
void show_bits(unsigned char);
void main()
{
   unsigned char operand = 0x55;                              /*1*/

   printf("\nOperand before: ");
   show_bits(operand);
   printf("\n    and after: ");
   show_bits(~operand);                                       /*2*/
   printf(" complement");                                     /*3*/
}
```

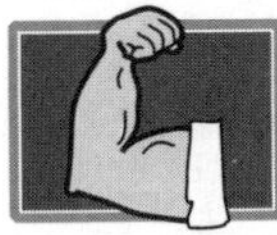

RESULT:

```
C:\>BITOP7

Operand before: 01010101
    and after: 10101010 complement
```

ANALYSIS:

1. Line /*1*/ initializes the operand so that every other bit is on.
2. Line /*2*/ displays the result of applying the complement operator—each bit is the opposite of the original value.

You can use the complement operator with masking to clear a selected bit pattern. For example, you could set the first nibble of one of the bytes in the above program to 0 with this statement:

```
pack[i] &= ~NIBBLE;
```

which is equivalent to:

```
pack[i] = pack[i] & ~NIBBLE;
```

The first representation, using the AND assignment operator (&=), is preferable. The result of *~NIBBLE* is 11110000, so ANDing this with any 8-bit pattern sets the 4 bits on the right to 0 and leaves the left 4 bits unchanged.

FLAGS AND BIT FIELDS

A flag is a data value that signifies an event or status; in programming, you often need to make a note that something occurred so that elsewhere in the program you can check on it. A flag can have a TRUE/FALSE value, or it can hold a range of integer values, or even characters. An example was introduced in Chapter 7 (Program 7.18,

NESTED4), in which a flag was used to exit from a nested loop. There you set a variable (a flag) in the inner loop to signal completion, then tested the flag in the outer loop to break and exit from the loop. This program devoted a whole variable (an *int*) to the flag, but it is possible to set flags with just one, or a few, bits. A group of flag bits within an integer is sometimes called a *field*.

Suppose you are a programmer for a large chain of hotels. The marketing department of the chain is conducting a study, and they want to track room usage closely for a period of 6 months. They are interested in the demand for rooms depending on what type of beds are in the rooms and whether smoking is allowed. Your task is to receive a daily report on room usage from each hotel. Because there are a large number of rooms and a large number of hotels, the central office wants to minimize communication costs by packing the information for each room into one 16-bit integer as follows:

Bits	Contents
0-9	Room number
10	1 = room was occupied the previous night
11	1 = smoking room, 0 = nonsmoking room
12-13	Bed configuration: 00 = one twin 01 = two twins 10 = one queen 11 = two queens
14-15	Not used

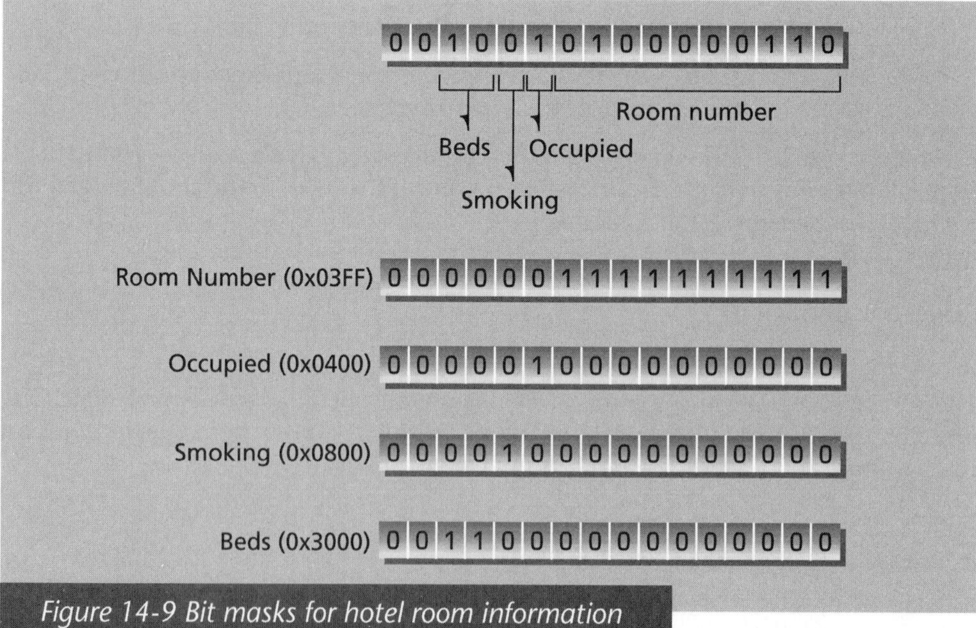

Figure 14-9 Bit masks for hotel room information

Your PC receives the information from a modem attached to a telephone line and writes it to a file. You can then read the integer values from the file and access the individual fields with the next program. Figure 14-9 shows how the mask bit patterns correspond to hexadecimal values and to the room information fields.

The program doesn't actually read a file to retrieve room information; instead, it initializes a variable to a likely bit configuration.

Listing 14.10 ROOMS.C Hotel room information

DO: • Enter, compile, and run ROOMS

```
#include <stdio.h>
#define NUMBER       0x03FF      /* Room number */
#define OCCUPIED     0x0400      /* Room occupied or not */
#define SMOKING      0x0800      /* Smoking or nonsmoking */
#define BEDS         0x3000      /* Bed configuration */
void main()
{
   unsigned int room = 0x2506;

   printf("\nThe room number is %d", room & NUMBER);

   if (room & OCCUPIED)
       printf("\nThe room was occupied");
   else
       printf("\nThe room was not occupied");

   if (room & SMOKING)
       printf("\nIt is a smoking room");
   else
       printf("\nIt is a nonsmoking room");

   printf("\nThe room has ");
   switch (room & BEDS)
   {
       case 0x0000:
              printf("1 twin bed");
              break;

       case 0x1000:
              printf("2 twin beds");
              break;

       case 0x2000:
```

```
                printf("1 queen bed");
                break;

        case 0x3000:
                printf("2 queen beds");
                break;
    }
}
```

RESULT:

```
C:\>ROOMS

The room number is 262
The room was occupied
It is a nonsmoking room
The room has 1 queen bed
```

ANALYSIS:

1. The program defines four masks, *NUMBER, OCCUPIED, SMOKING,* and *BEDS,* to select particular fields from the room data according to the scheme in Figure 14-9.
2. The program initializes the variable *room* to a bit pattern that represents a valid room configuration.
3. The program extracts each field value by ANDing the variable *room* with the appropriate mask. To display the information, the program uses the extracted values in three different ways:
   - When the field is an integer value (like room number), a printf() statement displays the result of the AND expression directly. The first printf() statement in ROOMS uses this technique.
   - When the field can be either TRUE or FALSE (occupied or not, smoking or nonsmoking), the program just tests the extracted value with an *if* statement to call the appropriate printf(). The next two statements in ROOMS represent this method.
   - The value of the bed configuration field is a code that must be deciphered to be meaningful. The program uses a *switch* statement to interpret the extracted code and display appropriate messages. The *switch* statement uses a hexadecimal constant for each *case*—

this is for readability; it is easier to visualize the matchup of hex code values than it is for decimal values.

Besides masking, C provides another way to reference groups of bits within an integer: *structure bit fields*. Bit fields are declared as part of a structure in the following manner:

```
struct tag
{
     field_type1 field_name1 : field_size1;
     field_type2 field_name2 : field_size2;
} name_list;
```

You can only declare bit fields to be type *int* or *unsigned int*; *unsigned* is the usual choice. Field names are identifiers used to refer to bit fields; the size of a field (the number of bits) is attached to the name with a colon (:). A bit-field structure starts at one end of the variable and assigns contiguous bit sequences to members in the order in which they are listed. C does not dictate which end represents the start, so the left-to-right or right-to-left order depends on the compiler. Figure 14-10 shows the layout of the room information integer for the bit-field structure declared in the next program; it reflects the right-to-left order imposed by Power C on an IBM PC.

You refer to members of a bit-field structure in the same way as for a regular structure, with the structure member operator (.). Bit-field members don't have addresses because they can be smaller than the smallest addressable memory element, the byte; therefore, you cannot use the address operator (&). A member of a bit-field structure returns the value of the bits as a right-justified integer, that is, the value is returned in the least-significant bits of the integer. For instance, if a member consists of bits two and three, both set to 1, then the value of the member is 3 (bit pattern 0011), not 12 (or 1100). Accessing bit values with a bit-field structure is often more convenient than with masking. It is not necessarily more efficient, though; the compiler simply does the work of masking and shifting for you and in the end generates basically the same executable code. The next program uses a bit-field structure to retrieve and display the hotel room information.

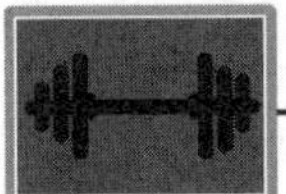

Listing 14.11 ROOMS2.C Hotel room information

DO:
- Convert ROOMS to use structure bit fields
- Compile and run ROOMS2
- Enter 2506

```
#include <stdio.h>
void main()
{
   struct info                                          /*1*/
   {                                                    /*2*/
      unsigned number:   10;                            /*3*/
```

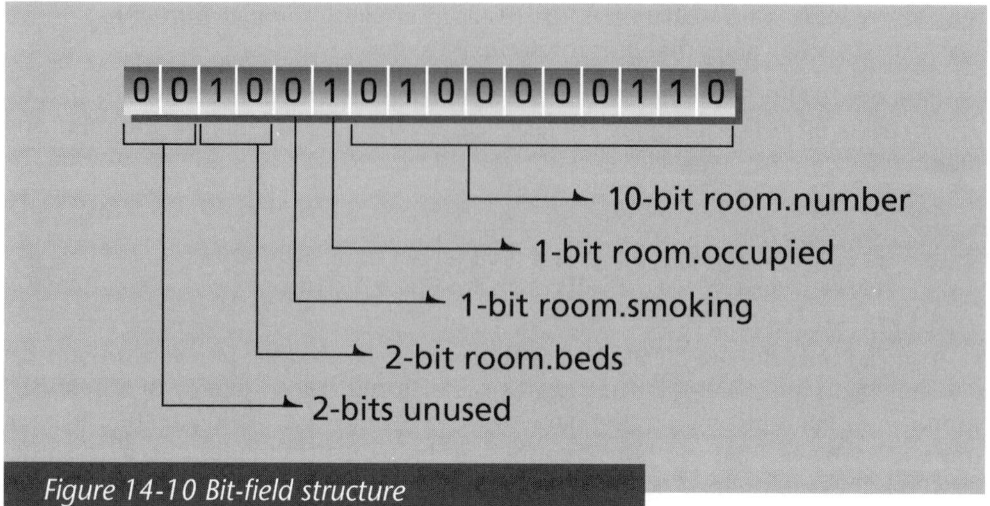

Figure 14-10 Bit-field structure

```
    unsigned occupied:  1;                                          /*4*/
    unsigned smoking:   1;                                          /*5*/
    unsigned beds:      2;                                          /*6*/
    unsigned:           2;                                          /*7*/
};                                                                  /*8*/

struct info room;                                                   /*9*/

printf("Enter a room information value: ");                         /*10*/
scanf("%X", &room);                                                 /*11*/

printf("\nThe room number is %d", room.number);                     /*12*/

if (room.occupied)                                                  /*13*/
    printf("\nThe room was occupied");
else
    printf("\nThe room was not occupied");

if (room.smoking)                                                   /*14*/
    printf("\nIt is a smoking room");
else
    printf("\nIt is a nonsmoking room");

printf("\nThe room has ");
switch (room.beds)                                                  /*15*/
{
    case 0:                                                         /*16*/
    printf("1 twin bed");
           break;

    case 1:                                                         /*17*/
```

```
                printf("2 twin beds");
                break;

        case 2:                                                     /*18*/
                printf("1 queen bed");
                break;

        case 3:                                                     /*19*/
                printf("2 queen beds");
                break;
    }
}
```

RESULT:

```
C:\>ROOMS2

The room number is 262
The room was occupied
It is a nonsmoking room
The room has 1 queen bed
```

ANALYSIS:

1. The program declares a bit-field structure template *info* on lines /*1–8*/. The statement declares a total of 16 bits; the last, unused bit field is unnamed because the program will not reference it.
2. Line /*9*/ uses the template *info* to define the structure variable *room*. You cannot initialize a bit-field structure at the definition, so lines /*10–11*/ prompt you to enter a value for the room configuration.
3. Lines /*12–15*/ use the flag values in the same way as in the previous program. However, now you don't have to extract them by masking; you just refer to them as members of *room*.
4. Note that the *case* constants on lines /*16-19*/ have changed because the structure bit fields automatically return values shifted to the least-significant bit.

GRAPHICS

The role of graphics in computers is expanding; Graphical User Interfaces (GUI) are widespread on PCs, and businesses are making increased use of computers to handle pictures, drawings, and photographs. One form of graphic image can be stored in a

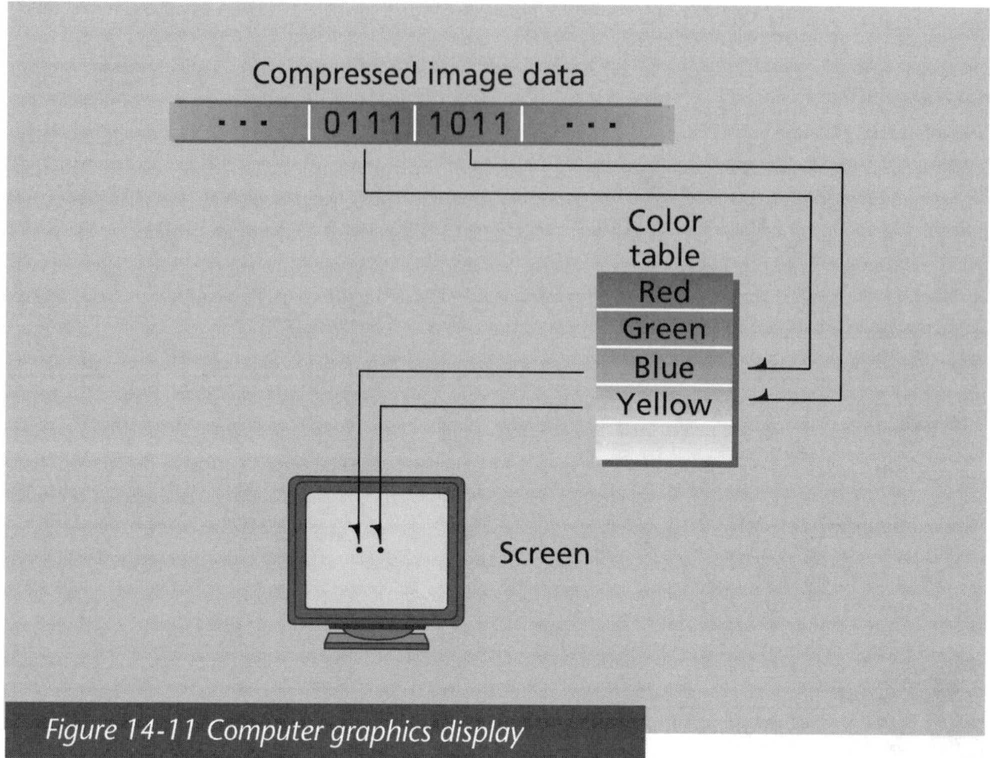

Figure 14-11 Computer graphics display

computer as a two-dimensional matrix of picture elements, or *pixels*. There can be thousands, even millions, of pixels in an image—more pixels yield a higher quality image. A standard VGA display for the IBM PC has a screen size of 640 x 480 pixels (a total of 307,200 pixels). In the world of graphics devices, this is not a particularly high quality display; a standard 8.5" x 11" page amounts to 8,415,000 pixels when printed on a 300 dot-per-inch laser printer. For a color display, each pixel is represented by a number giving the color of the image at a given point. If the display allows 16 colors, as the most basic VGA does, then an image will need 4 bits of storage for each pixel. Thus the total space requirement for a VGA image is 4 x 307,200 = 1,228,800 bits, or 153,600 bytes if all the data are packed and no bits are wasted.

A computer displays a graphic image on the screen by unpacking each pixel color number, looking up the color respresented by that number, and displaying that color at the correct place on the screen. Figure 14-11 illustrates this process.

These steps in displaying computer graphics are sometimes performed by a software program, and often these programs are written in C. We will end this chapter with an example of using bitwise operators to display a graphic image. In this case, the image pixels will be characters on the screen, so the image quality will be quite coarse, but the principles involved are the same as for high quality color images.

The following program illustrates the steps of unpacking pixel information, looking up the display intensity (color), and displaying the intensity at the correct screen location. With standard C functions, you don't have access to the actual pixels of your screen, so this program uses displayable characters to act as pixels. The program displays an image of size 16 x 16 pixels (characters), and it uses characters of different sizes to simulate colors. There are four colors (four different characters) in the image, so each pixel is represented by two bits of data. Thus, a 32-bit *long* integer can hold one row of the image (16 pixels times 2 bits per pixel), and an array of 16 *long* integers can hold the entire image. The program uses a two-bit mask to extract the individual color values from the image data.

Listing 14.12 IMAGE.C Display a graphic image

DO: Enter, compile, and run IMAGE

```
#include <stdio.h>
void main()
{
   int row;
   int col;
   char disp_char[4] = { ' ', '.', 'o', '@' };
   unsigned long mask = 3L;
   unsigned long image[16] = { 0x002AA800,
                               0x00955600,
                               0x02555580,
                               0x09555560,
                               0x25555558,
                               0xBF3F3F3F,
                               0xB3330C03,
                               0xBF330C3F,
                               0x83330C30,
                               0x833F0C3F,
                               0x95555556,
                               0x25555558,
                               0x09555560,
                               0x02555580,
                               0x00955600,
                               0x002AA800 };

   for (row=0; row<16; ++row)
   {
       printf("\n");
       for (col=0; col<16; ++col)
       {
               printf("%2c", disp_char[mask & image[row]]);
               image[row] >>= 2;
       }
   }
}
```

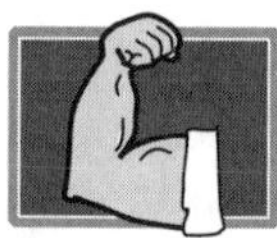

RESULT:

```
C:\>IMAGE

          o o o o o o
        o . . . . . . o
      o . . . . . . . . o
    o . . . . . . . . . . o
  o . . . . . . . . . . . . o
@ @ @   @ @ @   @ @ @   @ @ @ o
@         @     @   @   @   @ o
@ @ @     @     @   @   @ @ @ o
    @     @     @   @   @     o
@ @ @     @     @ @ @   @     o
o . . . . . . . . . . . . . . o
  o . . . . . . . . . . . . o
    o . . . . . . . . . . o
      o . . . . . . . . o
        o . . . . . . o
          o o o o o o
```

ANALYSIS:

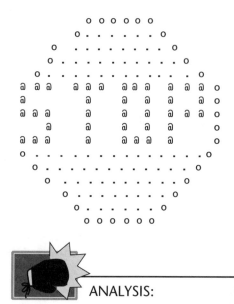

1. The program first defines three important quantities: *disp_char*, *mask*, and *image*. The array *disp_char* is initialized with four display characters, which are progressively larger; each character simulates a different pixel intensity on the screen. The *mask* has two bits set so that it can extract 2-bit pixel values. And finally, the program initializes the array *image* with hexadecimal values for the packed pixel numbers of a graphic image. The array is of type *unsigned long* (a 32-bit integer), and each row of 2-bit pixels is stored in one element of the array, so there are 16 pixels in each row. The array has 16 elements, so the number of rows is also sixteen.
2. The program begins with a *for* loop to increment down each row of the graphic image (each element of array *image*). The first printf() displays a newline character to move the cursor to the left side of each new row.
3. A nested, inner *for* loop displays each of the 16 pixels in a given row. The inner printf() statement selects one of the display characters in *disp_char* based on the result of masking the *image* array. The four possible index values (0, 1, 2, 3) select progressively larger character

sizes in *disp_char* (SPACE, '.', 'o', '@'), representing higher intensity pixels on the screen. The printf() statement gets index values from the image array by masking: *mask & image[row].*

4. Only the two least-significant bits of *mask* are set, so the program extracts pixel indexes from the image at these bit locations. The last statement in the inner loop shifts the *image* element right by two bits for each displayed pixel so that the next pixel will be located under the *mask* bits.

Figure 14-12 shows the central workings of the IMAGE program.

Array *disp_char* serves the same purpose as the color table in Figure 14-11; it determines the final display appearance for each pixel. You can alter the appearance of the image simply by changing the initialization of *disp_char*. Try it—replace the 'o' and '@' characters with '+' and 'X', then recompile and run IMAGE again.

You can animate the stop sign and make a part of the image move across the background by applying the exclusive OR operator, XOR (^). You can animate the letters, TO, and have them move upward and off the sign. To make this happen, you need to successively erase the subimage containing the letters, TO, and redisplay it in a new location. You can erase by applying XOR to the area where the subimage resides, and you can also redisplay the subimage by applying XOR again in the new location. This is conceptually the same operation as outlined previously in Figure 14-6. If you make the sequence of locations occur in a straight line, the letters will appear to "walk" across the main image. As the subimage "walks" across the background, the colors (characters) change because it blends differently with different areas of the background. Make the following modifications to the IMAGE program to see this happen.

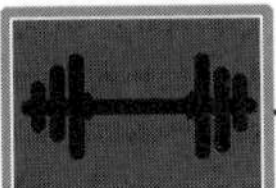

Listing 14.13 IMAGE2.C Animate a graphic image

DO:
- Add animation to IMAGE
- Compile and run IMAGE2

```
#include <stdio.h>
#include <bios.h>                                             /*1*/
void main()
{
   int i;                                                     /*2*/
   int n;                                                     /*3*/
   int row;
   int col;
   char disp_char[4] = { ' ', '.', 'o', '@' };
   unsigned long mask = 3L;
   unsigned long image2[16];                                  /*4*/
   unsigned long image[16] = { 0x002AA800,
                               0x00955600,
                               0x02555580,
```

```
                                       0x09555560,
                                       0x25555558,
                                       0xBF3F3F3F,
                                       0xB3330C03,
                                       0xBF330C3F,
                                       0x83330C30,
                                       0x833F0C3F,
                                       0x95555556,
                                       0x25555558,
                                       0x09555560,
                                       0x02555580,
                                       0x00955600,
                                       0x002AA800 };

   unsigned long subimage[5] = { 0x003F3F00,                   /*5*/
                                 0x00330C00,                   /*6*/
                                 0x00330C00,                   /*7*/
                                 0x00330C00,                   /*8*/
                                 0x003F0C00 };                 /*9*/

   for (n=5; n>-6; --n)                                        /*10*/
   {                                                           /*11*/

/* Display the image */

      clrscrn();                                               /*12*/
      for (i=0; i<16; ++i)                                     /*13*/
         image2[i] = image[i];                                 /*14*/

      for (row=0; row<16; ++row)
      {
         printf("\n");
         for (col=0; col<16; ++col)
         {
            printf("%2c",
                disp_char[mask & image2[row]]);                /*15*/
            image2[row] >>= 2;                                 /*16*/
         }
      }

/* Erase letters "TO" */

      for (i=0; i<5; ++i)                                      /*17*/
         if (n+i >= 0)                                         /*18*/
            image[n+i] ^= subimage[i];                         /*19*/

/* Move the letters "TO" */

      for (i=0; i<5; ++i)                                      /*20*/
         if (n-1+i >= 0)                                       /*21*/
            image[n-1+i] ^= subimage[i];                       /*22*/
   }                                                           /*23*/
}
```

RESULT:

```
C:\>IMAGE2

        o o o o o o
      o . . . . . . o
    o . . . . . . . . o
   o . . . . . . . . . . o
  o . . . . . . . . . . . . o
@ @ @   @ @ @   @ @ @   @ @ @ o
@         @     @   @   @   @ o
@ @ @     @     @   @   @ @ @ o
    @     @     @   @   @     o
@ @ @     @     @ @ @   @     o
o . . . . . . . . . . . . . . o
  o . . . . . . . . . . . . o
   o . . . . . . . . . . o
    o . . . . . . . . o
      o . . . . . . o
        o o o o o o

        .
        .
        .

        o o o o o o
      o . . . . . . o
    o . . . . . . . . o
   o . . . . . . . . . . o
  o . . . . . . . . . . . . o
@ @ @                   @ @ @ o
@                       @   @ o
@ @ @                   @ @ @ o
    @                   @     o
@ @ @                   @     o
o . . . . . . . . . . . . . . o
  o . . . . . . . . . . . . o
   o . . . . . . . . . . o
    o . . . . . . . . o
      o . . . . . . o
        o o o o o o
```

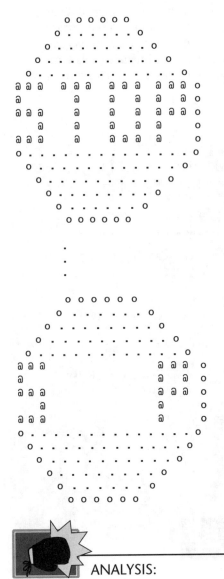

ANALYSIS:

1. Line /*1*/ includes a new header file that contains the prototype for function clrscrn() on line /*12*/. This is a nonstandard function sup-

plied by Power C that clears the screen before the program displays each new image.

2. Lines /*2–3*/ define a couple of new index variables, *i* and *n*, needed to control the sequence of events.

3. The nested *for* loop (that displays the image) shifts the image data as it extracts the color values, so the program needs to use a temporary image buffer for this operation. Line /*4*/ defines an array, *image2*, for this purpose. Lines /*13–14*/ copy the lasting image to this temporary buffer so that the program can use it on lines /*15–16*/ during the display sequence.

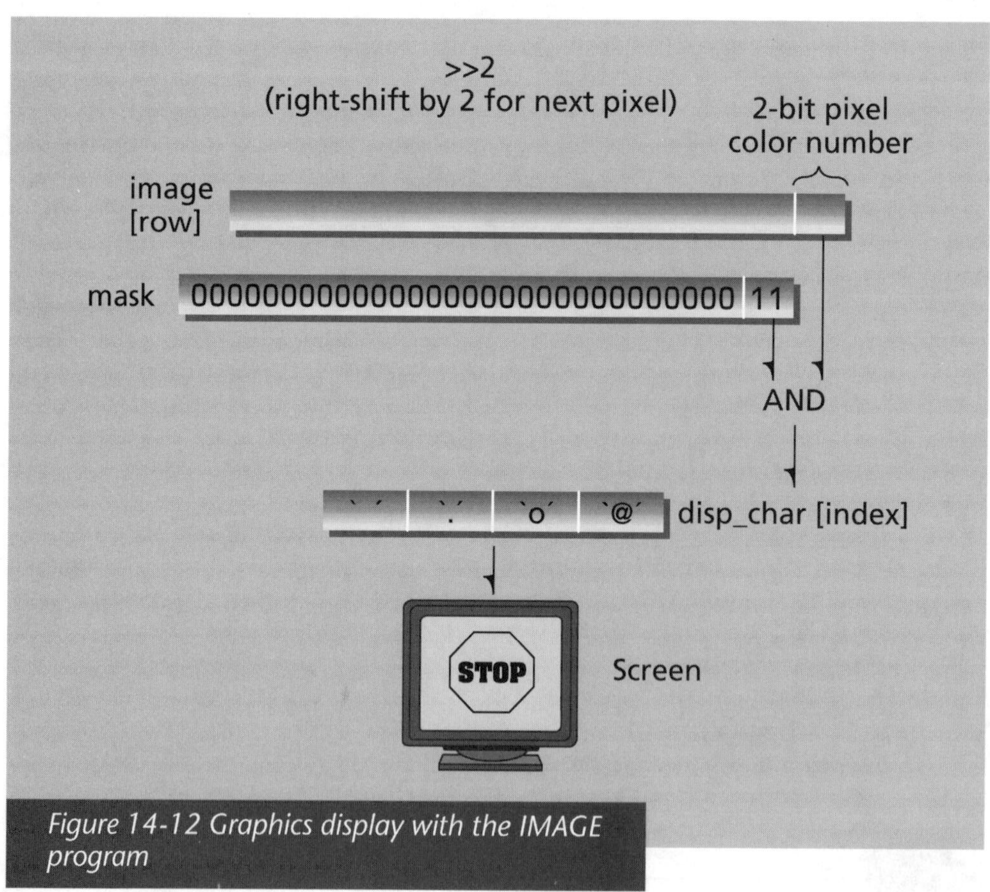

Figure 14-12 Graphics display with the IMAGE program

4. On lines /*5–9*/, the program defines and initializes the subimage array, *subimage*, containing the letters, "TO". Compare the initializer list for *subimage* to the initialize list for *image*; the *subimage* comes from the central portion of rows 6 through 10 of *image*—just the area where the letters "TO" reside.

5. Line /*10*/ starts a loop that controls the path of the letters as they "walk" off the sign. The index, *n*, starts at row 5 (the top of the letters in the sign) and decrements to -6 so that the tops of the letters move upward and off the sign far enough so that the bottom of "TO" disappears.

6. The heart of the animation process occurs on lines /*17–22*/. Lines /*17–19*/ erase the letters "TO" from the current location of the subimage. The *for* loop on line /*17*/ indexes from the top row of the subimage to the bottom row, and the statement on line /*19*/ XORs the *subimage* row with the corresponding *image* row and assigns the result (the background) to the *image*. The *if* test on line /*18*/ makes sure that the operation does not occur when the indexes go out of bounds (negative) and refer to a nonexistent array row.

7. The operation used to redisplay the letters on lines /*20–22*/ is exactly the same as that used for erasing them, except it operates at a different location, one row farther up—the index *n-1* controls the placement. The XOR operation merges *subimage* rows with *image* background rows in such a way that the next XOR will erase the subimage.

When you run IMAGE2, you can observe that the characters that form the subimage letters, "TO", change as they "walk" across the sign. This happens because the XOR makes composite colors from the foreground and the background. If you want to observe the image more closely at each step, you can insert a *getchar();* statement just after the program displays the image, and this will stop the action until you press (ENTER) each time. This demonstration of animation is relatively simple, yet the underlying techniques are the same as those used to create sophisticated color animations on high resolution displays.

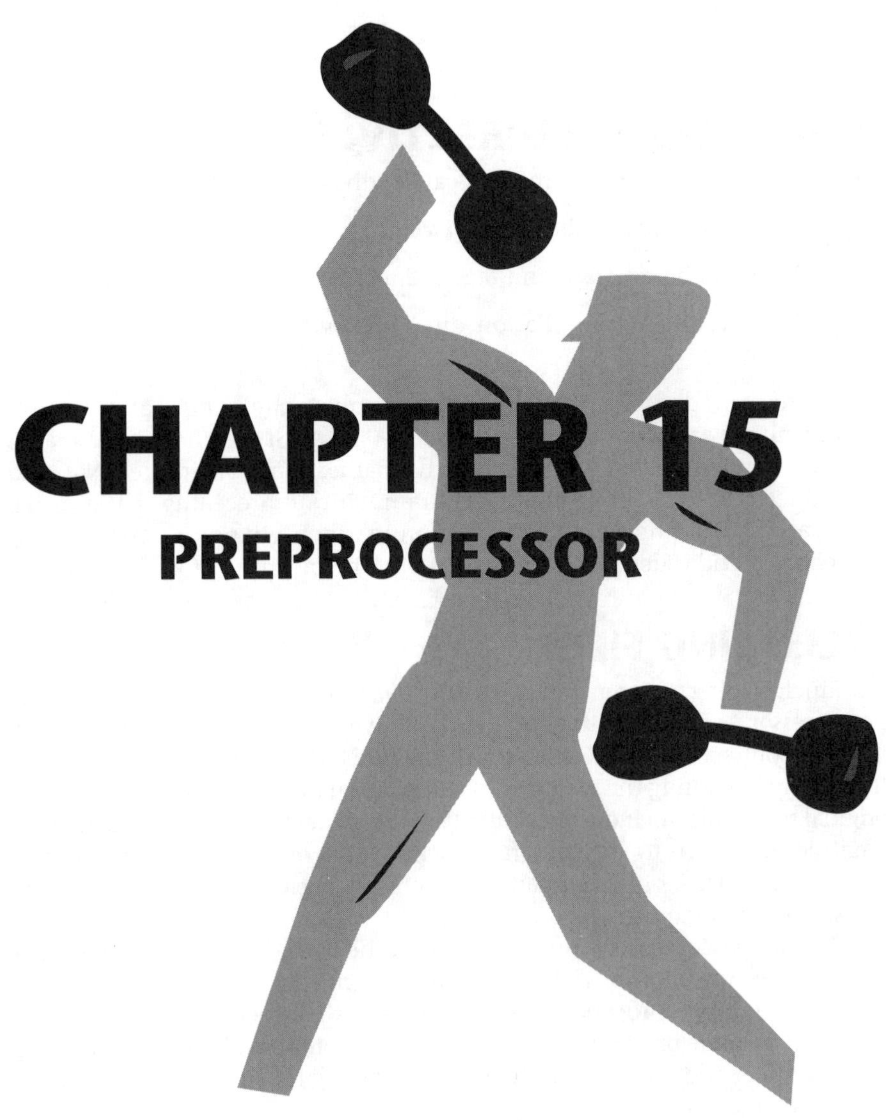

CHAPTER 15
PREPROCESSOR

The compiler *preprocessor* is true to its name—it processes program statements before the main compilation steps. The preprocessor is part of the compiler, and it alters source code statements according to directives that you insert into the program. You have made extensive use of a couple of preprocessor directives (#include and #define) in exercises throughout the book. In this chapter, you will learn about these directives in more detail, and you will gain experience with other preprocessor directives. You will learn how to use preprocessor directives to add and exclude statements, and you will cause statements to be altered in useful ways. You will also learn how to write *macros*—efficient alternatives to functions.

PREPROCESSOR DIRECTIVES

The principle preprocessor directives can be divided into three categories:

1. The file include directive (*#include*)
2. Symbolic constant and macro directives (*#define* and *#undef*)
3. Conditional compilation directives (*#if, #ifdef, #ifndef, #else, #elif, #endif*).

Preprocessor directives begin with the pound sign (#), and C allows you to precede the directives with space and tab characters. The ANSI specification also allows spaces between the pound sign and the directive name. Some older, pre-ANSI compilers require directives to begin in the first column with no preceding spaces or tabs and no spaces after the pound sign. You should ordinarily begin preprocessor directives in the first column and indent them only to clarify the meaning of nested directives.

INCLUDING FILES

The #include directive comes in two forms: *#include <header.h>* or *#include "header.h"*. The preprocessor responds to either of these directives by placing the contents of file *header.h* into the source code at the location of the #include directive. The additional lines are then compiled during the next step of compilation just as if you had typed them into the original source file. Included files are called *header* files because they usually contain statements located at the top of a program, such as other preprocessor directives and function prototypes. C header files normally have a file extension of **.h**; you can use other extensions, but **.h** is almost universal.

The difference between the two forms of the include directive is the expected location of the header file. If you enclose the header file name in double quotes, "header.h," the preprocessor will look for the file where you designate, and if you enclose it in angle brackets, <header.h>, the compiler will look in places designated by your compiler and operating system. The following list summarizes where the Power C compiler looks for header files:

Make a new header file, move it around to several different directories on your computer, and try including it from each of the different places. First, create a new directory especially for your own header files, and use the double quotes to attempt to include a header file located there.

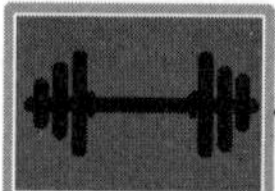

Listing 15.1 PREP.C Include a header file

DO:
- Make a new directory called *MYINCL*
- Make a header file named myhead.h with one line (use your editor):

  #define GREETING "Hello"

- Place myhead.h in the new directory and nowhere else
- Enter, compile, and run PREP

```
#include <stdio.h>
#include "myhead.h"
void main()
{
     printf(GREETING);
}
```

```
#include <stdio.h>
```

Header is located in a place designated by the compiler and operating system; use this form for standard C header files.

Search sequence for Power C:

1. directories defined by /i compile option
2. PATH directories
3. current directory

```
#include "myhead.h"
```

First search the current directory, then in the other locations; use this form for your own header files.

Search sequence for Power C:

1. current directory
2. directories defined by /i compile option
3. PATH directories

```
#include "C:\MYINCL\myhead.h"
```

Search the specified directory; use this form when you have a special directory for your own header files.

Search sequence for Power C:

1. C:\MYINCL

List 15-1 Preprocessor #include directives

RESULT:

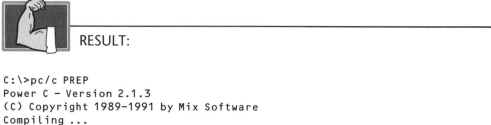

```
C:\>pc/c PREP
Power C - Version 2.1.3
(C) Copyright 1989-1991 by Mix Software
Compiling ...
PREP.C(2):#include "myhead.h"
********* ^ 77
     77: Error opening #include file
-----------------------------------------------------------------
PREP.C(5):    printf(GREETING);
*********                       ^104
      104: Undeclared identifier
-----------------------------------------------------------------
 113 lines compiled
   2 Compile errors
```

ANALYSIS:

1. If by chance you already have a directory called *MYINCL*, you should choose another name that is not a directory on your system.
2. As the error message indicates, the compiler could not find the header file; it is not located in the current directory.

In addition to the current directory, double quotes allow you to specify any directory path for the include file. For instance, you can explicitly designate directory C:\MYINCL.

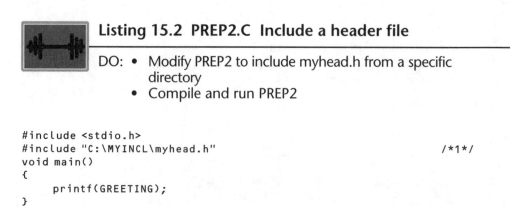

Listing 15.2 PREP2.C Include a header file

DO:
- Modify PREP2 to include myhead.h from a specific directory
- Compile and run PREP2

```
#include <stdio.h>
#include "C:\MYINCL\myhead.h"                                  /*1*/
void main()
{
    printf(GREETING);
}
```

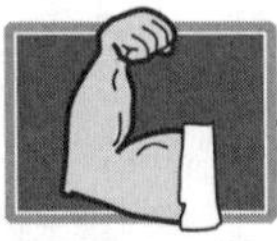

RESULT:

```
C:\>pc/c/e PREP2
Power C - Version 2.1.3
(C) Copyright 1989-1991 by Mix Software
Compiling ...
   113 lines compiled
Optimizing ...
   1 function optimized in 1 file
Linking ...
PREP2.EXE created

C:\>PREP2
Hello
```

ANALYSIS:

The compiler now finds myhead.h in the directory C:\MYINCL as instructed on line /*1*/

Change the #include directive to use angle brackets and experiment with how the compiler locates the file with this form of include.

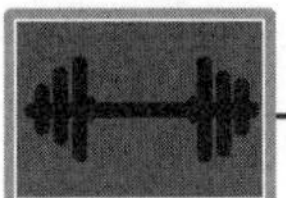

Listing 15.3 PREP3.C Include a header file

DO:
- Enclose myhead.h in angle brackets
- Compile PREP3

```
#include <stdio.h>
#include <myhead.h>                                              /*1*/
void main()
{
     printf(GREETING);
}
```

RESULT:

```
C:\>pc/c PREP3
Power C - Version 2.1.3
(C) Copyright 1989-1991 by Mix Software
Compiling ...
PREP3.C(2):#include <myhead.h>
*********  ^ 77
```

```
     77: Error opening #include file
------------------------------------------------------------
PREP3.C(5):    printf(GREETING);
*********                     ^104
       104: Undeclared identifier
------------------------------------------------------------
  113 lines compiled
    2 Compile errors
```

ANALYSIS:

1. The compiler could not find the header because it is in C:\MYINCL, not C:\WORKOUTC, as expected.

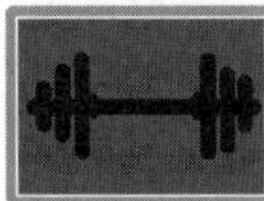

DO:
- Copy myhead.h to the directory where all the standard C header files (like stdio.h) are located (directory C:\WORKOUTC).
- Compile, link, and run PREP3

RESULT:

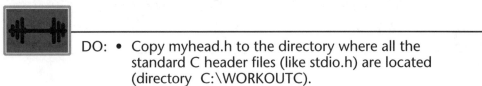

```
C:\>copy C:\MYINCL\myhead.h C:\WORKOUTC
        1 File(s) copied

C:\>pc/c/e PREP3
Power C - Version 2.1.3
(C) Copyright 1989-1991 by Mix Software
Compiling ...
  127 lines compiled
Optimizing ...
    1 function optimized in 1 file
Linking ...
PREP3.EXE created

C:\>PREP3
Hello
```

ANALYSIS:

Now the compiler can find the header file along with all the others, and it successfully locates the defined symbolic constant, "Hello."

If you are using Power C, you can work the next example to see how it uses the PATH environment variable to locate header files; otherwise, just follow along.

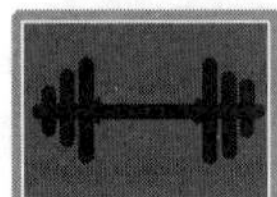

DO:
- Delete myhead.h from standard directory C:\WORKOUTC
- Add directory C:\MYINCL to the DOS PATH environment variable; first look at the current PATH setting, then add the directory to what is already there
- Compile, link, and run PREP3

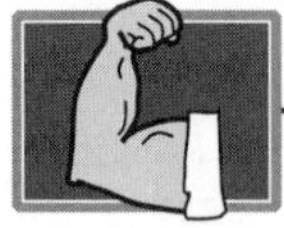

RESULT:

```
C:\>del \WORKOUTC\myhead.h

C:\>PATH
PATH=<current setting>

C:\>set PATH=<current setting>;C:\MYINCL

C:\>pc/c/e PREP3
Power C - Version 2.1.3
(C) Copyright 1989-1991 by Mix Software
Compiling ...
  127 lines compiled
Optimizing ...
    1 function optimized in 1 file
Linking ...
PREP3.EXE created

C:\>PREP3
Hello
```

ANALYSIS:

Now the compiler knows where to find the header file because the operating system environment variable PATH tells it to look in directory C:\MYINCL.

Program PREP3 illustrates the normally recommended method of including files, which is:

> Use angle brackets to include standard C header files, and use double quotes to include your own header files.

This keeps your header files separate from the C headers; yours are located with the source files, and the C headers are located with the compiler.

When you develop an application with many functions in separate files, you should place items that are common to multiple functions in a header file; then you can simply include the header in each file and avoid repetition. You should ordinarily **not** place executable source code statements in a header file; here is a list of the items normally found in header files:

Item	Syntax
Symbolic constants	`#define NAME value`
Function prototypes	`type func(arg list);`

Structure templates	`struct tag`
	`{`
	`/* members */`

Macros	`#define NAME(arg list) macro`
Typedefs	`typedef name type`

These are all nonexecutable statements that do not allocate memory; they are either preprocessor directives or type declarations. You have not yet learned about Macros and Typedefs (these topics are coming up later in this chapter and the next), but you can insert the other items (symbolic constants, function prototypes, and structure templates) in a header file, as shown in the next example.

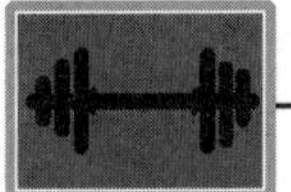

Listing 15.4 PREP4.C Include a header file

DO: • Modify myhead.h, as follows:

```
/*------------------ Symbolic constants ------------------*/

#define GREETING "Hello"

/*------------------ Structure templates -----------------*/

struct x
{
     char message[6];
};

/*------------------ Function Prototypes -----------------*/

void display(struct x);
```

ANALYSIS:

1. This header file is divided into three sections by comments. The first section holds symbolic constants; if you expand the program to use other symbolic constants, you should add them to the header in this area. The second section contains declarations for structure templates, and the third area is devoted to function prototypes.

2. The order in which items appear in the header file can be important. In this file, the prototype for function display() refers to the structure tag, *x*, so the structure must be declared first. There is nothing special about header files in this regard; these priorities are important in the same way in which they would be if you explicitly entered the statements into one of your C functions.

You have just created a header file. Now you can develop a program with two functions in separate source files. The header file contains declarations that both functions need, so you can include it at the top of each source file.

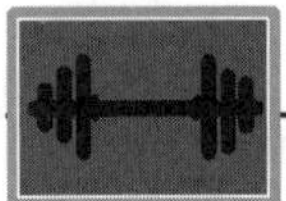

DO: • Enter the main function to file PREP4.C

```
#include "myhead.h"
void main()
{
     struct x hi = {GREETING};

     display(hi);
}
```

ANALYSIS:

The first statement includes the header, myhead.h, so that the program can declare variable *hi* by using the structure tag *x*, and so that it can initialize *hi* with the symbolic string constant *GREETING*.

DO: • Enter the following function into a separate file named DISPFUNC.C

```
#include <stdio.h>
#include "myhead.h"
void display(struct x hey)
{
      printf("%s", hey.message);
}
```

ANALYSIS:

1. This function simply displays a message transferred to it by the calling function.
2. The file needs to include the standard C header, stdio.h, to use the prototype for printf(), and it needs to include your header, myhead.h, to use the prototype for display(), and also to use the structure tag, *x*.

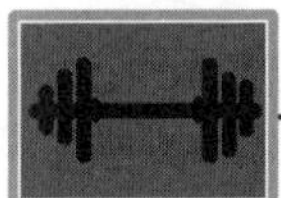

DO: • Compile and link PREP4 and DISPFUNC
• Run PREP4

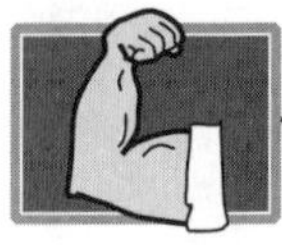

RESULT:

```
C:\>pc/c PREP4
Power C - Version 2.1.3
(C) Copyright 1989-1991 by Mix Software
Compiling ...
   21 lines compiled
Optimizing ...
    1 function optimized in 1 file

C:\>pc/c DISPFUNC
Power C - Version 2.1.3
(C) Copyright 1989-1991 by Mix Software
Compiling ...
  127 lines compiled
Optimizing ...
    1 function optimized in 1 file
```

```
C:\>pcl PREP4 DISPFUNC
Linking ...
Power C Linker - version 2.0.1
PREP4.EXE created

C:\>PREP4
Hello
```

ANALYSIS:

The preprocessor has combined the header with each of the two functions, main() and display(), to supply all the elements needed for a successful compile.

The PREP4 program is small and it is a contrived teaching example, but the division of source files and the design of the header file are both important concepts. This system of files will hold up well when applied to much larger, more complex software systems.

You can use the *#include* directive within a header file; thus, a header file can include other header files. This is sometimes desirable, especially with large software systems, because it gives you the ability to segregate and group header items in a logical manner. By placing related items in a common header, you can avoid repetition, and yet you can use multiple headers to keep unrelated items separated. You can then collect the headers in a master header, which can in turn be easily included by functions in many different source files.

#define DIRECTIVE

The *#define* directive provides a way to substitute any desired character sequence for a specified identifier. You have used the directive in many examples in previous chapters to define symbolic constants (like *#define TRUE 1*), but the *#define* directive also allows you to substitute executable statements for the occurrence of an identifier (used this way, a *#define* directive becomes a Macro, as explained later in this chapter).

Although you can use any legal form of C identifier, it is conventional C programming practice to use uppercase letters for *#define* identifiers. This makes it clear which identifiers the preprocessor will modify, and if there is any question in your mind about what is going on, you can refer to the *#define* directives at the top of the file or in a header file.

Symbolic constants

The simplest form of *#define* is:

```
#define IDENTIFIER substitution
```

This form instructs the preprocessor to replace every occurrence of *IDENTIFIER* with the *substitution* characters. The *scope* of a statement is the area where it is in effect;

the scope of a *#define* is from the point of the *#define* directive down to the end of the file—a *#define* directive does not affect other files unless it is in a header file included in those files. The principle use of this basic form of directive is to define symbolic constants (sometimes called *manifest constants*). A symbolic constant allows you to set and modify a single value that the preprocessor will substitute in any number of places in the program. Some examples of symbolic constants are:

```
#define PI 3.1416
#define FILENAME "PAYROLL.DAT"
#define TRUE 1
#define FALSE 0
#define INTEGER unsigned int
```

You can make the substitute character sequence anything you wish: it can be a constant of some valid C data type, it can be a C statement, or it can be something totally meaningless to C—but, of course, whatever you substitute must ultimately be acceptable to the compiler in the final context. Notice that the last *#define* has a space in the substitution sequence; this is OK because the preprocessor accepts all characters after the identifier to the end of the line. However, it removes leading and trailing spaces from the substitution sequence, so it will substitute the 12 characters, *unsigned int*, for *INTEGER*.

You can make interesting use of symbolic constants by substituting symbols for certain C operators. For example, some C programmers like to avoid the confusion between the assignment (=) and the equality (==) operators by substituting EQ for the equality. The next program shows how to do this; this example changes all of the relational operators to FORTRAN style symbols.

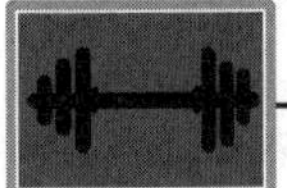

Listing 15.5 SYMBOLIC.C Symbolic constant

DO:
- Enter and compile SYMBOLIC
- Run SYMBOLIC and enter a

```
#include <stdio.h>
#define EQ ==
#define NE !=
#define GT >
#define LT <
#define GE >=
#define LE <=
void main()
{
     char letter;

     printf("Enter a letter: ");
     letter = getchar();

     if ((letter GE 'a') && (letter LE 'z'))
```

```
            printf("The letter is lowercase");

      if (letter EQ 'a')
            printf("\nThis is the first letter of the alphabet");
}
```

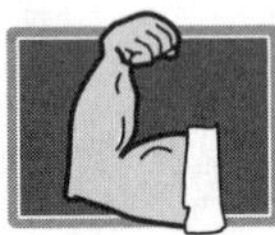

RESULT:

```
C:\>SYMBOLIC
Enter a letter: a
The letter is lowercase
This is the first letter of the alphabet
```

ANALYSIS:

1. The series of define directives establishes a two-character substitute for each of the six C relational operators.
2. The program asks you to enter a letter, then displays some messages that depend on which letter you enter.
3. The two *if* statements demonstrate the use of the new symbolic operator constants. After the preprocessor finishes, the compiler will see the first *if* statement as:

   ```
   if ((letter >= 'a') && (letter <= 'z'))
   ```

This statement tests whether *letter* is lowercase. The use of the symbolic constant EQ in the second *if* statement avoids the mistake of typing a single equal (=) in place of the relational operator (==). The preprocessor reliably makes the substitution of == for EQ so that the if test becomes:

```
if (letter == 'A')
```

Other substitutions are possible, such as these directives, which change the logical operators:

```
#define AND &&
#define OR  ||
```

The substitution of custom symbols for C operators is a controversial topic among programmers, but there is no question that this technique can alleviate errors arising from confusion about operators like '=' and '&'. Those against the technique argue that it violates the C standard and is less portable.

Macros

A more complex form of *#define* allows arguments:

```
#define IDENTIFIER(argument list) substitution
```

This form of define is called a *macro*, which provides for the inclusion of arguments into the substitution sequence. Consider the following macro:

```
#define ALPHA(n) 'A' + n
```

The value of this macro is the *n*th uppercase character, counting from 0. When the preprocessor encounters a reference to ALPHA in the program, it uses the argument in the substitution. Table 15-1 shows some statements that use the macro *ALPHA*, along with the preprocessor substitution.

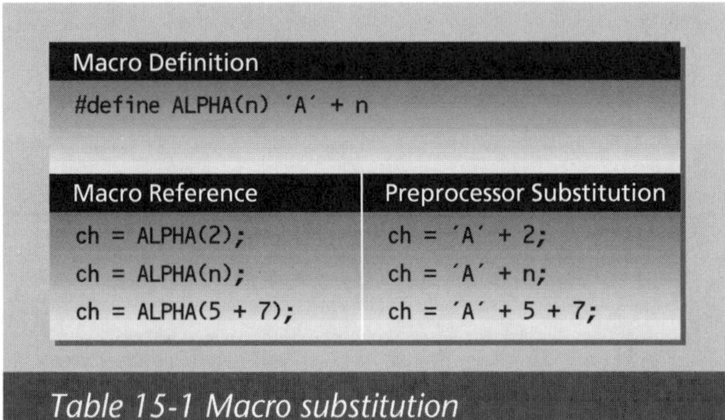

Macro Definition	
#define ALPHA(n) 'A' + n	

Macro Reference	Preprocessor Substitution
ch = ALPHA(2);	ch = 'A' + 2;
ch = ALPHA(n);	ch = 'A' + n;
ch = ALPHA(5 + 7);	ch = 'A' + 5 + 7;

Table 15-1 Macro substitution

A macro substitution is literal; the preprocessor substitutes arguments **exactly** as specified and lets the compiler evaluate expressions in the next compile step. Notice in Table 15-1 that the preprocessor carries the argument 5 + 7 directly over without evaluating the expression. If you do something illegal, the preprocessor does not care—it will make the substitution and let the compiler catch the error later. For instance, if you were to specify:

```
ch = ALPHA(!!!);
```

the preprocessor would substitute:

```
ch = 'A' + !!!;
```

and the compiler will generate an error.

The following program shows how to write a macro that yields the uppercase equivalent of a lowercase character.

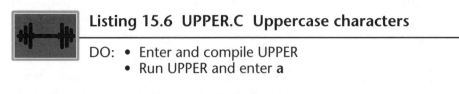

Listing 15.6 UPPER.C Uppercase characters

DO:
- Enter and compile UPPER
- Run UPPER and enter **a**

```
#include <stdio.h>
#define TOUPPER(ch) (ch >= 'a') && (ch <= 'z') ? ch - 32 : ch
void main()
```

```
{
     char letter;

     printf("Enter a letter: ");
     letter = getchar();

     printf("Here it is in uppercase: %c", TOUPPER(letter));
}
```

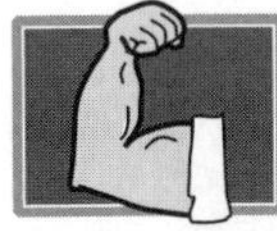

RESULT:

```
C:\>UPPER
Enter a letter: a
Here it is in uppercase: A
```

ANALYSIS:

1. The *#define* directive establishes the macro *TOUPPER* with the argument *ch*. The macro is a conditional statement that returns the uppercase version of the argument (*ch* - 32) if the argument is a lowercase character; otherwise, it returns the argument unchanged. The operation of the macro *TOUPPER* is equivalent to this *if* statement:

   ```
   if ((ch >= 'a') && (ch <= 'z'))      /* Is ch lowercase?      */
        ch -= 32;                       /* Make it uppercase     */
   else                                 /* Otherwise             */
        ch = ch;                        /* Don't change it       */
   ```

2. The program prompts you to enter a character, then displays the uppercase character as a result of applying the macro *TOUPPER* to the argument *letter*.

Your macro, *TOUPPER*, is very similar to the standard C library function, toupper(), in name, use, and operation—both accept a character argument and return the uppercase equivalent. A macro reference looks a lot like a function and it performs much like a function, but there are some very important differences. A macro accepts arguments and yields a value, like a function, but you don't really "call" a macro, and the macro doesn't really "return" a value because the program does not transfer control to a new location. A macro executes "in-line" code because it causes the preprocessor to substitute new statements right into the program. The preprocessor repeats the macro statements every time it finds a reference to the macro, and the repeated statements are compiled in place.

Figure 15-1 illustrates the difference between a function and a macro.

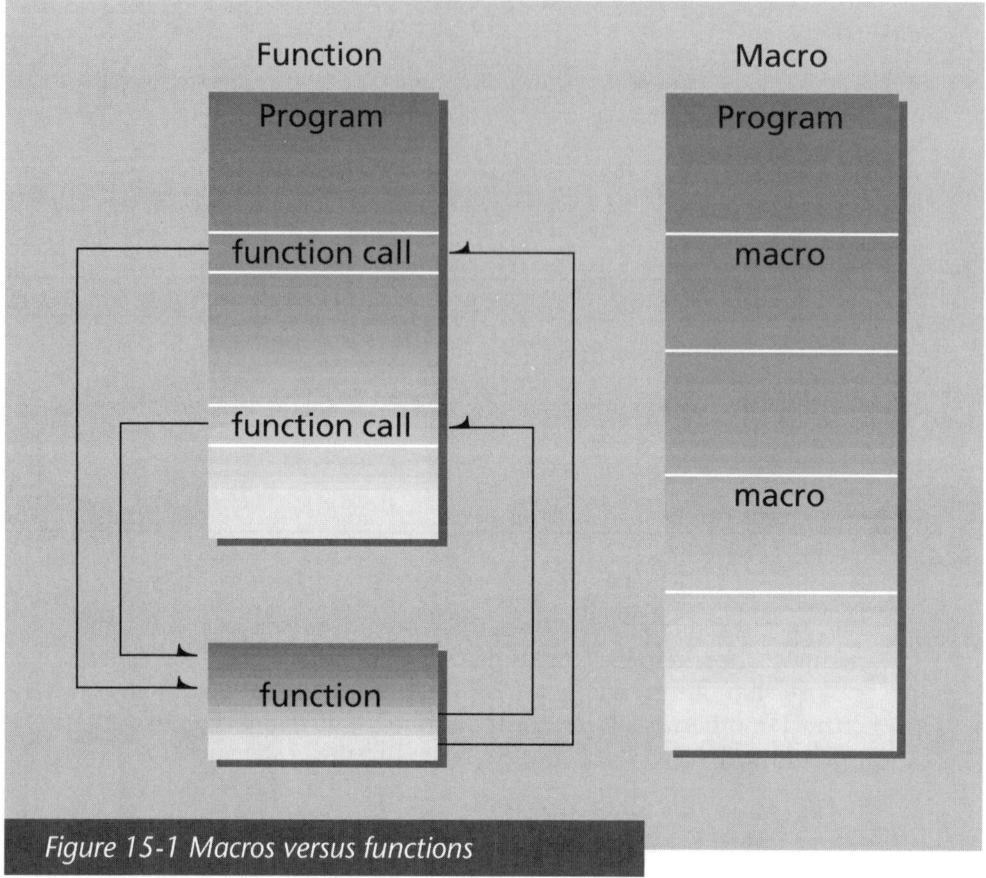

Figure 15-1 Macros versus functions

The main consequence of this difference is that macros are faster than functions. The program does not have to transfer control to a new location for a macro, nor does it have to pass data values back and forth. On the other hand, macros require more memory than functions because the compiler repeats the code every time you use a macro. Another difference is that a macro is not type dependent; you don't have to declare the argument or return types because macro parameters automatically take on the data types of arguments, and a macro value is automatically the data type inherent in the statements and expressions of the macro. You should use macros with restraint, because they can be tricky and they can obscure the meaning of program code. There are subtle traps with macros that can cause logic errors, as you will soon see in the ROUND2 program. In a nutshell, you should use a macro when speed is important in a short sequence of operations; otherwise, it is probably a better idea to use a function.

The next program combines some symbolic constants with the macro *TOUPPER* to show how you can use them in combination.

Listing 15.7 UPPER2.C Uppercase characters

DO:
- Add symbolics to UPPER
- Compile and link UPPER2
- Run UPPER2 and enter **a**

```
#include <stdio.h>
#define GE  >=                                                      /*1*/
#define LE  <=                                                      /*2*/
#define AND &&                                                      /*3*/
#define TOUPPER(ch) (ch GE 'a') AND (ch LE 'z') ? \
                              ch - 32 : ch                          /*4*/
void main()
{
    char letter;

    printf("Enter a letter: ");
    letter = getchar();

    printf("Here it is in uppercase: %c", TOUPPER(letter));
}
```

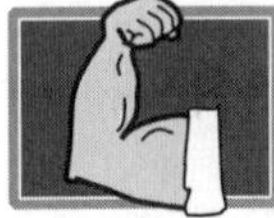

RESULT:

```
C:\>UPPER2
Enter a letter: a
Here it is in uppercase: A
```

ANALYSIS:

1. Lines /*1–3*/ define symbolic constants for three of the C operators that appear in the macro *TOUPPER*; the preprocessor will substitute these constants (&& for AND, <= for LE, and >= for GE) in the macro statement at the same time it substitutes the macro statement for *TOUPPER*.
2. Line /*4*/ shows how to continue a macro definition onto several lines if needed; you add a continuation character (\) to the end of a line, then just type the rest of the statement on the next line. You can use as many continuation lines as needed.

When you write a macro, do not end with a semicolon—this is a very common error that is all too easy to make. You are accustomed to ending statements with a semicolon, and it probably seems natural to put one at the end of your macro. But the semicolon belongs in the program statement that refers to the macro—not in the macro definition. If you add a semicolon to the macro *TOUPPER*, the compiler will generate an error.

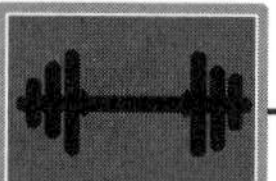

Listing 15.8 UPPER3.C Uppercase characters

DO:
- Add a semicolon at the end of the macro
- Compile UPPER3

```
#include <stdio.h>
#define GE  >=
#define LE  <=
#define AND &&
#define TOUPPER(ch) (ch GE 'a') AND (ch LE 'z') ? \
                                   ch - 32 : ch;                        /*1*/
void main()
{
    char letter;

    printf("Enter a letter: ");
    letter = getchar();

    printf("Here it is in uppercase: %c", TOUPPER(letter));
}
```

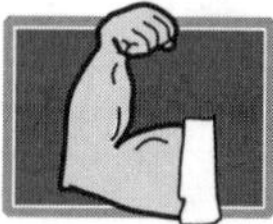

RESULT:

```
C:\>pc/c UPPER3
Power C - Version 2.1.3
(C) Copyright 1989-1991 by Mix Software
Compiling ...
UPPER3.C(14):    printf("Here it is in uppercase: %c", (letter >= 'a')
&&  (letter  <=  'z') ?  letter  - 32 : letter;);
************                                      ^ 4, 9
     4: ')' expected
     9: Right braces expected
------------------------------------------------------------------
 122 lines compiled
   2 Compile errors
```

ANALYSIS:

1. The macro definition on line /*1*/ contains the offending semicolon (;), but the compiler error shows up in the printf() statement that

references the macro. This is usually the case; the semicolon turns out to be extra, unwanted punctuation in the line where the preprocessor makes the substitution.

2. The compiler error shows the preprocessor in action; it displays the line after the macro substitution has occurred. Notice that *letter* has replaced *ch*, >= has replaced *GE*, <= has replaced *LE*, and && has replaced *AND*.

You must be cautious with macros, because macro substitution can lead to subtle logic errors. The next program defines a useful macro for rounding off integers, which we will use to demonstrate a trap. Then, we will introduce an easy method for escaping that trap. The program defines a macro to round off an integer to the nearest value of 10. If the ones digit of an integer is five or greater, then it will round up; otherwise, it will round down. For instance, the macro will round 14 down to 10 and 15 up to 20.

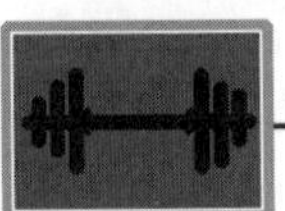

Listing 15.9 ROUND.C Round off

DO:
- Enter and compile ROUND
- Run ROUND and enter **14**

```
#include <stdio.h>
#define ROUNDOFF(n)  (n % 10 >= 5) ? \
                     (n - n % 10 + 10) : (n - n % 10)
void main()
{
     int number;

     printf("Enter an integer: ");
     scanf("%d", &number);

     printf("Rounded to the nearest 10: %d",
          ROUNDOFF(number));
}
```

RESULT:

```
C:\>ROUND
Enter an integer: 14
Rounded to the nearest 10: 10
```

DO: Run ROUND and enter **15**

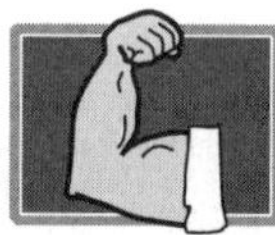

RESULT:

```
C:\>ROUND
Enter an integer: 15
Rounded to the nearest 10: 20
```

ANALYSIS:

1. The definition of the macro *ROUNDOFF* uses a conditional statement that is comparable to the following *if* statement:

   ```
   if (n % 10 >= 5)            /* 1's digit 5 or greater?      */
         n += 10 - n % 10;     /* Yes--round up                */
   else
         n -= n % 10;          /* No--round down               */
   ```

   The first expression finds the value of the ones digit (n % 10) and tests to see if it is greater than or equal to 5. If this is true, then the number must be rounded up and the conditional statement subtracts the units digit, adds 10, and returns this value. If the ones digit is 4 or less, the conditional statement returns the original number minus the ones digit. You have used the conditional statement for two macros in this chapter; this statement is often used in macros because it performs a conditional test, then returns a value.

2. The program prompts you for an integer, then displays the result of rounding by referring to the macro *ROUNDOFF* in the printf() statement.

Now let's trap ourselves by asking the program to add the number we enter to 100, then round off that sum.

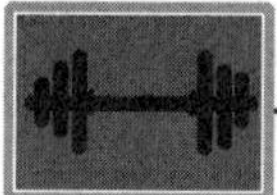

Listing 15.10 ROUND2.C Round off

DO:
- Modify ROUND to add 100 to the entered integer
- Run ROUND2 and enter **14**

```
#include <stdio.h>
#define ROUNDOFF(n)  (n % 10 >= 5) ? \
                     (n - n % 10 + 10) : (n - n % 10)
void main()
{
```

```
    int number;

    printf("Enter an integer: ");
    scanf("%d", &number);

    printf("Rounded to the nearest 10: %d",
         ROUNDOFF(100 + number));                             /*1*/
}
```

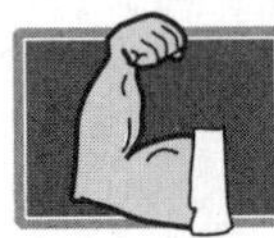

RESULT:

```
C:\>ROUND2
Enter an integer: 14
Rounded to the nearest 10: 28
```

ANALYSIS:

1. Line /*1*/ implements the new requirement by adding 100 to *number*.
2. But what happened!? The program is supposed to round 114 down and display 110; why did the macro yield a result of 28? If you carefully substitute the argument 100+14 into the macro, you will see why. The macro becomes:

   ```
   (100+14 % 10 >= 5) ?
          (100+14 - 100+14 % 10 + 10) : (100+14 - 100+14 % 10)
   ```

   The first expression, 100+14 % 10, evaluates to 104 because the modulus operator (%) has precedence over plus (+); similarly, the last expression, 100+14 - 100+14 % 10, evaluates to 18. Thus, the macro simplifies to: (104 >= 5) ? (28) : (18), and it yields a value of 28.
3. The program is working correctly, but the macro contains a logic error. The macro needs to evaluate the argument 100+14 first, and then apply the result, 114, in the remaining expressions. This is the subtle trap that we alluded to, and it is due to an undesired order of evaluation in expressions.

You can guarantee that a macro will receive correct parameters by forcing early evaluation of arguments with parentheses. As a general rule:

add an extra pair of parentheses around each argument in a macro definition.

The next example implements this rule.

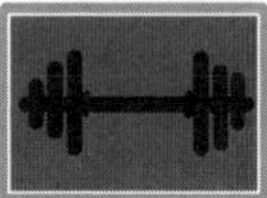

Listing 15.11 ROUND3.C Round off

DO:
- Add an extra set of parentheses for the argument
- Compile, and run ROUND3
- Enter **14**

```
#include <stdio.h>
#define ROUNDOFF(n) ((n) % 10 >= 5) ? \
                    ((n) - (n) % 10 + 10) : ((n) - (n) % 10)
void main()
{
     int number;

     printf("Enter an integer: ");
     scanf("%d", &number);

     printf("Rounded to the nearest 10: %d",
          ROUNDOFF(number));
}
```

RESULT:

```
C:\>ROUND3
Enter an integer: 14
Rounded to the nearest 10: 10
```

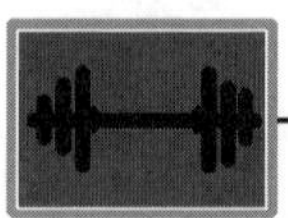

DO: Run ROUND3 and enter **15**

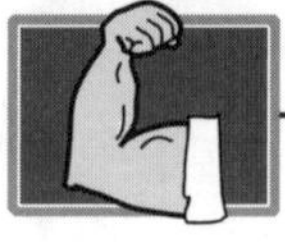

RESULT:

```
C:\>ROUND3
Enter an integer: 15
Rounded to the nearest 10: 20
```

ANALYSIS:

Now the macro performs as expected and it will correctly evaluate all arguments passed to it.

It is a good idea to be in the habit of using an extra pair of parentheses with each argument in a macro.

Here is another situation to avoid when using macros. Can you predict what will happen if you supply the argument *++number* to the macro *ROUNDOFF*? Modify the ROUND3 program to do this.

Listing 15.12 ROUND4.C Round off

DO:
- Add an increment operator to the argument
- Compile and run ROUND4

```
#include <stdio.h>
#define ROUNDOFF(n) ((n) % 10 >= 5) ? \
                    ((n) - (n) % 10 + 10) : ((n) - (n) % 10)

void main()
{
    int number;

    printf("Enter an integer: ");
    scanf("%d", &number);

    printf("Rounded to the nearest 10: %d",
        ROUNDOFF(++number));                                /*1*/
}
```

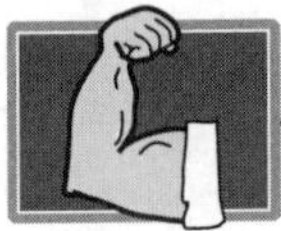

RESULT:

```
C:\>ROUND4
Enter an integer: 13
Rounded to the nearest 10: 9
```

ANALYSIS:

1. On line /*1*/, you have incremented the argument as if to pass a value one greater than the number entered from the keyboard, or 14.
2. The result is not 10, as you expected—it is not even 20! When the compiler makes the macro substitution, it replaces **every** occurrence of *n* with *++number*, so the program ends up incrementing *number* three times instead of only once. After substitution, the statement on line /*1*/ looks like this:

```
((++number) % 10 >= 5) ?
((++number) - (++number) % 10 + 10) :
((++number) - (++number) % 10);
```

The program evaluates the conditional expression on the left first, with a result of: (14 % 10 >= 5) or (4 >= 5) or 0. Since the conditional expression is false, the statement evaluates the third, or last, expression, and increments *number* twice more in the process, to yield: (15 - 16 % 10) = 9.

Because of the potential for repeated incrementing, you should observe another rule with macros:

Don't apply increment (++) or decrement (--) operators to macro arguments.

CONDITIONAL COMPILATION

C provides some conditional control directives for the preprocessor. The directives *#if, #ifdef, #ifndef, #else, #elif,* and *#endif* allow you to specify that certain groups of statements be included or excluded from a program depending on the value of defined symbolic constants. The model for conditional compilation directives (also known as conditional inclusion directives) is the familiar true/false test:

```
#if (constant expression)
        /* TRUE statements */
#else
        /* FALSE statements */
#endif
```

If the constant expression is true, the preprocessor includes the TRUE statements down to the *#else* directive; otherwise, it includes the FALSE statements down to the *#endif* directive. The preprocessor does not recognize curly braces { } for compound statements; instead, it accepts multiple statements sandwiched between directives. The *#if* directive causes the compiler to include the one set of statements and exclude the other, just as if you had not typed the excluded statements into the program. The constant expression can use actual constants or symbolic constants, and a result of zero (0) is FALSE and of nonzero is TRUE. The parentheses around the constant expression are not necessary—they only improve readability.

You can use conditional compilation to adjust a program for different environments (different computers, compilers, or operating systems), to set particular program options, or to match software delivery requirements. You will see examples of some of these applications of conditional compilation in this chapter. The first example of conditional compilation declares an array to be either of type *int* or of type *long*, depending on the data expected. You might use such a conditional compilation in a program that accepts data from several sources, in which the size of the numbers from each source is quite different. If all the data from one source will fit into 16 bits, then you would want to allocate an array of type *int*. However, if the numbers from another source are larger, then you would need to declare type *long*. The next program shows how to accomplish this kind of conditional compilation; it deliberately declares an invalid array identifier so that a compiler error message will display preprocessor substitutions.

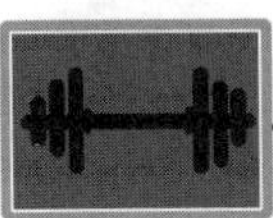

Listing 15.13 COND.C Conditional compilation

DO: Enter and compile COND

```
#include <stdio.h>

/* Define the data size */

#define LARGE      1
#define SMALL      2
#define DATA_SIZE SMALL

/* Remove this comment for LARGE data size
#define DATA_SIZE LARGE
*/

/* Define the type of symbolic INTEGER */

#if (DATA_SIZE == SMALL)
     #define INTEGER int
#elif (DATA_SIZE == LARGE)
     #define INTEGER long
#endif

void main()
{
     INTEGER !array[1000];  /* Deliberately invalid identifier */
}
```

RESULT:

```
C:\>pc/c COND
Power C - Version 2.1.3
(C) Copyright 1989-1991 by Mix Software
Compiling ...
COND.C(23):    int    !array[1000]; /* Deliberately invalid
**********             ^  2^104 ^138
       2: Identifier expected in a type declaration
     104: Undeclared identifier
     138: Type of variable is not array
--------------------------------------------------------------
```

```
131 lines compiled
  3 Compile errors
```

ANALYSIS:

1. The program first defines three symbolic constants, *LARGE, SMALL,* and *DATA_SIZE,* to designate the size of the data that the program will use. The program defines the symbolics *LARGE* and *SMALL* as integer constants; it doesn't matter what the values are as long as they are different.

2. The program defines *DATA_SIZE* to be *SMALL* in this instance, and it provides another inactive directive, *#define DATA_SIZE LARGE,* that you can use to change the array declaration. The surrounding comment delimiters render this directive inactive; to change the data environment, you would remove the comment.

3. Following the definition of *DATA_SIZE,* the program conditionally defines the symbolic *INTEGER* to be either of type *int* or of type *long* depending on the size of the data. The preprocessor *#if* directive determines which of the two *#define INTEGER* directives to keep while the other is excluded from compilation; in this case, the preprocessor keeps *#define INTEGER int.*

4. The *#elif* directive is the combination of else and if, so it implements an additional true/false test based on the attached expression (*DATA_SIZE == LARGE*).

5. The main function uses the symbolic constant *INTEGER* as the data type when it declares the variable *!array.* We have purposely used an identifier that illegally begins with an exclamation (!) so the compiler error message will show that the preprocessor has substituted *int* for *INTEGER.*

Now remove the comment for *LARGE* data and instead disable the directive for *SMALL* data, then recompile to see type *long* used to declare the array.

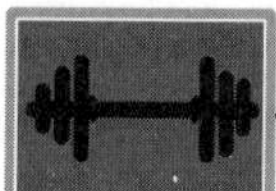

Listing 15.14 COND2.C Conditional compilation

DO:
- Designate LARGE data
- Compile COND2

```
#include <stdio.h>
```

```
/* Define the data size */

#define LARGE     1
#define SMALL     2

/* Remove this comment for SMALL data size
#define DATA_SIZE SMALL
*/

#define DATA_SIZE LARGE

/* Define the type of symbolic INTEGER */

#if (DATA_SIZE == SMALL)
     #define INTEGER int
#elif (DATA_SIZE == LARGE)
     #define INTEGER long
#endif

void main()
{
     INTEGER !array[1000];  /* Deliberately invalid identifier */
}
```

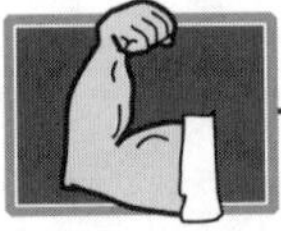

RESULT:

```
C:\>pc/c COND2
Power C - Version 2.1.3
(C) Copyright 1989-1991 by Mix Software
Compiling ...
COND2.C(24):    long   !array[1000];  /* Deliberately invalid
***********              ^  2^104 ^138
       2: Identifier expected in a type declaration
     104: Undeclared identifier
     138: Type of variable is not array
-----------------------------------------------------------
  132 lines compiled
    3 Compile errors
```

ANALYSIS:

The error message now shows that the symbolic constant *INTEGER* is the same as type *long*.

Different brands of C compilers use slightly different header files; sometimes the files have the same name, but the contents are different. Another use for the *#if* directive is to make a program more portable. Depending on the compiler, you can include different header files, or header files from a different directory.

The next example uses conditional compilation directives to select and omit C statements within the main function. Suppose you are with a software company that markets a custom application to two large corporations that are regular customers. The application software is pretty much the same for both customers, but some custom changes are included for each client before it is delivered. The legal contracts require that the program display a licensing message each time it runs. Here's how you can fulfill that requirement.

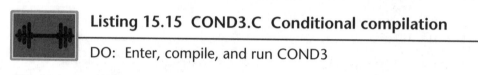

Listing 15.15 COND3.C Conditional compilation

DO: Enter, compile, and run COND3

```
#include <stdio.h>
#define ACME  'A'
#define ZEBRA 'Z'
#define CUSTOMER ZEBRA
void main()
{
#if (CUSTOMER == ACME)
     char owner[] = "Acme Mfg. Co.";
#elif (CUSTOMER == ZEBRA)
     char owner[] = "Zebra Services, Inc.";
#endif

     printf("This software is licensed to %s", owner);
}
```

RESULT:

```
C:\>COND3
This software is licensed to Zebra Services, Inc.
```

ANALYSIS:

1. The program defines two symbolic constants, *ACME* and *ZEBRA*, to represent the two customers, then it defines the current *CUSTOMER* to be *ZEBRA*. Notice that the first two *#define* statements use values that are character constants.

2. The *#if* preprocessor directive tests to see if the symbolic constant *CUSTOMER* equals *ACME*, and when it does not, the directive *#elif*

tests to see if it equals *ZEBRA*; it does, and so the preprocessor keeps the second declaration of array *owner* and discards the first one.

3. The printf() statement displays the appropriate licensing message whenever the program runs.

To change customers in this program, you must edit the directive, *#define CUSTOMER ZEBRA*, and recompile. However, most compilers (including Power C) provide a more convenient way to define symbolic constants. Power C has a **/d** option, which allows you to define symbolic constants on the command line when you compile a program; it has the form */dNAME=VALUE*, where *NAME* is the symbolic constant identifier and *VALUE* is its value. Eliminate the directive that defines *CUSTOMER* from the previous program and use the compiler option instead.

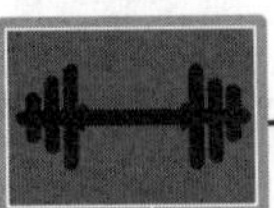

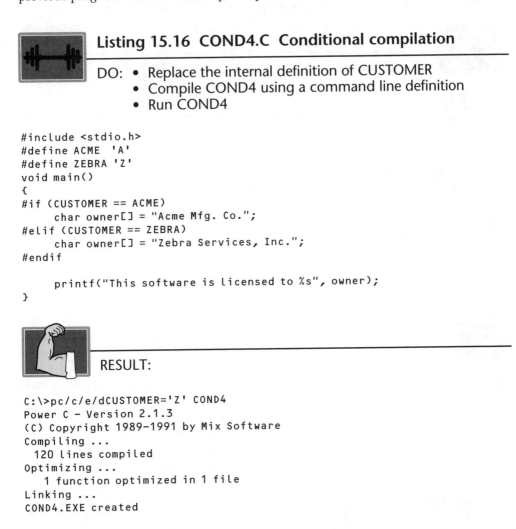

Listing 15.16 COND4.C Conditional compilation

DO:
- Replace the internal definition of CUSTOMER
- Compile COND4 using a command line definition
- Run COND4

```
#include <stdio.h>
#define ACME  'A'
#define ZEBRA 'Z'
void main()
{
#if (CUSTOMER == ACME)
     char owner[] = "Acme Mfg. Co.";
#elif (CUSTOMER == ZEBRA)
     char owner[] = "Zebra Services, Inc.";
#endif

     printf("This software is licensed to %s", owner);
}
```

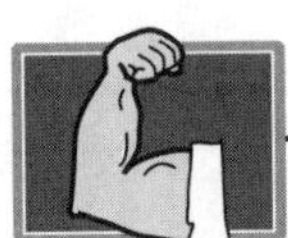

RESULT:

```
C:\>pc/c/e/dCUSTOMER='Z' COND4
Power C - Version 2.1.3
(C) Copyright 1989-1991 by Mix Software
Compiling ...
  120 lines compiled
Optimizing ...
   1 function optimized in 1 file
Linking ...
COND4.EXE created
```

```
C:\>COND4
This software is licensed to Zebra Services, Inc.
```

ANALYSIS:

To use the command line definition for this program, you have to know the possible values for *CUSTOMER*; in this case, you assigned the value corresponding to *ZEBRA*, which is 'Z'. We have purposely chosen two easily remembered values for these constants.

Now recompile without specifying a value for *CUSTOMER*.

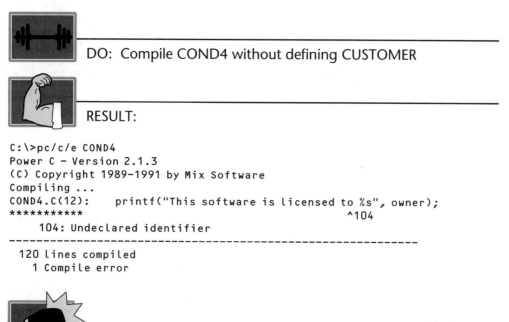

DO: Compile COND4 without defining CUSTOMER

RESULT:

```
C:\>pc/c/e COND4
Power C - Version 2.1.3
(C) Copyright 1989-1991 by Mix Software
Compiling ...
COND4.C(12):    printf("This software is licensed to %s", owner);
***********                                            ^104
     104: Undeclared identifier
---------------------------------------------------------------
  120 lines compiled
    1 Compile error
```

ANALYSIS:

The compile error occurs because both directives *#if* and *#elif* are false (*CUSTOMER* is not defined) and the program never declares the array *owner*.

You can define symbolic constants without values and use their mere existence or nonexistence to control conditional compilations. The directive *#define NAME* establishes that the symbolic constant *NAME* exists, but without a value. You can conditionally include statements based on the existence of *NAME* with the *#ifdef* (if defined) directive:

```
#ifdef NAME
```

```
        /* TRUE statements */
#endif
```

Or you can include statements based on the nonexistence of *NAME* with the *#ifndef* (if not defined) directive:

```
#ifndef NAME
        /* TRUE statements */
#else
        /* FALSE statements */
#endif
```

Use of the *#else* directive is optional, but here the preprocessor will keep the TRUE statements if *NAME* does **not** exist, and it will keep the FALSE statements if it does exist.

The next program puts a box around the previous license message. It provides for two kinds of boxes: one is based on the hyphen (-) and vertical line (|) characters available on any computer, and one is based on the graphic characters available in the upper range of ASCII codes for an IBM PC (codes 128–255, see Appendix G). With the graphic characters, you can generate a connected, higher quality box, while the normal characters present a broken outline.

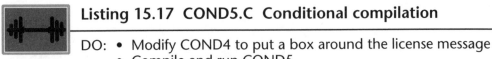

Listing 15.17 COND5.C Conditional compilation

DO:
- Modify COND4 to put a box around the license message
- Compile and run COND5

```
#include <stdio.h>
#define ACME  'A'
#define ZEBRA 'Z'
#define GRAPHIC                                                    /*1*/
void main()
{
#if CUSTOMER == ACME
     char owner[] = "Acme Mfg. Co.";
#elif CUSTOMER == ZEBRA
     char owner[] = "Zebra Services, Inc.";
#endif

/*****-------- Add new statements from here on...--------*****/

#ifdef GRAPHIC
     char horz_line =  196;
     char vert_line =  179;
#else
     char horz_line = '-';
     char vert_line = '|';
#endif
```

```
    int i;

    for (i=0; i<33+strlen(owner); ++i)
        printf("%c", horz_line);

    printf("\n%c", vert_line);
    for (i=0; i<31+strlen(owner); ++i)
        printf(" ");
    printf("%c\n", vert_line);

    printf("%c This software is licensed to %s %c",
        vert_line, owner, vert_line);

    printf("\n%c", vert_line);
    for (i=0; i<31+strlen(owner); ++i)
        printf(" ");
    printf("%c\n", vert_line);

    for (i=0; i<33+strlen(owner); ++i)
        printf("%c", horz_line);
}
```

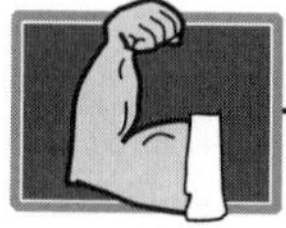

RESULT:

```
C:\>pc/c/e/dCUSTOMER='Z' COND5

C:\>COND5
```

```
 This software is licensed to Zebra Services, Inc.
```

ANALYSIS:

1. Line /*1*/ defines the symbolic constant *GRAPHIC*, and an *#ifdef* directive uses it to select the statements that initialize the variables *horz_line* and *vert_line* to graphic or nongraphic character codes. Because *GRAPHIC* is defined, the directive selects graphic characters.
2. The printf() statements in the balance of the program display the *horz_line* and *vert_line* characters in a pattern that forms a box around the license message.

You can switch to the other, nongraphic form of box by removing the directive *#define GRAPHIC*, or you can leave it and add a new *#undef GRAPHIC* directive beneath it—*#undef* (undefine) nullifies any preceding definition of a name.

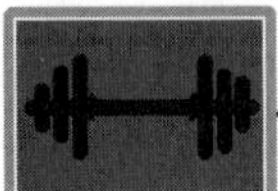

Listing 15.18 COND6.C Conditional compilation

DO:
- Undefine GRAPHIC in COND5
- Compile and run COND6

```
#include <stdio.h>
#define ACME  'A'
#define ZEBRA 'Z'
#define GRAPHIC
#undef  GRAPHIC                                                    /*1*/
void main()
{
#if CUSTOMER == ACME
     char owner[] = "Acme Mfg. Co.";
#elif CUSTOMER == ZEBRA
     char owner[] = "Zebra Services, Inc.";
#endif

#ifdef GRAPHIC
     char horz_line =  196;
     char vert_line =  179;
#else
     char horz_line = '-';
     char vert_line = '|';
#endif

     int i;

     for (i=0; i<33+strlen(owner); ++i)
          printf("%c", horz_line);

     printf("\n%c", vert_line);
     for (i=0; i<31+strlen(owner); ++i)
          printf(" ");
     printf("%c\n", vert_line);

     printf("%c This software is licensed to %s %c",
          vert_line, owner, vert_line);

     printf("\n%c", vert_line);
     for (i=0; i<31+strlen(owner); ++i)
          printf(" ");
     printf("%c\n", vert_line);

     for (i=0; i<33+strlen(owner); ++i)
          printf("%c", horz_line);
}
```

RESULT:

```
C:\>pc/c/e/dCUSTOMER='Z' COND6

C:\>COND6
```

```
This software is licensed to Zebra Services, Inc.
```

ANALYSIS:

You can also remove both the *#define* and *#undefine* directives, and control the graphics box from the compile command line as in the next example.

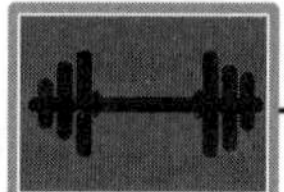

Listing 15.19 COND7.C Conditional compilation

DO:
- Remove define and undefine of GRAPHIC in COND6
- Compile and run COND7

```
#include <stdio.h>
#define ACME  'A'
#define ZEBRA 'Z'
void main()
{
#if CUSTOMER == ACME
     char owner[] = "Acme Mfg. Co.";
#elif CUSTOMER == ZEBRA
     char owner[] = "Zebra Services, Inc.";
#endif

#ifdef GRAPHIC
     char horz_line =  196;
     char vert_line =  179;
#else
     char horz_line = '-';
     char vert_line = '|';
#endif

     int i;

     for (i=0; i<33+strlen(owner); ++i)
```

```
        printf("%c", horz_line);

    printf("\n%c", vert_line);
    for (i=0; i<31+strlen(owner); ++i)
        printf(" ");
    printf("%c\n", vert_line);

    printf("%c This software is licensed to %s %c",
        vert_line, owner, vert_line);

    printf("\n%c", vert_line);
    for (i=0; i<31+strlen(owner); ++i)
        printf(" ");
    printf("%c\n", vert_line);

    for (i=0; i<33+strlen(owner); ++i)
        printf("%c", horz_line);
}
```

RESULT:

```
C:\>pc/c/e/dCUSTOMER='Z' COND7

C:\>COND7
```

```
This software is licensed to Zebra Services, Inc.
```

ANALYSIS:

The compile option, */dCUSTOMER='Z'*, defines the symbolic constant, *CUSTOMER*, to be the character 'Z', but the compile command line leaves *GRAPHIC* undefined. Therefore, the program displays the "Zebra Services" message in a nongraphic box.

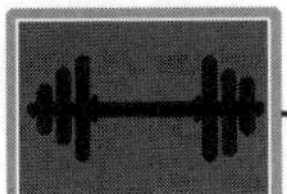

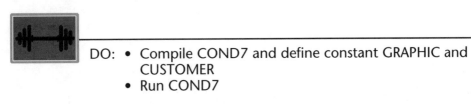

DO:
- Compile COND7 and define constant GRAPHIC and CUSTOMER
- Run COND7

RESULT:

```
C:\>pc/c/e/dCUSTOMER='Z'/dGRAPHIC COND7

C:\>COND7
```

```
This software is licensed to Zebra Services, Inc.
```

ANALYSIS:

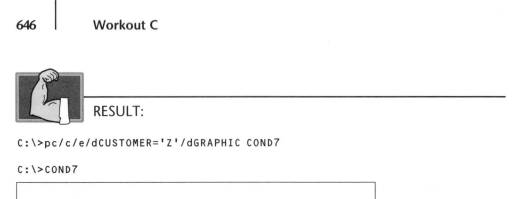

The compile command line defines *CUSTOMER* to be 'Z', and it also defines *GRAPHIC*, so the program displays the "Zebra Services" message in a graphics box.

You will make frequent use of the *#define* and *#include* preprocessor directives. You will certainly include standard header files (at least stdio.h) in every program, and you will often include some of your own header files. You should make maximum use of the *#define* directive to declare symbolic constants, and you may occasionally need to define some macros for efficiency. You will need the other preprocessor directives only in connection with special requirements to adjust a program prior to compilation.

CHAPTER 16
MORE ABOUT DATA TYPES

Each variable declared by a C program has a data type and it also has a *storage class*. The data type determines **how much** storage the variable will use and **what** kind of data it can hold; the storage class determines **where** the variable can be used, **when** it exists, and **how** it is initialized. In this chapter, you will learn about these vital aspects of declaring and using variables.

C provides a means for you to create names of your own choosing and assign them to data types with the *typedef* keyword. It also provides a way to assign a restricted set of names to the values of an integer variable with the *enumerated* data type. In this chapter, you will also learn and use these features.

STORAGE CLASSES

A variable is a dynamic element of a program, and as such it has an initial value, a lifetime, and definite boundaries of usability. The compiler may or may not initialize a variable when it allocates space for it—we'll refer to this as the initialization property. A program creates and destroys a variable at certain times during execution—this is the lifetime property. The third property of a variable is called its scope, which is the program area where a variable is accessible. These three properties (initialization, lifetime, and scope) are determined by the *storage class* of a variable. There are two storage classes in C, *automatic* and *static,* and the storage class is set either by the location of a variable declaration or by using one of four keywords with the declaration, *auto, extern, register, or static.* Table 16-1 summarizes the declaration and properties of variables in automatic and static storage classes.

Class	Variable Declaration: Location	Variable Declaration: Qualifier	Scope	Lifetime	Automatic Initialization
AUTO	Inside a function	none	function	function	none*
		auto	function	function	none*
		register	function	function	none*
					*except for partially initialized array
STATIC	Outside of functions	none	file	program	zero(0)
		static	file	program	zero(0)
		extern	across files	program	zero(0)
	Inside a function	static	function	program	zero(0)

Table 16-1 Automatic versus static storage classes

Automatic storage class

Variables in the automatic storage class are *local* to the function in which they are defined; the lifetime and scope of automatic variables is limited to that function. More precisely, the scope and lifetime of an automatic variable is controlled by the **block** (the curly braces) in which it appears; so the opening and closing curly braces of a function actually control the automatic variables declared inside the function. The variables come into being when the function begins execution, and they cease to exist when the function ends. This is the origin of the term **automatic**—a function automatically creates these variables every time it begins, and it automatically destroys them when it ends. Despite the name, however, the compiler does not automatically initialize automatic variables—you have to do that explicitly. Any variable declared within a function is automatic by default if not otherwise specified, or you can declare it outright with the keyword *auto*.

Variables declared with the qualifier *register* are also automatic; by specifying *register*, you can request that a variable be assigned to one of the high-speed hardware registers. This is no more than a request, however, because the compiler can ignore it if a register is not available or if the data type of the variable is not the proper one for a register. A compiler has access to only a few of the hardware registers, and it can use them as it sees fit; if the compiler refuses your request for a register, there is no harm—it simply assigns the variable to a memory location. You cannot use the address operator (&) with a register variable, because the variable may not be in memory; therefore, you cannot take the address of a register variable.

The following program shows three ways to declare automatic variables, and it demonstrates that the lifetime and scope of the variables is limited to the function in which they are defined.

Listing 16.1 CLASS.C Automatic storage class

DO: Enter, compile, and run CLASS

```
#include <stdio.h>
void different(void);
void main()
{
     int          x = 1;         /* Automatic by default  */
     auto int     y = 2;         /* Explicitly automatic   */
     register int z = 3;         /* register is automatic */

     printf("\nAuto variables in     main(): \
x = %d, y = %d, z = %d", x, y, z);

     different();

     printf("\nAuto variables in     main(): \
```

```
x = %d, y = %d, z = %d", x, y, z);
}

void different(void)
{
     int          x = 7;         /* Automatic by default  */
     auto int     y = 8;         /* Explicitly automatic   */
     register int z = 9;         /* register is automatic */
     printf("\nAuto variables in different(): \
x = %d, y = %d, z = %d", x, y, z);
}
```

RESULT:

```
C:\>CLASS

Auto variables in      main(): x = 1, y = 2, z = 3
Auto variables in different(): x = 7, y = 8, z = 9
Auto variables in      main(): x = 1, y = 2, z = 3
```

ANALYSIS:

1. This program has two functions: main() and different(). Each function declares three variables (*x, y, and z*) in the same way. The variables are separate even though the names are repeated, because you define them in separate functions. The scope of variable *x* in main() is limited to function main(), and the scope of *x* defined in different() is limited to function different(). The same is true of variables *y* and *z*.

2. Variable *x* is automatic by default. Inside each function, you declare *x* without a qualifying keyword, and so it defaults to the automatic class.

3. Variable *y* is automatic by virtue of the explicit *auto* qualifier used in each function.

4. Variable *z* is automatic because it is qualified by the *register* keyword. Presumably, the compiler will actually assign both *z* variables to hardware registers, because this program has so few variables.

5. This program explicitly initializes all variables, because the compiler does not automatically zero out automatic variables.

6. The printf() statements make it clear that the variables in the main function are separate from those in the function different(). The val-

ues in main() are not the same as those in different() and they do not change after calling function different().

You cannot declare a variable to be *auto* outside a function; try this by modifying the above program.

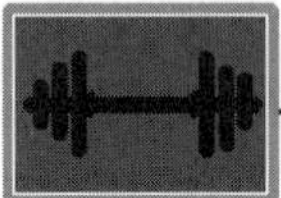

Listing 16.2 CLASS2.C Automatic storage class

DO: • Move the *auto* declaration outside of main()
• Compile CLASS2

```
#include <stdio.h>
void different(void);
     auto int      y = 2;      /* Explicitly automatic   */ /*1*/
void main()
{
     int             x = 1;      /* Automatic by default  */
     register int z = 3;      /* register is automatic */

     printf("\nAuto variables in main(): \
x = %d, y = %d, z = %d", x, y, z);

     different();

     printf("\nAuto variables in main(): \
x = %d, y = %d, z = %d", x, y, z);
}

void different(void)
{
     int          x = 7;        /* Automatic by default  */
     auto int     y = 8;        /* Explicitly automatic   */
     register int z = 9;      /* register is automatic */

     printf("\nAuto variables in different(): \
x = %d, y = %d, z = %d", x, y, z);
}
```

RESULT:

```
pc/c CLASS2
Power C - Version 2.1.3
(C) Copyright 1989-1991 by Mix Software
Compiling ...
CLASS2.C(3):auto int    y = 2;    /* Explicitly automatic */
***********      ^ 6
       6: Illegal symbol
-----------------------------------------------------------
```

```
149 lines compiled
  1 Compile error
```

ANALYSIS:

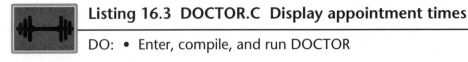

Line /*1*/ now attempts to declare an automatic variable outside of both functions. The compiler will not accept this attempt at illegal memory usage, and it reacts with an error message.

You can only use the keyword *auto* with variables that are automatic anyway, so about the only use for this keyword is to emphasize that you really intended that the variable be automatic.

Variables declared outside of functions belong strictly to the static storage class—our next topic of discussion.

Static storage class

Variables of the *static* storage class are sometimes referred to as *global* because they are not as restricted in scope and lifetime as are local, automatic variables. The lifetime of a static variable is the same as that for the overall program. When a program goes into execution, it allocates space for all static variables and initializes them (to 0 if explicit initialization is not specified). Only when the program ends do the static variables cease to exist. Static means stationary; therefore, the name is appropriate for variables that stay in place the entire time that a program executes.

The scope of a static variable (where it can be accessed) depends on how you declare it. There are basically three ways to declare a static variable, which we present in order of progression from narrower to wider scope: (1) When you declare a variable inside a function and qualify it with the keyword *static*, you restrict its scope to that function. (2) When you declare a variable outside of all functions in a file (whether you use *static* or not), then its scope includes the whole file—the variable is accessible to all the functions of the file, but not necessarily to functions in another file. You can prohibit access from other files if you declare it to be *static*. (3) You can make the scope of a variable extend to another file if you declare it outside of all functions in one file (without a *static* qualifier), and declare it with the qualifier *extern* in other files. The next three programs will illustrate the three basic methods of declaring static variables. The basic program used is a simple one that reports the next available appointment time at a doctor's office. The main function calls on another function to retrieve an appointment time from an array.

Listing 16.3 DOCTOR.C Display appointment times

DO: • Enter, compile, and run DOCTOR

```
#include <stdio.h>
```

```
char *next_appointment(void);
void main()
{
     printf("\nThe next available appointment is at %s",
          next_appointment());
     printf("\nThe next available appointment is at %s",
          next_appointment());
}

char *next_appointment(void)
{
static int  next;
static char appointment[8][6] = {" 8:00", " 9:00",
                                 "10:00", "11:00",
                                 " 1:00", " 2:00",
                                 " 3:00", " 4:00"};
     return(appointment[next++]);
}
```

RESULT:

```
C:\>DOCTOR

The next available appointment is at  8:00
The next available appointment is at  9:00
```

ANALYSIS:

1. The main function displays two appointment times; it calls the function next_appointment() from inside the two printf() statements to get the appointments.
2. The function next_appointment() returns the appointment time referenced by the current value of *next*, then postfix increments *next* for the next appointment.
3. The key ingredient of this program is the two statements defining variables *next* and *appointment* inside the function next_appointment(). The *static* qualifier gives the variables a lifetime that lasts as long as the program executes so that they can retain their values between function calls. The program automatically initializes *next* to 0 only once, when it starts up, and thereafter, the function next_appointment() will increment *next* each time it returns. The program will only have to initialize the array *appointment* once, and its values do not

change after that. The variables are limited in scope by the keyword *static,* so that they are not available outside of next_appointment(). Even though this program automatically initializes *next,* it would still be better to explicitly set it to 0 just to make the intended value clear.

Here is how to expand the scope of the variables so that they are accessible to main() by defining them outside the function.

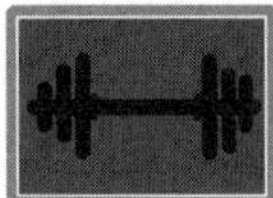

Listing 16.4 DOCTOR2.C Display appointment times

DO:
- Move the static variables outside the functions
- Compile and run DOCTOR2

```
#include <stdio.h>
char *next_appointment(void);

int  next = 0;                                                /*1*/
char appointment[8][6] = { " 8:00", " 9:00",                  /*2*/
                           "10:00", "11:00",
                           " 1:00", " 2:00",
                           " 3:00", " 4:00"};

void main()
{
     printf("\nThe next available appointment is at %s",
          next_appointment());
     printf("\nThe next available appointment is at %s",
          next_appointment());

     if (next == 7)                                           /*3*/
          next = 0;                                           /*4*/
}

char *next_appointment(void)
{
     return(appointment[next++]);
}
```

RESULT:

```
C:\>DOCTOR2

The next available appointment is at  8:00
The next available appointment is at  9:00
```

ANALYSIS:

1. You have removed the *static* qualifier from the statements that define *next* and *appointment* (lines /*1–2*/) and moved them to the top of the

program. The variables are still of the static storage class, because the program defines them outside of all functions. Line /*1*/ explicitly initializes *next* to 0; this is redundant, because the compiler automatically clears static variables, but now the intent is unmistakable. The lifetime of the variables is the lifetime of the program, but they are initialized only once. The scope of both variables extends to the entire file DOCTOR.C, so they are accessible to both functions.

2. The main function has a new duty: to reset *next* to the beginning of the appointment array when it reaches the end; this is implemented on lines /*3–4*/. This is now possible only because *next* has a wider scope and is accessible both from main() and from next_appointment().

The next program changes the scope of the variables once again, this time to extend to different files. To do this, you will need to use the keyword *extern* to link the declaration of a variable in one file to the definition of the variable in another. Figure 16-1 shows the linkage between declarations of the same variable in separate files.

You can establish linkage between variables in separate files with the following two steps: (1) define a static variable in one file outside of the functions of that file, and (2) declare a variable of the same type and name in another file with the *extern* qualifier. You can declare the *extern* variable either inside or outside of a function. Notice the important distinction between **define** and **declare** here: an *extern* statement does not allocate memory for a variable, so it is a declaration that simply establishes linkage. Not surprisingly, you cannot initialize a variable in an *extern* declaration. The statement that allocates memory defines the variable; you can only define it once, but you can declare *extern* linkage as many times as necessary. The next program modifies the scope of the variable *next* in DOCTOR2.C by splitting the program into two files and declaring *next* to be *extern* in one of them.

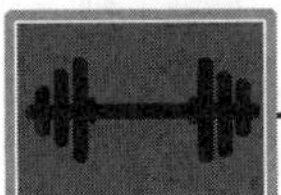

Listing 16.5 DOCTOR3.C Display appointment times

DO:
- Split main() into a separate file
- Compile DOCTOR3

```
#include <stdio.h>
char *next_appointment(void);

int next = 0;
char appointment[8][6] = { " 8:00", " 9:00",
                           "10:00", "11:00",
                           " 1:00", " 2:00",
                           " 3:00", " 4:00"};

void main()
{
```

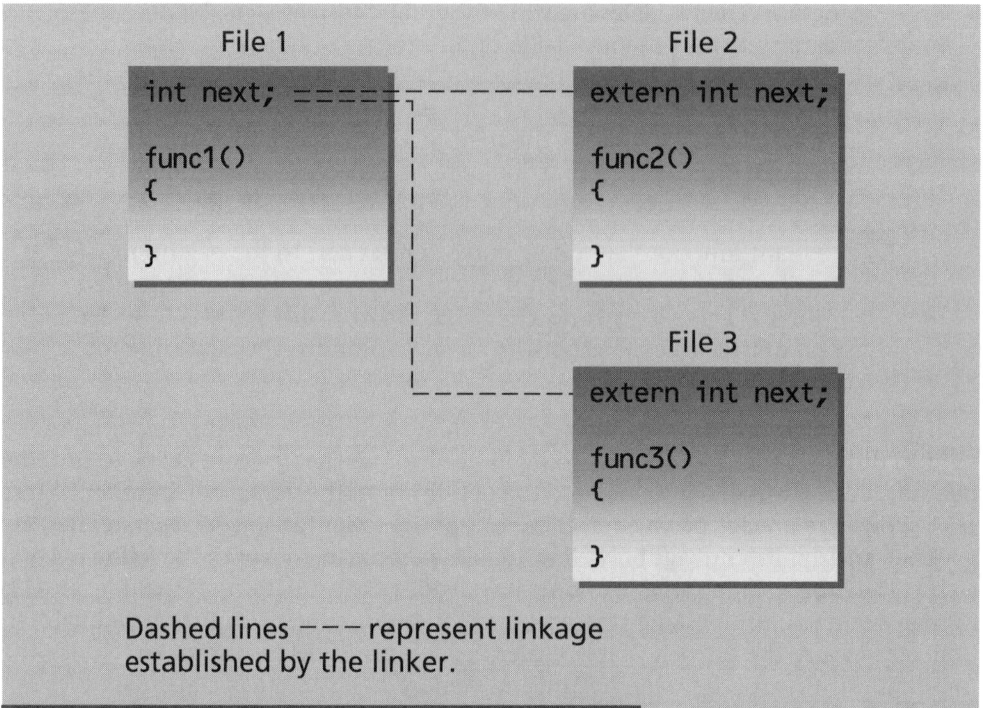

File 1

```
int next;

func1()
{

}
```

File 2

```
extern int next;

func2()
{

}
```

File 3

```
extern int next;

func3()
{

}
```

Dashed lines --- represent linkage established by the linker.

Figure 16-1 External linkage

```
    printf("\nThe next available appointment is at %s",
         next_appointment());
    printf("\nThe next available appointment is at %s",
         next_appointment());

    if (next == 7)
      next = 0;
}
```

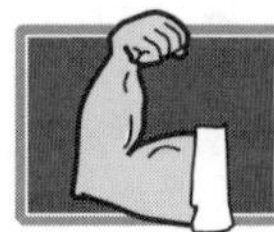

RESULT:

```
C:\>pc/c DOCTOR3
Power C - Version 2.1.3
(C) Copyright 1989-1991 by Mix Software
Compiling ...
 126 lines compiled
Optimizing ...
   1 function optimized in 1 file
```

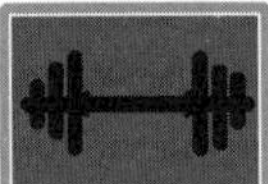

Listing 16.6 DOCTOR4.C Display appointment times

DO:
- Put next_appointment() into a separate file
- Declare the variables to be external
- Compile DOCTOR4

```
char *next_appointment(void)
{
     extern int  next;                                          /*1*/
     extern char appointment[8][6];                             /*2*/

     return(appointment[next++]);
}
```

RESULT:

```
C:\>pc/c DOCTOR4
Power C - Version 2.1.3
(C) Copyright 1989-1991 by Mix Software
Compiling ...
   7 lines compiled
Optimizing ...
   1 function optimized in 1 file
```

ANALYSIS:

1. Line /*1*/ declares *next* to be an external integer variable, so the compiler expects that another file will define *next* and that the linker will later make the connection between the two.
2. Likewise, line /*2*/ declares *appointment* to be *extern*; the main file initializes the array, so the declaration just has to be consistent with the type and dimensions of the array.
3. The scope of the variables *next* and *appointment* extends to both files, so once the files are linked, the variables will be accessible to all functions.

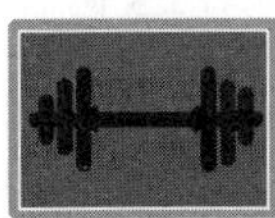

DO:
- Link DOCTOR3 and DOCTOR4
- Run DOCTOR3

RESULT:

```
pcl DOCTOR3, DOCTOR4
Power C Linker - version 2.1.3
DOCTOR3.EXE created

C:\>DOCTOR3

The next available appointment is at  8:00
The next available appointment is at  9:00
```

ANALYSIS:

The ability to establish linkage between variables in separate files is important for large programming projects. This mechanism makes it possible to keep files a manageable size and still share global (static) variables between functions.

A final word of caution about external variables: The C language specification only guarantees that compilers will use the first 6 characters of the names of external variables in the static storage class. It also does not guarantee that the compiler will recognize the difference between uppercase and lowercase characters for these names. This applies to all variables declared outside of functions in a file, or variables qualified with the keyword *extern*. This condition is imposed for reasons of compatibility—some computer systems (primarily mainframes) cannot deal with names longer than 6 characters. Most compilers will recognize at least 31 characters for external names, but if you need to write extremely portable programs, you need to keep this restriction in mind.

Static functions

The *static* qualifier is not confined to just variables; you can also declare functions to be static. You accomplish this by adding the *static* qualifier in front of the return type when you declare the function prototype and when you define the function:

```
static char *next_appointment(void);    /* Prototype */
static char *next_appointment(void)     /* Definition */
{
}
```

This action restricts the scope of the function to the file where it appears, that is, the function can only be called by another function in the same file. You can apply this feature when you want a function to be used in a very limited way. Perhaps you have a specialized function that has only a single purpose, and that purpose is totally meaningless except to other functions in the same file; in that case, you might declare it to be *static*. Or, perhaps a function accesses some data that should be protected against unauthorized or unnecessary access; you could protect the data by declaring the function to be *static*. This situation sometimes arises in libraries of utility functions that accompany database software or networking and communications software; it also arises in connection with object-oriented programming, in which some of the data for an object remains private. A static function within a software library would not be callable from an external program; it would only be used by other functions in the library. As an example, suppose you were asked to write a function to return the cost of an appointment made in a doctor's office so that the cost could be displayed along with an appointment time. This information might be considered private, and you would not want another program to be able to access it by calling your cost function. You could add a static function to file DOCTOR4.C that returns the cost, and yet protect it against external access as follows:

Listing 16.7 DOCTOR5.C Display appointment costs

DO:
- Add a static cost function to DOCTOR4
- Compile DOCTOR5
- Link DOCTOR5 with DOCTOR3
- Run DOCTOR3

```
static char *appointment_cost();                                /*1*/

char *next_appointment(void)
{
   extern int  next;
   extern char appointment[8][6];

   printf("\nAn appointment cost is %s",                        /*2*/
        appointment_cost());                                    /*3*/
   return(appointment[next++]);
}

static char *appointment_cost(void)                             /*4*/
{                                                               /*5*/
   return("$500.00");                                           /*6*/
}
                                                                /*7*/
```

RESULT:

```
C:\>pc/c DOCTOR5
Power C - Version 2.1.3
(C) Copyright 1989-1991 by Mix Software
Compiling ...
```

```
   16 lines compiled
Optimizing ...
    1 function optimized in 1 file

C:\>pcl DOCTOR3, DOCTOR5
Power C Linker - version 2.1.3
DOCTOR3.EXE created

C:\>DOCTOR3

An appointment cost is $500.00
The next available appointment is at  8:00
An appointment cost is $500.00
The next available appointment is at  9:00
```

ANALYSIS:

1. Lines /*2–3*/ display the cost of an appointment by calling the new function appointment_cost() from the printf() statement.
2. The prototype on line /*1*/ declares the new function to be *static,* as does the function definition on line /*4*/. The prototype appears only in this file (DOCTOR5.C), because this is the only place where the program calls the function; contrast this with the placement of the prototype for appointment_times() in the other file (DOCTOR3.C).
3. The method of accessing the cost information is known only within the file DOCTOR5.C; you could keep it a secret by hiding the source code to DOCTOR5.C, and nobody else would know how to get the information.

Try calling appointment_cost() from the main function in DOCTOR3.C to see how the compiler protects a static function from outside access.

Listing 16.8 DOCTOR6.C Display appointment times and costs

DO:
- Add a call to get an appointment cost
- Compile DOCTOR6
- Link DOCTOR6 and DOCTOR5

```
#include <stdio.h>
char *next_appointment(void);
```

```
int next = 0;
char appointment[8][6] = { " 8:00", " 9:00",
                           "10:00", "11:00",
                           " 1:00", " 2:00",
                           " 3:00", " 4:00"};

void main()
{
     printf("\nThe next available appointment is at %s",
          next_appointment());
     printf("\nThe next available appointment is at %s",
          next_appointment());
     printf("An appointment cost is ", appointment_cost());     /*1*/

     if (next == 7)
          next = 0;
}
```

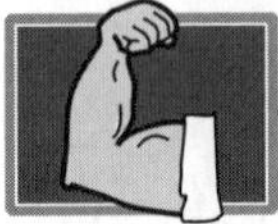

RESULT:

```
C:\>pc/c DOCTOR6
Power C - Version 2.1.3
(C) Copyright 1989-1991 by Mix Software
Compiling ...
  127 lines compiled
Optimizing ...
   1 function optimized in 1 file

pcl DOCTOR6, DOCTOR5
Power C Linker - version 2.0.1
** Unresolved references:
appointment_cost          ? in main      (DOCTOR6.MIX)
```

ANALYSIS:

A link error occurred indicating an unresolved reference to an external function; the function appointment_cost() is not available to any function outside of DOCTOR5.C.

Another reason for declaring *static* functions is so that you can freely use function names within a module without experiencing conflicts with names in system libraries or other modules. You can make up function names inside a file without worrying about whether the names are repeated elsewhere as long as you declare them to be *static*. Be aware, though, that this practice limits a function so that it cannot be used outside the file where it resides.

TYPEDEF

With the keyword *typedef*, you can assign your own names (C identifiers) to data types; this can be especially useful as a kind of shorthand for complex data declarations. It is a good idea to use uppercase letters in *typedef* names so that they are easily distinguishable. For example, you could assign the name BYTE to the data type *unsigned char* with this statement:

```
typedef unsigned char BYTE;
```

Then you could declare variables with the new name:

```
BYTE ch1;
BYTE ch2;
```

This has the same effect as if you had declared:

```
unsigned char ch1;
unsigned char ch2;
```

In this case, *typedef* acts a lot like the preprocessor *#define* directive. Basically, there are two reasons for using *typedef*: to make programs more readable, and to make them more portable. You can make a program more readable by assigning names to data types that are shorter and more meaningful in terms of the usage. This is similar to one of the uses of the preprocessor *#define* directive, in which you substitute a name like *TRUE* for the value 1. You can make a program more portable by assigning a name that you use to declare variables many times throughout a function or functions; then you only need to change the data type in one place when you move the program to another computer or compiler. Once again, this is similar to how you might apply the *#define* directive; however, *typedef* is different in some important ways.

Differences between #define and typedef

Typedef statements are different from *#define* directives because they are compiled rather than handled by the preprocessor, and you can only use *typedef* with names for data types. You can replace any C element with *#define* directives, but there are certain complex *typedef* constructions that a *#define* directive cannot duplicate. They are also different because syntactically, you **must** end a *typedef* statement with a semicolon (;), which you should not do with a *#define*, and the two commands put the new name (the identifier) in a different order. With *#define*, you put the name before the replacement text, and with *typedef*, you put it where the variable name would normally appear.

Fundamental and derived data types

There are two categories of data types in C: *fundamental* and *derived*. The fundamental types are the declarations provided for by C, such as *int*, *char*, and *float*, including qualified declarations like *unsigned*. The next program shows two examples of using *typedef* with fundamental data types.

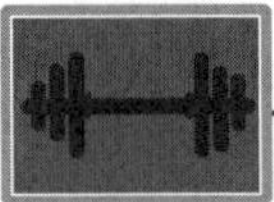

Listing 16.9 TYPES.C Assign new data type names

DO: Enter, compile, and run TYPES

```
#include <stdio.h>
typedef unsigned char UBYTE;
typedef int           INT16;
void main()
{
    UBYTE small_mask = 0x0F;        /* Bit pattern 00001111 */
    UBYTE small_number;
    INT16 large_number = 0x102;

    small_number = small_mask & large_number;
    printf("Small number is %X", small_number);
}
```

RESULT:

```
C:\>TYPES
Small number is 2
```

ANALYSIS:

1. The two *typedef* statements assign new names to two of the standard, fundamental C data types: the first assigns *UBYTE to unsigned char*, and the second assigns *INT16* to *int*. *UBYTE* is descriptive of a data type that is one byte in size that will be used to hold unsigned integer values, and *INT16* describes an integer data type that is 16 bits long.
2. Inside the main function, the new names declare some variables: *small_mask* and *small_number* are *unsigned char* variables, and *large_number* is type *int*. The program initializes the mask with the four least-significant bits set so that it can extract only these bits from a number.
3. The assignment statement applies the mask to the value of *large_number* with a bitwise AND operator (&), then assigns the result to *small_number*. The printf() statement shows that the assignment statement extracted the value 2 from the lower 4 bits of *large_number*.

You produce derived data types when you declare arrays, pointers, structures, unions, and functions. The *typedef* is particularly helpful with derived types because the name that you assign is a concise way of representing a complex declaration. You assign a name to a derived data type by declaring the type preceded by *typedef* and using the name where the variable identifier would be. In the next program, you can use *typedef* to assign new names for a pointer and an array.

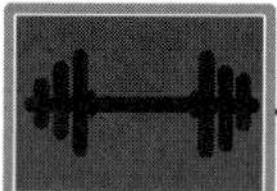

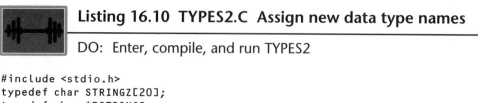

Listing 16.10 TYPES2.C Assign new data type names

DO: Enter, compile, and run TYPES2

```
#include <stdio.h>
typedef char STRINGZ[20];
typedef char *PSTRINGZ;
void main()
{
      STRINGZ  holiday;
      PSTRINGZ ptr = holiday;

      strcpy(ptr, "Thanksgiving");
      printf("%s", ptr);
}
```

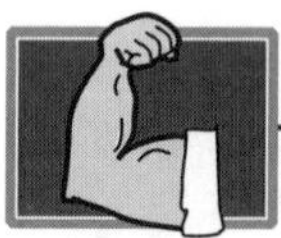

RESULT:

```
C:\>TYPES2
Thanksgiving
```

ANALYSIS:

1. The first *typedef* statement declares STRINGZ to be the name of a 20-byte character array (to hold zero-terminated strings), and the second *typedef* statement declares PSTRINGZ to be a character pointer.
2. The program uses the new name STRINGZ to define the variable *holiday*, a 20-character array. The statement *STRINGZ holiday;* is the same as *char holiday[20];*.
3. The next line, *PSTRINGZ ptr = holiday;* is the same as *char *ptr = holiday;* which defines a character pointer and initializes it to the address of array *holiday*.
4. The remaining two program lines copy a string constant to the array and display it.

You can use *typedef* to assign names to structures and unions just as easily as you do for arrays. Here is an example of using *typedef* for a structure. This example also shows that you can use a *typedef* name as part of another *typedef*.

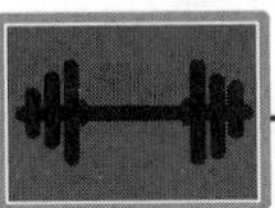

Listing 16.11 TYPES3.C Assign new data type names

DO: Enter, compile, and run TYPES3

```
#include <stdio.h>
typedef char STRINGZ[20];
typedef struct
{
      STRINGZ holiday;
      STRINGZ date;
} TIMEOFF;
void main()
{
      TIMEOFF day = {"Thanksgiving", "November 28"};

      printf("In 1991 %s is on %s.", day.holiday, day.date);
}
```

RESULT:

```
C:\>TYPES3
In 1991 Thanksgiving is on November 28.
```

ANALYSIS:

1. The second *typedef* statement assigns the name TIMEOFF to a structure that has two character array members, *holiday* and *date*. The members are declared as type STRINGZ, declared in the previous *typedef* statement as being synonymous with a 20-byte character array.
2. The *typedef* structure has no tag, although it could, and the new *typedef* name occupies the place ordinarily occupied by a structure variable name.
3. The program declares the structure variable *day* as type TIMEOFF and initializes the members, then displays the member strings as part of a sentence.

You can also use *typedef* to assign a name to a function type; the syntax for this is:

```
typedef return_type NAME(argument_type list);
```

With this statement, you assign an alias (NAME) that specifies the data types of all the arguments for a function and the return data type. The next program shows an example of using a function *typedef*.

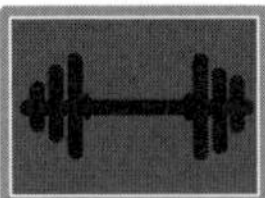

Listing 16.12 TYPES4.C Assign new data type names

DO: Enter, compile, and run TYPES4

```
#include <stdio.h>
typedef void FUNC(char *);           /* Declare FUNC data type */

FUNC show_day;                       /* Function prototype */
void main()
{
     show_day("Thanksgiving");
}

FUNC show_day(ptr)                   /* Function definition */
{
     printf("%s", ptr);
}
```

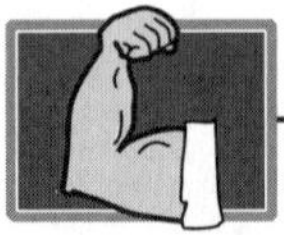

RESULT:

```
C:\>TYPES4
Thanksgiving
```

ANALYSIS:

1. The *typedef* statement declares the name FUNC to be a function with one argument (a character pointer) that does not return a value (type *void*).

2. The program uses the new *typedef* name FUNC both to declare a function prototype and to define the function itself. Because FUNC implies the argument and return data types, the prototype is declared simply by attaching the function name, show_day. Likewise, when the program defines the function, all it needs is the *typedef* name, FUNC, followed by show_day and the name of the parameter in parentheses.

3. This program executes a simple task; the main function calls function show_day(), passing a pointer to a string constant, and the function displays the string.

The preferred location for *typedef* statements is outside the main function, just after preprocessor directives like *#include* and *#define*, as shown in the four preceding program examples. A header is also a good place to put *typedef* statements because they are often needed in many functions that may be in different files.

THE ENUMERATED DATA TYPE

C provides the *enum* (enumerated) data type, which you can use to declare variables and associated collections of constant values. The syntax of an *enum* declaration is similar to a structure:

```
enum tag { enumerator list } variable_name;
```

It is not normal practice to line up the two curly braces in the fashion of a structure; to be more space efficient, the enumerator list is usually configured like an array initialization list. All of the items are optional except the keyword *enum* and the semicolon (;). The tag plays much the same role as a structure tag, and as with a structure, the best way to declare a variable of type *enum* is with two statements. First, you declare the template of the enumerated type, like:

```
enum day { SUNDAY, MONDAY, TUESDAY, WEDNESDAY,
           THURSDAY, FRIDAY, SATURDAY };
```

Then you define one or more variables using the template tag:

```
enum day workday, holiday;
```

The first statement names a data type, *enum day*, and it also declares a list of named constants that a variable of type *enum day* can have. The enumerator list (*SUNDAY, MONDAY, ...*) is a set of named constants with integer values—as if you had listed a series of preprocessor *#define* directives. The compiler assigns each item in the list a sequential integer value, starting with zero (0). Thus, *SUNDAY* has a value of 0, *MONDAY* is 1, and *SATURDAY* is 6. You can use either uppercase or lowercase letters for the enumerated constants; we prefer to use uppercase for consistency with our representation of symbolic constants in *#define* directives. The second *enum* statement defines two variables of type *enum day*, so that you end up with integer variables *workday* and *holiday* that can accept the seven values corresponding to *SUNDAY* through *SATURDAY*. The compiler assigns default values to an enumerated list that start with 0 and increment upwards, but you can control the sequence by assigning values within the list. You could start renumbering at *TUESDAY* and again at *FRIDAY* with this statement:

```
enum day { SUNDAY, MONDAY, TUESDAY=16, WEDNESDAY,
           THURSDAY, FRIDAY=-2, SATURDAY };
```

This declaration causes the numbering sequence to start over with 16 at *TUESDAY* and -2 at *FRIDAY*, so that the final list of values is:

```
SUNDAY              0
MONDAY              1
TUESDAY            16
WEDNESDAY          17
THURSDAY           18
FRIDAY             -2
SATURDAY           -1
```

Variables declared with *enum* are always of type *int*, so the named constants must always be values compatible with data type *int*—either signed integers or character constants.

There are two reasons for using enumerated types. One is to enhance the readability of programs—names are easier to read than arbitrary numbers. Enumerated data types are most often used with familiar sequences of items, such as colors, days of the week, or months of the year, in which the names are highly recognizable. Another reason is to provide automatic checking of values assigned to variables; some compilers will generate an error if you try to assign an unlisted value to an enumerated data type, but the C specification makes this an optional feature, and many compilers do not perform this check.

The next program queries your attitude about money, then uses an *enum* declaration to help check your response. As this example shows, you can assign character values to enumeration constants as well as integer values.

Listing 16.13 RESPOND.C Keyboard response

DO: Enter, compile, and run RESPOND

```
#include <stdio.h>
void main()
{
     enum acceptable { YES='Y', NO='N', MAYBE='M' };
     enum acceptable answer;

     printf("Would you accept a million dollar gift? \
(Y)es, (N)o, (M)aybe: ");

     do
     {
        answer = getchar();

     } while ((answer != YES) && (answer != NO) &&
              (answer != MAYBE));

     printf("\nI feel the same way.");
}
```

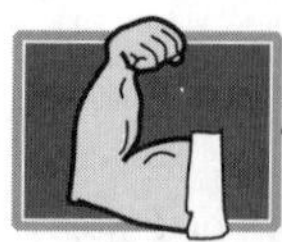

RESULT:

```
C:\>RESPOND
```

```
Would you accept a million dollar gift? (Y)es, (N)o, (M)aybe: Y

I feel the same way.
```

ANALYSIS:

1. The first *enum* statement declares the tag *acceptable* and a list of named constants, *YES, NO, MAYBE.* It also assigns character constants to the three named constants—these are the acceptable keyboard responses for the program.
2. The second *enum* statement defines a variable *answer* of type *enum acceptable* (which is also type *int*).
3. The program prompts you to enter one of the three acceptable characters ('Y', 'N', or 'M'), then reads your response in a *do while* loop. The *while* expression ends the loop only if your response matches one of the three enumerated named constants, *YES, NO,* or *MAYBE.*

The most important concept from this chapter is the difference between automatic and static storage. The two storage classes are best characterized by the three properties of each—initialization, lifetime, and scope. In general, static variables are automatically initialized, they last the lifetime of the program, and they have a wide scope. Automatic variables have no default initialization, they have a life that is limited to one function, and their use is also limited to that function.

CHAPTER 17

PROGRAMMING TECHNIQUE AND STYLE

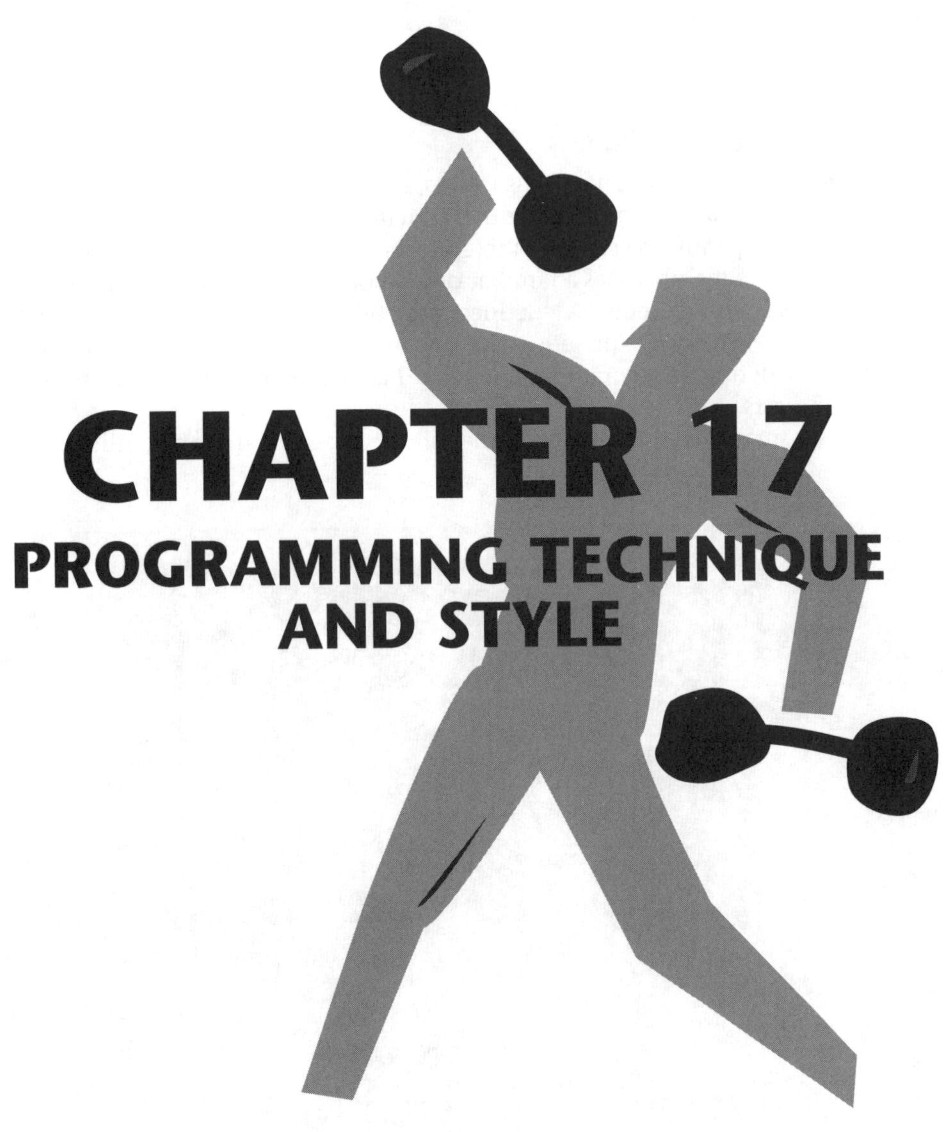

The C language gives you wide ranging freedom to write programs using many powerful constructions without strict layout requirements. You can make the best use of this privilege by observing the bounds of some established guidelines. By adopting proper programming techniques, you can save time, effort, and trouble, both for yourself and for others who work with your programs. This chapter summarizes many of the style recommendations presented throughout the book—most are widely recognized techniques that lead to programs that are readable, reliable, maintainable, and efficient.

PROGRAM LAYOUT

C programs are made up of several basic parts, such as *#define* directives, global variable declarations, the main function, and other functions. Most software projects involving two or more programmers establish a fixed sequence for these basic parts of a program so that each team member sees a familiar order when he or she looks at a source file. If you have to search for items (say defined symbolic constants) in a different place in every source file, you can experience a lot of confusion and wasted effort. Table 17-1 is a suggested ordering of program sections that has proven successful with some major software projects.

Here is a small example that embodies all the program sections outlined in Table 17-1.

Section	Contains
1. Includes	Preprocessor #include directives for header files
2. Defines	Preprocessor #define directives for symbolic constants and macros
3. Typedefs	typedef statements for new data type names
4. Prototypes	Function prototypes
5. Globals	Declaration of global variables
6. main () {	The main function
locals statics	Declaration of local variables Declaration of static variables
statements }	Program statements
7. Functions	Other function definitions

func1
{
}	

func2
{
}	

Table 17-1 Suggested ordering of program sections

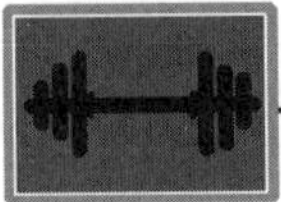

Listing 17.1 COMPARE.C Compare two character values

DO: Examine and match up the program sections with Table 17-1.

```
#include <stdio.h>

#define TRUE  1
#define FALSE 0

typedef char BYTE;

int same(char);

char omega = 'Z';

void main()
{
     BYTE alpha = 'A';

     if (same(alpha))
          printf("The letters are the same");
}

int same(char alpha)
{
     if (alpha == omega)
          return(TRUE);
     else
          return(FALSE);
}
```

ANALYSIS:

It is often better to place defines, typedefs, and prototypes into a header and use an *#include* directive for the header file.

COMMENTS

Comments are an essential ingredient of all programs; they document the purpose and operation of the code, and they also serve to separate and organize program sections. Most programs are modified frequently during their lifetimes, especially the best and most useful programs, and comments make it possible for either the original author or someone else to understand and modify a program long after it was written. You should adopt a certain style of commenting and use that style throughout. As a rough guideline, about 25% of the lines in a program should be comments. We will discuss three categories of comments: **information headers**, **variable comments**, and **code comments**.

Information headers

You should precede each function with an information header—a section of comments that explains the purpose and operation of the function. If a file contains several functions, you may choose to have a separate header for each function, or you may summarize the functions in one header at the top of the file, or you may even select some combination of the two. As a minimum, a header should contain the name of the function, an explanation of the function purpose, information about the calling arguments and return value, the programmer's name, and the date. It is also useful to include space for a revision history, a listing of files accessed (if any), global variables (if any), and an example of how to call the function. You should feel free to design your own headers, but here is a suggested format:

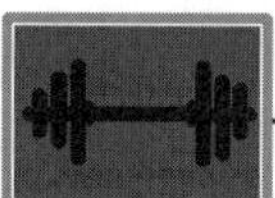

Listing 17.2 COMPARE2.C Compare two character values

DO: Examine the information headers

```
/****************************************************************
   Program: COMPARE

   Purpose: Test to see if two character values are the same.

      Call: compare
            (this is the main program)

   Globals: char omega;  One of the two characters.

Programmed: David P. Himmel, 22-October-1991

   Revised: Who        Date           Explanation
****************************************************************/
#include <stdio.h>

#define TRUE  1
#define FALSE 0

typedef char BYTE;

int same(char);

char omega = 'Z';

void main()
{
     BYTE alpha = 'A';         /* To be compared with global char */

     if (same(alpha))
          printf("The letters are the same");
}
```

```
/*************************************************************
 Function: same

  Purpose: Compare a global character to a character argument.

     Call:  ret = same(alpha);

 Arguments and Return values:

I/O     Type            Name            Usage
--      ----            ----            ----
I       char            alpha           Character to be compared.
O       int                             Return value of the function
                                              TRUE if character values match,
                                              FALSE otherwise.

  Globals: char omega;  One of the two characters.

Programmed: David P. Himmel, 22-October-1991

  Revised: Who          Date            Explanation
*************************************************************/
int same(char alpha)
{
      if (alpha == omega)
            return(TRUE);
      else
            return(FALSE);
}
```

Variable comments

A variable name should reflect its usage, but the name alone is rarely sufficient to explain its purpose. A brief phrase to the right of each variable declaration can be immensely helpful in clarifying how you intend to use the variable. These suggested comments would take the following form:

```
int age;            /* Age of each person as of 1-Jan-1990 */
```

Another example appears in the main function of the above program, where a comment explains that alpha will be compared with a global variable.

Code comments

You should sprinkle comments throughout a program to explain what is going on at every stage. We suggest that you use three different levels of comments: (1) major comments that precede and separate significant program sections, (2) minor comments that clarify blocks of code within major sections, and (3) local comments that explain particular details. These code comments might take on the following appearance:

```
/*---------------------- Major comment ----------------------*/
```

```
/* Minor comment */

Block of related statements

/* Minor comment */

Block of related statements /* Local comment */
```

A major comment should extend across the page to separate the subsequent section of code from preceding statements. The comment should briefly state the purpose of the subsequent section (like, "Read the file," or "Sort names alphabetically"). A minor comment should be smaller in size than a major comment, but it should still occupy an entire line. Minor comments should segregate and clarify smaller blocks of related statements with phrases like "Detect read errors," or "Initialize sort parameters." You should make the major and minor comment lines stand out by inserting a blank line before and after each one. A local comment does not need to be on a separate line; you can just place these brief notes to the right of any statement that needs some extra explanation.

It is all too tempting to put off commenting until later, thinking "I'll do it all at once when I finish the program," but then you never get back to adding the comments. The best time to insert comments is while you are programming the statements. This is true for two reasons: (1) the ideas are fresh in your mind so you can do it faster and more accurately than at any other time, and (2) the act of commenting can be a part of the programming task—an action akin to making a flow diagram. When you make comments, beware that you don't just repeat what the code says; compose comments that add to the information already in the statements. For instance, the following comment is totally redundant:

```
sum = 0;     /* Set the sum to zero */
```

Instead you might take the opportunity to say something significant about the event:

```
sum = 0;     /* Clear out previous accumulation */
```

INDENTATION AND SPACING

C statements are free form—you can place one or more statements anywhere on a line. Your choice of placement for statements can make the difference between a program that is confusing and difficult to maintain, and one that is clear and readable. You should generally only use one statement per line, and some control statements should even occupy two lines.

Without exception, you should indent statements controlled by looping and branching keywords (*if*, *for*, *while*), and nested control statements deserve different levels of indentation. You should also indent all statements inside the curly braces of a function. This program fragment that displays a sequence of characters that contains four levels of indentation:

```
while (n > 0)                                   <- 1st level indent
{
        scanf("%d", &n);                        <- 2st level indent
                                                <- blank line separator
        for (i='A'; i<n; ++i)
                if ((i >= 'A') && (i <= 'Z'))   <- 3rd level indent
                        printf("%c", i);        <- 4th level indent
}
```

All statements within functions need to be indented once, so this whole code fragment is indented to the first level. All of the statements controlled by the *while* are indented one more level, then the *if* statement (controlled by the *for*) is indented to the third level, and finally the printf() is indented to the fourth level. The printf() is really a part of the *if* statement, so this is an example of a statement that occupies two lines, and the *if* is a part of the *for* statement, making the *for* statement occupy three lines. You should indent enough to show a definite shift, but not so much as to shove statements out of visibility on an 80-character screen—four spaces is a practical amount.

C compilers will ignore blank lines in a program; you can use these spaces to segregate related statements and make a program more readable. In the above program fragment, a blank line appears just after the scanf() statement; this serves to separate the input section from the display section of this series of statements.

Without a header	With a header

`#include <stdio.h>`
 	
`#define TRUE 1`
`#define FALSE 0`
 	
`typedef char BYTE;`
 	
`int same (char);`
 	
`char omega = 'Z';`
 	
`main ()`
`{`
`.`
`.`
`.`
	`#include <stdio.h>`
	`#include <compare.h>`
	
	`char omega = 'Z';`
	
	`main ()`
	`{`
	`.`
	`.`
	`.`
	
	Header file (compare.h)

Table 17-2 Use of a header file

HEADERS

When the number of preprocessor *#define* directives, typedef statements, and function prototypes becomes large, or you use these same statements in more than one file, it is time to place them in a header file. The header file simplifies housekeeping for these items; you can avoid repeating the statements with a preprocessor *#include* directive for the header in each source file, and the programs become shorter and simpler. Of course, any statements that you put in a header file are somewhat "hidden," so if only a few such statements exist, you may choose to leave them in the program. Table 17-2 shows the beginning sections of the COMPARE program (program 17.1) without, then with, a header file.

CONSTANTS

Too often, you can look at the source code for a program and see lots of mysterious, meaningless numbers. In your programs, you can, and should, give meaning to numbers with symbolic constants. The COMPARE program, presented in Program 17.1, uses the symbolic constants *TRUE* and *FALSE* to clarify the return value for the function same(). Without these symbols, the return statements would be:

```
return(1); or return(0);
```

The numeric values are not really of interest here; the return value carries a true or false meaning, so the *TRUE/FALSE* symbolic constants are more appropriate. Our advice is to use symbolic constants as often as possible. They can often designate limits, such as the size of an array, or the minimum/maximum values of variables:

```
#define MAX_NUM_BRIDGES 1000
#define LOWEST_CLEARANCE  15
#define HIGHEST_CLEARANCE 50

char bridge[MAX_NUM_BRIDGES];
if ( (bridge[index] < LOWEST_CLEARANCE) ||
     (bridge[index] > HIGHEST_CLEARANCE))
```

This conveys more information than:

```
char bridge[1000];
if ((bridge[index] < 15) || (bridge[index] > 50))
```

In addition to making programs more expressive and readable, symbolic constants make them easier to maintain—you can use a symbolic constant many times in a program, yet to change it, you only need to modify the one statement that defines its value. It is also an advantage to centralize constants in a header file so that you always know just where to go to change or examine a value.

FUNCTIONS, SOURCE FILES, AND LIBRARIES

A hallmark of good programming style is the extensive use of functions. In Chapter 8, we listed five basic advantages of functions, which are worth summarizing here:

1. Function code is reusable.
2. Functions make programs smaller.
3. Functions make programs easier to write.
4. Functions lead to improved commenting and readability.
5. Programs with functions are easier to maintain.

You should form a function whenever it makes sense based on any of the following five criteria summarized from Chapter 8:

1. The operation is used in two or more places.
2. The operation can be used in more than one program.
3. The operation returns a single value.
4. The operation can be described as a distinct task.
5. A program is too long.

When you peel the unique, repeated operations out of a program and make functions out of them, then you have a further opportunity to group similar functions and place them in a file. You might place all I/O functions in one file, all data processing functions in another, and all general utility functions (like conversions, parsers, etc.) in yet another. By organizing functions in files, you shorten compile times and make the development process easier and more efficient. When you finish all the functions in one file, you do not need to recompile them again—just link them with your programs.

The organization of functions into separate files also facilitates the building of libraries. As outlined in Chapter 8 (see topic LIBRARIES), Power C provides for the linking of separate object files. Many compiler/operating system combinations (including Power C/DOS) also support object libraries wherein you can store a collection of compiled functions. A library makes sense at the point when you have finished a significant number of reusable functions and they are ready to be "put away."

VARIABLES AND STORAGE CLASSES

You should choose an identifier to reflect the intended purpose of a variable, but you can get caught between wanting to be descriptive with a longer name and wanting to keep the amount of typing to a minimum. A helpful rule is to use shorter names for control variables, like loop counters and indexes, and longer names for parameters.

Naming conventions for variables

In this book, we have used lowercase characters for identifiers with an underline (_) used to connect words within a name. For example, the ages of a worker and of the bridge that he is repairing might be: *worker_age* and *bridge_age*. Some alternative naming conventions are available; one that is in widespread use today capitalizes the first letter of each word and leaves the separating underline out, so the above age variables become: *WorkerAge* and *BridgeAge*. The names are clearly readable, and some programers prefer to type uppercase characters rather than the underline character (_). A third naming convention called *Hungarian* notation (after Charles Simonyi of Microsoft Corporation, who is of Hungarian descent) also capitalizes the first letter of each identifier word. Hungarian notation attaches a lowercase prefix to each identifier to signify the data type and/or usage of the variable. Using a lowercase 'i' to signify type *int*, the age variables would be *iWorkerAge* and *iBridgeAge*. There is no strict standard for the prefixes—programmers on different projects seem to adopt their own standards, but Table 17-3 lists a few common Hungarian prefixes.

Prefix	Data type
i	int
ui	unsigned int
l	long
ul	unsigned long
b	unsigned char (byte)
ch	char
sz	char array (string terminated by zero)
p	pointer (combined with any other prefix)

Examples

```
char  chAlpha;
int   iFinalValue;
int   *piValue;
char  szFilename[40];
char  *pszName;
unsigned uiByteMask;
unsigned char bFileExists;
```

Table 17-3 Hungarian notation

The advantage of Hungarian notation is that you can tell at a glance what kind of values are legal for a variable; this can prevent bugs from creeping into a program. For instance, when you assign a constant to a *long* variable, it is important that you attach an L to the number; the Hungarian prefix is a valuable reminder to do so.

You can take your pick of naming conventions—they all have merit. Just be sure to stick to a single convention on any given programming project.

Dos and Don'ts for variables

Here are two things **not** to do with variables:

1. Don't repeat names for different purposes. C allows you to have the same name for variables in different functions, but don't do it, except for the following reason: When you call a function, it can be desirable to use the same name for an argument as for the corresponding parameter in the function called.

2. A corollary to the previous rule is use variables for a single purpose only—don't muddle the meaning of a variable by reusing it with another meaning. For instance, you might be tempted to declare the variable *age* and use it in one part of a program to access the age of some bridge workers and in another part to access the age of the bridge itself. You should resist this kind of temptation; instead, declare two variables, *worker_age* and *bridge_age*. Rarely is program space so tight that you cannot afford separate variables for separate purposes.

Here are two things to go easy on with variables.

1. Use global variables sparingly; global (static) variables take up space for the entire time that a program executes. If a variable does not have to have a wide scope and be around the entire time that a program

runs, then declare it inside a function so that the program can discard it when it is not needed. Small variables may not make much difference, but arrays can take up a lot of memory. Another reason to go easy on global variables is that they tend to hide at the top of a file and not be as evident as local, automatic variables. And finally, global variables are susceptible to inadvertent changes; you can cut down the chances for logic errors by minimizing the number of global variables.

2. When you call a function, keep the number of arguments fairly small; otherwise, declare a structure and pass a pointer to the structure as a single argument (see Chapter 13). This does not mean that you should avoid passing necessary information to a function, only that it is better to keep the calls somewhat compact. A structure will tend to hide the parameters from view, so you should only use this technique when the number of arguments exceeds a half-dozen or so, or when it becomes awkward to type them in a function call.

ERROR HANDLING

Programmers frequently overlook the error handling requirements of a program and don't adequately cover them, or they even leave error handling out altogether. Error handling is important because, first of all, problems have to be fixed when errors occur, and secondly, without error handling, a program can react to an error unpredictably, sometimes with disastrous consequences. Imagine what might happen if a program fails to open a data file and continues to execute—it might attempt to read information from the file and end up writing "garbage" to another file, perhaps without even indicating that a problem had occurred. Imagine also what might happen if a program attempts to allocate memory when none is available—in trying to use the nonexistent memory block, it could cause a system to *crash* (a nasty occurrence that requires you to reboot the computer). These sorts of things don't have to happen in your programs; with a little planning, it is easy for you to do a nice job of trapping and reporting errors.

Here are some areas of programs that particularly deserve error checking attention:

- File operations (open, read, write)
- Memory allocations (calloc(), malloc())
- Arithmetic operations (divide, tan())
- Custom operations in your own functions

The following program is an example of incorrect (or no) error handling.

Listing 17.3 ERRORS.C Divide by zero error

DO: Enter, compile, and run ERRORS

```
#include <stdio.h>
void main()
{
     static int dividend;
     static int divisor;
     static int answer;

     answer = dividend / divisor;
     printf("The answer is %d", answer);
}
```

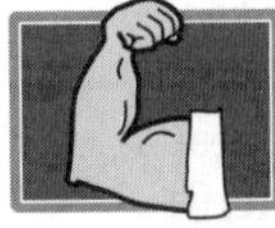

RESULT:

```
C:\>ERRORS

Divide overflow
```

ANALYSIS:

1. This program performs a simple division of some integer numbers, but the *static* declaration initializes *dividend* and *divisor* to 0, so the operation fails on an attempt to divide by 0. The message, "Divide overflow," comes from the operating system after it has aborted your program.

2. You should never permit a program to attempt to divide by 0. Check divisors for 0 values and avoid that circumstance either by performing another operation or by indicating an error.

One technique for handling errors is to use function return codes to indicate the success or failure of the operation of the function. You declare each function to be of type *int* so that it can return a value that indicates success (usually 0) or fail (nonzero). You can use different nonzero values to signify different error conditions, and you can assign these values to symbolic constants. Modify the previous program to detect the zero-divide error and exit more gracefully.

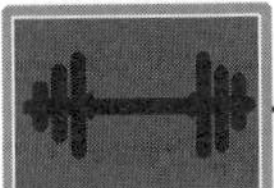

Listing 17.4 ERRORS2.C Divide by zero error

DO:
- Add error handling to ERRORS
- Compile and run ERRORS2

```
#include <stdio.h>
#define OK  0                                               /*1*/
```

```
#define ERR 1                                                   /*2*/
int main()
{
    static int dividend;
    static int divisor;
    static int answer;

    if (divisor == 0)                                           /*3*/
    {                                                           /*4*/
       printf("\nERRORS2: Cannot divide by zero...exiting");    /*5*/
       exit(ERR);                                               /*6*/
    }                                                           /*7*/
    answer = dividend / divisor;
    printf("The answer is %d", answer);

    exit(OK);                                                   /*8*/
}
```

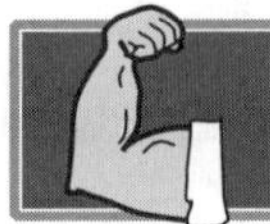

RESULT:

```
C:\>ERRORS2

ERRORS2: Cannot divide by zero...exiting
```

ANALYSIS:

1. The program defines *OK* (0) on line /*1*/ to indicate successful completion and *ERR* (1) on line /*2*/ to indicate that an error occurred.
2. The *if* test on line /*3*/ keeps the program from attempting to divide by 0; the act of detecting that an error is about to occur is called *trapping* an error.
3. Instead of letting the error occur, lines /*4–7*/ display a message that explains what is happening, then exit from the main function with an error code of 1 (*ERR*).

In the above example, you could just as well recover from the potential error and continue processing. Suppose a divisor of 0 implied an answer of 0. Then you could recover as shown in the next example.

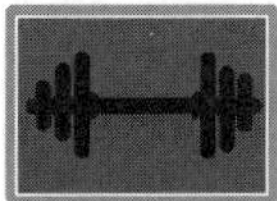

Listing 17.5 ERRORS3.C Divide by zero error

DO:
- Add error recovery to ERRORS2
- Compile and run ERRORS3

```
#include <stdio.h>
#define OK 0
#define ERR 1
int main()
{
    static int dividend;
    static int divisor;
    static int answer;

    if (divisor == 0)
        answer = 0;                                     /*1*/
    else                                                /*2*/
        answer = dividend / divisor;
    printf("The answer is %d", answer);

    exit(OK);
}
```

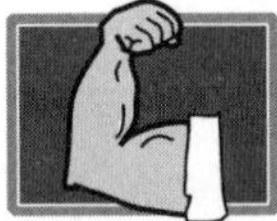

RESULT:

```
C:\>ERRORS3
The answer is 0
```

ANALYSIS:

1. Now if the divisor is 0, line /*1*/ assigns a value of 0 to answer; otherwise the *else* clause on line /*2*/ causes the program to compute the answer.
2. The program still traps the error, but it recovers and continues to execute to a normal ending even if the answer is wrong.

Another good way to accomplish error handling is to design a separate function devoted to trapping and reporting errors. When an error occurs, you can call this function with an argument that indicates the nature of the error and let it deal with most of the details of reporting, recovery, or exiting. Here's an example of an error function:

```
void error(int error_id)
{
    static char *message[] = {  "File open failure",
                                "Memory allocation error",
                                "Attempt to divide by zero",
                                "Invalid data"};

    printf("\nUnrecoverable error: %s", message[error_id]);
```

```
        printf("\nExiting the program...");
        exit(1);
   }
```

The argument to this function is an index to the static message array; a good way to provide these index values is to define a set of symbolic constants, like:

```
#define FILE_ERROR   0
#define ALLOC_ERROR  1
#define ZERO_DIVIDE  2
#define INVALID_DATA 3
```

The error messages themselves are local to the error function, with the advantage that they are centralized and reusable. You should compose error messages that use descriptive terms; you need to be brief, but there should be enough information to point out the nature of the error and a possible remedy.

The advantages of using a central error function are that you achieve consistency in error handling, you avoid repeating many error handling statements, software development is much easier, and because it is easier, you will do a more thorough job of error handling.

Now add this form of error handling to the ERRORS program.

Listing 17.6 ERRORS4.C Divide by zero error

DO:
- Add an error function to ERRORS
- Compile and run ERRORS4

```
#include <stdio.h>
#define FILE_ERROR   0                                                   /*1*/
#define ALLOC_ERROR  1                                                   /*2*/
#define ZERO_DIVIDE  2                                                   /*3*/
#define INVALID_DATA 3                                                   /*4*/
int main()
{
    static int dividend;
    static int divisor;
    static int answer;

    if (divisor == 0)                                                    /*5*/
        error(ZERO_DIVIDE);                                              /*6*/
    answer = dividend / divisor;
    printf("The answer is %d", answer);
}
void error(int error_id)
{
   static char *message[] = {      "File open failure",
                                   "Memory allocation error",
                                   "Attempt to divide by zero",
                                   "Invalid data"};
```

```
    printf("\nUnrecoverable error: %s", message[error_id]);
    printf("\nExiting the program...");
    exit(1);
}
```

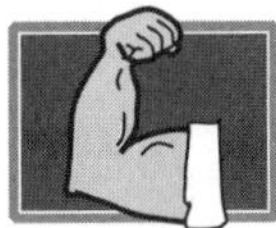

RESULT:

```
C:\>ERRORS4

Unrecoverable error: Attempt to divide by zero
Exiting the program...
```

ANALYSIS:

1. The symbolic constants defined on lines /*1–4*/ serve as argument values to tell the error function which error occurred; they are also indexes to the error messages. If there is a large number of these *#define* directives, you can place them in a header file.
2. The simple *if* statement on lines /*5–6*/ illustrates just how easy error handling is after you have written the reusable error handling function.

You can use both forms of error handling (function return codes, and an error handling function) together in a program. Use the error function to process errors detected in the return values from function calls.

Appendix A
Using the Editor

What is the Power C Editor?

Your Workout C disk includes the Power C Editor, a powerful text editor that you can use to write, revise, and run your C programs. If you worked through the introductory tutorial on the editor in Chapter 1, you already know the basic steps involved in writing and saving a C program. You really don't need to know much more about the editor to write short programs. Nevertheless, the Power C editor has a number of useful features that can make writing, revising, and running programs easier. This appendix will look at these features systematically and in greater detail. Additionally, we will provide tables that you can use as handy references to editor features, key combinations, and commands.

If you don't have much experience with text editing programs, you should note that the Power C editor is *not* a full-fledged word processing program. It doesn't have such features as word wrap, special effects such as boldface or italics, or the ability to change fonts or character sizes. Rather, the Power C Editor is designed for working with C programs, which are ordinary ASCII text files without special formatting or invisible control characters. Besides writing programs, you could use the editor to make simple notes or lists.

You don't have to use the Power C editor to write programs with Workout C. You can use any text editor (such as the Edit program that comes with DOS Version5.0), or you could use some word processors in "ASCII text mode." The Power C compiler doesn't care which editing program was used to create your program code.

The Power C editor does provide a number of useful features for programmers, however. You can take advantage of automatic indentation to keep your program code properly aligned for readability. You can edit two files at once using separate windows (screen areas), or write your program in one window while reviewing a header (include) file in the other window. Once you've written your program, you can compile it directly from the editor and view any error messages from the compiler or linker. You can also "shell to DOS" and run any DOS command or program that you wish, returning to the editor when you're done. These features make it worthwhile for you to explore the Power C Editor.

As a text editor, the Power C Editor provides many useful editing features such as cutting and pasting text and searching for and replacing strings—in fact, there are over 100 different editor commands you can use. Because the main focus of the Workout C package is to teach you the fundamentals of C programming, we will cover only the most useful and important editor commands here. The Power C Editor provides online help summarizing most of the editor commands. You can also obtain a complete manual from Power C software by buying the standalone Power C Editor product. The standalone product provides additonal capabilities such as the ability to customize the editor keys and to create "macros" that combine several editing commands into one operation.

Running the Power C Editor

The Workout C installation program places the editor files in the WORKOUTC subdirectory, unless you specify some other location for the Workout C files. The Power C Editor as distributed with Workout C uses the files listed in Table A-1.

File	Contains
EDIT.COM	The executable Editor program
SETUP.EDT	The Editor configuration for DOS systems
BLOCK.HLP	Help for cutting, pasting, and copying text
CURSOR.HLP	Help for cursor movement commands
DELETE.HLP	Help for keys and commands for deleting text
FILE.HLP	Help for loading and saving files, viewing directories, etc.
FUNCTION.HLP	Help showing commands assigned to function keys
HELP.HLP	Explains how to use the online help
INSERT.HLP	Help on keys and commands for inserting text
MACRO.HLP	Help on predefined macro commands

Table A-1 Files used by the Power C Editor in Workout C

To run the Power C Editor, change the current directory to the Workout C directory and type **edit** at the DOS prompt:

```
C:\>cd workoutc(ENTER)
C:\WORKOUTC>edit(ENTER)
```

The (ENTER) means to press the Enter key, as you normally do for DOS commands. It is important that you run the editor from the Workout C directory. If you aren't in that directory, typing **edit** may run another editor program such as the DOS editor instead.

The Editor Screen

In a moment you will see the screen shown in Figure A-1. The screen has no text, because you haven't written anything yet. The cursor is in the upper left hand corner of the screen, where you will begin typing text. The line below the cursor has the

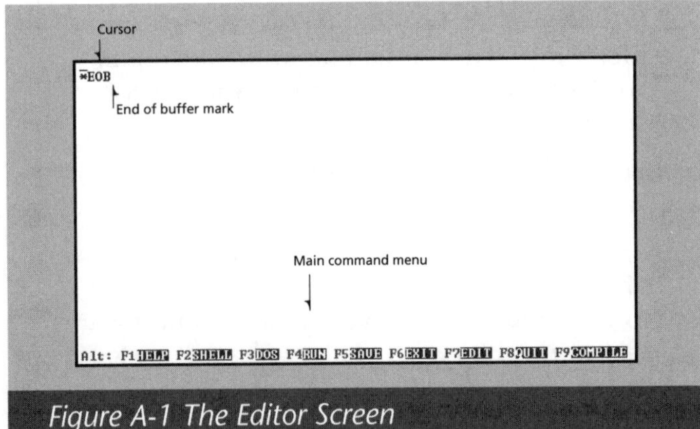

Figure A-1 The Editor Screen

designation *EOB. This means "end of buffer." The editor stores the text you enter in a temporary area in memory (a buffer) until you save the text to a disk file.

The Main Command Menu

At the bottom of the screen you will find a list of commands that are assigned to the various function keys. You execute one of these commands by holding down the ALT key, pressing the designated function key, and then releasing both keys. For example, you can quit the editor by pressing ALT and F8. A prompt appears at the bottom of the screen:

```
<QUIT>REALLY?
```

If you want to quit, enter y for yes and press ENTER. The editor will say goodbye and returns you to the DOS prompt:

```
Goodbye - Have a nice day ...
C:\WORKOUTC>
```

Because you don't want to quit now, type »n.ENTER instead, and you will remain in the editor.

Editing a Specific File

In the previous example we started the editor without specifying any file. You can also start the editor by typing **edit** followed by the name of a file:

```
C:\WORKOUTC>edit myprog.c(ENTER)
```

If the file MYPROG.C exists on the disk, the editor automatically loads it.

Another way to edit a file is to use the **Edit** command listed at the bottom of the screen. Press ALT-F7 followed by the name of the file you want to edit, and the editor will load that file.

The Status Line

The status line summarizes the editor's current position in the file buffer and in memory. When you first run the editor the status line isn't shown, but it appears as soon as you press a key. Here is what the status line might look like when you are just starting to create a new file:

```
1->no file  mem=491904 98% row= 1 col=  1 line=    1 insert indent
```

Starting from the left, the status line displays:

- The number of the buffer being used. You start out with buffer number 1. As you will learn later, you can use two buffers to edit two different files at the same time.
- The name of the current file. Here, because you haven't saved a file yet, the display says "no file."
- The amount of memory in bytes available in the buffer. The editor can use all the available system memory up to 640K (more than 650,000 characters), so you should seldom have a problem fitting a file in memory. You will learn later how you can load files that are too large to fit in memory.
- The percentage of memory still available—here, 98%.
- The row and column position of the cursor, and the current line number. The row and column refer to the location of the cursor within the editing window. The editing window can normally hold 23 rows (or lines) (when the status line is enabled). Up to 80 columns can be shown in the window at a time, but lines can actually be as long as 255 characters. We recommend that you keep the lengths of C program lines to 80 characters or fewer, so that no part of a line is hidden. The line number refers to the position of the current line in the file as a whole. Thus if the line number is 211, this means that 210 lines precede the current line in the file. Most of these lines won't be visible in the window, of course.
- The word "insert," indicating that the editor is in "insert mode." In insert mode, which is the default, the editor places characters that you type in front of any existing text at the cursor position. When this word does not appear, the editor is in "overtype" mode—the editor replaces any existing text at the cursor position.
- The word "indent," which means that each new line you type will automatically be indented under the preceding line. As you probably know, indentation is important for showing the structure of a C program. A block of C statements (such as the body of a loop or a branch of an **if** statement) is usually indented to show that it is a unit.

Entering Text

To enter text into the file, just start typing. The only thing you have to remember is that unlike word processors, the editor does not automatically "wrap" your text at the right margin. While such wrapping is convenient for regular written documents, program code is normally entered as a series of separate lines, not paragraphs.

Let's begin a new program by typing the following line of code:

```
#include <stdio.h>
```

If you make a mistake you can use the (←) key to move back to the mistake, then press the (DEL) key to delete the mistake, and then type in the corrected text. You will soon learn about other ways to move the cursor and to insert and delete text. Notice that you press (ENTER) to end each line and start the next line. Type in the rest of the program:

```
int main(void)
{
    printf("hello, world");
}
```

Notice that the line beginning with "printf" is indented. You indent a line by pressing the (TAB) key before typing it. You can indent an existing line by moving the cursor to the beginning of the line and pressing (TAB), provided the editor is in insert mode. By default, the editor indents 4 spaces when you press (TAB).

Control Key Commands

Many editor commands are executed by holding down the (CTRL) (Control) key while pressing one or two other keys. For example, to save your text to a file, you can hold down the (CTRL) key and press the (K) and (S) keys in succession, and then release the (CTRL) key. This key combination is listed in our tables as (CTRL)-(K)-(S). Note that while we show the K and S as capital letters for clarity, you do not need to capitalize them. (Indeed it would be awkward to use both the (CTRL) and (SHIFT) keys together.)

The editor provides a complete set of (CTRL) key commands that are compatible with WordStar, one of the first popular word processors. The advantage of (CTRL) key commands is that you can type them without your fingers leaving the "home area" of the keyboard. This feature is appreciated by touch typists. Some people, however, dislike (CTRL) key commands either because reaching for the (CTRL) key is awkward, or because it may not be easy to remember what key combination goes with a given command. Actually, most of the (CTRL) key commands do stand for their intended action. For instance, the (K) key is used for commands that involve files, buffers, or blocks of text. The (S) means "Save." Therefore the command as a whole means "Save the buffer." We will look at many groups of key commands that serve differing purposes, such as moving the cursor or cutting and pasting blocks of text. We will also present tables that will help you learn these commands.

In some cases a non-control key alternative is provided for a command. For example, you can also press (ALT)-(F5) (as shown at the bottom of the screen) to save your file. Where there is a choice, we suggest that you experiment to find out which style of command is easiest for you to remember and use.

Save your text now by pressing (CTRL)-(K)-(S). After you press the keys, the editor prompts you for a name under which to save your file:

```
(SAVE)FILE: hello.c(ENTER)
```

Type the filename "hello.c" and press (ENTER). The editor then asks if you want to make a second (backup) copy of the file:

SAVE BACKUP?

It doesn't hurt to have a spare copy in case you make a mistake later, so you might want to press ENTER to make the backup. If you do, the file on disk as it was before you began editing will be renamed with a .BAK extension, and the revised file will be saved under your original file name. Thus if you edit a file on disk called PROG.C, and save it with a backup, the original file will be renamed PROG.BAK and your newly edited file will be PROG.C.

You are asked for a filename the first time you create a file. Once you have saved the file under a file name, you can press ENTER at the file name prompt to save the file under the same name. Or you can use the ALT-F5 combination to save without any prompt at all.

Command Mode

There is yet a third way to send commands to the editor: by using command mode. To switch from text entry mode to command mode, press the ESC key or the CTRL-J key combination. The cursor moves to the bottom of the screen, where it follows a prompt that looks like this:

<>_

You type the two-letter command name and press ENTER, and the command is executed. For example, you can save your file by entering saENTER after the command prompt. You will be given the same prompts for the file name and for the backup file as you receive with the CTRL and function key versions of the command. The difference between the command mode version and the CTRL and function key versions is that you must first enter command mode with ESC or CTRL-J, and you must press ENTER to execute the command.

The editor actually provides a command mode equivalent for every control or function key command, plus some commands that don't have equivalent key combinations. For most commands, however, the key combination is faster and easier to use. For example, you wouldn't want to enter command mode and type **cl** to move the cursor one character left. Although you could do this, pressing the CTRL-S key combination or the ← key is much faster!

By the way, as with CTRL combinations we will show command names such as SA or CL in uppercase for clarity, but you may type commands in lowercase.

Ending Your Editing Session

The CTRL-K-S or SA command saves your text and keeps you in the editor, ready to continue work. It's a good idea to save your work every 15 minutes or so, as a precaution against serious mistakes, a hardware problem, or power failure. A similar command, CTRL-K-X or EX (exit) also saves your text (with the usual prompts), but exits the editor, returning you to DOS. If you don't like what you've written or revised, you can throw away your work but remain in the editor by using the CTRL-K-Q or Q/ (quit) command. (That last command consists of the letter q and a slash, followed by pressing ENTER as usual.) Finally, you can abandon your work and exit the editor by using the QT command. For both of these commands the editor asks for confirmation:

```
(QUIT)REALLY?
```

Type (y) (ENTER) if you really want to quit; otherwise type (n) (ENTER), and the editor will ignore the command and your changes or additions to the file will *not* be lost.

Note that the save, exit, and quit commands can also be executed from the main menu at the bottom of the screen by pressing (ALT)-(F5), (ALT)-(F6), and (ALT)-(F8), respectively.

Repeating a Command

The ability to execute a command more than once can be quite useful. For example, suppose you want to move the cursor down 10 lines. As you will learn in the section on Moving the Cursor, you can move the cursor down one line by pressing (↓) or the (CTRL)-(X) key combination. To move down 10 lines involves repeating this command 10 times. To repeat a command, start by pressing (CTRL)-(Q)-(Q). You are prompted for the number of times to repeat the command:

```
(REPEAT)TIMES:10(ENTER)
```

After you've entered the number of times to repeat, you simply enter the command to be repeated. In this case, press the (↓) key, and the cursor will move down 10 lines.

Using the Command Tables

Table A-2 summarizes the basic editing commands that we have discussed. Each discussion in this appendix will be accompanied by a summary table. Each table gives a series of tasks that you might want to accomplish with the editor, and the appropriate key combinations or command mode commands to accomplish that task.

Sometimes the instructions for entering a command have a word such as *file name* or *string* in italics. This means that you should substitute an actual file name or string at that point.

To do this...	Enter this...
Start the editor without a file	edit(ENTER) (at DOS prompt)
Start the editor with an existing file	edit *filename*(ENTER)
Enter a line of text	*text line*(ENTER)
Save current text to file and continue editing	(CTRL)-(K)-(S) *or* (ALT)-(F5) *or* SA
Save current file and clear buffer	(CTRL)-(K)-(D) *or* E/
Save current file and exit the editor	(CTRL)-(K)-(X) *or* (ALT)-(F6) *or* EX
Exit editor without saving text	(ALT)-(F8) *or* QT
Throw away changes but stay in editor	(CTRL)-(K)-(Q) *or* Q/
Execute a command-mode command	(ESC)*command*(ENTER) *or* (CTRL)-(J)*command*(ENTER)
Repeat a command	(CTRL)-(Q)-(Q)*times*(ENTER) *command*
Display status line	(F10)

Table A-2 Basic procedures for using the editor

Moving the Cursor

The most frequently used editor commands involve moving the cursor from one place to another in the text. There are two alternate approaches to moving the cursor: WordStar style control key combinations and the use of the arrows and other keys on the keypad. First we'll look at the control key approach. Table A-3 summarizes the keys you can use to move the cursor by character, word, or line, as well as commands for scrolling the text in the window up or down or moving to the beginning or end of the file. As listed in the table, these key combinations don't make any particular sense. When you look at Figure A-2, however, you can see that the position of the various keys on the keyboard does correspond to the direction of the movement commands.

Think of the S, D, E, and X keys as forming a diamond. Pressing the CTRL key together with one of these keys moves the cursor in the direction of that key. Pressing the CTRL key together with one of the four keys on the outer corners of the diamond (W, R, Z, and C) moves (W or Z) or scrolls (R or C) in the direction indicated. Moving means changing the cursor to a new location *within the window*, while scrolling means moving the text "under" the window so that new text appears.

Notice that you can also move the cursor to the beginning or end of the current line, or move it word by word to the left or right.

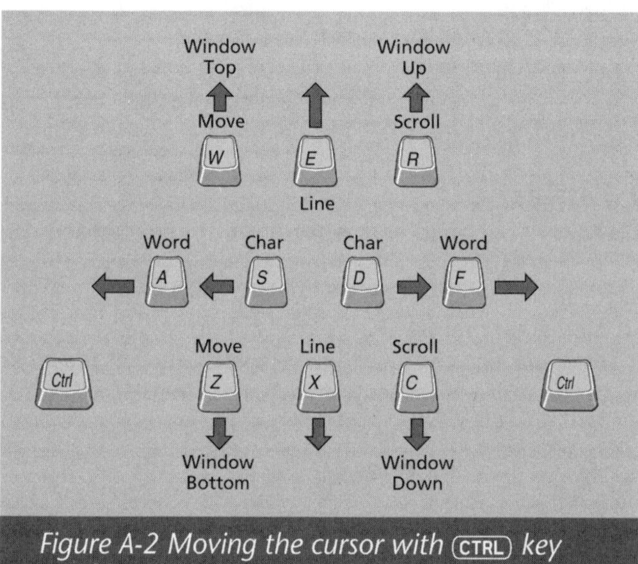

Figure A-2 Moving the cursor with CTRL key combinations

To do this...	Press this...
Move cursor one character right	CTRL-D
Move cursor one character left	CTRL-S
Move cursor one word right	CTRL-F
Move cursor one word left	CTRL-A
Move cursor to beginning of line	CTRL-Q-S
Move cursor to end of line	CTRL-Q-D
Move cursor up one line	CTRL-E
Move cursor down one line	CTRL-X
Move cursor up one paragraph	CTRL-Q-W
Move cursor down one paragraph	CTRL-Q-Z

Move cursor to top of window	CTRL-Z
Move cursor to bottom of window	CTRL-W
Scroll up one window	CTRL-R
Scroll down one window	CTRL-C
Move cursor to beginning of file	CTRL-Q-R
Move cursor to end of file	CTRL-Q-C

Table A-3 Moving the cursor with CTRL key combinations

The alternate approach to cursor control is to use the arrow keys and the PGUP, PGDN, HOME, and END keys. This layout is shown in Figure A-3. On the left of this Figure is the separate cursor keypad that comes with enhanced keyboards such as those found on most AT and PS/2 compatible systems. The right of the figure shows the traditional numeric keypad found on all PCs. You can use either or both of the keypads (if available), and you can combine the control key commands and key pad commands if you wish. Note that if you want to use the regular numeric keypad for cursor movement you must make sure the NUM LOCK setting is *off*.

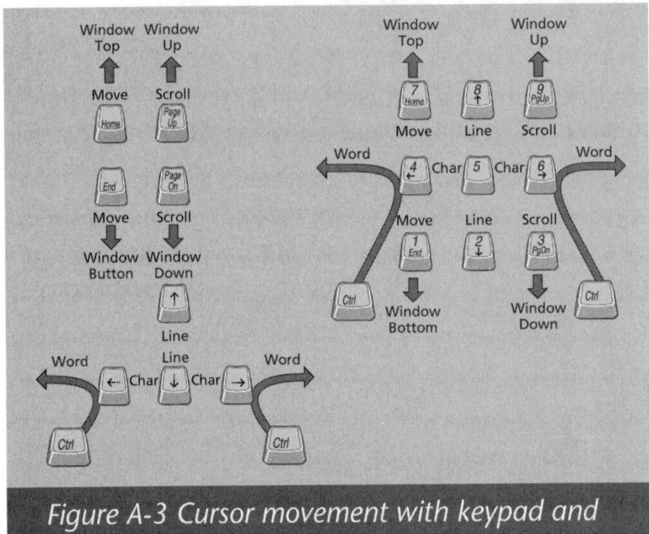

Figure A-3 Cursor movement with keypad and arrows

The choice between CTRL commands and use of the cursor pad is a matter of personal preference. You may want to try both if you're not already used to one or the other. The arrow keys are easier to press than CTRL key combinations, but moving to the cursor pad may interrupt your typing rhythm if you are a fast touch typist.

To do this...	Press this...
Move cursor one character right	→
Move cursor one character left	←
Move cursor one word right	CTRL-→ *or* F4
Move cursor one word left	CTRL-← *or* F3
Move cursor to beginning of line	SHIFT-F3
Move cursor to end of line	SHIFT-F4
Move cursor up one line	↑ *or* F1

Table A-4 (continued)

To do this...	Press this...
Move cursor down one line	↓ or F6
Move cursor to top of window	HOME
Move cursor to bottom of window	END
Scroll up one window	PGUP
Scroll down one window	PGDN
Move cursor to beginning of file	SHIFT-F1
Move cursor to end of file	SHIFT-F2

Table A-4 Moving the cursor with the cursor pad keys

Whichever system of cursor movement you use, you're likely to find that moving word by word along a line is faster than moving a character at a time. To the editor, a "word" is any group of characters that ends in a space. Thus in the line:

```
printf("hello, world")
```

if you start with the cursor at the beginning of the line and press CTRL-F or CTRL-→, the cursor will jump to the space after "hello." (If you had put a space after "printf," then the cursor would have stopped there.) Repeat the command and the cursor will go to the end of the line (the end of a line is also considered to be the end of a word.)

Making Corrections

Once you've written and run your program you're likely to find errors that need to be corrected—or perhaps you'll think of features that you want to add. The basic procedure for revising your program with the editor is to first move the cursor to the place where you want to make the correction. (The cursor movement commands were discussed in the last section). You then delete incorrect text and insert the corrections or additions. For small corrections, you may sometimes find it useful to turn off insert Mode (by pressing the INS key) and then type over the incorrect text to correct it. The commands for deleting text are summarized in Table A-5.

To do this...	Enter this...
Delete character under cursor	Delete
Delete word under cursor	CTRL-T or F5
Delete from cursor to end of line	CTRL-Q-Y or F8
Delete whole line under cursor	CTRL-Y or F6
Join line under cursor with next line	CTRL-Q-J or SHIFT-F7 or SHIFT-F7

Table A-5 Deleting text

Consider the program you typed in and saved as HELLO.C:

```
int main(void)
{
    printf("hello, world");
}
```

Looking at this program, you realize that you wanted to put a carriage return/linefeed after "hello" so any subsequent text will be printed on the next line. The easiest way to make the correction is to use the appropriate control or arrow keys to move the cursor to the beginning of the "printf" line. You can then use the arrow or control key combinations to move the cursor until it is right over the closing quote ("). Assuming you're in insert mode, you can then press \n to put in the CR/LF. The line will now look like this:

```
printf("hello, world\n");
```

As you can see from Table A-5, it is easy to delete all or part of the current line. (To delete several lines, you can also use the block manipulation commands discussed later.)

Besides deleting and inserting characters or typing over existing characters, you can also insert one or more new lines or break an existing line into two lines. These commands are summarized in Table A-6.

To do this...	Enter this...
Insert a character	*character* (Insert mode on)
Correct a character	*character* (insert mode off)
Insert a blank line	CTRL-N *or* F9
Insert several blank lines	CTRL-Q-N *number of lines or* SHIFT-F9 *number of lines or* IN *number of lines*
Open line (push rest of text to next line)	CTRL-Q-O *or* F7

Table A-6 Inserting text

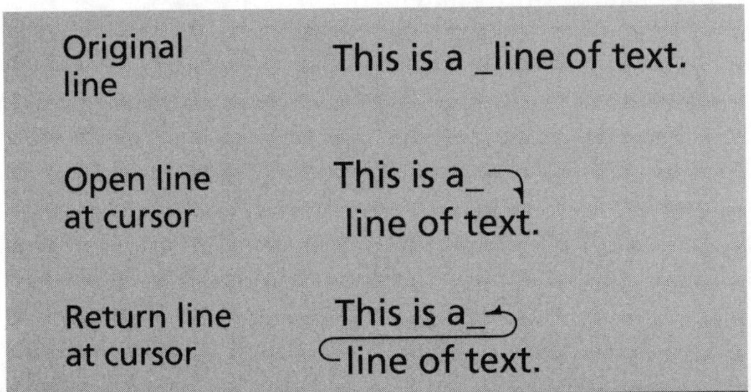

Original line	This is a _line of text.
Open line at cursor	This is a_ line of text.
Return line at cursor	This is a_ line of text.

Figure A-4 Opening and joining lines

Note that the command to insert more than one blank line will prompt you for the number of lines to insert. Also note that the "Join lines" command in Table A-5 and the "Open lines" command in Table A-6 are complementary. Lines opened with the open lineS command can be rejoined with the join lines command, although an extra space will be inserted at the join. Figure A-4 illustrates the open lineS and join lines commands.

Finally, note that opening a line is different from simply pressing ENTER while in Insert mode. Doing the latter also opens (breaks) the line, but moves the cursor down to the start of the second line.

Cutting, Moving, and Copying Text

Many corrections involve deleting or cutting and pasting chunks of text from one part of the file to another. A chunk (sometimes called a "block") might be a single line or several lines (perhaps a whole C function definition). Table A-7 shows how you can pick up and move a single word or a whole line.

To do this...	Enter this...
Pick up word	CTRL-T *or* F5
Put word in new position	CTRL-Q-T *or* SHIFT-F5
Pick up line	CTRL-Y *or* F6
Put line in new position	CTRL-Q-Y *or* SHIFT-F6
Undelete word	CTRL-Q-T *or* SHIFT-F5
Undelete line	CTRL-Q-Y *or* SHIFT-F6

Table A-7 Moving small amounts of text

The basic idea in moving a word or line is to combine the delete and undelete operations. Thus to move a word you first delete it (CTRL-T or F5), move the cursor to the place where you want to move the word, and then undelete the word by pressing CTRL-Q-T or SHIFT-F5. A similar procedure allows you to move a line. The undelete commands are also useful for restoring a mistakenly deleted word or line. However, you can only restore the last word or line. Finally, you could delete and then repeatedly undelete the same word or line in order to make several copies of the text. This can be a quick way to generate a series of blank printf() statements like this:

```
printf(" ");
printf(" ");
printf(" ");
```

You can then easily fill in additional characters for each printf().

But what about deleting, copying, or moving several words or lines at once? For this we turn to the block manipulation commands, shown in Table A-8. Note that these commands have only control key combinations. The basic idea, shown in Figure A-5, is quite simple. First you mark the beginning of the block of text you want to work with by pressing CTRL-K-B. (A block can be several words on one line or several lines, including a partial beginning or ending line.) The editor gives the message "marked beginning" at the bottom of the screen.

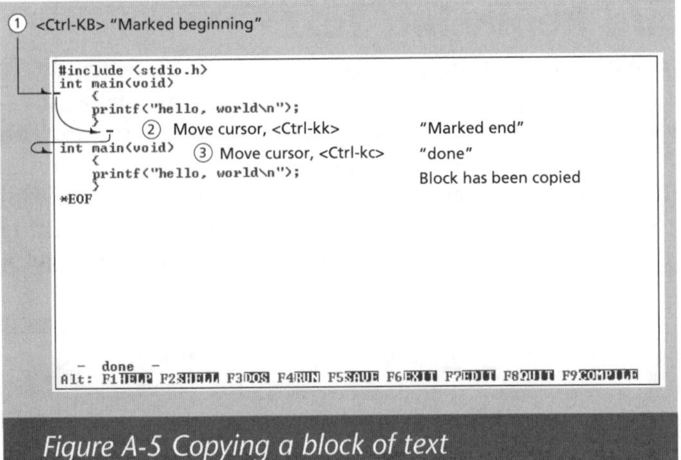

Figure A-5 Copying a block of text

You then mark the extent of the block by moving the cursor to the end of the block, using the usual cursor movement commands. (You should move the cursor to the character *after* the last character belonging to the block.) Once the cursor is at the end of the block, press CTRL-K-K to mark the end of the block. The message "marked end" will appear at the bottom of the screen.

The next step depends on what you want to do. You can simply delete the block (CTRL-K-Y) or you can move or copy the block. To move or copy the block, use the cursor commands to move the cursor to the location where you want the block inserted. Press CTRL-K-C to make a copy of the block at the new location (the original block remains unchanged). Press CTRL-K-V to *move* the block to the new cursor location. Moving the block places it at the new location and deletes the original block. The message "done" at the bottom of the screen announces the completion of any of these operations.

As you can see in Table A-8, you can do a number of other useful things with a marked block. You can save a block to a file, print the block, or change the characters in the block to all uppercase or all lowercase.

To do this...	Enter this...
Mark beginning of block	CTRL-K-B
Show extent of block	*move cursor to end of block*
Mark end of block	CTRL-K-K
Cut marked block	CTRL-K-Y
Copy marked block	*move cursor to new position,* CTRL-K-C
Move marked block	*move cursor to new position,* CTRL-K-V
Change marked block to lowercase	CTRL-K-L
Change marked block to uppercase	CTRL-K-U
Save marked block to a file	CTRL-K-O*filename*
Hide block (disable block commands)	CTRL-K-H
Print marked block	CTRL-K-P

Table A-8 Manipulating blocks of text

Searching for and Replacing Text

Another useful editor feature lets you search for a string of text. This can be handy for finding just where in your program a particular variable is defined, and what statements use this variable for something. The ability to search for and replace text can also be useful: suppose, for example, that you want to change all occurrences of the variable "Total" to "Sum." If you search for each occurrence by hand, you might well miss one. Automating the search/replace procedure makes it more likely everything will be accurately changed. Table A-9 summarizes the commands involved with searching and replacing text strings.

To do this...	Enter this...
Search for a string	CTRL-Q-F *string or FS* string
Find next ocurrence of string	CTRL-L *or* NS
Replace string with confirmation	CTRL-Q-A *search string, replacement string or* QR *search string, replacement string*
Replace next occurrence only	RS *search string, replacement string*
Replace all occurrences without confirmation	RG *search string, replacement string*

Table A-9 Searching for and replacing text

For example, suppose that the following text is currently in the editor:

```
int subtotal, total;
total = 0;
subtotal = 0;
total = total + subtotal;
```

and the cursor is at the start of the first line. To start a search for the word "total," press CTRL-Q-F or enter the FS (find string) command. The editor asks you for the string to find:

```
<FIND>STRING: total
```

The cursor moves to the "t" in "subtotal." This shows us that the editor will match not only the word being searched for, but a word that *contains* that word. If you want to match the exact word, put a space after the search string. Thus, if we typed "total" followed by a space, the cursor would have gone down to the word "total" at the beginning of the second line.

Once you've found and considered an occurrence of your search string, you can find the next occurrence by typing CTRL-L. Each time you do so, the cursor moves to the next occurrence of the search string until no more can be found or you reach the end of the file. (The search does not wrap around from the end of the file to the beginning.)

The safest way to replace strings is to use the "query replace" command. For example, with the cursor back at the start of the file shown above, we can press CTRL-Q-A: and enter the search string (FSTRING) and the replacement string (RSTRING):

```
QREPLACE FSTRING: total
QREPLACE RSTRING: sum
```

As each occurrence is found, the following prompt is displayed:

```
Replace? (y/n/q)
```

Press y to replace the occurence at the cursor, n to skip over this occurrence (making no replacement), or q to end the search and replace operation.

The "replace global" command is faster but more dangerous, because it replaces everything found without asking for confirmation. If you're going to use this command, it's best to save your file first and to examine the results to see if they are what you expected.

Using Tabs and Tab Stops

The TAB key is used fequently in C programming to indent a statement or group of statements under another. Earlier in the book you saw many suggestions for proper code formatting. By default, the editor tabs four spaces when you press TAB, and this is satisfactory for most purposes. As you can see in Table A-10, you can set a tab stop at the cursor location, or change the interval between tab stops to some number other than the default of four.

To do this...	Enter this...
Move cursor one tab stop right	TAB (Insert mode off)
Move cursor one tab stop left	SHIFT-TAB (Insert mode off)
Move text one tab stop right	TAB (Insert mode on)
Set tab stop at cursor	TSE
Clear tab stop at cursor	TCE
Set tab at specified intervals	TB number of *characters*
Set tabs at specific columns	TB *col#, ...*

Table A-10 Using Tabs

All of these commands prompt you for any required numbers.

Working with Files and the Disk

While developing your C programs in the editor, you are likely to need some of the facilities offered by DOS, such as viewing directories, copying files, formatting disks, and so on. You may even want to run a program. The editor allows you to accomplish all of these tasks and then return to the editor right where you left off. Table A-11 summarizes the file and disk-related commands.

To do this...	Enter this...
View a file on disk	SF *filename*
View current file directory	CTRL-K-F *drive or path*
Delete a file from disk	CTRL-K-J
Page through a large file	CTRL-P-P
Run a program	ALT-F4 *progname*
Run a DOS command	ALT-F3 *command*
Shell to DOS	ALT-F2

Table A-11 Working with files and the disk

To get a listing of the files in a disk directory, you can enter the DI command. The following prompt appears:

```
<DIR>PATH:
```

Type in the name of the directory or DOS path you want to use, or press ENTER to view the current directory (which is probably the WORKOUTC directory). You are shown a standard DOS directory list. If the directory is too long to fit in the editor window, the display pauses at the bottom of each screen and—more—is displayed. Press any key to see the next screen. When the last part of the directory is shown, the editor resumes where you left off editing.

If you want to see the contents of a particular file on disk, use the SF command. You will be asked for the file name: give the complete pathname if the file isn't in the current directory. The file will be shown in the editor window. Although the file is "read only" (you can't edit it), the regular scrolling commands do work, so you can move up and down in the file or read a screenful at a time.

The "run a DOS command" menu option (ALT-F3) prompts you for a DOS command:

```
<DOS>COMMAND: copy myprog.c b:
```

The command can be any legal DOS command: here we copied our program MYPROG.C to the floppy disk in drive B:.

The "DOS shell" menu option (ALT-F2)is similar, except that instead of executing just one DOS command, this option gives you a DOS shell with a standard DOS prompt:

```
Microsoft(R) MS-DOS(R) Version 5.00
            (C)Copyright Microsoft Corp 1981-1991.

C:\WORKOUTC>_
```

Work with DOS as usual, and then type "exit" when you want to return to the editor:

```
C:\WORKOUTC>exit
```

Note that if you use the "run a DOS command" option ((SHIFT)-(F3)) and press (ENTER) instead of typing in a command, the result will be the same as if you had used the "shell" option. The "run a program" option ((SHIFT)-(F4)) can be used to run any program that will fit in available memory. (You could use it to run the Power C compiler, but, as you will soon see, it's much easier to use the editor's "compile a program" for that option.)

Developing Programs

The final section of our discussion will deal with how to compile, run, and correct programs without leaving the editor. As you have seen earlier in this book, you can certainly develop programs by using and exiting the editor and then running the compiler and linker from the DOS command line. It is often easier to work directly from the editor, however. This lets you see your compiler errors, make corrections, and recompile, repeating the process until your program is correct.

Working with Two Files at Once

Thus far we have been working with only one file in the editor at a time. The Power C editor can also display two files in two separate buffers. Because program development often involves working with more than one source file (not to mention header files, sample data files, and so on), the ability to work with one more file buffer can be very useful. Table A-12 summarizes the simple commands you use to work with two files. Pressing (CTRL)-(O) moves you between the two buffers. (You can tell which buffer you are using by noting the first number in the status line at the bottom of the screen, which will be 1 or 2 depending on whether you are using the first or second buffer.) As far as the editor is concerned, the buffers are completely separate. When, for example, you are looking at the second buffer, any commands (such as loading or saving a file or searching for or replacing text) apply to that buffer only. Any "exit" command that would ordinarily exit the editor and put you back in DOS instead exits from the current buffer and switches to the other buffer (if the latter is in use).

To do this...	Enter this...
Split screen for use with two files	(CTRL)-(P)-(H) *or* (CTRL)-(P)-(V) *or* SS *row or column number*
Return to full screen	(CTRL)-(U) *or* SS 0
Switch between buffers (files)	(CTRL)-(O)

Table A-12 Working with two files at once

The ability to show both buffers on the same screen makes working with buffers even more useful. The (CTRL)-(P)-(H) command splits the screen horizontally with the first buffer in the top half of the screen and the second buffer in the bottom half. The (CTRL)-(P)-(V) command is similar, except the screen is split vertically, with buffer 1 being on the left side and buffer 2 on the right. These commands split the screen evenly between

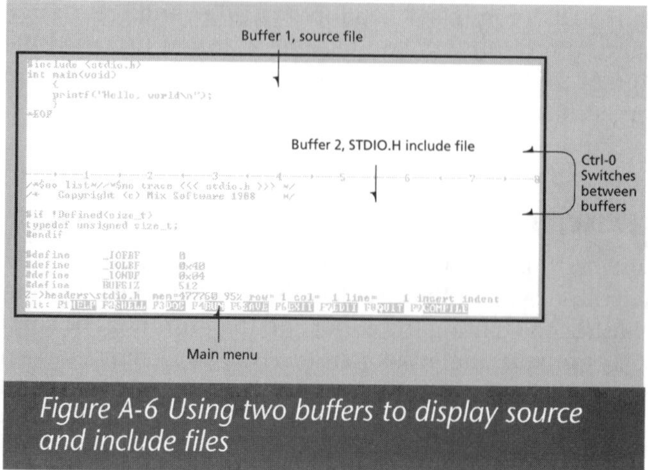

Figure A-6 Using two buffers to display source and include files

the two buffers. The SS command allows you to split the screen at a specific row (line) or column. You are first prompted for a row number. You can enter the number of the row (line) at which to split the screen, or press ENTER. If you press ENTER at the row prompt, you are then prompted for a column number and can split the screen vertically at the specified column.

Figure A-6 shows a useful application of the split screen. Buffer 1, at the top of the screen, has the source file HELLO.C. Buffer 2, at the bottom of the screen, is showing the STDIO.H include file. Being able to view an appropriate header file along with the source code can be useful if you're not sure how the definitions in the header file relate to the operation of your program.

Compiling and Running Your Program

Once you've written your program, it's time to run it and see what happens. The editor commands used in compiling and running a program and working with program errors are summarized in Table A-13.

To do this...	Enter this...
Compile, link, and run current program	ALT-F9
Show errors in separate window	ERR ENTER
Number lines to identify errors	LN ENTER
Link a compiled program	LINK ENTER
Run a compiled and linked program	EXEC ENTER
Trace program (requires Ctrace)	TRACE ENTER
Optimize program	SPEED ENTER

Table A-13 Compiling and running programs from the editor

To run your program, save it to a file and then press ALT-F9. The program will be submitted to the Power C compiler and linker. If the program has no errors, it will run and the results will be displayed on the screen. Here's what is displayed when we run

HELLO.C from the editor:

```
Power C - Version 2.1.3
(C) Copyright 1989-1991 by Mix Software
Compiling ...
  112 lines compiled
Optimizing
...
Power C Linker - Version 2.1.2...
hello, world

<Press any key to continue>
```

(We have left out some of the file names that flash by during the optimization and linking stages.)

As Table A-13 shows, you can peform the individual program development steps separately. You can use the SPEED command to optimize a previously compiled program, the LINK command to link a compiled program, and the EXEC command to run the compiled and linked program. It's usually easier to use the COMPILE option to do everything at once.

The TRACE command is available only if you use the CTRACE debugger, a product available separately from Mix software. This command allows you to debug the current program by tracing its flow of execution, setting breakpoints, and so on.

Viewing and Correcting Program Errors

The discussion thus far has assumed that your program has no errors. Realistically, errors often do occur. Fortunately the Power C Editor also helps you view and fix program errors.

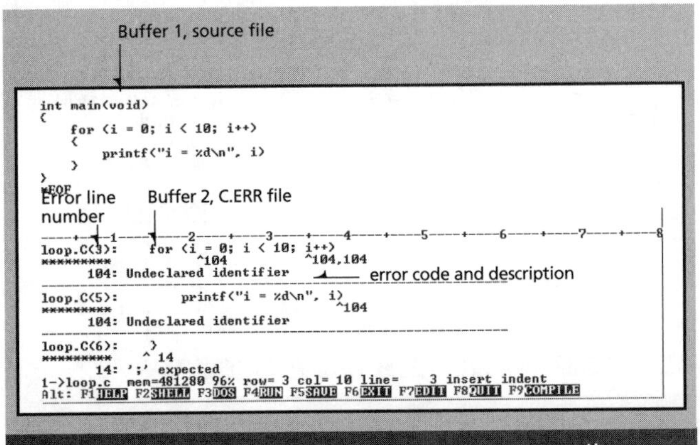

Figure A-7 Using two buffers to view compile errors

Consider the program in Figure A-7. As shown in the figure, the program itself is in buffer 1 at the top of the screen. This program has two errors (the variable is not declared, and the semicolon is missing from the end of the printf() statement.) When you first press ALT-F9 and compile this program, some error messages will flash by. You'll know something is wrong, but it will be hard to figure out just *what.* The solution is to enter the ERR command. This command splits the screen and loads the file C.ERR into the second buffer. The C.ERR file contains all the error messages from the last compilation.

As you can see in the figure, you can now switch to the second buffer ((CTRL)-(O)) and scroll through the error messages. Each error message gives the line number where the error occured, its approximate position within the line, the error code, and a brief description of the error. For example, line 5 has error 104: Undeclared identifier.

You can now switch back to buffer 1 to fix the error. If you're not sure just where the line number referred to in the error message is in your source file, enter the LN command while in the buffer containing your source file. This command numbers all the lines in the buffer, making it easy to find the erroneous line.

Using Online Help

We've about wrapped up our discussion of the Power C Editor. One more important feature is the editor's online help. The editor has seven help screens that summarize the key assignments and commands for different kinds of tasks, as shown in Table A-14. For example, there is a help screen on the subject of moving the cursor, and you can view this screen online by pressing (CTRL)-(F2). Alternatively, you can enter the HELP command followed by the word "cursor." Figure A-8 shows this help screen. Besides being useful for looking up or reviewing a command, the help screens list some commands that we did not have room to cover in this discussion.

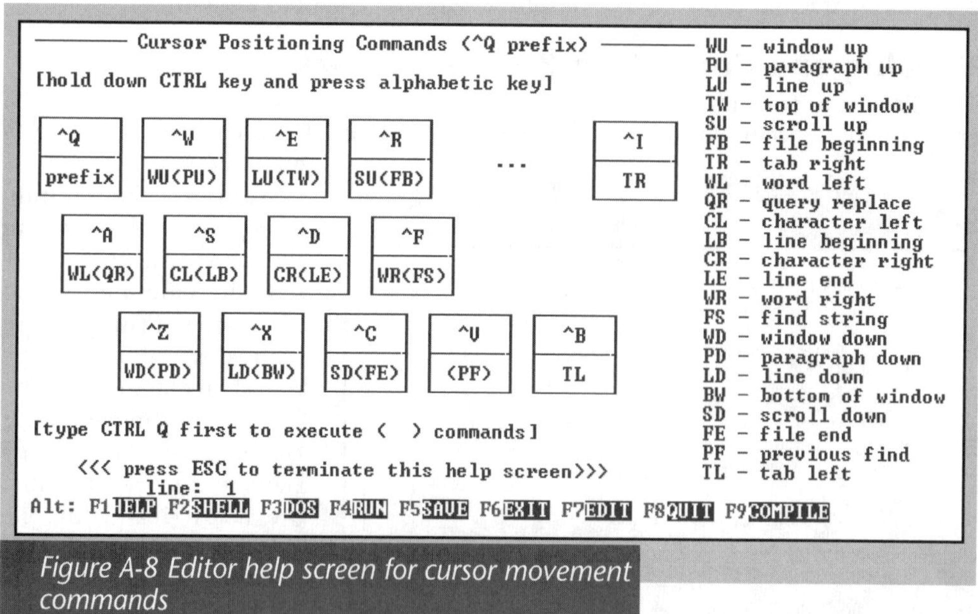

Figure A-8 Editor help screen for cursor movement commands

To do this...	Enter this...
Get help on a subject	HELP *subject* (in command mode; *subject* is one of those listed below)
Get help on function key assignments	CTRL-F1
Get help on cursor movement keys	CTRL-F2
Get help on inserting text	CTRL-F3
Get help on deleting text	CTRL-F4
Get help on manipulating blocks of text	CTRL-F5
Get help on file-related commands	CTRL-F6
Get help on macros defined in MACRO.TXT	CTRL-F7

Help subjects are: FUNCTION,CURSOR, INSERT, DELETE, BLOCK, FILE, and MACRO.

Table A-14 Using online help

You should now know your way around the Power C Editor. A little practice will soon have you speedily typing in, revising, compiling, and testing your programming efforts! Don't forget to consult the tables in this appendix or the online help if you get stuck.

Appendix B
Power C Command Line Options

This appendix explains how to use the command line to invoke the Power C compiler, then provides a reference for each of the command line options.

Using Power C on the DOS Command Line

The Power C compiler requires the PC.EXE and PCO.EXE files to be present in the directory C:\PowerC. PC.EXE is the compiler, and PCO.EXE is the optimizer. Together they construct object files with a .MIX extension from your source files.

The Power C compiler takes as its input one or more text source files and may generate as its output an object file, a list file, and an error file. You can control the behavior of the Power C compiler by using one or more command line options.

The command line form is the compiler name, pc, followed by any desired options, followed by source file names. An option is the slash character (/) followed by an option letter. As examples,

```
C:\WORKOUTC> pc
C:\WORKOUTC> pc test
C:\WORKOUTC> pc test.c
C:\WORKOUTC> pc /l test.c
C:\WORKOUTC> pc /l/y/e test.c,trial.c,attempt.c
```

When you invoke the Power C compiler with no command line parameters, it responds with a list of command line options.

When you invoke the Power C compiler with a file name without specifying an extension, the Power C compiler searches the current directory for a file with a matching name according to the following rules. The Power C compiler treats a file name with no extension or with a .PRJ extension as a "project" file (often called a "make" file); it treats file names with any other extensions as source (.C) files.

When the Power C compiler begins to work, it first searches the environment for an environment variable named PCOPTION. If you have set PCOPTION to equal a string of command line options, the compiler will operate as though you typed those options on the command line. To set PCOPTION, use the SET command. As an example,

```
C:\WORKOUTC> set pcoption=/l/y/e
```

The compiler will take its direction to display the name of each function as it compiles it (/y), display a list file on the screen (/l), and invoke the linker to make an executable file (/e).

You can override the environment variable settings by entering command line options on the command line. As an example,

```
C:\WORKOUT> pc /ltest.lst /y- test
```

If you have a file in your current directory named TEST or TEST.PRJ, the compiler treats that as a "project" or "make" file. If your file has any other extension, such as TEST.C or TEST.SRC, the compiler treats it as a C source file.

For a file named TEST.C, the compiler would create a list file named TEST.LST. It does not display function names as it compiles them, and it does invoke the linker to make an executable file.

Command Line Option Reference

/c The /c option directs the compiler to compile a source file even if the object file date is current.

/d The /d option lets you define a macro name on the command line, either with some value or with a null value. This is useful with the #ifdef or #ifndef preprocessor directives. As an example, /dWOW creates the same effect as #define WOW in your source code, and /dWOW=15 is the same as #define WOW 15.

/e The /e option directs the compiler to invoke the linker to create an executable file if the compile step successfully ends an object file.

/f The /f option has several forms, depending on how you want your program to handle floating-point calculations. The /fa option (the default) directs the compiler to use the PCAUTO.MIX floating-point library file for routines that use the 8087, or to create software emulation if the 8087 is not present. The /fb option directs the compiler to use the BCD business math library file (not included). The /fi option directs the compiler to use the PCIEEE.MIX library file. The /f8 option directs the compiler to use the PC87.MIX library (requires 8087 or 80287). The /f- option directs the compiler to disable the use of floating-point calls for any library file (used to compile functions with out floating-point calculations).

/j The /j option directs the compiler to treat char data types as signed char. The default is /j-, which generates unsigned char.

/k The /k- option (note the minus sign) directs the compiler to ignore all extended keywords (far, interrupt, near...). The default is /k.

/l The /l option directs the compiler to create a list file. The default is /l-, which directs the compiler not to make a list file. The /l option by itself generates a list file to stdout, the console display. You can specify a directory name, for instance, /lsweatit, for which the compiler will create a list file in the sweatit subdirectory of the current directory. You can specify a device, for instance /lprn, which prints the listing.

/m The /m option is used with the l, m, or s modifiers to specify a memory model for the object file. The /ml option directs the compiler to build the object file using the "large" model, with no limit to the amount of memory available for program instructions and no limit to the amount of memory available for program data. The /mm option directs the compiler to build the object file using the "medium" model, with no limit to the amount of memory available for program instructions and a maximum of 64K memory available for program data. The /ms option directs the compiler to build the object file using the "small" model, with a 64K memory limit for program instructions and a 64K memory limit for program data.

/n The /n option directs the compiler to respect nested comments (e.g., /* outer /* inner "nested" comment */ comment */).

/o The /o option directs the compiler to generate an object file if the source code compiles correctly. The default makes an object file. The /o- option directs the compiler not to make an object file (which makes for quicker compile time). The /odirname option directs the compiler to generate an object file (assuming a successful compile) and place it in the specified directory (in this case, dirname).

/q The /q option directs the compiler to generate object files that are compatible with those generated by the Microsoft C compiler.

/r The /r option directs the compiler to place register data types in available CPU registers (this is the default). The /r- option directs the compiler not to locate any register data types in any of the CPU registers.

/s The /s option directs the compiler to add code that checks for stack overflow every time a function is called. This produces a runtime error message, which is helpful for debugging, but slows down the program a bit.

/t The /t option directs the compiler to include debugging symbol information in the object file required by the Power C trace debugger.

/x The /x option directs the compiler to expand macros in the list file (see the /l option).

/y The /y option directs the compiler to display the name of each function as it compiles.

/1 The /1 option directs the compiler to generate code for the 80186 CPU.

/2 The /2 option directs the compiler to generate code for the 80286 CPU.

Using the Power C Linker

The PCL linker links the object file for your program with functions in library files as well as with other object files you can specify on the command line.

The linker searches for these files first by searching the current directory, then by searching directories specified by the LIBRARY environment variable, then finally by searching directories specified by the PATH environment variable. The following example shows how to set the LIBRARY environment variable, assuming you placed the libraries in a \lib subdirectory of the \workout directory.

```
C:\WORKOUTC> set library=c:\workout\lib
```

When you invoke the linker, it will first search the current directory for .MIX files, then it will search the LIB subdirectory of the WORKOUT directory, then it will search each of the directories specified by the PATH environment variable.

If the linker does not resolve all references, it displays the unresolved symbols to the console without making an executable file. If the linker can resolve all references, it makes an executable file with the same name as the first file in the file list and with an .EXE extension. It places the executable file in the current directory.

Command Line Use of the Linker

To invoke the linker, enter its name, PCL, on the command line with the following parameters: any command line options, numerical specifications for the stack, near heap, and far heap, and the names of the object (.MIX) files you want to link.

The simple form specifies the linker with a file name; the other parameters are optional. The following example shows the simple invocation of the linker.

```
C:\WORKOUT> pcl somefile
```

In response to the above command line, the linker will generate an executable file named SOMEFILE.EXE and locate it in the current directory. The executable file will have a stack space of 32K, a near heap space of 32K, and a far heap the size of whatever system memory is available. This is generally the best choice.

The following example shows how to use the /m option to direct the linker to make a “map” listing file.

```
C:\WORKOUT> pcl /m somefile
```

In response to the above command line, the linker will generate an executable file named SOMEFILE.EXE and a “map” file named SOMEFILE.MAP and place them both in the current directory.

The next example shows the order in which to use the other parameters.

```
C:\WORKOUT> pcl /m 8K, 16K, 32K, somefile, nudrfile
```

In response to the above command line, the linker will create a "map" file named SOMEFILE.MAP as well as an executable file named SOMEFILE.EXE that contains the executable code for both SOMEFILE.MIX and NUDRFILE.MIX. The executable file will have a stack space of 8K, a near heap space of 16K, and a far heap space of 32K. You can specify the stack, near heap, and far heap as a certain number of bytes, as the final example shows.

```
C:\WORKOUT> pcl /m/p- 256, 512, 0, somefile, nucrfile, thrdfile
```

In response to the above command line, the linker will create a "map" file named SOMEFILE.MAP, as well as an executable file named SOMEFILE.EXE that contains the executable code for SOMEFILE.MIX, NUDRFILE.MIX, and THRDFILE.MIX. The executable file will not be "packed" thanks to the /p- option. The executable file will have a stack space of 256 bytes, a near heap space of 512 bytes, and no far heap space.

Linker Command Line Options

/a The /a option directs the linker to search the PCAUTO.MIX library file for 8087 auto-sensing, floating-point function references.

/b The /b option directs the linker to search the PCBCD.MIX library file for Binary Coded Decimal, floating-point function references.

/d The /d option directs the linker to search the PCDMY.MIX library file for dummy floating-point function references.

/i The /i option directs the linker to search the PCIEEE.MIX library file for IEEE floating-point function references.

/m The /m option directs the linker to generate a "map" list file that shows functions and their locations in memory along with a list of symbols in the object file. The linker gives this file the same name as the object file but adds the .MAP extension.

/p The /p option directs the linker to create a packed executable file (this is the default). The /p- option directs the linker to create an executable file that is not packed.

/8 The /8 option directs the linker to search the PC87.MIX library file for floating-point functions that require an 8087 math coprocessor to be installed on the system where the program will run.

Appendix C
Power C Library Functions

This appendix presents descriptions of Power C library functions arranged in alphabetical order.

Each function description begins with a function prototype as it should appear in your program source file, usually above the main() function, with an attached semicolon (;). You can either do this explicitly, or you can do it by including header files as discussed in the next paragraph.

The #include statement(s) that follows the function prototype shows which files you should specify with the #include preprocessor directive in your program source file. We recommend that you print out all of the include files (files with an .h extension). Read each of the files and you will notice defined symbols and macros, as well as declared variables and prototypes for related functions.

The text that follows the include directives describes the argument list for the function.

The description for a function ends with a paragraph that discusses the return type and value for the function.

We recommend that you write small programs that exercise the include preprocessor directives. Use the identifier names that are contained in the .h (header) files in the argument list for the function. Alter and expand examples from related chapters. Know thy header files.

```
void abort(void)
   #include <process.h>
   #include <stdlib.h>
```

Takes no arguments. The abort() function terminates the program and displays an error message: "abnormal program termination." (ANSI)

Returns no values.

```
int abs(int)
   #include <stdlib.h>
```

Takes as its argument a signed integer. (ANSI)

Returns the absolute integer value of its argument.

```
int absread(int, int, int, void *)
   #include <dos.h>
```

Takes as its first argument an integer whose value specifies a disk drive (0 for A:, 1 for B:, 2 for C:, and so on). Its second argument is an integer whose value specifies the number of sectors to read. Its third argument is an integer whose value specifies the number of the first sector the absread() function is to read. Its fourth argument is a pointer to a memory area that is large enough to store the data that the absread() function reads from the disk (number of sectors times 512 bytes per sector).

Returns 0 upon success, -1 upon failure.

```
int access(char *, int)
  #include <io.h>
```

Takes a pointer to a character string that specifies a file name. Its second argument is an integer whose value specifies the mode (read, write, read/write) for the file.

Returns 0 if there is a valid file as specified. Returns 1 upon failure.

```
double acos(double)
  #include <math.h>
```

Takes an argument in the range from -1 to 1. (ANSI)

Returns the arc cosine value of its argument or 0 upon failure.

```
void *alloca(unsigned)
  #include <malloc.h>
```

Takes as its argument an unsigned integer that specifies the number of bytes that the alloca() function is to allocate from the program stack area.

Returns a pointer to the newly allocated memory area upon success. Returns NULL upon failure.

```
int allocmem(unsigned, unsigned *)
  #include <malloc.h>
```

Takes as its first argument an unsigned integer whose value specifies the number of bytes for the allocmem() function to allocate. Its second argument is a pointer to an unsigned integer in which the allocmem() function is to store the segment address of the newly allocated memory block.

Returns -1 upon success. If unsuccessful, the allocmem() function returns an integer whose value specifies the size in bytes of the allocated block.

```
char *asctime(struct tm *)
  #include <time.h>
```

Takes as its argument a pointer to a structure of type tm (defined in time.h) that contains the time. (ANSI)

Returns a pointer to a character string that expresses the time.

```
double asin(double)
  #include <math.h>
```

Takes as an argument a double floating-point value in the range of from -1 to 1. (ANSI)

Returns a double float whose value is the tangent of its argument upon success. Returns 0 upon failure.

```
void assert(/* logical expression */)
  #include <stdio.h>
  #include <assert.h>
```

Takes as its argument an expression that resolves to TRUE or FALSE. Generates an error message if the expression tests FALSE. (ANSI)

Returns no data.

```
double atan(double)
  #include <math.h>
```

Takes as its argument a double floating-point value. (ANSI)

Returns the arc tangent value of its argument upon success. Returns 0 upon failure.

```
double atan2(double, double)
  #include <math.h>
```

Takes as its first argument a double floating-point value. (ANSI)

Returns the arc tangent of the quotient of the first argument divided by the second.

```
int atexit(void (*function)(void))
  #include <stdlib.h>
```

Takes as its argument a pointer to a function that you wish to run upon program termination. (ANSI)

Returns 0 upon success, nonzero upon failure.

```
double atof(char *)
  #include <math.h>
  #include <stdlib.h>
```

Takes as its argument a pointer to an ASCII string that expresses a numerical value. (ANSI)

Returns a double float value corresponding to the valid numerical digits stored in the string.

```
int atoi(char *)
  #include <stdlib.h>
```

Takes as its argument a pointer to an ASCII string that expresses the numerical value of a whole number. (ANSI)

Returns an integer with a value corresponding to the valid numerical digits stored in the string.

```
long atol(char *)
  #include <stdlib.h>
```

Takes as its argument a pointer to an ASCII string that expresses the numerical value of a whole number. (ANSI)

Returns a long integer whose value corresponds to the valid numerical digits stored in the string.

```
int bdos(int, unsigned, unsigned)
  #include <dos.h>
```

Takes as its first argument an integer that specifies one of the DOS executive dispatcher (INT 21H) functions. Its second argument is an unsigned integer whose value the bdos() function sends to the CPU DX register. Its third argument is an unsigned integer whose value the bdos() function sends to the CPU AL register.

Returns an integer whose value is that of the CPU AX register upon termination. Returns -1 upon failure.

```
int bdosptr(int, void *, unsigned)
   #include <dos.h>
```

Takes as its first argument an integer that specifies one of the DOS executive dispatcher (INT 21H) functions. Its second argument is a pointer to a memory area that contains data to which the CPU data registers (DS:DX) must point. Its third argument is an unsigned integer whose value the bdosprt() function sends to the CPU AL register.

Returns an integer whose value is that of the CPU AX register upon termination. Returns -1 upon failure.

```
int biosequip(void)
   #include <bios.h>
```

Takes no arguments.

Returns an integer whose value is that of the DOS BIOS equipment flag (via INT 11H).

```
void box(int, int, int)
   #include <graphics.h>
```

Takes as its first argument an integer whose value specifies the width in pixels of a box which the box() function is to draw on the display screen with its upper left corner at the current cursor location, given that the video display is set in one of its graphics modes. Its second argument is an integer whose value specifies the height in pixels of the box. Its third argument is an integer that specifies the fill pattern. See the pen_color(), move_to(), and fill_style functions.

Returns no data.

```
char *brk(void *)
   #include <malloc.h>
```

Takes as its first argument a pointer to the memory address just beyond what you wish to be the upper address of the data (CPU DS register) segment.

Returns the address of the first byte above the new upper limit of the data segment upon success. Returns -1 upon failure.

```
void bsearch(void *, void *, size_t, size_t, int (*)(void *, void *))
   #include <search.h>
   #include <stdlib.h>
```

Takes as its first argument a pointer to a value that the bsearch() function is to find in a sorted array located as specified by the second argument. Its third argument is a size_t type (unsigned integer) that specifies the number of elements in the array. Its fourth argument is a size_t type that specifies the size in bytes of each element in the array. Its fifth and final element is a pointer to a function (one that you write or one of the library functions such as the strcmp() function) that itself takes the first two arguments of the bsearch() function and returns 0 for a match, a negative number if the first argument's item is less than the second, and a positive number if the first argument's item is greater than the second. (ANSI)

Returns a pointer to the first found occurence of the array element that matches that pointed to by the first argument of the bsearch() function.

```
void *calloc(sized_t, size_t)
  #include <malloc.h>
  #include <stdlib.h>
```

Takes as its first argument a size_t type (unsigned integer) that specifies the number of elements in an array. Its second argument is a size_t type that specifies the size in bytes of each element in the array. The calloc() function allocates a new memory area that will hold the specified array. (ANSI)

Returns a pointer to the beginning of the newly allocated memory area upon success. Returns NULL upon failure.

```
double ceil(double)
  #include <math.h>
```

Takes as its argument a double floating-point value. (ANSI)

Returns a double float whose value is that of the smallest whole number that is larger than the argument.

```
char *cgets(char *)
  #include <conio.h>
```

Takes as its argument a pointer to a character string buffer. The cgets() function reads input from stdin (the console keyboard) into the specified character array, beginning at the third byte position in the array, terminating at the end of a line (newline character), and places the terminating '\0' character at the end of the string.

Returns a pointer to the character string upon success.

```
int chdir(char *)
  #include <direct.h>
```

Takes as its argument a pointer to a character string that contains a path specification for a valid directory that exists on the current disk drive.

Returns 0 upon success, -1 upon failure.

```
int chmod(char *, int)
  #include <io.h>
```

Takes as its first argument a pointer to a character string that contains a file specification. Its second argument is an integer whose value specifies the read/write mode for the specified file (see S_IREAD, S_IWRITE, and S_IREAD|S_IWRITE in io.h).

Returns 0 upon success, -1 upon failure.

```
int chsize(int, long)
  #include <io.h>
  #include <errno.h>
```

Takes as its first argument an integer that is a file descriptor handle for a file previously opened in write mode. Its second argument is a long integer whose value specifies the number of bytes that the file will accommodate.

Returns 0 upon success, -1 upon failure.

```
void circle(int, int)
  #include <graphics.h>
```

Takes as its first argument an integer whose value specifies the length of the radius in pixels. Its second argument is an integer whose value specifies the color of the outline of a circle, assuming the video is in a graphics mode.

Returns no data.

```
void clearerr(FILE *)
  #include <stdio.h>
```

Takes as its argument a pointer to a file. The clearerr() function clears the DOS End-Of-File and Error flags for the file. See the feof() and ferror() functions. (ANSI)

Returns no data.

```
clock_t clock(void)
  #include <time.h>
```

Takes no arguments. (ANSI)

Returns a long integer of type clock_t (defined in time.h) whose value is the number of system clock ticks since your current program began execution. Returns -1 upon failure.

```
int close(int)
  #include <io.h>
```

Takes as its argument an integer whose value is that of a file descriptor handle that the close() function closes. See the fclose() function.

Returns 0 upon success, -1 upon failure.

```
void clrscrn(void)
  #include <bios.h
```

Takes no arguments. The clrscrn() function clears the video screen and sets attributes to 07H, given that the video is in text mode.

Returns no data.

```
void clrscrn2(int)
  #include <bios.h>
```

Takes as its argument an integer whose value specifies the video attributes to which the clrscrn2() function is to set the display screen after clearing it. The clrscrn2() function will work with video graphics modes.

Returns no data.

```
unsigned coreleft(void)
  #include <malloc.h>
```

Takes no arguments.

Returns an unsigned integer whose value specifies the number of bytes left in the near heap, i.e., the amount of unallocated memory remaining.

```
double cos(double)
  #include <math.h>
```

Takes as its argument a double floating-point value. (ANSI)

Returns a double float whose value is the cosine of the argument.

```
double cosh(double)
  #include <math.h>
```

Takes as its argument a double floating-point value. (ANSI)

Returns a double float whose value is the hyperbolic cosine of the argument.

```
int cprintf(char *, ...)
  #include <conio.h>
```

Takes as its first argument a pointer to a character string, typically a string literal delimited by quotation marks. Subsequent arguments must correspond to format specifiers embedded in the string of the first argument. The cprintf() function sends its output to stdout, the system console, and is similar to the printf() function, with the exception that the cprintf() function needs the \r\n escape characters instead of just the \n escape character. See the printf(), fprintf(), and vprintf() functions, as well as Appendix E, which lists the format specifiers for these and related functions.

Returns an integer whose value is the total number of characters the cprintf() function displays.

```
void cputs(char *)
  #include <conio.h>
```

Takes as its argument a pointer to a character string that the cputs() function writes to stdout, the console.

Returns no data.

```
int creat(char *, int)
  #include <io.h>
```

Takes as its first argument a pointer to a character string that specifies a file that you want the creat() function to create in the mode specified by its second (integer) argument. If the file exists, and if the file is set for read only, the creat() function will terminate as a failure. If the file exists and is set for other than read only, the creat() function destroys all data in the file as if it created a new file.

Returns an integer whose value is a file descriptor handle upon success. Returns -1 upon failure.

```
int cscanf(char *, ...)
  #include <conio.h>
```

Takes as its first argument a pointer to a format string, typically a string literal delimited by quotation marks. Subsequent arguments are addresses of variables that correspond to format specifiers embedded in the format string of the first argument.

Returns an integer whose value specifies the number of items successfully stored.

```
char *ctime(time_t *)
  #include <time.h>
```

Takes as its argument a long integer of type time_t whose value specifies the number of seconds since midnight, January 1, 1970, Greenwich Mean Time. (ANSI)

Returns a pointer to a character string that contains the abbreviated day and month with the date, time, and year, terminating with the newline and NULL characters.

```
void ctrlbrk(int (*ctrlbrk_handler_func)(void))
  #include <dos.h>
```

Takes as its argument a pointer to a function that itself takes no arguments and serves as a replacement for the DOS »CTRL»BREAK« handler. The called function must return an integer which is the argument value that determines the behavior of the ctrlbrk() function. A zero return value allows your program to continue. A nonzero return value terminates your program.

Returns no data.

```
void cursblk(void)
  #include <bios.h>
```

Takes no arguments. The cursblk() function sets the cursor to appear as a block (see the curslin() function).

Returns no data.

```
int curscol(void)
  #include <bios.h>
```

Takes no arguments.

Returns an integer whose value specifies the column position of the cursor. See cursrow().

```
void curslin(void)
  #include <bios.h>
```

Takes no arguments. The curslin() function sets the cursor to appear as an underscore line (see the cursblk() function).

Returns no data.

```
void cursoff(void)
  #include <bios.h>
```

Takes no arguments. The cursoff() function eliminates the cursor from the display (see the curson() function).

Returns no data.

```
void curson(void)
  #include <bios.h>
```

Takes no arguments. The curson() function restores the appearance of the cursor (see the cursoff() function).

Returns no data.

```
int cursrow(void)
  #include <bios.h>
```

Takes no arguments.

Returns an integer whose value specifies the row position of the cursor.

```
double difftime(time_t, time_t)
  #include <time.h>
```

Takes as its first argument a long integer of type time_t that specifies the number of seconds. Its second argument is of type time_t that specifies another time value in seconds. (ANSI)

Returns a double float whose value is the difference between the second argument and the first.

```
void disable(void)
  #include <dos.h>
```

Takes no arguments. The disable function sets the CPU Interrupt Flag (IF) via the CLI instruction to disable interrupts.

Returns no data.

```
div_t div(int, int)
  #include <stdlib.h>
```

Takes as its first argument an integer that the div() function uses as a numerator. Its second argument is an integer that the div() function uses as a denominator. (ANSI)

Returns a structure of type div_t that contains two integers, the first the quotient, the second the remainder, of the division operation of the numerator by the denominator.

```
time_t dostounix(struct date, struct time)
  #include <dos.h>
```

Takes as its first argument a structure of type date (defined in dos.h) that contains date information. Its second argument is a structure of type time (defined in dos.h) that contains time information.

Returns a long integer of type time_t (defined in dos.h) whose value is the elapsed seconds since midnight, January 1, 1970, Greenwich Mean Time.

```
double drand(int)
  #include <stdlib.h>
```

Takes as its argument an integer (see the srand() and the rand() functions).

Returns a double float whose value is a pseudo-random selection between 0 and the value of the argument, a fraction if the argument has a value of 1, and a whole number if the argument has a value greater than 1.

```
int dup(int)
  #include <io.h>
```

Takes as its argument an integer whose value is a file descriptor handle for a valid, open, existing file.

Returns an integer that is a unique, new file descriptor handle for the same file identified by the argument. Returns -1 upon failure.

```
int dup2(int, int)
  #include <io.h>
```

Takes as its first argument an integer whose value is a file descriptor handle for a valid, open, existing file. Its second argument is an integer whose value is a file descriptor handle. The dup2() function sets the second argument as a duplicate file descriptor handle for the first argument, closing whatever file may be referenced by the second argument.

Returns 0 upon success, -1 upon failure.

```
char *ecvt(double, int, int *, int *)
  #include <stdlib.h>
```

Takes as its first argument a double floating-point value. Its second argument is an integer whose value specifies the number of characters in the character string that the ecvt() function will create. Its third argument is a pointer to an integer where the ecvt() function will store a value specifying the location of the decimal point in the string: a value of 0 indicates the decimal point is immediately to the left of the first digit in the string, a positive value indicates the decimal position is so many digits to the right, a negative value indicates it is so many digits to the left. Its fourth argument is a pointer to an integer in which the ecvt() function stores the value for the sign: a value of 0 indicates a positive number, a nonzero value indicates a negative number.

Returns a pointer to a character string that expresses the value of the first argument.

```
void ellipse(int, int, int)
  #include <graphics.h>
```

Takes as its first argument an integer whose value specifies the x axis radius in pixels of an ellipse. Its second argument is an integer whose value specifies the y axis radius in pixels of the ellipse. Its third argument is an integer whose value specifies the color of the line that forms the ellipse. The video must be set to a graphics mode (see the pen_color() and setvmode() functions).

Returns no data.

```
void enable(void)
  #include <dos.h>
```

Takes no arguments. The enable function clears the CPU Interrupt Flag (IF) via the STI instruction to allow interrupts to occur (see the disable() function).

Returns no data.

```
int eof(int)
  #include <io.h>
```

Takes as its argument an integer whose value is a file descriptor handle for a valid, open, existing file.

Returns zero if the DOS End-Of-File (EOF) flag is clear. Returns nonzero if the DOS EOF flag is set, meaning that the file position indicator for that file has reached the end of the file (see the clearerr() and the feof() functions).

```
int execl(char *, char *, ..., NULL)
  #include <process.h>
```

Takes as its first argument a pointer to a character string that specifies the name of the file that is a program to load and execute. Its subsequent arguments are pointers to character strings that are in essence command line arguments for the called program. The final NULL argument serves as a delimiter to mark the end of the argument sequence.

Returns an integer whose value specifies the exit status of the called program. Returns -1 upon failure. Calling the execl() function terminates your program.

```
int execle(char *, char *, ..., NULL, char *)
  #include <process.h>
```

Takes as its first argument a pointer to a character string that specifies the name of the file that is a program to load and execute. Its subsequent arguments are pointers to character strings that are in essence command line arguments for the called program. The NULL argument serves as a delimiter to mark the end of the argument sequence. Its final argument is a pointer to an array of character strings that make up a new environment that the new program is to use.

Returns an integer whose value specifies the exit status of the called program. Returns -1 upon failure. Calling the execle() function terminates your program.

```
int execlp(char *, char *, ..., NULL)
  #include <process.h>
```

Takes as its first argument a pointer to a character string that specifies the name of the file that is a program to load and execute. The execlp() function will search the current DOS PATH to find the specified program. Its subsequent arguments are pointers to character strings that are in essence command line arguments for the called program. The final NULL argument serves as a delimiter to mark the end of the argument sequence.

Returns an integer whose value specifies the exit status of the called program. Returns -1 upon failure. Calling the execlp() function terminates your program.

```
int execlpe(char *, char *, ..., NULL, char *)
  #include <process.h>
```

Takes as its first argument a pointer to a character string that specifies the name of the file that is a program to load and execute. The execlp() function will search the current DOS PATH to find the specified program. Its subsequent arguments are pointers to character strings that are in essence command line arguments for the called program. The NULL argument serves as a delimiter to mark the end of the argument sequence. Its final argument is a pointer to an array of character strings that make up a new environment that the new program is to use.

Returns an integer whose value specifies the exit status of the called program. Returns -1 upon failure. Calling the execlpe() function terminates your program.

```
int execlv(char *, char *)
  #include <process.h>
```

Takes as its first argument a pointer to a character string that specifies the name of the file that is a program to load and execute. Its second argument is a pointer to an array of character strings that are in essence command line arguments for the called program.

Returns an integer whose value specifies the exit status of the called program. Returns -1 upon failure. Calling the execlv() function terminates your program.

```
int execlve(char *, char *, char *)
  #include <process.h>
```

Takes as its first argument a pointer to a character string that specifies the name of the file that is a program to load and execute. Its second argument is a pointer to an array of character strings that are in essence command line arguments for the called program. Its final argument is a pointer to an array of character strings that make up a new environment that the new program is to use.

Returns an integer whose value specifies the exit status of the called program. Returns -1 upon failure. Calling the execlve() function terminates your program.

```
int execlvp(char *, char *)
  #include <process.h>
```

Takes as its first argument a pointer to a character string that specifies the name of the file that is a program to load and execute. The execlp() function will search the current DOS PATH to find the specified program. Its second argument is a pointer to an array of character strings that are in essence command line arguments for the called program.

Returns an integer whose value specifies the exit status of the called program. Returns -1 upon failure. Calling the execlvp() function terminates your program.

```
int execlvpe(char *, char *. char *)
  #include <process.h>
```

Takes as its first argument a pointer to a character string that specifies the name of the file that is a program to load and execute. The execlp() function will search the current DOS PATH to find the specified program. Its second argument is a pointer to an array of character strings that are in essence command line arguments for the called program. Its final argument is a pointer to an array of character strings that make up a new environment that the new program is to use.

Returns an integer whose value specifies the exit status of the called program. Returns -1 upon failure. Calling the execlvpe() function terminates your program.

```
void exit(int)
  #include <stdlib.h>
  #include <process.h>
```

Takes as its argument a number which it returns to the operating system error-checking facility. A zero value indicates normal termination. Nonzero values should correspond to the DOS error messages. The exit() function terminates your program after flushing file buffers, closing files, and deleting any temporary files. (ANSI)

Returns no data.

```
void _exit(int)
  #include <stdlib.h>
```

Takes as its argument a number which it returns to the operating system error-checking facility. A zero value indicates normal termination. Nonzero values should correspond to the DOS error messages. The exit() function terminates your program without flushing file buffers, closing files, or deleting temporary files.

Returns no data.

```
void exitmsg(void)
  #include <memory.h>
```

Takes no arguments. The exitmsg() function terminates your program with a message that indicates how much memory your program required of the stack and the near heap.

Returns no data.

```
double exp(double)
  #include <math.h>
```

Takes a double floating-point value. (ANSI)

Returns the exponent of the natural logarithm base for the argument.

```
void *_expand(void *, int)
  #include <malloc.h>
```

Takes as its first argument a pointer to a previously allocated block of memory. Its second argument is an integer whose value specifies the total number of bytes that the memory block should store. In effect the _expand() function lets you adjust the size of a previously allocated memory block.

Returns a pointer to the re-sized memory area (the same value as its first argument. Returns NULL upon failure.

```
double fabs(double)
  #include <math.h>
```

Takes as its argument a double floating-point value. (ANSI)

Returns the absolute value of its argument.

```
void far *farcalloc(unsigned long, unsigned long)
  #include <malloc.h>
```

Takes as its first argument an unsigned long integer whose value specifies a number of data elements. Its second argument is an unsigned long whose value specifies the size in bytes of each unit (see the farfree() function).

Returns a far pointer to a memory area in the far heap that is as large as the product of the two arguments, with all locations initialized to 0. Returns NULL upon failure. Note the use of the far extended keyword.

```
unsigned long farcoreleft(void)
  #include <malloc.h>
```

Takes no arguments.

Returns an unsigned long integer whose value specifies the number of unallocated available bytes in far memory.

```
void farfree(void far *)
  #include <malloc.h>
```

Takes a far pointer to a previously allocated block in far memory. The farfree() function deallocates that memory block. Note the use of the far extended keyword.

Returns no data.

```
void far *farmalloc(unsigned long)
  #include <malloc.h>
```

Takes as its argument an unsigned long integer whose value specifies the number of bytes that the farmalloc() function is to allocate from the far heap.

Returns a far pointer to the newly allocated memory block. The farmalloc() function initializes all locations to 0. Returns NULL upon failure. Note the use of the far extended keyword.

```
XXX farmemXXXXX()
  #include <malloc.h>
```

The following functions that begin farmem... are similar to those that begin mem... with corresponding suffixes. The differences are that the farmem... functions take far pointers to the memory area known as the "far heap," which is memory not within allocation distance of the small and the medium model programs' memories, both of which have a data area limited to 64K. For clarity, we present a complete description of the first of the series of farmem... functions, the farmemccpy() function. To understand the other members of this series, refer to the mem... functions later in this appendix. Note the use of the far extended keyword.

```
void far *farmemccpy(void far *, void far *, int, size_t)
  #include <malloc.h>
```

Takes as its first argument a far pointer to a destination memory area. Its second argument is a far pointer to a source memory area. Its third argument is an integer whose value specifies the ASCII code for a character. Its final argument is of type size_t (unsigned integer defined in MALLOC.H> that specifies the maximum number of bytes that the farmemccpy() function is to copy from the source to the destination. The farmemccpy() function will cease when it reaches the maximum number of bytes as specified by the size_t argument or after it copies the first instance of the character specified by the third (integer) argument.

Returns a far pointer to the memory location one byte above the character specified by the third argument. Returns NULL if it copies the maximum specified number of bytes without encountering the character of the third argument.

Other farmem... functions:

```
void far *farmemchr(void far *, int, size_t)
int       farmemcmp(void far *, void far *, size_t)
int       farmemcpy(void far *, void far *, size_t)
int       farmemcmp(void far *, void far *, size_t)
int       farmemmove(void far *, void far *, size_t)
void far *farmemset(void far *, int, size_t)
```

```
void far *farrealloc(void far *, unsigned long)
#include <malloc.h>
```

Takes as its first argument a far pointer to a previously allocated memory area in the far heap. Its second argument is an unsigned long integer whose value specifies the number of bytes that the realloc() function will allocate at the location of the first argument (see the farfree() function). The realloc() function does not reinitialize or otherwise alter the values in the memory area specified by the first argument.

Returns a far pointer to the reallocated memory block (the first argument) upon success. Returns NULL upon failure. Note the use of the far extended keyword.

```
unsigned farsetsize(unsigned)
#include <malloc.h>
```

Takes as its argument an unsigned integer whose value specifies the number of 16-byte paragraphs that the far heap is to contain.

Returns an unsigned integer that specifies the number of 16-byte paragraphs in total available system memory, including program instructions, the near data area, and the far heap.

```
XXX farstrXXXXX()
#include <malloc.h>
```

The following functions that begin farstr... are similar to those that begin str... with corresponding suffixes. The differences are that the farstr... functions take far pointers to the memory area known as the "far heap," which is memory not within allocation distance of the small and the medium model programs' memories, both of which have a data area limited to 64K. For clarity, we present a complete description of the first of the series of farstr... functions, the farstrcat() function. To understand the other members of this series, refer to the str... functions later in this appendix. Note the use of the far extended keyword.

```
char far *farstrcat(char far *, char far *)
#include <malloc.h>
```

Takes as its first argument a far pointer to a character string. Its second argument is a far pointer to a second character string. The farstrcat() function appends (concatenates) a copy of the string of the second argument to the end of the string of the first argument.

Returns a pointer to the string of the first argument.

Other farstr... functions:

```
char   far *farstrchr(char far *, int)
int         farstrcmp(char far *, char far *)
int         farstrcmpi(char far *, char far *)
char   far *farstrcpy(char far *, char far *)
size_t      farstrcspn(char far *, char far *)
char   far *farstrdup(char far *)
char   far *farstristr(char far *, char far *)
size_t      farstrlen(char far *)
char   far *farstrlwr*char far *)
```

```
char    far *farstrncat(char far *, char far *, size_t)
int         farstrncmp(char far *, char far *, size_t)
char    far *farstrncpy(char far *, char far *, size_t)
int         farstrnicmp(char far *, char far *, size_t)
char    far *farstrnset*char far *, int, size_t)
char    far *farstrpbrk*char far *, char far *)
char    far *farstrrchr(char far *, int)
char    far *farstrrev(char far *)
char    far *farstrset(char far *, int)
size_t      farstrspn(char far *, char far *)
char    far *farstrstr(char far *, char far *)
char    far *farstrtok(char far *, char far *)
char    far *farstrupr(char far *)
```

```
long fartol(void far *)
  #include <malloc.h>
```

Takes as its argument a far pointer to a previously allocated memory area. Note the use of the far extended keyword.

Returns a long integer whose value is that of the argument.

```
int fclose(FILE *)
  #include <stdio.h>
```

Takes as its argument a pointer to a file. The fclose() function flushes file buffers and closes the file. (ANSI)

Returns 0 if successful, EOF if unsuccessful.

```
int fcloseall(void)
  #include <stdio.h>
```

Takes no arguments. The fcloseall() function flushes all file buffers and closes all files except for the DOS standard files stdin, stdout, stderr, stdaux, and stdprn.

Returns an integer value of the number of files successfully closed. Returns -1 if unsuccessful.

```
char *fcvt(double, int, int *, int *)
  #include <stdlib.h>
```

Takes as its first argument a double float value. Its second argument is an integer that specifies the number of digits that the fcvt() function should allow to the right of the decimal point. Its third argument is a pointer to an integer into which the fcvt() function should place a value that specifies where the decimal point resides (0 is to the immediate left of the first digit, a negative number is so many digits farther left, a positive number is so many digits to the right of the first digit). Its fourth and final argument is a pointer to an integer into which the fcvt() function places a value that specifies the sign (zero for a positive number, nonzero for a negative number). See the ecvt() and ftoa() and gcvt() functions.

Returns a pointer to a string of characters that is the ASCII representation of the double float value.

```
FILE *fdopen(int, char *)
  #include<stdio.h>
```

Takes as its arguments an integer specifying a particular file descriptor handle followed by a string constant that specifies the mode for which the file was previously opened ('r,' 'w,' 'a,' 'r+,' 'w+,' or 'a+').

Returns a pointer to an already opened file associated with the integer value; returns NULL upon error.

```
int feof(FILE *)
  #include <stdio.h>
```

Takes as its argument a pointer to an open file. (ANSI)

Returns zero if the file pointer associated with the specified file has not reached the End-Of-File, nonzero if it has.

```
int ferror(FILE *)
  #include <stdio.h>
```

Takes as an argument a pointer to an open file. (ANSI)

Returns zero if the DOS error flag for that file is clear (there has been no error), nonzero if the error flag is set (there has been an error).

```
int fflush(FILE *)
  #include <stdio.h>
```

Takes as an argument a pointer to an open file. The fflush() function flushes all buffers associated with the specified file, saving any unsaved data to disk. (ANSI)

Returns zero if successful, nonzero if unsuccessful.

```
void _ffree(void far *)
  #include <malloc.h>
```

Takes as an argument a pointer to a block of far memory that the _ffree() function releases from allocation (see the farfree() function, which is identical; see also the _fmalloc() function). Note the use of the far extended keyword.

Returns no data.

```
int fgetc(FILE *)
  #include <stdio.h>
```

Takes as its argument a pointer to a file. (ANSI)

Returns an integer whose value is the next available character if successful, EOF if End Of File.

```
int fgetchar(void)
  #include <stdio.h>
```

Takes no arguments.

Returns an integer whose value is the ASCII code of the next character from stdio (normally the console keyboard).

```
int fgetpos(FILE *, fpos_t *)
  #include <stdio.h>
```

Takes as its first argument a pointer to an open file. Its second argument is a pointer to a long integer of type fpos_t (defined in stdio.h) into which the fgetpos() function stores a long integer whose value specifies the current position of the file pointer for the specified file. (ANSI)

Returns zero if successful, nonzero if unsuccessful.

```
char *fgets(char *, int, FILE *)
  #include <stdio.h>
```

Takes as its first argument a pointer to a character string buffer. Its second argument is an integer that specifies the total number of characters in the character buffer. Its third argument is a pointer to a file that the fgets() function is to read into the character buffer of the first argument until it reads one less than the number of characters specified by the first argument or until it encounters EOF. The fgets() function places the terminating '\0' character at the end of the string. (ANSI)

Returns a pointer to the character buffer (the first argument) upon success. Returns NULL upon failure.

```
long filelength(int)
  #include <io.h>
```

Takes as its argument an integer whose value specifies a valid, open, existing file descriptor handle.

Returns a long integer whose value specifies the total number of bytes in the specified file, upon success. Returns -1 upon failure.

```
int fileno(FILE *)
  #include <stdio.h>
```

Takes as its first argument a file pointer to an open file (see the fdopen() function).

Returns an integer whose value is a file descriptor handle for the file specified in the argument.

```
void fill(int)
  #include <graphics.h>
```

Takes as its argument an integer whose value specifies a color (the video display must be set to one of the graphics modes and the cursor inside a region bounded on all sides, for instance a circle or a box). See the setvmode(), move_to(), pen_color(), box(), circle(), and ellipse() functions.

Returns no data.

```
void fill_style(char *, int, int)
  #include <graphics.h>
```

Takes as its first argument a pointer to a two-dimensional array of bytes the numerical values of which specify video colors, one for each pixel in the object that the fill_style() function will draw on the display screen. Its second argument is an integer that specifies the width of a rectangle in pixels. Its third argument specifies the height of the rectangle in pixels. See the fill() and flood() functions.

Returns no data.

```
int findfirst(char *, struct ffblk *, int)
   #include <direct.h>
   #include <dos.h>
```

Takes as its first argument a pointer to a character string that specifies a file name. Its second argument is a pointer to a structure of type ffblk (defined in direct.h) into which the findfirst() function will store information about the specified file. Its third argument is an integer whose value specifies the attribute (defined as FA_X... in dos.h) of the specified file.

Returns 0 upon success, in which case your function can inspect the structure members of the second argument. Returns -1 upon failure.

```
int findnext(struct ffblk *)
   #include <direct.h>
   #include <dos.h>
```

Takes as its argument a pointer to a structure of type ffblk (defined in direct.h) into which the findnext() function will store information about subsequent files specified by the findfirst() function. Use the findfirst() function first, then to find additional files with the same attributes, use the findnext() function.

Returns 0 upon success, in which case your function can inspect the structure members of the second argument. Returns -1 upon failure.

```
void flood(int, int)
   #include <graphics.h>
```

Takes as its first argument an integer whose value specifies the width in pixels of a rectangle. Its second argument is an integer whose value specifies the height in pixels of the rectangle. The flood() function draws a solid rectangle the upper left corner of which is at the current cursor position and the color of which is that of the border color.

Returns no data.

```
double floor(double)
   #include <math.h>
```

Takes as its argument a double floating-point number. (ANSI)

Returns a double equal to the largest whole number that can be contained in the argument.

```
int flushall(void)
   #include <stdio.h>
```

Takes no arguments. The flushall() function writes all unsaved data to disk for all open files.

Returns an integer whose value is the number of files the buffers of which the flushall() function has flushed.

```
void far *_fmalloc(unsigned)
  #include <malloc.h>
```

Takes as its argument an unsigned integer whose value specifies the number of bytes that the _fmalloc() function is to allocate from the far heap.

Returns a far pointer to the newly allocated memory block, all bytes of which the _fmalloc() function initializes to zeros. Note the use of the far extended keyword. Returns NULL upon failure.

```
double fmod(double, double)
  #include <math.h>
```

Takes as its first argument a double floating-point value that is to be divided by its second (double float) argument. (ANSI)

Returns a double float whose value is the remainder of the division.

```
unsigned _fmsize(void far *)
  #include <malloc.h>
```

Takes as its argument a far pointer to a previously allocated block in the far memory area.

Returns an unsigned integer whose value specifies the number of bytes in the memory block specified by the argument.

```
FILE *fopen(const char *, const char *)
  #include <stdio.h>
```

Takes as its first argument a pointer to a file name or a string constant specifying a file name. Takes as its second argument a pointer to an access mode specifier or a string constant specifying an access mode specifier (typically 'r,' 'w,' 'a', 'rb,' 'wb,' 'ab,' 'r+,' 'w+,' 'a+,' 'r+b,' 'w+b,' or 'a+b'). (ANSI)

Returns a value that is a file pointer (handle) if successful, 0 if unsuccessful.

```
unsigned FP_OFF(void far *)
  #include <dos.h>
```

Takes as its argument a far pointer to a previously allocated block in far memory.
Returns the CPU offset register value for the far pointer argument.

```
unsigned FP_SEG(void far *)
  #include <dos.h>
```

Takes as its argument a far pointer to a previously allocated block in far memory.
Returns the CPU segment register value for the far pointer argument.

```
int fprintf(FILE *, char *, ...)
  #include <stdio.h>
```

Takes as its first argument a file pointer that identifies a valid file opened in write mode. Its second argument is a pointer to a character string, typically a string literal in quotation marks. Its subsequent arguments are identifiers for values that correspond to the format specifiers embedded in the character string of the second argument. (ANSI)

Returns an integer whose value specifies the number of characters the fprintf() function writes to the file.

```
int fputc(int, FILE *)
  #include <stdio.h>
```

Takes as its first argument an integer whose value specifies the ASCII code for a character. Its second argument is a file pointer to a file opened for writing. The fputc() function writes the character to the specified file. (ANSI)

Returns upon success an integer whose value is that of the character it writes. Returns EOF upon failure.

```
int fputchar(int)
  #include <stdio.h>
```

Takes as its argument an integer whose value specifies the ASCII code of a character that the fputchar() function writes to stdout, the console keyboard.

Returns upon success an integer whose value is that of the character it displays. Returns EOF upon failure.

```
int fputs(char *, FILE *)
  #include <stdio.h>
```

Takes as its first argument a pointer to a character string. Its second argument is a file pointer to which the fputs() function writes the character string. (ANSI)

Returns zero upon success, nonzero upon failure.

```
size_t fread(void *, size_t, size_t, FILE *)
  #include <stdio.h>
```

Takes as its first argument a pointer to a buffer area in memory. Its second argument is an unsigned integer of type size_t (defined in stdio.h) that specifies the number of bytes in each data element. Its third argument is of type size_t that specifies the number of data elements. Its fourth argument is a file pointer that specifies a file opened in read mode from which the fread() function reads the number of data elements into the memory buffer of the first argument. (ANSI)

Returns a value of type size_t that specifies the number of elements that the fread() function read into the memory buffer.

```
void free(void *)
  #include <stdlib.h>
```

Takes as its argument a pointer to a previously allocated block of memory. The free() function deallocates the memory block specified by its argument. (ANSI)

Returns no data.

```
unsigned _freect(unsigned)
  #include <malloc.h>
```

Takes as its argument an unsigned integer whose value specifies the number of bytes in an unallocated block of memory.

Returns an unsigned integer whose value is the number of unallocated memory blocks of a size specified by the argument that are available in the near heap.

```
int freemem(unsigned)
  #include <malloc.h>
```

Takes as its argument an unsigned integer whose value specifies the value in the CPU DS register that is a segment address of a previously allocated block of memory.

Returns 0 if the freemem() function deallocates the memory block. Returns -1 upon failure.

```
FILE *freopen(char *, char *, FILE *)
  #include <stdio.h>
```

Takes as its first argument a pointer to a character string that contains the valid name of an unopened file that the freopen() function is to open. Its second argument is a character string the contents of which specify a read or write mode for the newly opened file. Its third argument is a file pointer that specifies an already open file that the freopen() function is to close. (ANSI)

Returns a file pointer for the newly opened file upon success. Returns NULL upon failure.

```
int fscanf(FILE *, char *, ...)
  #include <stdio.h>
```

Takes as its first argument a file pointer for a file opened in read mode. Its second argument is a pointer to a character string that contains a sequence of format specifiers. Its subsequent arguments are addresses of data elements that correspond to the format specifiers embedded in the character string. (ANSI)

Returns an integer whose value is the number of data elements that the fscanf() reads from the specified file into memory. Returns EOF upon failure.

```
int fseek(FILE *, long, int)
  #include <stdio.h>
```

Takes as its first argument a file pointer for an open file. Its second argument is a long integer whose value specifies the number of bytes that the fseek() function is to move the DOS file pointer for the specified file. Its third argument is an integer whose value specifies one of three values: SEEK_SET (beginning of file), SEEK_CUR (current file pointer position), or SEEK_END (end of the file). (ANSI)

Returns zero upon success, nonzero upon failure.

```
int fsetpos(FILE *, fpos_t *)
  #include <stdio.h>
```

Takes as its first argument a file pointer to an open file. Its second argument is a pointer to a data element of type fpos_t (long integer) whose value specifies an absolute byte location in the specified file to which the fsetpos() function moves the DOS file pointer. (ANSI)

Returns zero upon success, nonzero upon failure.

```
int fstat(int, struct stat*)
  #include <sys\types.h>
  #include <sys\stat.h>
```

Takes as its first argument an integer whose value is a file descriptor handle. Its second argument is a pointer to a structure of type stat (defined in SYS\stat.h) into which the fstat() function stores statistics about the specified file.

Returns 0 upon success, -1 upon failure.

```
long ftell(FILE *)
  #include <stdio.h>
```

Takes as its argument a pointer to an open file. (ANSI)

Returns a long integer whose value is the current absolute byte position of the DOS file position indicator. Returns -1 upon failure.

```
void ftime(struct timeb*)
  #include <sys\types.h>
  #include <sys\timeb.h>
```

Takes as its argument a pointer to a structure of type timeb (defined in SYS\timeb.h) into which the ftime() function will store the current time.

Returns no data.

```
void ftoa(double, char *, unsigned, unsigned, unsigned)
  #include <stdlib.h>
```

Takes as its first argument a double floating-point value. Its second argument is a pointer to a character buffer into which the ftoa() function will store the ASCII character representation of the first argument. Its third argument is an unsigned integer the bitwise value of which directs the ftoa() function as to the format. Its fourth argument is an unsigned integer whose value specifies the number of character place digits to the left of the decimal point. The fifth argument is an unsigned integer whose value specifies the number of places for digits to the right of the decimal point.

Returns no data.

```
size_t fwrite(void *, size_t, size_t, FILE *)
  #include <stdio.h>
```

Takes as its first argument a pointer to a buffer area in memory into which the fwrite() function will write a number of data elements. Its second argument is an unsigned integer (size_t defined in stdio.h) whose value specifies the number of bytes in each data element. Its third argument is a size_t value that specifies the number of data elements the fwrite() function is to read from a file specified by the fourth argument, a file pointer. (ANSI)

Returns a value of size_t that is the number of data elements written. Given success, the return value should equal that of the third argument; any different return value indicates failure.

```
char *gcvt(double, int, char *)
  #include <stdlib.h>
```

Takes as its first argument a double float that it will convert to a character string. Its second argument is an integer that specifies the number of digits in the string. The third argument is a pointer to a character buffer in which you want the string to reside.

Returns a pointer to the string buffer.

```
void geninterrupt(int)
  #include <stdlib.h>
  #include <dos.h>
```

Takes as its argument an integer that specifies which DOS interrupt service routine to execute.

Returns no data.

```
int getc(FILE *)
  #include <stdio.h>
```

Takes a pointer to a file stream. (ANSI)

Returns the integer value of the ASCII character code for the next available character in the file stream.

```
int getcbrk(void)
  #include <stdlib.h>
  #include <dos.h>
```

Takes no arguments.

Returns an integer with a value of NULL if the DOS »CONTROL+»BREAK flag is clear (off) and a value of 1 if the DOS »CONTROL+»BREAK flag is set.

```
int getch(void)
  #include <conio.h>
```

Takes no arguments.

Returns an integer that specifies the value of the ASCII code of the character entered at stdin, the console keyboard. This function does not echo the character on the console display.

```
int getchar(void)
  #include <stdio.h>
```

Takes no arguments. (ANSI)

Returns the integer value of the ASCII character code for the next available character from stdin, the console keyboard.

```
int getche(void)
  #include <conio.h>
```

Takes no arguments.

Returns an integer that specifies the value of the ASCII code of the character entered at stdin, the console keyboard. This function does echo the character on the console display.

```
int getcseg(void)
  #include <dos.h>
```

Takes no arguments.

Returns an integer that specifies the value in the code segment (CS) register of the CPU.

```
int getcurdir(int, char *)
  #include <direct.h>
```

Takes as its first argument an integer that specifies a disk drive (0 is the current drive, 1 is A:, 2 is B:, 3 is C:, and so on). Its second argument is a pointer to a character buffer in which you want the name of the current directory stored. This buffer must be MAXDIR bytes long or longer.

Returns 0 upon success, -1 upon failure.

```
char *getcwd(char *, int)
  #include <direct.h>
```

Takes as its first argument a pointer to a character buffer into which you want to store the name of the current working directory. Takes as its second argument an integer that specifies the length of the character buffer.

Returns a pointer to the character buffer in which the name of the current directory resides. This may be different from the first argument if the string is greater than the number of bytes specified by the second (int) argument.

```
void getdate(struct date *)
  #include <dos.h>
```

Takes as its argument a pointer to a structure of type date as specified in dos.h into which it loads an integer for the current year, a character for the current day, and a character for the current month.

Returns no value.

```
void getdfree(int, struct dfree *)
  #include <dos.h>
```

Takes as its first argument an integer that specifies a disk drive (0 for the current drive, 1 for A:, 2 for B:, 3 for C:, and so on). It takes as its second argument a pointer to a structure of type dfree as specified in dos.h into which it loads four unsigned integers, the first for the available clusters, the second for the total clusters, the third for the bytes per sector, and the fourth for the sectors per cluster of the specified drive.

Returns no value.

```
int getdisk(void)
  #include <direct.h>
```

Takes no arguments.

Returns an integer whose value specifies the current disk drive (0 for A:, 1 for B:, 2 for C:, and so on), and yes, these values are one less than for such functions as the getdfree() or getcurdir() function).

```
int getdseg(void)
  #include <dos.h>
```

Takes no arguments.

Returns an integer that specifies the value in the Data Segment (DS) register of the CPU.

```
char far *getdta(void)
  #include <dos.h>
```

Takes no arguments.

Returns a far pointer to a character string that is the Data Transfer Area (DTA) maintained by DOS.

```
char *getenv(char *)
  #include <stdlib.h>
```

Takes a pointer to a character string that specifies an environment variable, for example, PATH. (ANSI)

Returns a pointer to the first character of the string value of that environment variable, for example C:\WORKOUT;C:\DOS;C:\. Returns NULL upon failure.

```
void getfat(int, struct fatinfo *)
  #include <dos.h>
```

Takes as its first argument an integer that specifies a disk drive (0 is for the current drive, 1 is for A:, 2 is for B:, 3 is for C:, and so on). The second argument is a pointer to a structure of type fatinfo (defined in dos.h) into which the function stores File Allocation Table information: a byte value specifying sectors per cluster, a byte that is the identification byte, an integer that specifies the number of clusters, and an integer that specifies the number of bytes per sector.

Returns no data.

```
void getfatd(struct fatinfo *)
  #include <dos.h>
```

Takes as its argument a pointer to a structure of type fatinfo into which the function will store File Allocation Table information for the current drive (see explanation for the getfat() function).

Returns no data.

```
int getftime(int, struct ftime *)
  #include <dos.h>
```

Takes as its first argument an integer that is a file descriptor handle. Its second argument is a pointer to a structure of type ftime defined in dos.h that receives the datestamp of the file specified.

Returns 0 upon success.

```
int getkey(void)
  #include <conio.h>
```

Takes no arguments.

Returns an integer that specifies the ASCII value of the character code of whatever key is currently pressed. Returns EOF if no key is currently being pressed.

```
char *getpass(char *)
  #include <conio.h>
```

Takes as its argument a pointer to a character string that contains the text for a prompt of your choosing.

Returns a pointer to a character string that contains up to eight characters input from stdin, the console keyboard. This function temporarily disables character echo so that the input characters are not displayed on the console. Good for retrieving passwords.

```
int getpid(void)
  #include <process.h>
```

Takes no arguments.

Returns an integer that is the DOS Process ID (PID) for the current process that is running.

```
int getpixel(int, int)
  #include <graphics.h>
```

Takes as its first argument an integer that specifies the x coordinate of a pixel on the stdout console display. Its second argument is an integer that specifies the y coordinate of the pixel. Use this when the display is set to a graphics video mode.

Returns an integer that specifies the color of the pixel.

```
unsigned getpsp(void)
  #include <dos.h>
```

Takes no arguments. Requires MS-DOS Version 3.90 or higher.

Returns an unsigned integer that specifies the current Program Segment Prefix (PSP) for the current program.

```
char *gets(char *)
  #include <stdio.h>
```

Takes as its argument a pointer to a character string input buffer. Reads characters from stdin, the console keyboard, up to, but not including the newline or end-of-file character, then places a terminating NULL character at the end of the string. (ANSI)

Returns a pointer to the same character buffer. Returns NULL upon failure.

```
void gettime(struct time *)
  #include <dos.h>
```

Takes as its argument a pointer to a structure of type time (defined in dos.h) into which the function stores the current time.

Returns no data.

```
struct vconfig *getvconfig(struct vconfig *)
  #include <graphics.h>
```

Takes as its argument a pointer to a structure of type vconfig (defined in graphics.h) into which the function stores the current video configuration information.

Returns a pointer to the structure into which it has stored the current video graphics information.

```
void interrupt (far *getvect(int))()
  #include <dos.h>
```

Takes as its argument an integer whose value specifies a DOS interrupt service routine.

Returns an interrupt far pointer that yields the interrupt vector for the interrupt service routine specified. Note the use of the interrupt extended keyword.

```
int getverify(void)
  #include <dos.h>
```

Takes no arguments.

Returns an integer with the value of 0 if the disk write verify is cleared (off) and of 1 if the disk write verify flag is set.

```
int getvmode(void)
  #include <bios.h>
```

Takes no arguments.

Returns an integer that specifies the current video mode.

```
int getw(FILE *)
  #include <stdio.h>
```

Takes as its argument a pointer to a file that you opened in binary mode.

Returns an integer whose value is that of the next word in the specified file.

```
struct tm *gmtime(time_t *)
  #include <time.h>
```

Takes as its argument a pointer to a variable of type time_t (defined in time.h) which contains the time. (ANSI)

Returns a pointer to a structure of type tm (declared in time.h) that stores the elapsed time in seconds since midnight, January 1, 1970, Greenwich Mean Time.

```
void huge *halloc(long, unsigned);
  #include <malloc.h>
```

Takes as its first argument a long integer that specifies the number of array elements. Its second argument is an unsigned integer that specifies the size in bytes of each element.

Returns a pointer of type huge to the base point of a memory area that can store the array, which the function initializes to zeros. Note the use of the huge extended keyword. Use this return value with the hfree() function to deallocate the space.

```
void harderr(int *()(int, int, int, int)
  #include <dos.h>
```

Takes as its argument a pointer to a function that you want to use as a disk error handler that itself takes as its first argument an integer that specifies an error number followed by three integers containing the values of the AX, BP, and SI registers.

Returns no data.

```
void hardresume(int)
  #include <dos.h>
```

Takes as its argument an integer that directs the harderr routine to take the following actions: 0 ignores, 1 retries, 2 aborts via the »CONTROL+»BREAK interrupt. This function is properly used within the function used as the only (function) argument in harderr().

Returns no data.

```
void hardretn(int)
  #include <dos.h>
```

Takes as its argument an integer that represents an error code that is properly passed as the first (integer) argument of the function used as the only (function) argument of harderr().

Returns no data.

```
void hfree(void huge *)
  #include <malloc.h>
```

Takes as its argument a pointer to a huge array memory area. This function deallocates the space allocated by the halloc() function. Note the use of the huge extended keyword.

Returns no data.

```
double hypot(double, double)
  #include <math.h>
```

Takes as its first argument a double floating-point number that specifies one side of a right triangle. Its second argument is a double floating-point number that specifies the other side of the same right triangle.

Returns a double floating-point number whose value is that of the hypotenuse for the triangle.

```
int inp(unsigned)
  #include <conio.h>
```

Takes as its argument an unsigned integer that specifies a system hardware port.

Returns an integer that specifies the ASCII code for the character currently available from that port.

`int inport(int)`
`#include <dos.h>`

Takes as its argument an integer that specifies a system hardware port.

Returns an integer that it finds currently available from that port.

`int inportb(int)`
`#include <dos.h>`

Takes as its argument an integer that specifies a system hardware port.

Returns an integer that specifies the ASCII code for the character currently available from that port.

`int int86(int, union REGS *, union REGS *)`
`#include <dos.h>`

Takes as its first argument an integer that specifies which interrupt service routine to execute. Its second argument is a pointer to a structure of integers or characters (as defined in dos.h) that contain values you must first specify. Its third argument is a pointer to a structure of integers or characters that stores register values at the time the interrupt service routine terminates.

Returns an integer that contains the status of the AX register when the function returns control to your calling function.

`int int86x(int, union REGS *, union REGS *, struct SREGS *)`
`#include <dos.h>`

Takes as its first argument an integer that specifies which interrupt service routine to execute. Its second argument is a pointer to a structure of integers or characters (as defined in dos.h) that contain values you must first specify. Its third argument is a pointer to a structure of integers or characters that stores register values at the time the interrupt service routine terminates. Its fourth argument is a pointer to a structure of type SREGS (defined in dos.h) that contains unsigned integers with values of the CPU segment registers.

Returns an integer that contains the status of the AX register when the function returns control to your calling function.

`int intdos(union REGS *, union REGS *)`
`#include <dos.h>`

Takes as its first argument a pointer to a structure of integers or characters (as defined in dos.h) that contain values you must first specify. Its second argument is a pointer to a structure of integers or characters that stores register values at the time the interrupt service routine terminates. This function calls the DOS executive function handler INT 21h.

Returns an integer that contains the status of the AX register when the function returns control to your calling function.

`int intdosx(union REGS *, union REGS *, struct SREGS *)`
`#include <dos.h>`

Takes as its first argument a pointer to a structure of integers or characters (as defined in dos.h) that contain values you must first specify. Its second argument is a pointer to a structure of integers or characters that stores register values at the time the interrupt service routine terminates. Its third argument is a pointer to a structure that contains unsigned integers with values of the segment registers. This function calls the DOS executive function handler INT 21h.

Returns an integer that contains the status of the AX register when the function returns control to your calling function.

```
int ioctl(int, int, ... void *, int *)
  #include <io.h>
```

Takes as its first argument an integer that specifies a file or device descriptor handle. Its second argument is an integer that specifies an operation. Its third argument is a pointer to an integer that contains information associated with the CPU DX register, normally the location of a character array. Its fourth argument is a pointer to an integer associated with the CPU CX register. The function makes a call to DOS function 44h and takes action according to the value of its second argument as follows:

Operation value	Action taken
0	get information about the device or file
1	set device information according to the value of the third (integer) argument
2	get a number of bytes specifed by the fourth argument into a character array specified by the third argument
3	write the number of bytes specified by the fourth argument to the character array pointed to by the third argument
4	where the first argument specifies a disk drive (0 is current, 1 is A:, 2 is B:, 3 is C:, and so on), gets a number of bytes specified by the fourth argument into the character array specified by the third argument
5	where the first argument specifies a disk drive (see operation 4), performs similarly to operation 3
6	get the input status for the first argument (zero is ready, FFh is not ready)
7	get the output status for the first argument (zero is ready, FFh is not ready)
8	get information that device is removeable (i.e., is it a floppy drive) (must use DOS Version 3.0 or higher)
11	set number of times to retry sharing conflict (must use DOS Version 3.0 or higher)

Returns an integer whose value indicates the bitwise results as follows:

IO.H	#define	Meaning
ISDEV	0x0080	first argument represents a device
ISCTRL	0x4000	device responds to control strings
ISNEOF	0x0040	device file pointer is not at End Of File
ISBIN	0x0020	device is set in binary mode
ISCLK	0x0008	device is the system clock
ISNUL	0x0004	device is the null ("bit bucket") device
ISCOT	0x0002	device is stdout (console display)
ISCIN	0x0001	device is stdin (console keyboard)
ISDEV	0x0000	first argument represents a file
ISNEOF	0x0040	no write has taken place

To inspect these, and the return value with the appropriate value and test if it is true. Returns 0xFFFF upon error.

```
int isalnum(int)
  #include <ctype.h>
```

Takes an integer value specifying an ASCII character code. (ANSI)

Returns a nonzero value if the ASCII character code is alphanumeric. Returns NULL if the ASCII character code is anything else.

```
int isalpha(int)
  #include <ctype.h>
```

Takes an integer value specifying an ASCII character code.

Returns a nonzero value if the ASCII character code is alphanumeric. Returns NULL if the ASCII character code is anything else. (ANSI)

```
int isascii(int)
  #include <ctype.h>
```

Takes an integer value specifying an ASCII character code.

Returns a nonzero value if the character code is within range of the standard ASCII character set (0 to 0x7F). Returns NULL if the ASCII character code is anything else.

```
int isatty(int)
  #include <io.h>
```

Takes as its argument an integer that represents a file descriptor handle.

Returns a nonzero value if the file descriptor handle represents a character device. Returns a zero value if the file descriptor handle does not represent a character device.

```
int iscntrl(int)
  #include <ctype.h>
```

Takes an integer value specifying an ASCII character code. (ANSI)

Returns a nonzero value if the ASCII character code is a control character. Returns NULL if the ASCII character code is anything else.

```
int isdigit(int)
  #include <ctype.h>
```

Takes an integer value specifying an ASCII character code. (ANSI)

Returns a nonzero value if the ASCII character code is a digit from 0 to 9. Returns NULL if the ASCII character code is anything else.

```
int isgraph(int)
  #include <ctype.h>
```

Takes an integer value specifying an ASCII character code. (ANSI)

Returns a nonzero value if the ASCII character code is a printable character (other than the space character). Returns NULL if the ASCII character code is anything else.

```
int islower(int)
  #include <ctype.h>
```

Takes an integer value specifying an ASCII character code. (ANSI)

Returns a nonzero value if the ASCII character code is a lowercase alphabetic character. Returns NULL if the ASCII character code is anything else.

```
int isprint(int)
  #include <ctype.h>
```

Takes an integer value specifying an ASCII character code. (ANSI)

Returns a nonzero value if the ASCII character code is a printable character (including the space character). Returns NULL if the ASCII character code is anything else.

```
int ispunct(int)
  #include <ctype.h>
```

Takes an integer value specifying an ASCII character code. (ANSI)

Returns a nonzero value if the ASCII character code is a control character or the space character. Returns NULL if the ASCII character code is anything else.

```
int isspace(int)
  #include <ctype.h>
```

Takes an integer value specifying an ASCII character code. (ANSI)

Returns a nonzero value if the ASCII character code is a white space character (‘ ’ or ‘\f,’ ‘\n,’ ‘\r,’ ‘\t,’ ‘\v’). Returns NULL if the ASCII character code is anything else.

```
int isupper(int)
  #include <ctype.h>
```

Takes an integer value specifying an ASCII character code. (ANSI)

Returns a nonzero value if the ASCII character code is an uppercase alphabetic character. Returns NULL if the ASCII character code is anything else.

```
int isxdigit(int)
  #include <ctype.h>
```

Takes an integer value specifying an ASCII character code. (ANSI)

Returns a nonzero value if the ASCII character code is a hexadecimal digit (‘0’ to ‘9’ or ‘A’ to ‘F’ or ‘a’ to ‘f’). Returns NULL if the ASCII character code is anything else.

```
char *itoa(int, char *, int)
  #include <stdlib.h>
```

Takes as its first argument an integer whose value it will convert to a character string of digits in the location specified by the second argument, a pointer to a character string buffer. Its third argument is an integer that specifies the number base for the conversion (2 is binary, 8 is octal, 10 is decimal, 16 is hexadeximal, and so on, from 2 to 36).

Returns a pointer to the character string in which it has stored the conversion string.

```
int kbhit(void)
  #include <conio.h>
```

Takes no arguments.

Returns a nonzero value if the DOS keyboard buffer contains a character (the user hit a key). Returns zero if the keyboard buffer is empty (no key was hit). Nondestructive to the keyboard buffer (just reports, has no effect).

```
void keep(int, int)
  #include <dos.h>
```

Takes as its first argument an integer that specifies an exit code for a Terminate and Stay Resident (TSR) routine via a call to DOS function 31h. Its second argument is an integer that specifies the number of 16-bit paragraphs of memory to allocate to that function.

Returns no data.

```
long labs(long)
  #include <stdlib.h>
```

Takes as its argument a long integer. (ANSI)

Returns a long integer that is the absolute value of the argument.

```
double ldexp(double, int)
  #include <math.h>
```

Takes as its first argument a double float. Its second argument is an integer that contains the value of an exponent to which the number two is to be raised. (ANSI)

Returns the product of the first argument times two raised to the power of the second argument.

```
ldiv_t ldiv(long, long)
  #include <stdlib.h>
```

Takes as its first argument a long integer that the function uses as a numerator. Its second argument is a long integer that is the denominator. (ANSI)

Returns a structure of type ldiv_t (defined in stdlib.h) that has two members: a long integer that is the quotient followed by a long integer that is the remainder.

```
char *lfind(void *, void *, unsigned *, unsigned, int (*)(void *, void *))
  #include <search.h>
```

Takes as its first argument a pointer to an undefined data type having a specific value. Its second argument is a pointer to an array having one or more elements of the first type. Its third argument is a pointer to an unsigned integer that specifies the number of elements in the array. Its fourth argument is an unsigned integer that specifies the size of each array element in bytes. The fifth argument is a pointer to a function (such as the strcmp() function or your own function) that compares pointers to two data elements.

Returns a pointer to the first-found element in the array that matches that pointed to by the first argument.

```
void line_by(int, int)
  #include <graphics.h>
```

Takes as its first argument an integer that specifies the x offset of a point on the display. Its second argument is an integer that specifies the y offset of that same point. The function draws a line from the current position to the point described by the two arguments. (see the setvmode(), move_to(), line_style(), and line_to() functions.) Returns no data.

```
void line_style(char *, int)
  #include <graphics.h>
```

Takes as its first argument a pointer to an array of bytes that together specify the color makeup of the line drawn by the line_by() and line_to() functions. Its second argument is an integer that specifies the number of elements in the array. The array itself is composed of a comma-delimited series of character digits (0 to 9), each of which specifies a color in the form

```
  char line_make_up [M] = {N, N, N, ...}
```

where the first argument points to line_make_up, the second argument specifies *M*, and the value *N* can be whatever color number you wish. (see the setvmode(), move_to(), line_by(), and line_style() functions.)

Returns no data.

```
void line_to(int, int)
  #include <graphics.h>
```

Takes as its first argument an integer that specifies the x offset of a pixel on the display. Its second argument specifies the y offset of the same pixel. The function draws a line from the current cursor position and sets the cursor to the end of the line. (see the setvmode(), move_to(), line_style(), and line_by() functions.)

Returns no data.

```
struct tm *localtime(time_t *)
  #include <time.h>
```

Takes as its argument a pointer to a long integer that contains the value of the number of seconds elapsed since midnight, January 1, 1970, Greenwich Mean Time. Note that this function depends upon an environment variable, TZ, that the user should have set at run time to one of the following values: CST6, CST6CDT, EST5, EST5EDT, GMT0, MST7, MST7MDT, PST8, or PST8PDT. Without the TZ environment variable defined, as a default the function assumes a value of PST8PDT: Pacific Standard Time, 8 hours behind Greenwich Mean Time, and Pacific Daylight Savings Time. (ANSI)

Returns a pointer to a structure of type tm (defined in time.h) that contains the current local date and time.

```
int locking(int, int, long)
  #include <sys\locking.h>
  #include <errno.h>
  #include <io.h>
```

Takes as its first argument an integer that specifies a file descriptor handle. Its second argument specifies a mode that directs the function whether to lock or unlock the file or device specified by the first argument. Its third argument is a long integer that specifies the number of bytes affected (see the lseek() and fseek() functions). Requires MS-DOS 3.0 or above.

Returns an integer with a value of 0 upon success, -1 upon failure, in which case you must check values defined in errno.h, EACCES (file already locked or unlocked), EBADF (file descriptor invalid), EDEADLOCK (could not lock file with 10 tries), and EINVAL (second argument invalid).

```
double log(double)
  #include <math.h>
```

Takes as its argument a double float number. (ANSI)

Returns a double float with the value of the natural log exponent to which *e* (2.718281828) must be raised to generate the value of the argument.

```
double log10(double)
  #include <math.h>
```

Takes as its argument a double float number. (ANSI)

Returns a double float with the value of the exponent to which the base 10 must be raised to generate the value of the argument.

```
void longjmp(jmp_buf, int)
  #include <setjmp.h>
```

Takes as its first argument a value of a return destination of type jmp_buf (defined in setjmp.h), which must first have been used with the setjmp() function. Its second argument is an integer that is passed to the setjmp() function and becomes its return value. (ANSI)

Returns no data.

```
char *lsearch(void *, void *, unsigned *, unsigned, int (*)(void *, void *)
  #include <search.h>
```

Takes as its first argument a pointer to an undefined data type having a specific value. Its second argument is a pointer to an array having one or more elements of the first type. Its third argument is a pointer to an unsigned integer that specifies the number of elements in the array. Its fourth argument is an unsigned integer that specifies the size of each array element in bytes. The fifth argument is a pointer to a function (such as the strcmp() function or your own function) that compares pointers to two data elements (see the lfind() function).

Returns a pointer to the first-found element in the array that matches that pointed to by the first argument. If the value of the first argument is not present in the array, the function appends the value to the end of the array (assuming the array has sufficient unused allocated memory) and increments the value pointed to by the third argument.

```
long lseek(int, long, int)
  #include <io.h>
  #include <stdio.h>
```

Takes as its first argument an integer that specifies a file descriptor handle. Its second argument is a long integer that specifies the position in which the function must place the DOS file pointer in the file. Its third argument is an integer with a value of SEEK_SET (the second argument is relative to the begining of the file), SEEK_CUR (the second argument is relative to the current position of the file pointer), or SEEK_END (the second argument is relative to the end of the file), as defined in stdio.h.

Returns a long integer with a value that specifies the new position of the file pointer with respect to the beginning of the file. Returns -1 upon failure.

```
char *ltoa(long, char *, int)
  #include <stdlib.h>
```

Takes as its first argument a long integer. Its second argument is a pointer to a character buffer in which the function will store a character string that represents the value of the first argument. Its third argument is an integer, within the range of from 2 to 36, that specifies the number base that underpins the character string conversion (2 is binary, 8 is octal, 10 is decimal, 16 is hexadecimal).

Returns a pointer to the character buffer in which the character string resides.

```
void far *ltofar(long)
  #include <malloc.h>
```

Takes as its argument a long integer whose value is a 20-bit absolute memory address specification.

Returns the same address as specified by its argument, but in far pointer form (segment, offset).

```
int main(void)
int main(int, char *)
int main(int, char *, char *)
```

The main() function is not a library function but a user-written program. All C programs must include a main() function with which the compiler and linker coordinate a special set of startup routines that work with the operating system. You can write the main() function to receive none, two, or three arguments. The compiler and linker will adjust to your choice.

If you write main() to take no arguments, your program will have no access to command line parameters users might use when they invoke your program. (ANSI)

If you write main() to take two arguments, the first must be an integer that specifies the total number of arguments on the command line. The second argument is a pointer to an array of character strings, the first of which is the name of your program, with subsequent strings being space- or tab-separated command line parameters the users typed as they invoked your program. (ANSI)

If you write main() to take three arguments, the first two are as described in the previous paragraph. The third argument is a pointer to an array of character strings that reside in the environment.

Returns zero or whatever integer value you specify with a return statement.

```
void *malloc(size_t)
  #include <stdlib.h>
```

Takes as its argument an unsigned integer of type size_t (defined in stdlib.h) that specifies the number of bytes of uninitialized memory that the operating system should allocate to your program's use. (ANSI)

Returns a pointer to the base of the new block of memory if successful. Returns NULL upon failure.

```
int matherr(struct exception *)
  #include <math.h>
```

Takes as its argument a pointer to a structure of type exception (defined in math.h). The math library functions call this function upon an arithmetic error.

Returns a zero value upon error, nonzero upon success.

```
unsigned _memavl(void)
  #include <malloc.h>
```

Takes no arguments.

Returns an unsigned integer whose value specifies the number of unallocated bytes in the near heap.

```
void *memccpy(void *, void *, int, size_t)
  #include <string.h>
```

Takes as its first argument a pointer to a destination buffer. Its second argument is a pointer to a source buffer. Its third argument is an integer whose value is the ASCII code for a character. Its fourth argument is a size_t type (unsigned integer) that specifies the number of characters to copy from the source to the destination.

Returns a pointer to the byte location immediately above the last character copied into the destination upon success. Returns NULL upon failure.

```
void *memchr(void *, int, size_t)
  #include <string.h>
```

Takes as its first argument a pointer to a buffer that contains a set of byte (char) sized values. Its second argument is an integer whose value is the ASCII code for a character to be found in the buffer. Its third argument is a size_t type (unsigned integer) that specifies the number of characters in the buffer to search. (ANSI)

Returns a pointer to the byte location in the buffer that contains the first occurrence of the specified character. Returns NULL upon failure.

```
int memcmp(void *, void *, size_t)
  #include <string.h>
```

Takes as its first argument a pointer to a buffer that contains a set of bytes. Its second argument is a pointer to a second buffer that contains a set of bytes. Its third argument is a size_t type (unsigned int) that specifies the maximum number of bytes in each buffer. (ANSI)

Returns zero if the contents of the two buffers are identical. Returns an integer whose value specifies the arithmetic difference between the ASCII code values between the bytes at the lowest location at which the contents of the two buffers differ.

```
int memcpy(void *, void *, size_t)
  #include <string.h>
```

Takes as its first argument a pointer to a destination buffer. Its second argument is a pointer to a source buffer. Its third argument is of type size_t (unsigned int) and specifies the number of bytes that the function is to copy from the source location to the destination. Use the memmove() function if the storage blocks for the two buffers overlap. (ANSI)

Returns an integer whose value is the integer representation of the first argument (an integer equivalent to a near pointer value).

```
int memicmp(void *, void *, size_t)
  #include <string.h>
```

Takes as its first argument a pointer to a buffer that contains a set of characters. Its second argument is a pointer to a second buffer that contains a set of characters. Its third argument is a size_t type (unsigned int) that specifies the maximum number of bytes in each buffer.

Returns zero if the contents of the two buffers are identical. Returns an integer whose value specifies the arithmetic difference between the ASCII code values between the bytes at the lowest location at which the contents of the two buffers differ, a positive value if the character at the buffer for the first argument has a greater alphanumeric place than that of the second ('E' is greater than 'A,' and 'W' is greater than 'r').

```
int memmove(void *, void *, size_t)
  #include <string.h>
```

Takes as its first argument a pointer to a destination buffer. Its second argument is a pointer to a source buffer. Its third argument is of type size_t (unsigned int) and specifies the number of bytes that the function is to copy from the source location to the destination. This is different from the memcpy() function in that this will correctly handle overlapping blocks. (ANSI)

Returns an integer whose value is the integer representation of the first argument (an integer equivalent to a near pointer value).

```
void *memset(void *, int, size_t)
  #include <string.h>
```

Takes as its first argument a pointer to a buffer that can store one or more bytes. Its second argument is an integer that specifies the ASCII code for a character. Its third argument is of type size_t (unsigned int) and specifies the number of locations in the buffer that the function should set with the value of the second argument. (ANSI)

Returns a pointer to the base of the buffer location in memory.

```
int mkdir(char *)
  #include <direct.h>
```

Takes as its argument a pointer to a character string that specifies a directory name, which may include a valid existing drive and path specification.

Returns NULL if the function successfully makes a new directory. Returns -1 upon failure.

```
void far *MK_FP(unsigned, unsigned)
  #include ,dos.h>
```

Takes as its first argument an unsigned integer whose value you want to be a CPU segment register value. Its second argument is an unsigned integer whose value you want to be a CPU offset register value.

Returns a far pointer with a segment/offset value that corresponds to the first and second arguments.

```
char *mktemp(char *)
  #include <io.h>
```

Takes as its argument a pointer to a character string that specifies a valid file name that does not currently exist in the target directory. Your character string may specify a disk drive and directory path specification; the file name must terminate with six uppercase 'X' characters. The function creates a temporary file in which it converts the 'X' characters to a zero or alphabetical character followed by five digits that represent the DOS process ID for the program that calls the mktemp() function.

Returns a pointer to the character string upon success, NULL upon failure.

```
time_t mktime(struct tm *)
  #include <time.h>
```

Takes as its argument a pointer to a structure of type tm (defined in time.h) in which you specify the local time. (ANSI)

Returns a long integer of type time_t whose value specifies the number of seconds elapsed from midnight, January 1, 1970, Greenwich Mean Time to the time you specify in the structure.

```
double modf(double, double *)
  #include <math.h>
```

Takes as its first argument a double floating-point number. Its second argument is a pointer to a double float variable in which you wish to store the whole number portion of the first argument. (ANSI)

Returns a double floating-point number whose value is the fractional part of the first argument.

```
void move_by(int, int)
  #include <graphics.h>
```

Takes as its first argument an integer that specifies an x coordinate offset value from the current cursor position. Its second argument is an integer that specifies a y coordinate offset value from the current position. The function moves the cursor from its current position to the new position specified by the first and second arguments.

Returns no data.

```
void movedata(int, int, int, int, unsigned)
  #include <string.h>
```

Takes as its first argument an integer whose value is the segment register value for a source buffer containing a set of bytes. Its second argument is an integer whose value is the offset register value for the source buffer. Its third argument is an integer whose value is the segment register value of a destination buffer to which you wish to copy the bytes from the source buffer. Its fourth argument is an integer whose value is the offset register value for the destination buffer. Its fifth argument is an unsigned integer whose value specifies the number of bytes to copy from the source buffer to the destination buffer.

Returns no data.

```
void move_to(int, int)
  #include <graphics.h>
```

Takes as its first argument an integer whose value specifies the x coordinate of a graphics mode location on the display. Its second argument is an integer whose value specifies the y coordinate of the graphics mode location. The function moves the cursor to the specified location.

Returns no data.

```
void movmem(void *, void *, size_t)
  #include string.h>
```

Takes as its first argument a pointer to a source buffer that contains a set of bytes. Its second argument is a pointer to a destination buffer into which you want to copy the data in the source buffer. Its third argument is an unsigned integer (of type size_t, defined in string.h) that specifies the number of bytes the function is to copy. This function correctly handles buffers that may overlap in memory.

Returns no data.

```
unsigned _msize(void *)
  #include <malloc.h>
```

Takes as its argument a pointer to a location of a previously allocated memory area.

Returns an unsigned integer whose value specifies the number of bytes in the memory area specified by the argument.

```
void _nfree(void near *)
  #include <malloc.h>
```

Takes as its argument a pointer to the location of a block of memory previously allocated by the _nmalloc() function. Note the use of the near extended keyword. The _nfree function deallocates this block of memory, enlarging the near heap by the amount of the memory block.

Returns no data.

```
char near *_nmalloc(unsigned)
  #include <malloc.h>
```

Takes as its argument an unsigned integer whose value specifies the number of bytes of near memory you wish it to allocate.

Returns a pointer to the newly allocated block of memory. Note the use of the near extended keyword.

```
unsigned _nmsize(void near *)
  #include <malloc.h>
```

Takes as its argument a pointer to a block of memory previously allocated by the _nmalloc() function.

Returns an unsigned integer that specifies the number of bytes in the memory area specified by the argument.

```
int open(char *, int)
int open(char *, int, int)
  #include <io.h>
```

Takes as its first argument a pointer to a character string that specifies a file name for a new file that you wish to open. Its second argument is an integer that specifies the type of access as defined in io.h (beginning with O_). Takes as an optional third argument an integer that specifies the permission mode for the file.

Returns an integer whose value is the file descriptor handle for the new file. Returns -1 upon failure.

```
int outp(unsigned, int)
  #include <conio.h>
```

Takes as its first argument an unsigned integer that specifies an IO port number to which you wish to send a character. Its second argument is an integer whose value is the ASCII code for the character you wish to send to the port.

Returns an integer whose value is the ASCII code for the character specified in the second argument.

```
void outport(unsigned, int)
  #include <dos.h>
```

Takes as its first argument an unsigned integer that specifies a DOS IO port to which you wish to send a word-sized (integer) data element. Its second argument is an integer whose value you wish to send to the port.

Returns no data.

```
void outportb(int, char)
  #include <dos.h>
```

Takes as its first argument an integer whose value specifies a DOS IO port to which you wish to send a byte-sized data element. Its second argument is a char type data element whose value you wish to send to the port.

Returns no data.

```
int peek(unsigned, unsigned)
  #include <dos.h>
```

Takes as its first argument an unsigned integer whose value is that of a segment register. Its second argument is an unsigned integer whose value is that of an offset register.

Returns an integer which is that of the word-sized data element at the location specified by the two arguments.

```
int peekb(unsigned, unsigned)
  #include <dos.h>
```

Takes as its first argument an unsigned integer whose value is that of a segment register. Its second argument is an unsigned integer whose value is that of an offset register.

Returns an integer which is that of the byte-sized data element at the location specified by the two arguments.

```
int pen_color(int)
  #include <graphics.h>
```

Takes as its argument an integer that specifies a color that will be used by subsequent calls to graphics line drawing functions. The following table correlates values to colors:

Value	Color	Value	Color
0	black	8	gray
1	blue	9	light blue
2	green	10	light green
3	cyan	11	light cyan
4	red	12	light red
5	magenta	13	light magenta
6	brown	14	yellow
7	white	15	bright white

Returns an integer whose value specifies the previous color.

```
void perror(char *)
  #include <stdio.h>
  #include <errno.h>
```

Takes as its argument a pointer to a character string that you use as an auxilliary message to that associated with the errno variable, whose value is that of the last error to have occurred. You can access all error messages via an array of strings named sys_errlist. (ANSI)

Returns no data.

```
void pie(int, double *, int, struct fill_pattern *)
  #include <graphics.h>
```

Takes as its first argument an integer whose value specifies the radius of a circle in pixels. Its second argument is a pointer to an array of double floating-point values, each of which specifies a number that defines the size of a portion of the circle relative to the other array elements (for example, a circle with three portions sized 1.2, 2.3, and 3.4, or a circle with five portions sized 3.654, 7.127, 3.878, 9.442, and 1.773). Its third argument is a pointer to an array of structures of type fill_pattern (defined in graphics.h), each of which defines the fill pattern for its correlating element in the array of doubles.

Returns no data.

```
void plotch(int)
  #include <graphics.h>
```

Takes as its argument an integer whose value is the ASCII code for a character. The function draws the character at the current cursor location in whatever graphics mode is set for the video display.

Returns no data.

```
void plots(char *)
  #include <graphics.h>
```

Takes as its argument a pointer to a character string. The function draws each character in the string at the current cursor location in whatever graphics mode is set for the video display.

Returns no data.

```
void poke(unsigned, unsigned, int)
  #include <dos.h>
```

Takes as its first argument an unsigned integer whose value specifies the value of a CPU segment register. Its second argument is an unsigned integer whose value specifies that of a CPU offset register. Its third element is an integer whose value you wish to locate at the specified memory location.

Returns no data.

```
void pokeb(unsigned, unsigned, char)
  #include <dos.h>
```

Takes as its first argument an unsigned integer that specifies the value of a CPU segment register. Its second argument is an unsigned integer whose value specifies that of a CPU offset register. Its third element is an integer that specifies a byte value that you wish to locate at the specified memory location.

Returns no data.

```
double poly(double, int, double *)
  #include <math.h>
```

Takes as its first argument a double float that is the base of a polynomial expression. Its second argument is an integer whose value specifies the degree of the polynomial expression. Its third argument is a pointer to an array of double floats that correspond to the sequence of factor values, beginning with the 0 power of the polynomial expression. For example, if the first argument is 5.6, the second argument is 3, and the array would contain four double float elements, the first of which would be multiplied by 5.6 to the zero power, the second multiplied by 5.6 to the one power, the third multiplied by 5.6 to the two power, and the fourth multiplied by 5.6 to the third power.

Returns a double floating-point value that is the sum of the products described above.

```
void poscurs(int, int)
  #include <bios.h>
```

Takes as its first argument an integer that specifies a given row of the video display in text mode. Its second argument is an integer that specifies a given column on the display. The function positions the cursor at the specified position.

Returns no data.

```
double pow(double, double)
  #include <math.h>
```

Takes as its first argument a double floating-point value that is the base to be raised to a certain power. Its second argument is a double float whose value is the power to which the first argument is to be raised. (ANSI)

Returns the value of the first argument raised to the power of the second argument. Returns 0 if the first argument is 0 and the second is 0 or a negative number. Returns 0 if the first argument is a negative number and the second argument is not a whole number. Returns a value of HUGE_VAL (defined in math.h) if the result is larger than the largest possible double float value or smaller than the smallest possible double float value.

```
double power10(int)
  #include <math.h>
```

Takes as its argument an integer that the function will use as an exponent to raise the base of 10. (ANSI)

Returns the value of 10 raised to the power of the argument.

```
int printf(char *, ...)
  #include <stdio.h>
```

Takes as its first argument a pointer to a character string, typically a constant string pointer in the form of a string literal in double quotes. Takes a variable number of subsequent arguments depending upon the number of format specifiers embedded in the string of the first argument. The printf() function calls an internal formatting function that converts various internal data types to their ASCII character equivalents and permits you to specify the nature of the print field within which the arguments are displayed. (ANSI)

Returns an integer whose value specifies the number of characters displayed. Returns a negative number upon error.

```
int putc(int, FILE *)
  #include <stdio.h>
```

Takes as its first argument an integer that specifies the ASCII code for a character. Its second argument is a file pointer of type FILE (defined in stdio.h) that specifies a file to which the function is to write the character (remember, you must have opened the file in write mode). (ANSI)

Returns an integer whose value is that of the first argument upon success. Returns EOF upon failure.

```
void putch(int)
  #include <conio.h>
```

Takes as its argument an integer that specifies the ASCII code for a character it is to write to stdout.

Returns no value.

```
int putchar(int)
  #include <stdio.h>
```

Takes as its argument an integer whose value specifies the ASCII code for a character that the function is to write to stdout, normally the console display. (ANSI)

Returns an integer whose value is that of the first argument upon success. Returns EOF upon failure.

```
char *putenv(char *)
  #include <stdlib.h>
```

Takes as its argument a pointer to a character string that the function will locate as the next environment variable. Be sure to set the string in the proper format, "ENV_VAR_NAME=whatever..." The updated environment will not be reflected by using the envp() function.

Returns 0 upon success. Returns -1 upon failure, which generally reflects insufficient available environment memory space.

```
int puts(char *)
  #include <stdio.h>
```

Takes as its argument a pointer to a character string. The puts() function writes the character string to stdout, normally the system console. (ANSI)

Returns zero upon success, nonzero upon failure.

```
int putw(int, FILE *)
   #include <stdio.h>
```

Takes as its first argument an integer whose value the function will write to a file specified by the second argument, which is a pointer to a file descriptor handle.

Returns an integer whose value is that of the first argument upon success. Returns EOF upon failure.

```
void qsort(void *, size_t, size_t, int (*)(void *, void *))
   #include <stdlib.h>
```

Takes as its first argument a pointer to an array. Its second argument is an unsigned integer of type size_t that specifies the number of elements in the array. Its third element is of type size_t and specifies the number of bytes required by each array element. Its fourth argument is a pointer to a function that the qsort function calls to compare two array elements. You can write this function yourself, or you can specify it to be one of the library functions, for instance the strcmp() function. The called function must take as its two arguments pointers to two array elements and must return a value of 0 if the two elements match, return a negative value if the first argument is less than the second, and return a positive value if the first argument is greater than the second. (ANSI)

Returns no data.

```
int raise(int)
   #include <signal.h>
```

Takes as its argument an integer whose value is one of those defined in signal.h. Use this function to test the results of the signal() function. (ANSI)

Returns zero upon success. Returns nonzero upon failure.

```
int rand(void)
   #include <stdlib.h>
```

Takes no arguments.

Returns an integer of unpredictable value within the range of from 0 to RAND_MAX as defined in stdlilb.h. (ANSI)

```
int read(int, char *, unsigned)
   #include <io.h>
```

Takes as its first argument an integer whose value is that of a file descriptor handle for a file you have opened in read mode. Its second argument is a pointer to a character array into which you want to store byte-sized elements the read() function will read from the file. Its third element is an unsigned integer that specifies the maximum number of bytes the read() function is to read. The read() function will read the maximum number of bytes unless it encounters EOF.

Returns an integer whose value is the number of bytes the function reads from the file. Returns 0 if it reads no bytes (at EOF). Returns -1 upon error.

```
int readattr(void)
  #include <bios.h>
```

Takes no arguments.

Returns an integer whose value reflects the status of the video display, given that the video display is in text mode.

```
int readch(void)
  #include <bios.h>
```

Takes no arguments.

Returns an integer whose value is the ASCII code for the character at the current cursor position of stdout, normally the console display.

```
int readdot(int, int)
  #include <stdio.h>
```

Takes as its first argument an integer whose value specifies the row position for the video display, given that the video display is in graphics mode. Its second argument is an integer whose value specifies the column.

Returns an integer whose value is that of the pixel at the location specified by the two arguments (see the writedot() function).

```
void *realloc(void *, size_t)
  #include <stdlib.h>
```

Takes as its first argument a pointer to a block of memory. Its second argument is of type size_t (defined in stdlib.h), which specifies the number of bytes that the function should reallocate in the memory block. (ANSI)

Returns a pointer to the reallocated memory block. Returns NULL upon failure.

```
int remove(char *)
  #include <stdio.h>
```

Takes as its argument a pointer to a character string that specifies a valid and existing file, optionally including a drive and path specification, that the function will remove. (ANSI)

Returns zero upon success, nonzero upon failure.

```
int rename(char *, char *)
  #include <stdio.h>
```

Takes as its first argument a pointer to a character string that specifies a valid, existing file or directory name that the rename() function is to change. Its second argument is a pointer to a character string that contains a valid and nonexisting name the function will use as the replacement. (ANSI)

Returns zero upon success, nonzero upon failure.

```
void repmem(void *, void *, int, int)
  #include <string.h>
```

Takes as its first argument a pointer to a destination memory area. Its second argument is a pointer to a source memory area that contains initialized values. Its third argument is an integer that specifies the number of bytes in the source area that the function is to record. Its fourth argument is an integer that specifies the number of times the function is to repeat writing the block of recorded values to the destination memory area.

Returns no data.

```
void rewind(FILE *)
  #include <stdio.h>
```

Takes as its argument a file pointer. This function resets the DOS file pointer to the beginning of the file specified in the function argument. (ANSI)

Returns no data.

```
int rmdir(char *)
  #include <direct.h>
```

Takes as its argument a pointer to a character string that specifies a valid and existing name of an empty directory the rmdir() function is to remove.

Returns 0 upon success, -1 upon failure.

```
int rmtmp(void)
  #include <stdio.h>
```

Takes no arguments. This function removes temporary files created by the tmpfile() function.

Returns an integer whose value reflects the number of temporary files the function removed from the current directory.

```
char *sbrk(int)
  #include <malloc.h>
```

Takes as its argument an integer whose value specifies the number of bytes by which the function is to change the size of the data segment memory area.

Returns a pointer to the address of the first character past the end of the data segment upon success. Returns -1 upon failure.

```
int scanf(char *, ...)
  #include <stdio.h>
```

Takes as its first argument a pointer to a character string, typically a string literal enclosed in double quotation marks. Its optional subsequent arguments correspond in their order to the format specifiers embedded in the character string and are of the form of addresses into which the scanf() function is to copy data it reads from stdin (normally the console keyboard). See Appendix E for a description of format specifiers. Also see the cscanf() and fscanf() functions as well as the cprintf(), fprintf(), and printf() functions, all of which use a nearly identical set of format specifiers. (ANSI)

Returns an integer whose value specifies the number of values successfully input. Returns EOF upon failure.

```
char *searchpath(char *)
  #include <direct.h>
```

Takes as its argument a pointer to a character string that specifies a valid and existing file. The function searches the current directory. If it does not find a file with a name that matches that of the character string, it searches the directories specified by the PATH environment variable.

Returns a pointer to the full file specification upon success. Returns NULL upon failure.

```
void segread(struct SREGS *)
  #include <dos.h>
```

Takes as its argument a pointer to a structure of type SREGS as defined in dos.h. The function stores into the structure the current values of the CPU segment registers

Returns no data.

```
int setapage(int)
  #include <graphics.h>
```

Takes as its argument an integer whose value specifies the current active video page for the various graphics screen functions.

Returns an integer whose value specifies the previous active video page.

```
int setblock(int, int)
  #include <dos.h>
```

Takes as its first argument an integer whose value specifies a block of memory previously allocated by the allocmem() function. Its second argument is an integer whose value specifies the number of paragraphs (16 bytes per paragraph) that the block should contain.

Returns -1 upon success. Upon failure, the function returns an integer whose value specifies the maximum number of blocks available.

```
void setbuf(FILE *, char *)
  #include <stdio.h>
```

Takes as its first argument a file descriptor handle. Its second argument is a pointer to a character array that the function will use as an input buffer and which contains at least BUFSIZ bytes (defined in stdio.h). (ANSI)

Returns no data.

```
int setcbrk(int)
  #include <dos.h>
```

Takes as its argument an integer which, if its value is 1, directs the function to turn the »CONTROL»BREAK flag on, and if its value is 0, directs the function to turn the »CONTROL»BREAK flag off.

Returns an integer whose value is the current state of the »CONTROL»BREAK flag (0 or 1).

```
void setcolor(int, int)
  #include <graphics.h>
```

Takes as its first argument an integer whose value sets the background color. Its second argument is an integer whose value specifies the current color palette.

Returns no data.

```
void setdate(struct date *)
  #include <dos.h>
```

Takes as its argument a pointer to a structure of type date (defined in dos.h) that contains the values that you want the function to use in updating the system clock.

Returns no data.

```
int setdisk(int)
  #include <direct.h>
```

Takes as its argument an integer whose value corresponds to a disk drive (0 for A:, 1 for B:, 2 for C:, and so on). The setdisk() function sets the current disk drive to match the argument.

Returns an integer whose value is the total number of logical disk drives available to the system.

```
void setdta(char far *)
  #include <dos.h>
```

Takes as its argument a far pointer to a character buffer. The setdta() function sets the Disk Transfer Area (DTA) to be that memory area specified by its argument.

Returns no data.

```
int setftime(int, struct ftime *)
  #include <dos.h>
```

Takes as its first argument an integer whose value is that of a valid file descriptor handle. Its second argument is a pointer to a structure of type ftime (defined in dos.h) that contains the date stamp values you wish the setftime() function to apply to the file specified by the first argument.

Returns 0 upon success, -1 upon failure.

```
int setjmp(jmp_buf)
  #include setjmp.h>
```

Takes as its argument a buffer of type jmp_buf (defined in setjmp.h as an array of 32 integers) into which the setjmp() function stores the current CPU register information needed by the longjmp() function to effect a direct return to the next program statement in the function that calls the setjmp() function. Note that the function must be active, i.e., it must have called the functions that call the functions that contain the longjmp() function. This is a kind of "goto" workaround to avoid the overhead of backing out of nested function calls—use it carefully and beware of logic errors particularly those involving stack data (particularly auto variables). (ANSI)

Returns 0 or the value of whatever integer argument you passed to the longjmp() function.

```
void setmem(void *, int, char)
  #include <memory.h>
```

Takes as its first argument a pointer to a currently allocated memory area. Its second argument is an integer that specifies the number of bytes in that memory area to initialize. Its third argument is a character that is the byte value that the function is to use as the initialization value in the memory area.

Returns no data.

```
int setmode(int, int)
  #include <io.h>
  #include <fcntl.h>
```

Takes as its first argument an integer whose value specifies a valid file descriptor handle. Its second argument is an integer whose value specifies one of two modes as defined in FCNTL.H, O_TEXT, or O_BINARY, determining whether the specified file is a text file or a binary file.

Returns an integer whose value is that of the previous mode upon success. Returns -1 upon failure.

```
void setpixel(int, int)
  #include <graphics.h>
```

Takes as its first argument an integer whose value specifies an x coordinate of a pixel on the video display. Its second argument is an integer that specifies the y coordinate of the same pixel. The function sets the color of that pixel to be that of the current pen color (see the pen_color() function).

Returns no data.

```
void settime(struct time *)
  #include <dos.h>
```

Takes as its first argument a pointer to a structure of type time (defined in dos.h). This function sets the system clock to match those values you have stored in the time structure (see the gettime() function).

Returns no data.

```
int setvbuf(FILE *, char *, int, size_t)
  #include <stdio.h>
```

Takes as its first argument a pointer to a file descriptor handle. Its second argument is a pointer to a buffer that you wish to use for file input/output. Its third argument is an integer whose value is _IOFBF, _IOLBF, or _IONBF (defined in stdio.h for full, line, or no buffering). Its fourth argument is of type size_t (an unsigned integer, as typedef'ed in stdio.h) and specifies the size of the buffer area. (ANSI)

Returns zero upon success, nonzero upon failure.

```
void setvect(int, void interrupt (*)())
  #include <dos.h>
```

Takes as its first argument an integer that specifies an entry in the DOS interrupt vector table. Its second argument is a pointer to a function that you want to serve as the interrupt service routine, to be activated when the specified interupt is called.

Returns no data.

```
void setverify(int)
  #include <dos.h>
```

Takes as its argument an integer whose value specifies the state of the DOS disk write verify flag. A value of 1 directs DOS to verify that the data is written correctly. A value of 0 directs DOS to ignore verification (see the getverify() function).

Returns no data.

```
int setvmode(int)
  #include <bios.h>
  #include <graphics.h>
```

Takes as its argument an integer whose value specifies the video mode for the display, as shown in the following table.

Mode Number	Display Type	Rows	Columns	Description
0	CGA	40	25	B & W text
1	CGA	40	25	Color text
2	CGA	80	25	B & W text
3	CGA	80	25	Color text
4	CGA	320	200	4-color graphics
5	CGA	320	200	4-color (off)
6	CGA	640	200	B & W graphics
7	Mono	80	25	B & W text
13	EGA	320	200	16-color graphics
14	EGA	640	200	16-color graphics
15	EGA	640	200	B & W graphics
16	EGA	640	350	4- or 16-color graphics
17	VGA	640	480	2-color graphics
18	VGA	640	480	16-color graphics
19	VGA	320	200	256-color graphics
99	Hercules	720	348	B & W graphics

Returns an integer whose value specifies the previous video mode.

`int setvpage(int)`
`#include <graphics.h>`

Takes as its argument an integer whose value specifies the video page number for the display.

Returns an integer whose value specifies the previous video page.

`double sin(double)`
`#include <math.h>`

Takes as its argument a double floating-point value. (ANSI)

Returns a double float whose value is the sine of the argument.

`double sinh(double)`
`#include <math.h>`

Takes as its argument a double floating-point value that expresses a number of radians. (ANSI)

Returns a double float whose value is the hyperbolic sine of the argument.

`void sleep(unsigned)`
`#include <dos.h>`

Takes as its argument an unsigned integer whose value specifies the number of seconds to suspend program execution.

Returns no data.

`void sound(int, int)`
`#include <bios.h>`

Takes as its first argument an integer whose value specifies a frequency in Hertz within the range of 37Hz to 32767Hz. Its second argument is an integer whose value specifies the duration in clock ticks (18.2 ticks per second) of the period during which the system speaker will generate the frequency.

Returns no data.

`int spawnl(int, char *, char *, ..., NULL)`
`#include <process.h>`

Takes as its first argument an integer that specifies one of two modes: P_WAIT or P_OVERLAY (defined in process.h), which direct the program to wait until the child process terminates or to overlay the calling process with the child. Its second argument is a pointer to a character string that specifies the name of the file that is the child process. Its subsequent arguments are pointers to character strings that are in essence command line arguments for the called program. The final NULL argument serves as a delimiter to mark the end of the argument sequence.

Returns an integer whose value specifies the exit status of the called program.

`int spawnle(int, char *, char *, ..., NULL, char *)`
`#include <process.h>`

Takes as its first argument an integer that specifies one of two modes: P_WAIT or P_OVERLAY (defined in process.h), which direct the program to wait until the child process terminates or to overlay the calling process with the child. Its second argument is a pointer to a character string that specifies the name of the file that is the child process. Its subsequent arguments are pointers to character strings that are in essence command line arguments for the called program. The NULL argument serves as a delimiter to mark the end of the argument sequence. The final argument is a pointer to an array of character strings that make up the environment to be passed to the child process (instead of letting the child use the environment of the parent).

Returns an integer whose value specifies the exit status of the called program.

```
int spawnlp(int, char *, char *, ..., NULL)
  #include <process.h>
```

Takes as its first argument an integer that specifies one of two modes: P_WAIT or P_OVERLAY (defined in process.h), which direct the program to wait until the child process terminates or to overlay the calling process with the child. Its second argument is a pointer to a character string that specifies the name of the file that is the child process. Its subsequent arguments are pointers to character strings that are in essence command line arguments for the called program. The final NULL argument serves as a delimiter to mark the end of the argument sequence. This function directs DOS to search the current PATH for the specified called function.

Returns an integer whose value specifies the exit status of the called program.

```
int spawnlpe(int, char *, char *, ..., NULL, char *)
  #include <process.h>
```

Takes as its first argument an integer that specifies one of two modes: P_WAIT or P_OVERLAY (defined in process.h), which direct the program to wait until the child process terminates or to overlay the calling process with the child. Its second argument is a pointer to a character string that specifies the name of the file that is the child process. Its subsequent arguments are pointers to character strings that are in essence command line arguments for the called program. The NULL argument serves as a delimiter to mark the end of the argument sequence. The final argument is a pointer to an array of character strings that make up the environment to be passed to the child process (instead of letting the child use the environment of the parent). This function directs DOS to search the current PATH for the specified called function.

Returns an integer whose value specifies the exit status of the called program.

```
int spawnv(int, char *, char *[])
  #include <process.h>
```

Takes as its first argument an integer that specifies one of two modes: P_WAIT or P_OVERLAY (defined in process.h), which direct the program to wait until the child process terminates or to overlay the calling process with the child. Its second argument is a pointer to a character string that specifies the name of the file that is the child process. Its third argument is a pointer to an array of character strings that are in essence command line arguments for the called program.

Returns an integer whose value specifies the exit status of the called program.

```
int spawnve(int, char *, char *[], char *[])
  #include <process.h>
```

Takes as its first argument an integer that specifies one of two modes: P_WAIT or P_OVERLAY (defined in process.h), which direct the program to wait until the child process terminates or to overlay the calling process with the child. Its second argument is a pointer to a character string that specifies the name of the file that is the child process. Its third argument is a pointer to an array of character strings that are in essence command line arguments for the called program. The final argument is a pointer to an array of character strings that make up the environment to be passed to the child process (instead of letting the child use the environment of the parent).

Returns an integer whose value specifies the exit status of the called program.

```
int spawnvp(int, char *, char *)
  #include <process.h>
```

Takes as its first argument an integer that specifies one of two modes: P_WAIT or P_OVERLAY (defined in process.h), which direct the program to wait until the child process terminates or to overlay the calling process with the child. Its second argument is a pointer to a character string that specifies the name of the file that is the child process. Its third argument is a pointer to an array of character strings that are in essence command line arguments for the called program. Returns an integer whose value specifies the exit status of the called program. This function directs DOS to search the current PATH for the specified called function.

```
int spawnvpe(int, char *, char *[], char *[])
  #include <process.h>
```

Takes as its first argument an integer that specifies one of two modes: P_WAIT or P_OVERLAY (defined in process.h), which direct the program to wait until the child process terminates or to overlay the calling process with the child. Its second argument is a pointer to a character string that specifies the name of the file that is the child process. Its third argument is a pointer to an array of character strings that are in essence command line arguments for the called program. The final argument is a pointer to an array of character strings that make up the environment to be passed to the child process (instead of letting the child use the environment of the parent). This function directs DOS to search the current PATH for the specified called function.

Returns an integer whose value specifies the exit status of the called program.

```
int sprintf(char *, char *, ...)
  #include <stdio.h>
```

Takes as its first argument a pointer to a memory location to which the function will write formatted output. Its second argument is a pointer to a character string, typically a string literal delimited by quotation marks, that may contain format specifiers (see Appendix E for a description). Its subsequent optional arguments correspond in order to whatever format specifiers are embedded in the character string. The sprintf() function terminates by placing the null character at the end of the output data. (ANSI)

Returns an integer whose value specifies the number of characters written to the memory location, not including the terminating null character.

```
double sqrt(double)
  #include <math.h>
```

Takes as its argument a double floating-point value that is zero or a positive number. (ANSI)

Returns a double float whose value is the square root of the argument.

```
void srand(unsigned)
  #include <stdlib.h>
```

Takes as its argument an unsigned integer whose value the function uses to seed the start sequence for the rand() and drand() functions. Use different arguments to vary the initial and subsequent results of the rand() and drand() functions if your application requires unpredictability beyond that simulated by the rand() and drand() functions. (ANSI)

Returns no data.

```
int sscanf(char *, char *, ...)
  #include <stdio.h>
```

Takes as its first argument a pointer to a character string that contains formatted data such as that output by the sprintf() function. Its second argument is a pointer to a character string, typically a string literal delimited by quotation marks, that contains format specifiers (see Appendix E for a description of the format specifiers). Its subsequent optional arguments are addresses of data elements that correspond in their order to the format specifiers embedded in the string of the second argument. (ANSI)

Returns an integer whose value is the number of data elements successfully assigned.

```
unsigned stackavail(void)
  #include <malloc.h>
```

Takes no arguments.

Returns an unsigned integer whose value specifies the number of bytes available on the stack (see the alloca() function).

```
int stat(char *, struct stat *)
  #include <stat.h>
```

Takes as its first argument a pointer to a character string that is the path specification for a file or directory. Its second argument is a structure of type stat (defined in SYS\stat.h) into which the function stores statistics about the file or directory.

```
#define dev_t   short
#define ino_t   unsigned short
#define off_t   long
#define time_t  long
```

```
#define S_IFMT  0xf000        /* mode type masks v */
#define S_IFDIR 0x4000
#define S_IFCHR 0x2000
#define S_IFREG 0x8000
#define S_IREAD 0x0100
#define S_IWRITE 0x0080
#define S_IEXEC 0x0040        /* mode type masks ^ */

struct stat
{
    dev_t          st_dev;    /* drive number containing the file or
                                 file descriptor handle of the device */
    ino_t          st_ino;
    unsigned short st_mode;   /* one of the mode type masks */
    short          st_nlink;  /* always 1 */
    short          st_uid;
    short          st_gid;
    dev_t          st_rdev;   /* identical to st_dev */
    off_t          st_size;   /* number of bytes in the file */
    time_t         st_atime;  /* date and time stamp on file */
    time_t         st_mtime;  /* same as atime */
    time_t         st_ctime;  /* same as atime */
};
```

Returns 0 upon success, -1 upon failure.

```
unsigned _status87(void)
  #include <float.h>
```

Takes no arguments.

Returns an unsigned integer whose value is the status word that contains the interrupt exception mask values for the 80x87 math coprocessor chip (if one exists in the system). (See float.h for interrupt exception mask values.)

```
int stime(time_t *)
  #include <time.h>
```

Takes as its argument a pointer to a long integer of type time_t (defined in time.h) whose value is the time you want the function to set in the system clock.

Returns 0.

```
char *stpcpy(char *, char *)
  #include <string.h>
```

Takes as its first argument a pointer to a destination character string. Its second argument is a pointer to a source character string. The function copies the source string to the destination.

Returns a pointer to the destination character string.

```
char *strcat(char *, char *)
  #include <string.h>
```

Takes as its first argument a pointer to a character string area. Its second argument is a pointer to another character string. The strcat() function appends (concatenates) the second character string to the end of the first. Be sure that the first argument has sufficient memory allocated to receive the second. (ANSI)

Returns a pointer to the beginning of the first argument.

```
char *strchr(char *, int)
  #include <string.h>
```

Takes as its first argument a pointer to a character string. Its second argument is an integer whose value is the ASCII code for a character that the function is to locate in the contents of the character string. (ANSI)

Returns a pointer to a character string that is the location of the character whose ASCII code matches the second argument. Returns NULL upon failure.

```
int strcmp(char *, char *);
  #include <string.h.>
```

Takes as its first argument a pointer to a character string. Its second argument is a pointer to a second character string. The function compares the contents of the two strings character by character. (ANSI)

Returns an integer whose value is the difference between the ASCII codes for the first corresponding nonmatching set of characters. The value is negative if the character code in the string of the first argument is less than that of the second, positive if larger, and zero if the two character strings match exactly.

```
int strcmpi(char *, char *);
  #include <string.h.>
```

Takes as its first argument a pointer to a character string. Its second argument is a pointer to a second character string. The function compares the contents of the two strings character by character, but ignores case differences (thus it treats 'M' and 'm' as identical). (ANSI)

Returns an integer whose value is the difference between the ASCII codes for the first corresponding nonmatching set of characters. The value is negative if the character code in the string of the first argument is less than that of the second, positive if larger, and zero if the two character strings match exactly.

```
char *strcpy(char *, char *)
  #include <string.h>
```

Takes as its first argument a pointer to a destination character string area. Its second argument is a pointer to a source character string. The strcpy() function copies the source string to the destination. (ANSI)

Returns a pointer to the destination.

```
size_t strcspn(char *, char *)
  #include <string.h>
```

Takes as its first argument a pointer to a character string. Its second argument is a pointer to a comparison character string. The strcspn() function searches each string until it finds the first matching pair. (ANSI)

Returns a size_t type (unsigned integer) whose value is the number of characters in the string of the first argument that have no matching value in the comparison string. For example, a string "ABCDE" matched with a comparison string "DWXYZ" returns a value of 3, reflecting that the sequence of characters "ABC" is unique.

```
char *strdup(char *)
  #include <string.h>
```

Takes as its argument a pointer to a character string. The strdup() function makes a copy of the string in a new location in memory.

Returns a pointer to the new location of the duplicate character string.

```
char *strerror(int)
  #include <string.h>
```

Takes as its argument an integer whose value the function uses as an index into an array of DOS system error messages. (ANSI)

Returns a pointer to the indexed error message character string.

```
size_t strftime(char *, size_t, char *, struct tm *)
#include <string.h>
#include <time.h>
```

Takes as its first argument a pointer to a character buffer in you which to store a character string that represents the date and time. Its second argument is of type size_t (unsigned integer) and specifies the number of available bytes in the buffer. Its third argument is a pointer to a format character string that is typically a string literal delimited by quote marks and that contains embedded format specifiers shown in the following table. Its fourth argument is a pointer to a structure of type tm (defined in time.h) that contains the date and time values you wish to be converted and stored in the buffer. (ANSI)

Format Specifier	Meaning
%A	weekday name
%a	weekday name abbreviation
%B	month name
%b	month name abbreviation
%c	date and time
%d	numerical digit for day of month
%H	numerical hour of the 24-hour clock
%I	numerical hour of the 12-hour clock
%j	numerical day of the 366-day year
%M	minute of the hour
%m	numerical digit for the month of the year
%p	AM or PM for the 12-hour clock

%S	second of the minute
%U	numerical digit for the week of the year (begins Sunday)
%W	numerical digit for the week of the year (begins Monday)
%w	numerical digit for the day of the week (begins Sunday)
%X	current time
%x	current date
%Y	four-digit numerical year since 0 AD
%y	two-digit numerical year since 0 AD
%Z	name of time zone
%%	%

Returns a size_t type (unsigned integer) whose value specifies the number of characters stored to the buffer. Returns 0 upon failure.

```
char *stristr(char *, char *)
  #include <string.h>
```

Takes as its first argument a pointer to a string whose contents it inspects to find a substring matching the string to which its second argument points.

Returns a pointer to the beginning of the matching substring within the string of the first argument. Returns NULL upon failure.

```
size_t strlen(char *)
  #include <string.h>
```

Takes as its argument a pointer to a character string for which you want the size in bytes. (ANSI)

Returns a value of type size_t (unsigned int) that specifies the number of characters of the string, not including the terminating null character.

```
char *strlwr(char *)
  #include <string.h>
```

Takes as its argument a pointer to a character string whose contents the strlwr() function will convert to lowercase.

Returns a pointer to the character string.

```
char *strncat(char *, char *, size_t)
  #include <string.h>
```

Takes as its first argument a pointer to a character buffer that contains a character string. Its second argument is a pointer to a character string. Its third argument is an unsigned integer of type size_t that specifies the maximum number of characters in the second string that the strncat() function should append (concatenate) after the last character of the string of the first argument. (ANSI)

Returns a pointer to the beginning of the string of the first argument.

```
int strncmp(char *, char *, size_t)
  #include <string.h>
```

Takes as its first argument a pointer to a character string. Its second argument is a pointer to a second character string. Its third argument is an unsigned integer of type size_t that specifies the maximum number of characters in each string that the function is to compare. (ANSI)

Returns an integer whose value is the difference between the ASCII code for the first nonmatching character pair, a negative number if the ASCII code for the character in the first argument is smaller than that in the second, a positive if the code for the character in the first argument is larger than that of the second, and zero if the strings are a perfect match.

```
char *strncpy(char *, char *, size_t)
  #include <string.h>
```

Takes as its first argument a pointer to a target character buffer. Its second argument is a pointer to a source character string. Its third argument is an unsigned integer of type size_t that specifies the maximum number of characters that the strncpy() function is to copy from the source to the target. The strncpy() function pads the end of the copy with the NULL character if necessary. (ANSI)

Returns a pointer to the target character string.

```
int strnicmp(char *, char *, size_t)
  #include <string.h>
```

Takes as its first argument a pointer to a first character string. Its second argument is a pointer to a second character string. Its third argument is an unsigned integer of type size_t whose value specifies the number of bytes in each string to compare, irrespective of case.

Returns an integer whose value is the difference between the ASCII codes for the first nonmatching characters. The return value is negative if the character in the first string is less than that in the second string, a positive if the character in the first string is greater than that in the second, and zero if the strings match.

```
char *strnset(char *, int, size_t)
  #include <string.h>
```

Takes as its first argument a pointer to a character string or character buffer. Its second argument is an integer whose value specifies the ASCII code for a character that the function will use to initialize the bytes in the string area. Its third argument is an unsigned integer of type size_t that specifies the number of characters in the string area to initialize.

Returns a pointer to the character string area.

```
char *strok(char *, char *)
  #include <string.h>
```

Takes as its first argument a pointer to a character string. Its second argument is a pointer to a string of one or more characters that the function is to find in the string of the first argument. The characters in the string of the second argument are token separators. Characters not in the string of the second argument are therefore tokens. The string of the first argument is therefore a string of tokens delimited by characters found in the string of the second argument. (ANSI)

Returns a pointer to the next substring within the string of the first argument that is a token. Returns NULL upon failing to find additional tokens.

```
char *strpbrk(char *, char *)
  #include <string.h>
```

Takes as its first argument a pointer to a first character string. Its second argument is a pointer to a second character string. (ANSI)

Returns a pointer to the first character in the first string that has a match to any character in the second string.

```
char *strrchr(char *, int)
  #include <string.h>
```

Takes as its first argument a pointer to a character string. Its second argument is an integer whose value is the ASCII code for a character the strrchr() function is to find in the character string. (ANSI)

Returns a pointer to the last character in the string whose ASCII code matches the second argument.

```
char *strrev(char *)
  #include <string.h>
```

Takes as its argument a pointer to a character string. The function reverses the order of the elements of the string, leaving the terminating NULL character in place.

Returns a pointer to the beginning of the altered character string.

```
char *strset(char *, int)
  #include <string.h>
```

Takes as its first argument a pointer to a character string that ends with the NULL character. Its second argument is an integer whose value specifies the ASCII code for a character that the strset() function uses to reinitialize the elements in the character string.

Returns a pointer to the beginning of the altered character string.

```
size_t strspn(char *, char *)
  #include <string.h>
```

Takes as its first argument a pointer to a character string. Its second argument is a pointer to a second character string. (ANSI)

Returns an unsigned integer of type size_t whose value specifies the number of bytes in the matching substring.

```
char *strstr*char *, char *)
  #include <string.h>
```

Takes as its first argument a pointer to a first character string. Its second argument is a pointer to a second character string. (ANSI)

Returns a pointer to the beginning of a substring embedded in the first character string that matches the second character string.

```
double strtod(char *, char **)
  #include <stdlib.h>
```

Takes as its first argument a pointer to a character string that contains a valid expression of a double floating-point value. Its second argument is a pointer to a character pointer in which the strtod() function will store the address of the character in the numerical expression of the first argument upon which the strtod() function stops its evaluation. The second argument may also be NULL. (ANSI)

Returns a double float whose value corresponds to that expressed in the character string of the first argument.

```
long strtol(char *, char **, int)
  #include <stdlib.h>
```

Takes as its first argument a pointer to a character string that contains a valid expression of a long integer value. Its second argument is a pointer to a character pointer in which the strtol() function will store the address of the character in the numerical expression of the first argument upon which the strtol() function stops its evaluation. The second argument may also be NULL. The third argument is an integer whose value specifies the numerical base for the number expressed in the first argument (2 is binary, 8 is octal, 10 is decimal, 16 is hexadecimal). (ANSI)

Returns a long integer whose value corresponds to that expressed in the character string of the first argument.

```
unsigned long strtoul(char *, char **, int)
  #include <stdlib.h>
```

Takes as its first argument a pointer to a character string that expresses the value of a valid unsigned long integer. Its second argument is a pointer to a character pointer where the strtoul() function will store the address of the first character it ceases its evaluation. The second argument may be NULL. Its third argument is an integer that specifies the number base for the value expressed in the string of the first argument. (ANSI)

Returns an unsigned long integer whose value corresponds to that expressed in the string of the first argument.

```
char *strupr(char *)
  #include <string.h>
```

Takes as its argument a pointer to a character string. The strupr() function converts all characters in the string to uppercase.

Returns a pointer to the converted character string.

```
void swab(char *, char *, int)
  #include <stdlib.h>
```

Takes as its first argument a pointer to a source character string. Its second argument is a pointer to a destination character buffer. Its third argument is an integer whose value specifies the number of bytes the swab() function is to copy from the source to the destination. The swab() function copies pairs of bytes at a time, swapping their order. For example, the string "ABCD" will arrive in the destination as "BADC." Note that the third argument must be an even number.

Returns no data.

```
int system(char *)
  #include <stdlib.h>
```

Takes as its argument a pointer to a character string that the system() function passes to the DOS command interpreter (typically COMMAND.COM). (ANSI)

Returns an integer whose value reflects success or failure of the DOS command interpreter to execute the command; returns zero upon success, nonzero upon failure.

```
double tan(double)
  #include <math.h>
```

Takes as its argument a double floating-point value. (ANSI)

Returns a double float whose value is the tangent of the argument.

```
double tanh(double)
  #include <math.h>
```

Takes as its argument a double floating-point value that expresses radians. (ANSI)

Returns a double float whose value is the byperbolic tangent of the argument.

```
long tell(int *)
  #include <io.h>
  #include <errno.h>
```

Takes as its argument a pointer to an integer whose value is a file descriptor handle.

Returns a long integer whose value is the location of the operating system file pointer in the specified file. Returns EBABF (defined in errno.h) if the file descriptor handle is invalid (e.g., if the file is not opened).

```
char *tempnam(char *, char *)
  #include <stdio.h>
```

Takes as its first argument a pointer to a character string that identifies a directory on the current disk drive. Its second argument is a pointer to a character string that specifies a file name prefix. The tempnam() function will check the environment for the TMP environment variable, which, if it exists, specifies the directory the tempnam() function is to use. The tempnam() function checks for the existence of a directory defined in stdio.h by P_tmpdir. The tempnam() function checks for the existence of a directory named TMP. The tempnam() function creates a character string to concatenate onto the prefix specified by the second argument.

Returns a pointer to a character string that is the newly created temporary file name. Returns NULL upon failure.

```
time_t time(time_t *)
  #include <stdio.h>
  #include <time.h>
```

Takes as its argument a pointer to a variable of type time_t (a long integer as defined in time.h) into which the time() function is to store the current system time expressed in seconds elapsed since midnight, January 1, 1970, Greenwich Mean Time. (ANSI)

Returns type time_t whose value is the current system time expressed in seconds elapsed since midnight, January 1, 1970, Greenwich Mean Time.

```
FILE *tmpfile(void)
  #include <stdio.h>
```

Takes no arguments. (ANSI)

Returns a file pointer for a new file that the tmpfile() function has opened in binary read/write mode. Returns NULL upon failure.

```
char *tmpnam(char *)
  #include <stdio.h>
```

Takes as its argument a pointer to a character buffer that contains L_tmpnam number of bytes (defined in stdio.h) in which the tmpnam() function is to store a temporary file name that it creates. Your program may not call the tmpnam() function more than TMP_MAX times (defined in stdio.h). (ANSI)

Returns a pointer to the character buffer.

```
int toascii(int)
  #include <ctype.h>
```

Takes as its argument an integer whose value is the ASCII code for a character within the range of from 0 to FFh.

Returns an integer whose value is the ASCII code for a character, within the range of from 0 to 7Fh. Use this function to convert a character in the "extended character set" to its counterpart in the normal ASCII range.

```
int tolower(int)
  #include <ctype.h>
```

Takes as its argument an integer whose value is the ASCII code for a character within the range of from 'A' to 'Z.' (ANSI)

Returns an integer whose value is the ASCII code for the lowercase counterpart of the argument; returns the value of the argument if the argument is not within range.

```
int _tolower(int)
  #include <ctype.h>
```

Takes as its argument an integer whose value is the ASCII code for a character.

Returns an integer whose value is 32 (decimal) greater than that of the argument.

```
int toupper(int)
  #include <ctype.h>
```

Takes as its argument an integer whose value is the ASCII code for a character within the range of from 'a' to 'z.' (ANSI)

Returns an integer whose value is the ASCII code for the uppercase counterpart of the argument; returns the value of the argument if the argument is not within range.

```
int _toupper(int)
  #include <ctype.h>
```

Takes as its argument an integer whose value is the ASCII code for a character.

Returns an integer whose value is 32 (decimal) less than that of the argument.

```
void tzset(void)
  #include <time.h>
```

Takes no arguments. This function searches the environment for the TZ environment variable whose value must be CST6, CST6CDT, EST5, EST5EDT, GMT0, MST7, MST7MDT, PST8, or PST8PDT. If the TZ environment variable does not exist, the tzset() function uses PST8PDT as the default. The tzset() function sets the values of the daylight, time zone, and tzname external variables (defined in time.h) accordingly.

Returns no data.

```
char *ultoa(unsigned long, char *, int)
  #include <stdlib.h>
```

Takes as its first argument an unsigned long integer whose value the ultoa() function will convert to an ASCII character string at a location specified by the second argument, a character pointer. Its third argument is an integer whose value specifies the number base that the ultoa() function will use in its conversion.

Returns a pointer to the character string that contains the converted value.

```
int umask(int)
  #include <io.h>
  #include <stat.h>
```

Takes as its argument an integer whose value is a specific file mode of S_IREAD, S_IWRITE, or S_IREAD|S_IWRITE (defined in stat.h). The umask() function directs the fopen() function not to use the read, write, or read/write permissions when opening new files.

Returns an integer whose value is that of the previous mode.

```
int ungetc(int, FILE *)
  #include <stdio.h>
```

Takes as its first argument an integer whose value is that of an ASCII code for a character. Its second argument is a file descriptor handle. The function replaces the current last input character in a file with that specified by its first argument. (ANSI)

Returns an integer whose value is that of the first argument upon success; returns EOF upon failure.

```
int ungetch(int)
  #include <conio.h>
```

Takes as its argument an integer whose value is the ASCII code for a character. The ungetch() function stores the character corresponding to its argument in the keyboard buffer, effectively undoing the last keystroke.

Returns the value of its argument upon success, EOF upon failure.

```
void unixtodos(time_t, struct date *, struct time *)
  #include <dos.h>
```

Takes as its first argument a long integer of type time_t (defined in dos.h) whose value specifies a time and date in seconds elapsed since midnight, January 1, 1970, Greenwich Mean Time. Its second argument is a pointer to a structure of type date (defined in dos.h) into which the unixtodos() function will store date elements based on the first argument. Its third argument is a pointer to a structure of type time (defined in dos.h) into which the unixtodos() function will store time elements based on the first argument.

Returns no data.

```
int unlink(char *)
  #include <io.h>
```

Takes as its argument a pointer to a character string that contains the name of a file (which may be the relative or full path specification) that the unlink() function is to delete.

Returns 0 upon success, -1 upon failure.

```
int utime(char *, struct utimebuf *)
  #include <type.h>
  #include <sys\utime.h>
```

Takes as its first argument a pointer to a character string that specifies the name of a file. Its second argument is a pointer to a structure of type utimebuf (defined in SYS\Utime.h) that contains a new time for the datestamp of the specified file. If the second argument is NULL, the utime() function sets the file's datestamp to the current system time.

Returns 0 upon success, -1 upon failure.

```
int write(int, char *, int)
  #include <io.h>
```

Takes as its first argument an integer whose value specifies a file descriptor handle. Its second argument is a pointer to a character buffer which contains an array of bytes. Its third argument is an integer whose value specifies the number of bytes that the write() function is to write from the specified buffer to the specified file.

Returns an integer whose value is the number of bytes that the write() function wrote to the file; returns -1 upon failure.

```
void writech(int)
  #include <bios.h>
```

Takes as its argument an integer whose value is the ASCII code for a character that the writech() function is to place at the current cursor location.

Returns no data.

```
void writechs(int, int, int)
  #include <bios.h>
```

Takes as its first argument an integer whose value is the ASCII code for a character. Its second argument is an integer that specifies the video attributes to associate with the character. Its third argument is an integer that specifies the number of times the writechs() function is to copy the character to the display, beginning at the current cursor position.

Returns no data.

```
void writedot(int, int, int)
  #include <bios.h>
```

Takes as its first argument an integer whose value specifies the x coordinate of a pixel. Its second argument is an integer that specifies the y coordinate of the pixel. Its third argument is an integer that specifies the value of the pixel, depending upon which graphics modecurrently controls the display.

Returns no data.

Appendix D
Operators

Expressions in C are composed of operands and operators. For instance, the expression (a + b++) is composed of the operands a and b along with the (), +, and ++ operators. The operators combine the operands to produce a single value.

Every operator in the C language has a place in a "precedence" hierarchy. Operators may have higher, lower, or equal precedence than others. In case of equal precedence, each operator has a quality of "associativity" that determines whether evaluation is to proceed to the right or the left.

A C compiler evaluates an expression by applying operators in the order of precedence. In the case of an expression that contains two or more operators of the same precedence ranking, the C compiler resolves the expression according to the operators' rules of associativity.

The following table presents the operators of the C language in their order of precedence, with those with the highest precedence first, and it also notes the direction of association for each. L-R means apply the left operator first; R-L means apply the right operator first.

Operator	Type	Associativity
() [] . ->	Expressions and Members	L to R
++ -- ! ~ - * & sizeof + (typecast)	Unary Operators	R to L
* / %	Multiplication and Division	L to R
+ -	Addition and Subtraction	L to R
<< >>	Left and Right Shift	L to R
< > <= >=	Less than and Greater than Relations	L to R
== !=	Equal and Not Equal Relations	L to R
&	Bitwise AND	L to R
^	Bitwise XOR	L to R

Table D-1 (continued)

<table>
<tr><th>Operator</th><th>Type</th><th>Associativity</th></tr>
<tr><td>|</td><td>Bitwise OR</td><td>L to R</td></tr>
<tr><td>&&</td><td>Logical AND</td><td>L to R</td></tr>
<tr><td>||</td><td>Logical OR</td><td>L to R</td></tr>
<tr><td>? :</td><td>Conditional (if…else)</td><td>R to L</td></tr>
<tr><td>= += -=
*= /= %=
&= |= ^=
<<= >>=</td><td>Assignment</td><td>R to L</td></tr>
<tr><td>,</td><td>Sequence</td><td>L to R</td></tr>
</table>

Table D-1 Operator precedence and associativity

Appendix E
printf() and scanf() Format Specifiers

The Power C library contains a family of four input and four output formatting functions: cscanf(), fscanf(), scanf(), sscanf(), cprintf(), fprintf(), printf(), and sprintf(). An argument for each of these functions is a format character string that contains format specifiers with modifiers of various types. This appendix provides a reference for the format specifiers and their modifiers. See the specific function description in Appendix C to understand the difference between the related functions.

Type

The following table lists the format specifier characters that you can use in the format character string. Precede each with the % symbol, as in the following example.

```
printf("Here are a few good specifiers %% %d %X %lf", this that the other);
```

%	Displays the % character.
c	Specifies an unsigned char; can be used with any char or int argument.
d	Specifies a signed int to be displayed in decimal format; can be used with any int or char argument.
e	Specifies a double float in exponential format; can be used with any float or double argument (same as the f type for the scanf() function).
E	Same as the e type but with the E character prepended (same as the f type for the scanf() function).
f	Specifies a double float in fixed point format; can be used with any float or double argument.
g	Specifies a double float in either exponential or fixed point format, depending upon which is more compact; can be used with any float or double argument (same as the f type for the scanf() function).
G	Same as the g type, but with the ENTER character prepended if the value is displayed in exponential format (same as the f type for the scanf() function).
i	Specifies an integer that may be in octal, decimal, or hexadecimal form for the scanf() function (same as the d type for the printf() function).
n	Specifies a pointer to an integer that stores the total number of characters displayed to that point.

o	Specifies an unsigned integer in octal format.
p	Specifies a void * pointer in unsigned integer format.
s	Specifies a pointer to a character string that is to be displayed up to, but not including, the terminating null character for the printf() function. Specifies a character string input for the scanf() function.
u	Specifies an unsigned integer in decimal format.
x	Specifies an integer in hexadecimal format with lowercase alpha characters for the printf() function, and can be used with any integer or unsigned integer (same as the X type for the scanf() function).
X	Same as the x type, but displays uppercase alpha characters for the printf() function.
[...]	Specifies a series of characters for the scanf() function only that comprise a valid set of characters. The scanf() function will stop reading when it encounters a character not in the specified set.

Modifiers for printf() and scanf() Format Specifiers

The following table lists modifiers and the format specifiers with which they can be used.

F	Use the F modifier with types p or s to specify a far pointer type.
h	Use the h modifier with types d, i, o, u, x, or X to specify a short integer data type.
l	Use the l modifier with types d, i, u, o, x, or X to specify a long integer data type.
L	Use the L modifier with types e, E, f, g, or G to specify a long double floating-point data type.
N	Use the N modifier with types p or s to specify a near pointer type.

Precision Field Characters for the printf() Function

The following table lists the two types of precision field characters you can use with numeric format specifiers.

digits	For an integer you can specify the total number of digits to display. A value that requires fewer digits will begin with blank padding. A value prefixed with 0 will generate leading zeros. For a floating-point value of type e, E, or f, you can specify the total number of digits to the right of the decimal point. For a floating-point value of type g or G, you can specify the maximum number of digits to the right of the decimal point. The default is six. For a string you can specify the maximum number of characters to display. The default is to display the entire string.

*	Use the * character as a placeholder for the next argument in the optional argument list. This argument must be of type int, and it specifies the precision value.

Width Field Characters for the printf() Function

The following table lists the two types of width field characters that you can use with numeric format specifiers.

digits	You can specify the width of the print zone to contain a certain number of characters. If the value you print happens to require more characters, they will override this setting so that all characters are displayed. If the value you print happens to require fewer characters, they will rest within this field.
*	Use the * character as a placeholder for the next argument in the optional argument list. This argument must be of type int, and it specifies the print zone minimum width.

Flag Field Characters for the printf() Function

The following table lists the four flag field characters that you can use with numeric format specifiers.

–	For all types, left-justify within the print zone.
+	For types d, i, f, e, E, g, and G, prepend a + sign to positive values. Do not use with the space character flag.
space	For types d, i, f, e, E, g, and G, prepend a space character to positive values. Do not use with the + flag.
#	For type o, prepend a leading 0. For type x or X, prepend a leading 0x or 0X. For type f, e, or E, print the decimal point whether or not digits follow to the right. For type g or G, print the decimal point whether or not digits follow to the right and print all trailing zeros.

White Space and Suppression Characters for the scanf() Function

The scanf() function responds to white space characters by ignoring them in the input stream. Thus a format string with " %c %c" will ignore white space characters before and after the first character.

The asterisk (*) character is the suppression character. It directs the scanf() function to read the next input type without assigning it to a corresponding argument. Thus "%d%*s%d" directs the scanf() function to read an integer, skip an intervening character string, and read another integer.

Appendix F
C Keywords, Directives, and Global and Environment Variables

This appendix presents a reference for C language keywords, which are extended keywords that are unique to the Power C compiler, as well as the preprocessor directives, the global variables, and the environment variables.

Keywords

The C language is composed of keywords, operators, and the rules for their use. The following table references the C language keywords.

Keyword	Meaning
auto	declares a variable local to a function as temporary, i.e., it resides on the stack only for the time that its function is active.
break	exits from the loop body of a *do, while,* or *for* statement. Use with *case* statements to prohibit fall-through from one *case* to the next.
case	identify case labels in a *switch* statement
char	declares a variable or array to require 1-byte storage elements.

const	declare an object as nonmodifiable:
	`const int i;           /* constant int */`
	`const int *ip;         /* variable pointer to constant int */`
	`int *const *ip;        /* constant pointer to variable int */`

continue	used within the body of a loop; forces execution to skip the remaining part of the loop and to start the next loop cycle, generally depending on a condition.
default	used once in a *switch* statement identifying the default code as an alternative to multiple case statements.
do	used with *while* to declare a loop with trailing control expression.
double	declares double-precision floating-point variables (8-byte size for Power C) and arrays.
else	used with *if* to declare an alternative execution statement

Table F-1 (continued)

Keyword	Meaning

enum	declares an identifier with a list of enumerated constants and defines variables associated with the identifier. Enumeration constants are a way to generate sequential integer constants that can replace *#defines* in some contexts.
	`enum pal_list {Mary=1, Bess=2, Bill=3, Andy=4, Geronimo=5};`
	`enum pal_list pal`

extern	declare a variable or function that is defined in a separate module (in another file, and not declared as *static* or *extern*).
float	declares a variable or array to be single-precision floating-point (four bytes storage in Power C). Cannot be used with the *long* qualifier.
for	declares three expressions, the initializer, the controller, and the counter, and then the body of the loop.
goto	forces an unconditional jump to a label located within the current function.
if	used with a Boolean expression to permit or prohibit execution of a statement or set of statements. Can be followed by an *else* construct.
int	declares a variable or array to be type integer requiring two bytes of storage for Power C.
long	qualifier for the *int* keyword specifies a Power C data type of four bytes. ANSI C requires only that a *long int* data type be no shorter than an *int* data type.
register	declares that an integer data type should be stored in a register if possible. A register variable cannot have a memory address.
return	forces termination of function execution. Used with an argument, returns that argument to the calling function.
schar	declares an identifier of an ANSI-standard 1-byte element. It can be used for both characters and numbers (range -127 to 127).
short	qualifier for the *int* keyword specifies a Power C data type of 2 bytes. ANSI C requires only that a short *int* data type be no longer than an *int* data type.
signed	qualifier declares any integral data type to represent a negative number if the Most Significant Bit (MSB) of the character or integer data element is set, nor a positive number if the MSB is clear.
sizeof	operator that returns the storage requirements of a data type or structure in bytes.
static	declares that a data type or structure should be stored permanently in memory, whether or not the function to which it belongs is active.

struct	declares an identifier that represents a group of not necessarily similar data types that are stored contiguously in memory.
switch	followed by an argument, declares a set of case expressions, each with an associated statement to be executed if its expression matches the initial argument. Execution will fall through to the next case unless the execution statement is followed by a break.
typedef	declares a data type to be associated with a new identifier.

```
typedef struct
    {
      char *command;
      void (*function)(void);
    } cmd_entry;

   const cmd_entry table[]=
    {
      "help",    do_help,
      "reset",   do_reset,
      "quit",    do_quit
    };
```

union	declares several variables or structures and specifies their storage at the same memory location.
unsigned	qualifier specifies integer data types to be positive numbers only (without respect to status of MSB).
void	used as a type-specifier that declares a function that returns no values, a function that takes no parameters, or a "generic" pointer that can be used with any other data or pointer type.

```
void f(); /* A function without return value */
type_spec f(void);       /* A function with no parameters */
void *p;  /* Generic pointer. Can be cast to
          /* any other pointer and is assignment
          /* compatible with any pointer type */
```

volatile	qualifier that identifies a variable that may be modified by software or hardware not within the control of the final executable program. May be used with *const* to initialize the variable.
while	declares a loop with a controlling expression. Used alone it creates a loop with a leading control expression, used with *do,* it creates a loop with a trailing control expression

Table F-1 Keyword definitions

Extended Keywords

In addition to the ANSI C keywords, Power C includes five proprietary keywords that extend the language. These extended keywords may not be permitted by other compilers, so be warned that using these may limit the portability of your source code. Consider conditioning their use with #ifdef or #ifndef preprocessor directives (see the following section in this appendix). The /k command line option disables the effects of any of these extended keywords.

far	The *far* keyword is a qualifier that declares a pointer to far memory. A far pointer is a 32-bit pointer that allows full access throughout all available memory. Its normal use is as a pointer to the far data area, beyond the 64K near data segment, when compiling with the small or medium memory models (see command line options /ms and /mm).
huge	The *huge* keyword is a qualifier that declares a pointer to an array that is greater than 64K in size.
interrupt	The *interrupt* keyword is a qualifier that declares a function to be called via the interrupt mechanism rather than through the normal call mechanism. To use the *interrupt* keyword, be sure not to set the global variable _istksiz below its default value of 1K.
near	The *near* keyword is a qualifier that declares a pointer to near memory. A near pointer is a 16-bit pointer that permits access only to the current 64K data segment. If you are compiling using the large memory model (see the /ml command line option), data pointers are 32 bits by default. The *near* keyword allows near data access with smaller, nimbler pointers.
pascal	The *pascal* keyword qualifies a function such that its argument passing convention is reversed. Normally, the C compiler calls functions by pushing their last arguments onto the stack first, and their first arguments last. The *pascal* keyword directs the compiler to call a function by pushing its first argument onto the stack first, and its last argument last. The pascal calling convention allows you to specify functions written for languages other than the C language. It also provides a means of dynamically controlling variable parameters if the last argument is an integer that specifies the total number of arguments passed for that call. You must design the function itself to inspect that parameter and handle whatever number of arguments is specified.

Table F-2 Extended Keywords

Preprocessor Directives

The Power C preprocessor provides text-processing services that allow symbol, token, and macro substitution as well as file inclusion and conditional compilation. The preprocessor responds to defined directives.

Syntax rules for ANSI compatible preprocessor directives are:

- The first nonwhitespace character on the line must be the pound # sign.
- The directive immediately follows the pound sign.
- A space or tab character delimits an identifier or expression. Subsequent delimiters separate elements of the directive statement.
- A backslash (\) character allows text string continuation on the following line.
- Preprocessor directive statements do not end with a terminating semicolon.

Definitions of the preprocessor directives follow.

Directive	Meaning
#define	The #define directive associates a symbol with a value, a text string, or an expression that may contain variables (macro).
#elif	The #elif directive is equivalent to using the #else #if (expression) sequence of directives.
#else	The #else directive follows an #if directive and any associated statements and directs the preprocessor to enable its set of statements in the event that the Boolean condition for the preceding #if fails. Terminate control of the #if directive with the #endif directive.
#endif	Used to terminate control of an #if, #ifdef, or #ifndef directive condition.
#if	Use the #if directive with a Boolean expression followed by one or more C language statements. Terminate control of the #if directive with the #endif directive.
#ifdef	Use the #ifdef directive with a symbol followed by one or more C language statements. If the symbol is currently defined by the #define directive, the statements following will be active. Terminate control of the #ifdef directive with the #endif directive.
#ifndef	Use the #ifndef directive with a symbol followed by one or more C language statements. If the symbol is currently not defined, the statements following will be active. Terminate control of the #ifndef directive with the #endif directive.
#include	The #include directive followed by a file specification directs the preprocessor to open the file and insert its contents at the location of the #include statement. The -I compiler command line option permits similar file content inclusion at the head of the source file.
#line	Use the #line directive with an integer constant to renumber the following line in the source file. The #line directive also permits use of a new filename for subsequent source code.

Table F-3 (continued)

Directive	Meaning
#pragmA	The ANSI standard permits C compiler manufacturers to provide proprietary features yet maintain source code portability. The #pragma directive directs the preprocessor to inspect the subsequent "switch" keywords. If they conform to those permitted by that compiler, the preprocessor enables them. If not, the preprocessor ignores them. With the exception of the #pragma pagesize NN keyword, the form is always #pragma keyword or #pragma keyword- such that the - terminating character indicates that the feature is turned off. Note that the default settings specify those for which you need not use the keyword. Power C permits the following #pragma "switch" keywords.
convert	The default is #pragma convert. Use #pragma convert- immediately before a function call to disable type conversion. The effect in that case is that the compiler will not convert characters to integers nor floats to doubles.
extern8	The default is #pragma extern8-. Use #pragma extern8 to direct the compiler to recognize only the first 8 characters of function names rather than the normal 31 characters.
keywcase	The default is #pragma keywcase-. Use #pragma keywcase to direct the compiler to recognize C keywords in lower, upper, or mixed case spellings rather than in all lowercase, as is the normal rule.
List	The default is #pragma list. Use #pragma list- to direct the compiler not to make a listing file. This has an effect only when compiling with the /l command line option.
listmacr	The default is #pragma listmacr-. Use #pragma listmacr to direct the compiler to expand macros in its listing files. This has an effect only when compiling with the /l command line option.
nestcmnt	The default is #pragma nestcmnt-. Use #pragma nestcmnt to permit nested comments, for example, to allow /* one /* two */ one */, which by default would generate a compiler error.
pagesize	The default is #pragma pagesize 60. Use #pragma pagesize with any two-digit numeral to set the number of lines per printed page for the list file. This has an effect only with the /l command line option.
signext	The default is #pragma signext-. Use #pragma signext to direct the compiler to extend the sign of characters as it converts them to integers in expressions. By default, the compiler always converts a character to a positive integer.
stackchk	The default is #pragma stackchk-. Use #pragma stackchk to check stack overflow for every function call.

trace	The default is #pragma trace. Use #pragma trace- to direct the compiler not to generate debugging information in its object file. Such debugging information consists of symbol names required by the Power C trace debugging utility. This has an effect only with the /t command line option.
uppercas	The default is #pragma uppercas-. Use #pragma uppercas to direct the compiler to convert function names to all uppercase spelling rather than with the spelling that appears in the source file. Be warned that this will disrupt your program's ability to call supplied library functions.
#undef	Use the #undef directive with a symbol name to nullify previous #define definitions. The C compiler will report subsequent encounters with that symbol with "undefined symbol" warnings.

Table F-3 Preprocessor directives

Global Variables

The following table references the global variable identifiers with respect to the header files in which they are declared and their data type.

daylight	Declared in <time.h>. int daylight.
_doserrno	Declared in <errno.h>. int _doserrno.
environ	Declared in <dos.h>. char *environ.
errno	Declared in <errno.h>. int errno.
_fmode	Declared in <fcntl.h>. int _fmode.
_istksiz	Declared in <dos.h>. int _istksiz.
_osmajor	Declared in <dos.h>. unsigned char _osmajor.
_osminor	Declared in <dos.h>. unsigned char _osminor.
_psp	Declared in <dos.h>. unsigned int _psp.
sys_errlist	Declared in <errno.h>. char *sys_errlist[].
sys_nerr	Declared in <errno.h>. int sys_nerr.
timezone	Declared in <time.h>. long int timezone.
tzname	Declared in <time.h>. char *tzname[2].
_version	Declared in <dos.h>. unsigned int _version.

Table F-4 Global variables

Environment Variables

The following table references the evironment variables you use to direct the compiler and linker operations. See the environ global variable

LIBRARY	Use the LIBRARY environment variable to specify directories for the linker to search for library files. The linker will first search the current directory, then any directories specified by the LIBRARY environment variable, and finally any directories specified by the PATH environment variable.
PATH	Use the PATH environment variable to specify directories for the linker to search for library files. Before searching directories specified by the PATH environment variable, the linker will first search the current directory, then any directories specified by the LIBRARY environment variable.
PCOPTION	Use the PCOPTION environment variable to set default compiler command line option settings. The Power C compiler will first search the PCOPTION environment variable settings for its command line option directions, then it will refer to the options you used on the command line; any command line options will override the settings specified by the PCOPTION environment variable.

Table F-5 Environment variables

Appendix G
ASCII Table

IBM Character Codes

DEC	HEX	Symbol	Key
0	00	(NULL)	CTRL 2
1	01	☺	CTRL A
2	02	☻	CTRL B
3	03	♥	CTRL C
4	04	♦	CTRL D
5	05	♣	CTRL E
6	06	♠	CTRL F
7	07	•	CTRL G
8	08	◘	BACKSPACE
9	09		TAB
10	0A	◙	CTRL J
11	0B	♂	CTRL K
12	0C	♀	CTRL L
13	0E	♪	ENTER
14	0E	♫	CTRL N
15	0F	¤	CTRL O
16	10	►	CTRL P
17	11	◄	CTRL Q
18	12	↕	CTRL R
19	13	!!	CTRL S
20	14	¶	CTRL T
21	15	§	CTRL U
22	16	■	CTRL V
23	17	↨	CTRL W
24	18	↑	CTRL X
25	19	↓	CTRL Y
26	1A	→	CTRL Z
27	1B	←	ESC
28	1C	└	CTRL \

IBM Character Codes

DEC	HEX	Symbol	Key
29	1D	↔	CTRL]
30	1E	▲	CTRL 6
31	1F	▼	CTRL -
32	20		SPACEBAR
33	21	!	!
34	22	"	"
35	23	#	#
36	24	$	$
37	25	%	%
38	26	&	&
39	27	'	'
40	28	(	(
41	29	)	)
42	2A	*	*
43	2B	+	+
44	2C	,	,
45	2D	-	-
46	2E	.	.
47	2F	/	/
48	30	0	0
49	31	1	1
50	32	2	2
51	33	3	3
52	34	4	4
53	35	5	5
54	36	6	6
55	37	7	7
56	38	8	8
57	39	9	9

IBM Character Codes

DEC	HEX	Symbol	Key
58	3A	:	:
59	3B	;	;
60	3C	<	<
61	3D	=	=
62	3E	>	>
63	3F	?	?
64	40	@	@
65	41	A	A
66	42	B	B
67	43	C	C
68	44	D	D
69	45	E	E
70	46	F	F
71	47	G	G
72	48	H	H
73	49	I	I
74	4A	J	J
75	4B	K	K
76	4C	L	L
77	4D	M	M
78	4E	N	N
79	4F	O	O
80	50	P	P
81	51	Q	Q
82	52	R	R
83	53	S	S
84	54	T	T
85	55	U	U
86	56	V	V
87	57	W	W
88	58	X	X
89	59	Y	Y
90	5A	Z	Z
91	5B	[	[
92	5C	\	\
93	5D	]	]
94	5E	^	^
95	5F	_	_
96	60	`	`

IBM Character Codes

DEC	HEX	Symbol	Key
97	61	a	a
98	62	b	b
99	63	c	c
100	64	d	d
101	65	e	e
102	66	f	f
103	67	g	g
104	68	h	h
105	69	i	i
106	6A	j	j
107	6B	k	k
108	6C	l	l
109	6D	m	m
110	6E	n	n
111	6F	o	o
112	70	p	p
113	71	q	q
114	72	r	r
115	73	s	s
116	74	t	t
117	75	u	u
118	76	v	v
119	77	w	w
120	78	x	x
121	79	y	y
122	7A	z	z
123	7B	{	{
124	7C	¦	¦
125	7D	}	}
126	7E	~	~
127	7F	Δ	CTRL ←
128	80	Ç	ALT 128
129	81	ü	ALT 129
130	82	é	ALT 130
131	83	â	ALT 131
132	84	ä	ALT 132
133	85	à	ALT 133
134	86	å	ALT 134
135	87	ç	ALT 135

IBM Character Codes

DEC	HEX	Symbol	Key
136	88	ê	ALT 136
137	89	ë	ALT 137
138	8A	è	ALT 138
139	8B	ï	ALT 139
140	8C	î	ALT 140
141	8D	ì	ALT 141
142	8E	Ä	ALT 142
143	8F	Å	ALT 143
144	90	É	ALT 144
145	91	æ	ALT 145
146	92	Æ	ALT 146
147	93	ô	ALT 147
148	94	ö	ALT 148
149	95	ò	ALT 149
150	96	û	ALT 150
151	97	ù	ALT 151
152	98	ÿ	ALT 152
153	99	Ö	ALT 153
154	9A	Ü	ALT 154
155	9B	¢	ALT 155
156	9C	£	ALT 156
157	9D	¥	ALT 157
158	9E	₧	ALT 158
159	9F	ƒ	ALT 159
160	A0	á	ALT 160
161	A1	í	ALT 161
162	A2	ó	ALT 162
163	A3	ú	ALT 163
164	A4	ñ	ALT 164
165	A5	Ñ	ALT 165
166	A6	ª	ALT 166
167	A7	º	ALT 167
168	A8	¿	ALT 168
169	A9	⌐	ALT 169
170	AA	¬	ALT 170
171	AB	½	ALT 171
172	AC	¼	ALT 172
173	AD	¡	ALT 173
174	AE	«	ALT 174

IBM Character Codes

DEC	HEX	Symbol	Key
175	AF	»	ALT 175
176	B0	░	ALT 176
177	B1	▒	ALT 177
178	B2	▓	ALT 178
179	B3	│	ALT 179
180	B4	┤	ALT 180
181	B5	╡	ALT 181
182	B6	╢	ALT 182
183	B7	╖	ALT 183
184	B8	╕	ALT 184
185	B9	╣	ALT 185
186	BA	║	ALT 186
187	BB	╗	ALT 187
188	BC	╝	ALT 188
189	BD	╜	ALT 189
190	BE	╛	ALT 190
191	BF	┐	ALT 191
192	C0	└	ALT 192
193	C1	┴	ALT 193
194	C2	┬	ALT 194
195	C3	├	ALT 195
196	C4	─	ALT 196
197	C5	┼	ALT 197
198	C6	╞	ALT 198
199	C7	╟	ALT 199
200	C8	╚	ALT 200
201	C9	╔	ALT 201
202	CA	╩	ALT 202
203	CB	╦	ALT 203
204	CC	╠	ALT 204
205	CD	═	ALT 205
206	CE	╬	ALT 206
207	CF	╧	ALT 207
208	D0	╨	ALT 208
209	D1	╤	ALT 209
210	D2	╥	ALT 210
211	D3	╙	ALT 211
212	D4	╘	ALT 212
213	D5	╒	ALT 213

IBM Character Codes

DEC	HEX	Symbol	Key
214	D6	╓	ALT 214
215	D7	╫	ALT 215
216	D8	╪	ALT 216
217	D9	┘	ALT 217
218	DA	┌	ALT 218
219	DB	█	ALT 219
220	DC	▄	ALT 220
221	DD	▌	ALT 221
222	DE	▐	ALT 222
223	DF	▀	ALT 223
224	E0	α	ALT 224
225	E1	β	ALT 225
226	E2	Γ	ALT 226
227	E3	π	ALT 227
228	E4	Σ	ALT 228
229	E5	σ	ALT 229
230	E6	µ	ALT 230
231	E7	τ	ALT 231
232	E8	Φ	ALT 232
233	E9	Θ	ALT 233
234	EA	Ω	ALT 234

IBM Character Codes

DEC	HEX	Symbol	Key
235	EB	δ	ALT 235
236	EC	∞	ALT 236
237	ED	φ	ALT 237
238	EE	ε	ALT 238
239	EF	∩	ALT 239
240	F0	≡	ALT 240
241	F1	±	ALT 241
242	F2	≥	ALT 242
243	F3	≤	ALT 243
244	F4	⌠	ALT 244
245	F5	⌡	ALT 245
246	F6	÷	ALT 246
247	F7		ALT 247
248	F8	°	ALT 248
249	F9	•	ALT 249
250	FA	·	ALT 250
251	FB		ALT 251
252	FC	η	ALT 252
253	FD	^{2}	ALT 253
254	FE	■	ALT 254
255	FF	(blank)	ALT 255

Note that IBM Extended ASCII charcters can be displayed by pressing the »A..key and then typing the decimal code of the character on the keypad.

INDEX

B

G

T

U

V

W

About the Author

Dave Himmel is a graphics programmer for Boeing Computer Services in Seattle, Washington, and an independent software consultant. He holds a BS degree in Physics from the University of Illinois, an MS in Electrical Engineering from Washington University, St. Louis, and an MBA from Southern Methodist University. Dave has 28 years of experience with a variety of programming languages, including Assembly, BASIC, C, FORTRAN, and Pascal. He has also taught college courses in C.

Colophon

Production for this book was done using desktop publishing techniques and every phase of the book involved the use of computer technology. Never did production use traditional typesetting, stats, or photos, and virtually everything for this book, from the illustrations to the formatted text, was saved on disk. Only the cover used traditional techniques.

Although this book was written on a Dell 386 computer and a Zeos 386SX portable computer, Apple Macintosh computers were used for desktop publishing. The following method was used to go between machines: The author wrote the text for this book in Word for DOS 5.5. The finished documents were then saved in an RTF format and transferred directly to a Macintosh on a 3.5-inch DOS diskette, using Insignia's Access PC. These text files were then opened in Microsoft Word for the Macintosh, which interpreted the RTF formatting.

All book design and page formatting was done in Aldus PageMaker on the Macintosh, using the imported Microsoft Word files. Adobe Postscript and Paperback Software fonts were used. Line art was created in Adobe Illustrator and Aldus Freehand.

The cover was created as a photograph and was traditionally separated and composed. PageMaker 4.01 was used for cover design.

Final page files were sent on a SyQuest cartridge to the Courier Connection in San Mateo, California, where they were output on film through a Macintosh IIci and an Agfa 9800 imagesetter. Plates were then made from the film.

AS A PUBLISHER AND WRITER WITH OVER 360,000 BOOKS SOLD EACH YEAR, IT CAME AS A GREAT SHOCK TO DISCOVER THAT OUR RAIN FORESTS, HOME FOR HALF OF ALL LIVING THINGS ON EARTH, ARE BEING DESTROYED AT THE RATE OF 50 ACRES PER MINUTE ❧ AT THIS RATE THE RAIN FORESTS WILL COMPLETELY DISAPPEAR IN JUST 50 YEARS ❧ BOOKS HAVE A LARGE INFLUENCE ON THIS RAMPANT DESTRUCTION ❧ FOR EXAMPLE, SINCE IT TAKES 17 TREES TO PRODUCE ONE TON OF PAPER, A FIRST PRINTING OF 30,000 COPIES OF A TYPICAL 480 PAGE BOOK CONSUMES 108,000 POUNDS OF PAPER WHICH WILL REQUIRE 918 TREES ❧ TO HELP OFFSET THIS LOSS, WAITE GROUP PRESS WILL PLANT TWO TREES FOR EVERY TREE FELLED FOR PRODUCTION OF THIS BOOK ❧ THE DONATION WILL BE MADE TO RAINFOREST ACTION NETWORK (THE BASIC FOUNDATION, P.O. BOX 47012, ST. PETERSBURG, FL 33743), WHICH CAN PLANT 1,000 TREES FOR $250.

WA

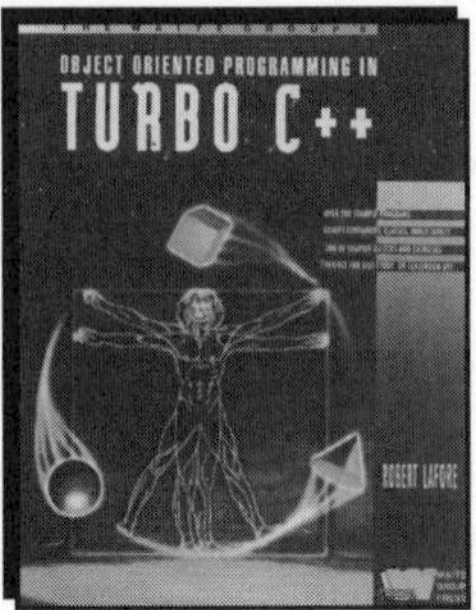

THE WAITE GROUP'S

OBJECT-ORIENTED PROGRAMMING IN TURBO C++

ROBERT LAFORE

Suitable for students, hackers, and enthusiasts, Lafore's practical, real-world lessons teach the basics of object-oriented programming, focusing on C++ as a separate language, distinct from C, and assuming no prior experience with C. Covers Turbo C++, Borland C++, and Borland BGI Graphics. Includes objects, classes, overloading, constructors, inheritance, and virtual functions. End of chapter quizzes and exercises.

ISBN 1-878739-06-9, TRADE PAPER,
776PP., 7 X 9, COMPANION DISK AVAILABLE **$26.95 US**

THE WAITE GROUP'S

C++ PRIMER PLUS

Teach Yourself Object-Oriented Programming

STEPHEN PRATA

Teaches "generic" AT&T C++ 2.0, and 2.1, in the same style as the author's best-selling New C Primer Plus (Winner of the CPA's Best How-To Computer Book Award), over 400,000 copies sold. Gentle, step-by-step lessons teach the basics of OOP including classes, inheritance, information hiding, and polymorphism. No C programming needed. Perfect for UNIX and DOS. "Prata makes a relatively complex subject—professional programming—clear and enjoyable." — Computer Press Association.

ISBN 1-878739-02-6, TRADE PAPER,
744PP., 7 X 9, COMPANION DISK AVAILABLE **$26.95 US**

THE WAITE GROUP'S

MASTER C

Let the PC Teach You C

MITCHELL WAITE, STEPHEN PRATA, AND REX WOOLLARD

Master C uses your computer to teach generic ANSI C from the fundamentals of C through advanced concepts, including prototyping, pointers, and data structures. Unique features of the IBM PC are covered. You can follow Master C's learning course that covers C in 15 comprehensive chapters. Or you can ask Master C for any standard concept word in its C glossary, and it will present the definition and follow it with a lesson. Both Master C and Master C++ turn your PC into a sophisticated interactive learning system.

ISBN 1-878739-00-X, TRADE PAPER,
3-5.25" DISKS, 231PP., 7 X 9 **$44.95 US**

THE WAITE GROUP'S

MASTER C++

Let the PC Teach You Object-Oriented Programming

REX WOOLLARD, ROBERT LAFORE, AND HARRY HENDERSON

Master C++ also uses your computer to teach AT&T Version 2 compatible C++, Turbo and Borland C++, and follows the proposed ANSI C++ standard. You'll find everything you need for writing your own Object-Oriented Programming (OOP); creating classes and member functions, mastering *cin* and *cout,* using polymorphism, inheritance, and containers. This package also covers the fundamentals of C that are common to C++, including loops, decisions, variable types, prototyping, pointers, and data structures. Similar to Master C, you can learn linearly or by concept word.

ISBN 1-878739-07-7, TRADE PAPER,
3-5.25" DISKS, 391PP., 7 X 9 **$39.95 US**

NO ONE CAN DO A BETTER JOB RAVING ABOUT OUR MASTER SERIES THAN OUR READERS.

Here are just a few of hundreds of comments we have received:

Please explain the one thing you liked MOST about this product.
VERY HELPFUL PRODUCT!

Please explain the one thing you liked MOST about this product.
The easiest way to work with it the examples and notes

Please explain the one thing you liked MOST about this product.
EXPLANATIONS ARE VERY PRECISE & AT A LEVEL FOR EASY UNDERSTANDING

Any other comments?
Excellent format, thorough, flexible, very effective!

Any other comments?
VERY GOOD, DON'T HAVE DOUBTS NOW AS IF I AM DOING IT RIGHT OR NOT.

Please explain the one thing you liked MOST about this product.
you can take your own pace slow or fast + review or skip as needed

Please give us any additional comments
VERY EASY to USE; VERY good INSTRUCTION

Please explain the one thing you liked MOST about this product.
Really "builds" well, a little at a time, until you find that you're actually learning C!

Any other comments? It's A great PRODUCT EVEN FOR beginners

Please explain the one thing you liked MOST about this product.
EXCELLENT FOR SOMEONE wanting to LEARN programming without going to College

Any other comments?
EXCELLENT PRODUCT / VALUE! WELL PLEASED

This is the most excellent Tutorial on "C" that I have ever used. Please send brochures on any other such products.

SOFTWARE LICENSE AGREEMENT

This is a legal agreement between you, the end user and purchaser, and The Waite Group, Inc. By opening the sealed disk package, you are agreeing to be bound by the terms of this Agreement. If you do not agree with the terms of this Agreement, promptly return the unopened disk package and the accompanying items (including the related book and other written material) to the place you obtained them for a refund.

SOFTWARE LICENSE

1. The Waite Group, Inc. grants you the right to use one copy of the enclosed software program (the program) on a single computer system (whether a single CPU, part of a licensed network, or a terminal connected to a single CPU). Each concurrent user of the program must have exclusive use of the related Waite Group, Inc. written materials.

2. The copyright in the Power C program and tools is owned by Mix software, Inc. and the copyright in the entire work is owned by The Waite Group, Inc. and is therefore protected under the copyright laws of the United States and other nations, under international treaties. You may make only one copy of the program exclusively for backup or archival purposes, or you may transfer the program to one hard disk drive, using the original for backup or archival purposes. You may make no other copies of the program, and you may make no copies of all or any part of the related Waite Group, Inc. written materials.

3. You may not rent or lease the program, but you may transfer ownership of the program and related written materials (including any and all updates and earlier versions) if you keep no copies of either, and if you make sure the transferee agrees to the terms of this license.

4. You may not decompile, reverse engineer, disassemble, copy, create a derivative work, or otherwise use the program except as stated in this Agreement.

GOVERNING LAW

This Agreement is governed by the laws of the State of California.

LIMITED WARRANTY

The following warranties shall be effective for 90 days from the date of purchase: (i) The Waite Group, Inc. warrants the enclosed disks to be free of defects in materials and workmanship under normal use; and (ii) The Waite Group, Inc. warrants that the program, unless modified by the purchaser, will substantially perform the functions described in the documentation provided by The Waite Group, Inc. when operated on the designated hardware and operating system. The Waite Group, Inc. does not warrant that the program will meet client's requirements or that operation of the program will be uninterrupted or error-free. The program warranty does not cover any program that has been altered or changed in any way by anyone other than The Waite Group, Inc. The Waite Group, Inc. is not responsible for problems caused by changes in the operating characteristics of computer hardware or computer operating systems that are made after the release of the program, nor for problems in the interaction of the program with other software.

THESE WARRANTIES ARE EXCLUSIVE AND IN LIEU OF ALL OTHER WARRANTIES OF MERCHANTABILITY OR FITNESS FOR A PARTICULAR PURPOSE OR OF ANY OTHER WARRANTY, WHETHER EXPRESS OR IMPLIED.

EXCLUSIVE REMEDY

The Waite Group, Inc. will replace any defective disk without charge if the defective disk is returned to The Waite Group, Inc. within 90 days from date of purchase.

This is Purchaser's sole and exclusive remedy for any breach of warranty or claim for contract, tort or damages.

LIMITATION OF LIABILITY

THE WAITE GROUP, INC. SHALL NOT IN ANY CASE BE LIABLE FOR SPECIAL, INCIDENTAL, CONSEQUENTIAL, INDIRECT, OR OTHER SIMILAR DAMAGES ARISING FROM ANY BREACH OF THESE WARRANTIES EVEN IF THE WAITE GROUP, INC. OR ITS AGENT HAS BEEN ADVISED OF THE POSSIBILITY OF SUCH DAMAGES. THE WAITE GROUP, INC.'S LIABILITY FOR DAMAGES HEREUNDER SHALL IN NO EVENT EXCEED THE PURCHASE PRICE PAID.

COMPLETE AGREEMENT

This Agreement constitutes the complete agreement between The Waite Group, Inc. and you, the purchaser.

Some states do not allow the exclusion or limitation of implied warranties or liability for incidental or consequential damages, so the above exclusions or limitations may not apply to you. This limited warranty gives you specific legal rights; you may have others, which vary from state to state.

Upgrade Your Power C Software
Full Commercial Version Plus Accessories

The compiler you received with Workout C supports the medium (640K code, 64K data) memory model. The full commercial version of Power C additionally supports the small (64K code, 64K data) and large (640K code, 640K data) memory models. The small memory model makes your programs more efficient, while the large memory model gives your programs access to more memory for data storage. The commercial version also provides two additional floating point libraries (IEEE software only and 80x87 hardware only support). The Power C manual (680 pages) includes a detailed C language reference section as well as a complete description of all the library functions (with examples). The Power C compiler is a three time winner of Computer Shopper's Best Buy award.

Power Ctrace is a state-of-the-art debugging tool designed for one purpose: To make it very easy for you to find your programming errors. The debugger is extremely simple to use. You can execute your program one statement at a time by simply pressing the *Space-Bar*, or press the *Enter* key to watch an animated display as each statement executes in sequence. You can automatically stop execution at a specific statement by simply moving the cursor to the statement and pressing the *Insert* key to insert a break point. The program output and a list of all the variable names/values may be viewed in separate windows. Quoting from Computer Shopper: *"The Ctrace debugger is where Mix really shines. It is magnificent".*

The Power C Library Source is the C and assembly language source code for all 400+ functions in the Power C library. The source code lets you see exactly how all of the functions are implemented and allows you to create new libraries. Also included is the Power C assembler, which you may use to write your own assembly language functions.

The Power C BCD Business Math is a special binary coded decimal floating point library designed for business applications (i.e. dollars & cents calculations). By linking your programs with this base-10 BCD library, you can transparently eliminate the roundoff errors that occur for the default base-2 IEEE library. Financial functions for calculating interest and depreciation are included.

Mix Software, 1132 Commerce Drive, Richardson, TX 75081 (Tel: 214-783-6001, Fax: 214-783-1404)

To order your Power C Software, please see tearout card at the back of this book.

Stamp

Mix Software, Inc.
1132 Commerce Drive
Richardson, TX 75081
USA

Waite Group Satisfaction Report Card

Please fill out this card if you wish to know of future updates to *The Waite Group's Workout C*, or to receive our catalog.

Company Name: ______

Division: ______ **Mail Stop:** ______

Last Name: ______ **First Name:** ______ **Middle Initial:** ______

Street Address: ______

City: ______ **State:** ______ **Zip:** ______

Daytime telephone: ( ) ______

Date product was acquired: Month ______ **Day** ______ **Year** ______ **Your Occupation:** ______

Overall, how would you rate *The Waite Group's Workout C*?

☐ Excellent ☐ Very Good ☐ Good
☐ Fair ☐ Below Average ☐ Poor

What did you like MOST about this product? ______

What did you like LEAST about this product? ______

Please describe any problems you may have encountered with installing or using Workout C: ______

How do you use this book (tutorial, reference, problem-solver...)? ______

How did you find the pace of this book? ______

Did you know C when you bought this book? ______

What computer languages are you familiar with? ______

What is your level of computer expertise?

☐ New user ☐ Dabbler ☐ Hacker
☐ Power user ☐ Programmer ☐ Experienced professional

Is there any program or subject you would like to see The Waite Group cover in a similar approach? ______

Please describe your computer hardware:

Computer ______ Hard disk ______
5.25" disk drives ______ 3.5" disk drives ______
Video card ______ Monitor ______
Printer ______ Peripherals ______

Where did you buy this book?

☐ Bookstore (name: ______)
☐ Discount store (name: ______)
☐ Computer store (name: ______)
☐ Catalog (name: ______)
☐ Direct from WGP ☐ Other ______

What price did you pay for this book? ______

What influenced your purchase of this book?

☐ Recommendation ☐ Advertisement
☐ Magazine review ☐ Store display
☐ Mailing ☐ Book's format
☐ Reputation of The Waite Group ☐ Other ______

How many computer books do you buy each year? ______

How many other Waite Group books do you own? ______

What is your favorite Waite Group book? ______

Additional comments? ______

☐ **Check here for a free Waite Group catalog**

NO POSTAGE
NECESSARY
IF MAILED
IN THE
UNITED STATES

BUSINESS REPLY MAIL

FIRST CLASS MAIL PERMIT NO. 33 MILL VALLEY, CA

POSTAGE WILL BE PAID BY ADDRESSEE

Waite Group Press, Inc.
Attention: *Workout C*
200 Tamal Plaza, Suite 101
Corte Madera, CA 94925

FOLD HERE

Waite Group Press Product Warranty Card

Make sure you hear about our future product updates and offerings. Register now!

Before using this Waite Group Press product please complete and return this registration card. Only original cards will be accepted. Please print all information.

This product was acquired by: ☐ Individual ☐ Business Other ______________________

If business, please complete this card using your business address.

Serial Number: ______________________

Company Name: ______________________

Division: ______________ **Mail Stop:** ______________

Last Name: ______________ **First Name:** ______________ **Middle Initial:** ______

Street Address: ______________________

City: ______________ **State:** ______________ **Zip:** ______

Daytime telephone: ( ) ______________________

Date product was acquired: **Month** ______ **Day** ______ **Year** ______

Store where product was purchased: ______________________

Please give us any additional comments

____

____

____

____

At The Waite Group we are always looking for ways to make our current products even better. As a registered Waite Group Press user you will be the first on our list to receive new product notices and updates when they become available. So fill out and mail your registration card today!

Workout C

Stamp

Waite Group Press, Inc.
Attention: Workout C Warranty
200 Tamal Plaza, Suite 101
Corte Madera, CA 94925

FOLD HERE